# Labour Law in India

# Labour Law in India

## Second Edition

**Chandra Kumar Johri**

This book was originally published as a monograph in the International Encyclopaedia of Laws/Labour Law and Industrial Relations.

General Editor: Roger Blanpain
Associate General Editor: Michele Colucci

Wolters Kluwer
Law & Business

*Published by:*
Kluwer Law International
PO Box 316
2400 AH Alphen aan den Rijn
The Netherlands
Website: www.kluwerlaw.com

*Sold and distributed in North, Central and South America by:*
Aspen Publishers, Inc.
7201 McKinney Circle
Frederick, MD 21704
United States of America
Email: customer.service@aspenpublishers.com

*Sold and distributed in all other countries by:*
Turpin Distribution Services Ltd.
Stratton Business Park
Pegasus Drive, Biggleswade
Bedfordshire SG18 8TQ
United Kingdom
Email: kluwerlaw@turpin-distribution.com



*Printed on acid-free paper*

ISBN 978-90-411-5326-5

This title is available on www.kluwerlawonline.com



Printed and Bound by CPI Group (UK) Ltd, Croydon, CR0 4YY.

# The Author

Chandra Kumar Johri is an economist by training and profession. He studied at the University of Allahabad, India and the University of Michigan, Ann Arbor. He has authored *India: Perspectives on Politics, Economy and Labour, 1981–2001* in two volumes: Vol. 1. *The Age of Gandhi, 1918–1957* (2011) and Vol. 2. *The Age of the Constitution, 1958–2007* (2012) published by Aakhar Books, Delhi.

**The Author**

# Table of Contents

# List of Abbreviations

| | |
|---|---|
| APSRTC | Andhra Pradesh State Road Transport Corporation |
| AITUC | All India Trade Union Congress. |
| BSNL | Bharat Sanchar Nigam Ltd |
| BIFR | Board for Industrial and Financial Reconstruction |
| CVC | Central Vigilance Commissioner |
| CDM | Clean Development Mechanism |
| CAT | Central Administrative Tribunal |
| CITU | Centre of Indian Trade Unions |
| CPC | Criminal Procedure Code |
| CPI | Consumer Price Index |
| CO | Conciliation officer |
| CSO | Certified Standing Orders |
| DA | Dearness allowance |
| CWA | Current weekly activity status |
| CDS | Current daily activity status |
| ESI | Employees' State Insurance |
| ESIC | Employees' State Insurance Corporation |
| HRA | House rent allowance |
| ID Act | Industrial Disputes Act |
| INTUC | Indian National Trade Union Congress |
| LAT | Labour Appellate Tribunal |

## List of Abbreviations

| | |
|---|---|
| MP | Madhya Pradesh |
| MRTU and PULP Act | Maharashtra Recognition of Trade Unions and Prevention of Unfair Labour Practices Act |
| NPA | Non-performing assets |
| MSO | Model standing orders |
| MWA | Minimum Wages Act |
| ONGC | Oil and Natural Gas Commission |
| PF | Provident Funds |
| SDM | Sub-divisional Magistrate |
| SC | Supreme Court of India |
| SO | Standing orders |
| SARFAESI Act | The Securitization and Reconstruction of Financial Assets and Enforcement of Security Interest Act |
| SLC | Standing Labour Committee |
| UP | Uttar Pradesh |
| NSS | National Sample Survey |
| UPSS | Usual Principal Status and Subsidiary Status Worker |
| VRS | Voluntary Retirement Scheme |
| PSU | Public Sector Undertakings |

# General Introduction

## Chapter 1. General Features

### §1. The Evolving Modern India

*1.* Modern India owes its origin to contacts with Europe which began with trade and later turned into wars, diplomacy and conquests. After the elimination of other contenders, principally France, and defeating rival Indian powers the British East India Company made this country a part of the still expanding empire. Rule by conquest and diplomatic stratagems received a severe military jolt in the great revolt in 1857, called the Sepoy Mutiny in the British annals, and as the first war of independence in nationalist India. It was savagely crushed by reconquest and reprisals. However, this led to a complete transfer of power to the sovereign in 1858 and direct governance by the British government under laws passed by Parliament. The long phase of political and constitutional development began about two decades later and led to the emergence of an organized nationalist movement. It formally ended in August 1947 when India was partitioned into India and Pakistan. The two countries became independent assuming full responsibility for their affairs, internal as well as external. The British rule had overcome the welter of India and created a united country under British laws, administration and judiciary. Together with the railway system, post and telegraph, ports and harbours, modern schools and universities, the British promoted trade and commerce, several industries and plantations and commercialized agriculture. These were bequeathed to the two succeeding nation states. Other important developments were the ideas of nationalism and secularism and India as a country with which people might identify and the concurrent belief that only through a democratic, tolerant and liberal polity could the enormous diversity of religions, ethnicity, languages and caste based divisions, principally among the Hindus, be brought together under political management.

*2.* India is ancient and modern at the same time. It is not a smooth coexistence, though both find contemporary voices, of affirmation and denial in religious discourses and political discussion. India's diversity seeks shelter under the common umbrella of an accommodative, modernizing constitution, while the people in various ways have let the modernizing forces proceed relatively unhampered by ancient beliefs or medieval customs. One of the strongest forces of modernization is India's openness to a wide swathe of influences from different sources in the world. Ironically these influences have also reinforced religious beliefs and practices even as people's lives are exposed to the world wide network of communications and news and ideas as never before. To the educated youth the Western world, especially the United States, exercises a great pull, partly for higher education and also for commercial opportunities and careers. Added to this is the development of organized tourism as a major industry and Indians' speedy emergence as avid travellers in the world. Modern India is forging commercial and industrial links with the rest of the world and at a faster pace with the newly industrialized countries, such as China, Thailand, Malaysia and South Korea. However, over the last six decades principal initiatives for international connections have been taken by the more developed countries which remained interested in India's development for political and economic reasons. This momentum has continued and has been reciprocated by Indian businessmen. At present the strongest integrating force is international finance capital, despite its inherently volatile nature. Thus far the range of its influence on the economy and lives of people has remained confined to a small population segment.

*3.* The modernizing trends are undoubtedly dominant, but their sweep is contained by older cultures which have demonstrated unexpected resilience and capacity for resistance on occasions and in certain parts of India. The primary source of cultural resistance among the Hindus is the ascribed status to caste, community, lineage and religion in marriages, from which is derived the principle that the individual rights of choice and free selection are subordinated to the power of the village collective as voiced by the society's leaders. Forces of tradition have met the challenge of democratic values by both accommodation and rejection. While the former works for modernizing society, the latter does not. Instances have come to light where a particular category of inter-caste marriages, of a (Dalit) boy and a girl of a middle caste (other backward castes), has produced violent reactions, resulting in the killing of one or both. Equally strong opposition has been voiced against marriages within a common lineage specific to a caste. These are disastrously regressive tendencies which have sprung up as a reaction against the rapid spread of the democratic, humanistic and freedom promoting values. Steadily over the last six decades the democratic doctrines of India's secular Constitution have made deeper inroads into society. Their liberating effect upon women, the lower castes and backward communities in general has unmistakably expanded in geographical coverage and percolated deeper. These have undermined the grip of traditional community forums, such as the village councils, called the *panchayats*, led by the elderly members of the powerful land-owning castes who have asserted the primacy of traditional village laws over the secular. Unfortunately a number of politicians have hedged on the issue and may be willing to concede the primacy of customary laws over the secular. In urban areas the legitimacy and primacy of civil laws as interpreted and enforced by courts has been accepted and in some form or other formal compliance is assured. Modern education has prompted this habit, and in families in which education is already accepted as the uppermost value respect for courts is ordinarily observed. But in two-thirds of the population which is still rural and bound to village society it is the command of police and courts which produce compliance.

§2. Identity at Birth

*4.* Caste and religion have found a new sanctity. Politics is increasingly centred on the issue of identity by birth which is conjoined with generalized notions of economic conditions to permit the grouping of entire people by castes and minority religions and to carve out appropriate political constituencies for the competing parties. Practically all the political parties have agreed to annul the hitherto observed maxim of precluding caste in the decennial censuses and to count only individuals as residing in households. This has been found to be a needless restriction since ever increasing communal, caste and tribe based communities have demanded political recognition and claims for privileged access to government employment, state funded schools, higher educational institutions and political influence. The idea of common citizenship regardless of birth and beliefs already counts for much less and has been sacrificed in several states of the north-east, the Punjab and Jammu and Kashmir. Further decline of common citizenship may be anticipated as the census data in 2011 are grouped, variously cross-tabulated and analysed for various purposes. This will be a far more challenging task for the census organization to conduct, since the state governments do not possess prior lists of existing caste names. Census enumerators will be asking an apparently straightforward question to every individual to disclose his caste identity. The enumeration may turn up thousands of caste, community, religion, tribe and village based names and surnames along with many mixed caste marriages with children having very diffuse identities. The political class is unconcerned about them; it is primarily focused on locating politically relevant groupings which can be used as electoral constituencies to collect votes and receive assured segmented political backing. In fact political parties have been doing this routinely in every election. While selecting candidates for contesting the election, their religion and caste affiliations are prominently noted and the number of the particular households in every constituency is counted or intelligently guessed. The probability of securing a satisfactory voter count would enable the party to make a rough estimate of the number of seats it may expect to win. These habits are so deeply entrencned in the political system that practically every party is known by its religion and caste-based electoral support, much less for what it says in the name of political and economic programmes. From their collective perspective the pretence of secularism, supposedly free from communal and casteist connotations, is best given up as an encumbrance and what they actually practise is accorded a formal, institutionalized political sanction. Accordingly the 2011 census of India would be unlike any previous census conducted since 1951, while huge problems of comparability and non-comparability may crop up as the demographic data are released and the numerous names and castes which may add up to about 100,000 are tabulated. Beginning with 2011, a new political era may commence for the post-independence India, with fewer things remaining in common with the past as wholly new features take shape and become politically established. The government has decided to conduct two separate censuses in 2011, separated by several months, so that the normal decennial census is freed from the avoidable confusion caused by caste contamination of the mixed up data.

## §3. National Leaders and Present Day Politicians

5. Contemporary India is vastly different from the partitioned political entity which began the unchartered journey of democratic governance under an elaborate Constitution against heavy odds. India was providentially fortunate in having a relatively large pool of dedicated, disciplined and selfless leaders in full control of country's affairs. They were led, trained and developed under Gandhi's moral discipline and his over-arching, indeed, super-leadership umbrella. Most of them ceased to be Gandhian in lifestyle and practice in due course but remained committed to serving India and its people through the state and laws enacted by elected legislatures. They had a vision of political future in which India would be substantially freed of its many divisions and the practice of democracy would teach people to practise tolerance and religious accommodation while the caste divisions slowly withered away. Sixty year later this civilizing mission of democracy has been abandoned in practice and the political class feels less hampered by professions of lofty ideals. The politicians now unhesitatingly affirm their loyalties to segmented identities and interests and may strive to transform the polity to subserve a more deeply communal and caste-based political system. The most glaring gap in national politics is the absence of widely respected and acclaimed leaders who can reach out to the masses and classes alike cutting across party lines and sectional divisions. At present the political class comprises a large body of active politicians and political workers whose chief aim in life is to make a living out of politics and use positions of power to acquire wealth and higher status. They are closer to the people, understand them better and conscious of the numerous frailties and circumscribed conditions in which people live. If people practise parochialism in their daily lives, prefer their own kin over more deserving ones of other castes and communities and experience no qualms about it, so do the leaders. If people are more materialist and money minded in outlook and care little for superordinal goals, or wish to stay affiliated with caste, community or religious bodies, so may the leaders be. The political classes are now far more mundane and down to earth in furthering their political careers than were their predecessors.

## §4. The Print Media

6. The changing profile of India is prominently reflected in the enormous growth and diversity reflected in the media. Beginning with the radio and newspapers it has expanded to cover the visual channel, most spectacularly seen in 24/7 news channels and includes both national and international TV companies. Unlike the radio and TV which were government monopolies for several decades, the print media was and continues to be in private hands. Newspapers, in English and Indian languages, reach out to millions of readers every day and are still the most important source of news and views to the reading public. Unlike the highly developed societies, like the USA, where print media is in decline, and has yielded first place to TV, in India newspapers continue to be in demand and generate steady profits for the owners. Since 2005 the number of newspaper titles has increased by 44 per cent to 2700. *The Times of India*, an English newspaper, has a circulation of 4 million,

and may be the world's largest English newspaper. All the Hindi newspapers have a combined circulation of more than 25 million. *The Economist* reported, 'as India's middle class swells, firms are splashing out on newspaper advertisements for property, mobile phones, cars and matchmaking services that promise your daughter a computer savvy hubby'.[1] It is expected that newspapers' revenue will grow by 9 per cent a year in the next four years to reach $5.9 billion. But all is not well in the print media. Journalists are hired on contract and know full well that contract renewal and a successful career require, in addition to competence, a willingness to toe the owner's line on policy matters, not independence, and they are not expected to be critical of the paper's advertisement business. The journalists union has been all but busted. The evil of paid news specially at the time of an election has raised the question of integrity of newspapers. In most of the papers the post of chief editor has been abolished; hence there is no internal monitoring and there is lack of balance between the owners policies and public interest in independent and objective news reporting.[2]

1. *The Economist*, 25 September – October 2010, p.77.
2. T.N. Ninan, 'The Newspaper Capital of the World', in *Business Standard*, India 2009. New Delhi, BS books 2009, pp. 205–220.

## Chapter 2. The UN Millennium Goals

*7.* World opinion is playing a hugely important rule in India's future. At the United Nations Millennium Summit in September 2000 the Millennium Declaration selected eight developmental goals to be achieved by 2015. There were 18 time bound targets and 48 progress indicators which could be monitored. These deal with substantial reduction in extreme poverty and hunger eradication over a period of time; achieving universal primary education for all children by 2015 and working towards this goal in order to raise the enrolment ratio to 100 per cent. Moreover, all children who enter the school at grade I are retained until grade V and complete the stage of primary education. Another important millennium goal is to eliminate discrimination against women and create conditions of gender equality. Yet another goal is to substantially lower child and maternal mortality. This would require a very large expansion in institutional care and the supply of skilled health personnel. Connected with health care are the goals on HIV/AIDS prevention, deaths due to malaria, incidence of tuberculosis and associated matters pertaining to improved sanitation, safe water and hygiene. These are essential prerequisites for realizing specific goals or targets and must move up in national and state wise planning exercises, specially allocation of funds in the annual budgets. It is important to recognize that in India the government has taken these goals seriously and reprioritized the Tenth and Eleventh five-year plans accordingly. Each of the millennium goals has required converting them into realizable targets for each state and engaging in the colossal task of institution building, training of manpower and providing the push and drive for overcoming inertia and resistance or reluctance to achieve the targeted outcomes.

The one goal that was and continues to be elusive of realization pertains to poverty reduction and elimination of extreme hunger. At a deeper level poverty and hunger are aspects of population growth. Reduction in poverty is crucially dependent on acceptance of lower fertility rates by the poor, specially among the backward classes of the less or least developed regions and subregions of India. Poverty and backwardness have been systemically reproduced along with the lowering of death rates but without a corresponding reduction in birth rates. Moreover in the long run several crucially important supply side factors in the economy would improve or deteriorate depending upon the annual increase in population, for instance, the availability of land and water for agriculture and urbanization. The efficiency of the entire supply chain which connects agriculture with the consumers is dependent on supply elasticity of agriculture. Furthermore, the welfare augmenting programmes of the centre have not yet succeeded in enthusing all state governments, particularly the lower organs of their bureaucracy at the delivery stage of each programme. This has affected the family planning programme as well. During the Tenth plan, it was reported that the state governments took almost 2–2½ years to prepare the district level programmes, though in the latter half of the plan period progress was more rapid. This problem is inherent in the political system, since practically all the MDG related subjects are in the state list in the Constitution. It is an implied aspect of planning in these subjects that at every stage at which the macro-plan is broken down to concrete realizable targets, the consent and cooperation of states are essential elements of performance. The state government should also raise resources and provide for enhanced allocations towards these goals in state budgets. An added complicating feature is provided by the constitutional amendments, numbering 73 and 74, by which new powers and responsibilities are entrusted to local bodies in rural and urban areas. Village councils and municipalities are expected to take on and share the commitment to provide primary education, health care and other services. However, actual progress is much less than was expected due to the extreme unwillingness of several state governments to pare down their responsibilities and transfer funds and powers to local bodies in a constitutional rearrangement of subjects.

## §1. Urban Poverty

*8.* Unlike rural poverty which affects large masses and entire regions, urban poverty is partly migratory and in some part reproduced within urban societies. However, regardless of origination, the urban poor can be viewed as a homogeneous segment of the growing urban population. The reason why special attention needs to be paid to the task of scaling down, if not eradication of urban poverty, is that the goal is set for significant improvement in the conditions of slum dwellers. They are already a large population of over 43 million in India. In 2001, according to the census count, the slum population lived in 640 cities and towns and comprised 15 per cent of the urban population. Greater Bombay is reported to have 54 per cent of its population living in slums, in Delhi it is about 19 per cent. It is not possible to generalize for all urban areas solely on the basis of Greater Bombay data, where more than 43 per cent slum dweller were migrants, mostly from backward regions and states. But it does not follow that urban poverty and migrant status are near synonyms. The data suggest that the non-migrants end up being poorer than the migrants.[3] Actually the slums provide dwelling places for the migrants as well as the non-migrants and for both classes of people, the poor and the non-poor. Income-poverty may not be the most discerning feature of urban slums. Slums are marked by appalling living conditions, low or very low per capita living space, intolerable congestion, indeterminate quality of infrastructure, poor sanitation and public hygiene and general squalor. The government is now involved in the enormously burdensome task of urban renewal and redevelopment through the Jawaharlal Nehru Urban Renewal Mission (JNNURM) and the integrated housing and slum development programme (IHSDP), and seems to be keen on addressing several Millennium Devolpment Goals (MDGs) on poverty, health and gender equality in urban areas. The economic rationale is that by augmenting the economic and physical infrastructure, the cities will turn into growth engines. This is achievable, but the more elusive goal is to find the means to provide more shelter to the poor, specially improved security of tenure on affordable terms.

*9.* The National Urban Housing policy 2007 views the urban future expecting that by 2041 nearly 50 per cent of India's population will be living in urban areas.

3. D.P. Singh, 'Poverty and Migration: Does moving Help?' in *India: Urban Poverty Report* 2009, Ministry of Housing and Urban Poverty Alleviation and UNDP, New Delhi, OUP, 2009.

Clearly this requires creating as many new integrated townships as may be feasible. In 2011 the urban population may have comprised 28 per cent of the estimated population of 1.2 billion. Nearly three-quaters of urban population lives in large cities. The task on hand is to create new humane cities and townships which will be free from slums. However, it is important to take note of the underlying reason why smaller towns are free of slums, while the poor cluster in the already congested slums of very large cities. They need to work and make a living and prefer a dwelling place in slums which are near the workplaces. Given this compulsion, future urban planning should focus on industrial cities or large trading centres on different criteria and not just humane conditions. Labour in search for employment may be expected to migrate from future townships to large cities and accept the low quality of life in slums as normal. Data show that the unemployment rate in million-plus cities tends to be higher than in the middle and small size towns. There may be a persistence of labour redundancy in the million-plus cities, but emigrants still come and stay on in the hope of finding work and improving their living conditions. The middle and small towns do not appear to show employment growth, and this may be an unchanging condition. Slums are also a function of the severely limited urban space. The middle class, upper and elite groups are able to claim a large part of the urban space and they are essential for the survival and prosperity of cities. Moreover, the collective voice in large cities is increasingly market-centred. It is the claim over parcels of land based an urban land prices and zoning policies of the government which ultimately determine the total land area on which the poor and the migrant may settle. Policies geared to eradication of urban poverty may find these facts inescapable.[4]

*10.* So far as the Eleventh Plan (2007-2012) is concerned, the realization of the MDG on urban poverty is at the preliminary stage of planning and action. The role of the central government is primarily as a facilitator of change, since the subject lies in the state list of the Constitution. Currently, the housing shortage is estimated at around 24.71 million, most of it for low income groups and the economically weaker sections of population. During the Eleventh Plan the total housing requirement including the backlog may be around 26.53 million. According to the Plan, 'it is for the state Governments to bring in the required institutional reforms and legislative measures to augment housing both by state agencies and the private sector'.[5] There are severe constraints which lie ahead. First, there is a severe shortage of the serviced land in urban areas. Second, even as existing cities expand and new townships are planned, the government does not want prime agricultural land to be acquired for the purpose. Instead, urban planning should focus on degraded lands. Third, while acquiring rural land, 'a suitable resettlement and rehabilitation policy for the displaced rural families' should be in place. This imposes a heavy cost constraint on urban extensions and new townships. Fourth, the investment required is very high, of the order of Rs 361,318.10 crores (10 million = 1 crore) over the plan

---

4. Darshini Mahadevia, 'Urban Land Market and Access to the Poor' in *Urban Poverty Report*, and *Eleventh Five Year Plan*, Vol. III, *Urban Infrastructure, Housing, Basic Services and Poverty Alleviation*, esp. pp. 402-419.
5. *Ibid.*, pp. 411–414.

period. It is not at all clear how this scale of urban housing can be financed, though a number of possibilities are suggested. Fifth, the technology constraint must also be overcome. Several technologies are at various stages of development, including demonstration houses. A flexible approach is preferred. Apparently, the stage has not been reached where urban planning, incorporating land use, new land acquisitions, technology selection, cost-pricing projections and modes of financing, will be ready for implementation. The MDG will have to be deferred.

## §2. Elementary Education

*11.* Education is a foremost need of every child, to be met by the parents and society working together. Unfortunately in India the poor have been slow in demanding greater access to good quality schools, mainly due to the low ability of parents to make a corresponding commitment to keep their children in school and not prematurely withdraw them for adding to family income, or with girls, to share their mothers' household chores. This is a vicious circle and to effectively break it consistent initiatives have to be taken both at the parent's end as well as at the government's. As a practical problem it has thus far defied the government policies on schooling. The data on school enrolment show, considerable growth at the primary level, age class 6–10, but a sharp reduction at the upper primary level, age class 11–13, and a further decline at the level of secondary schools. In fact the number of schools has increased faster than the population, though most of the increase has taken place at the upper primary level. This shows the effect of demand for schooling from the parents. The poor drop out of the school at first stage itself due to low staying power. In 2004 over 767,000 children were in primary schools, while the number at the next stage was 274,000; this shows heavy withdrawal of children by parents, presumably due to poverty.[6] The government should do more to improve the physical side of schools, also provide more trained teachers and greatly improve facilities. Free meals at the schools are an added attraction, though their provision casts a heavy responsibility on local governing bodies to ensure the quality of nutrititious foods as well as the health, hygiene and safety aspects at every stage of purchase, storage, cooking, transportation and delivery of cooked meals to the schools. The condition of school teachers has received much criticism, including complaints of teachers' absence during class hours, and by the teachers on the miscellaneous duties, not at all connected to school work, assigned to them by the government. This is another vicious circle which is hard to break. The state governments are known to be reluctant to hire permanent teachers as regular complements of the school system. Perhaps temporary teachers can be hired at lower cost to the government, but they can hardly provide the life-long commitment to school teaching which children need and parents may value.

*12.* School enrolment data are often inflated and largely unreliable. The attendance rate of children is much lower. The worst affected groups are the scheduled castes (SC), scheduled tribes (ST) and Muslims, particularly in the backward and

6. OECD, *Economic Surveys: India*, New Delhi, Academic Foundation, 2007, Table 8.1, p. 222.

least developed regions of India. In Bihar it was reported on school drop-out rates that the presence of pupils was less than 50 per cent of those enrolled. At the all India level, the figures for the year 2003-04 indicate that drop-out rates were 31.36 per cent from classes I to V, 52.2 per cent from classes I to VIII and 62.68 per cent from classes 1 to V.[7] The drop-out rates for girls were a little lower in the first two categories of classes, but higher at 64.92 per cent for classes Ist to Vth. In Bihar the drop-out rates were higher, the highest in India. The infrastructure in many schools was found to be in a dilapidated condition in 2007. The other side of the school system, viz. teacher education, is not any less unsatisfactory. The teaching institutions are in a run-down condition and the quality of teacher training way below the mark. They are unable to attract and retain competent staff, the curriculum is outdated and the training programmes low on vitality and realism – all signs of academic isolation and low connectedness with schools. At the state level there are centres for educational research and training. These are either sub-optimal or, as in Bihar, in a decrepit condition. Moreover, the school system suffers from all the shortcomings of Indian society, mainly socio-cultural discrimination against the SC, ST and the poor, in aggravated forms. Discrimination tends to perpetuate illiteracy, lack of opportunity, denial of equality and the consequent malaise of backwardness and poverty. This vicious circle is hardest to crack since it involves not just schools, teachers, related institutions but large populations as the perpetrators and the sufferers. Poverty, illiteracy, illhealth, low body weight, malnourished parents and children and low capacity to work are interrelated aspects of a phenomenon which militates against the realization of MDGs.

*13.* In the Eleventh Five-Year Plan (2007–12) the government has set targets for universal gross enrolment by 2010 and to cut down the drop-out rate from 50 per cent to 20 per cent. The basic policy tool for the former is to set up a school near every habitation and to make sure that none of the neglected habitations has been left out. Two policy instruments may help realize the second objective. These are the universalization of the mid-day meal scheme and greatly augmenting the stock of women teachers, especially in the backward states where this was lagging far behind. The latter rests on the plausible theory that the presence of women teachers will help in girls staying in school to complete elementary education. Experience in this regard is not particularly rewarding, because many girls continue to drop out to lend a helping hand to their mothers. Until fertility rates decline and the intrinsic worth of girl children rises in the community's scale of values and societies advance on a broad front, the problem of girls' education may persist in the backward regions of India. Meanwhile, another very serious problem has surfaced up together with the universal access to schools and the universal gross enrolment ratio for children. The Eleventh Plan reports: 'Lack of universal pre-schooling (early childhood care and education) and consequent poor vocabulary and poor conceptual development

---

7. Muchkund Dubey, 'School Education: a Constraint on the Sustainability of Growth Rate in India', in Manmohan Agarwal (ed.), *India's Economic Future Education, Technology, Energy and Environment*, New Delhi, Social Science Press, 2009.

of mind makes even enrolled children less participative in the class, even for learning by rote.'[8] This is early impairment and coupled with the poor quality of education children may still stay in the school out of sheer necessity but without acquiring basic literacy and numeracy skills. Premature drop-outs may be unpreventable, and from the point of view of good schools it may by even desirable. At present the government is focused on overcoming the weakest links of elementary education programme, which are teacher attendance, ability and motivation. These weaknesses may be viewed as forming part of the phenomenon of high drop- out rates at primary levels for the scheduled castes (34.2 per cent) and scheduled tribes (42.3 per cent), which are way above the national average (29 per cent).

## §3. The Energy Deficit

*14.* The commercial energy deficit is a major constraint on growth. It also slows down the expansion of the social sector, especially education and health in rural areas due to high cost of providing power and uncertainty of supply. Rural electricity and the social sector are highly subsidized and it is becoming progressively less likely that the government will be able to pass on the cost of subsidies to commercial users of power by charging highly discriminatory tariffs. Moreover, at present the economics of power generation and distribution is burdened by high transmission losses, which may be around 40 per cent. Most of these losses occur due to systematic theft of power and the accompanying corruption in the system. These cost around Rs 20,000 crore annually. If the goal of bringing down these losses to 15 per cent by the end of the Eleventh Plan is realized, the gain will immediately translate into greater availability of power and higher revenues. This is a task each state is expected to set for itself and put in place the needed reforms in laws, organization and the technological back-up. Realism does not warrant much optimism on this score and for the same reason it may not be feasible to provide dependable electricity access to all households which are below the poverty line. So far as capacity creation is concerned, separate targets were set for the central government, the state governments and the private sector in the Tenth Plan, though every sector under-achieved and the total expansion was barely above 50 per cent of the target. Instead of targeted expansion of 411,099.4 MW, the realized accretion in 2007 was only 21,080.24 MW. At the end of the Eleventh Plan the gross electricity requirement is estimated at 78,577 MW, which is three and a half times that achieved in 2007. The sources are hydro, thermal, nuclear, wind and renewables. The share of hydro is diminishing, that of nuclear is dependent on being able to overcome numerous technological and political obstacles and constraints, while the share of the fourth can be raised further provided the targets are backed by resources and leadership. The most dependable source is the thermal power based on coal and it provides the principal energy fuel resource in the country.

8. *Eleventh Five-Year Plan 2007-2012,* Vol. II, *Social Sector*, p. 4, also, Ch. 1, 'Education'.

*15.* India's dependence in energy fuels, mainly crude oil, gas and uranium is growing. In 2006–07 the domestic production of coal met 90.33 per cent of demand, of lignite, 100 per cent, oil 26.6 per cent, natural gas and LNG 82.08 per cent and hydropower 99.74 per cent. The difference between demand and local supplies was met by imports. In 2011–12 the dependence on coal may diminish, also on oil, while it may rise for gas and hydropower. The bulk of coal imports are used by power plants, and present little difficulty in international relations. In oil and gas the government is keen on developing local resources, because world politics and volatile price structure are inherent sources of instability and anxiety. The future of nuclear energy is almost totally dependent on the success of political negotiation with the United States and other countries which produce uranium and also have the appropriate technologies. At present nuclear power provides a mere 3.1 per cent of total production capacity. The capacity utilization has decline to 57 per cent due to low fuel availability. More progress can be made when the domestic R&D in nuclear power generation has achieved a break-through, specially in the technology of thorium based fast breeder reactors (FBR). According to the Eleventh Plan, 'The FBR technology is critical for developing the second stage of India's nuclear power programme. Without developing the wide-scale use of FBR technology, India would find it difficult to go beyond 10000 MW nuclear capacity based on known indigenous uranium resources.'[9] Future projections up to 2050 in the development of nuclear power installed capacity have been made on optimistic and pessimistic scenarios. In 2010 the two sets generated 11 GWe and 9 GWe, respectively, by 2020 the figures (in GWe) range between 29 GWe and 21 GWe; by 2040 the gap between the two widens to 131 and 104, and by 2050 farther to 275 and 208. It follows that on pessimistic projections India will have to look further and beyond its borders for alternative fuel supplies, especially gas and find ways for stabilizing gas prices, so that as a fuel it does not become economically unviable. At present gas based power production is more costly and so is less viable than coal. There is already considerable opposition to higher prices charged by gas based power plants.[10]

## §4. Environmental Concerns

*16.* In the Tenth Five-year Plan (2002–07), the government for the first time noted with alarm that 'Disasters can have devastating effects on the economy; they cause huge human and economic losses, and can significantly set back development efforts of a region or a state. Two recent disasters, the Orissa cyclone and the Gujarat earthquake are cases in point.' UN studies showed that these trends of destruction were rising and there was singular lack of preparation for disaster management.[11] In India, an important dimension of disaster is that high population density may result in escalating losses in lives. It followed that a multi-pronged strategy for total risk

9. *Eleventh Five-year Plan*. p. 356.
10. T.L. Sankar, 'India's Energy crisis. Threat or Opportunity', in S. Mahendra Dev and N. Chandrasekhar Rao (eds.), *India: Perspectives on Equitable Development*, New Delhi, Academic Foundation, 2009. p. 306.
11. *Tenth Five-year Plan, 2002–2007,* Vol. 1, p. 189.

management, including risk reduction and mitigation, was needed for sustainable development. Sustainability requires environmental protection, afforestation programmes, pollution control, construction of earthquake resistant structures, etc. and these should have high priority within the plans.[12] Quantitative targets were set for (i) increase in forest and tree cover, (ii) cleaning of major polluted rivers, and broad goals were laid down for (iii) monitoring air and water quality in cities and towns. In June 2005, a progress report forming part of the mid-term Appraisal of the Tenth Plan was prepared and it showed an all-round progress, also many gaps which needed additional resources. The government announced that following the ratification of the Kyoto Protocol by Russia in February 2005, it had come into effect and in India a National Action plan for operationalizing the clean Development Mechanism (CDM) has been put in place. Under the United Nations Framework Convention on Climate Change, (UNFCCC), the enabling countries, including India, use several innovative mechanisms to meet their targets of green house gases (GHG) emissions at lower cost during the first commitment period, 2008–2012.[13]

*17.* Fortunately the importance of environment and climatic change did not diminish with the change in government in 2004. Building on the Tenth Plan, the Eleventh Five-year Plan (2007–2012), decided to take the momentum forward. The first national environment policy was announced in May 2006. Practical steps were taken for re-engineering the environment clearance process and the environmental impact assessment notification review, for improving the quality of environmental governance. Similarly, a review of the Coastal Regulation Zone Notification was undertaken. In the Constitution, 'environment' is seen as a residual central subject. However, the central government alone cannot shoulder the responsibility for putting into effect the national policy on a wide-ranging subject and concurrent legislation by the state governments and notification of rules by the local authorities are needed. This may require amending the constitution to make 'environment and climate change' as a concurrent subject. The political consensus for the needed constitutional amendment is yet to be achieved and this forms part of the delayed common realization in the country of the importance of the subject for the long-run protection and well-being of our people. The pressure for action in climate change is largely international and so is the need felt for putting policies in place for implementing India's obligation under the Kyoto protocol. However, measures for reducing air and water pollution, increasing the forest cover, conservation of threatened species and disaster mitigation programmes are under the national five-year plans and do not require international obligations or monitoring. In the same class are other programmes, such as, urban solid waste management, mountain ecosystems, national lake conservation plan and coastal zone management, etc. In conducting these programmes the authorities should fully take into account local circumstances and vulnerabilities of the people. The participation of civil society is an essential component of any action plan though the funds may come from the central government and the state governments may provide the essential administrative support.

12. *Ibid.*, p. 201.
13. Mid-Term Appraisal of *Tenth Five-year Plan* (2002–2007), June 2005, p. 430.

As of now there is very little feedback and information on the actual experience of conducting these activities at the ground level.

## §5. Climate Change

*18.* International focus on global climate change has made it an urgent business of national governments to reach an agreement among the industrialized countries and the third world countries on reducing green house gas (GHG) emissions into the atmosphere. It is estimated that, due to the GHGs in the atmosphere, the earth's surface temperature has risen by $0.6 \pm 0.2^{\circ}C$ over the 20th century. In fact the earth's temperature has been rising at a faster rate in the last few decades and unless it is stopped and reversed, unpredictable climatic disasters may occur. The greatest threat is that the rising temperature will turn polar ice caps into water and at higher temperatures the sea level will rise and inundate many islands and coasts causing economic losses, damaging eco-systems and inflicting heavy loss of lives. In view of the urgency of taking action on matters pertaining to it, the government set up a council on climate change under the chairmanship of prime minister. Consequent to this, it was decided to prepare a national action plan for addressing the challenge of climate change. The government can respond by taking measures for mitigating the adverse effects of climate change and accord higher priority to adaptation. Strictly viewed the latter would require a reordering of development plans, especially of industrial activities which release CO2 and other gasses and raise earth's temperature or deplete the ozone layer. Climate research must have a high priority. 'The action plan will deal with key vulnerabilities of India to climate change and, in particular, the impact on water resources, forests, coastal areas, agriculture and health.' Agricultural technologies should be made a priority area in research. Internationally, India was expected to take concrete steps to bring down the GHG emissions to 1990 levels by the year 2000. This stage is already past. India's share of global emissions is about 4 per cent. No amount of mitigation by India will affect climate change. A substantial commitment to reduce emissions by the major industrialized countries will be required. Nonetheless, as contribution to the global reduction efforts, the Eleventh plan should focus on efforts to ensure that the emission intensity of India's GHG continues to decline.[14][15]

*19.* The national environmental policy, 2006 formulated the principle of, 'equal per capita entitlements of global environmental resources to all countries'. In July 2007, at an international forum, Prime Minster Manmohan Singh announced that the government would ensure that, 'India's per capita emissions never exceed the per capita emissions of the industrialized countries'. The change from total emissions to per capita emission appears fair, reasonable and realizable, but is unlikely to be accepted as a yardstick by the advanced countries which have smaller populations but higher emissions. It also stretches the principle of common but differentiated responsibility accepted by the industrially advanced countries. China has

14. *Eleventh Five-year Plan 2007–2012*, Vol. I, p. 205.
15. *Ibid.*, p. 206.

suggested the norm of emissions per unit of GDP produced. But this will affect faster growing economies far more than is justifiable in view of their underdeveloped economies. Yet it is probable that the current rate of GHG emissions is probably higher in China and India among other faster developing economics than in the USA. This will turn the argument of sharing the cost of reducing world wide emissions totally topsy-turvy and result in letting off lightly the developed countries which have caused cumulatively the greatest damage to climate. The international conference at Copenhagen was expected to produce an internationally binding settlement, but it failed to do so. The developed countries advanced the principle in terms of, 'global action and policies on preventing climate change must be consistent with economic growth and free market principles. Carbon trading naturally fits perfectly into the emphasis on market mechanisms.'[16] This leaves out the principle of entitlement and its corollary to developing countries, viz. the importance of transfer of green technologies being supported by capital movements into desired channels. These are political processes as between states and may not be compatible with the ITO's legally binding norms. Apparently, international conferences though attended by the heads of governments may not yet produce a binding settlement due to lack of consensus and sheer unwillingness to impose politically unpopular levies on standard of living of people without a corresponding pay-offs in ascertainable economic gains.[17] India has decided to make measured progress in national climate control consistently with the acquisition of climate favouring technologies and sustained economic development on a broad front. Labour will feel the impact of emission control measures most, as the existing technologies are phased out or punitive taxes are imposed on those industries which resist the change. The calculation of costs and benefits on industry by industry basis will be required if a smooth transmission is to be made in many industries which are currently run on climate unfriendly technologies. Altogether it is an uphill task and a major challenge for India's diverse, federalized, many parties-based political system.

16. See the Symposium on 'Climate Change Conundrum' in the Seminar, February 2010, esp. the article by Sanjay Joshi, 'The Shaping of Discourse', quote on p. 17.
17. See the comments on Copenhagen in *The Economist*, 2 January 2010, pp. 9–10.

# Chapter 3. Political Economy

## §1. Perspectives on Inclusive Goals

*20.* The Eleventh Five-Year Plan, 2007–2012 is different from previous five-year plans in respect of the prominence given to the concept of 'inclusive growth'. This is viewed as an essential complement to the strong market orientation and globalizing thrust imparted in the planning models. Market based faster economic growth need not be inclusive, in fact markets function efficiently by systematically excluding entire population segments which for various reasons are unable to produce, sell and buy into the market or do so profitably. Efficient markets seek creditable participants, especially those who have the capital, organization, skills and access to varied resources and require that the people be well informed and knowledgeable to understand the market trends and anticipate the future. Accordingly, markets give reward and punishment. If the latter is to be avoided, the government must step in with policies and programmes to render assistance to the many who are systematically excluded by the market participants and may be even denied assured access to essential supplies of goods and services to ward off poverty and distress. The Eleventh Plan began under favourable circumstances, but the government recognized that 'far too many of our people still lack the basic requirements for a decent living in terms of nutrition standards, access to education and basic health, and also to other public services, such as, water supply and sewerage'.[18] Subjects which have received increased attention and higher allocation of financial resources, expressed as enhanced shares of GDP, are 'education and skill development' as one targeted area, 'health and nutrition' as another and 'poverty, livelihood security and rural development' as yet another. In each subset of inclusive planning the government has developed specific schemes, programmes or missions. In all the three areas the government was already active and understood better the nature of challenges and hurdles which government schemes faced, when they intruded into peoples' lives and somewhat unsettled the established patterns of living, in particular the ordering of social relationships, allocation of time of adults and children between work and home, especially in rural areas. In promoting education, the Tenth plan had made creditable progress. As a result it was possible to claim that the number of out-of-school children dropped sharply from 32 million to 7 million, though the drop-out rate was still unacceptably high. The Eleventh plan decided to attack the problems in education and the health and nutrition; but the latter was found to be far more complex and reached beyond the institutional health care facilities to include clean drinking water, sanitation, diet, hygiene and feeding practices, all of which significantly affect the health status of people. The government had already launched the national rural health mission in 2005, and augmented targets were announced in respect of each of the nine programmes. Most of them should have achieved the targeted goals by 2008, 2009 and 2010. However, actual progress will be known better when the mid-term appraisal is published. The third

18. *Eleventh Five Year Plan 2007–2012*, preface, p. vi.

area is still more complex and has a very wide reach. It is inseparable from development of agriculture, though greater emphasis is placed on watershed development schemes in the dry land areas and a special focus on the category of small farmers. The national rural employment guarantee programme forms part of the endeavour. There is another scheme for building rural roads to provide all-weather connectivity to all villages with a population of over 1000 in plains and over 500 in hilly areas.

At the end of three years it should have been possible to bring out a report on the outcomes of enhanced outlays. This has been done for a few schemes, but not for most of them for which progress is implied in higher allocation of funds. Genuine progress is reported for technology mission for horticulture in the north-east. 'Up to 2008–09 an additional 4.94 lac hectares were brought under horticulture cultivation (i.e. Fruits 3 lac hectares, vegetables 0.78 lac hectares and spices 0.62 lac hectares) including plantation crops, medicinal/aromatic plants and flowers, etc.'[19] Low performance is reported in Bharat Nirman schemes. In four years, 2005–09, the rural roads were built to cover 54.2 per cent of the targeted habitations, new connectivity in kms was at 58.4 per cent, electrification of villages at 59.9 per cent and irrigation at 65.2 per cent. The telephone connectivity was higher at 85.9 per cent, upgradation of through-routes in kms, at 79.9 per cent, and total number of houses at 115.0 per cent. For Bharat Nirman projects the government provided a substantial increase in funding, by 45 per cent in 2009-10 budget over the previous year. The importance of Bharat Nirman projects in generating rural employment is considerable. Together these form the flagship programme of the government. Moreover, the effect on physical achievement is direct. [20]

## §2. Agriculture and Agrarian Crisis

*21.* Agriculture is a non-growth segment of Indian economy. It is stagnating. In 2008–09 it grew by 1.1 per cent, compared to 5.0 per cent in 2007–08. The rate of growth of agriculture, forestry and fishing at factor cost (at 2004–05 prices) was 5.2 per cent in 2005–06, 3.7 per cent in 2006–07, 4.7 per cent in 2007–08, 1.6 per cent in 2008-09 and -0.2 per cent in 2009–10. The production of coarse cereals, other cereals, pulses, food grains and oilseeds declined in 2009-10 as compared to 2007–08 by varying margins. In all the five segments, total output declined. It was the same with sugarcane production.[21] The government has put the decline down to the partial failure of the monsoon and rain fall deficit. These are disquieting trends. The government has launched a national food security mission to raise food grains production by at least 20 million tonnes by the end of the Eleventh plan. However, at the end of three years of the plan the trends are broadly negative, so only exceptionally good monsoon seasons in the next two years will enable the farm sector to realize the target. Recognizing that while major policy reforms are needed in a wide range of farming, the key agent is the farmer who should be addressed in many ways

19. Planning Commission, *Annual Report 2009–10*, pp. 27–29.
20. *Ibid.*, Table 4.3.1.
21. *Economic Survey 2009–10*, Chapter on 'Agriculture and food management'.

and motivated to accept changes for his own good as well as for the progress of Indian agriculture. The government announced a national policy for farmers in 2007. Provisions have been made for the National Agricultural Bio-security system, on one hand, and a comprehensive national social security scheme for the farmers, on the other. These policy imitatives demonstrate that at the intellectual level the government recognizes that the problems are deeper, of long-term in nature and require an all-round approach and, further, that they may not yield to routine methods of the government, of allocation of larger funds in the hope that the delivery at the ground level will be commensurate with the policy objectives. However, at the end of three years it is not at all clear the extent to which the mission goals and long-term programmes have been operationalized at the state and district levels and how these are being delivered.

*22.* Farmers, hence agriculture, suffer most from climatic woes. The irony is that the farmers' distress has increased, while the overall economy is on a high growth trajectory. This has widened the schism between agriculture and industry, also between rural and urban economies. The notable facts are: (i) with rising population the size of agricultural holdings is declining; about 82 per cent of farm holdings are too small for the subsistence of households; (ii) about 40 per cent of farmers are looking for an exit from farming; there has been a steady erosion of profitability in agriculture; (iii) in some areas, such as Rajasthan, the frequency of droughts has increased; in other areas receding water tables have curtailed availability of water for farming; in the irrigated areas serious problems of water logging and soil salinity have become endemic; (iv) rain fed agriculture comprises almost 60 per cent of the total cultivated area; rains are often erratic and produce unstable farm production; crop failures are frequent and lead to increased farmer distress; most cases of farmers suicide occur in drought-prone, rain-fed areas; the decline in rain-fed agriculture has prominently contributed to deceleration in agricultural growth and stagnation in output and investment. There are associated problems of insufficiency of credit availability at official interest rates, the continued dependence on the local money lender-cum-trader and increase in indebtedness. Farmers are unable to repay loans and forfeit claims on fresh loans from cooperative credit societies and banks, resulting in a vicious circle. To prevent extreme distress the government has announced schemes of cancellation of existing debts and provided cash grants. But it is very hard for marginal farmers to qualify for institutional credit because bad weather, failed inputs and poor crops occur too often. In large parts of India the cooperative credit system has collapsed. The problem is that the more input-intensive and diversified agriculture becomes, the heavier is the burden of indebtedness, indeed, there is greater dependence on the money lender though he may charge interest at 20-25 per cent or higher. The fear is that as climatic conditions worsen, or become less predictable, the agrarian crisis may also deepen.

## §3. Labour Force Unemployment

*23.* Data on labour force are generated by the NSS (national sample survey) organization at periodic intervals. It takes several years for publication, so current statistics usually refer to the most recent NSS, which at present is 2004–05. The NSS population data produce an under-count which lowers the size of labour force. Therefore, it is revised upwards to correspond to the census total. This may still leave out illegal immigrants who may or may not be included in either of the two counts, but engage in work. Hence the figures of labour force are approximate totals which are deemed to rise at the same rate as the population, while the labour participation rate is treated as given. People in the prime-age group, 15–59, and engaged in work or looking for it, are members of the labour force. In 2004–05 there were 413 million persons in the labour force in India. Given the demographic trends, the labour force is expected to grow faster over the decade than the population, which is increasing at a lower rate. It is estimated that over the next decade about 12 million persons will join the labour force every year. This may be higher, if more women decide to join the work force. Therefore, in 2010–11 the overall magnitude of the labour force may be around 485–500 million. Two factors may lower the total. One is withdrawal of some prime-age participants to obtain more education and the other is lower participation rates of women, also the discouraged people who are unable to find work. In 2004, more than a quarter of all workers worked in poverty, while an overwhelming majority of about 90 per cent worked in low productivity jobs. Not all the entrants to the work force will look for jobs, some will work as self-employed persons. Yet it may be assumed that about 8-9 million new entrants will look for jobs. In 2004-05 about 335 million persons worked in the informal or the unorganized sectors. These dominate the job markets and it is expected that the further growth of informal sectors will provide employment opportunities to most of the jobseekers.

*24.* The NSS employs several definitions of 'workers' or labour force participants. The most important is the term, 'usual principal status workers', which refers to the principal activity in the last 365 days in which the person was either engaged or looking for work. To this category may be added the 'subsidiary status workers', for which work was not a principal activity in the last 365 days but in which a person was employed or engaged for at least some time. Total employment is the sum of the two and described as UPSS workers. It includes paid or wage employment as well as unpaid work in house hold enterprises and casual workers. The sub-class of household work includes people who failed to find paid employment and instead chose to work at home to make a living. This could be a form of disguised unemployment or under-employment, but its statistical magnitude is a matter of guess work due to paucity of information in the NSS data. In the UPSS class of labour force of 412.9 million persons in 2004–05, males were 280.4 million and females 132.5 million. Open unemployment at 2.8 per cent refers to those UPS workers who spent more than six months looking for work and could not find it. This is long-term unemployment. Current unemployment should be based on yet another definition, the 'current weekly activity' status of a person, which uses the reference period of seven days. A person is employed as CWA worker if he worked for at least one hour on at least one day in the preceding week. There is also the 'current daily activity' status, which refers to employment as work for at least four hours on any day in the week in which the survey was done. The CWS unemployment was at 5 per cent, while the CDS unemployment was at 8.3 per cent. The last two are better indicators of the scale of unemployment, though the deemed employment by any of the aforesaid definitions includes varying margins of under-employment. Employed persons are classified as self employed, casual labourers and regular employees. Unemployment is highest among casual labourers; it is more among females than males. Long-term open unemployment is high among the youth, the better educated and in urban areas. 'Youth in the 15-29 age group account for an overwhelming proportion (over 80 per cent) of unemployed on the UPS status. This may in part be related to poverty.'[22]

## §4. Scope of Labour Market Intervention

*25.* There is a popular demand that the government should not be content with collecting and reporting data on unemployment but should be willing to intervene in labour markets to expand employment opportunities and reduce the duration of periods of unemployment. A notable feature of structure of unemployment is that the UPS data which capture long-term unemployment show that in urban areas (5.3 per cent) it is more than twice as high as in rural areas (2.5 per cent). Though the associated causes and demographic characteristics are not known, it is probably a reflection of migration of the predominantly illiterate and poor people from rural to urban areas, where their low employability is in stark focus. If at all it is possible to make a policy intervention to provide them direct support and redress, it would be necessary to have a reliable data set to work on and determine the administrative aspects of intervention. The difference between CWS measures (3.9 per cent) in rural areas and 6.0 per cent in urban areas and the UPS may be a truer indicator of intermittent unemployment. The CWS data show large differences between the rural and urban areas. In the latter intermittent unemployment is commonly observed among job seekers. By comparison, the CDS data show the rural (8.2 per cent) and urban (8.3 per cent) to be about equal. 'It captures the unemployed days of the chronically unemployed, the unemployed days of the usually employed who become intermittently unemployed during the reference week and unemployed days of those classified as employed according to the criterion of current weekly status.'[23] The government can make a large contribution in providing help to the intermittently unemployed and casual workers by greatly strengthening the labour market information system and the institution of employment exchanges in all urban areas. The government may also recognize that there are severe constraints on growth of urban population; specially the metropolitan cities which generate output and employment to disproportionate degrees. Severe limits need to be placed on further growth of employment based economic activities in large cities. So the desired policy option may be to discourage job seeking rural migrants into the large cities and instead encourage smoother and faster exits to other towns by promoting their development.

---

22. The World Bank, *India's Employment Challenge, Creating Jobs, Helping Workers*. New Delhi, OUP – World Bank, 2010, Ch. 1; quote on p. 42.
23. *Economic Survey 2009–10*, OUP, 2010, p. 275.

## §5. The National Rural Employment Guarantee Scheme (NREGS)

*26.* In India public works have been associated with famine relief. In the post-independence period public works began to feature more prominently with the Fifth and the Sixth Five-year Plans which aimed at reaching out to the neglected rural areas for building assets of economic value and provide employment. In the 1990s another policy shift took place to fight poverty and hunger with 'food for works' and related programmes. Experience of a decade showed that progress was minimal, partly due to underfunding and for the rest due to the leakages and poor delivery. Dependence on contractors emerged as a prime factor in the malpractices connected with poverty relief. The UPA government made a complete break with the past practices and decided to launch a scheme which conferred a right to work on fixed wages upon the beneficiaries as a government administered and financed activity free from any involvement of contractors. The National Rural Employment Guarantee Act, 2005 provides for not less than 100 days of employment per year at the notified agricultural minimum wage in the state for everyone who asks for it. Two ongoing programmes were subsumed in it. The scheme addressed chronic poverty associated with drought, deforestation and soil erosion and hoped to enhance the livelihood security of people. Beneficiaries have to volunteer to do unskilled work in the rural areas. By 2010 the scheme should have reached implementation stage in 600 districts and financed entirely by the Centre. In the first 18 months of its implementation, 66 million rural workers were issued job cards, and around 20 million persons were provided with work. In 2007–08 25.7 million households were provided wage employment. The labour market effect of the NREGS may be considerable. First, the scheme enforces the agricultural minimum wage and may produce a levelling up effect on rural wages. Second, it should reduce distress migration from rural areas in search of livelihood. Third, if the scheme succeeds in creating durable economic assets it should directly impact poverty and at least scale down the level of rural destitution. These expectations may have to be modified in view of reported high variability across states. Corruption at local levels will surely reduce the worth of the scheme for the targeted poor households and weaken its overall impact.

## §6. Employment in the Organized Sector

*27.* Combined public and private sectors employment declined between 1994 and 2005. In this period the government was keen on pressing on the public sector enterprises for greater efficiency and promoted the VRS and other incentives. The government was serious in turning around the many over-manned sick undertakings which regularly turned in losses and needed fiscal subventions to pay wage bills. The UPA government put an end to the drive, partly because the organized labour market was not creating new jobs even at the rate at which job losses had occurred. Though fresh jobs were being created in the private sector, the overall unemployment level rose. This was a disquieting development. The NSS data show that between 1993–94 and 2004–05, the total work force increased from 313.93 million to 384.91 million and the share of manufacturing in it rose from 11.10 per cent to

90 per cent. This is inclusive of rural industries and very small, small and .. dium size urban industries, or the unorganized sector. However, the unorganized sector is very different from the modern manufacturing and related industries. Job destruction in the modern sector is consistent with some growth in the former. Another set of data show that public sector employment peaked at 19.59 million in 1997 which dropped to about 18.00 million in 2005. By comparison, employment in private sector peaked at 8.75 million in 1998, which declined somewhat to 8.45 million in 2005. The arrival of the market economy created pressures for technological upgradation and higher productivity. As product market competition increased, industrialists had to shed the complacency and lethargy which the prolonged regime of import substitution and stifling controls had produced. The multinational companies which had arrived earlier as technical and business collaborators changed their stance and re-entered India as competitors with new products and new lines of production. Job destruction followed in established concerns. Most of the employment growth took place outside the organized sector, rising from 6 per cent to 9 per cent of total employment. Real wages fell due to excess supply of job seekers, while in the organized sector real wages rose following growth in productivity and profits.[24]

## §7. Globalized Growth Perspective

*28.* The Indian economy responded very well to the exposure to market pressures and freer investment. It took successive governments about 10–11 years to overcome objections, gather courage to reduce tariffs, dismantle the controls apparatus and lower bars on foreign investment. Thereafter the economy picked up steam while a favourable international environment spurred fresh investment. Beginning with 2003–04 GDP (at 1999–2000 prices) took off with 8.5 per cent in 2006–07 and 9.6 per cent in 2007–08, then dropped to 6.6 per cent in 2008–09. The set back was caused by a sharp global downturn in 2008. However, the economy recovered fast and has resumed to grow and in 2010–11 it may show acceleration again. Gross fixed capital formation (at 1999–2000) prices was at the same level in 2002–03 as in the previous five years, at 23.8 per cent of GDP, but it picked up the pace to reach 25.0 per cent in 2003–04, 28.4 per cent in 2004–05 and in 2005–06, 31.0 per cent in 2006–07, 32.5 per cent in 2006–07 and 34.0 per cent in 2007–08. Thereafter it declined by about 2.4 per cent, mostly in the private corporate sector in which the decline may be around 3.9 per cent. This was partly made up by the household sector where it rose by 0.7 per cent. Investment is no doubt the principal growth driver, but produces better results if labour productivity rises alongside. A better utilization of capital stock, even as capital intensity rises, would depend partly upon the levels of buoyancy in product markets, including export demand, and in part on labour productivity. These would lower the capital-output rates and raise the growth rates of output. Labour is often seen as a reluctant contributor mainly because higher productivity is historically associated with job destruction. Exports

24. OECD Economic Surveys: *India, 2007*, pp. 46–48 and *Economic Survey 2007–08*, pp. 248–249 and statistical appendix, pp. A-52 and A-53.

rose at a sluggish pace of 9.6 per cent of GDP in 2003–04, but started to rise in 2004–05 at 27.2 per cent followed by a 17.6 per cent increase in 2005–06 and 31.1 per cent in 2006–07, then to a low of 2.1 per cent in 2007–08 to revive at 12.8 per cent in 2008–09 and turning negative along with imports in 2009-10. Imports have risen even faster producing adverse trade balance which was financed by invisibles and capital imports. High domestic demand sustained rising imports.[25]

## §8. World Trade and India's Vulnerability

### I. India in the World Economy

*29.* India takes part in world economy in three ways. One is export and import of goods and services to trading partners. This has been slowly building up after at least three decades of decline and stagnation. In 1990 Indian exports accounted for a mere 0.5 per cent of world exports. In 2007 the share rose to 1.1 per cent. Exports reflect India's contribution towards meeting world demand in specific products or group of products. In order of importance, these are rice (17.9 per cent), spices (15.3 per cent), pearls, precious and semi-precious stones (13.3 per cent), iron ore and concentrates (11.6 per cent), tea and mate (8.6 per cent) and manufacture of leather or of composition leather (4.5 per cent). Textile yarn, fabrics and woven fabrics other than cotton or man-made fibres accounted for 4.0 per cent each. Together these represented 21.9 per cent of total exports. The importance of Indian tea in the world market has shown a steady decline over 40 years. In 1990 Indian tea accounted for 22.1 per cent of world demand. But as tea consumption rose, Indian exports failed to grow and their share declined. The exports depict the Indian economy as primarily a producer of agricultural, plantation and mineral products. Metal based manufactures are 4.0 per cent of world trade; apparel and clothing which include non-mill production added up to 2.8 per cent.[26] These essentially show the weak thrust of industrialization both pre-reform as well as post-reform. The second factor pertains to inflow and outflow of capital including foreign assistance and commercial borrowings. In 1990-91 total net foreign investment was only $103 million. In 2007-08 it rose to $ 43.326 billion. Inflows were $271.122 billion and outflows at $227.796 billion. In the next three years both declined due to world-wide downturn. By comparison external assistance has steadily declined, though in 2007-08 it was still at $2.114 billion. Commercial borrowings and repayments have risen from $3.329 billion in 1990-91 to $38.538 billion (net). Both inflows and outflows are quite large, being $77.951 billion and $39.413 billion in 2007–08. These too have sought lower levels.[27] The third factor is the movement of human resources, the entrepreneurial, skilled and other workers as well as the foreign travel. Export of services has risen faster than merchandise exports; though with the decline in world demand these have decelerated. In 2008 Indian export of computer and information

25. *Economic Survey 2008–09*, pp. 4–5 and A-4 and 2009–10, pp. 3–7.
26. *Economic Survey, 2009–10*, Table 7.5, pp. A102–103.
27. *Ibid.*, Table 6.2, pp. A72–73.

services accounted for 18 per cent of world exports/imports. All other services had a single digit share.[28]

## II. Indian Imports

*30.* Imports by India usually exceed exports. The volume of imports has risen, from $24.075 billion in 1990–91 to $251.654 billion in 2007–08 and exceeded $300 billion in 2008-09. As a result of excess of imports over exports, India's trade balance has shown a negative sign in every year in the last 30 years. From 2003–04 onwards in every year imports have risen faster than exports. In 2007–08 POL (petroleum oil lubricants) formed 31.6 per cent of total imports, capital goods 19.5 per cent and electric goods 8.0 per cent. These vary from year to year. In this respect the composition of imports has not changed significantly as compared to 1990–91. Despite self-sufficiency in food grains India imported six times more cereals and cereal preparations in 2007–08 (1848.000 tons) than in 1990–91 (308.30 tons). India does not grow all the food grains, especially pulses, that it needs to feed its population. Given the importance of varied imports it may be a notable fact that the single largest share in 2008–09 at 10.7 per cent was that of China, followed by UAE with a share of 7.8 per cent and USA of 6.1 per cent. In 2008-09, for some countries India's imports shrank so fast that their share fell to 0.0 per cent; the number of such trading countries was over 100. The same fate befell India's exports. The number is just below 100. Most of these countries exported to and imported from India in small quantities. These dismal statistics show the low reach of India's external trade with a large number of countries, also its volatile trait in the midst of fluctuating world trade.

## III. Exposure to World Prices

*31.* At present Indian economy is more exposed to world prices and financial flows than ever before. To cite trade related data, merchandise exports on a BOP basis posted a decline of 27.0 per cent in H1 (April-September 2009) of 2009–10 as against a growth of 48.1 per cent of the corresponding period of the previous year. Import payments declined by 20.6 per cent during April–September 2009 as against a sharp increase of 51.0 per cent in the corresponding period of the previous year. The decline in imports is mainly attributed to the base effect as well as the decline in oil prices.[29]

As the global recession deepened, exports fell at an accelerating pace. However, in December 2009 exports recovered. Exports include the services sector. Inclusive of services, like the IT services, the ratio of trade to GDP rose to 47 per cent in 2007–08. Volatility in trade renders the services sector highly vulnerable to fluctuations in the world economy. It is the same with movement of finance capital. In 2007–08 the capital inflows were at 9.3 per cent of GDP, these declined to

---

28. *Ibid.*, pp. 164–167.
29. *Economic Survey, 2009–10*, p. 13

1.8 per cent of GDP in 2008–09. Portfolio investment in 2008–09 show a negative sign–14.030 billion. This was completely reversed in April–Sept 2009, when the level rose to (net) $17.94 billion. Thanks to foreign exchange reserves of over $200.8 billion in 2008-09, this fluctuation was smoothly handled. As a result, in April-Sept 2009, foreign exchange reserves dipped by $9.533 billion. The reserves have exhibited considerable resiliency largely due to India's continued attractiveness as a destination for foreign capital.[30] The main problem India faces is the relatively low level of infrastructure which obstructs the direct productive employment of capital. On the other hand, the main task the monetary authorities face is to choose between the options of rupee appreciation and increased liquidity in the economy. The former slows exports growth, even as the rupee exchange rate would turn more volatile with the movement of foreign capital. The latter option, which is preferred, augments liquidity and fuels the inflation. Excess liquidity is partly neutralized by the trade deficits which are a normal occurrence in India. What affects the people most is the transmission of foreign fuel prices via higher retail prices of petrol, diesel, kerosene and petroleum lubricants to the general price level. There is very little the government can do to protect the standard of living of common people, if international prices of crude oil rise to abnormal levels, since Indian economy is heavily dependent on oil imports. In this respect the only option is to step up the pace of oil exploration wherever Indian presence is welcome.

30. *Ibid.*, Table 6.2, p. 126.

## Chapter 4. Political and Administrative Systems

*32.* India's political system derives its legitimacy from the Constitution, which is federal and unitary at the same time. Its basic design is federal but it provides for a strong centre and is subject to the overriding criteria of normalcy in centre–state relations and common acceptance of the implied rules of political conduct on the part of all the principal actors who might occupy the political space. Federal principles may be encouraged if the state government has the maturity to conduct its affairs within the four corners of the constitution and no state embarks upon the totally unacceptable path of breaking loose from the Union, or treading upon the toes of the centre in such matters as fall within the spheres of defence, foreign policy, communication, or any established national policy that is binding on all states. However, political maturity is not a deemed principle of the Constitution and it cannot be assumed to exist in every situation. Moreover, circumstances may arise in which states would by and large prefer to take centralized decisions though still enjoying delegated powers of implementation and administration. Taxation, distribution of revenue among the states, the broad frameworks of industrial policy, foreign capital, technology imports, labour policy, river water, forests, mineral wealth and protection of environment are among the obvious list of subjects on which the central government, acting through Parliament, may be considered as the appropriate constitutional agency for formulating policies. These would no doubt be backed by requisite enactments for enforcement, though even in respect of these subjects there may exist considerable scope for sharing of burdens and delegation of duties. On the other hand, if the state-level political leadership is found to be weak on bonafides and irresolute on national commitment, it would not matter much if it enjoyed considerable popular support within the state, or elsewhere, because the centre would have to intervene; in extreme cases it may even dismiss the state government and impose direct rule. It is on such occasions that the unitary principle comes into force and the overriding powers of the centre become apparent. However, both the federal and the unitary principles of the constitution must operate within the bounded parameters of the codified rules of parliamentary procedures, and rulings of the Supreme Court. If the unitary principle is extended too far, or in particular cases stretched to the limit by the government, it is permissible to mount the challenge in parliament as well as in the Supreme Court of India, and if it is successful, the decision found to be wrong is liable to be set aside or reversed.

*33.* There are several reasons for believing that the Indian Constitution can be stretched to adapt to unforeseen demands made upon it either by regional 'nationalism', or by the weak and the poor for greater justice. First, the Constitution is highly responsive to the 'public opinion' as articulated in the legislatures and outside. This has enabled the Supreme Court to adapt its judicial pronouncements so as to maintain reasonable accord with the progressive ideas of the government with only a minimum of friction. Second, the procedure for amending the Constitution is reasonably simple and can be put through if the party seeking it enjoys the support of a majority of the members in each house of parliament. The provisions relating to the federal system would, in addition, require ratification by a half of the state legislatures. Third, the constitution has made special provisions for dealing with problem of special nature. These range from the special political status of Jammu and Kashmir state, to the safeguards for minorities, backward classes, scheduled castes and tribes, to the procedure for allocation of financial resources between the centre and the states, and settlement of interstate disputes on river waters, etc. In principle, practically all disputes of federal nature can be resolved either within the existing constitutional machinery or by amending the constitution. Fourth, the Constitution does not pre-empt any ideology, nor does it block any political remedy to even the most persistent socio-economic problems, provided the political parties seeking them can secure sufficient electoral support to obtain a majority in Parliament. However, the Constitution has not been put to as much stress, nor stretched as hard as in the continuing political turmoil in several north-eastern states of India on the issues of citizenship, right to vote and residence of Bangladesh refugees and illegal immigrants, and the prior right of indigenous people to preserve their cultural identity and political dominance within the Indian union, as well as the right to protect their societies from deep encroachment, either by the Bangladeshi Muslim immigrants, or other outsiders who may be Indian migrants or settlers. The government has sent political signals that a new endeavour could be made provided armed confrontations are ended.

*34.* The administrative machinery of the government is a creation of the Constitution. The Constitution has entrusted 97 subjects to the central government and also all residual subjects that are not explicitly allotted to either the centre or the states. Even in the state sphere, the centre can legislate if the upper house (the *Rajya Sabha*), adopts a resolution to this effect. Moreover, during a national emergency, the centre can enact on any matter included in either the concurrent or the state list. The Constitution also empowers the centre to create new all-India services to administer any subject provided the *Rajya Sabha* favours the move with a resolution passed with a two-thirds majority. Another extraordinary feature of the Indian system is that the governor of a state may withhold assent to a Bill passed by the state legislature for the consideration of the President who, on the advice of the central government, may veto it. The governor may also return a Bill to the legislature with a message to reconsider it, but he cannot withhold assent, if with or without amendment the Bill is passed again. It is further provided that the governor shall not assent to any Bill which derogates from the powers of the High Court and endangers its position, reserving it for the consideration of the President. In every such case, reservation is obligatory; in other cases this is the alternative to assenting the Bill or refusing it. The governor enjoys discretion in this respect.

*35.* The signs of disarray in the institutions of governance of the country are matters of daily observance. The political system is under a great strain and the noticeable deterioration in the quality of political institutions is often discussed in public. There is the general phenomenon of growing class and caste conflicts which the political system is unable to resolve. These conflicts no doubt centre around deeper issues connected with sharing of political power and gains of economic development. The groups which are able to control power may also acquire grater access over economic resources and secure higher gains from the schemes of economic development. The poor have been mobilized but usually along caste and communal lines; and their political participation has frequently taken the form of breaking up of established political parties along narrow sectional lines. Several poor-centred parties have also emerged directly from the grass roots. As a result there are a large number of small parties none of which might be able to secure a majority in the state assemblies or Parliament and form a stable government. Non-governance follows, and the net outcome is the general decline in the moral authority of the political system. To sum up:

> this 'crisis of governability' takes multiple forms: unstable government, frequent elections and changes of political moods, inability to accommodate and reconcile contending demands and needs of different social groups and classes, weakening of law and order, growing civil discord and disturbance, sometimes reaching the proportions of insurgency, communal violence, increasing recourse of people to violent and extra- constitution agitations, growing corruption, and above all, the failure of the governments at the Centre and the states to implement their policies or to provide effective governance.

None the less, the basic resilience of India's democratic polity is not in question mainly because it is founded on a strong and flexible Constitution which can adapt to changing conditions. But the constitutional machinery can only work well and serve India's large and culturally and ethnically a very heterogeneous population, provided each limb, viz. the legislature, the executive and the judiciary, works reasonably well and functions within its carefully demarcated boundaries. This is not happening. Parliament is clearly on the downslide, and this is not due to any clever or mischievous government design to usurp power for the executive. Increasingly, it is due to the leaders of the numerous political parties which are represented there who have contributed to it by their irresponsible conduct, and treating Parliament as a forum for contentious and noisy demonstrations. The government proposes Bills but they cannot be enacted because for one reason or other the work of Parliament is stalled by agitational noises. On the other hand, India's higher courts are more active than ever before in giving directions to the governments to implement laws and to carry out their duties as per the provisions of the Constitution. But the judiciary at present is overloaded with work and there are enormous delays. The bureaucracy is unavoidably blamed for everything that goes wrong, but it appears to be too resistant to reform, and would rather not perform the cast iron role it once very ably discharged under the colonial administration; the other option is to play safe.[31]

*36.* Politics in India seems to have developed into a new phase, of which the most significant political characteristic is the entry of masses into the political space, with their demands, slogans and leaders seeking power for its own sake, or for control over the state machinery because of the belief that without it nothing can be achieved. National parties have responded by advancing populist policies and rebuilding their electoral bases by offering tickets to politicians with credible vote banks, though these may be formed of narrow caste, communal or ethnic lines. The politically aware electorate now expects their elected representatives to look after

---

31. Bipan Chandra *et al.*, *India After Independence*, Viking, 1999, Ch. 37, p. 47.

their constituencies, favour their factions, help their particular castes or communities and act out such roles as might be politically expedient in order to live up to their expectations. But the strategic change in the economic policy that commenced in 1991 has altered much, particularly the developmental role of the government and the scope of schemes that could be publicly funded. The liberalization of the economy, and its further progress towards globalization, are predicated upon slow downsizing of the role of the state and its ability to directly allocate resources among competing ends. In the last two decades the market mechanism has worked to a remarkable degree in favour of the educated urban classes, most of whom had been earlier edged out of the political process. There is an inherent contradiction between the politics of masses and the market driven economy which is critically dependent on the highly educated manpower and skilled workforce for its efficient functioning. Masses may participate in the market economy, or be excluded by it, depending upon their productive capacity, purchasing power and resilience. They cannot politically bend it to serve them. The contemporary political system has to serve two masters with contentious claims on scarce resources. If the political system cannot deliver the economic fruits to the various interests, classes and constituencies, the dissatisfied electorate and the large number of political parties which might become economically disenfranchised may react in unpredictable ways. The short-run response on the part of *Bhartiya Janata* Party (BJP) in 1998 and 1999 elections was to create political platforms of conglomerate coalitions, such as the NDA, and run the government as well as possible. The Congress has followed it with a similar structure and created the UPA. However, these alliances may reflect either the spirit of political accommodation on the part of some parties, or rank opportunism among others, or alternating combinations of both statesmanship and the art of sheer stratagem driving politics – it is difficult to tell. There is no doubt that the cabinet form of government has suffered from the coalition structure. Instances have come to light of some cabinet ministers deciding on policy matters ignoring the Prime Minister's advice. In 2010 the minister in charge of the communications portfolio pursued a preferred policy on a major issue, though the Prime Minister had asked him to change course. He persisted and had to relinquish the portfolio and leave the government on charges of corruption. The ex-cabinet minister, A. Raja of the DMK, is currently in detention and facing an investigation which may lead to his conviction.

## §1. Coalition Governments

*37.* The Congress supremacy finally ended in 1989 with the defeat of Rajiv Gandhi in the parliamentary election. Between 1989 and 2009 seven parliamentary elections have been held, while ten governments have been formed with eight prime ministers. Instability has become a common feature of political governance. Only three Parliaments have completed their full term of five years. Most coalitional parties are regional or sub regional in size with very small following in the electorate, but are still able to acquire a voice in coalition governments, due to the failure of the two leading national parties, viz. Congress and BJP to muster sufficient support from the electorate to secure a majority in Parliament. Yet these bigger national parties have claimed the right to rule by securing the support of regional parties. Coalition governments reflect the play of win-win game for both the national and smaller coalition partners. They share power, but the country in not the gainer; principles have been downgraded and a premium put on the unprincipled, opportunistic politics of convenience. Governance has suffered as coalition partners at first demonstrate loyalty and unreserved acceptance of the leadership of the Prime Minister, then brazenly cross the floor and look for greener pastures. There are also unresolved political contradictions. Often parties in coalition at the centre are bitter rivals in state assemblies' elections. For the state-based parties national political agenda is subservient to the compulsions of state politics. Moreover, on occasions, the leading coalition parties are confronted with terms of continued support which are either violative of laws or the accepted precepts of constitutional democracy. If these are unacceptable, the grieving partner may quit the coalition, destabilizing the government and with it the entire edifice of governance. This happened to the first NDA government in 1999. The only remedy is to dissolve the Parliament and call a fresh election. There is no assurance that at the end of it a more stable government will emerge. If this is to be avoided, the besieged Prime Minister must burn his time and energy in winning new supporters, or find some unprincipled remedy for the threatened instability. Some such game of very dubious political morality was played out in 2008 in which the UPA government won the no confidence vote.

## §2. Menace of Corruption

*38.* India has earned world notoriety as a corruption ridden country. The political system employs very large sums of money in running political parties, organizing rallies and demonstrations and contesting elections. Besides key political leaders have developed the habit of acquiring private wealth by tapping political funds, often at the source as commissions, or bribes or kickbacks. Party organizations in turn acquire the habit of politico-economic dependence on the leaders for financial support and the wherewithal at critical junctures. This can take institutionalized forms. Coalition parties demand portfolios with the cabinet rank in ministries which take decisions involving considerable financial stakes on the part of ambitious applicant businessmen. Ministerial corruption is either abetted or ignored by compliance oriented bureaucrats. A few join hands and facilitate the process, making helpful file notings and steer the path for the sordid moola collection. A deplorable game of corrupt practices and low standards of conduct is institutionalized and practised without fear of consequences. A particularly nasty aspect of this dirty and slimy practice is the public brazenness of politicians in casting slanderous accusations at rival political parties, implying that not just the ruling politicians but their predecessors in office and several others in office elsewhere in the country are no less foul and corrupt. The politics of engaging in loud slanging matches is not without a purpose. This is to stir up sufficient dust in the public domain to cloud the vision, distract attention and at the end of it, delay investigations, obfuscate findings, or more systematically transfer top officials, demoralize the team of investigators and so damage the enquiry in various ways that either the government will be persuaded not to press with the charges in court, or if forced to do so will ensure a failed, hopeless verdict. A more effective procedure is to obstruct the first essential step, viz. taking cognizance of a crime by an official agency, like the CBI which functions directly under the Prime Minister and will do only as much or as fast or with as much thoroughness as may be directed to do. It may also be possible to indefinitely prolong investigations, leave major gaps in collecting evidence and so complete the process that either there is no case made out against the accused ministers and officials or the court will find insufficient evidence to sustain the charge and let the arraigned persons go free. The corrupt politician would have demonstrated that he had acted within law and in conformity with the policy of the government and he was guilt free and could cast off the stigma of any wrong doing.

*39.* In 2010 massive corruption in the central Communications Ministry and the Commonwealth Games dwarfed all previous debates on the issue of corruption and systemically carried out malpractices in public view, directly under the government umbrella. Corruption charges against the minister, A. Raja, representing the DMK party of Tamilnadu in the UPA coalition, received added credibility due to the appointment of P.J. Thomas as the Chief Vigilance Commissioner against strong objections voiced by the opposition on the ground that he was already under a cloud of suspicion on corruption charges as a senior government official. Further it was found that a PR lobbyist, Nira Radia, was acting on behalf of her big corporate clients to influence key political appointments and policy related decisions. A. Raja was the preferred choice and his appointment as the cabinet minister with the communication portfolio had made the corporate bosses happy. These nasty facts entered the public domain with the leakage of Nira Radia tapes by a government agency which had been secretly recording them. The tapes made the shocking revelation that there were any number of political fixers in the Congress as well as the BJP and much that was done in important economic ministries could be manipulated to the advantage of favoured businessmen and their corporate entities. A. Raja's wrong doings were fully exposed by the independent government agency, the Comptroller and Auditor General of India which had audited the Department of Telecommunications' actions in awarding rights to mobile spectrum to various applicants for a price. The electromagnetic spectrum, or radio frequencies in airwaves, have become increasingly scarce and the demand far exceeds the supply. The CAG report cast huge allegations of wrong doings against the DOT, hence the minister in charge, specially for under-pricing spectrum licences. The CAG accused the minister for causing the government losses aggregating to the collosal sum of Rs 176,645 crore by the manipulated policy of first come first served and at 2001 prices. A particularly damaging aspect of wrongdoing was that the newly appointed CVC, P.J. Thomas, was earlier the secretary of the DOT.[32] The Supreme Court decided to examine the legal validity of his appointment and found it terribly wanting on the constitutionally vital principle of unimpeachable integrity, as a

32. See Paranjoy Guha Thakurta and Akshat Kaushal, 'Underbelly of the great Indian telecom revolution' *Economic and Political Weekly*, 4 December, 2010; also the editorial, 'Phone a Friend. Telecom Deregulation has led to a cozying up of government with the private sector, fuelling corruptions', p. 8 and Sukumar Muralidharan, 'Media: Stenographer to Power', pp. 10–14.

qualification on which the government could not compromise without undermining the constitutional edifice of governance. The government had admitted before the court that such a standard of integrity was no longer required and the primary qualification was acceptability to the government. The Supreme Court rejected the government's position and removed Thomas from the post. The Prime Minister accepted the judgment and admitted to being misled by his juniors in the council of ministers.

*40.* India has suffered huge losses due to prevalence of corrupt practices. *Business India* carried the following damaging information on money illegally taken out of India:

> Amount of money siphoned out of India primarily for tax evasion between 1948 and 2008, in billion dollars: 462.
>
> Ratio of illegal outflows between 1948 and 2008 to that of India's external debt as of end-2008, 2:1.[33]

What was done by A. Raja and his compliant officials in the DOT was in keeping with the sordid tradition of scams which have repeatedly occurred since India chose to liberalize the economy. A. Raja went farthest in disregarding policy norms in the DOT scam. He ignored the advice of the Prime Minister, the Finance Minister and the Law Minister on the advisability of auctioning of 2G spectrums. He flouted the cardinal parliamentary principal of collective responsibility of the Cabinet and respecting the Prime Minister's leadership in policy making and important decisions.[34] Instead he issued 122 new telecom licences in 2008 at the much lower 2001 prices. This may not damage the industry which is currently valued at Rs 120,000 crore with a subscriber base of 700 million. It has attracted foreign direct investment of $9 billion in the last decade and more was expected. However, the Raja scam has raised doubts on India's credibility and investors may be wary of entering the industry, though the market remains attractive. The Prime Minister's extreme reluctance in ordering the probe made the scam murkier and produced an opposition backlash resulting in total paralysis of Parliament in December 2010. Demanding a parliamentary probe into the DOT and two other scams, which broke out at about the same time, the opposition prevented the government from conducting any legislative business. A large part of the blame is cast on the unprincipled conduct of the DMK which has emerged as a party in the scam. Admittedly India suffers from an ethical deficit.

## §3. New Entrants in Indian Politics

*41.* Corporate India has emerged as an important player in politics taking advantage of liberalized policies and reduced say of the government in key economic decisions. The government still holds considerable power over allocation of scarce

33. *Business India*, 29 November – 12 December 2010, p. 18.
34. *Ibid.*, pp. 64–68.

resources wherein still lie important rent earning possibilities for the early participants. Corporate leaders have learnt to swing decisions favouring a few and denying others by encouraging obviously non-transparent policies and influencing ministerial decisions by the lure of money. Government is usually the loser as the unethical nexus formed between a select group of businessmen, the ruling politicians and the top echelons of bureaucracy make unholy decisions depriving it of revenue and the public of funds which could be spent on raising living conditions. Rent seeking corporates would like to take advantage of the delegation of power to the market to enhance the market valuation of their scrip's and corporate assets, once a naturally scarce resource has come into their possession.[35] Mining rights are one such resource which have given rise to several scams involving state level politicians, even chief ministers. The Karnataka government is in the limelight on this question. Huge fortunes are reported to have been made around mining and export of ores in Karnataka. Another major entrant to politics at the state level is the growing presence of the NRI factor (non-resident Indians), in state elections, and government formation. There are around 25 million Indians serving or doing business in about 130 countries. They have looked for a role in domestic politics and have been welcomed by several state governments. The governments want to attract the NRI money. The Gujarat government held a vibrant Gujarat summit in 2009 to attract Gujarati NRI's capital in industrial ventures in the state, especially in the SEZs. The state government has set up a separate ministry to attend to the needs of the diaspora Guajarati community. In 2006, according to one estimate, there were 800,000 NRI accounts in Gujarat totaling about $40 billion. Andhra Pradesh and the Punjab are the two other states in which the governments appear to be willing to accept NRI participation in elections and politics as well as investment related decisions. The NRI's are interested in promoting second generation reforms and cleaner politics. The regional diaspora is seen to be keen on organizing itself around regional parties and seeking closer linkages.[36]

## §4. Crisis of Governability and Anti-state Insurgencies

*42.* The state system is most organized at the centre, less at state levels though with wide variability among the states and least at the lowest levels. In many parts of rural India the state may not be present or visible at all. Connecting roads may be either non-existent or in such poor state of repairs as to be impassable through most of the year, the nearest police post at a considerable distance and mostly undermanned. Officials and the police may arrive in far-off villages from time to time to carry out routine inspections and other official tasks, but finding precious little time to listen to villagers' woes or attend to them. The core feature of the crisis is administrative non-governance, though electoral politics has enabled more voices to ask

35. Ajay K. Mehra (ed.) *Emerging Trends in Indian Politics: the 15th. General Election*, New Delhi, Routledge, 2010 article by Jyoti Srivastava, 'Contemporary Indian politics and the Corporate Sector'; article by Girijesh Pant, 'Diaspora in Indian Politics: Issues before the 15th. General Election'.
36. Srivastava, 'Contemporary Indian Politics', and Pant, 'Diaspora in Indian Politics'.

for justice against the perceived wrongs by the identified power wielding wrongdoers in the rural society, who are so well integrated in the politico-economic system that they cannot be touched. Over a period of time, the socio-political distance between the rulers and the masses has increased and produced crisis conditions. Political parties have obviously ceased to perform mediating roles. The Naxalite movement, born in north Bengal in the tribal Nexalbari area in 1967 around a peasant movement had been persecuted and its leaders incarcerated or killed by the police. It suffered a decline and at one point was virtually written off as a finished revolutionary movement. It broke up into feuding Marxist ideologues who gave varying interpretations to chairman Mao's teachings in their applicability to Indian conditions. They survived in pockets organizing share-croppers, landless workers, the tribal's and the youth. As a movement the Maoists gave voice to collective resentment and anger against identified policemen, village officials and politicians, turning it into a battle cry for class action against the society's enemies, accompanied by underground preparation for engaging in personalized attacks and violent reprisals against the state apparatus.[37] It has evolved into a violent revolutionary movement and has regrouped into a reckonable force in large parts of India.

*43.* In the last decate the Naxalites have carved up an occupied territory and a secure population base to militarily attack and defend themselves agaist their enemies. The initial collection of arms and ammunition was made by ambushing policemen on petrol or attacking near-empty police posts, then ransacking them for rifles and other arms. One of the outfits specialized in the use of landmines to cause heavy casualties among security forces, followed by looting of rifles, revolvers and ammunition. Several underground illegal factories making firearms also supplied the needed crude weapons against cash payment. The Naxalites soon learnt that the corrupt and demoralized police force and village officials preferred to retreat into safer areas than offer themselves as willing targets to a determined foe. As the state retreated, entire land areas and populations were acquired by the Naxalites who made actual progress towards realizing the principal goal of Maoism, to secure, defend and ably administer the liberated territory and turn it into a base for further guerilla actions and quasi-military attacks in order to expand the territory further. Militarily they are now better equipped, with light machine guns, assault rifles, grenades, etc. while the local police force may be, by comparison, severly ill-equipped with obsolete 303 rifles and poor leadership. On 6 May, 2010 the Maoists carried out the massacre of 78 men of the Central Reserve Police Force in the liberated area of the Dantewada district of Chhattisgarh state. They had gone there to implement a Home Ministry directive to initiate a concerted and coordinated drive against the Maoist violence, but unluckily were caught into an ambush and ended in a grim tragedy and utter failure.[38] There were other attacks in which more security personnel were killed. According to official estimates, the Maoists operate in 231 districts of the 626 districts in the country and have 20,000 armed activists to fight for the cause. The government could arrest two of their top leaders in 2009 and killed a few

37. Dr. P.K. Agarwal, *IAS, Naxalism. Causes and Cure*, New Delhi, Manas Publicatations, 2010, chs. 1, 7 and 8.

38. *Frontline*, 6 November, 2009 and 7 May, 2010.

more. The Maoists responded with more attacks, including a savage reprisal of beheading an abducted police inspector, thereby demonstrating that their striking power was undiminished. In the past five years their armed cadres reportedly have doubled in strength and now are also better trained and led.

*44.* Once the Naxalites are able to carve up liberated zones in contiguous areas of an ill-governed region, which is admittedly backward and poor and the people historically unprivileged and systematically excluded from the mainstream of economic development and democratic participation in the regional or sub-regional politics, hence providing a mass popular base for statehood, a qualitative change would occur. An insurgent Naxal state with popular backing and material resources to administer the population would come into existence. Based in a secure 'compact revolutionary Zone', the Naxalite power would seek extension of territory and larger population. The ultimate goal is usurpation of power over all India and overturning of the democratic state. The Naxalites hope to realize this dream goal by 2050. Naxalism would grow far beyond from being an ideology to reckon with, to a militarized state power capable of defense and attack and seizing new territories in adjoining areas.[39] This threat perception has been taken with utmost seriousness by the central government, but it is not shared by several state governments which are in the midst of the Naxalite menace. The question is, can a state like Jharkhand, in which 23 districts out of 24 are under the Naxalite influence and 14 are highly affected, where corruption among tribal politicians is already a chronic malady and its police force is poorly trained and ill-equipped, also demoralized, mount a security offensive against the Naxalite forces and emerge a winner? It is a most doubtful proposition and is better not pressed. The key issue is to reclaim the loyalty and support of an abandoned people for the democratic state. In West Bengal, in areas in which the Naxal influence was strong and they carried out almost on a daily basis, individualized killing, extortion and intimidation, people are seen to offer resistance and in several instances their diktat was not carried out.[40] The centre intends to follow a security centric strategy. 'It is a comprehensive operational strategy that would first seek to clear an area of Maoists, occupy it militarily and follow it up with socio-economic development activity. The understanding is that it would take 18-24 months in each of the phases to operationalise the strategy and implement it successfully.'[41] Meanwhile, the Maoists aim to expand in north Bengal, the plains of Bihar, the central districts of Orissa and eastern Chhattisgarh. These are backward areas and strategic for their movement.

---

39. Madhumita, 'Naxalism-Development or Discontent: A Study in Jharkhand', *South Asia Politics*, October 2010, Vol. 9, No.6.
40. Suhrid Sankar Chattopadhyay, 'Resisting Maoists', *Frontline*, 27 August, 2010.
41. *Frontline* 7 May, 2010, also 'Flawed operation', *Frontline*, 6 November, 2009.

## §5. The Crisis Mode of Indian Democracy

*45.* It is not unusual for the nascent democracy in India to fall into a crisis mode. Crisis conditions developed soon after the 1967 general elections in which the Congress Party lost a majority in several states, then schism among party factions weakened the organization and finally it broke into two parties in 1969 trading charges against each other. Indira Gandhi overcame the political crisis by aligning with the CPI and taking a leftward course in her policies. Later the Bangladesh war of 1971 and the massive refugee influx that preceded it raised the stress level on the economy enormously. The inflation that followed severely affected the masses and heavily contributed, at first, to the students' upsurge in Gujarat and soon thereafter the JP movement. The extraordinary aspect of this movement was that it placed large masses, mostly led by the discontented middle class youth, in a confrontationist relationship to the government, challenging its moral authority to govern and impose an unpopular rule. The crisis was never resolved; it was crushed under the emergency declared in June 1975. It nearly wiped out democratic freedoms, fundamental rights, independence of judiciary and the effectiveness of Parliament as the legitimate organ of popular moods and opinions, resting its political sanctity on recurring exercise of free vote at fixed intervals. The Constitution was amended and abridged in more ways than could be imagined. Lasting damage was done to the original, more thoughtfully crafted provisions in the Constitution pertaining to the role, status and powers of the President, which were severely amended and virtually excised. The President now can merely watch over a gathering crisis and see an unholy political mess go out of hand without being able to take any initiative to stem the rot. However, the present crisis that engulfed the centre in 2010 is entirely novel and quite unique in the manner it has been developing. But one important common feature is that the principal contestants are the same as then; these are the Congress, a greatly weakened party and unsure of the fleeting popular support received from the electorate and the stability of the coalition government, and the BJP, the reborn Jan Singh of pre-emergency period, in opposition, leading the assault. It finds occasional tactical support of the left front in a common offensive against the UPA government.

*46.* Among the political parties, the CPI was with the government supporting the emergency and repression, while the CPI-M was in opposition taking punishment from the government. At present both of them and the entire left is in opposition uncomfortably taking the some side as the deeply maligned BJP. Among other parties, the DMK as a coalition partner at the centre is facing the charge of becoming the centrepiece of the horrible scale of corruption and wrongdoing allegedly by its minister, A. Raja in cohort with other DMK leaders and key functionaries in the government. The second notable common feature is that the middle class, now more numerous and articulate, has expressed its disgust and utter disappointment at the shocking display of the total disregard for a fundamentally important premise of self-governance, that the ministers and officials have the character and moral stamina to stay clean and uncorrupted and capable of upholding public norms of honesty, probity and detachment from the many interests which hover around them with many temptations on offer. The crisis erupted due to the sequence of several improbable events. First, there was the inexplicable tardiness of the Prime Minister's initial reaction towards the demand for a parliamentary investigation without offering any cogent reason for the refusal and later his extremely slow, hence unappreciated decision to secure Raja's resignation, and later the perceptible lack of vigour in the delayed investigation conducted by the CBI, which is directly under the Prime Minister and will act with his prior approval not on its own initiative. The CBI showed energy only after the Supreme Court intervened and gave directions for more worthwhile investigations. This should not have been necessary at all, but the government virtually asked for it.

*47.* The key question is whether the elite group, which runs the structures of the state and its institutions and has fortified itself as a ruling caste, comprising powerful politicians in the government as well as in opposition, the bureaucratic-military apparatus and a thin segment of very wealthy and resourceful businessmen, can yet respond to the public opinion and serve common people of India. The baneful part is that the ruling caste governs and preserves the democratic façsect;ade with the active involvement of the print and electronic media. The present crisis shows, first, that the ruling caste is neither homogeneous nor monolithic and may be riven with internal dissensions, and second, that however powerful, without the assurance of renewed electoral support, it cannot satisfactorily govern the country. A subsidiary question is whether the political system, despite moral erosion, can still discharge the responsibility of introducing self correcting reforms and set a new ethical tone for itself? The multi-faceted threats that are faced by the democratic polity at present require foremost that the coalition government and the coalition opposition should together find a common agenda for purposive action to overcome the pressing crisis, restore public confidence in democratic governance and produce reforms in public administration and the conduct of parties and politicians. Restoration of ethical conduct is a prerequisite of deeper reforms. The issues were dramatically advanced towards finding a legal basis for fighting corruption by the extraordinary intervention of Anna Hazare's fast unto death and the government's capitulation in the face of the immense public support which was building up on a daily basis. The government agreed to set up a joint committee under Hazare's chairmanship to produce a draft bill on the subject. Success is not assured, but this is the very hesitatingly taken only the first step on a long journey.

## Chapter 5. Labour Policy and Industrial Relations

*48.* The policy related tasks pending before the government are, (a) consolidating the large number of labour laws with a vast array of definitions of terms applicable to labour as, workers, working men and employees, to cite the most common terms, into a common code in various uniform definitions, though with different scope and applicability of laws, (b) reforming the industrial relations statute to reduce their stringency and inflexibility and render them simpler, less legalistic and more friendly with the expanding nexus of market based social relations, and (c) enacting a body of laws to cover the unorganized and vulnerable segments of the working class, including those who are not employees and work as independent providers of goods and services. Unlike the organized workers, the unorganized add up to a large population and can be identified by many names of the customary caste-based occupations as well as the more modern industry-specific nomenclature. In so far as the first task is concerned, the labour bureaucracy has put up stout resistance on the ground that the task was beyond legal comprehension and intrinsically unattainable since a large body of case laws now existed around every law. Moreover, some laws are intentionally designed to have a far reaching coverage, such as, the Industrial Disputes Act, 1947, but are still not of a universal character. This task is achieved by restrictive definitions which simultaneously include those favoured, while excluding all others. Another difficulty springs from the constitution in which both the Centre and the states may legislate on labour and related fields, provide the former does not oust the latter's jurisdiction without their prior consent and the latter may not enact any laws which conflict with the existing central law on the subject. Several attempts made by the government in earnest to consolide the Trade Unions Act, 1926, the Industrial Employment (Standing Orders) Act, 1946 and the ID Act 1947 failed in securing the support of trade unions and were given up at the stage of legislation.

*49.* The second task was seriously proposed by the NDA government (1998-2004) and prior to it by the previous Congress Governments but it led to confrontational agitations by workers, principally the public sector employees and the left parties, and was given up. The government had hoped to receive support from the National Commission on Labour which it had appointed to report on labour. But the report (2002) was found equally disappointing by the leftist trade union centres, which formally rejected its findings, and the government, to which little of note was addressed which could be translated into suitable enactments, and the government just gave up. On the question of amending the Ch. V-B of the ID Act, the NCL ruled out bilateralism and instead recommended a very costly procedure that was also deeply contradictory. It said that the alternative then is to pay adequate compensation, offer outsourced jobs to the retrenched workers or their cooperatives; if any enterprise decided to close down, give workers or trade union a chance to take up the management of the enterprise before the decision to close is given effect; to underwrite facilities for medical treatment, education of children, etc. and provide for a third party or judicial review of the decision, without affecting the right of the management to decide what economic efficiency demands.

It is impossible to make any sense of it. The government has wisely shelved the report, which in any case failed to find support in any interest group, or the political parties, whether in the government coalitions or in opposition. Along with it the task of amending labour laws has also been indefinitely deferred. In the previous UPA government (2004–09) the left parties had the irony of supporting the government without joining it, and making it conditional, among other terms, that none of the laws which conferred job protection or wage security should be amended in any respect which affected labour adversely. The government obliged, hence no progress was made. Earlier the NDA government had given encouraging signals to the state governments to amend the central legislation in ways that suited them and two or three states did make progress in selected spheres. But the UPA government stopped the practice and imposed effective fetters on states which were slow in this regard. It rejected the idea of automatic hire and fire in a formal declaration of its policy. A significant change in the working of the ID Act was made by the enactment of the Industrial Disputes (Amendment) Act, 2010. The new law provides for setting up of Grievance Redressal Machinery in every industrial establishment employing 20 or more workers. Another change is to empower the workmen covered by Section 2A of the ID Act to make an application for adjudication directly to the Labour Court/tribunal after the expiry of 45 days from the date he made an application to the Conciliation officer. No reference by the government will be necessary. Yet another change is to secure the implementation of every award or settlement by obtaining the order and decree of a civil court. The civil courts will execute the awards.

*50.* The successor UPA government has remained committed to the idea of inclusive growth. The most effective way of combating poverty is by improving employment prospects along with acceleration in economic growth. In the organized sector there are few prospects of this happening. Most jobs have been created in the unorganized or the informal sector. The World Bank noted, 'Of the 413 million prime aged persons in the Indian labour force in 2004-05, the overwhelming majority, about 90 per cent, are employed in low productivity informal sector jobs', Moreover, unemployment and underemployment may be over 8 per cent of the labour force.[42] The government has come round to the view that the vast workforce in the informal sector must be provided with some form of social protection, preferably by reaching them directly. Several schemes have been launched. The insurance scheme, called Aam Admi Bima Yojana (Common Man's Insurance Scheme), provided cover against accidental death and disability to 82 million persons among rural landless labourers, beginning with 2 October 2007, up to 30 September 2009. The medical insurance scheme called Rashtriya Swasthya Bima Yojana (National Health Insurance Scheme) launched on 1 October 2007 aims to cover the below-poverty-line families with the insurance protection of Rs 30,000.00 per annum. The cost is shared between the centre and the states on a 75:25 basis. Beneficiaries are entitled to cashless transactions. About 10 million health cards have been issued. In 2008 the government enacted the Unorganized Workers' Social Security Act and it came into force on 16 May 2009. It may be too early for the government to report

42. The World Bank, *India's Employment Challenge, Creating Jobs, Helping Workers*, Delhi, OUP, 2010, p. 1.

on the progress made under its provisions. At the national and state levels, the Social Security Boards will recommend specific social security schemes for the unorganized workers and the respective governments will provide the financial and administrative support. A major problem is to determine the identity and addresses of beneficiaries, also their occupations, employment status and earnings. This hurdle may be eventually overcome when each person residing in India, non-citizens included, is provided with a unique identity. 'Once fully operational, the scheme will, besides facilitating financial inclusion ensure better governance and improved service delivery so that the targeted group of people is actually benefited by the schemes implemented by the Centre and States.'[43] It will be demand mandated, though the government may also require enrolment of prospective beneficiaries.

*51.* A notable contribution towards raising public awareness and government's responsibility towards the neglected sectors was made by the enormous work done by the National Commission for Enterprises on the Unorganized Sector. It was set up by the government in Setember 2004 under the chairmanship of late Arjun K. Sengupta. During four and a half years of its existence the NCEUS produced nine reports besides submitting policy oriented proposals to the government. The final report is entitled *The Challenge of Employment in India. An Informal Economy Perspective*, 2009. The NCEUS has produced a wealth of data and much sorted out information, including detailed analysis of particular features of selected employment sectors. A key dimension of its recommendations is the assumption of 9 per cent growth rate over a long period. This is compared with a possible scenario of 7 per cent growth rate and the statistical tables for the two sets show the percentage distribution of workers by formal and informal sectors, separately for agriculture, industry, services and total. According to the commission, the size of India's labour force in 2007 was 489 million which was greater than the total population of the country in 1961. In 2012 it is expected to grow to 538 million which would be about the same as the total population in 1971. Such a huge population will be more of a demographic burden than a dividend. There is considerable backlog of illiterate men and women as well as those with low levels of education that would hardly make for the ability to acquire skills and knowledge. To avoid the prospects of this demographic burden, focussed policies are called for. Two main elements of such a policy are: access to functional literacy and skill development and basic social security to take care of food/nutrition and health care.[44] The problems of access for women are acknowledged to be more serious and less tractable. As many as eleven states are called upon to develop region specific social policies to reach women workers and secure support of families towards these endeavour. It is a huge task.

*52.* Industrial relations, including working conditions and wages or earnings, are regulated by a large number of laws. The scale of labour legislation is best understood by examining the list of laws in force at the centre. In addition there are state laws. Laws are enforced through the rules which define the procedure and content

43. Government of India, *Economic Survey, 2009–10*, Delhi, OUP, February 2010, Ch. 11, pp. 278 and 286.
44. NCEUS, Government of India, *The Challenge of Employment in India*, 2009, p. 123.

of every dispute or grievance of workers, workmen or employees, depending upon the term employed in particular laws. The main laws are listed below:[45]

1. Apprentices Act, 1961.
2. Bidi and Cigar workers (Conditions of Employment) Act, 1966
3. Bidi Workers Welfare Cess Act, 1976.
4. Bidi Workers Welfare Fund Act, 1976
5. Bonded Labour System (Abolitioin) Act, 1976.
6. Child Labour (Prohibition and Regulation) Act, 1986.
7. Children (Pledging of Labour) Act, 1933.
8. Cine-Workers and Cinema Theatre Workers (Regulation of Employment) Act, 1981.
9. Cine Workers Welfare Cess Act, 1981.
10. Cine-Workers Welfare Fund Act, 1981.
11. Coal Mines Provident Fund and Miscellenceous Provisions Act, 1948.
12. Contract Labour (Regulation and Abolition) Act, 1970.
13. Dock Workers (Regulation of Employment) Act, 1948.
14. Dock Workers (Safety, Health and Welfare) Act, 1986.
15. Employees' Provident Funds and Miscellaneous Provisions Act, 1952.
16. Employees' State Insurance Act, 1948.
17. Employers' Liability Act, 1938.
18. Employment Exchanges (Compulsory Notification of Vacancies) Act, 1959.
19. Equal Remuneration Act, 1976.
20. Factories Act, 1948.
21. Fatal Accidents Act, 1855.
22. Industrial Disputes Act, 1947.
23. Industrial Employment (Standing Orders) Act, 1946.
24. Inter-State Migrant Workmen (Regulation of Employment and Conditions of Service) Act, 1979.
25. Iron Ore Mines, Manganese Ore Mines and Chrome Ore Mines Labour Welfare Cess Act, 1976.
26. Iron Ore Mines, Manganese Ore Mines and Chrome Ore Mines Labour Welfare Fund Act, 1976.
27. Labour Laws (Exemption from Furnishing Returns and Maintaining Certain Registers by Certain Establishments) Act, 1988.
28. Limestone and Dolomite Mines Labour Welfare Act, 1972.
29. Maternity Benefit Act, 1961.
30. Mica Mines Labour Welfare Fund Act, 1946.
31. Mines Act, 1952.
32. Minimum Wages Act, 1948.
33. Motor Transport Workers Act, 1961.
34. Payment of Bonus Act, 1965.
35. Payment of Gratuity Act, 1972.
36. Payment of Wages Act, 1936.

45. Bibek Debroy and P.D. Kaushik (eds.), *Reforming the Labour Market*, Delhi, Academic Foundation, 2005, pp. 39–41 and p. 414.

37. Personal Injuries (Compensation Insurance) Act, 1963.
38. Plantation Labour Act, 1951.
39. Public Liability Insurance Act, 1991.
40. Sales promotion Employees (Conditions of Service) Act, 1976.
41. Trade Unions Act,1926.
42. Weekly Holidays Act, 1943.
43. Working Journalists and Other Newspaper Employees (Conditions of Sevice and Miscellaneous Provisions) Act, 1955.
44. Working Journalists (Fixation of Rates of Wages) Act, 1958.
45. Workmen's Compensation Act, 1926.
46. Boilers Act, 1923.
47. Dangerous Machines (Regulations) Act, 1983.
48. Emigration Act, 1983.
49. Industries (Development and Regulation) Act, 1951.

A great deal of industrial relations is routinely conducted under these laws without producing agitations. The legal machinery and labour law administration at the centre and state levels implement these laws and sort out employment related workers' grievances without attracting public notice. These laws are amended from time to time in the light of judgments of higher courts or to correct anomalies and legal inadequacies usually without much fuss. However, there still remains a large body of wage earning people, either on regular employment or contract, especially in the IT sector, who work with minimal legal protection. Moreover, women have emerged as the most vulnerable segment of the wage earning class, party because they are least inclined to protest and have to defend their jobs against a number of insecurities at home and at work.[46] In fact, most people who work in the twilight zone between the organized and the unorganized sectors, may have formal laws granting them rights, but may be unwilling to invoke them for fear of losing their jobs. Actually the threat is more serious, as a considerable proportion of employing firms are capable of issuing wholly credible threats of moving out of present locations. The threat is believed because such employing firms carry out the work contracted to them by a foreign chain, each link of which is similarly constrained. Increased wage cost cannot be shifted forward or backward and its incidence must fall on the employing firm's well defined capacity to pay.

*53.* From the industrial relations perspective, five discernible segments are taking shape from the economic flux produced by partial liberalization and the global openness of policies. First, the totally protected government employment, of which the PSUs form an important part, has the most formal industrial relations. Workers, including white collar employees, are organized and represented by one or more unions in each establishment. The government treats unions as power centres, but deals with them or authorizes the managements concerned to negotiate with them within a set procedure and the policy parameters. Deviations are occasionally allowed and even settlements of an exceptional nature are politically permissible,

46. *Ibid.*, the article by Amaresh Dubey, Veronica Pala and Eugene D. Thomas, 'Economic Liberalisation and Women's Workforce Participation Rates'.

provided industrial peace is preserved and workers' discontent is kept within tolerable limits. Job security is assured even though some PSUs make losses, or simply cannot be turned around.

*54.* Second, the large scale private corporate sector also has organized industrial relations, but, with a curious phenomenon emerging, that at the enterprise level workers are often seen to be disengaging from the unions which have competing claims of representing them. The recurring subject matter of unions' agitations and confrontations is found to be of little relevance in resolving the day-to-day problems the workers face. They now better understand the force of market competition, consequently the importance of work, discipline, quality norms, wastage reduction and keeping the factory or business office in economically viable conditions. On reasonable assurances of jobs security by the employing firms, they might as well carry out their part of the industrial relations bargain. The firm's financial viability and workers' job security are contingent upon each other. This is a new paradigm of industrial relations.

*55.* Third, within the private corporate sector there is a sizeable conflict-prone segment. The companies may have obsolete technologies or products, or bad layout of factories, or simply a poor or uneconomic location and additionally some of them may be overmanned, so must carry the high cost of an aging labour force, which may be either predominantly unskilled, or has older skills which have become obsolete and redundant. The companies are unable to bring in any fresh financial infusion due to their inability to install more modern new machinery, which workers stoutly oppose. Redundancy is an obvious fact, but is still stubbornly opposed, because for most workers the alternative is quite stark, it is of low employment prospects, low wages and the non-affordability or low aptitude towards acquiring new skills. The consequent helplessness produces gloom and a feeling of being in a trap. The only remedy is to offer a VRS with the terminal benefits more generous than provided in the ID Act. While the factory is working the workers have the ID Act in their favour and the political support of parties, and may be local public opinion as well. In such companies the industrial disputes recur as a pattern, even as old issues are left unresolved or partially resolved. The ID Act requires that the company must continue to engage in production, that it cannot either cause lay-off or retrenchment or close down without government's permission, which though requested is usually declined. Stalemate in industrial relations results and industrial sickness follows. This paradigm is one of systematically unresolved industrial contradictions and perpetual distress.

*56.* Fourth, the medium and small-scale industries employ a large body of workforce working on simple, easy-to-man machines and the operating technologies which pertain to an earlier stage of industrialization. The division of labour is simple with a direct man-machine-output relationship. The scope of production is necessarily small and market determined. It is hard to unionize the labour force and promote the idea of workers solidarity, though workers may be organized around a general industrial union based on a particular location of a group of enterprises. A typical employer may either know each worker by face and some by name and encourage direct accessibility to him either individually or in groups. A good employer is expected to emphasize the qualities of loyalty, discipline, diligence at work, regular attendance and attention paid to raw materials, finished products and machines. Negligence is not tolerated. He pays market based wages, usually not below the legal minimum, an annual bonus or cash gifts once or twice a year and would like to treat them decently. The workers are his strength. The principal paradigm of industrial relations is that it is employer based and rests on workers' dependency, normally low penetration of unions and a peripheral relationship with the labour administration and labour laws. These features are complementary to small scale production of commodities for the market. Market determines the output, firm's growth or decline, prices, profits and wages.

*57.* Fifth is the unusual class of industries with anomy in industrial relations, or a general breakdown of the formal system either as a regular feature or as a transient phenomenon, which occasionally acquires threatening proportions. The key role is played by a large groups of industrial workers who decide to revolt simultaneously against their unions and leaders, the employers and the government machinery for poorly managing labour disputes. In 1967, in West Bengal, the syndrome of *gherao* (encirclement or confinement of individual managers of the targeted company) was its worst manifestation. In another form it erupted in 1982 in Bombay and produced the longest strike in memory in the cotton textile industry as a collective rebellion against the recognized trade union and the employers The strike failed, as it was bound to, but it produced disastrous outcomes both for the industry and the textile workers. Earlier in the mid 1950s, in this very industry, similar outbursts and breakdowns in industrial relations on the issue of rationalization of labour in Kanpur and Negpur had left both sides permanently weakened. The characteristic paradigm is the anarchic workers' rebellion against the system, especially the dispute settlement procedures, the established rules and laws accompanied by total erosion of trust. It is a product of underdeveloped institutions and immature attitudes towards industry as a source of livelihood and the politically drummed up clamour for job security and decent wages far in excess of the economy's capacity to pay.

# Part I. The Individual Employment Relationship

## Chapter 1. Definitions and Concepts

### §1. Worker, Workman, Employee, Employed Person and Related Terms

*58.* In Indian labour legislation several terms are used and denote the purpose for which the law has been enacted. The Factories Act, 1948 uses the term 'worker' to provide for his safety, health and welfare and now includes those 'employed directly or by or through any agency (including a contractor) with or without the knowledge of the principal employer, whether for remuneration or not, so as to protect the basic interests of not just regular employees but the contract and casual labourers and apprentices as well. A person is presumed to be employed in a factory, if he is found there at any time, except rest and meal intervals, when work is going on unless proved otherwise. This presumption is rebuttable and available only in relation to the Factories Act's penalties and procedures. The term 'workman' as defined in the Industrial Disputes Act, 1947, includes not only persons employed in any industry but also those who have been dismissed, discharged or retrenched and have raised disputes. This term also covers supervisors drawing wages not exceeding Rs 1,600 per month and do not exercise functions of a managerial nature. Certain other categories such as, military, police and prison personnel, etc. are excluded. The term workman includes anyone employed to do any manual, unskilled, skilled, technical, operational, clerical or supervisory work for hire or reward. Teachers and medical representatives are not workmen. An apprentice governed by the Apprentices Act, 1961 is not a workman. Other apprentices are workmen. A bank employed jewel appraisers for loans as the part-time staff. The Industrial tribunal, a single judge of the High Court and the Divisional Bench held that they were workmen. The Supreme Court allowed the bank's appeal and held that they were not workmen, as they had no fixed working hours, paid not monthly wages but commission by the borrowers of loan and could carry on other occupations. They were not subject to the direction by the bank as to the manner the ornaments brought by the borrowers were to be appraised.[47]

---

47. LLJ, 2006, Vol. 2, *Indian Overseas Bank* v. *Workmen, All India Indian Overseas Bank Employees Union*, Supreme Court of India, pp. 253–257.

*59.* In one case an employee hired by a bank in the junior management cadre was sacked barely two months after the appointment on account of improper behaviour and conduct with the customers, line, manager and fellow colleagues. The appellant complained to the Ministry of Labour, New Delhi and asked for conciliation proceedings. These were held and failed, thereafter, the Ministry declined to make the reference on the ground that the employee had not worked for 240 days in service, hence no dispute subsisted. This order was challenged in a writ petition which succeeded and the High Court held that mere non-completion of 240 days of service could not be a ground for refusal to make the reference. Thereafter, the reference was forwarded to the Industrial Court for adjudication. The appellant took the plea that her work was basically clerical in nature. She had no authority or power to take any decision to complete a transaction. Her work was not managerial or supervisory in nature. Hence she was a workman under Section 2(S) of the ID Act. The two witnesses of the bank admitted that the appellant did not have the power to sanction leave, that she did not supervise anyone's work and that nobody reported to her, that she did not have the power to initiate any disciplinary proceedings against any employee. The court accepted these facts of her work and decided that she came within the ambit of the definition of 'workman'. She was entitled to protection and her termination was bad in law. The bank was directed to reinstate the appellant on full back wages and continuity of service. The bank filed a writ petition against the award and the High Court admitted it. The Court came to the conclusion that the tribunal failed to consider material aspects of the evidence and to apply the tests which the Supreme Court laid down in deciding the question whether the appellant was a clerk or not. The Court decided that she was not a workman and the Industrial Court had no jurisdiction to entertain the reference. Its award was set aside. She filed an appeal against this order, which was heard by a bench of two judges of the High Court. The Court held that a workman must be employed to work within the stipulated categories, viz manual, unskilled, skilled, technical, operational, clerical or supervisory and it is not enough that she is not covered by either of the four exceptions to the definition. The burden of proving her status was on her and not on the employer. However, it is not the letter of appointment nor the nomenclature of her designation which mattered. This was not decisive in law. The Court examined the key responsibilities assigned to her and the submission that the responsibilities assigned to her were not necessarily those which she performed. This was held to be without any merit. She had admitted that she had to work with walk-in-customers and as a sales person sell the products of the bank. The bank has asserted that the appellant worked in the managerial category no. III. The Court noted the swift evolution of technology that has led to a quantum change in the business environment. The exigencies of managerial control over subordinates may be applicable in certain factual situations, but not in every conceivable case. It would be wholly inappropriate to apply the same test which governs the traditional form of manufacturing business to one founded on software, bio-genetics or business at the cutting edge of technology. The interpretation of Section 2(S) must be such as would not lead to the stultifying of innovations, development and change in managerial practice. Business managers should have a high degree of latitude in promoting efficiency in a competitive business environment. In the present case, it was not possible to accede to the submission that the work which was being done by the petitioner was essentially of a clerical or operational nature. Looking into the dominant nature of the duties and responsibilities performed by the appellant 'we are of the opinion that the appellant was appointed in the Bank's lower management cadre.' The appeal accordingly fails and the same is dismissed as such.[48]

*60.* In a case pertaining to Section 2(S) of the ID Act three courts, viz the Labour Court, the Industrial Court and the single judge of the High Court had held the complainant was not a workman. He filed an appeal which was heard and decided by a bench of the High Court in his favour. The appellant submitted that the findings of all the courts were based on totally erroneous test of facts required to be proved. They did not see 'what are predominant duties of the complainant.' They were misdirected on the nomenclature of the post on which he was appointed. The courts were misdirected due to six documents which, in fact, did not prove the predominant duties discharged and work performed by the complainant. On his behalf seven propositions were cited in as many cases. One of the proposition stated that occasional entrustment of supervisory, managerial or administrative work take a person mainly carrying out would clerical duties out of the purview of Section 2(S) of the Industrial Disputes Act. Another proposition held that the 'main feature, pith and substance of his employment must be manual or clerical before the definition of "workman" is attracted. The respondent's main line of defence was that the onus to prove that the claimant is a workman and to prove the test to satisfy all the ingredients lies on one who claims the said status.' Unless proof of such a fact emerges from the evidence, it cannot to held that he is a workman, The complainant had admitted that he was not getting the benefits which the workers who were party to the agreement between the union and the employer were getting. He was not a member of the union. Supervisors were barred from membership. He had signed gate passes for the non-supervisory employees. He had signed as an auditee in the audit reports.

*61.* The High Court bench formulated three questions to decide the issue. One, what is the quality and volume of evidence or proof of facts required to be brought by the complainant? And to have the onus of proof shifted on the employer, who denies the jurisdiction of the Court on the ground that the complainant is not a workman? Second, though the Indian Evidence Act does not apply in totality to the proceedings, it is not the basic rule that facts are to be proved by legal evidence? Whether the basic doctrine of proof of fact as to the nature of duties or work performed is applicable in labour adjudication? Answering the questions the Court said that while the complainant had proved various facts as to nature of duties, the management failed to disprove what the workman has proved. 'Had the complainant been working in supervisory capacity, it would be shocking to believe that he had signed only four documents in more than five years. They do not amount to proving predominance of work. The burden of proving facts was discharged by the complainant satisfactorily. The employer failed to bring substantive evidence, which was withheld inspite of the order. The employer has, therefore, to suffer the adverse

48. LLJ, Vol. 2, 2011, *Vandana Joshi D/o K.D. Joshi, Thane* v. *Standard Chartered Bank Ltd.*, High Court of Bombay, pp 261–270.

inference, that had evidence been produced it would have gone against the employer.' The result that follows, is that the findings of Labour Court and Industrial Court as confirmed by learned single judge, are based on erroneous foundation, namely, it is the nomenclature of post than the predominant nature of duties. Their judgments and orders deserve to be reversed and are hereby set aside. The complainant is a workman within the compass of the term as defined under Section 2(S) of the ID Act. The complaint is remanded to the Labour Court to hear and dispose of the remaining issues within three months of receipt of the order of this court. The cost is quantified as Rs 5000 only to be paid by the respondent within one month.[49]

*62*. The term 'employee' is used in several pieces of legislation but is not identically defined. In the Minimum Wages Act, 1948, this term is defined to include any employed person 'in a scheduled employment in respect of which minimum rates of wages have been fixed' and includes an out-worker who worked either at his house or some other premises, etc.; he may do any work, skilled or unskilled, manual or clerical, or may be an employee who has been declared to be one by the appropriate government, but does not include any member of the armed forces. This definition has been amended by several states to include dismissed, discharged and retrenched employees also, even those who have superannuated or retired, for the purpose at the Act. Under the Employees' State Insurance (ESI) Act, 1948, this term is given a very wide definition to include those directly employed as well as several other categories who may be indirectly employed. Earlier, casual workers were not deemed to be employees, but the Supreme Court has held that they too are covered. The term includes clerks, supervisors and managers whose salaries/wages do not exceed the level prescribed by the central government.

*63*. The EPF Act uses the term 'employee' to provide for wider coverage of the beneficial schemes formulated under the Act. In a case a government company, BSNL, petitioned the High Court against an order of the PF commissioner calling for PF contribution in respect of pre-induction trainees engaged by it. The trainees had voice a grievance that, though working as junior telecom officers or junior accounts officer, their training period was not counted for the purpose of coverage under the Act. The complaint was duly noted and the PF commissioner served notice to the parties. On hearing both sides, he issued the order to make the contesting employees members of the Provident Fund Scheme. In the hearing the so-called stipend was linked to their pay scales. They were recruited in terms of the requirement rules. Moreover, the period of training would be treated as duty for the purpose of promotion, fixing increments, eligibility for departmental examinations etc. Yet it was asserted that the pre-induction training period cannot be considered for the purpose of the EPF Act. The Court noticed that in 1988 Parliament amended Section 2(f) of the EPF Act to enlarge the definition of the term 'employee'. It included persons engaged as apprentices, but not those engaged under the Apprentices Act, 1961. A similar amendment was made in the ESI Act. As per the new definition, all the trainees are covered by these two Acts. It covers the pre-induction

49. LLJ, Vol. 1, 2011, *Chandrashekhar Chintaman Vaidya* v. *National Organic Chemical Industries Ltd.*, Akola, High Court of Bombay, pp. 200–210.

training period. In the joint agreement between the BSNL and the trainees they have agreed to cover the training period for the purpose of EPF. The Court dismissed the three writ petitions filed by the petitioner.[50]

*64.* In the Payment of Gratuity Act, 1972, the term 'employee' was linked to the level of wages. But by an amendment in 1994 this was omitted. Now 'employee' means any person, other than an apprentice, employed on wages in any establishment and includes managerial personnel, but does not include anyone who holds a post in the central or state government and is covered by any other Act or by any rules providing for payment of gratuity. In the Payment of Gratuity (Amendment) Act, 2009, the term 'employee' has been redefined to expand the coverage to include teachers. It means any person employed for wages, whether the terms are express or implied, in any kind of work, manual or otherwise, in a factory, mine, oilfield, plantation, port, railway company, shop or other establishment to which the Act applies, but excludes persons employed by the central or state government and to whom any other Act or Rules for payment gratuity apply.

*65.* In the Payment of Bonus Act, the term 'employee', while excluding apprentices, is linked to the level of salary or wage which has been periodically raised and in 1995 was fixed at Rs 3,500 per month. He may be doing any skilled or unskilled, manual, supervisory, managerial, administrative, technical or clerical work for hire or reward. The term expands the coverage of the Act to employees who are not workers. A worker on daily wages is covered by the term, provided he has worked in the establishment for not less than 30 days in that year.

*66.* In the Employees' Provident Funds and Miscellaneous Provisions (EPFMP) Act, 1952 the term 'employee' is defined to include any person who is employed for wages and includes those employed by or through a contractor as well as an apprentice, though it excludes one who is engaged under the Apprentices Act, 1961, or under the Standing Orders of the establishment. He may get his wages directly or indirectly from the employer and is covered from the date of joining the establishment. An employee must be a natural person who can be identified. A firm hired by the employer is not an employee.

*67.* The term 'employed person' is used in the Payment of Wages Act, 1936, and includes the legal representative of a deceased employed person. This term is left undefined and obviously means a person employed in an establishment, including a mine or an oilfield, to which the Act applies. Workers employed by a contractor, are covered by this definition. The liability to pay wages is that of the principal

50. LLJ, Vol. 4, 2011, *Bharat Sanchar Nigam Ltd.* v. *Union of India and Others*, High Court of Madras, pp. 874–898. The same judge had earlier decided another case in which the employing mill engaged 185 regular employees and 229 as apprentices and denied the latter the benefits of EPF. The mills writ petition was dismissed. LLJ, Vol. 3, 2011, *Sree Mangayarkavasi Mills (P) Ltd.*, v. *EPF Organization, Regional Office and another*, High Court of Madras, pp. 775–776.

employer. A person employed in a managerial or administrative capacity is not excluded by the Act.[51]

*68.* The term 'sales promotion employee' is employed in the Sales Promotion Employees (Condition of Service) Act, 1976, and includes any person by whatever name called (including an apprentice) engaged in any establishment for hire or reward to do any work relating to promotion of sales or business or both, but excludes a supervisor drawing a salary exceeding Rs 1,600 per month or engaged primarily in a managerial or administrative capacity. This term includes sales persons who work solely on a commission basis in addition to those who work for wages. A medical representative is a workman both under the amended provision of the ID Act as well as under the Sales Promotion Employees (Condition of Service) Act, 1976.[52]

*69.* The term used in the Motor Transport Workers Act, 1961 is 'motor transport worker' and means a person employed in a motor transport undertaking directly or through an agency, whether for wages or not, to work in a professional capacity or to attend to various duties in connection with arrival, departure, etc., of a transport vehicle, but excludes any such person employed in a factory as defined in the Factories Act, or who is covered by the Shops and Establishment Act or any such law in force. According to this very broad definition a motor transport worker need not be working for wages of reward though there must be some consideration to establish the basis for contract.

*70.* In the Building and Other Construction Workers (Regulation of Employment and Conditions of Service) Act, 1996, the term 'building worker' means, as in the ID Act, a person who is employed for hire or reward, and with similar exclusions, to work in connection with any building or other construction work. Since this is a controlling term it is given a detailed descriptive definition.

*71.* In the *Beedi* and Cigar Workers (Conditions of Employment) Act, 1966, both terms, 'contract labour' and 'employee' are employed to give as wide a scope to the protective legislation as seemed feasible. 'Employee' means a person employed directly or through an agency, whether for wages or not, in any establishment (or godown) to do any work, etc., and includes a 'home worker' and any person, though employed by an employer or a contractor (or both), but working with the permission of, or under an agreement with, the employer or contractor.

*72.* In the protective legislation of cinema workers, entitled, The Cine Workers and Cinema Workers (Regulation of Employment) Act, 1981, the term, 'cine-worker' means an individual who is employed directly or through any contractor or other person in or in connection with the production of a feature film, or works as

---

51. LLJ, 2006, Vol. 3, *Damodaran P. and Others* v. *M.K. Krishnan Kutty*, High Court of Kerala, pp. 407–408.
52. LLJ, 2006, Vol. 2, *German Remedies Ltd* v. *Presiding Officer, Labour Court, Bhopal*, High Court of Madhya Pradesh, pp. 8–13.

an artist, (including actor, musician or dancer), to do any work, etc., and whose remuneration does not exceed Rs 1,600 per month, or where it is by way of a lump sum, a sum of Rs 15,000. A person is a cine-worker and not an independent contractor if he has agreed to work personally.

*73.* In the Dock Workers (Regulation of Employment) Act, 1948, the term 'dock worker' means a person employed or to be employed in, or in the vicinity of any port, or work in connection with the loading, unloading, movement or storage of cargoes or work in connection with the preparation of ships or other vessels for the receipt or discharge of cargoes or leaving port. This definition provides no link with the principle of hire or reward and is yet sufficiently general to include all forms of stevedoring work.

*74.* In the Plantations Labour Act, 1951, the term 'worker' means a person employed in a plantation for hire or reward, whether directly or through any agency, to do any work, etc., but excludes a medical officer and any person whose monthly wages exceed Rs 750 per month, any managerial person even though his salary may not exceed Rs 750 per month, and any construction and building worker temporarily employed in the plantation for this kind of work.

*75.* In the Working Journalists and Other Newspaper Employees (Conditions of Service) and Miscellaneous Provisions Act, 1955, two terms are employed. The term 'newspaper employee', means any working journalist and includes any other person employed to do any work in, or in relation to, any newspaper establishment. The other term is 'non-journalist newspaper employee', who is employed to work in a newspaper establishment, but is not a working journalist, is not employed in a managerial or administrative capacity, or though a supervisor has the duties and the powers of a manager. The Act further defines a 'working journalist' as a person whose principal avocation is that of a journalist and includes an editor, a leader writer, news editor, sub-editor, feature-writer, copy-tester, reporter, correspondent, cartoonist, news photographers and proofreaders, but excludes persons employed in administrative or managerial capacities. Ex-employees too are covered by this definition. An editor who has additional duties as a manager or functions in an administrative capacity is none the less a working journalist.

*76.* In the Workmen's Compensation Act, 1923, which is a quasi-penal statute and provides for payment of damages by the employer, the term 'workman' is defined to mean any person other than a person who is employed otherwise than for the purposes of the employer's trade or business, who is (i) a railway servant (as defined), or (ii) a master seaman or other member of the crew of a ship, or (iii) a captain or other number of the crew of an aircraft, or (iv) a person recruited as a driver, helper, mechanic, cleaner or in any other capacity in connection with motor vehicle, or (v) a person recruited for work abroad by a company, etc., or (vi) employed in any such capacity as is specified in Schedule II of the Act and has a contract of employment. Apprentices are covered by this definition only if they have a contract of service. With effect from 8 December 2000 the Act is made applicable to all casual workers. The Act purposely omits to provide that only a workman who is employed in a factory can make a claim.

*77.* For the purpose of determining employer's liability in suits for damages the term 'workman' is defined more generally in the Employer's Liability Act, 1938, to mean any person who has entered into or works under a contract of service or apprenticeship with an employer whether by way of manual labour, clerical work or otherwise, and whether the contract is expressed or implied, oral or in writing. A similar definition occurs in the Personal Injuries (Compensation Insurance) Act, 1963. All direct employees and all contractors' employees are covered by the Personal Injuries (Compensation Insurance) scheme and not just workers as defined in the Factories Act, the Mines Act, the Plantation Labour Act, etc.

*78.* In a land mark legislation, the government expanded the scope of providing social protection to the unorganized sector. The term, 'unorganized sector' means an enterprise owned by individuals or self-employed persons and employs less than 10 workers. An 'unorganized worker' may be a home-based or a self-employed or a wage worker who is not covered by any of the Acts listed in schedule II of the Act. A 'wage worker' is employed on wages in cash or kind in the unorganized sector, either directly by an employer or through a contractor, and whether based on home, or as a temporary or casual or as a migrant or as a domestic worker, with a monthly wage of which the amount may be notified by the central or the state government. This definition leaves out of scope those enterprises which employ 19 workers without the aid of power. These are not factories under the definitions employed in the Factories Act, nor are they included in the class of unorganized enterprises due to the size of employment.

*79.* In the workmen's compensation (Amendment) Act, 2009 the term, 'employee' was substituted for the term 'workmen', wherever it occurs in the main Act, the Workmen's Compensation Act, 1923. It is defined to include railway servants, excluding those employed in an administrative capacity, a master seaman or other members of the crew of a ship, a captain or other crew members of an aircraft, drivers, helpers, mechanics or in any capacity in connection with a motor vehicle, any person employed by a company to work abroad in any capacity as may be specified in the schedule II of the Act and the ship, aircraft or motor vehicle is registered in India, but does not include members of the armed forces.

## §2. Wages and Remuneration

*80.* In the Payment of Wages Act, 1936, the term 'wages' means all remuneration that can be expressed in terms of money and includes any sum payable as a result of any award or settlement, or order of a court, overtime, paid leave or holidays, statutory bonus, termination pay, and 'any sum to which the person employed is entitled under any scheme framed under any law for the time being in force'. However, this term does not include profit sharing bonus (if excluded by the terms of employment), fringe benefits, such as, housing, water and electricity, social security benefits, travel allowance and special pay. This is the widest definition. In the ID Act there is an additional concept called 'average pay'. This varies with the monthly, weekly and daily rated workmen. It is the average wages of three months for the first, of four weeks for the second and of twelve full working days for the third. In the Minimum Wages Act while the same definition as in the Payment of Wages Act is followed, house rent allowance is specifically included, though several other factors (i.e. the value of any house accommodation, supply of light, water, etc.) are excluded.

*81.* In the Payment of Gratuity Act, 1972, 'wages' mean all emoluments earned on duty or on leave, in accordance with the terms of employment which are payable in cash but exclude bonus, commission, house rent allowance, overtime pay and any other allowance. Thus the value of food supplied by the employer is excluded. For piece rated workers daily wages are to be computed as the average of three months preceding the termination of employment.

*82.* In the social security legislation each Act has its distinctive definition. In the Employees' Provident Fund and Miscellaneous Provisions Act, 1952, the term employed is 'basic wages'. This means all emoluments which are earned in accordance with the terms of the contract of employment and are payable in cash but exclude (i) the cash value of any food concession, (ii) any dearness allowance, house rent allowance, overtime pay, bonus, commission or any other similar allowance. *Ad hoc* payments are excluded. Production bonus paid for extra production is also excluded. In the Employees' State Insurance Act, 1948, wages include not only all remuneration payable in accordance with the contract of employment, but also any payment made on account of a lay-off, lock-out and strike, which is not illegal, and any other remuneration paid at intervals not exceeding two months. If the additional remuneration is made on a quarterly basis it would be excluded from the coverage of the Act. Furthermore, wages should be actually paid and not classified as 'being payable'. Overtime wages are included. Incentive wages are included, but ex-gratia bonus is excluded. In the Maternity Benefit Act, 1961, wages are given a wide coverage and include cash allowances, like dearness allowance and house rent allowance as well as incentive bonus, and in addition, the money value of the concessional supply of food grains and other articles. However, bonus, overtime earnings and any deduction or payment made by way of fines are excluded.

*83.* Wages comprise a number of components. Often the least important is the 'basic wage' particularly in the older industries, the most important is the dearness allowance. The courts have held that once a dearness allowance, (i.e. pay connected with the cost of living index), is granted it cannot be taken back and must be treated as a part of the contract of employment. On the other hand, maternity benefit allowance is not wages, nor is the retaining allowance paid in seasonal industries. The facility of purchasing grains at concessional prices, although it can be expressed in money, does not form part of wages; it is just an amenity.

*84.* The Payment of Wages Act lays down detailed guidelines on permissible deductions from wages. A 'deduction' is defined as a payment made by the employees to their employers or their agents. It is legally possible to impose fines and deduct wages for absence, for causing damage or loss of goods, or for loss or money attributable to negligence. Deduction may also be made for providing housing, amenities and services to workers. In addition, deductions can be made with the written authorization of workers in respect of any valid purpose, subject however to the overall limitation that in any wage period the sum of all deductions should not ordinarily exceed fifty per cent of wages.

## §3. Employer, Principal Employer, Owner and Occupier

*85.* The aforesaid terms are defined to reflect the principle of ownership and control in the widest sense of the term and also include management personnel who have been delegated the responsibility for carrying out functions with which the law is concerned and are accountable to it. The oldest definition of the term 'employer' is in the Workmen's Compensation Act, 1923, and includes any body of persons, whether incorporated or not, and any managing agent of an employer and the legal representative of a deceased employer, and, when the services of a workman are temporarily lent or let on hire to another person by the person with whom the workman has entered into a contract of service or apprenticeship, means such other person while the workman is working for him.

The pervasive nature of this definition is meant to precisely fix the responsibility of the employers towards safety at the workplace and obligation to pay compensation in the personal injury or occupational disease suffered by any workman. A simpler and more direct definition of the term 'employer' is given in the Dangerous Machines (Regulations) Act, 1983. The term, 'employer' in relation to the operator of any dangerous machine means the person by whom such operator has been employed, whether for any remuneration or otherwise, for operating such a machine.

*86.* In the Employees' Provident Funds and Miscellaneous Provisions Act, 1952, the term 'employer' is defined in relation to factories as the owner or occupier of the factory, including the agent of such owner or occupier, the legal representative of deceased owner/occupiers, and also the manager of the factory, named under the Factories Act. In relation to any other establishment, the employer is the person who, or the authority which has the ultimate control over the affairs of the establishment and includes any manager, etc., to whom the said affairs are entrusted. However, anyone who is an employer by definition cannot be an employee, though he may be a salaried person. Directors/managing directors of a company are employers and cannot be treated as employees.

*87.* In the ESI Act, 1948, two terms are employed. The term 'principal employer' in relation to factories is linked to the Factories Act; in relation to any establishment under the control of the Government of India he is the authority appointed by the government, or the head of the department; and in any other establishment he may be any person responsible for its supervision and control. The managing director and other directors are not usually viewed as the principal employer. The other term is 'immediate employer', who is in a direct employment relationship with his employees and functions under the supervision of the principal employer or his agent and includes a contractor. He has the legal responsibility to maintain a register of employees and he may be paying the employees' contribution towards the ESIC to the principal employer.

*88.* In the Factories Act, 1948, the term employed is, 'occupier', which means the person who has ultimate control of the affairs of the factory. It is a lengthy definition specifying in different cases the level of authority of the person in the organization who is to be appointed as the occupier. For example, in the case of a dry dock which is available for hire, it is owner of the dock who is deemed to be the occupier, or it may be the owner of the ship, or his agent, or master, or other officer-in-charge of the ship, or any person who contracts with the owner, etc., to carry out the repair work who shall be deemed to be the occupier. In the case of a company, one of the directors has to be the occupier. The occupier is central to the purpose and scheme of the Act and has the statutory obligation to protect the workers, their health and safely against industrial and occupational hazards.

*89.* Unlike a factory where it is possible to locate the owner, employer or the occupier, it is very difficult to enforce norms of health and safety in an establishment which by its nature is unorganized and not a factory. In the *Beedi* and Cigar Workers (Conditions of Employment) Act, 1966, it has become necessary to define the terms 'contractor' as well as 'employer'; the latter also includes the term 'principal employer', and any other person to whom the affairs of the establishment are entrusted. In relation to contract labour the law refers to the principal employer and in relation to 'other labour' the employer is the person who has the ultimate control over the establishment; or, by reason of his advancing money, supplying goods or otherwise, he may have a substantial interest in the control of the affairs of the establishment. The long arm of the law cannot reach a person unless he can be identified in relation to an establishment as one discharging the functions of an employer, and in practice this has been very difficult to achieve. In order to overcome this handicap, the term 'employee' had to be expanded. In the state legislation, viz. the Kerala *Beedi* and Cigar Workers Welfare Fund Act, 1955 the term 'employee' has been enlarged to include 'any person not employed by an employer or a contractor but working with the permission of or under agreement with the employer or contractor; and any person employed by petty shop owners for making *Beedi* or Cigars'. This did not suffice, so the term 'self-employed person' has been included in the Act in order to expand its scope to bring within its ambit as many workers and families of workers engaged in this trade as might be feasible.

*90.* In the Unorganized Workers Social Security Act, 2008, the term 'employer' means a person or an association of persons who has engaged or employed an unorganized worker either directly or indirectly. Along with it the term 'home-based' worker in relation to the employer has also been defined, irrespective of whether the employer provides the equipment, materials or other inputs.

*91.* Under the Industrial Disputes Act the term 'employer' is defined only in respect of government owned industries. For the private sector the term is left undefined but this lacuna is made up by the very wide definitions of the terms 'industry' and 'industrial dispute'. In the public sector, even department heads can be treated as employers unless another person is duly notified. In the private sector it is the dictionary meaning of the word that would suffice. Obviously an employer would exist only in relation to his employees, which further implies that there must be in existence an employer-employee relationship. Where such a relationship has been found to be absent the employer too is non-existent. In Rajasthan state a new sub-clause has been added to include the term, 'the owner of the industry'.

## §4. Individual Disputes

*92.* Under the ID Act, 1947, Section 2A provides for an individual workman to raise an industrial dispute pertaining to termination of service on any ground by the employer though no other workman or any union is a party to it. He may make an application to the Labour Court for adjudication and the court shall have the jurisdiction to do so. All matters covered by the expression 'employment or non employment or the terms of employment or with the conditions of labour of any person' can be raised as industrial disputes', and by an individual workman if he has been refused employment. The Amendment Act 2010 provides for direct application to the Labour Court/Tribunal for adjudication of the dispute after the expiry of 45 days from the date he made an application for conciliation of the dispute and can expect adjudication proceeding to commence without any reference being made by the government. In this respect both the government and the union have become redundant.

*93.* The ID Act was amended in 1982 to provide for the setting up of grievance settlement authorities (GSA) and reference of certain individual disputes to them. The term employed is 'an industrial dispute connected with an individual workman' and excludes collective disputes. Such a dispute can be referred to the GSA both by the workman concerned and by any trade union of which he is a member. This provision bars the raising of individual disputes before the Labour Court. However, this enactment has not yet been notified and is not in force. In the new Industrial Disputes (Amendment) Act, 2010, it is provided to constitute a Grievance Redressal Machinery in every industrial establishment employing 20 or more workmen for the resolution of individual grievances.

*94.* The ID Act, Section 33C, specifically empowers an individual workman to recover money due from an employer under a settlement or an award or under the provisions in the Act for payment of compensation due to lay-off, retrenchment and closure, by making an application to the appropriate government; once an application is made and found valid, it becomes the responsibility of the government or the district collector to recover the amount as arrears of land revenue. Should there be a dispute on the calculation of the sum of money that is payable by the employer, the government may refer it to be decided by the Labour Court. The ID Act has also made a general provision for a workman to be properly represented in any dispute, to which he is a party or raised either by any union or by any other workman to the exclusion of the union.

## §5. Appointments

*95.* The contract of employment is usually issued by a letter of appointment, which expresses the conditions of employment in very general terms. The conditions of service were rarely spelled out and were meant to be implicit and could be changed to suit the needs of employers. The one- sidedness of contracts was an obvious fact and the tendency to change the terms of employment was evidently an act of arbitrariness devoid of fairness. The courts have also disapproved of discrimination amongst employees and have practically prohibited the practice of differential service conditions and terms of employment in the same establishment. So the contract of employment is partly a 'contract' and partly 'status' which is balanced in the interest of society. A contract of employment may be formed (i) by express written agreement, (ii) by express oral agreement and also (iii) be the conduct of the parties.

*96.* Under the Employment Exchange (Compulsory Notification of Vacancies) Act, 1959, the employment exchange sponsors unemployed candidates registered with it for the employer to consider and, if suitable, to hire them. The case arose by the refusal of the employer, the S.E. Railway, to employ a physically handicapped young woman who was selected by the competent authority in a written test for class III job and placed as no. 11 in the merit list. The denial rested on the ground that her candidature was not sponsored by the Employment Exchange. In her place the candidate on merit list 12 was selected and offered appointment. She and her father appealed to every administrative forum for justice, but on the same ground met with refusal. Her appeal to the Orissa High Court was heard by a Division Bench and answered in her favour. The Court observed: 'it needs to be reiterated that whereas physically handicapped candidates are required to be approached in a compassionate manner, the authorities seem to have acted in a callous and heartless manner'. The candidate had been selected in 1989 and more than 20 years have elapsed by now. It was a travesty of justice. The writ petition was allowed and the order impugned was quashed. The Railway was directed to issue the letter of appointment and give it effect from the date on which her juniors have been given appointment, also full back wages and seniority. The Central Government as Union of India appealed against the High Court order to the Supreme Court. The Apex Court expressed deep disappointment on the attitude displayed by the Government, quoted the Constitution (Article 41) and Part IV laying down the Directive Principles which reflect the aspirations of the people. The Court quoted Hellen Keller that 'Science may have found a cure for most evils, but it has found no remedy for the worst of them all, the apathy of human beings.' This appeal was illustrative of lack of sensitivity on the part of administrators entrusted with the task of doing justice. The Court found no merit in the arguments advanced by the Additional Solicitor General representing, the petitioner. There is nothing in the Employment Exchanges Act which obliges the employer to appoint only those who are sponsored by the Employment Exchange. The employer, though obliged to notify vacancies, is not obliged to recruit only those who are sponsored by the employment exchanges. The object of the Act is not to restrict but to enlarge the field of choice, so that the employer may choose the best and the most efficient and to provide an opportunity to the worker to have his claim for appointment considered without the worker having to knock at every door for employment.

> The South Eastern Railway Committed grave illegality by denying appointment to the respondent only on the ground that she did not get her name sponsored by an employment exchange. The appellant violated her right to equality in the matter of employment guaranteed under Article 16 of the Constitution. The appeal was dismissed and the appellant were required to pay her cost of Rs. 300,000 with two months from today. The High Court order was modified in as much as the pay would be notionally fixed from the date as already decided, but the actual monetary benefits will be given effect to from 5, September 2008, the date of the High Court order.[53]

## §6. Natural Justice

*97.* The principles of natural justice are bound by admissible rules of evidence. In one case the Supreme Court held that though absence of reasons in a disciplinary order might amount to denial of natural justice, the dismissal of a bank officer on facts was justified.

> Once the necessary material was placed on record and when the charge sheeted officer had no explanation to offer, the inquiry officer could not have taken any other view. The order of a bank officer may not be written in the manner in which a judicial officer would write. Yet what one has to see is whether the order is sufficiently clear and contains the reasons in justification for the conclusion arrived at. The High Court has ignored this aspect. Once the charges were found to have been established, the High Court had no reason to interfere in the decision. Even though there was sufficient documentary evidence on record, the High Court has chosen to hold that the findings of the inquiry officer were perverse. A perverse finding is one which is based on no evidence or one that no reasonable person would arrive at. Unless it is found that some relevant evidence has not been considered, or that certain inadmissible material has

53. LLJ, Vol. 2, 2011, *Union of India and Other* v. *Pritilata Nanda*, Supreme Court of India, pp. 305–312.

> been taken into consideration, the finding cannot be said to be perverse. Strict rules of evidence are not applicable to departmental enquiry proceedings. The only requirement of law is that the allegation against the delinquent officer must be established by such evidence acting upon which a reasonable person acting reasonably and objectivity may arrive at a finding upholding the gravamen of the charge against the delinquent officer. Mere conjecture or surmises cannot sustain the finding of guilt even in departmental enquiry proceedings.

The appeal was allowed and the impugned judgment and order passed by the division bench of the Allahabad High Court were set aside.[54]

*98.* The above principles mean that no tribunal can be a judge in its own case, that whoever is required to discharge a quasi-judicial function must not by conduct show that he is interested in any case, that witnesses should give evidence in the presence of the petitioner, and there should be an opportunity of cross-examining them, and that copies of documents used against the petitioner should be furnished to him. Furthermore, though an administrative body is not bound by the technical rules of evidence, it is yet bound by the rules of natural justice and it must be capable of reaching an independent decision. The inquiry officer should record his findings on the basis of plausible reasons based on the facts and evidence placed before him. An order passed in a writ appeal to the detriment of the appellants without notice to them, was set aside as it was in violation of principles of natural justice.[55]

*99.* In one case the High Court took a position that the order of the Labour Court that the onus to prove, whether the termination of service of the petitioner was justified, was on the workman, was legal. Both courts unsettled the principle, that when a domestic enquiry is found to be irregular, or improper, or is not at all conducted on the ground that it is not practical to hold it because of some compelling circumstances, the onus to prove that the termination was justified is on the management. 'In our opinion, in light of the settled legal position on the point, the judgment of the High Court is clearly indefensible.' In any proceedings the burden of proving a fact lies on the party that substantially asserts the affirmative of the issue, and not on the party who denies it. Therefore, it follows that where an employer asserts misconduct on the part of the workman and discharges him on that ground, it is for him to prove misconduct by the workman before the Industrial Tribunal, or the Labour Court, as the case may be, by leading evidence before it and it is open to the workman to produce evidence contra. In the first instance, a workman cannot be asked to prove that he has not committed any act tantamount to misconduct. Therefore, the order of the Labour Court shifting the burden to prove issue no.1 is fallacious and

---

54. LLJ, 2011, *General Manager, Punjab and Sind Bank and others* v. *Daya Singh*, Supreme Court of India, pp. 255–260.
55. LLJ, December 2010, *TVS Finance and Services Ltd* v. *S. H. Shiva Kumar*, Supreme Court of India, pp. 679–680.

the High Court should have quashed it. The appeals were allowed, the impugned judgments were set aside and the Labour Court directed to dispose of the references expeditiously. The appellants will also be entitled to costs, quantified at Rs 10,000 for each set of appeals.[56]

56. LLJ, 2011, *Amar Chakrabarty and Others* v. *Maruti Suzuki India Ltd.*, Supreme Court of India, pp 251–254.

# Chapter 2. Individual Contracts: Legal Limitations

## §1. Standing Orders

*100.* The regulation of terms of employment is done through the Industrial Employment (Standing Orders) Act, 1946. The standing orders are a written document spelling out with sufficient precision all the relevant aspects of employment, viz. hours of work and rest, shift system, including when a shift may be discontinued, attendance, holidays, compensatory holidays, leave of various kinds, including casual, medical, maternity, privilege and without pay, the procedure for granting leave, rules of discharge, lay-off and retrenchment, rules pertaining to involuntary stoppage of work, wage-payment system (sometimes the details of incentive schemes are also included), the fines and penalties along with the relevant rules, misconducts and the procedure of disciplinary action, etc. The certified standing orders have a statutory force and are binding upon the employer. 'Conditions of employment' have been taken to include terms of recruitment. The terms of employment specified in standing orders would prevail over the corresponding terms in the contract of service. The scope of standing orders has been expanded and includes, service record, confirmation, age of retirement, transfers, medical aid in case of accident, secrecy and exclusive service. Sexual harassment now also forms part of the Model Standing Orders.

*101.* The legal position of standing orders is that though not law in the strict sense, they nonetheless have the force of law. This is so in the sense that there cannot be any individual contract of employment which is in conflict with the provisions of the SO. In respect of all matters covered in the SO the Labour Court cannot disregard them; yet, this is possible if an industrial dispute is raised regarding their fairness or reasonableness. The SO have the force of law in that regardless of any express or implied terms of contract of employment the provisions made therein displace those provisions in the letter of appointment which are in conflict. The Act is applicable only to those industrial establishments which employ 100 or more workers, if the Central Act is applicable, or 50 or more in several states in which it has been accordingly amended. The certifying officer, if asked to interpret any clause in the standing orders, may do so, but not adjudicate on the material aspects which require evidence and arguments on facts pertaining to the dispute.

*102.* Section 13A of the Act provides for interpretation of a certified standing order by the Labour Court on an application by any employer or workman or a trade union and further that, having heard and decided the question referred to it, the decision of the Labour Court would be final and binding. It only provides a forum for interpretation of the meaning of any clause or term employed in any standing orders. The Supreme Court held that on certification the SO would not acquire a statutory force or become part of the statute. Any violation of the standing orders would result in the workman seeking relief either through the Industrial Disputes Act or taking recourse to the civil court. Earlier, the age of retirement was not on the list of subjects in the schedule to the Act, hence it did not form part of the company's certified standing orders. Later, in a settlement with the union 58 years was agreed to as the age of retirement. Accordingly a worker was retired at 58 years, though he contended that 60 years was to be the age of retirement under the subsequently revised CSO. The settlement came into force in 1978, while the revised CSO were put into effect on January 19, 1980. The court held that the settlement would prevail, more so since in a subsequent settlement this provision was left unchanged. The Court noted that in a notification issued in January 1983, age of superannuation was stated as 60 years. But it had no bearing on a subsisting settlement.[57]

*103.* In the new Schedule I-B, prescribed as the MSO, the record of age is specified in considerable detail. The date of birth once entered in the service card shall be the sole evidence of age in relation to all matters including the date retirement. On the question of confirmation, the MSO stipulates that in accordance with the terms and conditions given in the letter of confirmation, the employer shall confirm the eligible workman and issue a letter of confirmation. On age of retirement or superannuation, the MSO provides that it shall be as may be agreed upon between the employer and the workman under an agreement or a settlement or award which is binding on both the parties. But where there is no such agreed age the retirement age shall be on completion of 58 years. A sick public sector company decided to roll back the age of retirement from 60 years to 58 years. This was challenged in the High Court The court found that the SO provided for normal age of retirement at 58 years but also for the medically fit to retire at 60 years. The court held that this right had to be respected until the SOs were legally amended. However, there would be no interference with the policy of fixing the age of retirement at 58 years.[58]

*104.* Employing organizations, particularly in the public sector, often have in existence parallel conduct regulations which cover the same ground on misconduct as the standing orders. In one case, an employee had married another woman during the lifetime of his wife in violation of a particular conduct regulation which made it a misconduct. However, under the company's standing orders this act found no mention. The employer started the disciplinary proceedings, serving notice upon the employee as to why he should not be removed from service. This was challenged in a writ petition. The Madras High Court held that no disciplinary action could be taken in respect of an act which was not enumerated as an act of misconduct in the company's standing orders, and the show cause notice was quashed. In Madhya Pradesh, the Standard Standing Orders Rules provide for the definition of a 'permanent' employee as one who has completed six months' satisfactory service in a clear vacancy in one or more posts whether as a probationer or otherwise, or a person whose name has been entered in the muster roll and who is given a ticket of 'permanent employee'. A workman had completed more than six months service in the Public Health Engineering Department as a helper and prayed for regularization of his service because he had worked in a permanent vacant post. His pleadings were sympathetically heard and he received support at the Labour Court, the Industrial court and the High Court. The Labour Court did note that the workman had not

57. LLJ, 2006, Vol. 2, *Cochin Shipyard Ltd* v. *Iqbal*, High court of Kerala, pp. 1095–1099.
58. LLJ, July 2010, *ITI Ltd and others* v. *Venugopalan and others*, High Court of Karnataka, pp. 77–87.

been appointed to any permanent post by an appointment order, so he was not entitled to get the benefit of differences in wages, as he was a daily wager. But he was entitled to be classified in the permanent category. The state government's appeal before the Industrial Court was dismissed and so was the fate of the writ petition at the High Court. The Supreme Court admitted the appeal and held that all the lower courts failed to notice that he had not been appointed to any permanent and vacant position. The workman cannot be categorized as a permanent employee even though he may have completed six months of satisfactory service. The conditions are cumulative and not independent of each other. The orders of lower courts were set aside.[59]

*105.* A workman (general *mazdoor* category) occupied a residential quarter of the company without allotment. Allotment was by seniority and he was quite junior and could not have the allotment. He was served the eviction order and disciplinary action, inquiry and dismissal from service. The workman took the plea that failure to vacate the quarter was not listed as a 'misconduct' in the standing orders and he could not be charged of a misconduct. He succeeded in the industrial court in his defiance as well as before a single judge in the High Court. This led to an appeal to the High Court before a bench. The High Court held that the action of the workman amounted to criminal trespass. 'Non-adherence to lawful directions issued by the management squarely fell within the mischief of the Standing Orders for a clear act of misconduct, for which the management has rightly initiated disciplinary action. We hold that such an act would amount to misconduct.' The writ petition was allowed and the order of the industrial court set aside.[60]

## §2. Domestic Inquiry

*106.* Under law no disciplinary action against any workman can be contemplated before the satisfactory completion of a domestic inquiry. Only through an inquiry can an employer take disciplinary action for 'just and sufficient reasons'. The concerned worker must be given an opportunity to receive the charge, refute it and also 'to question the propriety and justice of a punitive or detrimental action taken against him'. The position of the individual workman has been reinforced by S-11A of the ID Act in 1971, by which the adjudication has been empowered to 'set aside the order of discharge or dismissal and direct reinstatement of the workman on such terms and condition, if any, as it thinks fit or give such other relief to the workman including the award of any lesser punishment in lieu of discharge or dismissal as the circumstances of the case may require'. However, adjudication cannot ask for fresh evidence and must go by the record adduced in the course of the domestic inquiry. This position has been repeatedly upheld by the higher courts. In

59. LLJ 2006, Vol. 1, *State of Madhya Pradesh and others* v. *Onkar Prasad Patel*, Supreme Court of India, pp. 683.
60. LLJ, 2006, Vol. 1, *G.M. Singareni Collieries Co. Ltd* v. *Presiding Officer, Industrial Court-1, Hyderabad and Another*, High Court of Andhra Pradesh, pp. 760–762.

one case, a bank clerk was charged of unruly behaviour towards customers and fellow employees. After a due enquiry he was dismissed from service. The Labour Court reduced the punishment to one of suspension for one year and denial of back wages. This was confirmed by a single judge of the High Court. On a writ petition the High Court bench held that once the enquiry was held to be proper and the charges proved, the Labour Court had to reach the finding that the punishment was shockingly disproportionate in order to interfere with it. The same rule applied to the High Court. The jurisdiction of the Labour Court is not to be exercised capriciously and arbitrarily. It is not unlimited. It had admittedly shown leniency by suspending him for one year instead of throwing him out to the street without a penny. The High Court held that this was done out of sympathy, not on valid judicial grounds. Section 11-A does not confer a jurisdiction of sympathy. The workman was not entitled to sympathy. The judgment was set aside. The learned single judge was wrong in affirming a faulty order. The writ appeal was allowed.[61]

*107.* The scope of domestic inquiry has been expanded by the Kerala High Court ruling that, on the facts of the case, a domestic inquiry would be considered validly held if the charge memo served on the worker mentioned his past record. In this case the worker had beaten a fellow worker and his past record was also not good. The past record, together with the finding of the misconduct, justified the dismissal.[62] In another case, the High Court of Punjab and Haryana held that if the charge of misconduct on which the workman had been retrenched had been proved on the basis of the records of the case, the holding of a domestic inquiry was not mandatory. But retrenchment was not a substitute for dismissal. This option did not exist in law. If there is a charge of misconduct, the authorities concerned with disciplinary action should conduct an inquiry and then proceed further. If the disciplinary authority disagrees with the findings of the inquiry, that the charges levelled against the workman were not proven, he was under a duty to serve a second show cause notice giving reasons for the difference of opinion and afford the opportunity of hearing to the employee. If no such opportunity was provided, the punishment inflicted was bad in law and liable to be set aside. The retrenchment order was bad and set aside.

## §3. Punishment

*108.* The punishment can take the form of (i) warning; (ii) fine; (iii) withholding of increments; (iv) demotion to a lower status and pay; (v) suspension; (vi) discharge; and (vii) dismissal. The first five are considered as minor and the last two as major punishments. A discharge connotes the termination of the contract of service and is considered less severe than dismissal, which implies the loss of additional benefits. An order of discharge does not carry any stigma for the employee. The court may decided to convert an order of dismissal into termination of service

61. LLJ, 2006, Vol. 2, *South Indian Bank Ltd* v. *V.G. Krishna Kumar and another*, High Court of Kerala, pp. 661–669.
62. LLJ, September 2010, *Sadashivam S.* v. *Managing Director, Head Office, Tamilnadu State Transport Corporation Ltd and another*, High Court of Madras, pp. 635–637.

with retirement benefits. In one case, an employee was removed from service in the Horticulture Department for non deposit of Rs 10 and Rs 20 to a total of Rs 600 over a period of one and a half years. He had rendered service for 21 years and had reached the age of superannuation. The Court held the punishment as disproportionate to the charges proved. The punishment was reduced to compulsory retirement.[63]

*109.* The company's standing orders would usually specify the quantum of punishment for different types of misconduct. For a number of offences it is permissible to deduct up to 2 per cent of wages in a month. If found guilty, a workman may be suspended for a period not exceeding four days at a time and also dismissed. But dismissal is an extreme penalty and should not be inflicted unless the misconduct deserves it. It is not necessary to list all possible misconducts in the SO. An order of dismissal may be justified, if the misconduct is serious even if it is not one listed. An act of grave misconduct would justify dismissal and in such cases the court should not lower the punishment by showing leniency. Section 11A of the ID Act vests the jurisdiction in the Labour Court to lower the punishment if it is found to be disproportionate to the offence committed by the workman. But this jurisdiction should not be arbitrarily exercised, but for good reasons only and with judicial discretion. The court/tribunal can reappraise the evidence and satisfy itself whether the evidence relied upon by the employer establishes the misconduct. The tribunal cannot interfere with the findings of the inquiry, unless the inquiry was bad and deserved to be disregarded. In one case, the punishment of 2 per cent cut in pension for loss caused to the government was contrary to evidence on record. The charges were not proved. The punishment was set aside by the Administrative Tribunal and the same was upheld by the High Court.[64]

## §4. Categories of Employees

*110.* The MSOs which serve as the basis for drafting the organization-specific SOs classify workmen as (i) permanent, (ii) probationers, (iii) *badlis*, (iv) temporary, (v) casual and (vi) apprentices. A permanent workman is one who has been engaged on a permanent basis and includes one who has completed a probationary period of three months in the same or another occupation in the industrial establishment, including breaks due to sickness, accident, leave, lock-out, strike, (not being illegal), or involuntary closure of the establishment. In the coal mines, a permanent workman is one who is appointed for an unlimited period or has satisfactorily put in three months of continuous service in a permanent post as a probationer. A probationer is one who is provisionally employed to fill a permanent vacancy and has not completed three months' service therein. A *badli* workman is appointed in the post of a permanent workman or probationer who is temporarily absent. Temporary

63. LLJ, February 2011, *K. Narayanaswamy* v. *Government of Tamil Nadu and others*, High Court of Madras, pp. 437–439.
64. LLJ, February 2011, *State of Andhra Pradesh* v. *S. Venkateswara Rao and another*, High Court of Andhra Pradesh, pp. 369–400.

and casual appointees are engaged for work which is essentially temporary or casual. An apprentice is a learner who is paid an allowance during the period of his training. He is not a workman. An employer is not obliged to offer employment to an apprentice who has completed his apprenticeship. His petition was dismissed.[65]

*111.* Appointments are made as per letters of appointment issued by the employer or his agent. Every workman should indicate his exact date of birth at the time of entering service of the establishment and produce evidence in support of the same. If it is not possible to produce an official document stating the date of birth, not even a certificate from a government medical officer indicating the probable age of the workman, an affidavit sworn in by himself, or his parents, or by a near relative before a first class magistrate, or oath commissioner may suffice. Once entered on the service card, the date of birth shall be the sole evidence of age in all matters pertaining to service, including retirement. Appointments of a contractual nature may be renewed, but will not result in a regular appointment merely on the length of service. Appointments made under a time bound contract and liable to end on a certain date are inherently contractual in nature.[66]

*112.* The letter of appointment should contain the terms and conditions for confirmation. The employer must issue a letter of confirmation to the workman in accordance with the stipulated terms and conditions. It is not common for the contents of a letter of appointment to be statutorily determined. The Sales Promotion Employees (Conditions of Services) Act, 1976, lays down all the important details that should be contained in a letter of appointment. These include the designation, date of appointment, the probation period, scale of wages, rate of increment, total wages as well as the conditions of service regulating the employees. In the public sector appointments are regulated by government policies on reservations based on caste or tribe membership and other considerations. These are open to judicial scrutiny if found to be violative of certain articles in the constitution or against well established principles of fairness and objective evaluation of facts.

## §5. Retirement

*113.* The age of retirement of a workman shall be (i) as may be agreed upon between the workman and the employer under an agreement, or, (ii) as specified in a settlement or award which is binding on both. It is not uncommon for workers covered by the Factories Act to be retired at the age of 55 years and for clerical and subordinate staff to retire at 58 years or 60 years as per the employer's policy in this regard. Many organizations have different rules for persons to be appointed on tenure posts and at the same time have an age of retirement. In one case the Supreme Court held that a person holding a tenure appointment of five years could not be

65. LLJ, January 2011, *Amar Singh* v. *Himachal Pradesh State Electricity Board and others*, High Court of Himachal Pradesh, pp. 34–38.
66. LLJ, 2007, Vol. 3, *Vijay Kumar and other* v. *State T.B. Control Society, Haryana and another*, High Court of Punjab and Haryana, pp. 918–922.

forced to retire on reaching the age of 62 years by curtailing his tenure. The age of 62 years is for superannuation and is irrelevant for tenure appointments. 'The concept of superannuation which is well-understood in service jurisprudence is alien to tenure appointments which have a fixed life span.' However, a person in government service can be compulsorily retired either as a punishment for serious dereliction of duty, or on attaining a certain age for reasons connected with management policy, such as, right sizing of manning a level which is overstaffed. Such a retirement though accompanied with incidental remarks about unsatisfactory service would not be held as stigmatic, hence not a punishment. In this case the employee had become dead wood. There was no place for natural justice in compulsory retirement.[67]

*114.* An internal senior auditor of a bank was compulsorily retired on charges of misappropriating funds and not discharging his duty with integrity. He received cash from 14 borrowers adding up to Rs. 46,790 and issued letters to the circle officer confirming adjustment of the accounts, but did not deposit the money so collected. He deposited the money only after the bank come to know about it and the lapel was pointed out to him. He received cash between 31 March 1995 and 7 April 1995 but returned the money to the bank on 27 February 2000. His defence was that he has inadvertently kept the money at his residence and in the meantime he was transferred to New Delhi. The Enquiry Officer held him guilty of the charge. He was suspended and later retired compulsorily. The High Court which heard his writ petition noticed that on two earlier occasions he had faced departmental proceedings and suffered the penalty of reduction in the time scale of pay and censure. The respondent bank took the plea that, having lost confidence in the petitioner, there was nothing wrong in dispensing with his services by imposing the penalty of compulsory retirement. The arguments advanced on his behalf were that there was no misappropriation since the amounts were returned, the penalty was too harsh and totally uncalled for the bank pointed out that the petitioner will be entitled to all retirement benefits and there was no case to interfere with the penalty under the Court's writ jurisdiction. More so, if the bank had not detected the misappropriation the petitioner would not have deposited the amounts. The court did not find any merit in the writ petition and accordingly dismissed it.[68]

*115.* The Supreme Court heard an appeal by a former Metropolitan Magistrate against the High Court Division Bench which dismissed her writ petition against compulsory retirement in terms of the Maharashtra Civil Services (Discipline and Appeal) rules, 1979. The charge was that she travelled in the local train without ticket on more than one occasion and asserted judicial immunity for such conduct. She asserted to the railway staff that the magistrates need not have a ticket. She had given threats to the railway staff and created unnecessary scene on the railway platform and this was viewed as a misconduct unbecoming of a judicial officer. On one

67. LLJ, 2009, Vol. 3, *National Aviation Co.* v. *S.M.K. Khan,* Supreme Court of India, pp. 40–44.
68. LLJ, 1, 2012, *Uma Kant Mili* v. *Punjab National Bank and others*, High Court of Gauhati, pp. 193–196.

occasion she was helped with money by another metropolitan magistrate who travelled by the next train and was informed of her plight. The disciplinary authority had a formal enquiry instituted and decided that the charges were proved. The disciplinary authority consisted of the Chief Justice and Judges of the Bombay High Court. They gave her opportunity to explain and defend herself. Finally the penalty of compulsory retirement was proposed. This was accepted by the State Government and the order of compulsory retirement was issued. The Apex Court held that it could probably interfere with the quantum of punishment only when it was shocking to the concience of the Court. In this case it could not be said that the punishment was disproportionate to the offence. In a country formed by rule of law, nobody is above the law, including judicial officers. A judge's official and personal conduct must be in line with the highest standards of propriety and probity. The Court found no reason to interfere with the findings arrived at by the High Court and fully agreed with its decision. The appeal was without merit and the same was dismissed.[69]

*116.* To retire voluntarily is the right of workmen. However, it has become a standard practice for employing organizations to formulate and put into effect voluntary retirement schemes usually in consultation with the unions. In one case a workman doing manual work was found to be suffering from chronic obstructive pulmonary disease and was given light duty. A voluntary retirement scheme provided for the retirement of old men and infirm workers with additional monetary benefits. At one stage the workman was informed that he had already availed of the facility of light duty and now he should take voluntary retirement, failing which his services would be terminated on medical grounds. The Delhi High Court which heard the workman's petition upheld the management's position. Where an employee retires under a voluntary retirement scheme before reaching the pensionable age, he has entitlement to an addition of five years of notional service, as per the regulations in force. Though the VRS did not envisage payment of pension, the court held that the bank was responsible for formulation of the scheme and must bear the risk of clarity if any.[70]

*117.* In a case the Labour Court adjudicated the grievance of an accountant who was directed to be retired on reaching the age of retirement at 58 years. The employee took the plea that since there were no service rules in the organization, he was entitled to work as long as he was hale and hearty. The employing organization, a Nidhi, told the Labour Court that it was the established practice of the management to superannuate people on completion of 58 years of age. Moreover, in the absence of service rules, the model standing orders would apply and in it 58 years of age is laid down as the age of superannuation. In the instant case, the employee was retired, not retrenched. He was the secretary of the union and there was an earlier settlement in which the demand for raising the age of retirement to 60 years was

---

69. LLJ, 2, 2011, *Arundhati Ashok Walawalkar* v. *State of Maharashtra*, Supreme Court of India, pp. 206–211.
70. LLJ, 2009, Vol. 3, *Bank of India and others* v. *K. Mohandas and others*, Supreme Court of India, pp. 609–623.

dropped. The Labour Court found supporting evidence in the documents produced, that the age of retirement in the Nidhi was 58 years. Accordingly the industrial dispute was rejected. The retired employee filed a writ petition against the Labour Court's order. The management informed the High Court that there was no life time employment to any one. Only in one case an employee was given a two years extension of service. The appellant had failed to prove that in three cases the employees continued to work beyond the age of 58 years. The petitioner was unable to give the dates of birth of these individuals. In the Group Gratuity Life Assurance Scheme of the Life Insurance Corporation of India, to the question on normal retirement age, 58 years is denoted. A permanent job does not carry the promise of life time employment. In the Nidhi there has been no practice to employ any workman till life time. The Labour Court's award is neither perverse nor illegal nor unsustainable accordingly. The writ petition was dismissed.[71]

*118.* In an unusual case the High Court found that the order of discharge from service on medical grounds was legal, though the medical board did not assign any reasons for declaring him medically unfit for duty. However, a voluntary retirement scheme was already in operation and the employer had extended the benefit of VRS to three other employees who were not found to be medically fit and discharged them from service. This was the result of writ petitions filed by them which were allowed by the court. This too was an identical case, and the court decided to grant him the same relief.[72]

*119.* In a unique case heard by the Supreme Court it deart with the right of the management to deny a request for voluntary retirement of a highly valued officer, though the bank in question had a voluntary retirement scheme in place since November 2000 and was ended five weeks later on January 2001. The Court observed that in case the bank undertakes manpower planning for downsizing the organization and reduces overhead costs, considerations that would apply would lead 'to adopt measures to have optimum human resources at various levels in keeping with the business strategies, skills profile to achieve the balanced age and requirement of the bank. 'The bank would not like to lose the best people. On the facts, the Court held, the bank's decision not to accept the respondent's request for voluntary retirement was legitimate and did not call for interference, earlier in 3, September 2003, the High Court had admitted a writ petition by the officer and quashed the decision of the bank rejecting the application for voluntary retirement and directed it to accept the same forthwith. The bank appealed to the Apex Court and secured a stay on the High Court order in February 2005. However, the officer reached the age of superamuation on 6 June 2009 and retired. The Court suggested to the two parties to try to come to some amicable settlement, since the officer had already received all his dues and was getting a monthly pension. The officer insisted

71. LLJ, 2, 2011, *T. Anantha Krishnan* v. *Management of Madras Purasawalkam Hindu Jonapakara Saswatha Nidhi or the Permanent General Benefit Fund Ltd., Chennai and Another*, High Court of Madras, pp. 557–561.
72. LLJ, 2009, Vol. 4, *D. Hanumatha Rao* v. *A.P. State Agro Industries Development Corporation Ltd*, High Court of Andhra Pradesh, pp. 96–98.

that the appeal be heard on merits, and in case it is dismissed, the Court may consider how to appropriately provide him the relief. The Court noted that the bank had reserved an absolute discretion, subject to recording the reasons, either to accept or reject the request for voluntary retirement. The respondent applied on 15, December 2000 for voluntary retirement though at that time he was working as Chief Manager of the bank in the city of Allahabad. The bank declined the request, considering the business/organizational requirements and administrative exigencies of the bank. The officer challenged the decision in the High Court. The bank informed the Court that there were 187 officers at scale IV and 80 had applied for voluntary retirement. The management accepted the applications of 22 officers and rejected others. The High Court took exception to the absolute discretion reserved by the management and found the explanation provided by the bank as very vague. The service record showed that the respondent had a highly merited service graph of promotions and dedicated service, therefore, the bank did not want to lose him. In an earlier judgment delivered in 2006, the Apex Court had unheld the principle of absolute discretion in accepting or rejecting an application for voluntary retirements, 'that a VRS was not a proposal or an offer but merely an invitation to treat, and the applications filed by the employees constituted an offer.' In the process of shedding surplus manpower no organization would like to lose its best people. However, absolute discretion cannot be completely uncontrolled, whimsical or capricious. In this case, the bank's decision was a legitimate to exercise of discretion that did not warrant any interference by the High Court. Its judgment is quite unsustainable. The appeal was allowed, the impugned judgment was set aside and the writ petition filed by the respondent was dismissed.[73]

*120.* In a case the High Court had to decide the question, whether the cessation of service brought about by resignation could be viewed as retirement for pensionary benefits. The petitioner, as an officer in the bank, wrote a letter requesting voluntary retirement after putting in 23 years of pensionable service. The Assistant General Manager informed her that her request could not be accepted as she had not completed 24 years of pensionable service, but, if she was agreeable, her application would be treated as resignation, if she would sign on the duplicate of the letter in token of her acceptance. She agreed and conveyed her consent. Following this, about a month later in January 1992, the order accepting her resignation was passed. Later the bank revised the pensionable service requirement to increase the eligibility to pension to those who had retired between 1 January 1986 and 1 January 1993. The petitioner thought that she qualified only if the letter seeking voluntary retirement was restored and the fact of resignation set aside for doing her justice. The bank refused, citing the fact of resignation which could not be treated as retirement. The appellant filed a writ petition in the High Court. The Court pointed out that if she had any questions to raise this should have been done when she received the

73. LLJ, 2, 2011, *Chairman and MD, Indian Overseas Bank and Others* v. *Tribhuwan Nath Srivastava*, Supreme Court of India, pp. 1-8.

order accepting her resignation. 'Without any reservation, she accepted the benefit', now the matter could not be reopened. The petition was dismissed.[74]

*121.* In an important case the Supreme court heard an appeal by Air India Cabin Crew Association against the High Court decision, rejecting the petition challenging the administrative order bringing. the female and male cabin crew at par in respect of age of retirement. The issue was whether the promotional avenues and other terms of service of the pre-1997 cadre of Assistant Flight Pursers could be changed to their prejudice despite the provision of the Air Corporation (Transfer of undertakings and repeal) Act, 1994 and also in view of several court judgments. and various agreements and settlements arrived at between the parties. A related question was whether a policy decision of gender neutralization, which was prospective in nature, could be applied retrospectively to the pre 1997 cadre of pursers, and whether this was contrary to the Articles 14, 19 and 21 of the constitution. The record showed that for several decades two distinct cadres, viz. male air flight pursers and female air hostesses existed with their own terms and conditions and promotional avenues. In 1980 several air hostesses had questioned the validity of such regulations as unconstitutional. The 1994 Act provided, that following the mergers of Indian Air lines with Air India, all the employees would have the same tenure, remuneration and conditions of service, including superannuation, as they had before the merger. Following the judgement in the *Air Hostesses case*, several devices for promotion were introduced by Air India Ltd. At the same time, separate promotional avenues, hierarchy and job functions on board an aircraft were maintained for the male and female cabin crew. In June 1997, a promotional policy was issued for all the cabin crew members, but treated the pre-1997 crew differently from post-1997 crew. In another case, the Bombay High Court held that the provision for air hostesses to end flying duties at the age of 50 years and thereafter they may accept ground duties upto 58 years was discrimination based on sex and violative of the constitution as well as the Equal Remuneration Act, 1976. In 2003 the management allowed air hostesses to fly up to the age of 58 years but the two cadres were continued separate, not merged. In 2005 it was indicated that the executive female cabin crew would be eligible for the position of In flight Supervisor along with the Executive Male Cabin Crew. The Delhi High Court, Division Bench, held in 2001, that the expression 'In-Flight Supervisor' was a description of a job function and not a post exclusively reserved for the male cabin crew. The Apex Court was appealed against the decision of the Delhi High Court. The High Court should not have accepted the proposal of merger of the two cadres without the consent of employees. It was wrong to allow air hostesses to continue to fly beyond 50 years. On behalf of the government, it was explained that in the new promotion policy, there was a merger of the male and female cabin crew, both the existing crew and the new crew recruits, to make them all eligible for the Career Advancement Scheme. Earlier, a majority of airhostesses had wanted to retire at the age of 50 years or opt for ground duties upto 58 years on a par with males. By increasing the flying age the complaint of discrimination was addressed and that the opportunities

74. LLJ, 1, 2012, *Vaidehi Rajagopalan* v. *Managing Director, State Bank of Hyderabad, Gun Foundry, Hyderabad*, High Court of Andhra Pradesh, pp. 142-144.

for male and female crew should be equal both to the level of workmen and the executive cadres. The Court held that the Management of Air India was always entitled to alter its policies with regard to their workmen, subject to the consensus arrived at between the parties in supersession of all previous agreements. Once an employee is placed in the Executive Cadre, he ceases to be workman and ceases to be governed by the settlements arrived at between the management and the trade union. The Apex Court decided not to interfere with the orders passed in the several writ petitions out of which the present appeal arose. These were dismissed.[75]

## §6. Increments and Promotion

*122.* The fundamental principle laid down by the adjudicators is that under normal circumstances annual increments cannot be withheld. However, employers can take disciplinary action and withhold one or more increments as a punishment if the misconduct is proved and the rules of natural justice observed. In one case the employer withheld ten annual grade increments as a punishment on the delinquent worker. This led to an industrial dispute and it was claimed that the punishment was harsh and highly excessive. The Labour Court accepted the contention and reduced the penalty to one of stoppage of three annual grade increments. This was challenged, but the Rajasthan High Court held that the adequacy of the penalty could be gone into by the tribunal and an unnecessarily harsh one could be reduced.[76] In another case the High Court set aside the harsh punishment of removal from service and substituted for it the penalty of stoppage of three increments without cumulative effect and with continuity of service.[77] Promotion can be withheld or kept in abeyance only in terms of valid rules. The constitutional scheme of equality should not be violated.

*123.* Promotion is a management prerogative. But no employee can be forced to accept it because a new contract would be substituted for the old and it is conceivable that in certain respects the promotee would stand to lose. If promotion is accepted, the employee would no doubt retain continuity of service, but he cannot claim benefits which arise out of the conditions of service he would he relinquishing. Overtime is one such benefit. On the other hand, an employee cannot claim a right to promotion unless there is a settlement or an award or the SO have made a provision to this effect. The employer may exercise his discretion on promotion provided he does not take any malafide action which amounts to an unfair labour practice. The rule is that, where merits are equal, the more senior employee is promoted. In this context seniority refers to a particular job and not the total length in service. Settlements may also determine the rule of seniority for promotion and eligibility. These may also cover minor misconducts and punishments. Where there is a

75. LLJ, Vol.1, 2012, *Air India Cabin Crew Association and others* v. *Union of India*, Supreme Court of India, pp. 305-320.
76. LLJ, Vol. 1, 1994, *Rajasthan State Road Transport Corporation* v. *Labour Court and Others*, High Court of Rajasthan, pp. 542–545.
77. LLJ. Vol. 3, 2000, *Tej Singh Manavat* v. *Bank of Rajasthan Ltd*, High Court of Rajasthan, pp. 153–154.

subsisting settlement which covers promotions and entitlement to it, if the employee suffers minor punishment and there is a bar on promotion for a fixed period of time, such as six months, his claim to it cannot be denied on the expiry of the period.[78]

*124.* On a question of whether officers who are under suspension, or facing disciplinary proceedings, can be passed over for promotion merely for these reasons, the Central Administrative Tribunal held that, though promotion was not a right, government servants were entitled to be considered for promotion as per rules and any non-consideration solely on the ground of pendency of disciplinary or criminal proceedings would be violative of the constitutional provisions of equality before law and non-discrimination. It also held, that pending the result of such proceedings, the decision of the departmental promotion committee to promote the suspended officer should be placed in a sealed envelope and action taken on it only after he has been exonerated. Promotion should be backdated and all the benefits including higher pay due on promotion should be awarded as arrears. The Supreme Court has laid down the rule that the courts should be extremely careful in exercising the power of judicial review in dealing with promotions, while the executive is also to bear in mind that in exceptional cases the assessment of merit made by them is liable to be scrutinized by courts.

*125.* Service rules provide for accelerated promotion in appreciation of outstanding performance and may include a provision removing the criterion of minimum service for eligibility to a higher post. In Andhra Pradesh the police officers were given this incentive to volunteer for the hazardous job of combating extremists who were viewed as a menace. This was challenged on the ground of being arbitrary and discriminatory and allowed for the practice of favouritism, hence violative of articles on equality, etc. of the Constitution. The Apex Court upheld the rule by providing for two classes in the same category which differed on the willingness to take risk on one's life. It is true that some may get an opportunity to serve and some may not, but that is exigencies of service. Wooden equality is not possible.[79]

## §7. Transfer

*126.* The right to transfer an employee is a management prerogative and, if exercised as incidental to the efficient working of the enterprise or establishment, it is unfettered. Tribunals may not interfere with transfers except, as with promotion, on the grounds that they have been actuated by bad intention and amount to victimization. In one case it was proved that the transfer was in the nature of punishment and it was set aside.[80] This exception to the rule is no doubt based upon experience

78. LLJ, 2009, Vol. 1, *Bank of Maharashtra* v. *Bank of Maharashtra Karamchari Sangh*, High Court of Bombay, pp. 579–589.
79. *AIR Supreme Court Weekly* 17 April 2007, *Government of Andhra Pradesh and Others* v. *Jaya Parasad Rao and others*, Supreme Court of India, pp. 2030–2045.
80. LLJ, September 2010, *Shyam Babu Bhatnagar* v. *U.P. Power Corporation Ltd and Others*, High Court of Allahabad, pp. 833–834.

that transfers are sometimes made as a form of punishment to inconvenient locations or as acts of riddance of union activists. The burden of proof of victimization, or malafide action is on the employee. If the allegation of malice is not proved the petition is liable to fail, as it happened in one case.[81] Transfer not due to exigency of service or to any genuine administrative reason but made as a punitive measure may be set aside. Transfers do not require notice of change. In another case the court held that 'the allegations of the appellant against the orders were not worthy of acceptance'.[82]

*127.* Other than the colourable exercise of power, the right of transfer is further restricted by a number of considerations. These are:

- the terms of service do not negate this right, or the SO prohibit transfers;
- a transfer should not be to the detriment of a worker and should not entail any losses;
- one cannot be transferred to an inferior position or made to perform an onerous duty not accustomed to, and
- one cannot be transferred to a new concern started subsequent to the employment of the said workman without his consent. Consent is also required if the transfer is from one state to another, unless there be a specific provision to this effect in the letter of appointment.

Such a transfer would not amount to alteration of conditions of service.[83] Refusal to accept a bonafide order may result in termination of service. It would warrant no interference. In one case a daily rated employee as a librarian was transferred to another city on the basis of service rules. A full bench heard the writ petition and held that a 'daily rated employee not appointed to a post cannot be transferred'. He was not subject to service rules governing suspension, transfer, etc. The appointment was purely contractual. The librarian was found acting unbecoming of an employee, photocopying certain documents in an unauthorized manner.[84]

## §8. Continuity of Service

*128.* The question of continuity of service arises if there is a break in service, as may occur if the business is sold or transferred to another owner. Any break in service does not affect continuity; it must be a substantial break. The change of ownership does not affect continuity. In one case it was found that the new owners tried

81. LLJ, Vol. 3, 2008, *Ms Bakarupanda Padmavathi* v. *Bank of India*, High Court of Andhra Pradesh, pp. 463–466.
82. LLJ, September 2010, *All India State Bank of Indore Officers' Coordination Committee* v. *State Bank of Indore*, High Court of Madhya Pradesh, pp. 859–861.
83. *Yearly Supreme Court Civil Digest*, 1999, *Management of Cipla Ltd* v. *R. Jayakumar*, p. 503.
84. LLJ, November 2010, *Ashok Tiwari* v. *MP Text Book corporation and another*, High Court of Madhya Pradesh, pp. 589–595.

to terminate services only to reemploy the same workers again on new contracts. So long as there is continuity of service and identity of the business is unchanged, there can be no break in service and the employees cannot be denied the benefits that accrue by virtue of length of service. However, if the employees accept termination, settle accounts and re-enter employment with the new owner, they cannot also claim continuity in service. Continuous service is inclusive of holidays. Continuity in service is not broken by a strike which is not illegal. If a workman works for 240 days in a year he is in continuous service. Workers are entitled to relief against certain kinds of mischief of interpreting the statutes against their social objectives. Weekly off and other holidays in which workers are paid wages must be included in continuous service even in seasonal industries or plantations. The issue involved the application of the Tamilnadu Industrial Establishments (Conferment of Permanent Status to Workmen) Act, 1981. The petitioners were required to pay costs.[85]

*129.* Resignation is the right of the employees. A resignation becomes effective if it is a voluntary act and the job is legally terminated. On acceptance of resignation the contract of service is mutually discharged. The contract of service also ends if a job is abandoned. According to the Supreme Court, a job cannot be deemed to have been abandoned unless the employee has a motive to do so. Where the relevant clauses in the SO have made an explicit provision as to what will constitute abandonment, viz. unauthorized absence for the specified number of consecutive days, the absentee worker can be automatically discharged. In one case a clerk in a bank was retired from service as per the settlement due to absence without leave for 980 days. His petition was dismissed.[86]

*130.* An employee forwarded a letter of resignation on 3 May 2006 but withdrew it on 5 August 2006. The employer apparently accepted the letter of resignation on 21 July 2006 but failed to communicate the same, nor was the employee relieved from service. The employer declined the second request of withdrawing the resignation. In the Labour Court to which the dispute was referred for adjudication the employer said that the employee was irregular in attendance and was unauthorized by absent from 5 July 2005 to 15 November 2005 and leave was refused, instead a show cause notice was issued on 15 April 2006; he submitted the resignation letter. The resignation was accepted with effect from 2 June 2006. The Labour Court held that the employee had the legal right to withdraw the proposal of resignation before the communication of its acceptance. The Labour Court directed reinstatement with continuity of service and 50 per cent back wages from 5 August 2006 to the date of reinstatement. The employer filed a writ petition against this award. The High Court referred to a judgment by the Apex Court which answered

85. LLJ, June 2010, *Tata Tea Ltd and Others* v. *State of Tamilnadu and Others*, High Court of Madras, pp. 762–778.

86. LLJ, September 2010, *Jaswinder Singh* v. *Regional Manager, Punjab National Bank, Karnal and Another,* High Court of Punjab and Haryana, pp. 702–704 also LLJ, 2008 Vol. 2, *Tata Engineering Locomotive Co. Ltd* v. *Ishwarchand Tarachand Jain and Another,* High Court of Bombay, p. 1146 (brief resume).

the question, whether it was open to a person having exercised, the option of voluntary retirement to withdraw the said offer after its acceptance, but before it was made effective. It held that the resignation, inspite of its acceptance, can be withdrawn before the effective date and allowed the employee to continue in service with all consequential benefits. The employee is deemed to have the locus poenitentiae to withdraw the letter of resignation. This was the ground taken by the Labour Court in the instant case. Unless the employee is relieved of the duty, the jural relationship of the employee and the employer does not come to an end. The petition was rejected.[87]

## §9. Abandonment of Job

*131.* The legal position on abandonment is that it must be proved and the workman who has been on unauthorized absence but reports for duty should be given a chance to explain his conduct. If it is negligence on his part it would not be fair to treat his absence as abandonment. In one case the employee fell ill and his request for medical leave was declined, and his services terminated. This order was set aside.[88] In another case the termination due to abandonment of job was not upheld though the plea taken, that, it was an order of dismissal but without holding an inquiry and observing rules of natural justice, was also rejected. Termination was treated as retrenchment.[89] In another case a workman, a clerk, disobeyed the order of transfer and his job was terminated on the ground of abandonment of job. The plea of illegal termination was rejected and he was not entitled to relief. [90]

*132.* The service of employees who have gone on a strike, though it may be illegal, cannot be terminated on the ground of voluntary abandonment of jobs. The SC has defined it to mean, 'voluntary relinquishment', implying that the failure to perform the duties must be with actual or imputed intention to abandon and relinquish the office or job. The authority who has to take a decision in the matter 'should act fairly, justly, reasonably and impartially'. Action taken should not be arbitrary, fanciful or oppressive.[91] The doctrine of natural justice was an in-built requirement of the standing orders. A workman lost his job on the ground of remaining absent without leave for four days and the SO provided for automatic termination. Termination

87. LLJ, January, 2012, *Managing Director, Compco Ltd., Mangalore* v. *B. Vishnu Murthy, Mangalore*, High Court of Karnataka, pp. 819-823.
88. LLJ, Vol. 2, 1994, *Joginder Chand* v. *Punjab Electricity Board,* High Court of Punjab and Haryana, pp. 113–115.
89. LLJ, Vol. 1, 2000, *A.B.L. Ltd, Durgapur, Burdwan* v. *Radha Gobinda Ghatak and Others*, High Court of Calcutta, pp. 686–694.
90. LLJ, 2008, Vol. 2, *State of Gujarat* v. *Dinesh S. Raval C/O All Gujarat General Mazdoor Sangh*, High Court of Gujarat, pp. 27–29.
91. Supreme Court opinion quoted in the Calcutta High Court judgment cited in ftnote 2 in para. 112, LLJ, Vol. 1, 2000, p. 692.

was held as illegal since it was not preceded by a departmental proceeding and hearing. But instead of reinstatement, a compensation of Rs 15,000 was ordered.[92] In another case the termination was found justified since the inquiry officer's findings showed that the charge was upheld. Earlier too he was issued charge sheets and given punishment for unauthorized absence. Punishment was not disproportionate to the gravity of misconduct.[93]

92. LLJ, 2007, Vol. 2, *Chandra Pal Shukla* v. *Labour Court (V), Kanpur and Other,* High Court of Allahabad, pp. 644–646.
93. LLJ, 2009, Vol. 2, *Shyambada Bouri* v. *Eastern Coalfields Ltd and Others,* High Court of Calcutta, pp. 588–589.

# Chapter 3. Settlement of Individual Disputes

## §1. What is an Individual Dispute?

*133.* In Indian statutes the term 'individual dispute' does not occur. In the ID Act the common term employed is 'industrial dispute' for both individual and collective disputes. When an industrial dispute is sponsored by the union it is of course a collective dispute. However, the courts have taken the view that where a dispute between a workman and the employer has the possibility of becoming a collective dispute it should be covered under the ID Act. Individual disputes need not turn into a collective dispute because they arise from individual workman's relationship with his supervisor or may pertain to a real or perceived grievance of unfairness by the employer. The lacuna in the statute has been corrected by the Industrial Disputes (Amendment) Act, 2010. It permits a workman to make a direct application to the Labour Court/ Tribunal for adjudication of a dispute after the expiry of 45 days from the date of his application to the conciliation officer. If there is delay in conciliation, the workman need not be delayed. He may bypass the government as well as the union in pressing his dispute for adjudication. Such a provision already exists in Andhra Pradesh and Tamilnadu.

## §2. Termination of Service

*134.* A dispute pertaining to termination of service can take the form of an individual dispute which the concerned workman can raise under Section 2A of the ID Act, or it may be sponsored by the union and become a collective industrial dispute under Section 10. In several state amendments (as in Andhra Pradesh), it is clearly stipulated that on receipt of an application from the aggrieved workman the Labour Court shall have jurisdiction to adjudicate upon any matter in the dispute, as if it had been referred to it by the government. In Tamil Nadu the amendment stipulates that adjudication may commence only after the failure of conciliation proceedings. In West Bengal the Act has been amended to provide for cases of the employer refusing employment, which goes well beyond the issue of termination of services. Section 2A is viewed as a legal fiction, or a narrow exception to the general definition of the term, 'industrial dispute'. This section does not bar the Labour court from adjudication in a dispute which has been sponsored by a union and it does not mean that as soon as other workmen have joined in the dispute it goes out of the purview of Section 2A.[94] Section 10 and Section 2A operate in different fields. Section 10 operates where the union or other workman espouse the dispute, while Section 2 (Andhra Pradesh) operates where the union does not do so.[95]

94. LLJ, Vol. 1, 1995, *Maharashtra General Kamgar Union* v. *State of Maharashtra and Others,* High Court of Bombay, pp. 841–844.

95. LLJ, Vol. 1, 2000, *Nutrine Confectionery Co. Ltd Chittoor* v. *Government of Andhra Pradesh and Others,* High Court of Andhra Pradesh, pp. 655–659.

*135.* Contracts of employment which are governed by the standing orders and the ID Act are subject to restrictions as provided therein. Section 25-F stipulates conditions precedent to retrenchment of a workman which will apply if he has been in continuous service for not less than one year. Section 25B defines 'continuous service' to include interruptions caused by sickness, or authorized leave, or an accident, or a legal strike or lock-out, or a cessation of work which is not due to any fault of the workman. Furthermore, one year means that he should have been employed below ground in a mine for 190 days and 240 days in any other case. Should there be an illegal strike, the benefit of Section 25F would still be applicable, if excluding the period of illegal strike the workman actually worked for more than 240 days in the year. This period is to be counted form the date of joining though on an *ad hoc* duty. A workman who has been in service for 240 days in a year cannot be retrenched without retrenchment compensation. There are a large number of cases on the applicability and scope of Section 25F. The burden of proving engagement for 240 days is on the workman. This was not proved in one case, so his complaint of violation of Section 25F failed.[96] He was not entitled to retrenchment compensation. Section 25F provides for three rules. First, that a notice will be served upon the workman or wages paid in lieu of notice. Second, that compensation at the rate of 15 days of wages for every completed year of service has been paid. Third, that a notice is served on the government. While the first and second conditions are mandatory, the third is merely directory, not mandatory. The hardship suffered by the workman is partially redressed by fulfilling the two clauses, but not the third which does not protect the workman. The order of the Labour Court for ordering reinstatement due to breach of the third rule was quashed and the petition was allowed.[97]

*136.* If legal stipulations have not been scrupulously followed the termination may be set aside and the workman reinstated. The normal rule is reinstatement with back wages. In one case the Labour Court while ordering reinstatement decided that the worker was entitled to only 50 per cent of his usual wages from the date of termination to the actual reinstatement. This was contested. The High Court held that there had occurred a wholly irregular exercise of jurisdiction by an arbitrary denial of half of back wages to the workman who was otherwise entitled to full wages. Payment of back wages is a matter of discretion, to be decided having regard to the facts and circumstances of the case, but it should be judicious. The Labour Court is the final court of facts and it may come to the conclusion that payment of 60 per cent wages would be just and proper. Recent court judgments have changed the law in as much as payment of full back wages has become less common. In several cases back wages were reduced to 30 per cent.[98] Some punishment was considered necessary in the case. Moreover, a workman in unemployment has to plead that he was

96. LLJ, September 2010, *Sumer Singh* v. *Chief Conservator of Forests, Haryana* and *Others,* High Court of Punjab and Haryana, pp. 834–836.
97. LLJ, September 2010, *Simplex Electronics* v. *Vimlaben Atmaram Yadav and Another,* High Court of Gujarat, pp. 841-848.
98. LLJ, 2006, Vol. 4, *Gujarat State Road Transport Corp.* v. *Narmadashanker G. Joshi,* High Court of Gujarat, p. 1033 (NOC).

not employed in order to claim back wages.[99] In one case the order of back wages was set aside. The petitioner had invoked the remedial jurisdiction after more than 10 years. Back wages were denied.[100]

*137.* Although the principle that employers have a right to terminate the service of workmen with a simple notice of discharge without giving any reasons has survived, the question whether any termination is tantamount to retrenchment has also survived, and this necessitated an amendment to the ID Act in 1984. Previously, the term 'retrenchment' was defined to mean termination of service for 'any reason whatsoever' and covered every termination other than the ones that had been explicitly excluded. Hence, discharge of workers at the end of contract was also covered. The amended Act has widened the scope of the term 'retrenchment' and excludes termination due to non-renewal of contract of employment on its expiry and due to continued ill-health. In a recent case a workman was appointed with a fixed period, which was extended twice and thereafter it was terminated. The letter of appointment carried the stipulation that it was upto a certain date or of a suitable candidate being available. The process of advertisement and appointment was already initiated. His plea for retrenchment compensation under Section 25F was rejected by Labour Court as the case came under Section 2(oo) (bb) which meant that the termination was due to the expiry of contract of employment, hence excluded from the scope of the term, 'retenchment'. The single judge of the High Court disagreed and set aside the order of the Labour Court. The High Court bench which heard the writ petition reversed the order of the single judge and restored that of the Labour Court. In this case Section 25F was not applicable.[101]

*138.* Recent case law has established a few modifications in the aforesaid principles in relation to facts. The jurisdiction of Labour Court cannot travel beyond the scope of reference made by the appropriate government. It cannot enlarge the reference on the pleading of the appellant. The government knowing the full facts and the contention of the union that the employer, against whom the dispute had arisen and as a result there was closure, was merely an agent of the real employer, or that he was a benami (unnamed) owner, yet chose to limit the reference to determine whether the closure was justified or not and if not to what relief the workman would be entitled. The Labour Court wrongly admitted the pleas and travelled materially beyond the scope of reference.[102]

*139.* The government is not expected to consider the merits of the industrial dispute once its existence is accepted and should refer it to the Labour Court with an order of reference. However, in one case the government decided on the nature of the dispute and declined the reference. The union filed a writ petition against the

99. LLJ, 2006, Vol. 4, *UP State* v. *Brahm Singh and Another*, High Court of Allahabad, p. 980 (NOC).
100. LLJ, 2008, Vol. 3, *Davendra Sahu* v. *Industrial Tribunal Cum-Labour Court, Visakhapatnam and Another*, High Court of Andhra Pradesh, pp. 466–470.
101. LLJ, January 2011, *Gujarat Water Supply and Sewerage Board & Another* v. *Bipin Chandra N. Ramanuj*, High Court of Gujarat, pp. 84–86.
102. LLJ, June 2010, *Management of Premier Mills Ltd* v. *Labour Court, Coimbatore and others*, High Court of Madras, pp. 757–761.

said order. The court held that the dispute existed when the union signed the settlement, agreeing not to make any further fresh demands or claims in future during its pendency and seek a reference for fresh adjudication. It revived the old dispute in a new guise. The petition failed.[103]

*140.* A bus conductor was found to be collecting fares but not issuing the tickets. The passengers were found travelling without tickets. He was charge sheeted, a show cause notice served on him and subsequently a domestic enquiry was instituted in which the chargesheeted conductor took part and cross examined several witnesses. He was found guilty of a grave misconduct and dismissed. The Labour Court to which the dispute was referred considered all aspects and held that the enquiry was strictly in accordance with law, the dismissal was proper and the employee not entitled to any relief whatsoever. On appeal the High Court found fault with the Labour Court and quashed it mainly on the ground that the passengers were not examined, nor was the cash checked. On an appeal, the Supreme Court said that in a domestic enquiry complicated principles and procedures laid down in the code of civil procedure and the Indian Evidence Act do not apply. On these grounds the domestic enquiry cannot be faulted. The High Court was not right in overturning the findings of the domestic tribunal. The appellate courts ought not give non-reasoned conclusions. 'Reason is the heart beat of every conclusion. Without the same it becomes life less'. The High Court's judgment was set aside and the award of the Labour Court restored.[104]

*141.* In one case the enquiry was found to be fair and proper by the Labour Court, but misconduct not established in the enquiry officer's report. It denied the opportunity to the management to adduce evidence to sustain the charges. Yet it came to the conclusion that the charges were not proved and set aside the enquiry report. Thereupon it gave the award of reinstating the workman with benefits. This was appealed. It was a rare case where the management adopted a conciliatory approach, while the conduct of workman was of defiance. The charge against the workman was that he deliberately disobeyed the lawful and reasonable order, it was a misconduct according to the standing orders, and the enquiry officer submitted a report with factual evidence which was reappraised by the Labour Court. The court held that a defective enquiry was on the same footing as no enquiry. But a fair and proper enquiry cannot be set aside as perverse. Even in such a case the Labour Court cannot direct the reinstatement of the employee without letting the employer lead additional evidence. It has no power to refuse. Moreover, the punishment cannot be interfered with except when it is too harsh and suggests victimization. The Labour Court is not an appellant body. Section 11A of the ID Act allows the tribunal to substitute a lesser punishment in place of dismissal. In this case the workman was not entitled to any indulgence and it was irrelevant that he was an active member of the

103. LLJ, June 2010, *Chemplant Employees' Union* v. *Government of Tamilnadu*, High Court of Madras, pp. 824–826.

104. LLJ, July 2010, *UP State Road Transport Corporation and Another* v. *Suresh Chand Sharma and Another*, Supreme Court of India, pp. 278–283.

union. The award of the Labour Court was set aside. However, there shall be no recovery of the wages already paid to him on the basis of the award.[105]

*142.* In a case two workmen were found guilty of theft of tea bags and selling them for personal gain. In the enquiry only the act of theft was inquired into and the omission of date in the charge sheet against one of them was ignored. The Labour Court found it to be a fatal flaw. Similar flaw existed in the other charge sheet where the place where teabags were sold was omitted. The Labour Court noticed other shortcomings in the evidence recorded against the charged workmen. According to the High Court the Labour Court could not have set aside the findings solely on technical grounds. 'The proceedings involved being not a criminal proceeding, what was required to be established is the preponderance of probability.' In view of these shortcomings the order of the Labour Court was set aside. 'The matter will now go back to the Labour Court for deciding afresh on the basis of evidence on record keeping in mind the observations made in this judgment and order.'[106]

*143.* In an intra-court letters patent Appeal the High Court posed the questions of law which arose for consideration. (i) What is the scope of Section 11-A of the ID Act? (ii) Whether the Labour Court was justified in altering the punishment of dismissal into reinstatement in service though the charge of misbehavior and misconduct were proved? (iii) Whether the approval of dismissal granted by the Labour Court/Tribunal could not be reopened by it? (iv) Whether the dismissal order, found guilty of misconduct, could be converted into reinstatement without back wages only on the ground that in the past no misconduct was committed by the workman? The employer had earlier filed a writ petition against the order of the Labour Court on reinstatement and the single judge allowed it, setting aside the Labour Court order. This appeal was filed by the workman against the order of the single judge. The court referred to the Apex Court's judgments on Section 11-A, which permits the Labour Court to modify the order of dismissal, it is disproportionate to the charge and award a lesser punishment or even set aside and order reinstatement. The law as it stood was that the jurisdiction of Labour Court under this section is not unlimited and can be exercised only if the punishment is disproportionate to the gravity of misconduct, and not on a compassionate ground. It cannot be exercised capriciously and arbitrarily. The court below cannot undermine the discipline of the organization by condoning an act of physical violence, not even the use of abusive language. 'To support its conclusion the Industrial Tribunal or the Labour Court, as the case may be has to give reasons in support of its decision.' Mere use of the words 'disproportionate' or grossly disproportionate' by itself will not be sufficient. It is not an appellate body. The Industrial Tribunal should be very slow in interfering with the findings arrived at in a domestic inquiry. The court cannot interfere on the ground that another view is possible on the material on record. On the second question, the Court found that the Labour Court had not recorded any

105. LLJ, August 2010, *GoodYear India Ltd* v. *D.N. Trikchija and Another,* High Court of Punjab and Haryana, pp. 476–486.

106. LLJ, September 2010, *Management of Dayang Tea Estate* v. *Secretary, Assom. Chah Karamchari Sangha,* High Court of Gauhati, pp. 622-626.

finding except that it was a first offence and poor financial condition of the appellant to alter the punishment. It had directed reinstatement in service without back wages whimsically. 'When the charges were proved *vis-à-vis* the establishment, interference with the punishment was not justified. The leniency shown on the ground of poor financial condition was unwarranted and would infect encourage indiscipline. On the next question, the Court said that prior to the adjudication by the Labour Court, the Industrial Tribunal had granted approval to the dismisal. This was because a reference was pending under Section 33(2) (b) of the Act and an approval application was moved by the employer. It proceeded in accordance with law and it did not preclude the jurisdiction of Labour Court. The last question pertains to the fact that in the past no misconduct was commited by the workman. The Court held that the past conduct could be a relevant consideration, if the Labour Court is not satisfied with the finding of the disciplinary authority or the quantum of punishment and after recording a further finding that the circumstances of the case require a lesser punishment. In the case of minor misconduct which is proved, the Labour Court, under its discretionary power under Section 11-A of the Act, can consider past record of the deliuquent workman and hold that the punishment of dismissal was shockingly disproportinate to the charges. The Apex Court had held in a case that 'the fact that the misconduct now alleged is the first misconduct again is no ground to condone the misconduct.' The Court held, 'the reprehensible behaviour of the appellant and serious misconduct commited by him was not pardonable and the dismissal from service in such a case was the appropriate punishment. We do not find any illegality in the impugned judgement passed by the learned single judge'. The appeals failed and were dismissed.[107]

*144.* In this case the petitioner, the Bangalore Metropolitan Transport Corporation, petitioned the High Court against an award of the Industrial Tribunal which interfered with the punishment to the driver of a bus for the occurrence of a traffic accident resulting in death of the scooter its and injuries to two children. In the Enquiry report the driver was held responsible to the extent of 20 per cent. He was punished by withholding of three increments with cumulative effect. On an appeal, the punishment was to withhold two annual increments with cumulative effect. He raised an industrial dispute which was referred to the Industrial Tribunal. The Industrial Tribunal examined the case with regard to proportionality of punishment, and taking note of the fact that earlier he received a cash prize, Appreciation letter and the Chief Minister's Gold Medal for having driven the bus for seven years, without any accident, held that the punishment was not justified and reduced it to the withholding of two increments without cumulative effect. The Court observed that the Tribunal had no jurisdiction to exercise power under Section 11-A of the ID Act, as it was not a case of dismissal or discharge of the workman. The Court noted that the Industrial Tribunal did not record that the findings of the domestic enquiry were perverse. Section 11-A had no application to the case. It committed an illegal act in interfering with the punishment. The writ petition was allowed and the impugned

107. LLJ, Vol. 1, 2012, *Madhav Singh Nagsibhai Solanki* v. *Gujarat Electricity Corp. Ltd.* and Another, High Court of Gujarat. pp. 811-818.

award quashed. The punishment imposed by the appellant authority was restored.[108]

*145.* In the instant case 16 workmen were dismissed following an industrial dispute on the disbanding of the quality control team, comprising a manager, a supervisor and 10 workmen and work was reorganized. There was no workload settlement with the union on production norms. In 1998, as the union saw it, the workload was increased without notice. An industrial dispute was raised which was still pending in 2010 when the writ petition was filed by the company. The management did not permit workers who reported to work as they used to do, which the management declined. There after 16 workers were suspended, charge memos were issued and domestic enquiries conducted in respect of 13 workers only. Two workers were straightaway dismissed without being afforded any opportunities. It was alleged that the enquiries were held against the principles of natural justice. Another dispute was raised and referred for adjudication in March 2002. Before the Industrial Tribunal 14 workers examined themselves individually. Workers filed 151 documents, while the management filed 248 documents, justifying the dismissals. The Industrial Tribunal framed six issues, ranging from violation of Section 33 (1)(a) of the ID Act, to unfair labour practices. On penalties, the Tribunal found that the management did not take into consideration the magnitude, nature and degree of misconduct and the circumstances in which it occurred. Awarding of major penalties for minor misconducts was liable to be construed as an unfair labour practice prohibited under Section 25-T of the Act. The Tribunal decided that since the case was pending for more than 10 years, the penalty of denial of one increment for one year would be a sufficient punishment. The order of dismissal was set aside and workers were deemed to be in service and entitled to 50 per cent of back wages from the date of dismissal. One worker had resigned and settled his accounts, so not eligible for any benefit. Two more had settled their accounts and were excluded. Three had reached the age of superannuation and were entitled to 50 per cent back wages till the date of superannuation. Earlier, the Court had ordered the payment of monthly pay under Section 17-B of the ID Act with liberty to management to move the Court in case any workman was engaged in gainful employment. The Tribunal's award was challenged by the management on the ground that a soft glove treatment to the delinquent workers would result in chaos, ultimately harming and damaging beyond repair the national discipline. The Labour Court ought to have gone into the evidence and then decide the matter. Back wages should not be granted mechanically, even if the termination was held to be invalid. The Court decided that the only question that needed to be considered was whether the Tribunal had correctly exercised its power under Section 11-A of the ID Act and whether it was legal and justified. The Court held that, while awarding 50 per cent of back wages the Tribunal had really struck a balance. All that the concerned workers had sought from the management was that they should be paid separately for the extra work introduced by the management. The mere fact that, while some workers started doing the extra work without damanding extra payment, and it is only the dismissed workmen who

108. LLJ, Vol. 11, 2011, *Bangalore Metropolitan Transport Corporation, Bangalore* v. *BMTC and State Transport Noukarara Sangh*, Bangalore, High Court of Karnataka, pp. 400-101.

insisted on extra payment, was not a justifiable ground for inflicting a serious punishment on them. The fact that the union has failed to prove the illegality of such a move of management can be a good ground to deny a portion of the back wages. Not only the Tribunal denied 50 per cent of the back wages, it also imposed a minor penalty viz. increment cut for one year as a sufficient punishment. The award of the Industrial Tribunal was upheld and the writ petition dismissed.[109]

*146.* Section 17B of the ID Act is in two parts. The first part makes it obligatory on the employer to pay the workman, reinstated in his job by the award of the Labour Court Tribunal, full wages last drawn by him, as if there was no termination. If the employer prefers an appeal or a writ petition against the award in the higher courts, during the pendency of such proceedings. The condition is that the workman should file an affidavit in the court that he had not been employed anywhere else. The second part stipulates that if it is proved before the court that such workman was employed fully or partly on adequate remuneration, the court shall order that no wages shall be payable for such period. In one case, the employer raised several contentions on the meaning of the Section 17B, as the respondent to an appeal by the union to secure payment of wages to the six workmen who had not been reinstated. The employer had succeeded in securing a stay on the award in an earlier writ petition. The first contention was that the workman must aver in the affidavit not only that he has remained unemployed during the period but that he sought employment but did not get any and furnish particulars. This was rejected by the Court because the affidavit merely required an averment that he was and is presently unemployed and nothing more. Once the workman files an affidavit, he has discharged the onus on him. Thereafter, the burden of proof shifts to the employer. Evidence has to be led in proof thereof. Section 17B is a benevolent provision. If the employer succeeds in disproving the averments in the affidavit, it would be for the workman to file further affidavits to rebut employer's contentions. The employer's second contention was that the workmen must prove, how without employment, they managed their life style, such as, educating their children, providing food, clothing and other necessities. The Court declined to accept it because the section did not require it, besides then, the workman must explain particulars of every conceivable fact. Acceptance of such submission would result in reversal of the legislative intent and the scheme of Section 17-B. The employer's third contention was that the term 'gainful employment' includes self employment. The Court did not agree with the meaning attached to self-employment, that this would disentitle a workman from benefits of Section 17B, even if he received an income though not working in a family venture. The court held's, it is not any employment or any remuneration that disentitles a workman to relief under Section 17B, it must be in respect of employment obtained an account of or as a result, or in lieu of, or due to, his being kept out of employment, which is the subject matter of the proceedings.' It was further contented that, if a person can survive on an amount less than the wages he is entitled to the Court must grant only that amount. The Court held that there was nothing in Section 17B that justified this interpretation. Moreover, the

109. LLJ, Vol. 4, 2011, *Management of Sundaram Industries, Ltd. Madurai* v. *Industrial Tribunal and Another*, High Court of Madras, pp. 575-578.

entire approach would be speculative and arbitrary. It would prolong the proceedings, defeating the very purpose of Section 17B. The Court declined another contention of the employer that relief under this section may be granted from the date on which the Court stays the award granting reinstatement, not from the date of the award. The Court read the statement of objects and reasons, which clearly state that wages should be paid from the date of the award till the case is finally decided in the Supreme Court or High Court. The employer is bound and liable to comply with the award and pay full wages from the date of the award, i.e. 13 December 2007 till the date of the stay order dated 2 January 2009. The Court also awarded cost of Rs. 2000 to be paid to each of the six workmen who had filed the affidavits. The civil appeal was allowed.[110]

*147.* In another case dealing with Section 17B, the appellant, a reinstated workers was found to be sitting back and doing nothing to enforce the award since there was no stay on the award. It was found that the workman had not gone to resume his duties and it was clear that he was not willing to work though the respondent, employer, had offered work. His application, resting on his assertion that he was ready and willing to resume work, had survived for five years. During this period he could have waited the proceeding for contempt of court, breach of the award or its implementation. Not having done so clearly subtracts bonafide from his asterisms. It was argued that the appellant possessed a car, lived in a joint family in a banglow, earned more than adequate remuneration, from his construction business and political activities and the litigation was carried on with an ulterior motive. He contested an election and was a member of a Gram Panchayat. The court found his statements on being unemployed and merely sitting in the office of an acquaintance as too self-contradictory to be believed. The court held that it must adopt a pragmatic approach to sub serve the original purpose and to draw necessary inferences the materials on record. The court decided that, despite his denials, the appellant was employed, received more than adequate remuneration and his claim to the benefit of Section 17B was not bonofide. The appeal was dismissed and he was ordered to pay cost of Rs. 5000 to the respondent within one month.[111]

*148.* The Additional Chief Engineer of the Bhabha Atomic Research Centre was confronted with three articles of charges. One was that in connivance with a subordinate officer and a contractor he cheated the government of Rs 158,801 by technically sanctioning non-existent works, thereby committing fraud. Second, that in connivance with the same contractor he cheated the government of Rs 260,667 by sanctioning non-existent works and issuing tender notices calling for sealed tenders for the said works. He carried out false inspections and completion certificates in respect of the said non-existent works. He also passed the first and final bills in favour of the contractor. There were 13 such non-existent works. The third charge was of misuse of financial powers and cheating the government to the tune of Rs

---

110. LLJ, Vol. 1, 2011, *Kirloskar Pneumatic Kamgar Sangh, Pune*, v. *Kirloskar Pnenmatie Co. Ltd. Pune*, High Court of Bombay, pp. 622-636.

111. LLJ, Vol. 2, 2011, *Rauf Mohmed Sheikh* v. *Prajati Glass Works Pvt. Ltd.*, High Court of Gujarat, pp. 433–436.

34,114 by fraudulently passing the contractor's final bill on fixing 167 Godrej Locks on the basis of false measurements. There was also a fourth charge of issuing gate passes to the contractor to enable him to remove empty scraps out of the BARC. The Inquiry officer found that charges 1, 2 and 3 were proved, but not the fourth. On its basis he was dismissed from service. He filed a revision petition against the penalty, but it was dismissed. He then appealed to the CGIT, which gave no relief. He then filed a writ petition in the High Court. The High Court said that the petitioner was afforded a reasonable opportunity to defend his case. The inquiry report gave detailed reasons and it was neither a cryptic report nor one that was not a speaking one. The penalty of dismissal from service was not disproportionate to the scale of misconduct. His petition was dismissed.[112]

## §3. Unfair Labour Practices

*149.* In one case the social welfare department of the government of Rajasthan issued a circular saying that part-time and daily wage employees should not be allowed to complete 240 days of service. The High Court held that the very idea of issuing such a circular deserves to be condemned and deprecated.[113] A similar circular issued earlier by the Reserve Bank of India was held to be an unfair labour practice. The circular was quashed.

*150.* The onus of establishing victimization is on the person pleading it. The charge must be established by safe and sure evidence. The charge of unfair labour practice cannot be sustained if it is an afterthought. In one case, following a long history of legal battle a workman was taken back in service. His company transferred him from Guahati, Assam, to Chindwara, Madhya Pradesh. Management informed the court that 17 employees were likewise transferred from various locations to Chindwara in connection with company's work. The workman, a driver earning petty wages, complained of victimization as he was being sent on deputation with a clear likelihood that at the end of deputation period he will be taken back in service only if the management's requirement warranted him to be reverted to the company. He may lose his position as a regular employee under a regular establishment. The matter went to the Labour Court which held that the management's decisions were not sustainable in law and viewed them an unfair labour practice. This was challenged, but the High Court upheld the Labour Court.[114]

*151.* Under the Maharashtra Recognition of Trade Unions and Prevention of Unfair Labour Practices Act, 1972, an action in breach of a settlement and award is an unfair labour practice. The law requires the Industrial Court constituted under the Act to issue an order to the management if it is found guilty of an unfair practice to

112. LLJ, February 2011, *Madhukar G. Wagh* v. *Union of India, Secretary Deptt. of Atomic Energy, Mumbai and Another,* High Court of Bombay, pp. 359–370.
113. LLJ, Vol. 2, 1994, *Kanhaiya Lal* v. *State of Rajasthan and others,* High Court of Rajasthan, pp. 474–488.
114. LLJ, 2009, Vol. 1, *Indian Potash Ltd* v. *State of Assam and other,* High Court of Guahati, pp. 673–677.

cease and desist from the practice and take affirmative action as directed. Under a settlement, the company used to pay Rs 480 as a non-recoverable advance every year to the workmen 10 days before the local Ganesh Festival. Later a fresh demand was made to raise this amount to Rs 800 every year. This was agreed to, but the company viewed it as a recoverable advance, not as an allowance. This led to the dispute travelling before the industrial court which agreed with the workmen and viewed the company's action as an unfair labour practice, and gave the award to refund the amount already recovered within 60 days or in default pay 9 per cent interest on the same. The High Court had to decide several related issues. On an important point of contention, the Court held that where the Industrial Disputes Act and the Maharashtra Act overlap, 'the choice is that of the employee to select either of the remedies. The remedies provided under the MRTU and PULP Act are much wider, as the courts are empowered to prevent the indulgence by an employer into an unfair labour practice by granting temporary reliefs, and it is open for the workmen to resort to speedier remedy, if such remedy is available to them.' On the substantive issue the court decided that Rs 480 payable under the earlier settlement continued to subsist and it was non-recoverable. It was an existing benefit which was not taken away by the award and could not be recovered. It upheld the award of the Industrial Court that the entire advance was not refundable.[115]

*152.* In one case the union was involved in an agitation on the issue of the overtime allowance and short payment of wages, etc. A settlement followed but shortly thereafter the company transferred several employees who were either office bearers of the union or its active members. The case travelled to the High Court. The Court held on facts the transfers to be malafide and set them aside.[116]

*153.* In one case the state government took cognizance of an offence listed under the unfair labour practices and served notice on the factory 'occupiers' that the labour commissioner has been authorized to lodge a complaint against them in the court of the magistrate I class. There were 70 other cases of a similar nature in the writ petitions to the High Court. Individual complaints of 70 workmen for violation of Section 25T of the ID Act led the government to take action. They were under an order of transfer to another town, where according to workmen no unit of factory had been yet established, and it was malafide of the law. The petitioner company took the plea that, save Section 2A pertaining to discharge and dismissal, no individual workman could make a valid complaint against the transfer order. Moreover, the government itself could not decide the question but refer it to the Labour Court for adjudication. The second petitioner denied being the 'occupier' under the Factories Act and said that he had not transferred any workman and so there was a complete non-application of mind in the matter. Furthermore, principles of natural justice were violated, because he had not been served any notice at all. However, the standing orders did not provide for transfer of any worker to any other location,

115. LLJ, 2009, Vol. 3, *Biddle Sawyer Ltd* v. *Chemical Employees Union*, High Court of Bombay, pp. 749–757.
116. LLJ 2009, Vol. 2, *Jayapandi T.* v. *State Express Transport Corp. Ltd* and Others, High Court of Madras (Brief Resume), p. 744.

nor did the appointment letters. The Act clearly provides that, 'to transfer a workman malafides from one place to another, under the guise of following management policy' is an unfair labour practice. Section 34 provides for cognizance of offences and that a specified court shall try any offence punishable under the Act. The court held that the complaints of unfair practices could originate with the individual workman. Moreover, a prima facie finding of unfair labour practice is only a prerequisite. At this stage no final proof is necessary and the government does not have the authority to impose any penalty which is always left in the hands of the judiciary. 'In this case it shall be the judicial magistrate who shall decide whether it is a fit case to take cognizance of the case and issue summons'. The petitions were dismissed.[117]

## §4. Notice of Change

*154.* Under the state government the Dairy Development Corporation issued fresh instructions that the leave rules in existence should not apply to the workmen who are governed by the Factories Act and are covered by the Industrial Employment (standing orders) Act. Accordingly, the earned leave rules were changed to one day per every 120 days of work. By comparison the office staff enjoyed 32 days of earned leave per year. The workmen complained against the reduction of earned leave by 18 days per year. The intimation was done by a Notice in English on the Notice Board and this was deemed to satisfy Section 9A of the ID Act on Notice of Change. The Industrial Tribunal gave an award in favour of workmen on merits, that the management could not have two sets of leave rules. Moreover, a notice on the notice board was not known to most workers. The notice was invalid. This award was implemented by the organization in due course. The writ petition of the management of 1999 was heard on 27 January 2010. It was dismissed.[118]

*155.* In another dispute involving the government, the hours of work were increased from 37½ hours per week to 44 hours in respect of the ministerial staff in Indian Security Press, as recommended by the Fourth Pay Commission. A notice under Section 9A was issued. To this, the union served a notice of strike and the matter was admitted for conciliation. The CO submitted a failure report, but the government declined the reference for adjudication. This led to a writ petition by the staff union, which was dismissed with the direction that instead the Central Administrative Tribunal be approached. The union approached the CAT as directed and secured a favorable verdict, and the government order was set aside. The government then referred the dispute to the central government's Industrial Tribunal for adjudication. The CGIT too upheld the workers' claim on Section 9A. More appeals followed, and thereafter it led to the writ petition filed by the government of India. The plea that the workmen were not industrial workers, but civil servants was

---

117. LLJ, June 2010, *Adarsh Gupta* v. *State of Haryana and others*, High Court of Punjab and Haryana, pp. 751–756.
118. LLJ, August 2010, *The Management of Salem District Corp. Milk Producers Union Ltd* v. *Industrial Tribunal, Chennai and another*, High Court of Madras, pp. 436–438.

rejected. Moreover, a notice under the Factories Act was not a Notice under Section 9A of the ID Act. The argument that the workmen had accepted the benefits of the recommendation of the Pay Commission and they had given an undertaking to abide by its recommendations was viewed as flawed on the ground that compliance with the Notice of Change was a statutory prerequisite for implementation of the increased hours of work. The Tribunal was held to be right in concluding that the petitioners had illegally changed the service conditions of workmen. The government was directed to pay overtime over a period of 20 years which the dispute took; the amount deposited by the government in the court and held in a fixed deposit was released in favour of the workman. The government was penalized with the cost quantified at Rs 10,000 to be paid to the staff union.[119]

## §5. Inquiry and Punishment

*156.* Cases of flawed inquiry and unjustified punishment continue to recur. A contractual employee serving as a store keeper in a government organization was charged with the misconduct of throwing the books in his custody into a ditch. A show cause notice was served on the employee, but he was given only one day to file his reply and thereafter final orders were passed. It was said that he had not acquired the status of a government servant and could not claim protection and parity with them on removal from the service. However, the tenure of contract was not over and the show cause notice did not give a reasonable time to file his reply, which was unfair. This plea of the employee was admitted by the court and he was given two weeks of time to make his reply; within three weeks thereafter the authority could pass the final order. Until then the impugned order should remain in abeyance.[120]

*157.* In a case pertaining to the alleged loss caused to the Irrigation Department, Uttar Pradesh in 1990, there was inordinate delay in proceedings conducted by the state government and in the meantime the employee retired, but his retirement benefits were blocked. He petitioned the High Court of the newly created state of Uttarakhand in which he was now resident. The facts showed that the employee, as a store keeper, was charged with cheating, forgery and faced departmental proceedings as well as in the criminal court. In the former, he was found guilty and punished with stoppage of two increments to recover the loss of about Rs 4.6 lakhs. The trial court convicted him, but on appeal he was acquitted of all charges. The state government's appeal against acquittal was dismissed on grounds of limitation. The state then approached the Apex Court which declined the leave and dismissed the petition. The workman appealed against the order of punishment in the departmental proceedings, and for quashing the punishment citing the order of acquittal. This

---

119. LLJ, January 2011, *Union of India through the Secretary, Government of India* v. *The Secretary, The Staff Union of India Security Press*, High Court of Bombay, pp. 78–83.

120. LLJ, December 2010, *Dhananjay Kumar Singh* v. *State of Bihar and others*, High Court of Patna, pp. 759–760.

remained pending and the government declined to release his pension and other retirement benefits. The Uttarakhand High Court observed, that though the two proceedings were different, but there was no excuse for not completing he Departmental proceedings. In 2004 the Court in a writ petition had advised the respondent, the UP government to review the case and proceed according to law. Nothing happened though the employee had already retired. Following a contempt petition, the state government passed an order on 9 March 2007 holding the petitioner guilty of all charges and imposed the punishment of stoppage of two increments with emulative effect and to recover the loss of Rs 466,928 from the petitioner from his retirement dues. The Court agreed that merely because one proceeding is pending there is no bar for the other to proceed and it is also true that, if one has been acquitted in a criminal case, ipso facto, one is not liable to be exonerated in a departmental proceeding. The two proceedings are separate and distinct. However, this case was unique. The department chose to sleep over the matter for more then 15 years and only proceeded with the matter after the contempt proceedings were issued by the Court. 'That delay on the part of the State of Uttar Pradesh is fatal in the present case. It has caused undue hardship to the petitioner.' In a case the Apex Court held that in case the departmental proceedings and criminal proceedings are on the same set of charges, then if an employee is acquitted in the criminal case, the departmental proceedings should follow the same. This has not happened in the present case in spite of the same set of charges in the two proceedings, the entire proceedings are perverse in nature. Consequently, the order dated 9 March 2007 is liable to be set aside and is hereby set aside. The respondents are directed to fix the pension of the petitioner and release the same including the arrears and post retirement benefits forthwith. The writ petition was allowed.'[121]

*158.* In another case the Industrial Tribunal held that the departmental inquiry against the workman was invalid and illegal because it was against the principles of natural justice. He was found guilty of several misconducts, such as, physical assault and use of abusive language against the superior officer and attempt to molest and misbehave with female apprentices. He was punished with demotion instead of dismissal. In the industrial dispute raised by the workman, the legality and validity of the departmental inquiry was challenged. The Industrial Tribunal agreed with the workman and gave the opportunity to the management to prove misconduct by leading evidence before the Tribunal. It was held that 'whenever the Labour Court or the industrial tribunal decides the validity of the departmental enquiry at the interlocutory stage, a writ petition challenging the said order would not be maintainable'. The decision at this stage cannot be appealed even after the final award. The High Court may refuse to intervene at that stage. There should be no undue delay in industrial adjudication. The challenge to the interlocutory order was rejected. On merits it was found that the enquiry officer relied upon the statements of three women who were never examined. While the company engaged an

121. LLJ. 3, 2012 *Kallu Singh* v. *State of Uttar Pradesh and Others*, Uttarakhand High Court, pp. 143-145.

advocate, the same request made by the workman was rejected. The petitioner company lost the case and the petition was dismissed.[122]

*159.* The Supreme Court's constitutional bench had observed in 1994 that mere absence of furnishing the copy of the inquiry report would not vitiate the inquiry unless a clear prejudice was shown by the employee. In this case it was not merely that the copy of the report was not furnished, but even the show cause notice for misconduct was not given to the workman before inflicting the punishment. Three workmen were dismissed. The Labour Court took the view that the actual prejudice caused to the workmen had not been established by specific pleadings in the claim statement, hence rejected their contention of not being furnished the enquiry report. The High Court held that taking a technical view of imparting strict rules of pleading in labour jurisprudence was uncalled for, especially when the reference itself was on the ground that the enquiry was not proper and the dismissal of service was not justified. The order of the Labour Court was set aside and the matter remitted to the Labour Court for fresh consideration.[123]

*160.* In a case of fraud involving a bank manager it was proved to the satisfaction of the bank that there had occurred very serious breach of conduct rules. The manager was charged with withdrawals of large amounts of cash in the name of fictitious persons, so after holding an inquiry the bank dismissed him. He was arrested along with the cashier on criminal charges and remained in judicial custody for some time. There were five charges. One that he sometimes sanctioned loans against 20 non-existent fixed deposit receipts to fictitious persons. Second, that he left the branch without handing over charge to anyone. Third, that he left his station without authorization and remained absconding from the services. Fourth, he was a guarantor to a loan at another branch. He stood surety in it without obtaining prior permission and did not make sincere efforts to recover the loan amount and the account had turned into a NPA. Fifth, he had given guarantee for his wife, who took a loan from another bank in Delhi, without seeking permission of the competent authority for standing as a guarantor. All the charges were proved and the cashier deposed during the inquiry. The manager participated in the inquiry, but could not explain the 20 loans he had sanctioned. The High Court set aside the dismissal order on the ground that the inquiry report was too sketchy as the evidence was not analysed and the documents were not detailed. This was viewed as a breach of natural justice. The bank was ordered to reinstate the employee and hold the inquiry afresh. The bank appealed to the Supreme Court against the High Court order. The Supreme Court held that 'The High Court has clearly erred in holding that the documents produced were neither detailed nor their nature was explained.' The present case did not show absence of reasons in the disciplinary order. Once the charges were established, the High Court had no reason to interfere in the decision. The Court cannot embark upon reappreciating the evidence or weighing the same as an appellant

122. LLJ, January 2011, *Gujarat State Fertilizers and Chemicals Ltd and Another* v. *Industrial Tribunal and Another,* High Court of Gujarat, pp. 225–238.

123. LLJ, September 2010, *Chandre Shekhar* v. *State of Haryana and others,* High Court of Punjab and Haryana, pp. 855–859.

authority. The appeal was allowed and the High Court order set aside. The contempt proceedings initiated against the bank for not implementing the High Court order was also dismissed.[124]

*161.* There are a number of reasons why a domestic enquiry against an alleged misconduct does not lead to firm conclusions and to imposition of penalty on the delinquent workman. Among others, these are:

- improper reporting by the officer;
- non-availability of evidence;
- defective charge-sheet;
- delay in starting the inquiry;
- lack of knowledge of rules by the departmental officer;
- lack of knowledge of rules by the inquiry officer;
- dilatory tactics in delaying submission of explanation, making allegation against the management or enquiry officer, etc.; and
- the impatience of management to punish the workman without observing the full procedure; denial of reasonable opportunity to the delinquent worker to defend himself in the inquiry that amounts to violation of a principle of natural justice.

It is a very basic rule that 'no penalty can be imposed even upon a very bad and dishonest employee without following principles of natural justice or procedures prescribed by law'.[125]

*162.* In another case, two directors of a society were instrumental in charge-sheeting the workman, also participated in the committee and board meetings which imposed the penalty. It was held that the inquiry was vitiated, as rightly held by the Labour Court. The order of dismissal was bad and the two persons who were penalized were entitled to reinstatement in their posts at 50 per cent of back wages. The writ petition file by the society was dismissed.[126]

## §6. Back Wages

*163.* Back wages in the ID Act wages are defined in Section 2(rr) and cover ground which is not identical to the Payment of Wages Act. For instance the value of house accommodation is included in the former, but excluded in the latter. Gratuity is excluded in the former, but included in the latter. Moreover, there is a clause in the Payment of Wages Act, 'any sum to which the person employed is entitled under any scheme framed under any law for the time being in force', which gives the term a very wide coverage, though it does not occur in the ID Act. Similarly, an

---

124. LLJ, January 2011, *General Manager, Punjab and Sind Bank and Others* v. *Daya Singh,* Supreme Court of India, pp. 255–261.
125. LLJ, Vol. 2, 2000, *Amal Kanti Bose* v. *W.B. State Co-operative Bank Ltd and Others,* High Court of Calcutta, pp. 171–176.
126. LLJ, July 2010, *Secretary, Chennai Corporation Societies Employees Cooperative Thrift and Credit Society (X-158)* v. *R. Paneerselvam and Others,* High Court of Madras, pp. 128–131.

ex gratia payment cannot form part of Section 2(rr). Under the ID Act, any sum due from an employer can form the basis of an individual wage dispute under Section 33(c). This may arise due to the wage arrears or any lay-off or retrenchment or closure compensation payable by the employer under its provision. However, this section will not operate if any question arises as to the amount of money due, or as to the amount at which such benefit should be computed. Then the question may be first decided by the Labour Court. A workman's termination order was set aside and awarded back wages along with reinstatement. The employer did not pay back wages and put up every hindrance possible to the claim of back wages. He lost at every stage of litigation, up to the High Court. The workman's plea of contempt of Labour Court for recovery of back wages under Section 33c(2) of the ID Act was allowed. The employer took the plea in the High Court that the claim was time-barred. This was rejected due to the continuity of cause of action. There is no specific limitation to apply for back wages under Section 33c(2). The Labour Court has quantified the wages to be paid and also the interest payable on it. As a court of equity it can award payment of interest from the date of the order. The writ petition was dismissed with cost.[127]

In another case the Labour Court held the termination order as illegal and awarded reinstatement with back wages. Employer preferred an appeal to the High Court and did not pay back wages. The workman appealed for back wages under Section 17B, which directs employer to pay full wages during the pendency of such proceedings unless the workman was employed and received adequate remuneration. His petition was allowed and the employer directed to pay the wages last drawn from the date the writ petition was filed within a period of four weeks.[128]

*164.* In a case of a doctor, an assistant professor in a medical college was dismissed from service by the state government for not returning to his job on the completion of his training and remaining absent without leave. The doctor said the he sent several applications for extension of leave, but these were ignored. He challenged the order in the High Court which held that the termination was violative of the principles of natural justice and set it aside and awarded full back wages from the date of the writ application. On an appeal, the division bench upheld the quashing of termination order, but set aside the order on payment of back wages of the High Court. Thereafter, the aggrieved doctor approached the Supreme Court which was heard in 2009, about 22 years after the order of termination, and about 11 years after it was set aside. The Supreme Court held that the payment of back wages has a discretionary element in it and there is no statutory sanction to direct the payment of back wages in its entirety. This was done during the 1970s and 1980s, but there is a change in the legal approach. The relief of reinstatement with back wages is not automatic and may be wholly inappropriate in a given situation. Each case would

127. LLJ, 2009, Vol. 4 *Managing Director, Kannad Sahkari Sakhar Karkhana Ltd* v. *Vishwanath Jagannath Kshirsagar,* High Court of Bombay, pp. 342–344.

128. LLJ, 2009, Vol. 4, *Suresh Mahato* v. *G.E. Industrial Pvt. Ltd and others,* High Court of Calcutta, pp. 489–491.

stand on its facts and circumstances and the court should exercise discretion on reasonable grounds and judiciously order back wages. In the case of the doctor appellant, the Apex Court awarded him 50 per cent of back wages until the age of superannuation.[129]

*165.* In a case the workman succeeded before the Labour Court and the High Court in the challenge of termination of his services, but the question was whether the award of full wages was justified. The Supreme Court held that the termination, unjustified though it was, did not create the right *inter alia* to full back wages. However, the factory remained closed for several years and ultimately it was declared a sick unit. At present the new management is involved in its rehabilitation and reconstruction. The appellant company said that it will suffer irreparable loss and injury if it has to employ a contractor-workman with full back wages even for the period when the establishment was closed. Section 11A of the ID Act vests a wide discretion in the Tribunal in the matter of awarding proper punishment and in the matter of the terms and conditions for reinstatement, including the award of back wages. The Court decided to award 50 per cent of back wages up to the date of reinstatement.[130]

*166.* In one case a workman driver was dismissed from service on charges of abusing and assaulting the conductor. The Labour Court held the dismissal unjustified and directed his reinstatement with benefits but without back wages. This was challenged in the High Court on the grounds that the Labour Court failed to notice that the conduct amounted to indiscipline as per the standing orders, that the evidence of the workman that he was not at all present on that day was not examined against the record and that once it found the enquiry as fair and proper, it ought not to have interfered with the punishment. The High Court said that the use of abusive or threatening language would not warrant the punishment of dismissal from service; 'it shocks the conscience of the court and the same is disproportionate to the proven charges. But since the event occurred in 1986, after 15 years, at this juncture, I do not propose to remit the matter to the disciplinary authority or to the Labour Court to consider the punishment in terms of S-11A of the Act.' The appropriate punishment would be reinstatement with continuity of service but the petitioner had to forgo his entire back wages.[131]

## §7. Non-payment of Salary

*167.* The employer company did not pay salary for eight months to its business development manager on the ground that he was not entitled to get any salary since he was not working for the company during this period and had not achieved the

---

129. LLJ, 2009, Vol. 4, *Malla C.N.V. State of Jammu & Kashmir and others*, The Supreme Court of India, pp. 667–669.
130. LLJ, 2009, Vol. 2, *P.V.K. Distillery Ltd* v. *Mahendra Ram,* Supreme Court of India, pp. 513–517.
131. LLJ, 2009, Vol. 3, *Managing Director, Tamilnadu State Transport Corp.* v. *Ezhilarasan and Another,* High Court of Madras, pp. 151–154.

performance standard as agreed upon. Moreover, he was a manager, not a workman. The manager approached the Labour Court under Section 33C(2) of the ID Act for payment of salary. The Labour Court allowed the application and issued the order to pay the salary to the company. The company filed a writ petition against the Labour Court. The High Court observed that the appointment order did not stipulate any performance level, nor an agreement by the employee to forgo his salary on this failure to achieve the said standard, nor was their any material to show the number of days he was absent. The Court upheld the finding of the Labour Court on his status as a workman, though he supervised the work of four employees, but there was no evidence that he sanctioned leave or could take any disciplinary action. None of the employees working in his section reported to him. Having regard to the nature of work and circumstances the employees was covered under the definition of workman under Section 2(S) of the ID Act. The petition was dismissed.[132]

*168.* Under the bipartite settlement between the banks and the award staff it was provided that the bank will pay the special allowance to the workman for performance or discharge of special functions over and above the routine duties and functions to a permanent incumbent even when he is a leave; including Sundays and holidays. The special allowance is also paid to a temporary workman when he is asked to do such duties, but the bank refused to pay the special allowance when he is on leave. This was raised as a dispute and was taken up for conciliation. On the failure of conciliation the issue was referred to the industrial tribunal which decided in favour of the temporary workman on the ground that no discrimination should be practiced. The bank appealed to the High Court. The Court found that whereas the bipartite settlement provides that a workman on casual leave is entitled to special allowance as if he is on duty, it does not provide that a temporary workman would have the same entitlement. A temporary incumbent on leave cannot be said to be occupying the post as such, the Court decided to modify the award by holding that the bank is not liable to pay special allowance to a temporary incumbent on the dates on which he is on leave.[133]

*169.* In an altogether unusual case a society registered under the Assam Cooperative Societies Act 1949 was actually formed by the state government to run its cattle development project and its board of directors, including the managing director were appointed by the government. All its staff were initially drawn on deputation from various government departments and in a phased manner they were reverted back to their parent departments. The replacement staff was recruited through a selection board set up by the state government on the posts sanctioned by it. The state grant met its expenses including the salaries of the staff from 1982–83 to 1994–95 when the sanctioned grant was not received and as a consequence the society (called CAMUL) failed to disburse salaries. In a writ petition the High Court

---

132. LLJ, February 2011, *Pan Network Ltd, Bangalorise* v. *B. Balakrishna*, High Court of Karnataka, pp. 596–599.
133. LLJ, June 2010, *Union Bank of India, Mumbai* v. *Union Bank of India, Employees Union, Pune and Another*, High Court of Bombay, pp. 692–695.

directed the state government to sanction the financial assistance to enable the society to disburse salaries and allowances, etc. It was contented that by lifting the veil the cooperative society would be treated as a department of the state government because it had pervasive control over its management. The state government preferred an appeal to the Supreme Court. The government listed the sums of money and the subject heads under which these were given as grants, but despite such assistance CAMUL became defunct and stopped all its activities. Moreover, at no time the state government made any commitment or agreed to bear the salaries of CAMUL or any other similar society, that CAMUL had to generate its own funds and pay the salaries of its staff, and further, that there was no relationship of employer and employees between the state government and the staff of CAMUL, and so it was not responsible to pay any amount on this score. The Apex court made a fine distinction between the term 'state' under Article 12 of the Constitution and the state government. Merely because a corporate body or a cooperative society answers the definition of state does not make it part of the state government, nor will the employees of such a body become holders of civil posts or employees of the state government. Consequently the state government is not liable to pay the salaries of CAMUL's employees. CAMUL was an independent juristic entity with power to hold property and enter into contracts, institute and defend suits, and it had a common seal. The state government had provided it financial assistance for many years, but it cannot be made liable for financial assistance for all times to come. The government companies and societies cannot bind the government for all their acts, liabilities and obligations as the agents of the centre/state government, whether under any central or state Act or under private law. The appeal was allowed and the orders of the High Court set aside.[134]

*170.* In a case the single Judge of the High Court set aside an award of the Labour Court and ordered compensation in lieu of reinstatement. The State Government as the employer filed of writ petition against the order. The single judge had awarded a compensation of Rs 25,000 and with regard to payment of wages under Section 17B of the ID Act held that as an affidavit to the effect that the workman was not gainfully employed. The amount payable as wages be paid together with the compensation money within a period of two months. The High Court bench noted that no plea was raised by the establishment that the workman was employed on a public post in contravention of statutory provisions governing the service. No plea was taken that white filling the past of a meson some statutory rules were required to be observed or that the provisions of Articles 14 and 16(1) of the Constitution were violated. Accordingly, no finding was recorded by the Industrial Tribunal-cum-Labour Court on the subject. It is recorded as a fact that there was no violation of Section 25-F of the Act since the workman did not complete 240 days in service. However, the Section 25-H on the principle, 'last come first out' has been violated because three workmen who were engaged after the appellant workman were continued in service. On this basis the Labour Court ordered reinstatement

134. LLJ, 2009, Vol. 4, *State of Assam* v. *Barak Upatyaka D.U. Karamchari Sanshtha*, Supreme Court of India, pp. 279–286.

with continuity of service but without back wages. The bench referred to the Apex Courts decisions and the law stated therein. The High Court could set aside the award of the Labour Court, if there is any jurisdictional enter to error of law apparent on the case of the record or there was violation of rules of natural justice. To substitute the award of the Labour Court by the learned single judge on the basis of his view concerning reinstatement of the workman, would not be within the scope of certiorari jurisdiction of the workman, would not be within the scope of *certiorari* jurisdiction. Following this judgment, this appeal succeeded the impugned judgment of the learned single judge was set aside and the award of the Industrial Tribunal-cum-Labour Court resorted. The workman shall be reinstated in service as a daily wager on the some terms and conditions at which he was working an 1 August 1996 with continuity of service. He would not be entitled to back wages until 5 October 2006 when the award was made, but he has to be paid full back wages from. The date of the award till the date of his reinstatement.[135]

*171.* In a complicated case a single judge of the High Court dealt with pleas for injunction against the company, the legitimacy of a strike which was seemed to be legal and the permission granted by the Industrial Court to the company to respite from the statement made by its advocate on not removing plant and machinery as urged by the union. The writ petition was filed by the union against the order of the Industrial Court allowing the company to reside from the promise that it would not remove plant and machinery from the printing establishment earlier the company was restrained by the Industrial court from removing the raw material and plant and machinery from the factory premises. First there was an application for interim relief seeking permission to remove raw materials, which was heard. It permitted the company to remove semi-finished goods and the machinery which was underutilized. The company would not retrench and employee, nor close down or shift the factory without following the law. This done, the application for interim relief was rejected. Thereafter the union commenced the strike following a notice to that effect and a complaint of unfair labour practices under the MRTUt PULP Act. The Industrial Court had held that the complaint of unfair labour practices was not proved. against this order the union filed a writ petition which was admitted and the single judge held that prima facie the company was engaged in unfair labour practices and the company was restrained from recruiting any person whether (i) from the open market or from its own establishment (ii) transferring raw materials, semi-finished goods and finished goods laying in the establishment and (iii) removing the plant and machinery during the pendency of the strike. On an appeal the bench of the High Court modified the order, and allowed to the company to reside from the statement or not removing plant and machinery with the permission of the Industrial Court granted the prayer of the company and allowed to shift the five machines as requested. The union again appealed to the High Court and it was heard by the some single judge who had restrained the company. The question was, could the company be allowed to reside from its earlier statement. The single judge held that no

135. LLJ, 3, 2011, *Chet Singh* v. *Secretary to Government of Punjab, PWD CB/R/Branch, Chandigarh and Others*, High Court of Punjab and Haryana, pp. 592-574 also LLJ, 2, 2010, *Harinder Singh* v. *Punjab State Warehousing Corporation*, Supreme Court of India.

new facts were placed on record by the company for it to be permitted to reside from its statement. The reason given by the Industrial Court in support of its order was rejected by the High Court judge mainly on the ground that there was a strike in progress which, prima facie, was legal.

> By allowing the application, the Industrial court has permitted the company to renege on its earlier statement and not merely to resile. Now it is not importable that the company would again seek to renege from the statement about bringing back the machinery or new machines, once the strike is withdrawn. Therefore, it is difficult to accept this statement mode on behalf of the company.

The company was not allowed to retract from the statement and this excluded any question of allowing it to remove any machinery. 'In my opinion, if the company is not restrained from removing the machinery, the strike would be frustrated.' An injunction would have to follow if the strike is prima facie legal, as in this case. 'Where a legal strikes in progress, in my opinion, the court cannot stultify the result of such cessation of work resorted to by the workers by permitting the company to remove its plant and machinery that would in effect make the strike a futile weapon.' The very purpose of declaring a strike is to ensure that the demands of the workers are met. The judge further said that though 29 demands out of 30 were admitted in conciliation, one, of demanding the abolition of contract labour still remains. Though this demand could not be considered under the Industrial Disputes Act, yet this demand would still become an industrial dispute under Section 2(K) of the Act. 'Prima facie, the strike which commenced continues to be legal in respect of this demand, although the other demands have been admitted in conciliation'. Under the MRTUR PULP Act, Section 24, the strike was not illegal. 'neither in its commencement nor its continuation today can be considered to be an illegal strike, prima facie.' The contention that the strike was not justifiable is not a matter which falls within the ambit of the MRTU & Pump Act. in any event, the employer has not bothered to approach the court for a declaration that the strike is illegal. In such circumstances the Industrial Court erred in allowing the Company to reside from its statement merely because of the high value of machines or that the company would incur great losses and hardship can be accepted as a valid ground to reside from its statement without granting an injunction to the workmen. Permitting the company to reside would mean that the interim relief sought by the union in respect of removal of plant and machinery has been rejected without hearing the parties on that count. 'In my opinion, therefore, the order of the Industrial Court is incorrect and must be set aside. The writ petition is allowed.'[136]

136. LLJ, Vol. 3, 2011, *Thomson Press Kamgar Sangathana, Thane* v. *Thomson Press (India) Ltd, Navi Mumbai and Another,* High Court of Bombay, pp. 409–420

## §8. Overtime Pay

*172.* Under Section 59 of the Factories Act, it is provided that a worker is entitled to overtime when he works for more than nine hours in any day or more than 48 hours in any week. The overtime rate should be twice the ordinary rate of wages. A factory worker includes those directly connected with the manufacturing process and others in any kind of work incidental to or connected with the manufacturing process. Such other work must have a nexus to or be proximate with the manufacturing process, for instance, by contributing to or facilitating the manufacturing process. Accordingly, the class IV employees in the dispensary of the hospital on the premises of the India Security Press were held to be factory workers and entitled to overtime allowance.[137] For price-rated workers the government in consultation with the concerned employers and workers should fix an equivalent time-rate which may form the basis for calculation of overtime wages. This is now fixed equal to the daily average of the previous month or week. By 'ordinary rate of wages' is meant the sum of basic wage and such allowances to which a worker is entitled, (this means principally the dearness allowance), and the equivalents of benefits in kind, such as, subsidies on foodgrains sold to workers or other articles admissible to a 'standard family'. The government has the authority to establish the cash equivalents of food concession and other admissible benefits. Bonus is not included in 'ordinary rate of wages', nor is overtime pay.

*173.* In one case the civilian employees of Kochi Naval Establishment petitioned the High Court against withdrawal of overtime wages on HRA, CCA, TA and small family norms allowance as 'ordinary rate of wages' at twice the rate. The government viewed the practice of overtime as a mistake and directed recovery of excess amount paid after July 2009. The Court held that though not defined in the Factories Act, the term 'ordinary rate of wages' should be interpreted in literal meaning as payable to each and every employee engaged for work without any discrimination. But, house rent allowances is paid to those who do not own a house, the transport allowance is paid on the particular travelling facilities in various cities, the city compensatory allowance varies with the size and location of city where one works and the small family allowance is an incentive to the family with less number of children. All such allowances are either compensatory for extra cost incurred by the employee or an incentive payment. These vary for the same type of employees. Though stationed in different cities, the basic wage is one and the same, Section 59(2) does not visualize discrimination among employees. So the court did not find any ground to deviate from the view taken by the Tribunal, which dismissed the applications against the instructions issued by the Ministry of Defence, disentitling the employees from overtime on compensatory allowances. On the plea, that by recalling existing benefits the order violates Section 9 A of ID Act, the Court held that a mistake can always be corrected at any time, and in this case, what is done is correction with future effect. The decision is not adverse to the terms of

137. LLJ, August 2010, *Union of India through the Secretary GOI* v. *Arun Vithal Bande and Others*, High Court of Bombay, pp. 535–540.

employment including overtime allowance, only the inadmissible benefits are to be recovered. The petition was dismissed.[138]

*174.* Basically the same principle is applied in the Mines Act. The difference is that the working time of eight hours a day below ground is equated with nine hours above ground. Moreover, a miner can have his ordinary wage calculated either on a weekly or a daily basis, whichever is more favourable to him. Furthermore, ordinarily a miner may not work for more than 10 hours in any day inclusive of overtime. However, persons holding positions of supervision, or employed in a confidential capacity, are exempted from all provisions of hours of work, including overtime, subject to the proviso that, if they are entitled to overtime pay under any award, agreement or contract of service, no exemption can be given. In the Plantations Labour Act, Section 19(2) states that where a worker works on any day in excess of the number of hours constituting a normal working day, or more than 48 hours a week, he shall in respect of such overtime work be entitled to twice the rate of ordinary wages.

*175.* Overtime is also an important subject in collective bargaining. What would constitute overtime work is not only dependent upon the relevant provisions of labour laws but also the scheduled hours of work determined by the management. If these are lower than 48 hours due to an agreement with the union, or a result of an award, or a decision of the management, the Factories Act will not apply and the excess over and above the scheduled hours will constitute overtime. A company had not paid overtime beyond the scheduled 39 hours a week on the ground that the law stipulated the excess over 48 hours only as overtime. The Supreme Court held that any decision by the management on extending the agreed hours of work would result in a loss of compensation to workers and would amount to altering the conditions of service. The payment of overtime was ordered but, because the company pleaded lack of capacity to pay the arrears, the court allowed it two years to make the payment in tweleve equal instalments.[139]

*176.* Under the Minimum Wages Act, Section 14 provides for overtime pay as fixed by the appropriate government. These vary depending upon the minimum wages being fixed by day, by the hour, or by such a longer wage period as may be prescribed. The state government may also fix the limit for overtime work or subject it to such conditions and restrictions as may be laid down. Under this Act the payment of overtime can be claimed only by those workers who are employed on minimum wages as prescribed under the Act. Those employed under other statutory rules cannot claim overtime wages under this Act.

*177.* Under the Factories Act, every adult worker, on completing 240 days in a calendar year, is entitled to annual leave at the rate of 1/20 days, and a child at the rate of 1/15 days of work. Any days of lay-off are deemed to be days worked. For

138. LLJ., Vol. 2, 2012, *V.E. Jossie and Other* v. *Flag Officers Commanding in Chief and Another*, Kerala High Court, pp. 195–197.
139. *Workmen of Calcutta Electric Supply Corpn. Ltd* v. *Calcutta Electric Supply Corpn. Ltd* 1973.

women workers maternity leave up to 12 weeks is likewise included. Under the Mines Act, 190 days of attendance below ground and 240 days above ground are deemed to be equal to one calendar year's services. Below ground workers are entitled to annual leave at the rate 1/15 days of work, whereas in all other cases it is 1/20 days.

*178.* On quitting employment, or on being discharged or dismissed, an employee retains his legal right to earned leave. The earned leave not availed of by the employee is allowed to accumulate provided the leave per year carried forward does not exceed 30 days for an adult and 40 days for a child. However, if leave applied for has not been sanctioned, he shall be entitled to carry forward the leave refused without any limit. A worker may avail of leave with wages by making an application not less than 30 days before the date the leave is to begin in a public utility, and not less than 15 days in any other factory. He is allowed to take his earned leave not more than three times in any year.

### §9. Cine-workers and Cinema Workers

*179.* An entirely new device was forged for regulating working conditions of the cine-workers and cinema theatre workers. Under the Cine-Workers and Cinema Theatre Workers (Regulation of Employment) Act, 1981 it is provided that every producer of a feature flim, before engaging cine-workers, will be required to enter into a written agreement with each one of them in the prescribed form and the same must be registered with the competent authority; and if the benefit of provident fund is also provided the said agreement should also be deposited with the Regional Provident Fund Commissioner. In case the cine-workers are engaged through a contractor the agreement must be executed by the producer and such contractor or other person. The Act prohibits employment of cine-workers without agreement. Under the agreement the producer agrees that a working day means a period not exceeding eight hours including one hour for rest and refreshments. A working week will be of six days, Monday to Saturday and the cine-workers will not be liable to work on Sundays and public holidays. They will not be required to work for more than five consecutive hours without break and a period of not less than 12 hours shall elapse between their release from the work place and the next succeeding call. Extra wages for working extra time are provided in the agreement. No such provision is made for the cinema-theatre workers. The benefits extended them are in respect of the laws on provided funds and payment of gratuity.

### §10. Conditions of Employment of *Beedi* Workers

*180.* In a writ petition before a High Court the *Beedi* workers represented by the Salem District *Beedi,* Cigar and Tobacco General Workers Union pleaded for minimum wages and justice since the management had orally terminated their services. The management denied that they were his employees, consequently the question of oral termination of their services did not arise. The identity cards produced by the *beedi* workers were issued by government inspectors but were not valid legal documents because under the relevant rules such ID card should be issued by the trade mark owner or the contractor, not by the Inspectors of the Labour Department. The management took the plea that once the legality of this document was rejected on a point of law, there was no material evidence to show the existence of master-servant relationship. On behalf of workmen it was pointed out that they have been making representations to the authorities to compel the employers to provide the ID cards and that they were maintaining fake master rolls. These had led them to conduct an investigation and issue the ID cards to the real workers, not to the *benami* (unnamed) workers. Each worker made a deposition in person, while on the side of the management there was no satisfactory rebuttal of evidence. The court decided to accept the ID cards as valid pieces of evidence to prove their employment status. Management failed to produce the annual returns which would have revealed the quantity of *beedi* rolled by the home workers. The self-serving registers produced by the contractors showed the bonus paid to their workers, but none of then had complained before the authority. The court rejected the contention of the management that the contesting workmen were employed by the contractors. The writ petition of the employers against the findings of the appellate authority was dismissed. The writ petition of workers against the orders of the Labour Court on claim petitions seeking minimum bonus, wages for national and festival holidays and earned leave totaling Rs 1452.30 was upheld. The Labour Court had rejected the claim petition on the ground that the ID cards were not valid pieces of evidence. Its orders were set aside. The workmen's claim for Rs 1452.30 was upheld as valid and the management was directed to pay this sum to each worker within a period of eight weeks from the date of receiving this order. The appellate authority had earlier found that the services of workmen were arbitrarily terminated and they were liable to be reinstated with back wages and all other attendant benefits. The court decided not to interfere with its orders.[140]

## §11. Absorption – Principle of Legitimate Expectation

*181.* On the closure of the watch assembly unit at Ajmer of the Rajasthan State Industrial Development and Investment Corporation Ltd, the employees were retrenched, which was challenged in a writ petition. Relief was declined which led to appeals before the division bench. The High Court held that in so far as the company reserved to itself the right to transfer its employees, it was bound to act fairly at the time of closure of its unit to protect the right to employment by absorbing them in its other 30 units. Principles of legitimate expectation were applicable in the present case. The appeal was allowed.[141]

---

140. LLJ 2009, Vol. 1, *Management of D.C. Diwan Mohideen Beedi Factory, Saleem* v. *Appellate Authority, Beedi and Cigar Workers (Conditions of Employment) Act, 1966, Labour Officer, Salem and Others,* High Court of Madras, pp. 616–622.
141. LLJ 2009, Vol. 3, *Kanta Kumari Banafal (Smt.) & Others* v. *Rico and others,* High Court of Rajasthan, p. 795 (NOC).

*182.* In another case a retrenched employee appealed to the High Court that despite the state government's orders that all retrenched employees should be absorbed in other departments on equivalent posts, he was not absorbed. Keeping in view the government order and other statutory rules and regulations the writ petition was allowed by the single judge and the government directed to consider the petitioner's case in view of the order.[142]

142. LLJ 2009, Vol. 3, *Mohd. Ibrahim* v. *State of UP and others,* High Court of Allahabad, p. 827 (NOC).

# Chapter 4. General Conditions of Service I

*183.* The Border Road Organization has been employing casual and temporary workers for many years and by discontinuing their employment at the expiry of employment contract, but with a short break reemploys them. This has been a regular practice. The trade union of such worker through writ petitions and appeals to the High Court sieved a writ of mandamus from the division bench to implement a scheme or the proposal of a scheme and consider the case of those employees who have put in more than five years of service for the purpose of regularization of their services. The court also directed that the casual workers working in the organization shall continue to work till they attain eligibility within the purview of the circular for being considered. The Supreme Court heard an appeal from the Government against this order and sent the matter on removed to the Division Bench for a closer secreting of the circular and related aspects while setting aside its order. The High Court conducted a fresh hearing and reached the finding that the government had formulated a scheme for the welfare of casually paid employees on a rational basis and again directed the central government of implement it. the government again appealed to the Apex Court against it. It was admitted and the court held, citing more than half-a-dozen of cases decided by it. That the said scheme was merely an inter-department communication which did not have the sanction of law creating an enforceable right. The union claim for regularization of casual workers could not be granted. A temporary or casual worker would not be entitled to be absorbed in regular service or made permanent, if the original appointment was not in terms of the process envisaged by the relevant rules. The impugned order was not sustainable. However, the court expressed anguish at the practices of terminating employment on completion of employment period.[143]

*184.* In an appeal against an order of a single judge which was upheld by the division Bench dismissing the writ appeals by the state government, the Supreme Court referred to the law stated in its earlier, judgments, especially, *Secretary of State of Karnataka* v. *Uma Devi* (2006, Vol. 2, LLJ) and related it point by point. High Court in exercising power under Article 226 of the constitution will not issue directions for regularization, absorption or permanent continuous illness the employees claiming regularization had been appointed in pursuance of a regular recruitment in accordance with relevant rules in a open impeditive process against sanctioned vacant posts. The equality clause in Articles 14 and 16 should be scrupulously followed and courts should not issue a direction which would be volatile of constitutional scheme. While something that is irregular can be regularized, back door entries, appointments contrary to the constitutional scheme and for/or appointment of irregular candidates cannot be regularized. Mere continuation of a service by a temporary, ad hoc or daily-wage employee, under cover of interim orders of the court, would not confer upon him any right to be absorbed into service, as such service would be litigious employment. 'sympathy and sentiment cannot be grounds

143. LLJ, 2, 2011, *Union of India and Others* v. *Vartak Labour Union*, Supreme Court of India, pp. 295–300.

for passing any order of regularization in the absence of a legal right.' Consequently, under no stretch of imagination could persons employed by the aided hostels be termed as persons employed by the state government. Hence the writ petitions by such persons were not maintainable and the decisions of the High Court grouting any relief to then cannot be sustained. Decisions relied upon the High Court were no longer good law. Further, even if there was an one time scheme for regularization of these who were in service prior to 1 May 1995, there cannot obviously be successive directions for scheme after scheme for regularization of irregular or part time appointments. Therefore, none of the respondents is entitled to any relief. The appeals were allowed and the order of the High Court set aside.[144]

*185*. In one case the Supreme Court set aside the High Court direction to the central government to implement a scheme under an office memo for the welfare of casual workers employed by the Border Road Organization for about 30 years. The High Court allowed the writ petition of the trade union to regularise the services of those workers who had been in service for more than five year. The government made a writ appeal before the Apex Court against the writ of mandamus issued by the High Court on regularization. The Apex Court held that inter-departmental communications and nothings on files do not have the sanction of law, creating an enforceable right. The Court held that the union's claim for regularization merely on the length of service cannot be granted because casual employment terminates when the same is discontinued and the casual laborers would not be entitled to be absorbed in regular service or made permanent if the original appointment was not in terms of the process envisaged by the relevant rules. The Court cited the judgement made in *Secretary, State of Karnataka and Other* v. *Uma Devi* (3) and other (2006) in support, that the state cannot frame a Scheme of regularization of ad hoc / temporary / daily wagers in violation of the doctrine of equality or the stipulation that such appointment will not confer any right to seek regularization or absorption in the regular cadre. The writ of *mandamus* could not be issued for regularization or absorption of such appointees. In the case of BRO the Court directed the government to consider enacting an appropriate regularization scheme for absorption and regularization of casual workers engaged in its going projects. The appeals were allowed and the impugned judgement and order were set aside.[145]

*186*. Taking an independent position, the Rajasthan High Court admitted a writ petition of daily wage employees who had worked for 20–25 years in the public sector company, the Indian Telephone Industries Ltd. The Court felt that the ITI's reliance on the judgments of the Supreme Court was only to justify its own wrong. If the respondents gave appointment to petitioners without there being statutory rules, against non-existent parts, without advertisement of the post, and without prescribing pay scale, it was none of the fault of the petitioners and it was grave misconduct

144. LLJ, 2, 2011, *State of Rajasthan and Others*. v. *Daya Lal and Others*, Supreme Court of India, pp. 193–198.
145. LLJ, 2, 2011, *Union of India and Other* v. *Vartak Labour Union*, Supreme Court of India, pp. 295–300.

of any instrumentality of the state, which amounted to exploitation of weaker section of the public. The petitioners relied on another judgement of the Supreme Court wherein it was held that the employees were entitled to a dignified life. The respondents took the plea that no vested right was created in temporary employment and a direction could not be given to regularize such employees in the absence of any existing vacancies, nor a direction could be given to the state to create posts in a non-existent establishment. The Court held that it was a clear case of non-application of mind of the employer to foresee their need of employees.

> It appears that all the judgements against regularization of the employees are used by the employer to protect their own wrong and are not used to learn the lesson of not indulging in such type of practice of giving appointment without making proper rules and providing appropriate pay scales.

The Court allowed the writ petitions in terms of the judgement delivered by this Court in *Ganpat Lal Prajapat* v. *ITI Ltd.* and others (2008) and the respondents were directed to consider the case of the petitioners in the light of directions issued by the Supreme Court in the case of *State of Karnataka* v. *Smt. Uma Devi* for regularization on the posts appropriate to the job of petitioners upon which they were initially appointed and further they were directed to grant regular pay scale of the post to the petitioners.[146]

*187.* In another case the court recalled the Supreme Court ruling: 'The principle of natural justice is attracted whenever a person suffers a civil consequence or a prejudice is caused to him by an administrative action.' The procedure to be followed is not a matter of secondary importance and in the broadest sense natural justice simply indicates the sense of what is right and wrong. There should be a fair procedure and a man's defence must always be fairly heard. In the instant case a manager was found to be negligent and also of several irregularities. He was placed under suspension and 15 charges levelled against him. He was later dismissed from service. His first writ petition was dismissed by a single judge. The second writ petition met the same fate.[147]

*188.* An employer is entitled to ask for loyalty. Employees, including workmen, are expected not to make defamatory and false statements about an employer. An act of disloyalty is a serious offence and could result in some form of punishment. However, going on strike, go-slow, or any other form of industrial action cannot be construed as disloyal acts. Furthermore, though employees are expected to adhere to standards of good and righteous conduct, it is not reasonable for an employer to seek to improve their moral or ethical tone in relation to outsiders by the use of disciplinary procedures. Giving evidence against the employer in an industrial adjudication is not an act of disloyalty. An employee may not write offensive letters to

146. LLJ, Vol. 2, 2011, *Jetha Ram Deora* v. *Indian Telephone Industries Ltd, Jodhpur and others*, High Court of Rajasthan, pp. 231-236.
147. LLJ, February, 2011, *R. 'deceased' Pattabhi and Others* v. *Tamil Nadu Minerals Ltd*, High Court of Madras, pp. 555–566.

directors of the company, abuse his superior, make a false complaint against superior officers to the police, sleep in his office during duty hours, and engage in rowdy conduct. But a private quarrel outside the premises of work cannot be constructed as subversive of discipline. It is also legitimate for a workman to demand the removal of a particular person from his post on valid grounds. If pursuant to this demand speeches are made against the officer, such action cannot be viewed as insubordination or indiscipline provided the speeches are not inflammatory or lead to violence.

*189.* In one case the charged workman had assaulted the staff members of the company about 50 metres from the gate of the factory during a strike. These were non-striking employees and had reported for duty.[148] An inquiry was held and the workman was dismissed from service. Later eight more workmen were found guilty of the same misconduct and dismissed. The High Court upheld the dismissals on the ground that a punishable misconduct need not take place within the factory premises.[149] In another case the Mills' Officers' Regulations prohibited employees from approaching the media in relation to matters pertaining to day-to-day functioning of the company. These rules were broken and the management initiated disciplinary action. The office-bearers of the Officers Association went to the High Court claiming rights of freedom of speech, expression and association, etc. The challenge failed and the service rules were upheld.[150]

## §1. Loyalty and Obedience

*190.* In the case of workmen the disciplinary rules are subordinated to the mandatory provisions of the ID Act. Under Section 33(2)(b) it is provided that, during the presidency of any proceedings before a Labour Court/tribunal/national tribunal in respect of an industrial dispute, the employer may punish a workman with a discharge or dismissal due to any misconduct in accordance with the standing orders, provided he has paid wages for one month and an application is made to the authority before which the proceedings are pending for approval. These two acts must form part of the same transaction. If the approval is not granted, the employer's order of discharge or dismissal is wholly invalid and inoperative. In the instant case it was further held that the same person could function as a conciliation officer and as the authority under Section 33(2)(b) though the powers and duties of the two were distinct and different from each other. The employer dismissed two workmen who were union officer bearers on the charge that they forced their way into a room where a meeting was in progress and assaulted the senior general manager with fist blows in the presence of other officials without any provocation. The management did not conduct any inquiry because the offending workers along with others had

148. LLJ, 2000, Vol. 3, *Management 2 of Madura Cement Pvt Ltd* v. *Presiding Officer, Principal Labour Court, Madurai and Other,* High Court of Madras, pp. 955–959.
149. LLJ, Vol. 2, 1995, *Khandu Krishna Bhyogade* v. *Kalyanai Steel Ltd and Others,* High Court of Bombay, pp. 314–318.
150. LLJ, Vol. 2, 1995, *Mysore Paper Mills Officers' Association* v. *State of Karnataka,* High Court of Karnataka, pp. 228–230.

unleashed a reign of terror at the factory site and everyone was mortally afraid of them. Since no one would come forward as a witness and depose against the offending employees the employer did not conduct any enquiry. The workmen denied before the conciliation officer that they were offered payment of salary for one month at the time of the order of dismissal, though several days later their bank accounts were credited with all the sum of money due to them. It was held that merely signing the cheque on the same day was not conclusive evidence of offer of payment of money. The cheque should have been duly served upon them. Moreover, under the standing orders, a chargesheet should have been drawn up and an enquiry held. Only if the workmen were found guilty in such a proceeding could the employer order their dismissal. The permission sought was declined, so the dismissal order lost validity. The High Court upheld the decision of the conciliation officer and dismissed the writ petition.[151]

## §2. Suspension

*191.* Under the service rules a government servant can be suspended pending disciplinary proceedings or in contemplation of disciplinary provceedings. The disciplinary authority is expected to consider the gravity of misconduct alleged or the nature of evidence placed before him for taking a decision whether it would be expedient to keep the employee under suspension. An officer was found to be in possession of disproportionate assets and a case was registered under the Prevention of Corruption Act, 1948. The order of suspension passed by the state government was, however, put in abeyance by the State Administrative Tribunal on an application by the employee. The Supreme Court upheld that suspension was not a punishment but only one of forbidding the employee from discharging the duties of office, that he may not have further opportunity for perpetrating the allged misconduct, or to have the enquiry against him scuttled or to win over the witnesses, etc. It was held that the order of the Tribunal staying suspension was not justified, it had acted in too much haste. The general principle is that an authority which can appoint a public servant would also be entitled to suspend him pending an enquiry into his misconduct. This power is either the creation of a statute or an express term in the contract.[152]

*192.* Another view is that suspension is an interim punishment during which the contract of service is held in abeyance and the employee is debarred from discharging his duties. However, suspension may be ordered only if there is a serious allegation of misconduct, or there is sufficient material for prima facie satisfaction of authorities. In the usual case, suitable investigation must follow and on the results thereof appropriate disciplinary action should be taken. During the period of suspension the employee should be paid a subsistence allowance which may be lower

151. LLJ, February 2011, *Orissa Power Generation Corp. Ltd* v. *Conciliation Officer-cum-Asstt. Labour Commissioner and Another,* High Court of Orissa, pp. 467–476.
152. LLJ, 1995, Vol. 1, *State of Orissa through its Principal Secretary, Home Department* v. *Bimal Kumar Mohanty*, Supreme Court of India, pp. 568–573.

than the normal wage earned by him. Suspension suspends the claim to salary. The enquiry should be concluded within a reasonable time because the expression, 'subsistence allowance' has an undeniable penal significance.[153] Employes cannot challenge the order of suspension on the grounds that the order is arbitrary, punitive and malafide, because the power to suspend falls squarely in the domain of the disciplinary authority and unless the same was a patent abuse of power, it can hardly be subjected to a judicial review.[154]

*193.* Employees of public sector banks are subject to rules and regulations laid out in considerable detail on matters pertaining to misconduct of wrong doing, fraud, or any serious breach of personal character and conduct. They are also covered by the Article 311(2) which provides for a procedure of an enquiry and affording reasonable opportunity of being heard in respect of charges which may result in the punishment of dismissal or discharge from service. Before the amendment to the constitution in 1976, such an employee was afforded a second opportunity of presenting himself in respect of the proposed penalty. But by the amendment the second defence was removed. He can no longer have the opportunity of making a representation on the penalty proposed. In a case the employee of a nationalized bank was suspended from service together with stoppage of two increments for one misconduct and punished again with the stoppage of two increments in another charge. Both charges were proved, but the authority awarding punishment decided that the loss of two increments will be suffered concurrently. This meant that he will lose two increments only, not four. It was also decided to treat the period of suspension as spent not on duty. Was this permissible under the rules? The Court decided that as soon as the police decided not to prosecute the employee on the criminal charge of fraud, there was no case for prosecution and the management was bound to treat the period of suspension as spent on duty. The only penalty that the employee must suffer was stoppage of two increments. Earlier the Labour Court had upheld the bank's order in respect of both penalties, and affirming that the delinquent employee would suffer the stoppage of four increments, not two. Not being on duty meant that during the period of suspension he would not earn any increment. The elaborate rules provide that, if after an enquiry it is decided not to take any action against the employee, he shall be deemed to be on duty through out the period of suspension and entitled to full salary and all other privileges. If some punishment is imposed, other than dismissal, a whole or part of period of suspension may be treated as spent on duty, at the discretion of the disciplinary authority. Other rules refer to the employee being convicted by a court, then dismissal may follow; if he is merely acquitted giving the benefit of doubt, not an honourable acquittal, some action departmentally may be taken, and the period of suspension shall not be

---

153. LLJ, Vol. 2, 2000, *Purushothaman Potti V.N.* v. *State Bank of Travancore and Others*, High Court of Kerala, pp. 635–637.
154. LLJ, 2008, Vol. 1, *BEST Workers Union & Another* v. *BEST Undertaking and Another*, High Court of Bombay, pp. 1058–61.

treated as spent on duty. The order of the Labour Court was set aside and the bank directed to reread the service rules.[155]

## §3. Discharge and Dismissal

*194.* In a case the bank manager was charged with breach of discipline, for several acts of omission and commission in respect of reckless sanction and disbursement of loans without observing the bank's guidelines, blatant misuse of his discretionary lending power, for making wrongful gains to himself and demanding and accepting bribe. The enquiry established each and every charge. The inquiry officer found that the pre-sanction inspection was made casually, the economic viability was not taken care of, margins were not ensured and civil constructions were not verified. As a result, a number of accounts have turned NPA and the bank had been caused losses due to bank manager's habit of not observing bank's guidelines. The inquiry officer found that the officer accommodated the defaulter borrowers and did not care to ensure that fresh loans to them could not be granted. All the procedural steps were taken before declaring him guilty and the penalty of dismissal was imposed. The court declined to intervene and dismissed the petition.[156]

*195.* In another case 13 workmen of a hospital were dismissed from service for going on strike, stoppage of work and riotous behaviour, etc. The Labour Court held the findings of the enquiry officer as perverse except on points,[157] and 6 on going on the illegal strike. Parties were invited to lead evidence. In the final award the Labour Court directed the hospital to reinstate the employees in service with back wages. This was challenged in a writ petition. The single judge allowed the petition and set aside the award of the Labour Court. This was followed by another writ petition filed by the union. The union took the plea that the strike was not declared illegal by a competent court; moreover, though a total of 85 workers proceeded on strike but only 13 were charged with misconduct. This was discriminatory. Furthermore, the punishment was too harsh and disproportionate to the misconduct. The court held that the hospital was a public utility service; that the workmen refused to work without any notice and indulged in assaulting the officers of the hospital and disrupted its smooth working. The plea that it was not declared an illegal strike was without any substance because the Labour Court had found it to be illegal. The charge of misconduct was proved. In any case, a court of law will not be justified in making an order which will result in sending all such employees back to work in the hospital because their conduct shows that they are unfit to work in any hospital as they have no regard for the welfare of the patients. 'The court had enquired whether the hospital would make any ex-gratia payment to the workers and the hospital had offered to pay two years of wages to each of the 13 workmen. This offer

155. LLJ, July 2010, *Anil Kumar Jaggi* v. *Industrial Tribunal Cum Labour Court, Chandigarh and Another,* High Court of Punjab and Haryana, pp. 193–199.
156. LLJ, July 2010, *Ram Avtar* v. *Bank of Baroda & Others*, High Court of Allahabad, pp. 298–313.
157. LLJ, December 2010, *Bombay Labour Union* v. *Bhartiya Arogya Nidhi and Others,* High Court of Bombay, pp. 783–785.

was rejected by the union. However, the hospital would make the payment even if at this stage they came for it. Appeal was dismissed. The order of the single judge was upheld.'

*196.* In a case of wrong dismissal, the chief pharmacist of a hospital connected with the Corporation of Madurai was charged of not handing over the key of the hospital before proceeding on leave. The second charge was that he failed to maintain the income and expenditure accounts and the third that he obstructed a doctor from performing his official duty. About one month before framing the third charge he was suspended from service and later served a single show cause notice calling him to explain why he should not be removed from service. All the aforesaid three charges which arose on different dates were combined in the show cause notice. The suspended employee filed a writ petition to direct the Madurai Corporation to pay subsistence allowance. While this was pending, the enquiry officer who was asked to enquire into the second and the third charges was promoted and became the Commissioner of the Corporation. In this capacity he passed the final order of removal of service of the suspended employee, though he had not completed the enquiry. This led to second writ petition praying to quash the order of dismissal. The Court asked the Corporation to pass appropriate orders on the basis of the enquiry instituted against the employee. The response was that a Chief Accountant was appointed as the enquiry officer. But he simply adverted to each charge and noted the reply given by the petitioners and concluded the enquiry and submitted the report. The earlier enquiry officer had examined witnesses and they were cited in the final order. The petitioner's plea was that no fresh enquiry was conducted, while the first enquiry was mid-way and never completed. That report was not submitted before the Court. The final orders did not refer to the first report, but only to the second report. The Court held that it could not be considered as the report, because it failed to give reference to the rival parties by the witnesses examined on either side. Moreover, the enquiry reports were not circulated to the punished employee before making the final orders. The Court found the impugned order as completely perverse. Unfortunately the petitioner died before the completion of proceedings, so he could not be directed to face yet another enquiry. Instead he was reinstated in service and the Corporation was directed to pay all back wages from the day of suspension till he attained superannuation and the pensionary benefits to the legal heirs.[158]

*197.* In another case an employee of the Indian Airlines was dismissed from service on the charge of producing a false document for visa to Australia. He had faked the signature of Senior Chief Manager. He had a uniformly good career of 27 years. At the Supreme Court he pleaded to modify the order of dismissal to one of termination of service, so that he may seek employment elsewhere. The Indian Airlines consented to this request and the Apex Court modified the order accordingly.[159]

---

158. LLJ, September 2010, *Nagsrathinam A. (deceased) and Commissioner* v. *Corporation of Madurai and Others,* High Court of Madras, pp. 803–806.
159. LLJ, 2008, Vol. 1, *Shiva Anand* v. *Indian Airlines Ltd and Others,* Supreme Court of India, pp. 666-667.

## §4. Rights of Protected Workmen

*198.* Subsection 3 of Section 33 of the ID Act confers special protection on a specified number of union functionaries. It imposes a blanket ban upon the employers from taking any action against any protected workman during the pendency of an industrial dispute with which he may be concerned, including discharge or dismissal or any form of punishment save with the express permission in writing of the authority before whom the dispute is pending. A 'protected workman' is a member of the executive or office bearer of a registered union in the establishment which has been recognized as such. Under this section the union is provided with complete protection against any threat of victimization, and assurance of freedom in conducting industrial disputes. Every registered trade union should write to the employer before the stipulated date, 30 April, under the rules, every year the names and addresses of the officers of the union who should be recognized as protected workmen by the employer, and the employer should do so in writing. In one case these rules were not observed. The General Secretary of the BEST Workers Union was charge sheeted, under the relevant standing orders for assaulting fellow workers with a bamboo stick outside a bus station, after a period of six months, as provided in the BIR Act. The incident occurred on 6 May 1995 while the chargesheet was served in January 1996. The enquiry commenced soon thereafter and concluded in June 1996, with the recommendation of punishment by dismissal. This was implemented in October 1997. The permission to punish the workman was sought in June 1996 and it was granted. The workman's appeal to the Labour Court was rejected in February 1998. The workman approached the Second Labour Court, Mumbai, but by an order the Court decided in March 2002 that the petitioner was not entitled to reinstatement and continuity of service. He then approached the industrial court but the appeal was dismissed. This led to a writ petition in the High Court. The Court decided that in view of the concurrent findings of the authorities in confirming the dismissal order based on a duly conducted enquiry there was no reason to interfere with the order. It was within the framework of law and 'there is nothing to interfere in such matters.' His protected status was of no avail.[160] In another case the company dismissed two office bearers of the union while exempting two others who tendered an opology. The charge was misconduct of instigating the contract workers, riotous and disorderly behaviour. An enquiry was conducted, the charges proved and two union leaders were dismissed from service. The tribunal upheld the order of dismissal and this led then to appeal to the High Court. The issue was whether the company's action was contrary to Section 33(3) of the ID Act, also whether the tribunal's award was perverse and whether it was a case of victimization.[161] The company had not granted them the dates of protected workmen, but the Asstt. Labour Commissioner did so and later reiterated this decision. The management questioned this order in a court but lost. So the two workmen were protected under law and the company's action was bad in law. On the second issue that

---

160. LLJ, 2006, Vol. 3, *General Secretary, BEST Workers' Union, Mumbai* v. *General Manager, BEST Undertaking and Another*, Bombay High Court, pp. 924–928.
161. LLJ, 2006, Vol. 3, *Bagalkot Cement Company Workers' Union* v. *Management of Kanoria Industrial Ltd*, Karnataka High Court, pp. 656–662.

the tribunal gave the award without examining the standing orders and had failed to notice that the findings of the enquiry were not supported by legally acceptable evidence. The Court held that the approach of the tribunal was bad in law and had resulted in the perversity of the award. On victimization, the court said that it connotes a person who becomes a victim of the employer's wrath by reason of his trade union activities. These two workmen were protected workmen but proceeded against while dropping charges against two other workmen. This was a clear case of unfair labour practice. The writ petition was allowed, the tribunal's award was quashed and the company was directed to reinstate the two workmen with back wages, continuity of service and all consequental benefits.

*199.* In one case the recognized union wrote to the employer nominating its general secretary as a protected worker. This request was not accepted as disciplinary proceedings pertaining to a memo of charges were pending against him. Recognition would stop the employer from taking any action against him without the prior permission of the authority. The court held that even if a union action is facing disciplinary action it does not render him ineligible for being recognized as a protected workman. It was a statutory right and the employer cannot refuse a request by the union.[162]

*200.* In one case the Transport Corporation of the Karnataka government transferred a driver who was an office bearer of the recognized staff and workers' union. The subsisting settlement laid down that the office bearers of the union shall not be transferred from the place of work during the term of their office. However, the driver faced the article of charges that he took part in a gate meeting and that he attempted to assault the Depot Security Officer. An enquiry was instituted and he was found guilty. The disciplinary Authority reduced the pay by one increment permanently and he was served an order of transfer. The driver raised an industrial dispute which was heard by the industrial tribunal. The tribunal set aside the punishment and the Corporation was ordered to pay arrears. It treated the transfer as an alteration in the condition of service and recognized the driver as a protected workman. In an appeal to the High Court, the tribunal's order was challenged as an interference in an administrative order. The Court held that in government service a transfer was an incident of service and often a corrective measure and no interference in such administrative matters should occur resulting from an industrial dispute. Moreover, the tribunal's reliance on the settlement was tentamount to administrative interference, since no clause of the settlement could be inconsistent with law which provided for transfer in the exigencies of service. Ordinarily the contract of service should provide for the right of the employer to affect transfer, but in this case it had no application. The incident of transfer is implied and it is not a contingency. Furthermore, there was no material on record to show that he was recognized as a protected workman. Therefore this contention was rejected. In effect

162. LLJ, September 2010, *HLL Life Care Ltd* v. *Hindustan Latex Labour Union (AITUC) and Another,* High Court of Kerala, pp. 811–815.

the High Court set aside this clause of the settlement. The petition succeeded and the order of the tribunal was set aside.[163]

## §5. Grievance Procedure

*201.* In India the MSOs provide for a grievance procedure to be set up to hear complaints arising out of employment but it is a recommendatory provision. The model grievance procedure envisages the constitution of a grievance committee, (i) where the union is recognized and (ii) where the union is not recognized but a works committee exists. In the former case the grievance committee may consist of two management representatives, one union representative and one union representative of the department where the concened workman works. In the latter case, there are two management representatives, workers are represented by the representatives of the department where they work and the secretary/vice president of the works committee. The grievance committee is deemed to be the appropriate forum for taking up grievances after the first step of grievance procedure has been exhausted.

## §6. Compassionate Appointments

*202.* On compassionate appointments the Supreme Court has held that the public authority concerned has to examine the financial condition of the family and only if satisfied that it would not be able to meet the crisis, that a job is to be offered to the eligible member of the family. Moreover, only a post in class III and IV, being the lowest posts in non-manual and manual categories, can be offered on compassionate grounds. No other posts are expected or required to be given by the public authorities for the purpose.[164] In one case the dependent applicant had the relevant qualifications as provided in the scheme for appointment on compassionate grounds. The Court held that possession of relevant qualifications does not create any vested right in the applicant. The availability of pension to the family is one of the financial parameters for determination of the financial condition of the family. Taking this into account the bank declined the request for compassionate appointment. Thereafter the applicant filed a writ petition in the High Court and secured an order to the bank to make the appointment on compassionate grounds. This was challenged in the Apex Court. The Court faulted the High Court for failing to notice that the bank had an elaborate scheme for the purpose; further, that its judgment would open a pandora box of litigation and all persons who are denied compassionate appointment would take recourse to it. There were also other errors in the judgment. It was

163. LLJ, 2006, Supplement, Vol. 4, *Karnataka State Road Transport Corporation, Bangalore* v. *S.D. Bandi,* High Court of Karnataka, pp. 352–356.
164. LLJ, Vol. 1, 1995, *State of Haryana and Others* v. *Umesh Kumar and Nagpal and Anil Malik,* Supreme Court of India, pp. 798–800.

held that the dependent acquired a right to preferential treatment subject to the discretion of the bank. The appeal was allowed and the orders of the High Court were set aside.[165]

*203.* Once a person has been appointed on compassionate grounds, no further consideration on this ground would ever arise. The Supreme Court has held that a direction should be issued for consideration and not a direction to appoint. It is open to the government to consider the mater and come to a conclusion one way or other. The Court pointed out that the eligibility of a person to be appointed to a given post (in this case, the sub-inspector of police), is one thing, the process of selection is yet another thing. Merely because a person is eligible, the High Court should not issue a direction.[166] In another case an employee of the Electricity Board died on duty leaving his widow and three children in destitution and she sought an appointment on compassionate grounds. But no action was taken for over 11 years, so she made a writ petition to the High Court. The Court held that a compassionate appointment has to be provided immediately to redeem the family in distress In the instant case directions were issued to appoint the petitioner widow in a part-time post, if necessary, by creating a supernumerary post. The Court relied on an earlier Supreme Court ruling that if there be no suitable post for appointment a super numerary post should be crated to accommodate the applicant.[167]

*204.* A widow secured compassionate appointment as a temporary clerk in the Institute of Science, Bangalore but the Institute terminated her job on learning that she had remarried and so was no longer entitled to compassion. She won at the Labour Court which directed the Institute reinstate her at the original post, but lost at the High Court which quashed the Labour Court award. The Institute contended that penury or financial distress did not continue on remarriage and that an appointment on compassionate ground did not vest in her an indefeasible right which could not be annulled. The Court said that in the normal course all appointments should be in accordance with the recruitment rules. Otherwise they would be violative of Article 14 of the constitution. Compassionate appointment is an exception to the general rule of recruitment. It cannot be another source of recruitment. The Apex Court had laid down the contours under which such claim should be examined and considered. This cannot be treated as a bonanza and also as a right to obtain government service. She contended that her appointment letter does not mention compassionate consideration. But only as temporary clerk. There was no vacancy in the quota for compassionate appointments and claims of several deceased employees family members who were senior to the deceased employee were pending consideration. Facts recorded by the Labour Court show that though married again her 'marriage has not been legally solemnized.' The Court held that 'penury or financial distress under which the family members of the deceased were placed at the time of

165. *AIR Supreme Court (Weekly)* 2006, Vol. 5, *Union Bank of India* v. *M.T. Lathesh,* Supreme Court of India, pp. 4626–4639.
166. LLJ, Vol. 1, 1995, *State of Rajasthan* v. *Unrav Singh,* Supreme Court of India, pp. 908–910.
167. LLJ, Vol. 1, 1995, *Sarabibi Usman Khan Pathan* v. *Supt. Engineer, Gujarat Electricity Board and Others,* High Court of Gujarat, pp. 776–780.

the death did not continue but got vanished or extinguished or evaporated by virtue of her remarriage to Shri M.V. Krishnan working in Indian Telephone Industries.' If the family of the deceased employee has tied over the financial distress for a considerable period, the claim of appointment on compassionate grounds would cease to exist. Her writ petition was dismissed.[168]

*205.* The Apex Court restated the law on compassionate appointment in a case where the application for such appointment seven and a half years after the employees death. The Division Bench of the High Court had granted the request and directed the employing establishment to provide appointment within three months from the date of the order. The Municipality had rejected the claim on two grounds. First, on the employees, death his widow did not make any request for an appointment and this showed that the death had not caused a serious financial crisis in the family second, the family was given Rs 26,674 as terminal benefits besides family pension to the widow. The High Court rejected the second reason, and on the score it could not be faulted. But it also rejected the first reason she had not the first reason. She had not applied sensibly because she suffered from anemia and law blood pressure. The Apex Court saw this ground as an after though and could not be accepted. Moreover, the Division Bench took a view that was completely divorced from the object and purpose of the scheme of compassionate appointment. An appointment made may years after the death of the employee or without due consideration of the financial resources available to the dependents simply because the clement happened to be one of the dependants of the deceased employee, would directly conflict with Articles 14 and 16 of the constitution, hence be illegal. The Municipality was clearly right in holding that with whatever difficulty, the family had been able to tide over the death of the employee. The impugned order of the Division Bench was unsustainable in law and was set aside.[169]

*206.* Judicial discretion: compassion with justice. A worker employed by the government owned Transport Corporation suffered from epilepsy and died. Shortly before his death the Corporation had discharged him from service, but failed to serve the discharge order on the employee and merely put it on the Notice Board. His illiterate widow applied for benefits under Group insurance and Family Pension under Section 33C(2) of the Industrial Disputes Act, which brought the reply that these claims are admitted when the employee dies while in service, but since he was discharged 19 days before his death, no claim benefits under the aforesaid schemes arise. The Labour Court which heard her petition agreed with the management and held that the petitioner failed to prove that the employee died during employment. The management had apparently secured a letter from the widow written in Tamil that described herself as the wife of the driver discharged or medical grounds. She gave her thumb impression on the letter. The Labour Court accepted it as valid evidence. In the writ petition she challenged the order of the Labour Court, that no

168. LLJ, 3, 2012, B. *Vijayakumari Pillai, Bangalore*, v. *Management of Indian Institute of Science, rep. by its Registrar*, Bangalore, Karnataka High Court, pp. 627–637.

169. LLJ, 3, 2011, *Local Administration Department and Another* v. *M. Selvanayagam @ Kukaravelu*, Supreme Court of India, pp. 10–12.

relief could be granted to her as the petitioner. The Court decided that the only dispute was whether he was in service on the day he died, 18 March 1995. On behalf of the petitioner it was pointed out that there was no proof that the discharge order was served on the employee. The burden of proof was on the management, not on the petitioner. They must also prove that the discharge was following the process of law. The settled law was that the order would take effect only if it was communicated to the concerned party. In this case there was no service of discharge order on the employee, so the aggrieved party could seek remedy and there was violation of principles of natural justice, as he was not afforded fair and adequate opportunity. The finding of the Labour Court that the workman died after discharge from service is vitiated by error of law on the face of record. 'Therefore this Court holds that the order of discharge dated 27 February 1995 did not take effect, as it was not communicated.' It held that the workman continued to be in service on the date of his death. On the letter which carried the widow's thumb impression the Court said that by no stretch of imagination can the show cause notice and the letter can be deemed to be an admission on the part of the first respondent as erroneously found by the Labour Court. The letter is unreliable and cannot be put against the petitioners to deny them relief. Management failed to produce them before the court. Therefore, the finding of the Labour Court in this regard is based on no evidence and is liable to be set aside. Assuming that on medical grounds the workman was unfit to do his usual duties, the management is required to act as per G.O. No. 746 dated 2 July 1981 which directs that in Transport undertakings those who have eye defect or other ailments and are found unfit on medical grounds be discharged and subsequently be provided with alternative employment in the posts like Helpers, depending upon their qualifications, without consulting the Employment Exchange- This was marked as an exhibit and the officials could have given alternative employment to the workman. As the employee died during employment, a family member of the petitioner is entitled to compassionate appointment as per G.O. Ms. No. 680, Transport Department dated 28 December 1977. The Court directed the petitioners to give representation to the second respondent Corporation, who shall consider their claim as if the application was made during 1955. Though the petitioners have only sought quashing of the Award and payment of Rs 247,000 under the Schemes, the case also compels this Court to grant more relief by moulding the relief. 'The power to mould relief is always available to the Court possessed with the power to issue high prerogative writs.' Further delay and laches do not bar the jurisdiction of the Court. It is a matter of discretion and not of jurisclistion.' Exercising this discretion this Court holds that : (i) The employee was not discharged as per law. (ii) The employee was deemed to be in service till his death. (iii) Therefore, the petitioners are entitled to salary payable from the date of discharge till his death. (iv) The petitioners are entitled to all benefits which are available to the family of the driver within 12 weeks from the receipt of the copy of the order. (v) The respondents should have given alternative employment to workman as per G.O. No. 746. (vi) The corporation shall give a compassionate employment to any member of the family of the deceased employee as per G.O. No. 680, treating the application for such compassionate employment was made during 1995, after getting the necessary application within two weeks from the eligible family member of the workman. Further, the Court awarded a sum of Rs 10,000 as compensation payable by the Corporation to the petitioner within four weeks of the receipt of the copy of the order. Writ petition was allowed with costs.[170]

170. LLJ, 3, 2012, *M. Sundarammal and Others* v. *Presiding Officer, Labour Court, Madurai and Another*, Madras High Court, pp. 57-63.

# Chapter 5. General Conditions of Service II

## §1. Hours of Work

*207.* The Factories Act 1948, is the principal standard setting legislation in India. Under this Act the maximum hours of work for an adult are prescribed at 48 hours per week and 9 hours per day. Inclusive of rest intervals he should not work for more than 10½ hours in any day. But the Act authorizes the Chief Inspector to allow a maximum spread-over, inclusive of rest intervals, of up to 12 hours. The Act also empowers the state governments to permit the periods of work to be so fixed that the legal limit of five hours, before an interval of rest, may extend to six hours in given cases. In 1997 for all seamen the ordinary hours of work were prescribed at 48 hours in a week (with effect from 26 September 1997).

*208.* Whereas Sections 51 to 56 lay down standards on hours of work, the power to grant exemptions and dilute these standards is given by Section 64. The state governments are provided with sweeping powers to grant exemptions from all or most of these sections in certain categories of work.

Exemptions from even the diluted standards may be granted to workers engaged on continuous operations to enable a shift worker to work the whole or part of the subsequent shift if necessity arises. Beyond this step, Section 65 empowers the state governments to modify or altogether drop the statutory provision for the display of 'notice of period of work for adults (Sec. 61)' and exempt any factory, or group or class of factories, from any or all the provisions pertaining to hours of work. In such an event the standards would be further lowered to:

- daily hours of work not to exceed 12;
- the spread-over, inclusive of rest intervals, not to exceed 13 hours in a day;
- overtime limited to seven days at a stretch and overtime work in any quarter not to exceed 75 hours;
- all of the above to be limited to 60 hours in any week.

In so far as women are concerned no exemptions can be made from the statutory limit on daily hours. Furthermore, no woman can be allowed to work in any factory except between 6.00 am and 7.00 pm. These hours can be changed to 5.00 am and 10.00 pm provided the state government issues a notification to this effect. Exemption may be granted for women working in fish-curing and fish-canning factories to prevent damage or deterioration in the quality of fish. The IT sector which employs people including women at all hours is currently free from the restriction on hours of work. As yet there is no law governing hours of work and working conditions applicable to this rapidly growing employment segment.

*209.* The Officers Association petitioned the High Court challenging the employer for increasing working hours for the officers from 42 to 48 hours per week with one day weekly off as against two days weekly off and to quash the notice dated 6 September 2011. The corporation is a public sector undertaking owned by the government of India. The order affected officers working in the general shift and those in three shifts. The policy aimed at adopting the working hour pattern of the Indian Oil Co. which is the holding company. The order was passed unilaterally; it was arbitrary, unreasonable and violative of Article Z1 of the Constitution, particularly affecting the health of employees as they worked in a polluted area. In the counter affidavit, the corporation related the history of working hours, which were 48 hours until 1970 and then these were reduced to 44 hours and again in 1979 to 42 hours. The Board of Directors decided to align various business processes and HR related policies with that of IOL, taking note of the interests of employees as well as the growth of the undertaking. Certain benefits were enhanced, to ensure parity with IOC employees. An additional benefit, in the form of 36 days of encashable compensatory off was on offer. This will enable them to earn additional income. Having heard both the parties at length, the Court held that before changing the service conditions, the members of the petitioner association were bound to be heard in compliance with the principles of natural justice. No hearing was given from 1 October 2011 before implementing the decision taken as per the resolution passed in February 2005. If civil rights are affected, hearing must be given to the persons likely to be effected. The natural justice rule can operate only in areas not covered by any law validity made to prevent miscarriage of justice. The action of the state, whether administrative or executive, has to be fair when rights of parties are to be effected. This was the principle laid down by the Supreme Court. In this view the impugned order cannot be sustained and was set aside. The respondent can very well convene a meeting and negotiate with the petitioner association to impress upon the members of the petitioner association to increase the working hours, etc. even though consensus is not required an increasing the working hour and for reduction of weekly holidays.' 'The matter is remitted to the respondent to convene a meeting for discussion and proceed further in accordance with law.' 'This order need not be construed as accepting the contentions of the petitioner association on merits.' The petition was disposed of accordingly.[171]

## I. Children and Adolescents

*210.* A child who has not completed his or her 14th year is prohibited from working in any factory or mine. However, a child is one who has not completed his 15th year of age. An adolescent is a person who has completed his 15th year but not his 18th year of age. A 'young person' is one who is either a child or an adolescent. In the mines there is a general prohibition of employment as well as presence of persons below 18 years of age, though even in mines, apprentices and trainees between 16 and 18 years are allowed to be employed under proper supervision and with prior permission. Non-adult workers should also be certified for fitness for work before they can be employed. If an adolescent is granted a certificate of fitness to work as an adult, he shall be deemed to be an adult for all purposes, but

171. LLJ, Vol. 2, 2012, *Chennai Petroleum Officers Association, Manali, Chennai* v. *Chennai Petroleum Corporation Ltd. rep. by its General Manager, (HR)*, Chennai, Madras High Court, pp. 514–520.

only if he has completed 17 years of age can he be permitted to work at night. Adolescents, both male and female, who have not attained the age of 17 years are only permitted to work between 6 am and 7 pm.

*211.* Under the Factories Act, child workers cannot be permitted to work for more than four and a half hours in any day or during the night. No child can be allowed to work in any factory on any day if he has already worked in another factory. If the Inspector is satisfied that any person without a certificate of fitness is a young person, or a young person is no longer fit to work, he may take action to arrange for a medical examination or forbid his employment until he has been examined. The Child Labour (Prohibition and Regulation) Act, 1986, prohibits the engagement of children in any occupation or workshop wherein the designated processes are carried on. In 1994 the list of occupations was expanded to include selling of crackers and fireworks in shops and slaughter houses. In 1998 the schedule to the Act was amended to substantially expand the list of prohibited occupations, and in 2001 it was again amended to include building industry, electroplating, diamond cutting and polishing and several others. Different laws employ varying age definitions for employing child labour. The ILO has adopted a standard, specifying 18 years of age below which employment in factories, mines, docks, railways, road transport and hazardous occupations among others is declared illegal. In India this may not be possible in the foreseeable future, mainly due to resistance from parents who cannot afford to keep their children in schools for that many years and must ask them to work and contribute to family income.

## II. Semi-organized Sector

*212.* Under the Plantations Labour Act, 1951, as amended in 1981, the maximum weekly hours of work for adults have been fixed at 48 hours and for children (below 15 years of age), and adolescents at 27 hours. The Act does not prescribe daily hours of work, though work should be so arranged that, inclusive of rest intervals and time spent in waiting for work, it does not extend beyond nine hours a day and 54 hours in a week. Rest intervals must be provided after five hours of work. No woman or child worker can be employed during hours other than between 6 am and 7 pm. Work done on the weekly day of rest must be treated as overtime. But no worker may work for more than ten days without a day of rest. There is no entitlement to a weekly day of rest if in any week a worker has worked less than six days.

*213.* Under the Motor Transport Workers Act, 1961, the hours of work are the same as under the Factories Act, but with the difference that on certain occasions work up to 10 hours a day and 54 hours a week can be taken; in case of a breakdown or dislocation of service, etc., work for more than 8 hours in any day or 48 hours in any week can be taken. But adolescent workers are not allowed to work for more than six hours, inclusive of rest intervals, and also between 10 pm and 6 am. Adolescent workers must also be certified for fitness by a medical officer.

*214.* Under the *Beedi* and Cigar Workers (Conditions of Employment) Act, 1966, a child is defined as one who has not completed 14 years of age, and is prohibited from working in any industrial premises. Women and young persons are allowed to work between 6 am and 7 pm only. The Act prohibits work in excess of 48 hours a week, or 9 hours a day. However, these rules and prohibitions do not apply to the category of 'home workers'. They are workers who work at home and not in any industrial premises. The Act does not apply to self-employed persons who work in private dwelling houses. Under state laws, the Tamil Nadu Building and Construction Workers (Conditions of Employment and Miscellaneous Provisions) Act, 1984, as amended in 1986, makes strict provisions on hours of work, etc. For an adult, work is limited to 9 hours in any day and 48 hours in any week. For adolescents, the limit is set at 6 hours a day inclusive of rest intervals. Overtime wages must be paid if work in excess of the statutory limit is taken or if a worker works on the day of rest.

*215.* Under the Minimum Wages Act which applies to all scheduled employments the appropriate government fixes the hours of work which constitute a normal working day inclusive of one or more specified intervals. Under the Central Rules, the hours of work for an adult are 9 hours and for a child 4½ hours. The working day of an adult should not exceed 12 hours. For an adolescent, the rule is that if he is certified to work as an adult, the adult hours of work will apply and if he works as a child, he cannot work for more than 4½ hours. A weekly day of rest must be allowed provided the employee has worked for the same employer for a continuous period of 6 days. The law provides for substitution of a rest day for work provided that he must not work for more than 10 days consecutively without a rest day. Rest days are paid days at overtime rates. The scheduled employments include practically the entire unorganized sector which falls outside the scope of the Factories Act, and includes various mines and quarries. The state governments' amendments cover shops and establishment, restaurants and eating houses, printing presses, metal foundries, engineering workshops, petrol pumps, carpet weaving, etc. These lists are periodically revised. In law an anomalous situation has developed on the question of overtime rate in the scheduled occupations and industries where the minimum wages paid are above the notified minimum. The latest position in law is that the regulation on overtime as per the MW Act loses its relevance where the minimum wages are above the notified minimum for the category of work.[172]

*216.* Under the Apprentices Act 1961, apprentices are trainees and not workers and the provisions of any law with respect to labour do not apply to them. They are not subject to any statutory daily hours of work. The weekly hours of work for trade apprentices are fixed in a range of 42-48 hours inclusive of time spent on instruction. Only in the third and subsequent years of apprenticeship are they required to work for the same number of hours per week as workers in the trade in the establishment. The rules also provide that no trade apprentice should be engaged in training between 10 pm and 6 am except with the prior approval of the apprenticeship

172. LLJ, November 2010, *National Airport Authority* v. *Sudershan Kumar and Others*, High Court of Delhi, pp. 557–562.

advisor. However, graduate or technician apprentices are required to work according to the normal hours of work of the department to which they may be attached. An apprentice will not qualify for training unless he has attained the age of fourteen years and he satisfies the prescribed standards of education and physical fitness; furthermore, if he is a minor, unless his guardian has entered into the contract of apprenticeship with the employer.

## III. Cine-workers and Cinema Theatre Workers

*217.* The Cine-workers and Cinema Theatre Workers (Regulation of Employment) Act, 1981, has the object of regulating working conditions as well as conciliation and adjudication of disputes. Under the Rules, an agreement between the two parties must be signed in accordance with the prescribed form and content. Under the statutory agreement, the Producer agrees that:

- a working day will comprise a period not exceeding eight hours including one hour for rest and refreshment;
- a working week means a six days week, and a cine worker is not liable to work on Sundays and public holidays:
- there must be a break after five hours of work;
- not fewer than 12 hours must elapse between the cine-worker's release from the work place and the next call; moreover, if required, the cine-worker will attend to work earlier than the scheduled time of shift provided he is paid extra wages at an agreed rate for early attendance, and that he will work beyond the working day with a one hour break provided he is paid extra wages at the agreed rate for work during the extended hours together with refreshments and transport facilities.

*218.* The agreement consisting of 20 clauses would cover most of the matters which need to be regulated. This is an unusual legislation inasmuch as it combines the features of standards setting legislation through the instrument of statutory agreement, with limited collective bargaining and also, in the event of disagreement, with conciliation and adjudication. In addition, the statutory agreement provides that the Employees' Provident Funds and Miscellaneous Provisions Act, 1952, will be applicable to the agreement. Thus some social security protection is also assured. Moreover, the producer is required to get the cine-worker insured for an injury, damage to person, or death caused by accident, etc., in the course of employment or during the period of assignment under the agreement. Under the Act, no person can be employed as a cine-worker without an agreement in writing and such an agreement is registered with the competent authority.

## IV. Working Journalists

*219.* The Working Journalists (Conditions of Service) and Miscellaneous Provisions Act, 1955, provides that no working journalist shall be required or allowed to work for more than 144 hours during any period of four consecutive weeks exclusive of the time for meals. Moreover, during any period of seven consecutive days, rest intervals of not less than 24 consecutive hours shall be provided, the period between 10 pm and 6 am being included therein. Under the rules, it is further provided that a normal working day exclusive of the time for meals shall not exceed 6 hours per day during the day shift and 5½ hours during the night shift; and, furthermore, no working journalist will be allowed to work for longer than the number of hours constituting a normal working day. The rule on interval for rest provides for its determination by such agreement as may be arrived at between the management and the working journalist employed in the establishment. Ordinarily he should work for not more than four hours in a day shift and three hours in a night shift. On night shifts the rule provides that a journalist should not be given work for more than one week at a time or more than one week in any period of 14 days. This limit may be exceeded in special circumstances.

### V. Mines, etc.

*220.* Under the Mines Act, the usual provision of working for not more than six days in a week exists. However, in the interest of safety, or for urgent work to be done to machinery, plant or equipment, etc., exemptions from the provision of law may be permitted. In such cases workers must be given compensatory days of rest within the two months following the month in which they were deprived of rest.

In mines, the hours of work below ground are normally limited to eight hours in a day and above ground to nine hours, subject to 48 hours in any week. Night shifts are treated at par with day shifts. Women workers are allowed to work only above ground and between 6 am and 7 pm; moreover, they must have an interval of not less than 11 hours between work on any two consecutive days.

*221.* The Weekly Holidays Act, 1942 provides for the grant of weekly holidays to persons employed in shops, restaurants and theatres. The purpose of this legislation is now reflected in other protective laws.

*222.* The Shops and Establishment Acts in states where these are applicable provide that every shop shall remain closed on one day a week, which shall be specified by the owner of the shop in a notice prominently exhibited in the shop. In addition the state government may require that shops be closed at the specified hour in the afternoon of one week-day every week. No deduction in wages can be made on these accounts.

## §2. Overtime and Minimum Wages Act

*223.* The overtime rate should be twice the ordinary rate of wages. For piece-rated workers the government may fix an equivalent time rate to form the basis for calculation of overtime wages. This is fixed at equal to the daily average of the previous month or week. The ordinary rate of wages mean the sum of basic wages and such allowances to which a worker is entitled, principally the dearness allowance.

The equivalents of benefits in kind, like subsidy on foodgrains and other admissible benefits, are included, but not bonus, nor overtime earnings.

*224.* Under the Mines Act, eight hours of work below ground is equated with nine hours above ground. A miner can have his ordinary wage calculated either on a weekly or a daily basis, whichever is more favourable to him. A miner may not work for more than 10 hours in any day inclusive of overtime. Under the Plantations Labour Act, any work in excess of the number of hours which constitute a normal working day, or more than 48 hours a week, is treated as overtime. The overtime pay is twice the rate of ordinary wages.

*225.* Where the scheduled hours of work are less than 48 hours a week, under an agreement with the union or the result of an award, the Factories Act will not apply and work in excess of the scheduled hours will constitute overtime. Any decision of the management on extending the agreed hours of work would result in a loss of compensation to workers and overtime pay would be payable to workers.

Litigation on overtime related issues has become infrequent. Overtime pay can be claimed under Section 33C(2) of the ID Act, provided the employer does not contest the claim. In a case where there is a dispute on the claim, it should be raised under Section 10 of the ID Act and an award obtained from the Labour Court. In one case the employees made a claim of overtime at the rate of Rs 60 per hour on the consolidated salary of Rs 5000 per month. The employer contented that the basic salary was only Rs 2500 per month, but adding the house rent allowance and other allowances raises it to Rs 5000 per month. He was liable to pay overtime only at the rate of Rs 30 per hour. The issue was adjudicated by the Labour Court and an award made in favour of the employees on the ground that the workmen received a consolidated salary of Rs 5000 per month and it did not include other allowances. In the High Court the writ petition of the employer failed, because he could not produce any evidence in support of his contention that the basic pay was only Rs 2500 per month.[173]

*226.* In another case the validity of the award made by the Labour Court was challenged on the ground that the Court did not have jurisdiction to adjudicate a case under (Section 33C(2)) of the ID Act, because the claim was disputed and was not already adjudicated by the court. The High Court agreed, since the proceedings were illegal without the force of law. The impugned award was set aside and quashed.[174]

*227.* In another case it was held that the employees governed by the central government rules and drawing more than the prescribed minimum wages were not entitled to overtime under the Minimum Wages Act and the Rules framed thereunder. The National Airport Authority was ordered by the Authority appointed under

---

173. LLJ, 2009, Vol. 3, *Management of Hardy Exploration and Production, India Inc.* v. *Presiding Officer, II,* Additional Labour Court, Chennai and Others, Madras High Court, pp. 553–554.

174. LLJ, 2006, Vol. 4, Supp., *Mining Engineer, Mines and Geology Deptt.* v. *Malu Ram and Another,* Rajasthan High Court, p. 854 (NOC).

the Minimum Wages Act to pay overtime at double the rate of wages being paid by the employing organization on the application of the 74 employees. The employer in his writ petition contended that though 'employment in the construction and maintenance of runways' is a scheduled employment the employees were not engaged in any scheduled employment and were not coverd by the Minimum Wages Act. The authority found that the 74 employees were doing the same work as they did as work-charged employees of the Central Public Works Department (CPWD) on absorption by the National Airport Authority. This was a finding of fact and the scope of writ jurisdiction to interfere in it was very limited. However, the Court upheld the other contention that on absorption, the workers would be eligible for payment of overtime as per the said regulations and not in accordance with the Act and its Rules. The employees enjoyed better terms of employment, earned much more than the minimum-wages notified under the Act and their working hours were lesser than those prescribed under the Act. The Minimum Wages Act is applicable to the unorganized sector, whereas the employees are in a regular employment and they cannot claim double benefits at the cost of the employer. Earlier the Supreme Court had ruled that under the MW Act overtime at double the rate was applicable only to the employees who received the minimum wages fixed under it. The problem arose since in an older judgement the Supreme Court had held that the employer of a scheduled employment had to pay double the rate of wages paid by him, not merely double the minimum wages. Clarifying the issue the Court held that the MW Act was not meant to govern the contract of employment between an employer and an employee drawing more than the minimum-wages even in a scheduled employment. It will have no application to such cases.[175]

## §3. Annual Leave with Wages and Other Entitlements

*228.* Protective laws provide for annual leave with wages. Under the Factories Act, every adult work, on completing 240 days in a calendar year earns annual leave with wages at the rate of 1/20 days and a child at the rate of 1/15 days of work. Any days of lay-off are deemed to be days worked. Under the Mines Act, 190 days of attendance below ground and 240 days above ground are deemed equal to one calendar year's of service. Below ground workers earn annual leave at the rate of 1/15 days of work, while for above ground workers it is at the rate of 1/20 days. In addition, women workers are entitled to maternity leave up to 12 weeks.

*229.* On quitting employment, retirement or discharge or dismissal, the workman or employee retains his right to earned leave. Accumulation of earned leave is allowed, provided the leave carried forward does not exceed 30 days for an adult and 40 days for a child. It leave applied for is not sanctioned, the leave refused is carried forward without any limit. He may take earned leave not more than three times in a year. In public utilities the application for leave should be made not less

175. LLJ, November 2010, *National Airport Authority* v. *Sudershan Kumar and Others,* High Court of Delhi, pp. 557–562 (cited in para. 165).

than 30 days before the date the leave is to begin and in other factories, not less than 15 days.

*230.* The Factories Act requires that crèches be provided by the employers where more than 30 women are ordinarily employed. The rules have made the 'competent authority', who may be the Coal Mines Welfare Commissioner or the Chief Inspector of Mines, or any other person duly authorized, to exercise the supervisory and investigating power in respect of crèches, their standards, and the ancillary amenities and facilities. Trained women may be appointed as crèche-in-charge who will have the responsibility of keeping the crèches in clean and sanitary conditions and to look after the children. The Plantation Labour Act also provides for crèches in every plantation wherein 50 or more women are employed on any day of the preceding 12 months or where the number of children of women workers is 20 or more.

## §4. Safety

*231.* Safety in industry, mines and office buildings has become a major concern with the government. State governments had systematically diluted standards, weakened the penal aspects of the Factories Act and allowd a general slackness in the observance of safety norms to set in, consequently, terrible disasters, of which the Bhopal gas tragedy is the best-known, have occurred in India. Explosions in chemical factories have affected not only the employees working therein, but also the larger urban population. The government has now taken a number of measures to raise safety norms, for fixing responsibility for slackness which may lead to accidents and for creating an organizational climate in which prevention of accidents will receive high priority. The Factories Act, the Mines Act, the Plantations Labour Act now provide for stricter measures for preventing accidents and increased power of enforcement of the inspectors.

*232.* Chapter IV of the Factories Act is devoted to safety. The state government is given the power to make rules, grant exemptions and to legislate new provisions and added safeguards in the interests of safety. The law requires that the occupier of the factory should comply with the safety provisions without waiting to be told by the Inspector. The legal responsibility cannot be shared, not even with the negligent workers who might show disregard for safety rules, and it rests solely upon the employer, the occupier, the manager, or by whatever name he is called. A senior manager of a firm of civil contractors undertaking civil work in the cement factory of a company could not be considered to be an occupier, because he did not have ultimate control over the affairs of the factory, though he had control over the factory work. Negligence of safety provisions resulting in the death of a worker employed by the contractor could not result in any criminal offence pertaining to safety.[176] The doctrine of contributory negligence cannot be invoked by the

176. LLJ, August 2010, *Dutta H. (a) Hiramanya Datta* v. *State of Jharkhand and Another*, High Court of Jharkhand, pp. 561–564.

employer, nor is the defence of common employment available. Safety measures should provide 'for protection of not only the diligent but also those who act inadvertently, or even inefficiently or foolishly'. Chapter IVA, dealing with provisions relating to hazardous processes, provides for compulsory disclosure of information and specific responsibility of the occupier in relation to the hazardous processes.

*233.* Section 23 of the Factories Act specifically forbids the employment of young persons on 'dangerous machines' which may be designated by the state government, unless they have been instructed as to the dangers, trained sufficiently to operate them and work under adequate supervision. Section 22 likewise restricts the employment of women and children on cleaning, lubricating or adjusting any part of a moving machinery or work between fixed and moving parts and also empowers the state government to designate factories for this purpose.

*234.* The bulk of safety provisions of the Factories Act, 1948, pertain to striking gear and devices for cutting off power, self-acting machines, casing of new machinery, revolving machinery, pressure plant, floors, stairs, and means of access, pits, sumps, openings in floors etc., and excessive weights, protection of eyes, precautions against dangerous fumes and explosive or inflammable dust, gas, etc. These provisions were made more up-to-date by the Amending Act in 1976 and further revised resulting in stricter standards by the Amending Act in 1989.

*235.* The 1976 Amendment to the Factories Act made a novel provision in Section 40B for the appointment of safety officers in factories employing 1,000 or more workers, or where, in the opinion of the state government, there is 'any risk of bodily injury, poisoning or disease, or any other hazard to health' to the employees. The duties, qualifications and conditions of service of the safety officers are to be laid down by the government. The inspector has been given the authority to order repairs and maintenance of buildings which might otherwise 'lead to conditions detrimental to the health and welfare of the workers'.

*236.* The Factories Act is a penal act. In one case two labourers while cleaning the boiler met with an accident and one of them died of burns. The owner and manager were convicted by the lower court for violating Section 36(5) of the Gujarat Factories Act, but were acquitted by the sessions judge. The two labourers had been hired by the contractor who had instructed them to enter the boiler in the afternoon when it would have cooled down. Section 3(5) specifically restricts the entry of anyone to boiler furnace, etc. or other confined space until it had been sufficiently cooled by ventilation, or was otherwise safe for persons to enter. The High Court held that there was not sufficient material for inferring that a permission to the entry into the boiler room existed during the morning hours when the accident took place. The High Court further observed that the Inspector should work out the risk and/or danger factors with regard to the timing for entering into a boiler room, or the occupier/manager ought to display the appropriate notice regarding restrictive timing; and, furthermore, that the carelessness, indolence, inadvertence or even disobedience of a workman may result in ill-fated accidents and the occupier/manager should provide against such hazards.[177]

*237.* The Factories Act, Section 92 provides for general penalty for offences. Section 94 provides for enhanced penalty after previous conviction. In one case the factory inspector came to notice that a serious accident had taken place and he filed a complaint before the magistrate. The respondent admitted his guilt, but prayed for mercy. The magistrate, while accepting the plea, convicted the respondent but imposed a fine below the minimum provided for in the Act. This was appealed against on the ground that the order of sentence was *ex facie* illegal.The High Court viewed the order as a gross defiance of the legislative mandate. It was a serious dereliction of duty, unbecoming on the part of the magistrate. The High Court totally rejected the idea of plea-bargaining, because it undermined the rule of law and might result in eradicating the very object of legislation.[178] Though the Factories Act provides for stringent penalties, their impact is reduced by providing for compounding of offences, as has been done in Uttar Pradesh under Section 106A. It provides that on realization of such amount of composition fee as the Inspector thinks fit, (on orders of the state government), the offence is compounded and the offender shall not be liable to prosecution and, if in custody, shall be set at liberty. If the prosecution has been already instituted the composition shall amount to acquittal of the offender.

## §5. Medical and Other Facilities

*238.* Medical facilities provided under the standards setting legislation are only a small part of the overall medical-cum-health services available to workers. The basic instrument for this purpose is the ESI Act 1948. In the Factories Act, there are provisions for:

- medical examination of young persons;
- certification of fitness issued by the certifying surgeons to all non-adult workers;
- checking certain diseases connected with industry and requiring medical treatment of such patients (a new Section 89, introduced in 1987);
- conducting inquiries into accidents and diseases (new Sections 90 and 91);
- requiring workers to observe rules of sanitation, to refrain from spitting except in spittoons, to observe the prohibition of entering any confined space with dangerous fumes, and other requirements on safety, cleanliness, medical fitness, etc.

---

177. *The State of Gujarat* v. *Dilip Kumar Dahyabhai Patel and Another* (1994), The Gujarat High Court, F.I.R., Vol. 87, Parts 4 and 5, 1995, pp. 109–115.

178. *State of Gujarat* v. *Ishwarbhai Harkhabhai Patel*, The High Court of Gujarat, LLJ, Vol. I, 1995, pp. 793-797. For the scope of Section 92 and related rules see *State of Gujarat* v. *Maganlal Gordhandas Merchant*, The High Court of Gujarat, LLJ, Vol. I, 1995, pp. 206–213.

In addition, the rules require that the District Medical Officer of Health, or a similar authority, should inspect drinking water, to take samples for chemical and bacteriological analysis, to specify the standards of purity of drinking water, and to make reports to the government. Furthermore, if any worker is absent from work, due to illness, he may be required to produce a medical certificate from a medical practitioner stating the cause of absence. Additional rules have been made requiring the occupier of factories to provide for medical examination of all workers engaged in certain industries, such as, electroplating or oxidation of metal articles, electric accumulators, glass manufacture, treatment of lead and certain compounds of lead, and so on.

*239.* A new provision in the Mines Act, also introduced in the Factories Act, gives the Inspector the power to require medical examination of any peson, other than an apprentice, to determine whether he is fit to work, and also to conduct safety and occupational health surveys (Section 91A). Any person who has been found to be medically unfit is now entitled to undergo medical treatment at the cost of the employer with full wages. If he continues to remain medically unfit even after the treatment, the nine owner/manager is statutorily obliged to find him an alternative employment for which he is medically fit. If this canot be done he must be paid a disability allowance, determined in accordance with the prescribed rates.

# Chapter 6. General Conditions of Service III

## §1. Section 17A of ID Act

*240.* In a dispute the petitioner to the High Court obtained an award from the Industrial Tribunal for revision of wages. The Puducherry government declined to enforce the award by issuing an order under Section 17A of the ID Act. This section provides unrestricted power to the appropriate government to decline to enforce an award, where it is a party, on the ground that it will be inexpedient on public grounds affecting national economy or social justice to give effect to the whole or any part of the award, and to issue a notification to this effect on the expiry of thirty days from the date of its publication, when it becomes enforceable. This was challenged in the High Court. The government had reserved for itself the power to judge and decide whether to accept an award or modify it or reject it, thereby rendering a court order into a nullity. The decision of the state government to take shelter under it was an affront to the independence of the judiciary, which has been interpreted by the constitutional bench of the Supreme Court, in a famous case decided in 1973, as a basic feature of the Indian Constitution. Earlier in 1997, the High Court of Andhra Pradesh had struck down this section as void under the constitution. It was argued that the jurisdiction of each High Court is the particular state and beyond it its judgement and order had only persuasive force. These were not binding on the Puducherry government. This plea was rejected. Once a High Court declares any law or part of it as unconstitutional, it ceases to be part of the statute. Quoting Justice Y.V. Chandrachud, the Court took the same position: 'Where a Statute is adjudged to be unconstitutional, it is as if it had never been. Rights cannot be built up under it, contracts which depend upon it for their consideration are void; it constitutes a protection to no one who has acted under it and no one can be punished for having refused obedience to it before the decision was made.' The High Court decided that Section 17A is no more in force in the union territory of Puducherry, also throughout India. The impugned notification was set aside. The award was enforced.[179]

## §2. The Securitization and Reconstruction of Financial Assets

*241.* Section 13(8) of this Act pertains to transfer of an undertaking, but affects Section 25 FF of the ID Act on the rights of labour, particularly the date at which wage dues are payable by the transferor company. The issue arose from a court order, that no valid transfer of the undertaking took place until the sale certificate for immovable property was issued by the secured creditor, in a proceedings under the SARFAESI Act and its liability to pay wage dues continued till then. This was appealed. The assets of the company were sold in an auction and the sale confirmed on 24 March 2005, the sale certificate for plant and machinery was issued on 10

179. LLJ, January 2011, *Textile Technical Tradesmen Association and Others* v. *Union of India*, represented by Secretary, Ministry of Labour, New Delhi and Others, Madras High Court, pp. 297–304. Also *Kesavananda Bharthi* v. *State of Kerala*, 1973, Supreme Court of India.

August 2005. However, the sale certificate for immovable property could be registered on 24 August 2006. It was held that the ownership of the undertaking stood transferred on 10, August 2005. Accordingly, the workmen were entitled to the benefits under Section 25FF of the ID Act upto this date. The delay in registration was due to the order of attachment under the Pondicherry Protection of Interests of Depositors in Financial Establishment Act, 2004. When the attachment of the property was lifted, the sale certificate of the immovable assets could be executed and registered on 24 August 2006. The Supreme Court had ordered on 31 August 2009 that the workers' dues will be paid out of the sale proceeds lying with the Indian Bank and the auction purchaser, EID Parry India Ltd, will have no liability. It later clarified that the computation of the sums payable to workers will be the compensation payable under Section 25FF, together with other dues as well. All amounts due to workers will be payable. The individual workman submitted his claim statement to the Labour Commissioner for computation and the appellant company agreed to pay dues upto 31 December 2004. The contending claim was that dues were payable till the date of deemed retrenchment on 1 October 2006. The Court decided that the ownership of the undertaking stood transferred on 10, August 2005 when the sale certificate in respect of plant and machinery was issued. The benefits to workmen would be computed only upto this date.[180]

## §3. The Persons with Disabilities (Equal Opportunities, Protection of Rights and Full Participation) Act, 1995

*242.* Under this Act on entirely new series of labour disputes have emerged in the courts. The Indian Oil Corporation decided in August 1995 to retire a person on medical grounds in accordance with a scheme on premature retirement on medical grounds with adequate monetary compensation to the concerned employees. The Medical Board was the competent authority to take decisions. Retirement would not be a punitive or disciplinary action and had no bearing on the employee's past record or conduct. The scheme appeared to be contrary to the Persons with Disabilities Act. It was pointed out that the Act came into force on 7 February 1996, hence it would not be applicable to the petitioner. Earlier the High Court had decided in another case that the new Act will cover the pending proceedings as well. The Court took note of, the Proclamation on the Full Participation and Equality of the People with Disabilities in the Asian and Pacific Region, adopted in December 1992. It requires that no establishment shall dispense with the services or reduce the rank of an employee who acquires a disability during his service. The Indian law was enacted to give effect to this proclamation. Section 47 of the Act provides for this protection and is mandatory in its reach. The Court decided to extend the benefits under the Act to the petitioners. The petitioner would have retired on 31 December 2002, if he had stayed in service. The Court struck down the retirement order of the IOC. In addition to the cash compensation already paid, the petitioner will get pension on the basis of his age at superannuation. He will also get 60 per

180. LLJ, January 2011, *New Horizon Sugar Mills Ltd* v. *Commissioner of Labour, Government of Puducherry and Others,* Madras High Court, pp. 291–296.

cent of the emoluments he would have earned if he had not been retired, as arrears of pay.[181] He was also awarded cost of petition of Rs 2000.

*243.* In Nagaland, a person who was physically handicapped and working on contract basis applied for a post of English lecturer and sought a writ commanding the Nagaland Public Service Commission to consider him under the quota of reservation provided in the Act. The Nagaland government responded that it had not applied its mind to this question. The Court directed the state government to carry out an exercise for making reservation to disabled persons under Sections 32 and 33 of the Act.[182]

*244.* In this case, the cause of action arose in February 1994 when the workman was prematurely retired on medical grounds. He had met with an accident and suffered grievous injuries in June 1991. He raised an industrial dispute under Section 10 of the ID Act and it was referred to the Labour Court for adjudication. The Labour Court gave an award on 18 February 2002, directing his reinstatement with continuity of service and full back wages. The court said that if he could not be retained as a security guard, the management should deal with him in accordance with Section 47 of the Persons with Disabilities Act, 1995. The award was upheld by a single judge of the High Court. This was appealed against and came up before a division bench. The first question was whether the said Act could have retrospective operation; moreover, Section 47 was not mandatory. Ordinarily, the rights of the parties crystallize on the date the Act commences, and it cannot apply to any pending litigation. The Courts do not have the power to legislate. The Courts cannot read words in the statute which are not there. The court agreed that the Act cannot be given retrospective effect, but chose to read it together with the proclamation made in 1992 to which India was a signatory. It invoked Article 41 of the constitution and the judgements of the Apex Court made prior to the enactment of the said Act. The Court decided that the Labour Court's award carried the same benefits as conferred by Section 47 of the Act. While upholding that the provisions of Section 47 cannot be given retrospective effect, yet in a pending proceeding the benefits of the Act can be certainly extended. This is also the mandate of Article 41 of the constitution. The appeal was dismissed.[183]

## §4. Right to Equality

*245.* In an appeal against the dismissal of their writ petition by the High Court, the trade union and typists-cum-computer clerks invoked Article 14 (Right to equality) in challenging their longer duty hours compared to those already in employment and sought a direction for parity in working hours or overtime pay. The Court

181. LLJ, November 2010, *Satija J.K.* v. *Indian Oil Corporation and Another,* High Court of Delhi, pp. 484–488.
182. LLJ, 2006, Vol. 4, *Vector Vero* v. *State of Nagaland and Others,* High Court of Gauhati, (NOC), pp. 851–852.
183. LLJ 2009, Vol. 2, *Delhi Transport Corporation* v. *Harpal Singh,* High Court of Delhi, pp. 475–487.

said that the High Court should have dismissed the writ petition on the ground that a clear alternative remedy was available by raising an industrial dispute under the Industrial Disputes Act. It showed lack of judicial discipline and an overly liberal approach in some high courts. Further, Article 14 is slippery slope and a fine balancing act must be done by the court to avoid slipping down the slope. The courts do not have ready made answers; the judicial process may ease the endless flux of social tensions. The Bombay Port Trust faced competition with other port and as a policy to raise efficiency and control costs, it decided that the existing working hours for indoor establishment, at seven hours per day including half an hour lunch break, should be limited to the employees recruited before 1 November 1996. Those recruited after this date were clearly told, prior to their appointment, that they will have to work for eight hours including half an hour of lunch break. The policy decided on was to have uniform working hours for both the indoor and outdoor establishments. This avoided litigation with the existing staff. With their retirement the working hour will be uniform for all employees. Since the working conditions of existing staff were left undisturbed, there was no need to serve a notice of change under Section 9A of the ID Act. The Court held that the Port classified persons working in the indoor establishment in two classes, the basis of classification being the date of their appointment and the objective being to become more competitive in business. Article 14 does not takes away the power of classification, which to some degree is bound to produce some inequality. Differential treatment, *per se*, does not constitute violation of Article 14. It denies equal protection only when there is no reasonable basis for differentiation. It is not abnoxious to deal equally with members of a well defined class. In order to pass the test of reasonable classification, two conditions should be met. That the classification must be founded on an intelligible differential, which distinguishes persons or things that are grouped together from others left out of the group; that the differentia must have a rational relation to the object ought to be achieved by the statute in question. Article 14 is not offended if the classification has a rational or reasonable basis. The Court then listed broad guidelines to test whether a classification or differentiation is reasonable or not. 'One test which we are laying down and which will be useful in deciding this case: is it conducive to the functioning of modern society? If it is, then it is certainly reasonable and rational.' In the modern world, business have to face competition and for this purpose longer working hours and greater efficiency may be needed. From this point of view the classification in question is clearly reasonable. 'We have to take a practical view of the matter, instead of relying on abstract, a priori, notions of equality. It was a bonafide decision, hence no fault can be found with the said decision and it cannot be said that it violates Article 14 of the constitution. It is well settled that the courts should not ordinarily interfere with policy decisions. Avoidance of labour disputes is a reasonable basis of classification. There is no merit in this appeal and hence it is dismissed.[184]

---

184. LLJ, 1, 2011, *Transport and Dock Workers Union and Others* v. *Mumbai Port Trust and Another*, Supreme Court of India, pp. 1-10.

*246.* The Mines Act, the Motor Transport Workers Act, the Plantations Labour Act and the *Beedi* and Cigar Workers (Conditions of Employment) Act have provisions similar to the Factories Act on canteens. For mine workers, extensive supervisory powers have been given to the Central government to supply food and drinks to workers on a non-profit basis. Under the Motor Transport Workers Act, canteens should be set up wherever 100 workers are employed. The general philosophy is that the canteens should be managed by joint committees; the standards of construction and cleanliness should be laid down by the authorities, and pricing of food items should be on a non-profit basis. Canteens may be supplemented by fair price shops wherever possible, but largely at the initiative of the employers.

*247.* The occupier is required to provide and maintain a canteen under Section 46 of the Factories Act, but if a canteen run by a cooperative society becomes defunct, the occupier is not bound to provide employment to canteen workers. Section 46 does not enjoin the occupier to become the employer of canteen workers. Workers of the factory can themselves run their canteen on a co-operative basis and then the law governing co-operative societies will govern the society.[185] In such a case it is not necessary to appoint a canteen managing committee.

*248.* Workers employed in canteens are often employed through contractors, who demand regularization of service as being part of the establishment. In respect of statutory canteens, the Supreme Court has held that they are part of the establishment, and therefore, the workers employed therein are the employees of the management for the purposes of Factories Act only. In respect of non-statutory but recognized canteens, the Court held that though it is not the statutory obligation to provide a canteen, it is still an obligation to do so. In such a case the canteen becomes a part of the establishment and the workers working therein are employees of the management. In respect of statutory canteens workers can claim benefits under the Factories Act only and not for any other purposes. This rule does not depend upon the abolition of contract labour system in the factory, but only on the provisions of the Factories Act, particularly the definition of the term worker.[186] The claim of non-statutory recognized canteen workers for regulation of their services was not upheld.

*249.* Establishments which are not factories still run canteens and cafeterias, as part of their overall management responsibility as an obligation under their organizational regulations. In a case, the cafeteria employees of a residential university demanded regularization, because the students were required to obtain food from them and the authorities maintained tight control over their finances and functioning. It was argued on their behalf, that there was a statutory and legal obligation to maintain residential accommodation and the existence of the cafeteria together with

185. *Digest of Labour Cases*, January 1992, *Workmen of Ashok Leyland Ltd and Ashok Leyland Co-operative Conteen Ltd* v. *Ashok Leyland Ltd and Others,* Madras High Court, pp. 2–3.

186. LLJ, Vol. 1, 2001, *Steel Plant Canteen Employees' Union, Vishakhapatanam and Others* v. *Chairman-cum-Managing Director, Vishakhapatnam Steel Project, Vishakhapatanam and Others,* High Court of Andhra Pradesh, pp. 1270–1278. Also LLJ, 2009 Vol. 2, *Kerala Electrical and A.E.O. Ltd* v. *Leemns D'Crize,* High Court of Kerala, pp. 94-104.

its staff members cannot but be a part of such accommodation and arrangement. The legal responsibility could not be shifted to students, who through the Food Committee had a specific role in the matter of management and control over the cafeteria. The Labour Court had earlier accepted the claim of employees and given an award in their favour. The High Court found the award to be perfectly justified in the facts and circumstances of the case and free from any error in law. The Supreme Court concurred, dismissing the appeal, clothing the judgment with a powerful plea in favour of cafeteria employuees who needed succour for livelihood.[187]

## §5. Environment

*250.* The Environment Protection Act, 1986 and the rules made thereunder are applicable to all factories and impose new responsibilities upon the occupier and the 'person' who has control over the affairs of the factory. The employer's obligations include (i) control of emission or discharge of environmental pollution, (ii) compliance with procedural safeguards, (iii) furnishing of information, (iv) providing assistance to inspectors, (v) on receipt of notice to provide all facilities to the officer for collecting samples of air, water, soil or other substances, and (vi) obtaining environmental clearance for projects. He should also submit an environmental statement under the Water (Prevention and Control of Pollution) Act, the Air (Prevention and Control of Pollution) Act and the Hazardous Wastes (Management and Handling) Rules every year. These provisions do not apply to the small scale industrial sector and to several other cases which are listed in the notification issued under the Act. The Supreme Court has cautioned the courts not to deal with the prosecution for offences in a casual or routine manner. The courts should share the parliament's concern on the escalating pollution level of our environment.[188]

*251.* In another piece of public litigation, an environmentalist organization succeeded in securing the Supreme Court's direction to the government and the State Pollution Board to perform their statutory duties in respect of several industrial units which were causing ecological fragility in the area. A number of chemical factories controlled by the same group of individuals located in Udaipur, Rajasthan were operating without obtaining clearances from the authorities and also disobeying orders. The Court held on facts that the principles of 'strict liability' and 'polluter pays' were applicable. Once the activity carried on is hazardous or inherently dangerous, the person carrying on such activity is liable to make good the loss caused to any other person by his activity, irrespective of the fact whether he took reasonable care while carrying on his activity. This rests on the premise that the enterprise engaged in hazardous activity alone has the resources to discover and guard against hazards or dangers and not the person affected, and the practical difficulty on the part of the latter in establishing the absence of reasonable care, or that the damage

187. LLJ, Vol. 2, 2000, *G.B. Pant University of Agriculture and Technology, Nainital* v. *State of Uttar Pradesh and Others,* Supreme Court of India, pp. 1109-1115.

188. *The Supreme Court Annual Digest,* 2000, *Uttar Pradesh Pollution Control Board* v. *Mohan Meakins Ltd,* Supreme Court of India, pp. 859–860.

to him was foreseeable by the enterprises. Furthermore, the responsibility for repairing the damage is that of the offending industry.[189]

*252.* The Apex Court has upheld the 'precautionary principle' and said that the corresponding burden of proof should be on the person who wants to change the status quo. If due to lack of data there is uncertainty about the extent of damage or pollution that may result, the burden of proof that the ecological balance would be maintained must be necessarily on the industry or the unit which is likely to cause it. On the other hand, where the effect of setting up of an industry on ecology or environment is known, then the issue is what mitigating steps can be taken to offset the same. The principle of sustainable development would come into play when the effect of the project is known. Sustainable development means that type or extent of development which can be sustained by nature with or without mitigation.[190]

*253.* The Supreme Court has upgraded the status of safety and protection against occupational hazards to the level of the constitutional right to life and this right to include the right to means of livelihood and the quality of life. This implies that the Court can issue directions on making the right to life meaningful; to prevent pollution of the work place; for protection of the environment, protection of the health of the workmen, or to preserve free and unpolluted water for the safety and health of the people. The Court noticed that there were yawning gaps in the effective implementation of safety rules under the Factories Act. It directed that the safety rules framed by the ILO, on the use of asbestos, shall be binding on all the industries. To all those workers found to be suffering from the disease, the compensation of Rs 100,000 would be payable by the factory or establishment concerned.[191]

## §6. APPRENTICESHIP

*254.* Apprentices engaged under the Apprentices Act, 1961, are not employees and are not protected by the ID Act. The courts have drawn a distinction between trainees and apprentices. The relationship between a corporation and an apprentice is not that of, 'master and servant'. It is a contract of apprenticeship, under which training in the designated trade for a specified period is given. Even apprentices, who are not engaged under the Act and are employed for one year and then relieved according to the terms and conditions of employment, cannot claim to have become employees. In a given case, the apprentices claimed that the work they were doing was still available, and was going to be available, so they were entitled to continue in the employment of the corporation irrespective of the terms and conditions of the original contract. This plea was rejected and the Court held that, 'it is inherent in the word "apprentice" that there is no element of employment as such in a trade or

189. Supreme Court Cases, 1996, Vol. 3, *Indian Council for Enviro-Legal Action and Others* v. *Union of India and Others*, Supreme Court of India, pp. 212–252.

190. Supreme Court Annual Digest, 2000, *Narmada Bachoo Andolan* v. *Union of India*. Supreme Court of India, p. 1271.

191. *Labour Law Journal*, Vol. 2, 1995, *Consumer Education and Research Centre and Others* v. *Union of India and Others*, Supreme Court of India, pp. 768–789.

industry'. Apprentices are not workmen under the ID Act, or workers under the Factories Act, and the stipend paid to them is not wages.[192]

*255.* The Apprentices Act clearly provides that it is not obligatory on the part of the employer to offer any employment to the apprentices on the completion of their training. But there are instances where the apprentices have continued to work, though without any letter of appointment. The courts have taken the view that, if the work done by them fits the definition of 'workman' in the ID Act and the period of apprenticeship is over, the employer cannot take cover behind the Apprentices Act. However, an apprentice, undergoing a training which continues beyond the period of express contract, does not get an employee status in the establishment. In order to become an employee, he must enter into a fresh contract with the employer. Should there be a termination and a dispute is raised on the status of the person, the Labour Courts can examine the facts and decide the issue.[193] In another case the SC held that, without a letter of appointment on the completion of training the apprentice could not become a workman.[194]

*256.* In a case, *Kanpur Jal Sansthan*, a corporate body created under the UP Water Supply Act, 1945, filed a writ petition in the High Court Challenging the award of the Industrial Tribunal in favour of a plumber holding him entitled to reinstatement, though an apprenticeship trainee. He was admittedly appointed as an apprentice, but there was a dispute on the apprenticeship period. According to the respondent plumber, it was one year, while the petitioner organization held that it was two years, from 16 March 1994 to 15 March 1996. The plumber was able to secure a reference for adjudication on the question, whether the services of workman, as he was called, were rightly and legally terminated, and if it was not so, to what relief the workman was entitled? The Court found that the Industrial Tribunal refused to decide the legal pleas raised by the petitioner, on the ground that these pleas were not substantiated before it. It took the argument that the apprentice was appointed for two years instead of three years as provided in the Apprenticeship Act, 1962 and worked up to 28 March 1996. He completed 240 days in a year as a workman and so he could not be disengaged without a notice or wages in lieu of notice. This was illegal and he was entitled to reinstatement with continuity of service and salary from the date of the award. The Court held, that as per the Tribunal's award he was an apprentice for two years and obviously could not acquire the status of 'workman' even if he has worked for a few days thereafter. Section 18 clearly says that the apprentices are not workmen and 'the provisions of any law shall not apply or in relation to such apprentices.' The Apprentices Act precludes the application of any other law, i.e. the UP Industrial Disputes Act and the Industrial Disputes Act, 1947. Hence the Labour Court/Industrial Tribunal do not have any jurisdiction to entertain any dispute arising there from. In this case, there is not even a whisper that

192. *Labour Law Journal*, 1993, Vol. 1, *Patel Pravin Kumar Somnath and Others* v. *Gujarat State Land Development Corporation Ltd and Others*, High Court of Gujarat, pp. 916-931.
193. LLJ, Vol. 1, 2000, *Textile Traders Co-Operative Bank Ltd* v. *Jagdish Bhai Natwarlal Patel*, High Court of Gujarat, pp. 235–241.
194. LLJ, Vol. 2, 2000, *Factory Manager, CIMMCO Wagon Factory* v. *Virendra Kumar Sharma and Another*, Supreme Court of India, pp. 773–775.

after the completion of training period, (may be one year or two years), the plumber was employed as a workman or there was a donors contract. There is not enough pleading that a contract of employment came into existence between the parties by their conduct … Moreover, the government undertaking cannot appoint any person without following the process of selection and inviting applications from public at large. The plumber was not selected through some selection process. In an earlier case, the High Court decided that a person who has got apprenticeship training cannot claim recruitment without competing in any direct recruitment selection. The Tribunal had approached the matter from a wrong angle and failed to consider the relevant aspects of the case. It wrongly treated the apprentice as a workman. The Tribunal posed wrong questions, resultantly committed the mistake in passing the impugned award. The award was set aside.[195]

*257.* In another case an apprentice who had completed the apprenticeship training made a petition to the High Court, seeking a direction to the Himachal Pradesh State Electricity Board to offer an appointment to him. The Court referred to Section 22 of the Apprentices Act and the Apprenticeship Rules, 1992 to observe that it was not obligatory for the Board to offer employment to the petitioner on completion of apprenticeship training. Moreover, there was great delay on the petitioner's part in seeking relief and the petition was liable to be dismissed on the ground of delay and laches. Under Rule 22(1), it is provided that, where there is a condition in the contract of apprenticeship that, on completion of apprenticeship training period, the apprentice shall serve the employer, then the employer is bound to offer a suitable employment to the apprentice and the latter is bound to serve the employer for such period and on such remuneration as may be specified in the contract. However, in the instant case there was no such condition in the contract of apprenticeship. No doubt, the government has formulated a policy that, 'other things being equal, trained apprentices should be given preference in case of employment' and that the government wants to promote chances of employment to qualified apprentices, because otherwise it would amount to destruction of developed human resources. But a promise could not be read in the policy. To be enforceable, the promise has to be clear and unequivocal. 'We do not read any such promise in the aforesaid three documents. The direction in question could not be issued by the High Court.' The petition was dismissed.[196]

*258.* In a review petition the High Court dealt with the question whether an apprentice was a workman for purposes of Verification of Membership and Recognition of Trade Union Rules, 1994, despite the Section 17 in the Apprentices Act, which excludes apprentices from the category of workman. Earlier this Court had decided that an apprentice was a workman in view of the definition of 'employee' in Rule 3(c) of the 1994 Rules. Under this Rule, an employee is a workman as

195. LLJ, Vol. 1, 2011, *Kanpur Jal Sansthan* v. *Presiding Officer, Industrial Tribunal and Another*, High Court of Allahabad, pp. 600-604

196. LLJ, Vol. 1, 2011, *Amar Singh* v. *Himachal Pradesh State Electricity Board and Others*, High Court of Himachal Pradesh, pp. 34-38.

defined in Section 2(S) of the ID Act, 1947. A workman means any person (including an apprentice) employed in any industry to do any manual, skilled, skilled, technical, operational, clerical or supervisory work for hire or reward. However, an apprentice is not a workman under the Apprentices Act. The Court formulated the question whether the Rules 994 as well as the ID Act are a special statute and the same should prevail over the Apprentices Act, while considering the issue whether an Apprentice was a workman or not for the purpose of verification of membership and recognition of trade unions. The Court referred to the opinion formed by the Supreme Court on the question: what do we mean by a special statute and, in the scheme of the two enactments in question, which can we regard as the special Act and which the general? In determining, whether a statute is a special or a general one, the focus must be on the principal subject matter plus the particular perspective. The ID Act is a special statute devoted wholly to investigation and settlement of industrial disputes. Relative to the subject matter, the LIC Act is but a general law. Accordingly, the Rules, 1994 is a special statute because it specifically deals with verification of membership and recognition of trade unions, while the ID Act would override a general law like the apprentices Act, 1961. Thus the definition of Section 2(s) of the ID Act must prevail over Section 2(r) and Section (18) of the apprentices Act, as the ID Act is a special Act. The Rule 3(c) of Trade Union Rules, 1994 would prevail over the Apprentices Act as regards an Apprentices status as a workman. The Special Rules, being later in point of time, would prevail over the General Rule. The petition was dismissed.[197]

## §7. Seamen's Employment

*259.* The seamen's employment, apprenticeship and welfare are regulated by the Merchant Shipping Act, 1958 which is a complete code under which the application of the ID Act is barred. Should a dispute arise or is apprehended between seamen and the owners of ships in which they are employed and the dispute relates to any matter connected with or incidental to the employment of seamen, the central government by notification may constitute a tribunal and refer the dispute to it for adjudication. This Act also provides for the engagement of boys who have attained the age of 15 years to enter into a contract, through their guardians with the shipping masters or owners, which should be in accordance with the rules made by the central government in this behalf. The courses of training, the vocational standards or the tests etc., are prescribed by the central government in the rules under the Act.

## §8. Sick Industries

*260.* The Sick Industrial Companies (Special Provisions) Act, 1985, was enacted for securing the timely detection of sick and potentially sick companies owning industrial undertakings and the speedy determination of preventive and remedial

197. LLJ, Vol. 4, 2011, *Larsen & Toubro Ltd., Mumbai* v. *State of Orissa*, High Court of Orissa, pp. 705-711.

measures to deal with their problems which had produced conditions of sickness. The Supreme Court interpreted this Act in terms of affording maximum protection of employment, optimizing the use of financial resources, salvaging the assets, realizing the amounts due to the banks and to revitalize and rehabilitate sick industries. Under this Act is constituted the Board of Industrial and Financial Reconstruction (BIFR), with requisite powers to enquire into the causes of sickness and devise suitable remedial measures through appropriate schemes and their implementation. Once the Board starts an enquiry, it acquires overriding powers into the affairs of the company. No proceedings for the winding up of the company, or for execution, distress or the like against any of its properties can be proceeded with, without the consent of the BIFR. Once a company has been declared sick, all its property would come under the direct control of the BIFR. The effect of this Act on other laws is that, all the labour laws, including the ID Act, cease to have any effect and the Board may proceed to revive a sick unit through its schemes without being burdened by the provisions of other laws. The Board may ask for sacrifices to be made by labour, regardless of the operation of subsisting awards and settlements.

*261.* In a case the court held that the declaration of sickness in respect of the company does not by itself affect the rights of workmen as this is only a jurisdictional fact that is decided by the BIFR. However, if the workmen and employees are heard before a scheme is finalized, that is more than sufficient to protect their interests. In a complicated case, an industrial undertaking had applied for closure and the same was rejected, then followed it with a reference to the BIFR which was accepted. The management had in the meantime announced a voluntary separation scheme and also reached on agreement with one union under Section 18(1) of the ID Act. The BIFR in the meantime also prepared a scheme through the operating agency, but the same was challenged by workers, who also made allegations against the agency. The Court said that, having taken a negative attitude towards the Board, the petitioner union could not contend that the finalized scheme was unsustainable. It also held that the provisions of the SICSP Act were overriding and the prior settlement under the ID Act could not be put up against the scheme finalized under its provisions. Repelling the union's contention, the Court observed that the doctrine of legitimate expectation would not apply in the present case and the workers could not legitimately expect, that the earlier scheme proposed by the state government in March 1992 and the settlement that followed, should be accepted by the BIFR as the scheme for the rehabilitation of the company. There were no justifications to interfere with the scheme finalized by the Board.[198]

*262.* Section 22 of the SICSP Act provides for the suspension of legal proceedings, contract, etc., where an enquiry is pending, or any scheme is under preparation, or a sanctioned scheme is under implementation, or where an appeal relating to an industrial company is pending. This bar affects proceedings under the Companies Act and any suit for the recovery of money or advances granted to the sick

198. *Indian Factories Journal* and *Factories Journal Reports,* 1996, Vol. 89, Parts 17, 18 and 19, *Madras Labour Union* v. *Binny Ltd (Buckingham and Carnatic Mills) and Others,* Madras High Court, pp. 516–601.

company. But the High Court hearing a case under the MRTU and PULP Act, alleging unfair labour practices, decided that a complaint was not a suit because it could not be the subject matter of a civil suit, since the jurisdiction of the civil court was barred under it. Failure to implement an award, settlement or agreement is listed under the Act, as an unfair labour practice. The Court noted the fact that the BIFR bench had already decided not to intervene in the litigations between the company and the workers regarding payment of latter's dues. Under these circumstances, there was no bar in proceeding with the petitioner's complaint regarding non-payment of wages and terminal dues in the Industrial Court.[199]

## §9. Contract Labour

*263.* The Contract Labour (Regulation and Abolition) Act, 1970 provides for abolition of contract labour system following the procedure laid down in it. Workers agitating for abolition and absorption by the principal employer faced a major hurdle on the right to absorption, because they were not deemed to be 'workmen' as defined in the Industrial Disputes Act and were barred from raising an industrial dispute in as much as a reference for adjudication was definitionally excluded. Contract workers carry out the contracted out duties agreed to by the contractor and never become the employees of the company. They were employed outside the establishment and no industrial dispute between them and the company could arise unless they were absorbed. There could be no industrial dispute between the employer and the persons seeking employment. The contractor was their employer who lent them to the company and was responsible for paying wages and other amenities. Section 10 of the CLRA Act provides for abolition of contract labour if it is established that there is a genuine contract and the appropriate government may do so by issuing a notification to this effect. Courts are not empowered to do so. However, if there was no genuine contact and the so called contract was a sham and a camouflage, the CLRA Act will be inapplicable. The Apex Court noted that the CLRA provides for abolition, but not for absorption of contract labour. The Court held that absorption must follow abolition. In a later case the Apex Court held that, by definition, the term 'contract labour' was a species of workmen. A workman may be hired by an employer or by a contractor. In the former case, master-servant relationship exists but in the latter case he is a contract laborer, not an employee of the employer. When the contract is alleged to be a sham and a camouflage, the contract labour can raise an industrial dispute themselves. They must have the legal remedy to prove that the contract for contract labour is sham and bogus. The legal question that needed to be answered was that, even if the contracts are held to be a sham, do such workers acquire a right to be absorbed. It was held that, despite supervision and control exercised by the employer's establishment, the contract labour cannot be allowed a back entry into employment, because they lack qualifications and cannot be employed as permanent workmen. They are the workers, supplied by the

199. LLJ, 2000, Vol. 2, *Carona Ltd* v. *Sitaram Atmaram Ghag and Others*, High Court of Bombay, pp. 296–304.

contractors, who would otherwise not be able to secure any employment whatsoever for the work they do for the establishment of the principal employer. The contract labourers action is misdirected and ill advised. The industrial establishment may not renew the contract for supplying these labourers. In one case, the award proceeded to consider the agreement as sham on the ground that the relevant documentation was maintained by the officers of the petitioner, the duties of contract labours were of permanent nature, the entire supervision and control was of the officers of the establishment; though the wages and statutory benefits were paid by the contractors. Consequently, the award directed to treat the contract labours as permanent employees at par with the petitioners own employees. It proceeds on the premise that the nature of the work brings the contract labouers within the scope of the term 'workman' under the ID Act. 'That basis suffers from a fundamental error and disregards the ground realities of such work making it in fact counterproductive for the very persons in whose favour apparently and ostensibly the relief is granted. The award is, therefore, required to be and is set aside.' The order was stayed for four weeks.[200]

*264.* The issue of privatization come up for consideration in a case where the central government, by a notification, abolished the contract labour system, but subsequent to it, the main work was leased out to a private organization, which decided, that it was an independent establishment and, to be operative, the notification on abolition of contract labour would have to be issued again. Till then it was free to engage contract labour. This plea was upheld by a single judge of the High court, but on appeal it was set aside and the law stated, that there was no need to reissue the notification since the original notification covered the leased entity. This was appealed and the Apex Court upheld the Division Bench's judgment and order. The Court held that the petitioner, Delhi International Airport Pvt. Ltd. was leased out a large portion of the airports Authority of India, but it has incomplete control and DIAL is nothing more than a contractor for AAI establishment. So DIAL is not a principal employer of an independent establishment. It falls under AAI establishment. In fact, the Operation, Management, Development and Agreement, (OMDA) agreement, between the AAI and the DIAL makes it clear that not only the functions and powers of AAI stand transferred, but the statutory obligations too are vested in the DIAL. DIAL had raised two issues. First, the central government's 2 July 2014 notification was inapplicable to DIAL. It was directed at AAI, not meant for the privatized operation handled by DIAL. Second, it was contented that, for DIAL, the appropriate government was the state government, not the Centre. The Apex Court examined both issues at length and held that in both respects the Division Bench had reached correct conclusions. The notification was applicable to DIAL, because it was an 'establishment' under the CLRA Act, and the appropriate authority was the Central Government. Meantime, the old contractor was replaced by a new entity who had brought in new workers for trolley retrieving. The erstwhile 136 trolley retrievers would not be regularized, because they were replaced.

200. LLJ, 1, 2011, *Airports Authority of India, Mumbai* v. *Indian Airports Kamgar Union and Others*, High Court of Mumbai, pp. 211–223.

They would be paid Rupees five lac each as compensation. New workers would be regularized. The appeals were dismissed.[201]

## §10. Welfare Officers

*265.* In an important case, the High Court decided, on a writ petition, the issue whether the jurisdiction of the Industrial Court to try a complaint of unfair labour practice under the MRTU & PULP Act was ousted, once the petitioner company denied the existence of employer-employee relationship, on the ground that the complainants were workers engaged by the contractor, not by the petitioner company. The Apex Court had earlier stated that if the workers admit the fact that they worked under a contractor, the Labour Court or industrial adjudicating authorities would not have any jurisdiction to deal with the matter. But if workers assert, that they were directly employed by the company and the contract was a mere camouflage, the matter would need to be adjudicated. In such a case, the workers repudiate the contract and the relationship with the contractor and claim to be employees of the company. This question can be examined by a regular industrial tribunal under the ID Act. The fact situation will have to be examined. Once a direct relationship is established before the tribunal or the court, the complaint under the MRTU & PULP Act would be maintainable. However, the jurisdiction is not ousted merely on the strength of denials by the employer. In the instant case, the workers were able to produce documentary evidence to support their claim and prove the denial by the company as false, though the contractor had given evidence in its support and asserted that the complainants were engaged by him. Evidence falsified the statement made by the contractor. He failed to show the signature / thumb impression of each worker on the register of wages, to be duly certified by the authorized representative of the principal employer. Moreover, the petitioner had admitted the employer-employee relationship in another legal forum, viz. Dy. Commissioner of labour in the process of conciliation of an industrial dispute. The Court declined to interfere, since the issue was purely a question of facts. The findings of the Industrial Court were not perverse or arbitrary and interference in the findings was uncalled for. The petition was dismissed.[202]

*266.* The Institute of Technology, Madras filed a writ petition challenging the order of the single judge of the Court that the cooks, cleaners, servers and servants employed by the Hostel Management of IIT were employees of IIT. The petitioner took the plea that they were under the exclusive control and management of the hostel establishment. Hostel management was the appointing authority of all its employees. Earlier, the Labour Court had held that the petitioners were not the employees of IIT, but on the issue of overtime wages held that they were entitled to it for 2½ hours in a day for the period of work. The IIT preferred a writ petition

201. LLJ, 4, 2011, *Delhi International Airports Pvt. Ltd.* v. *Union of India and Others*, Supreme Court of India, pp. 511–529.

202. LLJ, 3, 2011, *Indo-Europen Breweries Ltd.* v. *Dayaneshwar S/o Shyamrao Dhanwate*, High Court of Bombay, pp. 527–536.

which was heard by a single judge. The single judge held that the wages of hostel staff were paid by the IIT and since the appointment, terms and conditions of the hostel staff and control, supervision and payment of wages were made by the IIT, the contention that they had nothing to do with those employees could not be countenanced. Before the Division Bench the IIT pointed out that in 1985 the Division Bench of this Court had held that the Hostel employees were not the employees of IIT and this judgment had become final. However, in this writ petition the Division Bench confirmed the findings of the single judge. It was not in dispute that the employees of the hostel management enjoyed all the benefits on a par with the employees of IIT. From the materials on record. The hostel employees could not be denied the status on employees of IIT. The bench did not express any opinion on the earlier writ petition decided in 1985. On the plea that the Hostel employees had flexible working hours and could not claim overtime wages as they were not the employees of IIT, the Court said that the terms of employment and conditions of service already provided for payment of overtime allowance. Since the Hostel employees were the employees of IIT, their claim of overtime allowance cannot be refused. The respondent employees had worked beyond the working hours meant for them. This was the finding of the Labour Court. It was a factual finding and the court could not interfere with it. It was confirmed. The petition was dismissed.[203]

*267.* The duties of a welfare officer include working for harmonious relations between labour and management, grievance handling, understanding labour's point of view and communicating with both sides, advising the management of its obligations under the Factories Act, and for this purpose to maintain a liaison with the factory inspector, etc. and a host of other duties pertaining to joint committees, canteen, housing, apprentices, and so on. His is an advisory job and his effectiveness depends upon the education and skills he can bring to bear upon the complex problems of management of labour. Although appointed by law, the welfare officer remains an employee of the organization and must integrate fully with the management team.

### §11. Minimum Wages

*268.* In a case, the Court answered the question, whether the appellant society, engaged in imparting education to the deaf community and also running a printing press, could pay less than the minimum wages fixed under the MW Act, 1948. The court observed that in view of the notification dated 13, August 1965, bringing with in the Schedule of the Act, shops under the Delhi Shops Act 1954, and since the appellant society was covered by it, its employees were entitled to get the benefits under the Minimum Wages Act. The appeal was dismissed. In another case, the petitioner, the Sirpur Paper Mills Ltd, challenged the notifications fixing minimum wages for persons employed in the manufacture of paper and paper boards in so far

203. LLJ, 3, 2011, *Indian Institute of Technology, Madras* v. *Presiding officer, Principal Labour Court, Chennai and Others*, High Court of Madras, pp. 438–445.

as contract labourers engaged by it were concerned. The Court observed that section 12 of the Contract Labour (Regulation and Abolition) Act, 1970 provides for grant of licence to the labour contractors, which may contain conditions, such as the hours of work, wages, etc. as the appropriate government may decide. The appellant's plea that the stipulation of minimum wages came under the exclusive purview of the MW Act and the same could not be undertaken under the C.L Act came for review. The Court observed that there existed a dichotomy of opinion, whether a contract labourer answers the description of the term 'employee' under Section 2(i) of the MW Act. However, this matter does not come for consideration since there is no claim that the contract labourers are direct employees of the company. The Court agreed with the appellant that the notifications issued under the MW Act, prescribing the minimum wages do not apply directly to the contract labour, but if the contract labour discharges the same functions as any other regular worker, he shall be entitled to be paid the wages for such work, if prescribed. Thus the MW Act becomes applicable to the contract labour indirectly in some cases. The Court held that to enforce minimum wages on contract labour it is not necessary to treat the activity of labour contractor as 'scheduled employment', but by the process of enforcing the conditions of license. The writ petitions were dismissed.[204]

*269.* In one case the central government recategorized workers employed in an open cast mine at par with those working below the ground for fixing the minimum wage. The labour law separately provides for open cast and underground mines irrespective of the depth of the mine. Merger of the two categories led to the objection that the notification had made two unequals as equals. This was contrary to and inconsistent with the statutory provisions of the Act as well as the Mines Act, 1952. The Minimum Wages Act does not confer unbridled power to provide for benefits for certain employees in the style of benevolent despotism. The objection was upheld by the High Court, and it was held that the employees working in two different classes of mines would be entitled to their respective minimum wages and that part of the notification which merged them would cease to have any effect.[205]

*270.* In another hard fought case, a part time water bearer working for six hours per day in a government organization sought redress from the High Court. The Court referred to the agency and grievance voiced by the applicant in this civil application. Twice were her services terminated and twice she succeeded in having them set aside through writ petitions. She now sought direction for regularisation of service and also prayed for direction for payment of minimum wages as per the notification of the Gujarat government dated 11 February 2009. The Court observed that as per the said notification, the part time employees working for more than four hours were entitled to receive full minimum rate of wages plus special allowance. The petitioner was working for six hours a day and yet she had not been paid at the

---

204. LLJ, Vol. 3, 2011, *Multipurpose Training Centre for the Deaf* v. *Government of NCT of Delhi and Others*, High Court of Delhi, pp. 832–835; LLJ, Vol. 2, 2011, *Sirpur Paper Mills Ltd. And Others* v. *Government of Andhra Pradesh rep. by its Secretary, LET & P. Deptt and others*, High Court of Andhra Pradesh, pp. 646–652.

205. LLJ, 1989, Vol. 2, *Essel Mining Industries Ltd and Another* v. *Union of India*, High Court of Orissa, pp. 316–324.

above rate. The denial of minimum wages would be squarely hit by Article 14 of the Constitution of India. The Court said, that the voice of the petitioner, even though routed through the court, has fallen on deaf ears. In view of these facts the Court issued specific directions to the state of Gujarat, (i) to pay the wages at full rate of minimum wages plus allowance as applicable to part time employees, or (ii) to pay fixed monthly wages of Rs 3500 p.m. from the date of this application, (iii) the arrears of wages from the date of application till its actual payment be worked out and paid on or before 1 March 2011. And in case it is not paid, the interest on arrears at the rate of 8 per cent p.a. till the same is paid. (iv) In case wages are revised for part timers, then it would be open to the state to pay wages to the present applicant on that basis.[206]

206. LLJ, Vol. 4, 2011, *Manjulabehn Punjalal Dabhi* v. *State of Gujarat and Another*, High Court of Gujarat, pp. 758-765.

# Part II. Remuneration, Bonus and Benefits

## Chapter 1. Wages and Earnings

### §1. Wage Regulating Laws

*271.* There are three Acts which directly regulate payment and determination of wages. These are the Payment of Wages Act, 1936, the Minimum Wage Act, 1948 and the Payment of Bonus Act, 1965. The Payment of Wages Act was enforced in 1937 and amended in 1982 and 2005. It provides the most extensive definition of the term 'wages' in order to regulate its payment by the due dates and prevent illegal and unauthorized deductions from wages, as defined, earned by industrial workers over the wage period. This Act effectively brought the industrial wage payment system within the rule of law and eliminated a vast number of inequities and irregularities from the modes adopted for paying wages. The Minimum Wages Act, 1948 is a substantive law and establishes the floor below which wages ought not to fall. It has its set of definitions which only partly overlap with those of the Payment of Wages Act. Whereas the latter aims at total coverage, the minimum Wages Act has a more restricted purpose and its definitions reflect the limited scope of the legislation. By comparison, the Payment of Bonus Act has an altogether different aim. It is to establish a statutory right of workers in the prosperity of a company, hence a claim on earnings payable out of statutorily determined profits, present and future, in accordance with a set formula. The Act lays down a minimum and a maximum, but is rigid and flexible at the same time. Given the purpose, it has a set of definitions.

*272.* The social security legislation has created its own universe of definitions and each enactment, by its very nature, leads an independent life with no legislative links among them. Together, they deeply impact the employers' costs and prices, hence their business prospects and decisions on future plans. On the other hand,the well-being of workers and their families coupled with the collective endeavour to stay above the poverty line depends upon the scope and reach of the social security laws; hence the more expanded the coverage or wider the scope, the better for the target population. As with the Payment of Bonus Act, these laws raise divisive issues, providing ample room for public policy interventions and in the matter of settling disputes, for courts to adjudicate and make case laws.

*273.* Yet another set of definitions occur in the Industrial Disputes Act, 1947. All wage disputes that are not resolved through collective bargaining must go through the legal process of conciliation and adjudication as provided under the Act. Other than the statutory minimum wage, all wage disputes attract the principle of employer's ability to pay. It is for the court/tribunal to decide the questions of ability-to-pay in the light of the facts presented by the two parties and arrive at a fair settlement. The definition of wages in this Act reflects the purpose of dispute resolution. It is sufficiently wide in scope to be of general use for resolving disputes, yet flexible to enable the courts to interpret given facts in particular disputes and arrive at settlements.

*274.* Under the Minimum Wages Act, a state government can add to the schedule, any employment where persons are employed for hire or reward to do any work, skilled or unskilled, manual or clerical. If the persons do not fall in these categories, it would not be possible to fix minimum wages for them. On this ground teachers are excluded and the government is not competent to bring them under the purview of the Act. Similarly the detective and security services are excluded. These services could not be evenremotely linked to any of the notified scheduled employments. The Minimum Wages Act is not a complete code and it might be necessary to invoke the ID Act if any issue connected with the fixation of minimum wages requires adjudication. The authority under the Act functions like a judicial officer and not a court. Notifications have been successfully challenged on the grounds of their being arbitrary, unfair and unreasonable, or based on the advisory board's recommendation which did not rest on observed data on prevailing wages in the area, or could be put to non-application of mind, etc. Under Section 22F, the Payment of Wages Act is applicable, at the discretion of appropriate government, to wages payable under the Minimum Wages Act to the scheduled employments. A notification should be issued to this effect.

## §2. Definitions and Rules

*275.* The term 'wages' is defined in the various statutes to serve the specific purpose of law. These have been amended from time to time in order to widen the coverage and to confer the intended benefits upon workmen. The most general definition is under the Payment of Wages Act, 1936 as amended in 1982. Thus wages include:

- any remuneration payable under any award, settlement or order of a court;
- any remuneration payable for overtime work on holidays or any leave period;
- any additional remuneration payable under the terms of employment, whether called a bonus or by any other name;
- any sum payable under law on termination of employment even though the time within which the payment is to be made is not specified; and
- any sum to which the person employed is entitled under any scheme framed under any law for the time being in force. The wages for the period of lay-off fall within the definition of wages. However, if wages exceed Rs 1,600 per month (Rs. 6,500 since 2005) the Payment of Wages Act does not apply. A subsistence allowance is wages. It was a nickname for reduced wages.In one case subsistence

allowance was not paid during the pendency of disciplinary, proceedings. The workman filed a claim application under 5-15 of the Payment of Wages Act. The employer took the plea that subsistence allowance was not a wage and could not be covered under the Act. The Prescribed Authority under the Act held that it was a part of wages and the non-payment amounted to a wrongful deduction. This was appealed in a revised petition which was dismissed. This led to a writ petition. The court said that subsistence allowance is paid when the workman is under an enquiry, though he is not working. It is wages. The petition was dismissed.

The exclusions are:

- any bonus (such as profit sharing bonus) which is not covered by (iii) above as part of remuneration;
- the value of house accommodation or the supply of light, water, etc., or any amenity which has been excluded from the calculation of wages by an order of the state government;
- employers' contribution to any pension or provident fund and the interest accrued thereon;
- any travelling allowances or the value of any travelling concession;
- any sum paid to defray special expenses; and
- any gratuity payable on termination other than those listed above.[207]

*276.* Under the Minimum Wages Act, 1948, wages means any remuneration, capable of being expressed in money, which would be payable in respect of a person's employment or of work done in such employment. It includes house rent allowance, but excludes the following:

- the value of any house accommodation, supply of light, water, medical attendance or any other amenity or service excluded by the government;
- employer's contribution to any pension fund, provident fund or any scheme of social insurance;
- any travelling allowance or the value of any travelling concession;
- any sum paid to defray special expenses entailed on him by the nature of his employment;
- any gratuity payable on discharge.The Act lays down a procedure for fixing and revising minimum wages. It is mandatory and its disregard may result in nullification of the notification. The government is required to consult and seek advice of the interested parties before fixing minimum wages for the first time or on revising them. It should consider all representations received from the concerned parties and should be well informed on facts before the notification fixing wages. In one case the government appointed an Advisory Committee while the Act

207. LLJ, 2009, Vol. 4, *Khetriya Sri Gandhi Ashram, Gorakhpur* v. *Dy. Labour Commissioner/ Prescribed Authority and another*, High Court of Allahabad, pp. 866–870.

required it to constitute a more representative Advisory Board. This was patently illegal and on this count the notification was quashed.[208]

*277.* The definition under the ID Act broadly covers the same ground but it is more general and includes:

- such allowances (including dearness allowance) as the workman is entitled to;
- the value of house accommodation or the supply of light, water, etc; and
- any travelling concession (excluded in the Payment of Wages Act); and
- any commission payable on the promotion of sales or business (not mentioned in the Payment of Wages Act).

The ID Act excludes any bonus, or any contribution paid or payable to any pension fund or provident fund or gratuity payable on termination.

*278.* Under the social security legislation the term used is 'basic wages' because the purpose is to determine the rate of deduction and employer's contribution. Thus in the Employees' Provident Funds and Miscellaneous Provisions Act, 1952, 'basic wages' is defined to exclude any dearness allowance, house rent allowance, overtime, bonus, commission or any other allowance as well as the cash value of any food concessions, though for the purpose of determining the contribution to be made to the provident fund the dearness allowance (DA), the cash value of food concession and retaining allowance, if any, are added to basic wages.

*279.* Under the Payment of Gratuity Act, 1972, wages are defined to include all emoluments earned by an employee, while on duty or on leave, payable in accordance with the terms and conditions of his employment in cash and include dearness allowance but exclude any bonus,commission, house-rent allowance, overtime wages and any other allowances. This concept includes all types of wages earned by an employee. Piece rate earnings should also be included. An attempt was made to treat piece rate earnings as similar to overtime wages and excluded for the purpose of calculating gratuity. The Court held that piece-rate incentives are paid only when the employee completes the work given to him within his working hours and this may include any extra work done by him. This cannot be viewed as overtime, which is payable for working extra hours. However, incentive payments are not to be included in wages, on the same basis as their exclusion, for the purpose of leave wages, overtime wages, or in lieu of notice, provident fund contribution, bonus and other allowances. In order to remain in the realm of 'basic wages', the workman is paid an amount for the output given by him in a shift which is up to the norms prescribed for his output.[209]

---

208. LLJ, November 2010, *Ujjain Charitable Trust Hospital and Research Centre* v. *State of MP and Another*, High Court of Madhya Pradesh, pp. 345–349.
209. LLJ, November 2010, *Board of Trustees of Chennai Port Trust, Chennai* v. *Assistant Labour Commissioner and Another*, Madras High Court, pp. 544–552.

*280.* The Employees State Insurance Act, 1948 employs a wide definition of the term 'wages'. It is in three parts. The first part includes whatever remuneration is paid or payable to an employee under the terms of contract, express or implied, and covers the terms of original contract as well as the terms of a settlement arrived at later between the employer and the employees which too become part of the contract of employment. The second part includes whatever payment is made in respect of a period of authorized leave, lock-out, strike which is not illegal or lay-offs and the third part refers to other additional remuneration, if any, paid at intervals not exceeding two months. This too is wages, though it need not be under the contract of employment-but outside it. Hence house rent allowance, incentive allowances, 'heat, gas and dust allowance', medical allowance and driver's allowance are included as wages. The issue raised before the Court was whether conveyance allowance and washing allowance were wages or not. The industrial tribunal came to the conclusion that any remuneration paid under these terms must be included as wages. These are covered by the third part of the definition, which covers the amounts as paid instead of payable. The High Court confirmed this opinion.[210]

*281.* In the Workmen's Compensation Act the terms employed are 'monthly wages' in addition to 'wages'. The latter includes any privilege or benefit which is capable of being estimated in money, other than a travelling concession or a contribution paid by the employer towards any pension or provident fund or a sum paid to a workman to covey any special expenses entailed on him by nature of his employment. There terms are to be interpreted in the light of definitions provided in this Act and not the Payment of Wages Act. The words 'privilege or benefit' include free accommodation which being capable of estimation in money are included in wages. Section 5 of the Act provides for the method of calculating wages and defines monthly wages as the amount of wages deemed to be payable for a month's service and calculated by the prescribed method.

*282.* Wage claims arising from deductions or delay or penalty can be made under Section 15 of the Payment Wages Act. Under the central law, the Act imposes a ceiling of Rs 1,600 per month (Rs 6,500 p.m. since 2005) for eligibility. This has been abolished in West Bengal by an amendment to the Act in 1993. As a result, for the applicability of the Act, the amount of wages is unlimited. On deductions, the courts have clarified that no deductions can be made from wages unless these are authorized by law or by the employee in writing. In one case the government owned BSNL issued a notification that due to the cash withdrawal tax of 0.1 per cent on cash withdrawn of Rs one lakh or more on a single day, all employees should receive wages either by cheque or direct payment into their bank accounts. Those who desired to be paid in cash would be subjected to a proportionate deduction of the tax from their wages. This notification was challenged in the High Court. The Court admitted the petition and quashed the notification as illegal. No taxes could be imposed save by authority of law.

210. LLJ, 2009, Vol. 4, *Deputy Director, ESI Corp. Hyderabad* v. *Amrutanjan Ltd, Hyderabad and Others*, High Court of Andhra Pradesh, pp. 167–179.

The authority notified by the state government may direct the refund of the amount together with compensation without prejudice to the penalty to which the employer or the other person may be liable. Under Section 33C of the ID Act there is an altogether different machinery provided for recovery of wages, etc. If any money is due under a settlement/award or under the provisions pertaining to lay-off, retrenchment and closure, the workman or any person authorized by him may make an application to the government and then money may be recovered as arrears of land revenue by the collector of the district. A workman has two options viz. under the Payment of Wages Act and under the ID Act. Both are designed to produce the same result.[211]

*283.* Workmen hired by a contractor are covered by the Payment of Wages Act, though the employer denied the existence of the employer-employee relationship, hence questioned the jurisdiction of the Act. The case arose from the inspector's report on violations of the Act for not paying 11 workers their wages in full and making illegal deductions of over Rs 60,202 by the employer. The Prescribed Authority agreed and served a legal notice on the employer and directed him to make the payment together with the penalty at three times the money deducted. It led to a writ petition. The employer said that the said workmen were employed by the contractor. It was said on behalf of the workmen that under the Factories Act, workers employed by the contractor were protected and covered by the Payment of Wages Act. The Court decided that instead of going into incidental facts, essential facts should be examined. The First Appellate Court had already concluded that the workers worked as mazdoors in the sugar mill in their individual capacity, not on the basis of a contract or under an agreement and they used to sit outside the premises of the mill. The contractor was not registered as a contractor of the mill, though this was the law, On the basis of factory evidence on record which showed that all the workmen were shown as mazdoors of a workshop in shift 'D', it followed that the employer had wrongly deducted their wages.The appeal was dismissed.[212]

*284.* The Payment of Wages Act permits deduction from wages for absence from duty in proportion to the wage period. In a case, the union served notice for one day of token strike alongwith employees of other public sector undertakings for redressal of demands in the entire country. Following the principle 'no work no pay', which forms part of the Act, the employer, the Singareni Collieries Co. Ltd. decided to impose penal deduction of wages at the rate of two days of wages for each day of illegal strike. The deduction was made under the PW Act. This was challenged in the High Court on the ground that the Act was not applicable to the workers drawing more than Rs 6500 per month, while all the affected workers were drawing wages above this limit. Hence the order was illegal and invoking the jurisdiction of

---

211. LLJ, 2007, Vol. 7, *National Federation of Telecom Employees (BSNL) and another* v. *Bharat Sanchar Nigam Ltd and Others*, High Court of Calcutta, pp. 877–881.
212. LLJ, 2007, Vol. 3, *Triveni Engineering and Industries Ltd* v. *Khataulivs. Ist. Additional District Judges, Muzaffarnagar and Others*, High Court of Allahabad, pp. 491–494.

the Act as flawed, since the Act had no application. It was arranged by the respondents that by mutual understanding the provisions of the Act can be extended and that all the unions had agreed to the application of the PW Act in all respects and now they cannot turn around and say that the Act had no application. Moreover, the Certified Standing Orders prescribed penalty for absenteeism, though in view of a mass strike it was not possible to give individual notice so as to comply with the principles of natural justice. Moreover, it would have been an empty formality. The Court held that a contract in violation of mandatory statutory provision of law can only be read and enforced in the terms of law and in no other way. There can be no estoppel against the statute, nor can there be an excess of statutory power by acquiescence. The writ petition succeeded and the impugned order set aside. However, the respondent company will not be precluded from taking appropriate action under the law or the Certified Standing orders.[213]

*285.* In a case the Supreme Court had to decide several legal issues pertaining to industrial jurisprudence while determining the justness of workmen's claim for wages, though they had not worked on the ground that unpaid leave and holidays were illegally imposed upon them, pursuant to a government notification to this effect. 64 daily rated labourers employed by the Gujarat Agricultural University were given holiday on second and fourth Saturday of every month and 11 days on Diwali as holidays. No work was taken and no wages paid. This amounted to a change in their service conditions during the pendency of a reference before the Industrial Tribunal without following the proper procedure and was illegal. They were given forced leave and forced holiday which was illegal. Under the law they were entitled to a weekly day of rest on full pay. The employer should pay wages in lieu of forced leave and holidays. The Industrial Tribunal upheld their demand as just and ordered the university to pay. Its petitions to the High Court were dismissed. Hence the appeal to the Supreme Court. The Apex Court decided that merely because the daily wagers do not hold any post does not mean that there are no conditions of service. These were settled under a settlement which had expired, but still had legal validity until a new settlement or award replaced it. There could not be a void in industrial law. The term,'conditions of service' is not restricted to the holders of posts. Moreover, reducing the numbers of days worked would affect workers deeply and may disentitle them from several benefits, including regularization and permanency. At the same time the university had acted bonafide in enforcing a government order as applicable to everyone employed by it. In these peculiar circumstances, the principle of 'no work, no pay' cannot be given a go by. Instead the employer was directed to pay 50 per cent wages in lieu of the leave/holidays granted to workers. The appeal was partly allowed.[214]

*286.* In a case, the Authority under the Payment of Wages Act had ordered the Ramala Sahkari Chini Mills Ltd. to pay the workmen the wages wrongfully

213. LLJ, Vol. 1, 2012, *Singareni Collieries Workers Union and Other* v. *Singareni Collieries Company Ltd and Another*, High Court of Andhra Pradesh, pp. 493-500.
214. LLJ, 2009. Vol. 4, *Gujarat Agricultural University* v. *All Gujarat Kamdar Karmachari Union*, Supreme Court of India, pp. 382–391.

deducted with compensation, though it was not complied with for more than one and a half decade and the company preferred a writ petition against it, since the deduction from wages was made due to the loss caused by workmen. However, on enquiry, the Court learnt that it was not supported by any order of punishment of recovery. Hence the plea, that there was no wrongful deduction and the Authority had no jurisdiction, failed. There was no jurisdictional error, nor were the findings perverse, warranting interference with the impugned order. Moreover, the petitioner did not avail of the statutory remedy of appeal under Section 17 of the PW Act, but chose to file the writ petition. The Court condemned the employer seeking to prolong the litigation, stretching the plight of poor workmen to the point of breaking them. 'An individual poor workman may not withstand the prolonged litigation and consequential cost upon the petitioner, so that in future he may ponder over the matter twice before opting for the litigious hobby, just for the sake of harassment of individual worker.' The petition was dismissed with a cost Rs 20,000.[215]

*287.* In an unusual case, an employee was terminated from his service as the gate keeper of a cinema house due to misconduct, but on adjudication the Labour Court restated him to his previous employment. Against this award, the employer filed a writ petition, which was pending in the High Court, but an interim order was passed under Section 17B of the Industrial Disputes Act. The order said that in case the petitioner deposits the back wages with the Registrar of the Court within one month and pays the workman his wages at wages last drawn and continue to pay the some during the pendency of the writ petition the award shall remain stayed 'However, it will be open for the petitioner to take work or not from respondent no.2'. This was done on 1 October 1997. After this the employer started taking work from the employee at the rate of wages last drawn. Meanwhile, the minimum wages were revised upwards and the workman filed an application before the Prescribed Authority under the MW Act claiming difference between the minimum wages payable and the actual wages. On 20 November 2000, the case was decided in his favour directing the employer to pay the actual difference together with five times of the said amount as compensation. This, was challenged in a writ petition. The Court held that, the interim order in terms of Section 17B of the ID Act, the employer had the option of continuing to pay at wages last drawn and not take work from him or to take work and pay the normal wages which cannot be less the minimum wages. The interim order was passed 18 years ago and it would be enormous exploitation of the workman to ask him to work at wage last drawn. However, as the petitioner was only misrepresenting the interim order, no compensation could be directed to be paid. Accordingly, the impugned order was set aside in respect of compensation payable at five times of the balance between the minimum wages and the actual wages paid. In future normal wages must be paid.[216]

---

215. LLJ, Vol. 1, 2012, *Ramala Sahkari Chini Mills Ltd.* v. *Authority, under the Payment of Wages Act, 1936 and Others*, High Court of Allahabad, pp. 549–550; LLJ, Vol. I, 2000, *Ahmedabad Industrial and Other Employers Union* v. *State of Gujarat*, High Court of Gujarat, pp. 1424–1438.

216. LLJ, Vol. 1, 2012, *Natraj Picture Palace* v. *Prescribed Authority, Minimum Wages Act, Asstt. Commissioner, Mirzapur and Others*, High Court of Allahabad, pp. 52–54.

*288.* In a case it was claimed that the authority under the Minimum Wages Act failed to secure for the claimant earned wages for a period when the employment continued, but work was not done, hence the wages paid fell below what was earned. The authority declined to issue the order on the ground that wages were not earned when the petitioner did not work. Moreover, the Act did not empower the Authority to go into the merits or validity of the wages claimed and the petitioner could seek remedy in some other forum as advised. However the payment of one day's salary and penalty for late payment was ordered. In a subsequent writ petition the petitioner submitted that wages as defined in the Act mean 'remuneration capable of being expressed in terms of money, which would have been payable to the employee if the contract of employment had been fulfilled'. The Court said that 'wages' should be distinguished from 'earned wages'. The only meaning that can be given to the word 'earned' is the wages that have been earned by actual working. The Authority cannot go into other questions raised by the petitioner. He is not a substitute for a Labour Court or a civil court. The petition was dismissed.[217]

*289.* In a complicated case the High Court had to decide several issues of law pertaining to the Minimum Wages Act and the Contract Labour (Regulation and Abolition Act) and the rules framed thereunder. The Steel Authority of India Ltd (SAIL) owned a limestone mine in which a large workforce employed by a registered contractor worked. In March 1993 the central government by a notification abolished the employment of contract labour in limestone and dolomite mines in the country. The Ispat Khadan Labour Mazdoor Union demanded that the contract labour was without the employer and they should be declared as employees of the SAIL, as the principle employer. This was contested by SAIL. The union also demanded that wages paid should be at par with the regular employees. In a case (*Air India Statutory Corporation* v. *Labour Union*, decided in 1997), the Supreme Court had decided that on a notification abolishing contract labour, a direct relationship between the contract labourers and principal employer is created. In a later case (*Steel Authority of India and Others* v. *National Union of Waterfront Workers and Others*, decided in 2001) the constitutional bench of the Supreme Court ousted the earlier judgment. It decided that, on notification the contract labour is not unemployed but continues in the employment of the contractor, since the notification, does not severe the relationship of master and servant between the contractor and the contract labour. Consequently the principal employer cannot be required to absorb the contract labour. The contract between the principal employer and the contractor is snapped. It becomes extinct. Actually, the contract labour continued to work in the mine and was paid wages up to 1996 by the principal employer through the contractor. On this matter the central government referred the dispute to the industrial tribunal in January 2003, whether the termination of 3604 workers in March 1996 was legal, fair and justified, and if not, what relief the concerned workmen were entitled to and two other related issues. Meanwhile, the Apex Court had already decided in a related appeal that the question whether the employment of labour through a contractor was a sham and bogus could not be decided by a writ

217. LLJ, 2007, Vol. 2, *Mala Bhandari Dr. (Mrs.)* v. *Authority under Delhi Shops and Establishment Act and Another*, High Court of Delhi, pp. 464–466.

court, but will require adjudication before an appropriate forum. Accordingly, the central government referred the dispute to the industrial tribunal. The issue of minimum wages had also been raised before the competent authority, whether the difference between the wages paid by the contractor between 1993 and 1996 and the regular wages paid by SAIL, amounting to about Rs 8 crore can be directed to be paid. The workers were unemployed and in the last 13 years 300 had died. The rest were starving. In the end, the competent authority decided that only the minimum wages were payable. The compensation of five times this amount of more than Rs 21 crore was also awarded This was successfully challenged at the High Court. The compensation money was axed, substituted by the rate of interest at 6 per cent payable on the assessed minimum wage. This was again contested on the ground that the award of payment of interest was alien to the Minimum Wage Act. The Court decided to read the definitions under the Act and disposed of a number of related questions. It axed the 6 per cent rate of interest and substituted the amount of compensation of Rs 5 crore payable by SAIL. It would have to pay not the notified minimum wages under the Act, but the wages as agreed between the SAIL and its union. The workers had worked under SAIL over the relevant period.[218]

*290.* The UP State Forest Department had engaged daily wage earners at wages below the minimum wage. The High Court order to pay the minimum in the pay scale of government employees in the department was not carried out and led to contempt proceedings for non-payment of wages. This was appealed which was dismissed. The government desired that the order to pay the minimum of government pay scale but without any increments or allowances, should be limited to those workers who had approached the Court. This was declined. Instead the Court directed that the daily wagers were entitled to equality of pay with regular employees on the basis of 'equal pay for equal work'. There was no scope for mini-classification.[219]

*291.* In a complicated case, minimum wages for the contract labour, working for a government of India undertaking, Bharat Sanchar Nigam Ltd., in Tamilnadu had to be decided, taking into account the notifications on minimum wages payable to the specified categories of contract labour and the minimum wages fixed by the state government and the provisions of the contract labour (Regulation and Abolition) Act, 1970 had to be taken into account. The petitioner, BSNL filed a writ petition praying for a writ of certiorari to call for the records of the first respondent, Deputy Chief Labour Commissioner (Central), Chennai and to quash the same. The petitioner was registered to engage contract labour through the contractors for doing non-core work. The contractors are obliged to pay the minimum wages fixed by the district collectors from time to time. The petitioner ensures that this is done. But any deviation by way of enhanced rate of payment during the tenure of the subsisting agreement between the petitioner and the contractors will put the whole system in

218. LLJ, 2007, Vol. 2, *Steel Authority of India Ltd and Others* v. *Authority Under The Minimum Wages Act, 1948 and Others*, High Court of Madhya Pradesh, pp. 750–764.

219. LLJ, February 2011, *Chanchal Kumar Tiwari and Others* v. *Hari Shankar and Others*, High Court of Allahabad, pp. 581–587.

jeopardy. The Ministry of Labour and Employment issued a Notification dated 14 September 2006 on minimum wages pertaining to the telephone / telegraph and other departments. It presented little difficulty since the Fixed by the District Collector were better. The union representing contract labour made a representation seeking fixation of wages on par with the regular workmen. This representation was forwarded by the Chief Labour Commissioner, New Delhi to the Deputy Labour Commissioner, Chennai for adjudicating upon the matter. This he did and passed the impugned order. This order was erroneous, unjust, illegal and without jurisdiction. The Court held, that the Dy. Labour Commissioner is the competent authority to determine the wage rates, holidays, hours of work and acted within his jurisdiction. On the contention that the minimum wage rates fixed by the District Collector would be applicable and not the minimum wages notified by the government of India dated 7, August 2008 and a further notification dated 20 May 2009, the Dy Chief Labour Commissioner fixed the date for enforcement of his award as 1 January 2008. The petitioner pleaded that the date could not be prior to 20 May 2009, the date of notification. Against this the contract labour union argued that the Authority arrived at the conclusion based on the contract agreement between the principal employer and the contractor taking note of the notification dated 7 August 2008. Therefore the effect of the order shall not be less than the earliest notification as above. The Court decided that fixing of wages with effect from 1 January 2008 cannot be permitted. It will come into effect on 7 August, 2008. Finally, the Court said that the workers concerned in this writ petition belong to the lowest strata of the society, who do menial jobs in the establishments of the writ petitioner, and they deserve to be treated with dignity so that they are able to keep their body and soul together while working, in which situation, interfering with the impugned order, except the date of the effect of the same in this writ petition, is not warranted. The writ petition was dismissed.[220]

*292*. In a challenge before the High Court it was urged on behalf of the employer that, while fixing the minimum wages for the *beedi* industry, the state government had not borne in mind the relevant factors. The increase in wages was far greater than the requirement of neutralization and this amounted to arbitrariness. Moreover, the workers had signed a settlement on the minimum wages payable which were lower than the notified wages. The Court found that the impugned fixation did not demonstrate that the government had kept in mind the effect of the steep rise in wage cost upon the industry and its effect on the consumer. The process of consultation cannot be equated with concurrence. 'But if it is demonstrated that there was never any meaningful consideration of the representation of the aggrieved, and it is demonstrated so, then certainly the Court cannot take refuge under the theory that there need be only consultation and no concurrence.' The records did not show that the consultations held were intelligible, rational and candid. In this case it was not shown that the government had kept an open mind and the representation of the employer was meaningfully examined and considered. However, on the matter of the settlement in question, the Court rejected it as not being sustainable in law. The

220. LLJ, Vol. 1, 2012, *Bharat Sanchar Nigam Ltd. rep. by its Chief General Manager, Chennai* v. *Deputy Chief Labour Commissioner (Central)*, Chennai, High Court of Madras, pp. 784–792.

Court held that the notification had not been issued in compliance with requirement of Sections 3 and 5 of Act and therefore quashed the same. The government was directed to revise and refix the minimum wages for the *beedi* industry.[221]

## §3. Wage Fixation Machinery

*293.* Under the Minimum Wages Act the appropriate government may fix minimum rates of wages for any scheduled employment (i) for the first time, or (ii) revise wages so fixed. For these purposes it may appoint as many committees or subcommittees as it considers necessary for holding enquiries and ask for advice, or publish its proposals by a notification in the Official Gazette and seek comments and advice from those likely to be affected thereby and then issue a notification fixing or revising the minimum rates of wages. The Act makes provisions for the constitution of an Advisory Board for advising the government. The Act requires that representatives of employers and employees should be represented in equal numbers, and the independent members should not exceed one-third of total membership. In practice the government often issues notifications on the proposals, receives comments, makes up its mind and issues a second notification prescribing the minimum wages. The committee method is also used, but it takes more time to arrive at common acceptable rates of minimum wages.

*294.* The Working Journalists and Other Newspaper Employees (Conditions of Service) and Miscellaneous Provisions Act, 1995 provides for the setting up of statutory wage boards which shall follow the prescribed procedure in seeking representations in writing from the concerned parties and then make its recommendations to the central government. Section 10(4) provides that the Board shall have regard to the cost of living, the prevalent rates of wages for comparable employments, the circumstances relating to the newspaper industry in different regions and to any other circumstances which it may consider relevant. The Board may at its discretion make recommendations for fixation or revision of wages on all-India basis. The Supreme Court has held that the Wage Board would be bound to consider the capacity of the industry to pay. On receiving the recommendations of the Board the central government may fix the wage rates, if necessary, with retrospective effect.

*295.* Under the ID Act, the industrial tribunals have the authority to adjudicate wage disputes and revise wages in all industries other than industries of national importance or those located in more than one state. In such cases national tribunals are appointed. The Third Schedule of the ID Act lays down the subjects that fall within their jurisdiction. These include wages, including the period and mode of payments, allowances, bonus, provident fund and gratuity, manning, retrenchment and a host of other matters covering practically the entire area of wages and earnings. However, a tribunal can only go into the issues that have been raised in a dispute and referred to it by the government. It is not for the Labour Court/tribunal to

221. LLJ, Vol. 1, 2000, *Management of Jyothi Home Industries and Others* v. *State of Karnataka and Others*, High Court of Karnataka, pp. 596–609.

fix the minimum rates of wages. This is done by the government. They merely ascertain what the minimum rates of wages are for the purpose of deciding 'fair wages'.

*296.* Collective agreements have become increasingly common in the large-scale industries both in the public and the private sectors. In the public sector a collective agreement becomes effective when it is approved by the government. In the private sector it becomes legally binding if it takes the form of a 'settlement' under the ID Act and properly filed with the appropriate government. The subjects that dominate collective agreements are the pay packet, welfare and leave. The Supreme Court has tended to support collective settlements signed by unions and backed by a majority of workmen. The Supreme Court has held that, 'unless it can be demonstrated that the objectionable portion is such that it completely outweighs all other advantages gained, the Court will be slow to hold a settlement as unfair and unjust'. Yet wage disputes arise and reach higher courts. In a case pertaining to house rent allowance the Apex Court said, both the tribunal as well as the High Court have ignored the vital aspect of the matter, i.e. the effect of the awards and settlements arrived at between the bank and its employees and their effect thereon in determining their *inter se* rights and obligations. The Tribunal has completely ignored this basic issue and the High Court has also given short shrift thereto. The Tribunal was asked to reexamine the issue.[222]

*297.* Wages are paid for work done. It is not enough for the employees to attend the place of work; they must put in the work allotted to them. Wages are payable pro-rata for the work done and hence deductible for work not done.Wages are payable only if the contract of employment is fulfilled and not otherwise. Consequently, in a strike, whether legal or illegal, workers are liable to lose wages for the period of strike. During the period of strike the contract of employment continues, but they cannot expect to be paid.

*298.* The Supreme Court forms part of the wage fixing machinery in an unusual sense. It has had to decide matters pertaining to wage structure. DA, etc., arising from appeal petitions against the awards made by the tribunals. In one case, the industrial tribunal conceded the demand of the management for placing a ceiling on dearness allowance, because the neutralization factor exceeded 100 per cent. The workmen challenged the award,but the High Court upheld the award of the DA ceiling,while modifying it in certain other respects. However, the division bench of the High Court decided in favour of workers on the DA question, but found fault with the other parts of the award. The issue of upward revision of wages was remanded back to the tribunal to examine afresh. The Tribunal gave a fresh award on wage scales, and the matter then on led to appeals being heard by the Apex Court. The Court held that merely because the salary level of clerks could exceed those of junior executives was no ground for placing a ceiling on their DA. It is for the company to make the junior executive grade more attractive rather than deny the

---

222. LLJ, 2008, Vol. 2, *Andhra Bank through Regional Manager* v. *I.T-cum Labour Court and Another*, Supreme Court of India, pp. 957–959.

workers what is due to them. The Tribunal was also faulted for not revising the wage structure on certain well-settled principles and the same was set aside. The Tribunal was directed to once again re-examine the wage structure and determine the question of revisions.[223]

*299.* In the public sector the most important wage fixation authority is the pay commission. Once the pay commission makes its final recommendations, and if they are favorable to the employees, much political debate, even agitations, centre around the report and demands made to accept the recommended pay scales, allowances and other benefits. Experience shows that the pay commissions' recommendations are accepted by the centre first, then by the state governments and eventually by all the public sector managements where they are applicable. In the public sector, profits or losses matter little, nor does the capacity to pay carry much weight in deciding the question, whether at a particular juncture, in a particular industry or undertaking, wage increases on a substantial scale could be granted on rational economic grounds. The government takes the overall decision, taking the responsibility for paying the wage-bill, if required, and the management of each public undertaking sector is directed to implement the same.

## §4. Principles of Wage Determination

*300.* The judicial principles for wage fixation and revisions in wage structures are partly derived from the economic theory and partly from management doctrines and blended with the criteria of equity and fairness. The adjudication has sought to reconcile the conflicting demands of social justice with the claims of national economy and of capital for reasonable profits. The adjudicator must also take into account the increase in prices in order to determine the adequacy of proposed wages as well as the additional burden the wage bill might impose upon the consumers. However, it is seldom for the higher courts to spell out specific weights attached to the various principles; indeed they have avoided any kind of specific commitment to any formula for deciding wage issues.

*301.* It is a judicial doctrine that the employers who cannot afford to pay minimum wages may quit, if they please, but their point of view will carry no weight. Beyond the level of the minimum, the employers can argue on the ground of limited ability to pay. They are entitled to ask for a fair return on capital. The practical method evolved by courts is to apply the principle of industry-cum-region; it is neither of the whole industry, nor of the undertaking only. Then an attempt may be made to project the effect of a revised and improved wage structure upon costs, prices and profits over a period of two to three years, in order to determine whether or not a reasonable burden is being imposed upon the industry. Finally, on the basis

223. *Hindustan Lever Ltd Bombay* v. *B.N Dongre*, Supreme Court of India, *Reported Cases on Indian Labour Laws*, Vol. I. (ed: Colin Gonsalves, Ramesh Bhatt, Mini Mathews), Friedrich Ebert Stiftung, New Delhi, 1995, pp. 486–502.

of fairness and reasonableness, and as a measure of just compromise the adjudicator may give his award. The employer must produce evidence to show that he cannot afford higher wages demanded by the workmen and tribunal must provide real and effective opportunity to the employer to produce evidence and plead his case. The tribunal is required to give its finding on whether the employer has the capacity to pay higher wages. In the absence of a definite finding, the tribunal cannot award higher wages. Nor can higher wages be awarded when the prevailing wages are already higher than in other comparable concerns in the region. Wages cannot be revised merely on the ground that they had been fixed a long time ago, without considering other relevant factors.

*302.* Although the Supreme Court has advanced the doctrine that uniformity in wage scale on an industry-cum-region basis is to be preferred, it may not be possible to realize this objective because of different financial capacities of different concerns. In such cases the tribunals have been advised to lay greater stress on the industry, if there are a large number of concerns, but emphasize the region more, if the number is small. In the cases of clerical and subordinate staff, even inter-industry comparisons within a region are permissible, because there is not much difference in their work in different industries.

*303.* A considerable body of law on wages is devoted to defining terms. 'Rates of wages', implies the manner, mode or standard of payment for work done and includes the scale of wages. Tribunals are expected to categorize workers in different pay scales on the basis of the nature of work done. The classification of workmen is deemed to be incidental to the more important task of wage fixing and falls within their jurisdiction. However, whereas the classification of jobs, if in dispute, may be undertaken by the tribunals, that of fitment of individual workmen is best left to the managements to be done in consultation with unions.

*304.* By standardization of wages is meant the leveling up of the terms and conditions that are below the standardized ones. If wages are standardized in any industry, in a region, there is practically no scope for exceptions. However, wages of individual workmen that may be higher than the standardized wages can be protected.Where such wage islands are protected, the protection ceases with the retirement of the said workmen. Their successors cannot claim them. It is also possible that the higher wages may be gradually absorbed in future increments and the phenomenon is phased out. Furthermore, there can be no further raising of wages of such workmen until they are equalized with the standardized rates.

*305.* On DA, the judicial view is somewhat unclear. Usually there may not be any ceiling on DA to workmen, while the executive staff may be subject to one. There is a possibility of grave anomalies developing in the wage-cum-salary structure inasmuch as a junior person may draw higher earnings than his senior. In such cases the slab system of DA may be abolished or modified on the orders of the court to avoid huge distortions of wage differences. The Supreme Court has said that'the DA mainly protects real earnings from the ravages of inflation, and in most cases the workers only earn 'subsistence wages'; it would be inadvisable to tinker with the wage structure except under compelling circumstances'. In a case involving a cooperative sugar mill, the workers filed a suit for permanent injunction restraining the cooperative mill from withdrawing the VDA (Variable Dearness Allowance). It met with legal hurdles.[224]

224. LLJ, 2006, Vol. 3, *Morinda Cooperative Sugar Mills Ltd* v. *Morinda Cooperative Sugar Mills Workers Union*, Supreme Court of India, pp. 559–563.

# Chapter 2. Dearness and Other Allowances

## §1. Purpose of Dearness Allowance

*306.* DA is that component of the pay packet which bears some discernible connection to the cost of living. It is an additional wage to either wholly or partially compensate the rise in the cost of living. In India the DA has come to occupy a special place as distinct from basic wages, incentive pay, bonus and other components of pay. It reflects the evolution of the doctrine that it is not the wages but the DA that should rise and the fall with the CPI. This ensures complete flexibility and reduces wage disputes to clearly defined causes which in turn facilitate their settlement. Industrial adjudication has preferred to deal with wage disputes by separate categories and has laid down principles for the determination of each of them.

*307.* Though there is no law requiring the employers to pay the DA, nor on how the formula for payment of DA should be designed, some form of wage indexation is common in most industries. 'Under this system wages keep pace directly, by virtue of a prior decision and as automatically as desired, with an index (usually a price index) selected as being representative of price trends confronting the target households.' The number of formulas is very large but may be grouped into four classes:

(i) according to a given CPI;
(ii) flat rate;
(iii) pay scale/slab system; and
(iv) others.

In the public sector there are two systems of DA, the industrial DA (IDA) and the central DA (CDA). The presence of two systems in the same organizations has produced pay disparities amongst similarly placed employees. This is because those who come on deputation from the Centre are governed by the CDA. Employees also have the option to choose any one system of DA.

*308.* In a number of industries, largely due to bilateral settlements and tribunal awards, the DA system has been split into two components. These are:

- a common fixed dearness allowance usually pegged to an agreed level of CPI;
- a variable dearness allowance (VDA) which is revised periodically, let us say, every quarter according to the variation in the CPL.

In a large number of states the practice of paying DA and VDA has also been introduced under the Minimum Wages Act. The dearness allowance may be linked to a particular CPI for the year with so many points, and for any future rise of every one point over and above this level, an increase of so many paise or rupees to be paid as DA.

*309.* Under a special Act in Maharashtra, the benefit of dearness allowance was extended to unprotected workers. The Maharashtra Mathadi, Hamal and other

Manual Workers (Regulation of Employment and Welfare) Act, 1969 provides for the constitution of tripartite boards on which the registered employers, employees and the state government are represented. There are about 22 boards with which around 200000 workers in the state are registered. The Grocery Markets and Shops Board is one such board with which a company manufacturing food colours was registered. It reached a series of wage settlements with the union on the piece rate wage payment, but the issue of dearness allowance though discussed, was left open. In 2003, the settlement provided for the dearness allowance as decided by the High Court. The Board fixed the DA payable to all the Mathadi workers which the company ignored. The Board served it a notice to pay a sum of Rs 78,086.74 paise, failing which coercive steps would be taken. This led the company to the High Court on the plea that, as per the settlement, the workers were entitled to the agreed piece-rates and nothing else. Moreover, it was situated in the district of Raigarh, so the CPI based on the cost of living in Bombay was not applicable. The DA was fixed once in a year in November by the Board and it was not a statutory allowance. The Court held that the Board was set up under Section 25 of the Act. 'Having regard to the scheme of Section 25 of the Act, any contract or agreement which has the effect of a registered unprotected workman relinquishing any right conferred by the Act or the Scheme is void and of no effect whatever in so far as it purports to deprive the workman of such right or privilege or concession.' The plea was rejected. Raigarh had a higher cost of living than Bombay, and in any case the CPI was applicable. [225]

## §2. Judicial Principles

*310.* Under the ID Act, wages are defined to include the DA, if it is paid in any industry. It is included in the term 'salary' or wage in the Payment of Bonus Act. The DA allowance paid to neutralize the cost of living would form part of 'wages', under the Payment of Wages Act. Likewise the scope of the Payment of Gratuity Act includes all employees who earn the stipulated wages inclusive of dearness and other cash allowances. If, in any establishment, workers are not receiving a DA, they can lay a claim on it by raising a dispute and securing an award in their favour. If workers are already receiving it, a dispute can be raised on its quantum, method of calculation, or any part of the formula and they can seek an adjudication on it.

*311.* The Supreme Court has decided that full neutralization may be granted only to the lowest class of wage earners; that the neutralization should be on a sliding scale, that it should be flexible in the upward as well as in the downward direction, depending upon the behaviour of prices, and the basis of fixation should be industry-cum-region. Moreover, employees drawing the same pay should get the same DA even though they belong to different categories. Thus white-collar and blue-collar employees are to be treated at par if they earn the same amount. Furthermore, the

225. LLJ, 2007, Vol. 2, *Roha Dyecheml Ltd Mumbai* v. *State of Maharashtra, Industries and Labour Deptt*, High Court of Bombay, pp. 929–954.

tribunal must be careful to see that the financial burden is within the means of the employer to bear.

*312.* In a number of cases the Supreme Court has taken a more liberal view of DA in protecting real wages than hitherto. But the local flavour of DA must be preserved.

> a man is exposed to vagaries of the market where he resides and works, even though he may be an employee of a national, multi-national or transnational industrial empire … In the matter of dearness allowance especially, the court should lean in favour of adjudication of disputes on the principle of industry-cum-region, because the dearness allowance is linked to cost of living index of a particular centre which has a local flavour.

The Court did not favour all-India uniformity because then unequals would be treated as equals and this would be fatal to adjudication based on industry-cum-region principle.

## §3. Other Allowances

*313.* In the category of 'other allowances' are included three kinds of payment. One is the incentive pay which in some manner may be linked to productivity; the other is a special pay or an allowance paid because the employee has agreed to take on an additional duty or does extra work which is not normally included in the work for which basic wages are paid; and the third can be best described as a fringe benefit. These are not always special payments made for specific work or responsibilities, but usually additional concessions secured by labour, or granted ex gratia by the employer to improve the conditions of work, or enhance the earnings of employees. Social security benefits and amenities required to be provided under various legislation are excluded from this broad category.

*314.* On a rough count, 16 different allowance or wage payments may be included under this heading. These are:

(i) incentive wages or production bonus;
(ii) overtime wages;
(iii) tiffin allowance;
(iv) halting allowance and running allowance;
(v) transport allowance or conveyance allowance;
(vi) clothing and uniform allowance;
(vii) retaining allowance for off-season
(viii) compensatory special allowance;
(ix) medical allowance;
(x) acting allowance;
(xi) moving staff allowance;
(xii) vacation allowance;

(xiii) housing accommodation and house rent allowance (HRA);
(xiv) retirement allowance;
(xv) consolidated pay;
(xvi) subsistence allowance;

## I. Incentive Wages

*315.* Incentive wage plans usually rest upon a guaranteed time wage which reflects standard output or labour performance under normal conditions. Higher labour earnings are a reward for greater than the stipulated standard output and, under normal conditions, are based on the principle of sharing of gains in productivity.

## II. Overtime Allowance

*316.* The Bombay Shops Act has virtually extended the Factories Act to shops covered by it. Thus in Maharashtra, the overtime rate would be payable even to those employees working in a factory who are not 'workers' under the Factories Act. Where an industry is not a factory but is covered under the Shops Act of the State, the rules framed under it would apply, if in the Act itself a provision has been made for overtime. Where this is not done, the adjudicator must decide and fix the rate. The principles that should be followed are:

(i) the overtime allowance should be related to the total daily wage packet inclusive of DA; and
(ii) it should be fixed in relation to the prevailing practice in the area and the financial ability of the employer. It is an implied term of contract under the Factories Act and the Mines Act, that for the overtime work a worker is entitled to wages at the rate of twice his ordinary rate of wages which term includes basic wages plus such allowances including the cash equivalent of the advantage accruing through concessional sale of food grains and other articles. Under the Mines Act the term 'ordinary rate of wages' includes any dearness allowance and underground allowance plus compensation in cash accruing through the free issue of food grains and edible oils which a worker may be entitled to receive. Broadly the same definition is used in the Building and Other Construction Workers Act, though it is limited to basic wages and other allowances only.

*317.* In a flimsy petition to the High Court certain employees of the Chennai Port Trust asked for the restoration of the fixed overtime allowance because now it was being offered on a rotational basis. This was done partly in view of the union's demand that in place of just one set of persons getting a fixed overtime allowance system a rotational system should be introduced on an experimental basis for one year, so that everyone in the section may share it. The Court found no fault in the new policy because the petitioners did not have a vested right in the fixed overtime allowance. The petiton lacked merit and was dismissed.[226]

*318.* In a case of bureaucratic miscarriage of justice, a workman was denied overtime pay for working more than 50 hours per quarter because the Factories Act, Section 64 prohibits it without the permission of the Chief Inspector of Factories. Since this was not done, though such payments were earlier given without the permission of the Chief Inspector, because this time Finance Department of the state declined to sanction payment. The Court held that there was no justification for withholding the payment because it was the responsibility of the employer to obtain the permission, not the employee. The Court ordered that the payment should be made quickly, within two months, else for the delay the amount would earn interest at 6 per cent.[227]

*319.* In a decision the Gujarat High Court decided that under the Payment of Wages Act, the term 'wages' did not include the overtime allowance, because it was not a contractual wage. The amount claimable by way of overtime allowance would depend on the additional work done beyond the specified hours. This has no connection with the wage period. Once the contractual wage over a period of one month has been worked out, it would be payable under the Act. The overtime wage fell outside it. It was also held that when an employee remained on the premises of the employer to be at this beck and call and was not free to attend to his private work, he should be deemed to be on duty and has a right to overtime pay, even though he did not work.

*320.* In one case workers claimed that the computation of their overtime wages be done in terms of Section 59 of the Factories Act and under Section 33C(2) of the ID Act. The company contested this claim on the ground that wages of workmen were regulated by the provisions of the Tripartite Settlement, signed in March 1997, according to which the workers were entitled to Sunday allowance, not overtime. The settlement should prevail over the Factories Act, because it had been voluntarily entered into and had a binding force, and the company had acted upon it for more than a decade and a half. The High Court accepted the applications filed by workmen and directed the payment of overtime in accordance with Section 59 of the Factories Act. The Court said that any interpretation which restricted or curtailed the benefits admissible to workers under the Factories Act had to be avoided. The employees cannot be permitted to volunteer to work beyond the prescribed hours. The settlement contravened the mandatory provisions of the Act, so it cannot operate to the prejudice of workers.[228]

---

226. LLJ, 2007, Vol. 2, *Deendayalan S. and others* v. *Chairman, Port Trust, Chennai and Others,* High Court of Madras, pp. 776–777
227. LLJ, 2008, Vol. 2, *Nepal Chandra Das* v. *State of Tribura and Others*, High Court of Gauhati, pp. 877–879.
228. LLJ, Vol. 2, 1993, *Hindustan Machine Tools Ltd, Ajmer* v. *Labour Court and Another,* High Court of Rajasthan, pp. 1219–1224.

## III. Tiffin Allowance

*321.* Tiffin allowance is a fringe benefit provided by the employers in the form of free tea and biscuits. In one company workers demanded cash in lieu of tiffin saying that the tiffin was unsatisfactory. The Supreme Court upheld the claim on the ground that, once it is granted, the tiffin allowance becomes an implied condition of service and workers could claim a cash allowance in lieu of tea and biscuits as a right. However, in another case, the demand of workers that they be provided tiffin along lines given to the head office employees was rejected. It was argued on behalf of the employers that the tiffin formed part of the wage structure and that, in the Calcutta area, the constituent member companies of the Bengal Chamber of Commerce provided tiffin at the head offices only. Furthermore, canteens had been already provided on a no profit no loss basis and workers could not lay automatic claim on the employer's generosity. In yet another case, workers could succeed in establishing a claim for a lunch allowance for all of them, instead of for only a few of them who were required to go outside the city limits in connection with work. The practice of doing it in Calcutta and refusing it elsewhere was not accepted by the tribunal, since it amounted to discrimination.

## IV. Halting Allowance and Running Allowance

*322.* The workmen who claimed a halting or travelling allowance to attend the proceedings of the tribunal were not entitled to it in advance, under Section 11(7) of the ID Act. This section lays down the power of the Labour Court/tribunal to determine as to who, and to what extent, will bear the cost of proceedings. Similarly the workmen of the Calcutta Port Commissioners' Railways demanded a running allowance and free passes, among others, which were payable to similar employees doing comparable work in the railways. These claims were rejected on the grounds that the comparison was without any basis.

## V. Transport Allowance/Conveyance Allowance

*323.* The workers' claim to a transport allowance to enable them to travel between places of residence and the places of work has featured in a number of Supreme Court judgments. Some workers had claimed a bus allowance, others a cycle allowance, yet others a train allowance, depending on how they travelled. As the Supreme Court saw it, the demand was for free transport or, in lieu thereof, for a transport allowance. It decided that the employers had a responsibility to provide transport although the prevailing public transport facilities and the cost of travelling on them must be considered before deciding on the merits of the demand. The financial capacity of the concern could not be ignored, nor could it become the sole basis for deciding the issue in favour of workers. It upheld the tribunal's award of granting a transport allowance, while rejecting the employer's plea that they did not owe it and the union's claim for its enhancement.

*324.* At one stage the city of Nagpur lost its standing as a class A city and became a class B-1 city. The ESIC paid Transport Allowance to its employees in Nagpur as a class A city. In 2002 it decided to recover the excess payment, being the difference between A and B-1 city, for the period 1 August 1997 to 22 February 2002, from the salaries of employees in Nagpur. The latter appealed against this order to the Central Industrial Tribunal and secured a favourable verdict. The Corporation went to the High Court against it on the ground that, once the government reclassified the city as B-1 class, the employees should not have received it, and the excess payment can be claimed back by it. This plea was rejected by the Court on the ground that the Office Memorandum came into effect on 22 February 2002, so payments made prior to it could not be deducted from the employees' salary. Moreover, it provides that though reclassified as B-1 city, the city of Nagpur, along with other reclassified cities, will retain the existing status till further orders. This was for the purpose of City Compensation Allowance (CCA) and the House Rent Allowance (HRA). The Court found no rationale in not extending this principle to Transport Allowance. The ESIC's petition was dismissed.[229]

## VI. Clothing and Uniform Allowance

*325.* A tea estate had been providing a blanket allowance up to 1949 and then discontinued it. Six years later the workers demanded the restoration of this right. It was held that the blanket allowance had become a condition of service, that its discontinuance was unlawful, and therefore, it should be restored with retrospective effect. In another case, it was decided that there was a difference between uniforms and protective clothing. The latter was provided under the Factories Act, whereas uniforms had a different purpose. Workers could not claim uniforms as a matter of right. In yet another case the union demanded four sets of uniforms every year, because in the course of work their clothes became dirty and did not consider the management's offer of aprons as adequate. The Supreme Court upheld the tribunal award that if the clothes did get dirty the company should provide as many sets of uniforms as it deemed fit. This principle was reaffirmed in a later case.

## VII. Retaining Allowance

*326.* A retaining allowance is paid to seasonal workers to compensate them for the period of unemployment and to ensure that they report for duty when factories resume work. The sugar industry pays this allowance as an accepted industrial practice. The issue was whether unskilled workers should be paid any retaining allowance. It was not questioned that workers needed the relief, but whether it was the duty of the employer or of the government to provide it. Employers paid this allowance to the skilled and the semi-skilled workers in the interest of industry. The

229. LLJ, 2006, Vol. 2, *ESIC* v. *ESIC Officers Association and others*, High Court of Bombay, pp. 383–384.

Supreme Court favoured an increase in wages to the payment of a retaining allowance. In another case, it was found that the company was paying the allowance to half of a section of workmen and denying it to the other half. This was an unreasonable practice. The Court held that where it had become a condition of service, it must be extended to all workmen of that section.

## VIII. Compensatory Allowance and Special Allowance

*327.* Compensatory allowance is paid for work done on holidays or weekly rest days and generally at twice the normal rates of wages. If an alternative day of rest is provided, the compensatory allowance may be calculated at the lower rate, i.e. at half the normal wage. Compensatory allowance may be also given to equalize the wages of one category of workmen with a comparable category.

*328.* Special allowance is sometimes paid as a substitute for the DA but with no formal link with the CPI and determined either as a pay policy or the result of bilateral agreements with the employees. It may be also paid for discharging the duties of the immediate superior. In a case the issue was whether all employees of the bank who were asked to perform duties attracting special allowance would be entitled to it even on a day on which one was on leave. The bipartite settlement provided for it, but not payable for casual or occasional performance or discharge of such duties. The union claimed that even those who are temporary are entitled to it on Sundays, holidays and when on leave. The Industrial Tribunal agreed to the union stand and gave an award to this effect. This was confirmed by a single judge of the High Court. On appeal the Division Bench modified the award. Special allowances are payable to a permanent incumbent even when he is on leave or holiday, but not one who is asked to work temporarily in a post. A temporary staff member cannot be said to be occupying the post as such.[230]

## IX. Medical Allowance

*329.* This allowance is payable to employees who are not covered by the ESIC and do not have either direct access to hospitals, or the panelled, medical doctors with provision for covering medical expenses, or a group insurance policy. Only large business organizations have elaborate medical and surgical benefit policies as a part of the employees compensation plans. It is not uncommon to provide for employees to share the cost of medical care and also provide for medical leave. Given so many options, the scope of providing for a medical allowance as a cost limiting device is quite limited. Organizations may set the limit of medical reimbursement to one or two months salary.

230. LLJ, June 2010, *Union Bank of India through its Chairman and Managing Director* v. *Union Bank of India Employees Union, Pune and Another*, High of Court Bombay, pp. 692–695.

## X. Acting Allowance

*330.* Acting pay or allowance is a common practice in government owned or aided organization, when an employee is asked to occupy a vacant higher post without promotion, but on an acting basis on the lowest salary which the higher post carries. The acting employee should earn a higher pay and additional benefits subject to a maximum. This may be set at 25 per cent of the basic pay drawn. Disputes arising from the fixation of acting allowances rarely travel outside the government system.

## XI. Moving Staff Allowance

*331.* Travelling staff are usually provided with special facilities and pay benefits. They may get a day off for every two nights spent consecutively on travel, receive overtime pay for work done on holidays, and so on. In one case the tribunal decided that the mechanic who was required to travel and work on holidays should get a day off for every two nights spent consecutively in travel as well as overtime at double the rate for work done on holidays. Travelling allowance is a common practice among organization in which employees are transferred to other cities. Marketing personnel receive it as a part of their pay packet.

## XII. Vacation Allowance

*332.* Vacation allowances are granted in a number of industries. The principal beneficiaries are managers and officers and the benefit is rarely extended to workers. In one case the tribunal upheld the demand of workers that they too should receive a vacation allowance at par with the officers. But the Supreme Court found the tribunal to be in serious error, because it had not considered the other allowances and benefits allowed to workers. The total wage packets of various categories of employees and the nature of their duties must be considered in deciding whether parity in benefits can be established in law. This could, of course, be done, as in the refineries, on the basis of a collective agreement, but not through adjudication replying solely on the basis of the financial ability to pay of the company.

## XIII. Housing Accommodation and House Rent Allowance

*333.* The need for housing accommodation is widely felt. The government owned companies have taken this responsibility seriously, though they too have not been able to provide housing to everyone. In the private sector it is more common to pay a house rent allowance than to provide housing accommodation. Where industrial housing is provided, the rents charged are usually low and there is an element of subsidy provided by the company. In one case, the government raised the status of Vishakhapatnam as a group 'A' city. The staff of a bank demanded additional benefits, like house accommodation and house rent allowance. Several banks extended these benefits, but not the Andhra Bank, which referred to several subsisting awards and the bipartite settlement, and declined the demand. It was also running into huge losses. Protracted conciliation proceeding failed to resolve the dispute and it was refrred to the industrial tribunal. The tribunal gave the award in favour of bank staff on finding that the State government and other banks were paying 20 per cent HRA subject to a maximum of Rs 1000. The Andhra Bank was asked to do the same. The High Court found no infirmity in the award and confirmed it. The bank appealed to the Supreme Court. It held that both the tribunal and the High Court have ignored the vital aspect of the matter, viz. the awards and settlements and their effect in determining the *inter se* rights and obligations. The High Court's judgment was set aside and tribunal was asked for a fresh decision. It had already take more than 25 years, so the Court asked the tribunal to take a decision within six months.[231]

## XIV. Retirement Allowance

*334.* In a settlement between the management and workers, provisions were made for gratuity and retirement allowance. Employees were demanding that any person who claimed retirement allowance was entitled to it, whether or not he satisfied the conditions of eligibility. They also demanded payment of retirement allowance on the basis of average rate of dearness allowance paid during the preceding 12 months prior to May 1989. The company had reserved its discretion to grant proportionate retirement allowance in certain specified circumstances, particularly to those who had completed more than 20 years in service but had not completed 30 years in service. The Court upheld the Board's right to exercise discretion. It was not a right of the employees. It also decided that the employees were not entitled as of right to claim annual review of the retirement allowance. It was a matter entirely within the discretion of the Board.[232]

## XV. Consolidated Pay

*335.* The custom of paying consolidated pay in offices and shops is still quite common. In these establishments no DA is paid though the pay structure may be revised as often as necessary in accordance with the provisions of the bipartite agreements between the management and the employees. This system provides for a higher basic pay structure with corresponding higher benefits under the Provident Fund Schemes, the HRA and any other factors connected with the basic salary/wage. The system protects the employer from the liability of unplanned increases in pay bill on account of CPI indexed dearness allowances.

231. LLJ, 2008, Vol. 2, *Andhra Bank, Vishakhapatnam* vs. *I.T-cum- Labour Court and Another*, Supreme Court of India, pp. 957–959.
232. LLJ, Vol. 1, 1995, *General Manager, EID Parry (India) Ltd., Ranipat* v. *Presiding Officer, Labour Court and Others*, High Court of Madras, pp. 757–769.

## XVI. Subsistence Allowance

*336.* The Model Standing Orders provide by payment of subsistence allowance to a workman who is suspended from service pending the completion of domestic enquiry. In Tamil Nadu it was discovered that many industrial establishments had not secured the revision of the CSO and did not provide for payment of this allowance. As a remedial measure, the Tamil Nadu Payment of Subsistence Allowance Act, 1981 was enacted. It provides for the employer to pay 50 percent of the wages for the first 90 days, 75 per cent if it does not exceeds 180 days and thereafter to full pay of the period of suspension. The term used is 'employee', though it corresponds to the definition of 'workman'. By comparison, the Tamil Nadu Cooperative Societies Act, 1983, provides for suspension allowance at 25 per cent only. In a case, an officer of a Primary Cooperative Bank was suspended from service for misconduct. He was paid 25 per cent of his pay as subsistence allowance. He applied for subsistence allowance under the TN Payment of Subsistence Allowance Act, which was rejected on the ground that he was not an 'employee' under the Act. He appealed to the High Court, where the single judge upheld the view that he was not an 'employee', but an officer.[233] In another case, it was found that the employee's right to this allowance was not granted and in the end refused, because he was removed from service. The High Court held that though terminated from service, the employee had the right to get subsistence allowance, as per the Act for the period of suspension.[234]

*337.* An upper division clerk of the Public Works Department was suspended from service and a suspension allowance was provided for in the order. He was simultaneously transferred to another city, where he did not join duty. There were several procedural lapses, as a result of which he collected suspension allowance for the period, 4 September 1982 to 20 September 1982 in January 1985 and thereafter until September 1984, paid in February 1987. The State Administrative Tribunal which considered his application held that he himself was responsible for the delayed payment, not the PWD or the Chief Engineer, as the Appellate Authority. On appeal, the division bench of the High Court held that non-payment of subsistence allowance amounted to violation of principles of natural justice. Until it was paid in proper time, the delinquent employee could not be faulted for not being able to defend himself in the departmental enquiry. The Court set aside the tribunal's order as well as the order terminating his service. He was reinstated in service. Earlier, in another case the Apex Court had held that the payment of subsistence allowance in accordance with the rules was not a bounty. It was right. In this case the Court decided that the High Court committed a serious error in holding that the question of prejudice was not relevant. It was not established that communication in relation to subsistence allowance was in fact served on him and despite repeated

---

233. LLJ, 2006, Vol. 2, *Management of Thekkalur Primary Coop. Bank (K-2019) represented by its President* v. *Asstt. Commissioner of labour, Coimbatore and others,* High Court of Madras, pp. 610–615.

234. LLJ, 2006, Vol. 2, *Jeychandran K.* v. *Special officer, V. Kurumtapatti Agricultural Coop. Bank and Others,* High Court of Madras, pp. 609–610.

requests, the allowance could not be paid. The High Court was required to arrive at a correct finding of fact in order to base the right question for arriving at a right decision. The judgment was set aside and the matter was remitted back to the High Court for consideration afresh. The state was directed to pay Rs 50,000 to the respondent by way of litigation costs. The case had already taken 20 years.[235]

235. LLJ, 2008, Vol. 2, *State Government of M.P. and Others* v. *Shankar Lal,* Supreme Court of India, pp. 289–293.

# Chapter 3. Bonus and Related Payments

## §1. Bonus as a Justifiable Right

*338.* The transformation of bonus from an ex gratia payment into a legal right occurred as a result of adjudication of a dispute in 1946. The Bombay Industrial Court justified bonus when:

- wages fell short of the living standard; and
- the huge profits of industry were due to the contribution made by workers through increased production.

The same court in 1948 in another bonus dispute in the cotton textile industry devised a formula for determining bonus after deducting prior charges. These were:

- depreciation;
- bonus paid to workmen;
- bonus paid to clerks and other staff;
- taxes; and
- reserves.

*339.* The balance may be used for declaring dividends. This principle underwent two judicial modifications;first in 1949 and the second in 1952. In 1949 the Industrial Court exempted the loss-making textile mills from any liability to pay bonus thereby converting it into a profit-sharing bonus. In 1952 the Labour Appellate Tribunal modified the concept of 'prior charges' to include a fair return on paid-up capital (normally at 6 per cent), and reserves employed as working capital, (at 2 per cent). The original LAT formula was modified in subsequent awards and had the effect of lowering the proportion of surplus allocated to workers. In 1960 the Supreme Court decided that, where no evidence as regards the relevant factors has been adduced, the distribution of surplus between the employer and the workers should be approximately equal. This led to padding of debit entries in the profit and loss account. Taking note of these practices the Supreme Court directed that:

- debit entries that were wholly unrelated to the determination of trading profits should be ignored; and
- income to which worker have not contributed, viz. book profits on account of revaluation of assets should also be excluded.

Now the prior charges were:

- depreciation;
- income tax that was considered payable;
- returns on paid-up capital and reserves; and
- expenditure for replacement and modernization, but not including expansion or addition to the machinery.

However, the formula failed to satisfy either party and fresh disputes continued to arise. These related to the determination of allocable surplus, the share of workers as well as broader questions, such as, where several undertakings form part of a company, of which some made profits and other not, can workers employed in the loss-making units claim bonus or not? On these questions conflicting judgments were given. Moreover, the purpose of the LAT formula was judicially ascertained and this gave rise to fresh disputes.

## §2. The Bonus Commission

*340.* In view of the Supreme Court's judgments the government raised the subject of appointing a Tripartite Bonus Commission before the SLC in 1960 and secured its approval. A Commission was appointed in December 1961 with wide terms of reference, and it reported in 1964. Workers' representatives argued within the Commission as well as outside to have bonus declared as a deferred wage. But, despite pleadings, the Commission only said that bonus was a share in the prosperity of the establishment, and neither accepted nor rejected the theory of 'deferred wage'. It also accepted the LAT formula in all essential respects thereby establishing a firm connection with profits. On the other hand, the Commission did not accept the doctrine that bonus was a means of bridging the gap between the actual and living wages. Instead, the Commission advanced the doctrine that bonus could only become the means for achieving a lower target viz. the need based minimum wage when profits exceeded a certain base. On the controversial issue of treating rehabilitation as a prior charge, the Commission excluded it along with a number of accounting malpractices; thus a major source of arbitrariness in the calculation of allocable surplus was removed, The Commission also established the share of workers and employers in the ratio of 60:40. The distinction between wages and dearness allowance was abolished. The Commission fixed the minimum bonus at 4 per cent of the annual wage and a maximum at 20 per cent subject to certain conditions and procedures. The principles of 'set-on' and 'set-off' were devised to cope with situations when there were either no profits or when they were in excess.

## §3. The Payment of Bonus Act

*341.* The Payment of Bonus Act, 1965 modified the LAT formula to provide for;

- a minimum as well as a maximum bonus;
- a set-on and a set-off to reinforce the provisions on the minimum and maximum; and
- elimination of rehabilitation as a prior charge.

The Act is applicable to every factory or establishment employing 20 or more persons on any day in an accounting year. However, the term 'bonus' is not defined in the Act. It has been amended a number of times in respect of provisions on accounting year, wages/salary level for determining eligibility to bonus, linking bonus to production and productivity; and to provide for employers and workers to enter into an agreement for payment of bonus on a formula different from the Act, etc. The Act is a complete code in respect of the right to bonus, but not to remedies.

*342.* Sections 5 and 6 lay down the method of calculating the available surplus, depreciation and development rebate/allowance, as under the Income Tax Act, and direct taxed as prior charges. Other heads of expenses are also included in the term 'prior charges'. These are interest on capital employed of different description and partners' remuneration in case of partnership firms, The balance is the available surplus.

*343.* Form A (Rule 4A), specifies the method of computation of the allocable surplus. This is derived, first by calculating gross profit as per the First, the Second and the Third Schedules of the Act, then deducting from it the total of sums deductible under various heads. The difference between the two is called the available surplus for the accounting year The allocable surplus is for distribution among the employees as bonus, subject to a minimum of Rs 100 or 8.33 per cent, whichever is higher, and a maximum of 20 per cent of the annual wage/salary. However, the minimum must be paid whether or not the employer has any allocable surplus. If this fraction exceeds the maximum, the excess, subject to a limit of 20 per cent of salary/wage, shall be carried forward for being set-on in the succeeding accounting year and so on, up to and inclusive of the fourth accounting year for the payment of bonus. Likewise, if there is a deficiency in respect of minimum bonus, the deficiency may be carried forward to be set off in the next four years.

*344.* The annual wage/salary is to be adjusted for the number of days worked in the year. A worker to be eligible must have worked for a minimum of 30 days in the year. But if an employee, for no fault of his and involuntarily, is prevented from working in the establishment for the prescribed number of days, he does not lose eligibility to bonus. Illegal dismissal orders cannot deprive workers of their eligibility. In a dispute three issues were raised. It travelled up to the Supreme Court of India and recommended back to the High Court for review and disposal in the lights of its findings. These pertained to:

- the applicability of Section 33(c) (2)of the ID Act;
- the jurisdiction of the Labour Court to decide the matter; and
- applicability of the Bonus Act to the daily wagers.

The dispute arose from a claim made by daily wage workers of the HP State Electricity Board and HP State Forest Corporation and similar public sector undertakings for bonus which was declined on various grounds.

*345.* The workers approached the Labour Court asking for computation of bonus under Section 33(c)(2) of the ID Act and secured a favourable verdict. This led to an appeal to the High Court on the grounds that daily wage earners could not get bonus; that the Labour Court lacked jurisdiction and its award was illegal' and that Section 33(c)(2) of the ID Act was not applicable to the determination and payment of bonus. Only the employees drawing monthly salaries/wages were eligible. Section 33(c)(2) relates to a pre-existing right as an execution application and under it the claim to bonus could not be made. Moreover, there was no claim for interest to be paid, yet it was decided that interest was payable at 12 per cent. The Apex Court upheld the High Court on the applicability of Section 33(c)(2) to the issue. But the Labour Court could not have admitted the dispute; it should have been referred to the Industrial Tribunal as the competent court for bonus. On remand, the High Court affirmed the maintainability of Section 33(c)(2) of ID Act. Since the dispute, the Labour Court was notified as the Industrial Tribunal. Under the ID Act, only the latter can adjudicate bonus disputes. The Court also upheld the claim of daily wage earners who had worked for 30 days in a year for entitlement to bonus.[236]

*346.* The provision pertaining to the wage/salary of the eligible employees has been gradually raised. The Act also provides for the computation of the number of working days under Section 14. An employee is deemed to have worked on days on which he was laid off under an agreement, or under the standing orders, or under any other law, and when he has been on leave with pay, or when the absence was due to a temporary disablement caused by an accident during the course of employment, and when she is on maternity leave. Section 14 is exhaustive and not merely illustrative. Subsistence allowance cannot be considered as wages and no bonus is payable on it. First, the employee does not work during the period of suspension and secondly, it is not wages for work done.[237]

*347.* An employee who has been dismissed from service on grounds of:

- fraud;
- riotous or violent behavior while on the premises of the establishment; and
- theft, misappropriation or sabotage of any property is disqualified from receiving bonus, notwithstanding anything contained is this Act.

The Section 9 deals with the disqualification and it is in stringent terms. It contains a total disqualification for bonus which may have accrued but has not been paid. The disqualification is not limited to the accounting year, as is the case with Section 18, and has an overriding effect. This is not so with Section 18, by which the financial loss resulting from the employee's misconduct can be deducted from the bonus payable. Bonus carries with it the obligation of good behaviour which helps in sustaining the industry. However, if the employee receives excess amount by way of bonus, not due to any misrepresentation by him, it cannot be legally deducted from the bonus due and payable in subsequent years. The employer was required to pay the sum deducted on account of excess payment. The order of the Labour Court to

236. LLJ, January 2011, *Himachal Pradesh State Electricity Board and Others* v. *Krishan Dutt,* High Court of Himachal Pradesh, pp. 115–119 and LLJ, 2008, Vol. 2, *HP State Electricity Board and Another,* v. *Ranjeet Singh and Others*, Supreme Court of India, pp. 629–632.
237. LLJ, 2008, Vol. 2, *Deccan Merchant Corporation Bank Ltd* v. *Avdhoot Marutirao Rane and Another,* High Court of Bombay, pp. 40–41.

this effect was challenged in the High Court, but failed. The petition was dismissed.[238]

*348.* The Payment of Bonus Act, Section 20, specifies that only those establishments in the public sector which sell goods or render services in competition with the private sector and whose income from these activities is not less than 20 per cent of their gross income in the accounting year are liable to pay bonus under the Act. All other public sector establishments are excluded from the purview of the Act. In a case pertaining to Broadcasting Corporation of India, Chennai, a claim on bonus was raised by casual labourers employed in Prasar Bharti, to be paid under Section 33c(2) of the Act. The Labour Court allowed the claim. This led to a writ petition in the High Court. The Court held that though the casual labourers were workmen under the ID Act, they did not automatically come within the purview of the Bonus Act. Prasar Bharti functioned under the authority of the central government and it was not covered by the Bonus Act, Section 32(4)(iv). The claim for bonus rested on the fact that they had worked for more than 30 days in a year from 1995 to October 2000. Moreover, the Department, had paid bonus of 8.3 per cent to other employees, but denied it to them. It was a commercial establishment. The plea failed on both courts. Section 33c(2) was not applicable to the determination of bonus. The order of the Labour Court was set aside.[239]

*349.* In another case the controller of a private company which had been brought under the control of the government, under the Industries (Development and Regulation) Act, 1951, sought exemption under this provision. But the Supreme Court ruled against it on the ground that the company continued to be governed by the Companies Act, and its business had not changed, so a mere change in management did not change its character. In yet another case persons who had been appointed on daily wages but had worked continuously for more than six months and denied bonus, as per the state government circular, were held to be entitled to the minimum ad hoc bonus declared for the employees.[240]

*350.* A new Section 31A provides for employers and employees to reach agreements or settlements for the payment of an annual bonus linked with production or productivity in lieu of one based on profit, subject to the condition that no such agreements can deprive the employees of their right to the minimum bonus of 8.33 per cent as provided in Section 10. Furthermore, under Section 31A, employees cannot get more than 20 per cent of their annual salary as bonus. Even public sector establishments, which are debarred from paying the statutory bonus based on profits, can consider paying bonus based on production and productivity, as settled between the management and the union concerned.

---

238. LLJ, September 2010, *Sahkari Ganna Vikas Samiti Ltd Hardwar* v. *Dy. Labour Commissioner, Dehradun and Others*, High Court of Uttarakhand, pp. 657–659.
239. LLJ, August 2010, *Management, Broadcasting Corp. of India, Chennai* v. *Presiding Officer, Central Government Labour Court, Chennai and Another*, High Court of Madras, pp. 541–544.
240. LLJ, Vol. 1, 1993, *Lokesh Kumar Pareek and Another* v. *State of Rajasthan and Another*, High Court of Rajasthan, pp.1219–1221.

*351.* Under Section 36, the government, having regard to the financial position and other relevant circumstances, can exempt any establishment or any class of establishment from all or any of the provisions of the Act for such periods as it deems necessary. The power granted by this section is of a quasi-judicial nature; it is a conditional legislation which must be exercised in the light of principles laid down in it. This section was challenged on the ground that it delegated the authority of parliament to the government, and it was void. But the plea fell. Under this section the government does not have absolute discretion to grant exemption or refuse it. It must give reasons for coming to any conclusion in respect of any case and these should form part of the official notification. In one case, the state government suspended the operation of all the provisions of the Act with the intention of containing the erosion of capital, in public interest, for the year 1990-91 onwards until the public sector undertaking returned to the condition of having wiped out all accumulated losses and provided for its bad and non-performing assets. This was found to be a case of non-application of mind, etc., and the order was quashed. Suspension of an Act of Parliament by the executive is not permissible. If an employer proves that losses were being suffered for several years continuously and the entire capital had been wiped out, the state government cannot refuse to grant exemption under Section 36. But the mere fact that recurring losses have been suffered is not a sufficient ground to warrant the application of this provision.[241]

*352.* In a case the Pondicherry Housing Board, set up under the PHB Act, 1973 sought exemption under Section 32 of the Bonus Act from the liability to pay bonus to its employees. The section provides that nothing in the Act shall apply to 'institutions (including hospitals, chambers of commerce and social welfare institutions) established not for the sake of profit.' It had also applied for exemption under Section 36 of the Bonus Act but without any success. The Housing Board took the plea that it did not run its business on commercial lines; its main business was to provide for the execution of housing schemes, not to earn profit. Moreover, the unions should have raised an industrial dispute under the ID Act, rather than approach the High Court. The Court held that as decided by the Apex Court in similar cases, the Housing Board was liable to pay the statutory minimum bonus of 8.33 per cent. There was no necessity to raise an industrial dispute regarding the quantum of bonus payable to employees. Any ex gratia gift of bonus paid can be adjusted against the statutory minimum bonus. If the employees want something more, the only remedy is to raise an industrial dispute in terms of Section 22 of the Bonus Act.[242]

*353.* The Bonus Act is applicable to all factories and establishment in which on any day, twenty or more persons are employed. Under Section 1(3b) the appropriate government can extend the application of this Act to any establishment or class of establishments in which fewer than 20 persons are employed on any day provided

241. LLJ, Vol. 1, 2001, *Andhra Pradesh State Forest Development Corporation Ltd Employees' Union* v. *Government of Andhra Pradesh, Environment, Forests, Science and Technology Dept. and Another*, High Court of Andhra Pradesh, pp. 1002–1013.

242. LLJ, 2009, Vol. 4, *Pondicherry Housing Board Employees Union and Another* v. *Government of Pondicherry and Another*, High Court of Madras, pp. 359–364.

this number is in no case less than 10. In Kerala the Act has been notified for shops and commercial establishment employing 10 or more persons. This raised the question of applicability of the Act and the claim of employees to bonus in smaller establishments. The Supreme Court has held that it is not open for the tribunals to adjudicate on questions of bonus as payable under the Act, if the establishments do not lie within its scope. In one case the employer claimed that he employed less than 10 persons but the tribunal found that he did employ more than 10 persons. However, the employer did not produce the profit and loss account and the balance sheet despite being pressed to do so. In the absence of financial statements bonus could not be calculated as per the Act. The tribunal gave the award of 20 per cent of bonus for the disputed years. This was the subject of a petition to the High Court. The Court directed that the accounts be produced before the tribunal in order to ascertain the allocable surplus and awarded a cost of Rs 10,000 to be paid by the employer within two months; further, the tribunal should re-adjudicate the matter. The award of 20 per cent bonus was set aside since the allocable surplus was not found out. But if the accounts were not submitted to the tribunal within two months, the award would stand confirmed.[243]

*354.* Employees of a government establishment were aggrieved that the one month's salary paid as ex gratia in lieu of bonus paid from 1984-85 to November 1993 was stopped. They filed a writ petition for relief which was allowed and the same was upheld in the writ appeal. The establishment appealed to the Apex Court and it was allowed. It was run by the Andhra Pradesh government to supply nutritious food to schools and pre-school children, pregnant women and lactating mothers and such other beneficiaries as the government may decide as per its social welfare programmes. It was a non-profit establishment by an order of the Labour Commissioner in January 1983 and the factory producing foods was held to be outside the purview of the Bonus Act. Yet, in November 1984, as per the government policy, the factory made an ex gratia payment in lieu of the bonus. This was formalized as an annual payment in January 1986, as applicable to other public sector undertakings. In November 1993, as per the government circular on the subject, the ex gratia payment was stopped until further orders. This led to a writ petition to the High Court, and the single judge admitted it turning down the plea of the establishment that the Act did not apply to it. He also found that the stand that it was working without the profit motive was factually wrong. The division bench upheld the single judge. The plea taken before the Apex Court was that the High Court should not have entertained the writ petition in view of Section 22 of the Act which provided for an industrial dispute to be raised under the ID Act. The Apex Court agreed that since disputed questions of facts were involved, it was wrong to admit the petition. The questions were passed on by the Supreme Court and remanded to the state government to be decided by the appropriate tribunal. On merits no opinion was expressed.[244]

---

243. LLJ, Vol. 1, 2001, *N.S. Hospital and Maternity Home, Kollam* v. *The Industrial, Tribunal, Kollam and Another*, High Court of Kerala, pp. 60–62.
244. LLJ, 2006, Vol. 3, *A.P Foods* v. *S. Samuel and others*, Supreme Court of India, pp. 18–22.

*355.* In another case the Industrial Tribunal directed the state owned APSRTC to pay the difference between the ex gratia payable in accordance with the amended payment of Bonus Act, 1995 and the actual paid in accordance with the pre-amended Act. The Corporation paid the ex gratia pursuant to the settlement dated 15 June 1966 and the ex gratia payment rose with every amendment to the Act, raising the wage limit and the minimum payable. In addition the Corporation agreed to pay Rs 2000 as Transport Minister's goodwill amount for the years 1994-95 and 1995-96 to each employee whose pay exceeded the statutory limit of Rs 3500 per month. However, additional ex gratia was not paid for 1993-94 and the union served a strike notice in March 1997. The dispute was referred to the industrial tribunal. A question referred to was whether the minority union could raise a dispute, since a settlement with the majority union was signed. The tribunal found that the union represented between 7,000–8,000 workers in the state and so could raise a dispute, particularly on 21 October,1997 because the issue in question was left to be decided later, as per the award of the tribunal. It held that there was no meaning in not paying the ex gratia for 1993-94 as per the amended Act. This led to a writ petition to the High Court. The Court held that a minority union was competent to rise an industrial dispute. On the question whether the tribunal had exceeded the terms of reference, the Court held that the tribunal had no right to travel outside the reference, and adjudicate on matters not referred to it. Where a tribunal lacks jurisdiction to entertain any matter, neither acquiescence nor consent of the parties can confer jurisdiction on it. The Court said that the settlement signed in June 1966 was still in force as it was not duly terminated and replaced by another settlement or an award. According to it, the Corporation agreed to pay 4 per cent as ex gratia to all employees, other than casual employees, every year and the settlement of March 1997 had not given it a go-by. It has become a condition of service. The tribunal should not have examined the profitability of the Corporation, because it was beyond the scope of reference. The award was set aside to a limited extent and sent back on remand to examine other matters, particularly Section 9A of the ID Act in relation to the conditions of service.[245]

*356.* In the case of *Indian Oil Corp. (Assam Div.)* a dispute was raised on the payability of bonus for 1975 in terms of the amendment to the Bonus Act on 25 September 1975. The reference was made in 1978. The workmen claimed that bonus was paid from 1947 to 1974. It could not be denied in 1975 irrespective of the amendment to the Act. The tribunal found that the workers had made claim to bonus right from 1944, 1945 and 1946 and 1947 which was referred to the industrial tribunal. The tribunal by its a ward in 1949 rejected the claim for the years 1944, 1945 and 1946, but for 1947 it was payable as one month's salary. The claim was adjudicated on several occasions and bonus was payable as a link to basic pay of the workmen. The same principle was incorporated in several settlements including for the years, 1971, 1972, 1973 and, by an agreement, for 1974. The vital difference with the scheme of the Bonus Act was that it was linked to profit, not basic pay. For the year 1975 the tribunal found that there was no allocable surplus, so no bonus

245. LLJ, 2009, Vol. 1, *Management of APSRTC* v. *Workmen of the APSRTC and Another*, High Court of Andhra Pradesh, pp. 439–456.

was payable under the amended Act. Nevertheless, they were entitled to the minimum bonus at 4 per cent of the wage earned for the accounting year and the amount will carry an interest of 6 per cent till the date of payment. The Company appealed against the award. The workmen chose the amount will carry an interest of 6 per cent until the date of payment. The Company appealed against the award. The workmen not to appear and the Court decided to appoint a lawyer as the *amicus curiae* to represent and defend them. The amended Act provided for payment of 4 per cent as bonus for the year 1974, whether or not there was any allocable surplus, but was silent for the year 1975. According to the Court, 'The intention of the legislation by way of amendment is clear that no minimum bonus is payable in respect of subsequent accounting years, if there is no allocable surplus in these accounting years.' It follows that if there is no allocable surplus, the employer is not under any statutory obligation to pay the bonus at 4 per cent. In the result the tribunal's award was set aside. The employees were not entitled to any bonus at 4 per cent under the Bonus Act. In view of the grievances of workers, the Act was amended again in 1977 and the minimum bonus of 8.33 per cent for the year 1976 and onwards was provided. This case was decided in December 2006.[246]

*357.* The head load workers of the godowns of Kerals State Civil Supplies Corporation won the right to bonus in an award given by the industrial tribunal. On appeal to the High Court made by the Corporation the single judge upheld the award on reading in it that the Corporation, the appellant, was the employer of headload workers. The Division Bench which heard the writ petition noticed that the tribunal had found that the headload workers were engaged not only by the appellants but also by others in the same period. The practice was that they were engaged only when work was available at the depot and the payment was made to one of the headload workers who shared it with the others. The same workers had worked for others during the relevant time. Whenever the workers were not available, goods were sent to other depots for unloading there. They were casual workers on a rate contract and engaged on this basis. The tribunal had held that every employer under whom a worker had worked for not less than 30 days in a year was responsible to pay bonus to such employees. The bench found it anomalous on grounds of wages earned for eligibility to bonus. The correct position is that for eligibility to bonus, an employee should be under the same employer on an exclusive basis for 30 days in a year, therefore price-rate employment on a non-exclusive basis does not meet the requirement for bonus under the Act. The tribunal has to decide a dispute on statutory considerations, not for maintaining sound industrial relations. The appellants did not have the liability to pay the bonus. The writ petition was allowed by vacating the impugned award of the tribunal.[247]

*358.* In one case the organization paid the statutory minimum bonus at the rate of 8.33 per cent of the wages to its industrial employees but to the federation

246. LLJ, 2007, Vol. 2, *Indian Oil Corporation* v. *Presiding Officer, Central Government Industrial Tribunal and Others*, High Court of Gauhati, pp. 597–603.
247. LLJ, 2007, Vol. 2, *Kerala State Civil Supplies Corporation* v. *Industrial Tribunal*, High Court of Kerala, pp. 884–887.

employees it paid 20 percent. The employees' association contested this policy on the grounds of discrimination for which there was no justification. The Supreme Court agreed with the petitioners and held that all employees who were entitled to the payment of bonus under the Act were a class by themselves and there could not be discrimination within the class.[248]

*359.* A workman was dismissed from service but was ordered to be reinstated with 90 percent back wages with retrospective effect from March 1976 and this was interpreted to mean that he was reinstated at Bombay, where he used to work. The company decided to reinstate him at Pune. This was set aside and the company was found to be engaged in unfair labour practices. His claim for bonus became an industrial dispute because, according to the company, he had not worked for the minimum period required under the Act and was not entitled to it. The Court held that when the workman was ordered to be reinstated, it meant that he had been restored to the original position; hence he would be deemed to be in continuous service. Accordingly, he was entitled to all his claims connected with employment, including the bonus, for the period of his involuntary and forced unemployment.[249]

*360.* A customary or pooja festival bonus paid over an unbroken period of nine years had ripened into a condition of service and into a claim for customary or traditional bonus on the occasion of the pooja festival. The management took the plea that statutory bonus would now take the place of the customary bonus. On appeal, the High Court found that the traditional bonus was not dependent upon earnings and profits. The Supreme Court held that the Bonus Act was confined to profit oriented bonus only. This Act cannot affect the rights and obligations belonging to a different world of claims and conditions not relevant to its provisions. Referring to Section 17 of the Act, the Court decided that the employer was entitled to deduct any customary bonus before calculating the statutory bonus.[250]

## §4. Productivity Bonus-related Issues

*361.* A production bonus is usually considered as a form of an incentive payment. It is unrelated to profits, and may have no connection even with basic wages. However, in the revised scheme of the Bonus Act, under Section 31A and Section 34, it is possible for the two parties to come to a settlement providing for a production bonus with a minimum as well as a maximum, the amounts being percentages of annual pay. Such a scheme of production bonus would be simultaneously enforceable under the ID Act, inasmuch as it is a collective agreement, as well as under the Bonus Act. Employees with whom there does not exist an agreement in respect of payment of productivity bonus cannot take advantage of Section 31A.

---

248. Supreme Court Cases, 1995, Supp. (3), *CFFP Employee's Association (AITUC) and Another* v. *Chairman and Managing Director and Others*, Supreme Court of India, pp. 685–686.

249. LLJ. Vol. 2, 1994, *Vittal Venkatesh and Others* v. *Patheja Forging and Auto Parts Manufacturers Pvt. Ltd* and Others, High Court of Bombay, pp. 1015–1021.

250. LLJ, Vol. 1, 1995, *Workmen of Kettlewell Bullen & Co. Ltd* v. *Kettlewell Bullen & Co. Ltd and Others*, Supreme Court of India, pp. 1201–1209.

*362.* A production bonus is distinct from basic wages, in the sense that whereas the latter are fixed and uniform for all workmen, the former varies with the quantity of work done and the productivity of each worker or group of workers. Production bonus or incentive bonus becomes part of wages under the Payment of Wages Act only when it forms part of the terms of employment or payable under any award or settlement. In the ID Act the expression 'wages' does not include bonus.

*363.* In one case the Company challenged the Industrial Tribunal's award to make payment of 19 per cent of wages as bonus on the basis of productivity. The company had offered to pay at the rate of 8.33 per cent, but this was not accepted by the workmen. The company had suffered a loss in 1988-89, so only the minimum bonus could be paid. There had been an earlier settlement which was considered to be still binding because it had not been terminated. The Court held that Section 31A made a special provision and created an exception to the general rule on the payment of bonus. There must be a settlement or agreement every year, if the bonus with productivity is based on the profit and loss account of the respective accounting year. But the settlement could not become the basis for a similar bonus for the year in question. Accordingly the tribunal's award was set aside and quashed.[251]

*364.* In one case the company reached a settlement with the union under Section 18(1) of the ID Act to pay 20 per cent of basic wages, dearness allowance, etc., as bonus in full and final settlement of all the claims made by the union for the year 1984 and the same was paid on the due date. In 1985 the wage ceiling in the Act was Rs 1,600 per month. But bonus was to be calculated as per the wage limit of Rs 750 per month. It was on these bases that the settlement was executed. In 1985 the Act was amended raising the eligibility limit to Rs 2,500 per month and the wage ceiling for calculating bonus to Rs 1600 and it was retrospectively applicable for 1984. Thereupon the union made a fresh demand for bonus in respect of the employees who now became eligible. This was rejected by the company and the matter was referred for adjudication. The award was given in 1992 and it accepted the union claim that the amended Act had created a right and this would override the executed settlement. This led to the writ petition by the Company, that a concluded contract could not be reopened. The Court, relying on Section 34 of the Act, held that the amended Act must have effect, because this section provides that notwithstanding anything inconsistent therewith contained in any law, award, agreement or settlement, bonus must be paid as per its provisions. Workers were entitled to more statutory bonus as per the Amended Act because it was deemed to be in force for 1984 retrospectively. But the union claim for recalculation of bonus at the maximum rate of 20 per cent was rejected, because the settlement had already closed the matter insofar as Sections 4 to 7, 10 to 15 and 18 of the Act were concerned. The said settlement was not arrived at with reference to these sections, but under Section

251. LLJ, Vol. 2, 1999, *S.G Pharmaceuticals* v. *Sarabhai Chemical Staff Association and Others*, High Court of Gujarat, pp. 436–441.

18(1) of the ID Act. The tribunal was asked to readjudicate the rate of bonus payable in the light of the amended provisions of the Act.[252]

## §5. Other Bonus-related Issues

*365.* In one case the dispute related to the scope of incentive bonus. The Punjab State Electricity Board devised an incentive scheme applicable only to the workers directly connected with the repairs of transformers and denied to those working in ministerial and drawing establishment sections. The issue was whether the latter class of workmen could claim the benefit on the ground that without their help the transformers could not be repaired. Their plea was supported by both the executive engineer and the superintending engineer. Their opinion was that the nature of the work and the duties performed by the ministerial drawing staff were part and parcel of the entire work carried out by the other employees as a unit. In fact under an earlier scheme they had been getting the same incentive bonus. The Court held that the position taken by the tribunal was correct, that though the clerical and subordinate staff did not directly produce goods like the manual workers, and this may be a reason for treating them somewhat differently in the matter of incentive bonus, yet they cannot be altogether kept out of its scope.[253]

*366.* The Act allows exempt status during the infancy period of five years. Though this period was not over, the workmen of a defence establishment claimed the bonus on the ground that it had earned income on a commission as the agent of a French company. The industrial tribunal gave the award in favour of workmen, and this led to the writ petition and counter petitions. Section 16 (various subsections) provides that bonus is payable only for the accounting year in which the goods are sold or service is rendered in which the employer derives profit. If any profit is earned by it not by either selling its goods or its services but otherwise, the profit is not earned by it qua the establishment and for this reason bonus would not be payable. The rendering of service should be with the contemplation of earning profit. The company acted as a commission agent during the period the commercial production had not started, and, once it started, the work as a commission agent stopped. This activity was never intended to be a permanent one. That being so, the liability to pay bonus, as claimed under Section 16(1-B), would not arise. Though bonus had already been paid, and it was recoverable, yet the Court directed that only 50 per cent of the amount paid be recovered from the workmen to whom any ex gratia payment in lieu of bonus would be payable in future.[254]

---

252. LLJ, Vol. 1, 2000, *Ashok Leyland Ltd Ennore* v. *Industrial Tribunal*, Madras and Another, High Court of Madras, pp. 1234–1247.
253. Factories Journal Reports, Vol. 89, Parts 12 and 13, 1996, *Punjab State Electricity Board and Another* v. *Industrial Tribunal and Another*, Punjab and Haryana High Court, pp. 381–385.
254. LLJ, Vol. 3, Supp., 1999, *Mishra Dhatu Nigam Ltd, Hyderabad* v. *Industrial Tribunal A.P. Hyderabad and Another,* High Court of Andhra Pradesh, pp. 1189–1194.

# Chapter 4. Social Security Benefits

## §1. Introduction

*367.* The statutory social security schemes are of two kinds:

(i) contributory; and
(ii) non-contributory.

Barring the medical benefits these schemes cover only workers and employees below the managerial level. Unemployment benefit as provided under the ID Act takes the form of lay-off and retrenchment compensation. This is discussed in the next chapter. All permanent and semi-permanent government employees and those of semi-government establishments fall outside the scope of social security legislation. They are covered by government schemes under which they receive either comparable or greater benefits. The consideration of a comprehensive social security for all employees in general has not reached the discussion stage yet. This reticence is also a reflection of the fact that the only social security convention of the ILO which India has ratified is on Equality of Treatment (Social Security) of 1962, which is essentially procedural in nature.

## §2. Workmen's Compensation

*368.* Workmen's compensation is provided under the Workmen's Compensation Act, 1923 as amended in 2009. Compensation is paid for accidents that lead to death or total or partial disablement for more than three days. The accident should hae occurred in the course of employment. Compensation is also payable for a number of occupational diseases which workers may contract in the course of employment. Compensation is payable if:

- injury has been caused to a workman by an accident;
- the accident has arisen in the course of employment; and
- the injury has resulted in death, or permanent or temporary, or total or partial disablement.

In the amended Act the word 'employee' is substituted for 'workman'. It is for the workman/employee to prove that the accident arose out of and in the course of employment. The existence of a contract of employment between the employer and the injured workman must also be established. However, in cases of petty workmen, documentary proof of such a contract is not necessary. The Supreme Court has held that in a proceeding under the Act, the provisions of the Code of Civil Procedure or the Evidence Act are not applicable. The Comissioner could lay down his own procedures for arriving at the truth and rely upon such documents which are produced before it.[255]

*369.* Ordinarily the employment of a person commences when he reaches the place of his duty and ceases when he leaves it. However, exceptions to this rule have been made in deciding cases of accidents which occur when the employee is proceeding to or returning from his place of duty. The following points have been considered in deciding such cases:

- whether at the time of the accident the employee was required to be at that place;
- whether he was there as an employee;
- whether the employer had directed the employee to be there;
- whether his presence at the place of the accident was incidental to his employment; and
- whether there was a proximate or even causal connection between his employment and the accident.

A helper workman who was in employment of the Road and Building Development of the state died in an accident and his heirs were awarded compensation. The fact which the Commissioner ignored was that the deceased did not figure in the list of names of employees who were on duty. Moreover, he was not a workman in the workshop or the logistic section, so he would not be required to travel with the vehicle in question for its delivery to the workshop. In any case it was a Sunday and an 'off duty' day for the deceased. He had boarded the vehicle on his own and without any request from any one. The inference that he was on duty was without any basis. The liability to pay compensation arose only if the accident and death occurred in the course of employment. This was not the case. So the question of paying compensation did not arise. The award was set aside.[256]

*370.* The law makes an important distinction between a contract of service and contract for service. The injured/deceased must be employed on a contract of service to be entitled to compensation. In a 'contract of service', the employer can not only order the employee on what is to be done but also how and in what manner it is to be done. In a 'contract for service', the employer can only require what is to be done, but not how it should be done. In the latter case the employee is under no obligation to obey each and every order. The agreement is only to get the desired work done. Under the former there is an agreement for personal labour. A contract of work or service must form the basis of contract of employment. A husband and wife team working together could not raise the claim for compensation under the Act, when the husband died in an accident while driving an insured vehicle, on the theory that the wife owned the tractor and lived separately from the husband and

255. LLJ, 2008, Vol. 3, *Om Prakash Batish* v. *Ranjit @ RanbirKaur and Others*, Supreme Court of India, pp. 599–603.

256. LLJ, November 2010, *State of Gujarat* v. *Fattu Fakru Bhuria and Other*, High Court of Gujarat, pp. 427–432.

the latter worked for the former, though without any contract of work between them. The award of compensation was set aside.[257]

*371.* Whether a workman was employed on the day of the accident, hence under a contract of service to his employer, is a question of fact which has to be determined by the Commissioner on the basis of evidence. Once a finding has been given the High Court cannot interfere, unless it is shown that the finding is perverse in any manner. Contractors employing labourers on a day-to-day basis sometimes deny the existence of employer–employee relationship and may not produce the wage and attendance register, though asked by the Commissioner to do so. In one case, the Commissioner reached an adverse inference against the contractor. The Commissioner recorded that on the day of the accident the deceased had been taken by the contractor on a scooter. The widow had given the evidence that her husband was employed as a labourer to build a temple in the village where he died of an electric shock. This was accepted by the High Court and the contractor (appellant) was ordered to pay the compensation.[258]

*372.* Under Section 3(I) it has to be established that there was some causal connection between the death of the workman and his employment. If a workman dies as a natural result of the disease from which he was suffering, or while suffering from the disease, as a result of wear and tear of the employment, no liability would be fixed upon the employer. But if the employment is a contributory cause or has accelerated the death, or if the death was due not only to the disease, but also the disease coupled with the employment, then it can be said that the death arose out of the employment and the employer would be liable. There must be a causal connection between the injury and the accident, and the accident and the work done in the course of employment. The onus is upon the applicant to show that it was the work and the resulting strain which contributed to or aggravated the injury. Further, if the evidence on records establishes a greater probability which satisfies a reasonable man that the work contributed to the causing of a personal injury, it would be enough for the workman to succeed, but the same would depend upon the facts of each case.[259]

*373.* A workman truck driver died due to a heart attack while driving the truck. Suddenly the deceased felt chest pain and became senseless on his seat. Another driver drove him to a hospital where he was declared dead on account of heart attack. The employer denied that the deceased was employed by him, or that he was getting any salary as claimed. It was pleaded that the death had taken place due to

257. LLJ, 2007, Vol. 2, *Gottumukkala Appala Narsimha Raju and Others,* v. *National Insurance Co. Ltd,* Supreme Court of India, pp. 531–536.
258. 2000, LLJ, Vol. 3, Supp., *Bisumal Nagraj Oswal (Jain)* v. *Kunda Ashok Shinde and Others*, High Court of Bombay, pp. 1382–1386.
259. LLJ, 2006, Vol. 3, *Jyothi Ademma* v. *Plant Engineer, Nellore*, Supreme Court of India, pp. 324-326. This case was cited in the case, LLJ, June 2010, *Ram Dev Puri* v. *Trishla Devi and Others,* High Court of Himachal Pradesh, pp. 652–567.

a heart attack, not as a result of an accident and therefore the petition was not maintainable under Section 22 of the Act. The crucial link between the causal connection of employment with death was not a matter of surmise or conjecture. In this case there was nothing on record to show that due to stress of the work, the deceased died. The Court agreed and the order passed by the Commissioner granting excessive compensation was set aside.[260]

*374.* In one case, an electrician and his son were engaged through a contractor by a bank to repair the signboard as the lights of the board failed. When he was checking the board there was a short circuit and he fell to the ground with burn injuries. He died in hospital. The Commissioner on recording the evidence decided that since the deceased died while attending to the work of the bank, compensation was payable in accordance with Section 4(1)(a) of the Act as amended in 2000. The manager of the bank denied engaging any one for repairing the signboard or instructing anyone to get the repairs done. The amended Act included in the definition of, 'workman', any person 'employed for the purpose of making, altering, repairing, ornamenting, finishing or otherwise adapting for use, transport or sale any article or part of an article in any premises wherein or within the precincts whereof twenty or more persons are employed.' The Court decided that though the employment of the deceased was of a casual nature but he was engaged for the purpose of employer's trade or business, he must be termed as a 'workman'. Accordingly, the challenge to the Commissioner's award failed and the appeal was dismissed.[261]

*375.* In another case, a workman died while demonstrating a tractor due to the tractor overturning. He worked for the dealer. He had no relation with the manufacturer of tractors. Yet the dealer was not asked to produce his accounts or to demonstrate that the deceased was not his employee. Instead the manufacturer was saddled with the liability, as the employer of the deceased. The conduct of the dealer was questionable leading to an adverse inference. There was no evidence to show the employer-employee relationship with the manufacturer. The Act provides for the definition of employer to include the term, 'managing agent', which covered the dealer as his representative for the purpose of his trade or business. As the principal, the manufacturer was liable initially to pay the claim, but in terms of Section 12(2) he was entitled to be indemnified by the dealer. The manufacturer was bound to satisfy the award with the right and recourse to indemnification by the dealer. The order was set aside. Instead a new order was passed.[262]

*376.* Whenever an injury/disease is suffered by a workman and it has arisen out of and in the course of employment, he becomes entitled to compensation even though his capacity to work remains unimpaired. The Act is not limited to physical disablement and extends to any reduction in earning capacity. Moreover, the loss of

---

260. LLJ, February 2011, *Oriental Insurance Co. Ltd* v. *Bimla Devi @ Bindu and Another*, High Court of Himachal Pradesh, pp. 457–462.
261. LLJ, September 2010, *Branch Manager, Oriental Bank of Commerce, Karimnagar,* v. *Shaik Madar and Others*, High Court of Andhra Pradesh, pp. 705–711.
262. LLJ, November 2010, *Mahindra Gujarat Tractor Ltd, Gujarat* v. *Shabana W/o Abdul Rauf Pathan and Others*, High Court of Bombay, pp. 445–448.

earning capacity may be determined by considering, first, the diminution or destruction of physical capacity and, second, its effect on the extent of disablement suffered by the workman in the performance of his duties. Even if there is no immediate loss of earning capacity as a result of partial disablement, the entitlement to compensation will not be affected because the workman's eligibility as an employee may be diminished or lost. Compensation for partial and total disablement is provided in Schedule I of the Act. Permanent partial disablement in cases of injury not specified in the Schedule should be assessed by a medical practitioner and he should state the percentage of earning capacity of the injured workman. In one case the doctor assessed the loss of earning capacity as ranging between 65-80 per cent. The High Court raised it to 100 per cent but without giving any reason for it. This was not maintained and the Commissioner's order was restored.[263]

*377.* In another case of partial disablility the injury was listed in the Schedule I and the rate of compensation at 11 per cent was provided in it. Instead the Authority awarded compensation of 25 per cent based on the doctor's assessment of loss of earning capacity. This was not permissible because the Authority could not substitute the doctor assessment for the listed injury. The Court reduced the awarded compensation from 25 per cent to 11 per cent.[264]

*378.* The responsibility for the payment of compensation rests with the principal employer. No compensation is payable if the accident is caused by the fault of the worker, e.g. due to the influence of drinks, drugs and wilful disobedience of an order, etc. Whenever an injury of the kind specifically mentioned in Schedule I is suffered, the worker concerned is instantly entitled to compensation prescribed by the schedule without any further investigations. The compensation payable has to be calculated in terms of the percentage of monthly wages linked to the age of the workman. Factors for working out the lump-sum equivalent of compensation in case of permanent disablement and death are given in Schedule IV. If the completed years of age on the last birthday of the workman immediately preceding the date on which the compensation fell due is not more than sixteen years, the factor applicable is 228.54, (the highest factor) and, if it is 65 years or more, the applicable factor is 99.37 (the lowest factor). By an amendment to the Act, in 2000, the minimum amount payable on death was increased from Rs 50,000 to Rs 80,000. The ceiling on eligible monthly wage was also raised from Rs 2,000 to Rs 4,000. These rates have been revised upwards in the amendment Act, 2009. The minimum is raised to Rs 120,000 for death and to Rs 140,000 rupees for permanent disability. The Act empowers the central government to enhance the minimum rates form time-to-time.[265]

263. LLJ, 2007, Vol. 1, *National Insurance Co. Ltd* v. *Mubasir Ahmed and Another*, Supreme Court of India, pp. 1035–1038.
264. LLJ. 2007, Vol. 1, *New India Assurance Co. Ltd Vishakhapatnam* v. *T. Narsimha Murthy Raju and Another*, High Court of Andhra Pradesh, pp. 925–927.
265. LLJ, July 2010, 'Statutes', pp. 13–16

*379.* In all cases of fatal accidents in respect of which the employer has admitted his liability, the full amount of compensation must be deposited with the Commissioner. It is the latter's responsibility to inform the dependents, who are defined in the law, and pay the amount. The Commissioner is the key authority under the Act for determining the nature of the accident or illness, the extent of disablement and the amount of compensation in all cases of partial disablement. All disputes under this Act are settled by the Commissioner. No court has any jurisdiction on any matter under this Act that requires to be settled, decided or dealt with by a Commissioner. A Commissioner may, if he thinks fit, submit any question of law for the decision of the High Court, and, if he does so, shall decide the question in conformity with such decision. The Commissioner is vested with the power of a civil court. He can exercise his discretion in a proper and sound manner.[266]

*380.* An employee was murdered in a communal clash while coming to the rice mill to attend to his work. Death had occurred before the commencement of his work and outside the work place, while the cause of death bore no relationship to the employment, and so it was contended that the widow was not entitled to compensation. However, the workman was wearing the mill uniform and he was coming to the rice mill. It was held that he had died in the course of employment. The test is that there must be a casual connection between the employment and the accident. If the employee has to be in a particular place, and while there he has to face a peril, and the accident is caused by reason of that peril, then a casual connection between the accident and the employment is established. Accordingly, the appellant was entitled to compensation. The doctrine of notional extension is applicable in such cases. The expression 'arising out of' has a wider connotation than 'caused by'.[267]

*381.* Applications can be made for the review of half-monthly payments payable due to partial disability by either the employer or the worker for legitimate reasons. Reviews can also be sought by either party if fraud or improper means are alleged to have been used and if there is a mistake or error apparent on the face of the record. The Commissioners have the added authority to invest the compensation money for the benefit of dependants in the approved manner. Any half monthly payment may, on review (under Section 6 of the Act), be continued, increased, decreased or ended; or if the accident has resulted in permanent disablement, be converted into a lump-sum to which he is entitled less any amount he has already received.

*382.* The reach of the Act has been extended by another state law providing for the determination of the justness of claim for social security payment by incorporating the WC Act within it. The Tamil Nadu Manual Workers (Regulation of

266. LLJ, September 2010, *Kolandhayee* v. *Deputy Commissioner of Labour (Commissioner for WC Act)*, High Court of Madras, pp. 768–773.
267. LLJ, Vol. 1, 2000, *Parle Products Ltd* v. *SubirMukerjee* (2000), High Court of Calcutta, pp. 864–868.

Employment and Conditions of Work) Act, 1982 provides for formulation of welfare schemes. The Tamil Nadu Manual Workers Social Security and Welfare Scheme 2001 provided for Group Personal Accident Relief. The main Act, Section 26, applies the provisions of the Workman's Compensation Act, 1923 to the manual workers in any scheduled employment. The workmen under the Tamil Nadu Act are deemed to be workmen under the WC Act, and the benefits under the Group Insurance Policy are applicable to the manual workers.[268]

## §3. Sickness Insurance

*383.* The ESI Scheme under the ESI Act, 1948, is the principal social security scheme with all India coverage to provide the insured employees with a wide range of benefits and medical care in case of sickness, injury or death. It provides for the granting of cash benefit to the employees in the recognized contingencies of sickness, maternity and employment injury. The Act is applicable to non-seasonal factories and certain other establishments which have been brought under its purview by notification. State governments have expanded the coverage of the Act to certain classes of shops and businesses to which the state level Shops and Establishments Acts apply. Thus even places where services are sold on a retail basis are deemed to be covered by the Act. The establishment of a company engaged in the business of clearing and forwarding of documents at the Custom House under licence was covered by the Act. An advertising agency is also a shop. In respect of factories the Act becomes applicable as soon as it fulfils the conditions laid down in Section 2(12) which defines the term, 'factory'. The term, 'shop', includes premises where any economic activity is carried on having a nexus with purchase or sale of goods. Where there was no notification extending the coverage to the diagnostic centers, the effort of the ESIC to bring them under its purview failed at the High Court. A diagnostic centre is not a factory.[269]

*384.* The Act does not apply to a factory or establishment belonging to the central or state government whose employees are otherwise in receipt of benefits substantially similar or superior to those provided under its scheme. The Act has empowered the appropriate government to exempt any factory or establishment, single or as a class, in any specified area from the operation of this Act for a period not exceeding one year at a time. Similarly, subject to such conditions as it may deem fit to impose, the government may exempt any person or class of persons employed in a factory or establishment from the operation of the Act. If such a contention is made in respect of an establishment, the government should not reject it without giving a hearing to the employer and the union. The ESIC is entitled to be heard (Section 89), and make a representation, before the government grants exemption to any factory or establishment or person, either single or as a class.

268. LLJ, 2007, Vol. 2, *Maheswari V* v. *Secretary, Tamil Nadu Manual Labour Social Security Board, Chennai and Others*, High Court of Madras, pp. 963–968.

269. LLJ, 2006, Vol. 2, *Vijaya Diagnostic Centre and Another* v. *Employees State Insurance Corp, Hyderabad*, High Court of Andhra Pradesh, pp. 443–448.

*385.* The ESI Act and the Workmen's Compensation Act are substitutes. Where the former is in force the latter ceases. The provisions of the WCA stand repealed qua the employers and the employees of the establishments which are governed by the ESI Act. Furthermore, Section 61 of the Act has created an absolute bar on an insured person on receiving any similar benefit admissible under any other enactment. But the bar does not apply in respect of a person not covered under the ESI Act and the insurance premium not paid. In a case the father of the deceased worker approached the Commissioner for Workmen's compensation, with the complaint that his son died in a fire in a chemical factory where he was a direct employee. The factory and the worker were covered by the ESIC and he had a registered number. Yet, though the ESIC was informed, there was no response and then he decided to approach the Commissioner. The case was referred to the Labour Court which decided in the deceased's favour on the ground that the ESIC insurance cover was post-death, and for this reason it had not responded. Perhaps inadvertently a wrong registration number was produced in the Court's proceedings and it declared that the deceased was not a member of the ESIC. At this the ESIC filed a writ petition assailing the order. Section 53 of the ESIC Act placed an absolute bar and no claim could be made under the Workmen's Compensation Act. There were allegations of collusion between the employer and the Corporation officials to have the deceased worker insured after his death. The correspondence between the ESIC and the employer showed that the dependents of the deceased worker would not be entitled to receive any compensation either from the Workmen's Compensation Act or any other person. The Court held that under the ESIC Act the employer is liable to pay the contribution on behalf of the insured, workers, whether the certificate was issued prior to his death or after. Fraud vitiates every thing and must be probed. The Commissioner's Order could not be sustained. It was set aside and the ESIC offered to entertain the application of the deceased's father. The dependants could also make a claim against the New India Assurance Co. on merits and in accordance with law.[270]

*386.* In a case the factory was registered with the ESIC, but the employer failed to deposit the ESIC contributions in respect of the employer and the employees. A worker was injured losing two fingers and suffering a fracture in his thumb while working on a lathe machine. He sent a notice to the employer but no compensation was paid. He then filed a claim petition before, the Commissioner, Workmen's Compensation Act. The employer took the plea that the worker never worked for them. The facts of the accident and receiving of notice were also denied. At the same time the employer said that the workers were covered under the ESIC Act, so the claim petition under the Workmen's Compensation Act of the injured worker was not maintainable. The ESIC said that the name of the injured workman was not in the list of labourers working in the factory. Moreover, on the day of the accident he was not insured. Therefore the ESIC was not liable to pay any compensation. The Commissioner granted compensation to be paid by the employer. He appealed against it

270. LLJ, 2007, Vol. 3, *Crescent Catalyst and Chemicals* v. *Vithal Shankar Bhoir and Others*, High Court of Bombay, pp. 147–154.

to the High Court. It should have been rejected. The liability was that of the Corporation. It could not absolve itself of the liability merely on the ground that the employer did not make any contribution. The Court read through the Act. The Court held that merely because. The Factory was registered with the Corporation it would not *ipso facto* impose a duty on it to grant medical benefits upon the employee. Until an unless the employer fulfils his part of legal duties under the Act, the Corporation cannot be held liable to pay the benefits under the Act. He has failed to discharge his legal duties under the Act and so the Corporation cannot be held liable to pay the benefits under the Act. He has failed to discharge his legal duties under the Act, however he wants to take advantage of Section 53 of the Act, which imposes a bar on the Workmen's Compensation Act. He cannot invoke this prohibition. Section 53 does not provide an escape route from the liability to pay compensation for an erring employer. The appeal had no force and was dismissed.[271]

*387.* The application of the ESI Act to home and casual workers has met with obstacles. In one case the High Court held that though the work may be done outside the factory premises, so long as there was sufficient control and supervision over their work they were covered by the term 'employee', and the employer was liable to pay the contribution. Supervision in such cases does not mean day-to-day supervision, but the right to accept or reject the work done by these employees. From this it is inferred that the relationship of master and servant exists between them, and accordingly, the 'home workers' are included in the definition of the term 'employee'. In another case, the tanning company covered under the ESI Act declined to admit any liability to pay contributions in respect of its temporary, casual and other employees. It had not sent the returns in form 6 in respect of various categories of employees who were covered under the Act. The order issued by the ESI Corporation for recovering the contributions payable by the company under the Revenue Recovery Act was held to be in due observance of the provisions of law and procedure contemplated in the statute.[272,273]

*388.* A company engaged in manufacturing rubber articles employed about 200 direct workers and paid contributions to the ESIC for several years. But the employees engaged by a contractor for cutting and polishing rubber items, outside the premises of the factory, were also deemed to be employees of the company through the contractor on whom the term 'immediate employer' was fastened. The ESI Court heard the case and decided it in favour of the Corporation. This led to an appeal to the High Court. The Court referring to the Supreme Court's judgment in *CESC Ltd and others* v. *Subhash Chandra Bose and others (1992),* held that 'to supervise' means to direct or oversee the performance of operation of an activity and to oversee it, watch over and direct it. It is the work under the eye and gaze of someone who can immediately direct a corrective and tender advise. Since these activities

271. LLJ, 2007, Vol. 3, *Allied Industries* v. *Mool Chand and Another*, High Court of Rajasthan, pp. 737–742.
272. LLJ, Vol. 2, 2000, *Prakash Match Industries* v. *Employee State Insurance Cooperation,* High Court of Madras, pp. 49–52.
273. LLJ, Vol. 2, 2000, *Shalimar Tanning Co.* v. *ESI Corporation and Another*, High Court of Madras, pp. 937–941.

were not done by the appellant company and these were done totally by the contractors, their workers, could not be viewed as indirectly employed by the company. Therefore the company was not liable to pay contributions to the ESIC. The appeal succeeded. The impugned order of the ESI Court Act was set aside and the demand notice of the Corporation quashed.[274]

*389.* In another case which reached the Apex Court, the appellants, the Hassan Cooperative Milk Producers' Society Union Ltd, were ordered by the Corporation to pay contributions in respect of workers employed by the contractors for transporting milk from the member societies to the federal milk society and return empty cans back to member societies. The appellants failed in their contest at the ESI Court and the High Court. The Apex Court held that the conditions for treating the workers of the contractor to be employees of the principal employer were that, either they should be employed in the premises of the factory or establishment or that they worked under the supervision of the employer. Neither of the two sets of conditions was fulfilled in the present case; consequently the impugned orders were set aside.[275]

*390.* The Act was amended in 1989 to remove the specific wage ceiling for eligibility and to provide for the central government to prescribe it from time to time. By this Amendment Act, the term 'family' includes a child who is receiving education up to the age of 21 years and infirm children without any age restriction in order to be eligible for medical benefits. The term 'insurable employment' has been amended to mean, an employment in a factory or establishment to which this Act applies. An important new provision has expanded the scope of the medical benefit in respect of an insured person who ceases to be in insurable employment on account of permanent disablement, subject to the payment of contribution and such other conditions as may be prescribed, until the age of superannuation, had he not sustained permanent disablement. Insured persons may remain eligible to receive medical benefit even in post-retirement years provided they continue to make their contributions. The Act was amended in 2010 and came into force on 1 June 2010. The list of beneficiaries has been expanded. In chapter VA the central government is empowered to frame a scheme for other beneficiaries and the members of their families for providing medical facilities in any hospital established by the Corporation in any area which is under utilized on payment of user charges. The user charges shall form part of the Employees State Insurance Fund. On coverage, the Amendment Act provides for the inclusion of accidents happening while commuting to the place of work and vice versa, provided the nexus between the circumstances, time and place 'where the accident occurred is established'.

*391.* The 1989 Amendment Act has imposed new restrictions. The disablement benefit cannot be commuted into a lump sum. No person can claim sickness benefit

274. LLJ, 2007, Vol. 3, *National India Rubber Works Ltd* v. *ESI Corporation through its Regional Director and Another*, High Court of Madhya Pradesh, pp. 1014–1017.

275. LLJ, June 2010, *Managing Director, Hassan Cooperative Milk Producers Society Union Ltd* v. *Asstt. Reg. Director, ESIC*, Supreme Court of India, pp. 860–869.

or disablement benefit for temporary disablement on any day on which he works or remains on leave or on a holiday in respect of which he receives wages, or on any day on which he is on strike. Furthermore, the Act has made more stringent provisions for securing repayment of benefits improperly received. To curb excessive litigation on the part of principal employers, the new Section 75(2-B) provides that no dispute in respect of any contribution or dues demanded by the ESI Corporation can be raised in the Employees Insurance Court unless 50 per cent of the amount due has been deposited with the Court. Under a new Section 45A in the Amendment Act 2010, it is provided that if an employer is not satisfied with the order under Section 45A, he may prefer an appeal to an appellate authority within 60 days of such order after depositing 25 per cent of the contribution so ordered or the contribution as per his own calculation, whichever is higher, with the Corporation. If the appeal succeeds, the Corporation shall refund such deposit with interest as may be specified in the regulation. Another change is that the designation, 'Inspector', is abolished and replaced by 'Social Security Officer'.

*392.* The innocuous term 'insured person', which is in addition to the term 'employee', means a person who is or was an employee in respect of whom contributions are or were payable and entitled to the benefits provided by the Act. In one case the Insurance Court and the High Court said that no contribution in respect of contract labour was leviable on the company. The Supreme Court disagreed and held that the two Courts had misconceived both the object of the Act and the purpose of the insurance scheme under it. The contribution levied on the employer, in respect of the employees engaged by him directly or through another agency, is for the benefit of all workmen in general who are covered by the Act and is irrespective of the fact whether any particular group of employees obtain the said benefit or not. There is no quid pro quo between the persons insured and the benefit provided. Moreover, the employer is liable to pay the contribution in respect of even those employees who have left employment and are unidentifiable. They were employees in the sense that they were employed for wages 'in connection with the work of a factory or establishment to which this Act applies'.[276]

*393.* In a case the issue was whether the security guards employed though an agency were 'employees' of the establishment and came within the purview of Section 1 (9) (ii) and (iii) of the Act. The establishment had 18 direct employees and two security guards and together the number added up to 20 and the establishment was covered by the Act and liable to pay contributions for all of them, but not if the security guards were excluded. The ESI Court held that they were not employees. On appeal the High Court held that, in an earlier case decided in 2002, the Apex Court had laid down the provisions of law on the security guards in cinema halls employed through an agency. They were employees within the meaning of Section 2 (9) of the Act. In this case the Agency had already paid its contribution to the Corporation on the two security guards. The only question was whether the establishment can avoid the entire liability in respect of the other 18 employees. The ESI

---

276. Supreme Court Cases, 1995, Supp. 3, Regional Director, *ESI Corporation* v. *Kerala Drugs and Pharmaceuticals Ltd and Others,* Supreme Court of India, pp. 148–149.

Court was required to examine the evidence. If contributions have been paid by the Agency, the establishment will be liable to pay for the other 18 employees.[277]

*394.* The disablement benefit is payable in two situations: first, where temporary disablement is sustained for not less than three days, excluding the day of the accident, and second, where permanent disablement, whether total or partial, is sustained. In both cases, periodical payment is made to the insured person, at such rates and for such periods and subject to such conditions as may be prescribed by the central government. The Act stipulates that an accident arising in the course of an insured person's employment shall be presumed, in the absence of evidence to the contrary, to have arisen out of that employment. The insured person's protection is maintained even if the accident happens in breach of regulations or instructions from the employer, etc., provided he was acting for the purpose of and in connection with the employer's trade or business. The dependant's benefit is payable if an insured person dies as a result of an accident. The beneficiaries may be his widow, sons or unmarried daughters and anyone listed in the definition of the term 'dependant' under Section 2(6-A), and the benefit may be at such rate, and for such period and subject to such conditions as may be prescribed by the central government. Finally, a provision is made for funeral benefit payable to the eldest surviving family member of the deceased, as funeral expenses, on terms which the central government may decide from time to time. An employee died of cardiac arrest at the mill gate 5 minutes before the commencement of the first shift. The Court held that his death was not caused by any injury in course of employment. Another person met with an accident while returning to his house. He too was held to be not covered.[278]

*395.* A night watchman was murdered in the premises of the cinema while on duty. The Corporation took the view that the death did not occur in the course of employment, that murder fell outside the definition of accident or employment injury, as per the Act. The deceased had the key to each room and they were found on the body of the deceased. The ESI Court held the murder as an employment injury and decided in favour of the claimants. The High Court held that the murder occurred in course of employment and dismissed the appeal. The ESI Court did not commit any error, as claimed in the appeal. The dependant benefits were payable by the ESIC.[279]

*396.* Section 40 of the Act imposes the liability to pay contributions, in the first instance, on the principal employer. Thereafter, he can deduct the employees contribution from their wages. The amount deducted is an entrustment. In respect of the amount deducted the employer is a trustee. But he cannot contend that since he had

277. LLJ. 2007, Vol. 3, *Regional Director, ESIC, Bangalore*, v. *Falcon Trading Association, Mangalore and Another*, High Court of Karnataka, pp. 81–82.

278. LLJ, Vol. 1, 2001, *Regional Director, Employees State Insurance Corporation* v. *Narsabai, w/o Naran Pantji*, High Court of Gujarat, pp. 1488–1490; LLJ, Vol. 1, 2000, *Regional Director, ESI Corporation and Another* v. *Ram Singh and Another*, High Court of Madhya Pradesh, pp. 791–793.

279. LLJ. August, 2010, *Regional Director, ESI Corporation* v. *Shakeenabibi Munarash Khan Pathan and Another*, High Court of Gujarat, pp. 571–584.

not deducted the employee's contributions, he cannot be made liable for the same. That would negate the object of deeming entrustment of Section 40(4). The questions to be decided were, (i) whether the employer could be asked to pay contributions even after closure of business? And (ii) whether he could escape liability on the ground that he had not deducted the contribution from wages? The Supreme Court held that on these grounds the scheme of ESIC would not be promoted and, indeed, it would perpetuate the mischief and the beneficial provisions of the Act would be set at naught. Once coverage is admitted and there is no dispute on the number of employees and wages paid to them, it is a statutory duty to remit contributions. Failure to pay attracts punishment under Section 85.

*397.* The 1989 Amendment Act plugged a loophole, by providing that the 'immediate employer' shall maintain a register of employees employed by or through him and submit the same to the principal employer in order that he may settle the amount payable in respect of these employees. The principal employer has been given the power to recover the amount so paid from the immediate employer, either by deduction from any amount payable to him or as a debt. In such cases the immediate employer is entitled to make the deductions from wages. However, under Section 42, no contribution shall be payable by or on behalf of employees whose daily wages, being below the level prescribed by the central government, are in the category of 'exempted employees'. The role of immediate employer comes in the way of direct nexus being established between the employees and the principal employer. For all practical purposes he is the employer in respect of the persons directly employed by him. The term 'employee' as defined under the Act includes such employees. They receive the benefits under the Act because they pass the test in respect of the contribution paid and their names appear in the returns filed with the ESI Corporation. It is necessary that the employees be on the premises or be under the supervision of the principal employer or his agent. The work should not be irrelevant to the purpose of the establishment. It is sufficient if it is incidental to it. In a departmental store there were different counters given on contract basis to different trading concerns. In all 24 persons were employed in the establishment. The Insurance Court had found that the employees of the counter holders were not employees under the Act. This was held to be perverse and the Act was found to be fully applicable to the establishment.[280]

*398.* There are instances of the ESI Corporation trying to block the insured persons from receiving the benefits of insurance as provided in the Act. In one case a woman working in a slate works contracted silicosis. Being an insured person she was permitted to take leave for seven days, but was not paid the benefit of such absence. She appealed to the ESI Court for compensation, which decided in her favour. The ESI Corporation appealed against this order on the technical ground that she had not worked for six months continuously prior to contracting silicosis as provided in Section 52A. The Court held that, as provided in the Third Schedule, silicosis was an occupational disease peculiar to the employment. It further provides

280. 2000, LLJ, Vol. 2, *Deputy Regional Director* v. *Virgilio Velho*, High Court of Bombay, pp. 355–364.

'that the contracting of the disease shall, unless the contrary is proved, be deemed to be an 'employment injury' arising out of and in the course of employment. The Court pointed out that silicosis was a process which continuously grew in the body, as if a hidden enemy was growing, and the disease developed into silico-tuberculosis. In this background how was it to be accepted that an employee working in the slate industry should prove that she was in continuous employment prior to the day when she noticed the symptoms of the disease? The objection raised by the ESI Corporation was seen to negate the very purpose of a beneficial enactment like the Act. The attitude expressed by the Corporation deserved to be deprecated. The appeal was dismissed with costs.[281]

*399.* An employee who was covered under the ESIC Scheme, hence an insured person, met with an accident during the contribution period. But his salary exceeded the wage limit then prevailing, of Rs 1600 per month, and he ceased to be eligible for ESIC protection. The ESI Court held that he had paid the contribution and continued to be an insured person, so his claim to the benefits was fully justified. The Corporation appealed to the High Court which upheld its contention and set aside the ESI Court's order. The claimant appealed to the Supreme Court, which decided against him. The entitlement to benefits is with reference to Section 46 (C) of the Act. It specifically provides for two cumulative conditions for its applicability, (i) the claimant must be an insured person, (ii) and such an injury must be sustained when he was an employee. The Court held that he would not be entitled to any benefit of disablement, notwithstanding the fact that he was still an insured person. The Corporation had already decided that the benefit of sickness for the period covered by the contribution will be paid.[282]

*400.* Under the provisions of the Amendment Act, 1989 the coverage of the Act was extended to employees drawing wages up to Rs 6,500 per month in 1996. In a particular case, the company decided to withdraw the medical allowance which was introduced in 1972 to compensate those workers who were not covered by the Act. Then the wage ceiling was Rs 1,000 per month. Every time the wage ceiling was raised the company withdrew the allowance from the employees to whom the Act was extended. But this time the unions made a writ petition against the company because its action adversely affected 1759 employees out of a total of 1815. Section 72 of the Act prohibits the withdrawal of any benefit already enjoyed by the employees by reason only of their liability to pay any contributions under the Act. This action of the employer was seen to violate this provision of the Act. Moreover, the medical allowance had become a part of their service conditions and it could not be unilaterally withdrawn without serving a notice under Section 9A of the ID Act. Ordinarily a writ petition is not admitted for the enforcement of contractual obligations. But the Court held that if there was a statutory violation, or if an action was opposed to statutory provisions, the aggrieved person can approach it by way of a

---

281. 1999, LLJ, Vol. 2, *ESI Corporation Indore* v. *Siara (Smt.) and Another*, High Court of Madhya Pradesh, pp. 394–397.
282. LLJ, 2008, Vol. 2, *Krishnankutty Nair, P.B.* v. *Regional Director, ESI Corporation* and *Another*, Supreme Court of India, pp. 997–1000.

writ petition for appropriate relief. The Court further held that the existence of an alternative remedy (such as provided by Section 75, to approach the Insurance Court), was no bar for entertaining a writ petition, when the merits of the case warranted it. The Court had already issued an interim injunction upon the company, considering that the members of the unions would be seriously prejudiced and put to heavy loss and hardship if the injunction was not granted: it was made absolute.[283]

*401.* In one case the High Court had to decide whether the employment injury sustained by a workman had resulted in permanent total disablement or permanent partial disablement, because the Medical Board had assessed his loss of earning capacity at 20 per cent, but the cooperative society where he was employed to do the weaving work declined to assign him lighter work. In view of this, the Insurance Court, which heard the appeal, enhanced the loss of earning capacity to 100 per cent. The ESI Corporation went on appeal with the plea that the Insurance Court ought not to have reached a conclusion different from the assessment of the Medical Board. The safe test was whether the employee could do some other work. Permanent total disablement in the Act meant incapacitation for all work which he was capable of performing at the time of the accident, while partial permanent disablement should have reduced his earning capacity in the employment concerned. The High Court held that the former need not have any bearing on his readiness to acquire skill or dexterity to do some other new work. Therefore, the legal position was that it was not necessary that the employment injury should render the employee totally unfit do any work whatsoever, for holding that he had suffered permanent total disablement. The Insurance Court was directed to consider the question afresh in the light of the legal position stated by the Court.[284]

*402.* In a government owned textile mill there was a lock-out and the mill did not function at all. Some employees fell ill and received treatment as out-patients. In order to claim sickness benefit, the sick employees should produce a sickness certificate from the medial officer certifying the nature of the disease and that the sick employee should be allowed to remain absent from work. He would be then entitled to receive sickness benefit due to temporary disablement. In view of the tock-out, the Labour and Employment Department had issued instructions not to issue sickness certificates to insured employees, though the use of the OPD treatment was provided. The ESI Court had given the order to issue the sickness certificate. It also decided that the lock-out was illegal. Consequently the employees were entitled to sickness benefit and the hospital should do its part. This was appealed. The High Court held that during the period the insured persons neither attended to the work, nor allowed the officers to enter into the officers. Under these circumstances, the question of remaining absent from duty due to sickness did not arise. Having absented from work voluntarily they cannot take the plea that the absence was due

283. 2000, LLJ, Vol. 3, Supp., *Seshashayee Paper Mills and Other* v. *Seshasayee Paper* and *Boards Ltd*, High Court of Madras, pp. 617–624.

284. 1995, LLJ, Vol. 2, *Regional Director, Employees' State Insurance Corporation* v. *K.P. Gopi and Another*, High Court of Kerala, pp. 235–237.

to sickness and claim entitlement to sickness benefit. Non-issuance of sickness certificate did not appear to be illegal or unjustified. Furthermore, the ESI Court lacked jurisdiction to declare the lock-out illegal. He could not have exercised the jurisdiction beyond the scope of the Act. The order was not sustainable and it was set aside.[285]

*403.* A bus conductor felt dizzy and fell down in the bus. He was taken to a hospital where after several days of treatment he died. His dependents filed a claim for dependents benefits, and for disablement benefit for an earlier period. The ESI Court held that his disease might have accelerated due to the strain of work and therefore it was an employment injury. The ESIC appealed against the order on the ground that the findings of the ESI Court were perverse. The employee died of a natural disease and his work had not accelerated it, leading to his death. The Court said that in order to claim dependent's benefit, one has to prove that (i) the deceased employee was an insured employee, (ii) the claimants are dependents, (iii) the injury occurred during the course of employment, and (iv) the injury occurred due to an occupational disease or an accident arising out of an employment. There was no dispute on the first three conditions. The medical certificate showed that he had an advanced liver disease and the death was due to it. His work as a conductor did not aggravate the liver disease which he had. The stress and strain of work had not caused any worsening of the existing condition of illness. He suffered from cirrhosis of liver, portal hypertension, vericeal bleeding, encephalopathy and ascitis. The ESI court did not accept the opinion of the medical officer and as to the basis on which he issued the medical certificate. The Court concluded that the death was due to an employment injury and the claimants were eligible for dependant's benefit. The High Court rejected the reasoning of the ESI Court. Admittedly the deceased person did not die due to an occupational disease. A causal connection with the employment must be established. In this case only sickness benefits and funeral benefits were payable. No disablement benefits or dependants benefits were payable. The order of the ESI Court was set aside and appeal allowed.[286]

*404.* An insured employee was a permanent operator with the Escorts Tractors Ltd. On 24 October 1985, while coming for duty from his house he took a lift in a car which met with an accident with a DTC bus. He suffered a fracture and stayed in the hospital up to 6 December 1985. His fractured leg was shortened by 2 inches and he became permanently disabled. His claims for payment of compensation, pension, medical benefits were rejected by the Corporation on the ground that the injury he suffered was not during the course of employment. Moreover, the report of the accident was sent on 17 June 1986 as an after thought to making a claim. The ESI Court noted that the company provided a free bus at Dhaula Kuan. The statement on the route taken was discrepant. The discrepancy raised doubt whether the petitioner was on his way to the factory or going somewhere else. On this account the injury did not get linked with his employment. The case was decided against him.

285. LLJ, 2007, Vol. 2, *State of Orissa and Others* v. *Kailas Chandra Nayak and Others,* High Court of Orissa, pp. 675–678.
286. LLJ, 2006, Vol. 1, *ESI Corporation* v. *Sainaba*, High Court of Kerala, pp. 320–323.

He appealed to the High Court. The plea was that the journey from his village to Dhaula Kuan was also a journey taken to reach the place of employment. The Court cited two similar cases and held that the settled principle of law was that for any injury or death caused during the course of employment, while coming from his home to his place or work, the employee would be entitled to the amount of compensation as provided under the Scheme of the Corporation, if he was insured with it. The appeal was allowed and the order of the ESI Court set aside. The matter was remanded back to the Court to constitute a board of doctors for assessing the permanent disability of the appellant for the purpose of granting compensation and pass orders in accordance with law within a period of three months from the date of appearance of parties before him.[287]

## §4. Retirement Benefits

*405.* The principal legislation providing for provident funds and various schemes for family pension, deposit-linked insurance schemes and employee's pension scheme is the Employees Provident Funds and Miscellaneous Provisions Act, 1952. An older legislation, the Provident Funds Act, 1925 with restricted application is still on the statute. However, the EPF Act is of universal applicability and its scope and coverage have gradually expanded since its inception. It combines features of a social security scheme with those of government sponsored personal savings schemes with tax advantages, and facility of nomination, survivorship benefit, etc. Nonetheless, in the event of premature death the accumulations in the PF have often been too meager to support the family of the deceased. Therefore, the Family Pension Scheme based on the Family Pension Fund created out of a portion of contributions to the PF with subsidy from the Central Government was launched. The Employee's Pension Scheme, 1995, which replaced, the Employees Family Pension Scheme, 1971, has advanced the purpose of social security further. The Scheme applies to the employees of all factories and establishments to which the Employees Provident Funds and Miscellaneous Provisions Act, 1952 applies. In addition the government launched the Employee's Deposit-Linked Insurance Scheme in 1976. Its purpose has been enlarged under the Employees Deposit- Linked Insurance (Amendment) Scheme, 2010.

*406.* The Coal Mines Provident Funds and Miscellaneous Provisions Act, 1948, had the purpose of promoting thrift among the employees of coal mines and to stabilize the labour force. Four schemes are in operation under this Act. These are:

(i) the Coal Mines Provident Fund;
(ii) the Pension Scheme;
(iii) the Deposit-linked Insurance; and
(iv) the Bonus scheme; and are applicable to all coal mines and ancillary organizations throughout the country.

287. LLJ, 2009, Vol. 4, *Swaraj Yadav Alias Suraj Yadav* v. *ESI Corporation and Another*, High Court of Punjab and Haryana, pp. 273–275.

The Pension Scheme has been renamed as the Coal Mines Pension (Amendment Scheme, 2001. The Act provides that the accumulated balance in the PF of any member cannot be assigned or charged and shall not be liable to attachment under any decree or order of any court in respect of any debt or liability of the member. In the event of death, the amount will vest in the nominee, subject to deductions authorized under the Scheme but free from any other liability. Full refund is made on superannuation and earlier, in the event of retrenchment, total incapacity to work or death. Non-recoverable advances are permitted for approved purposes, which include purchase of a dwelling site or house construction, marriage of daughters and post-matriculation education of children. The definitions employed in the Act are now identical or at par with the principal EPF Act. The Coal Mines Bonus Scheme, which is the distinctive feature of the Act, provides an incentive to workers to be more regular in attendance and rewards workers for being more regular and for not taking part in illegal strikes. The Coal Mines Provident Fund and Miscellaneous Provisions (Amendment) Act 1996 enacted through un Ordinance on 31 March 1996 provides for superannuation pension, retiring pension or permanent total disability pension to the persons employed in coal mines and also for widow or widower pension, children pension or orphan pension and life insurance benefits payable to the beneficiaries of such employees. Under the new scheme, the term 'average emoluments' means the average of the notional salary payable to the employee for the last 10 months before retirement. The Coal Mines Pension Scheme came into force on 31 March 1998.

*407.* The Assam legislature enacted the Assam Tea Plantations Provident Fund Act, 1955, and the Parliament, the Seamen's Provident Fund Act, 1966. Over the years parallel provisions have been made in enactments. The principal enactment, the EPF Act, 1952, is of the widest scope and covers the largest number of workers. The Act applies to any factory or establishment employing twenty or more persons and engaged in industries named in Schedule I. Once the government issues a notification specifying the industry or class or establishments to be covered under the Act, it will become applicable on the date so notified. On giving a notice of two months the government may also extend the coverage of the Act to establishments employing less than twenty persons. However, newly established factories and undertakings are exempted for three years. The Act gives the central government discretionary power, having regard to the financial position of any class of establishments or other circumstances of the case, to grant exemption for such period and on such conditions as may be specified. Once an establishment is covered by the Act, it cannot be withdrawn even if the employment falls below twenty. The Act does not apply to any establishment registered under the Cooperative Societies Act, 1912, or under any other law pertaining to cooperative societies which employ fewer than 50 persons and work without power. Under the Employees Provident Fund (Amendment) Scheme, 2008 and Employees Pension (Amendment) Scheme, 2008, special provision are made for the employees under the Persons with Disabilities (Equal Opportunities, Protection of Right and Full Participation Act, 1995, and the National Trust for Welfare of Persons with Autism, Cerebral Palsy, Mental Retardation and Multiple Disabilities) Act, 1999, taking the added responsibility to contribute the employee's share up to a maximum period of three years of their joining the Fund.

*408.* Under the Employees' Provident Funds Scheme, as amended in 1985, every employee of a factory/establishment to which the Act applies is required to join the PF whose pay per month, inclusive of basic pay, dearness allowance, cash value of food concessions and retaining allowance, if any, does not exceed the level fixed by the government from time to time. Once a member, the employee continues to be a member even though the pay may exceed the pay limit. The scheme covers all contract labour, though his pay may exceed the pay limit. In respect of contract labour, the responsibility for complying with the provisions of the Act is that of the principal employer. What is included in basic wages has been a subject of disputes. The Supreme Court has clarified that production bonus is not included. A flat *ad hoc* allowance paid to all the employees, pursuant to an agreement between the management and the union, does not partake of the character of basic wages. The emoluments to constitute 'basic wages' must be earned by an employee while on duty. The question as to who is an employee and who is not has also been disputed. The Supreme Court has decided that a 'home worker in the *beedi* industry', by virtue of the fact that he rolls beedis, and is involved in an activity connected with the work of the factory, is an employee for the purpose of the Act. In another case it was decided by a High Court that so long as an employee was employed for the establishment's regular work, the period for which he was employed is not to be considered and he should be considered an employee. A substitute employee hired in the place of a regular employee who is on leave is not covered under the Act.

*409.* In a case the dispute started with the decision of the EPF commissioner to include the canteen subsidy and performance linked compensation as chargeable for making contribution under the EPF Act. Under a settlement with the union, it was agreed that the payments made by the employer would not attract provident fund contribution. The canteen subsidy was an alternate to providing a canteen and it could be withdrawn at the will of the employer. The PF Commissioner said that the settlement could not override the Act, specially when it was a beneficial legislation. The Court held that any such amount which is capable of earning must be as per the contract of employment, and that it is legitimate for the employees, while settling the dispute, to come to a settlement that certain payments shall not be reckoned for the purpose of provident fund, etc.[288]

*410.* Section 6 of the EPF Act mandates an employer to contribute 10 per cent of the basic wages which include dearness allowance and retaining allowance, if any, and the employees contribution shall be equal to that, or if he so desires it can be an amount exceeding 10 per cent of the above, but the employer shall not be under any obligation to exceed his contribution as provided in this section. The government is authorized to substitute the words 12 per cent for 10 per cent at both the

288. 2009, Vol. 4, *Regional Provident Fund commissioner* v. *Wipro Ltd and Another*, High Court of Madras, pp. 513–521.

places where they occur. For the purpose of this section, the term, 'dearness allowance', shall be inclusive of the 'cash value of any food concession' allowed to the employee. The problem arose from the definition of the term 'basic wages' which excluded (i) the cash value of any food concession, (ii) any dearness allowance, house rent allowance, overtime allowance, bonus, commission or any other similar allowance payable to the employee in respect of his employment or of work done in such employment, (iii) any presents made by the employer. The employer is charged to pay his contribution not only on basic wages but also dearness allowance and retaining allowance. The dearness allowance is inclusive of the cash value of any food concession and it creates a conflict between Section 2 (b) and Section 6 of the Act. The term, 'emoluments', refers to cash payments or payable in cash, while the cash value of food concession, excluded from basic wages, was not payable in cash. The Supreme Court observed in another case that the exception (i) to (iii) did not seem to follow any logical pattern which would be in consonance with the main definition. The exceptions suggest that though the main part of the definition includes all emoluments which are earned in accordance with the terms of contract of employment, certain payments which are in fact the price of labour and earned in accordance with the terms of contract of employment, are excluded from the main part of the term, 'basic wages'. Dearness allowance is excluded from 'basic wages' at one place and included for determining the employer's contribution. In search for a rationale, the Apex Court said,

> It seems that the basis of inclusion in Section 6 and exclusion in clause (ii) is that whatever is payable in all concerns and is earned by all permanent employees is included for the purpose of contribution under Section 6, but whatever is not payable by all concerns or may not be earned by all employees of a concerns is excluded for the purpose of contribution. To this rule the exclusion of dearness allowance in clause (ii) is an exception, though it has been corrected by including dearness allowance for the purpose of contribution.[289]

*411.* In a case it was agreed by the appellant company that the lump sum payment made to workers under a settlement did not partake of the meaning of the term 'basic wages', so it would not quality for contribution under the EPF Act. The settlement had a provision that such payment would not be classified or attract any statutory provisions, that the settlement was arrived at under the ID Act, and it was a valid settlement. The Court examined the records and found that the demands raised by the Indian National Cement Workers Federation on the Cement Manufacturers Federation were referred to arbitration under Section 10A of the ID Act. One of the demands was that an interim relief should be given and this was granted by the arbitrators to be adjusted against the award. Later, another interim award was passed and finally a settlement was arrived at. The interim advance was paid on the basis of the number of days worked in a month. The Court held that the payments were made to meet the demands made by the workers and they amounted to increase in

289. LLJ, 2009, Vol. 4, *Regional Provident Fund Commissioner* v. *Wipro Ltd and Another*, Madras High Court, pp. 513–521; Case relied on, LLJ, 1965, Vol. 2, *Bridge and Roof Co. (India) Ltd* v. *Union of India*, Supreme Court of India.

'basic wages' as defined in Section 2(b) of the Act. The Court reviewed its judgment in an earlier case, in which it held that, as per the settlement, the flat adhoc allowance and incentive earnings shall not be reckoned for provident fund and other statutory contributions. In this case the settlement did not provide for an *ad hoc*, one time payment. The writ petition failed.[290]

*412.* A company gave its employees, food allowance, not related to any rise in cost of food. The EPF Commissioner viewed it as the cash value of food allowance. The union claimed that the food allowance should be included for the purpose of employer's contribution to the provident fund. The Commissioner held that the food allowance was merely a compensation to meet the expenses of food and it formed part of the dearness allowance, even if the food was not provided by the employer. The Court found that the food allowance was payable under a settlement and it was like any other allowance payable to the employees. In the Act, the value in regard to food is the value by which the price of food is reduced. This presupposes that food is provided to the employees as part of the terms of employment. But, without the supply of such an amenity, the value of any food concession allowed to the employees cannot be calculated. There being no supply of any food, the payment of food allowance cannot be treated as the cash value of food concession allowed to the employees. The petition succeeded and the orders were set aside.[291]

*413.* A workman was terminated from service on 7 June 1982. In the ensuing litigation, by an award published on 27 September 1991, the workman was directed to be reinstated in service and to the payment of 75 per cent of the back wages. The employer did not deduct the amount the employees contribute to the provident fund, nor did he make any contribution on his part. At this the workman lodged a complaint and an enquiry was instituted by the Asstt. Provident Fund Commissioner. It was held that the back-wages were 'basic wages' and deduction should be made from the back wages as the employee's share together with employer's contribution and paid into the EPF account. He appealed to the Appellate Tribunal which decided to remand the matter to the Commissioner to be decided afresh under Section 7A. While the enquiry was underway, the Commissioner gave orders to conclude it and start a fresh enquiry under paragraph 26B of the Scheme, and thereupon he decided that back-wages were basic wages and the employer was liable to make the contribution. This led to the High Court with a petition against the order. The Court held that if 'continuity and service' was the period spent on duty, then the workman would be entitled to receive the entire salary and both the employee and the employer would be liable to make contributions to the provident fund. But in this case this was not so. The purpose of continuity in service is that such period is not to be treated as a break in service for the purpose of pay increments, leave, allowances, pension, etc. Since only a part of wages was awarded, it means that the period of absence from duty was not intended to be treated as spent on duty. What the

---

290. LLJ, 2009, Vol. 1, *Dalmia Cement (Bharat) Ltd v. Regional Provident Funds Commissioner*, Madras High Court, pp. 257–263.

291. LLJ, 2008, Vol. 1, *Tata Power Co. Ltd and Others* v. *Regional Provident Fund Commissioner*, High Court of Bombay, pp. 992–996.

Court does is to award damages assessed in terms of the whole or part of the wages the workman would have earned had he been in service without any interruption. It is not the same as payment of wages for duties performed for the period. The amount of damages or compensation awarded by a Court would not constitute 'basic wages' as envisaged in the Act. The petitioner is under no obligation to make statutory contribution to the provident fund under the Act. The order of the Commissioner was quashed and set aside. The enquiry initiated under paragraph 26B of the Scheme was also set aside.[292]

*414.* On the question of whether the encashing of the earned leave was 'basic wage', as argued by the EPF Commissioner, or not, the Appellate Tribunal held that it was not a part of basic wages. The Bombay High Court took a different view, holding that it was a part of basic wages. The Karnataka High Court merely followed the Bombay High Court's judgment. In the mean time the Madras High Court, following the Bridge and Roof Co, case and the opinion of the Apex Court, held that it was not a part of basic wages. The Apex Court went over the same ground and reiterated the position, that what was earned in accordance with the terms of employment, but it may not be earned by all the employees of a concern, would be excluded from 'basic wages'. Where the wage is universally, necessarily and ordinarily paid to all employees across the board, such emoluments are basic wages. Where the payment is available to be specially paid to those who avail of the opportunity is not a basic part of wages. In all the cases of encashment of leave, the option may be available to all employees, but some may avail of it and some may not do so. The inevitable conclusion is that 'basic wage' was never intended to include amounts received for leave encashment.[293]

*415.* The definition of basic wages provides for inclusion as well as exclusion of certain allowances based on an implicit it criterion which has to be ascertained and gives rise to industrial disputes. The test decided by the Supreme Court in *Bridge and Rcof Co. Ltd* v. *Union of India* (1962) still holds good. This test was applied in deciding a writ petition against the EPF Appellate Tribunal and the earlier order passed by the Asstt. Provident Fund Commissioner. The Company was not deducting provident fund contribution on house rent allowance + special allowance + management allowance and conveyance allowance while deducting it on Basic + VDA. The PF Comissioner noticed that the company was paying wages in the guise of allowance to limit the PF liability and issued a summon for determination of PF dues under Section 7A of the 1952 Act. The Authority held that special allowance was being paid as a part of monthly salary, so it should be included in basic wages. Likewise other excluded allowances were also part of basic wages. The company was liable to deposit Rs 1,254,269 for a period of less than four years. The company field an appeal which was dismissed. The court read the statutory definition

292. LLJ, 2008, Vol. 2, *Swastik Textile Engineers Pvt Ltd* v. *Vrijbhai Mavjibhai Rathod and Another*, Gujarat High Court, pp. 533–536.

293. LLJ, 2008, Vol. 2, *Municipal Academy of Higher Education* v. *Provident Fund Commissioner*, Supreme Court of India, pp. 667–691. Covering the same ground is LLJ, 2008, Vol. 1, *Thiru Arooran Sugars Ltd* v. *Asstt. Provident Fund Commisioner (ENF), Trichirapalli and Another*, Madras High Court, pp. 806–813.

and recalled the cases cited by the two parties. The bridges and Roof case is definitive on the subject. It is the rule that whatever is payable in all concerns and is earned by all permanent employees is included in basic wages, but whatever is not payable in all concerns, or may not be earned by all employees of a concern, is excluded for the purpose of contribution. In this view the wages which are universally, necessarily and ordinarily paid to all employee are included for contributions, and where the payment is made specially to those who avail of the opportunity is not basic wages and should be excluded. The company paid conveyance allowance to the non-executive category, to all employees and similarly with the Special Allowance paid to all the workers. Consequently, we do not find any merit in this petition. It is hereby dismissed. [294]

*416.* In another case a group of employers filed ten writ petitions against the PF authority that allowances paid to employees, such as, conveyance, educational allowance, food concession, etc were basic wages and attracted deductions. The Court found that some of the petitions should not have been filed, since the matter could be decided by a hierarchy of authorities and relief sought as provided under the amended Act. The petitioners have sought relief at the stage of show cause notice under Section 7A of the Act. Under this section no orders can be passed unless the employers are given a reasonable opportunity of representing their case. They were directed to produce various records to decide the question whether various allowances would be covered by the tern. 'basic wages'. If an adverse order is passed, the employer can file a review under Section 7B. Thereafter, appeal lies in the Appellate Tribunal under Section 7I in the five petitions filed at the show cause notice the issues raised are not purely legal issues, but mixed questions of facts and law. The petitioners' plea is that they are seeking an authoritative ruling that certain allowances will not constitute wages under Section 2(B) and then it will be binding on the authorities. The Court held that though the request may look attractive, but 'this court exercising powers under Article 226 of the constitution of India cannot clutch on to a jurisdiction which it does not have'. The Court does not have an advance ruling authority. It cannot give a ruling based on apprehension or on academic issues. The limited power of judicial review can be exercised only when a statutory authority makes an order and still requires on appropriate correction by way of Judicial review. Before a writ petition is entertained facts must be marshalled and findings given by the PF commissioner. The appeal powers are comprehensive and the Tribunal can go into both questions of law and fact based on relevant materials, to be decided by the authorities on the basis of records and they can enforce attendance of persons. The petitioners must avail the remedies under the Act. In view of these reasons this court is not inclined to entertain these five writ petitions. In the other five petitions the petitioners failed to convince the appellate Tribunal and have come to this Court. Each case will be dealt with on merits. An advertisement company gave food and entertainment allowance in place of canteen facilities. Hence it was not basic wages. The Authorities decided that the petitioner

294. LLJ,1, *2012 Montage Enterprises Pvt Ltd* v. *Employees Provident Fund, Indore and Another*, Madhya Pradesh High Court, pp. 371–377.

was liable to pay contributions in respect of education allowance, special allowance, conveyance allowance and food concession as they were part of basic wages. The Tribunal found that since these allowances were paid to all employees and no PF deduction was made, the company was bound to pay. In the case of a software company, on an earlier writ petition, the Court has granted interim stay pending find disposal. In another software company also an interim stay was granted. The third petitioner ran a machine tool factory and failed before the Tribunal but secure an interim stay while a notice of motion was ordered. In this case the Division Bench observed that the PF authorities have not given any reason for holding that the Special Allowance should be deemed to be dearness allowance. The officer has no power to deem something to be something else which it is not, it being the prerogative of the legislator? The petitioners' counsel also contended that if parties in terms of contract of employment agree that a particular sum should be excluded, then the Court cannot include those amounts. The Court recalled the Supreme Court's judgment in which it was held that it is only on combined reading of Section 2(B) and Section 6, the basis for computation can be arrived at. There cannot be contracting out of the statute at the whims of the parties. The counsel pointed out that in the Coal Mines Provident Fund Scheme the term 'basic wage' excludes payment of food concession, dearness allowance, house rent allowance and other similar allowances, besides overtime, bonus, commission, presents and donations, which were excluded. That definition can be taken as an internal aid for construing the definition of 'basic wage' under the 1952 Act. The Court rejected the suggestion. The provisions of the Act have to be interpreted in a purposive manner and the principles set out in Directive Principles of State Policy must be kept in mind.

If the employer neglects to remit the combined contributions of employee and his own or diverts the money for alien purposes the fund gets dry and the retirees are denied the meager support when they most need it. This demoralizes the working class and frustrates the hopes of the community itself. The whole project gets stultified, if employers thwart contributory responsibility. In the some spirit, if the employers and employees have a settlement to keep out certain payments from the purview of the term 'basic wages' and the authorities cannot go into the said settlement, there will occur a contracting out of the statute. This cannot be permitted. 'In essence there cannot be estoppels against the statute.' Any settlement and the award between the parties cannot be binding on an Authority under the Act, who can arrive at a conclusion based on all materials available including settlements, if any, produced before him. He can lift the veil to determine the issue. The Supreme Court has held that incentive earnings are not included in basic wages, nor overtime and leave encashment. These may not be earned by all the employees of the concern, only by those who avail of the opportunity. Deductions towards PF cannot be based on different contingencies and uncertainties. Payments made on monthly basis and labeling it as various types of allowances is not contingency payment. This can never be allowed. The Court discussed several judgments pronounced in connection with the ESI Act and decided that the term wages should be liberally construed as the Act is a welfare piece of legislation. 'If it is seen in this context, then the orders passed by the Tribunal which are under challenge cannot be found fault with.

The contentions raised by the petitioners are misconceived and bereft of legal reasons.' Hence all the five petitions are bound to fail in the result all the 10 petitions stand dismissed.'[295]

*417.* The Employees Pension Scheme, 1995 replaced the Family Pension Scheme, 1971 in the Act. This has been replaced by the Employees' Pension (Amendment) Scheme, 1999. As with the coal mines' employees, this scheme provides for superannuation pension, retiring pension or permanent total disablement pension to the employees of any establishment to which the Act applies and also for widow or widower's pension, children pension or orphan's pension payable to the beneficiaries of such employees. For this purpose a pension fund is to be created into which shall be paid from time to time, in respect of every employee who is a member of the pension scheme, specified sums from the employer's contribution not exceeding 8.33 per cent of the employee's pay. The central government's contribution is equal to the contribution payable at specified rates. A woman worker retired on 31 December 1995 on reaching 60th year of age. She contributed to the PF until 1995. But the Regional PF Commissioner denied her pension on the ground that, as per the records, she should have retired on 31 December 1992. The eligibility to the 1995 scheme was restricted to those employees who retired after the cut-off date, namely April, 1993. Accordingly she was not entitled to the benefits under the 1995 Scheme. She applied to the Consumers Disputes Redressal Forum for securing the release of the pension. One of the pleas taken by the Commissioner was that she was not a consumer under the Act. The Act executed such services as are rendered free of charge or under a contract of personal service. The services rendered by the Commissioner were free of charge. The Court rejected the position taken by the Commissioner. The date of birth as recorded in the Company's register was to be accepted. She was eligible for pension. She was a consumer under the Consumer Protection Act, and the position of the Commissioner was that of a service giver. She was fully entitled to approach the Forum for assistance and the pension should be released.[296]

*418.* A widow claimed family pension on the death of the employee under the Employee's Family Pension Scheme, 1971. This was denied. She approached the High Court which took it up for hearing almost 12 years later and the judge enquired whether her case could be considered sympathetically and the family pension provided to a widow now about 65 years of age. The Court was informed that there were several such cases pending with the PF Authorities and any indulgence shown in one case, contrary to statutory provisions, would result in a large number of similar claims being made. It was heard on merits. Her petition was rejected on the ground that there was an earlier break of more than one year in the reckonable service of the deceased worker, from 8 November 1985 to 30 December 1986, and also

295. LLJ, 1, 2012, *Management of Reynolds Pens India Ltd, Sriperumbdur Taluk, Kancheepuram and others*, v. *Regional Provident Fund Comissioner-II, Employees' Provident Fund Organisation, Mugappair, Chennai and others*, Madras High Court, pp 381–397.

296. LLJ, 2008, Vol. 2, *Regional Provident Fund Commissioner* v. *Bhavani*, Supreme Court of India, pp. 1079–1083.

during January and February 1987. Hence petitioner's request could not be acceded to. He was absent without wages. Absence for one year continuously from the first day of absence results in a loss of membership in the Scheme. Any shorter period of absence was condoned at the Commissioner's, discretion. In 1988 this clause (of one year's, absence without wages) was deleted. But the advantage could not be extended to the petitioner. The writ petition was dismissed.[297]

*419.* A sales manager met with an accident and both of his legs were amputated. The medical board certified the disability at 90 per cent. His application for permanent disability person was rejected in view of the medical board's opinion. The Commissioner did not notice that the same board had answered 'yes' to the question, whether the member was permanently and totally unfit for employment and to another related question too the answer was 'yes'. In view of these facts the Court decided to ignore the certification of 90 per cent of permanent disablement. Instead the Court read the Workmen's Compensation Act, Schedule 1, in which permanent total disablement is described in terms of loss of earnings capacity of 100 per cent, where a workman has had amputation of both legs. This was also the judgment of Andhra Pradesh High Court in a case decided in 2002, in which an employee had sustained permanent disability of 75 per cent to 80 per cent and was denied the pension. In that case the Court viewed the disability at 100 per cent of earning capacity. The rule that if the disablement renders the employee incapacitated for all work which he was capable of performing at the time of disablement, it is 100 per cent loss of earnings. So the disability would be 100 per cent. The Bombay High Court decided, 'we respectfully concur with the view of The Andhra Pradesh High Court'. Moreover, the denial of disablement pension to the petitioner was unjustified. The cost needed to be imposed for unnecessarily and unjustifiably opposing the just claim of the petitioner. The writ petition was allowed with a cost of Rs 5000 on the Commissioner. The communication dated 15 January 2003 was set aside. This was the date of passing the impugned order.[298]

*420.* In an unusual case, an employee resigned from his post and applied for withdrawals of provident fund benefits on 9 August 2000. This was sanctioned by the authorities on 24 August 2000, but the former employee suddenly died on 25 August 2000. His widow applied for family pension, which was rejected on the ground that the husband of the petitioner had applied for withdrawal of PF benefits and it was allowed an 24 August. Once the sanction order was issued, the employee ceased to be a member of the Scheme. The Court read the paragraph 6A of the Scheme and decided that the question was, whether he had availed of the withdrawal benefit or not. If not, and merely because the application of the deceased husband was allowed for withdrawal of PF dues, it could not be said that he had factually availed of the withdrawal of Provident Fund dues. Consequently the case of the husband did not fall within the ambit of paragraph 6A of the Scheme. The

297. LLJ, 2006, Vol. 1, *Laxmibai K* v. *Provident Fund Commissioner, Hyderabad*, High Court of Andhra Pradesh, pp. 27–32.
298. LLJ, 2006, Vol. 1, *Avinash Anant Vaidya* v. *Regional Provident Fund Commissioner, Thane and Others*, High Court of Bombay, pp. 489–493.

petition was allowed and the Commissioner directed to grant Family Pension as per the Employee Pension Scheme, 1995.[299]

*421.* The claim to family pension to a member was denied on the ground, that as per paragraph 10 of the 1995 Scheme, it is provided that a member who on attaining the age of 58 years superannuates and has rendered pensionable service of 20 years, his pensionable service shall be increased by a weight-age of 2 years. The plaintiff did not complete 20 years of service, nor did he complete the requisite 10 years to be entitled to the benefits of the Scheme. He took the plea that he had contributed to the Scheme for 9 years and if the benefit of weight-age of 2 years was awarded to him, he would complete 11 years and become entitled to the benefit of the Scheme. His claims were upheld by the Appellate Court, but the Commissioner persisted in denying him the benefit and filed a regular second appeal, though it was barred by a delay of 21 days. The appeal was dismissed on merit as well as on the point of delay. The Commissioner had initially waived off the period form 1982 to 1990, enabling the employees to become members of the Scheme without depositing the amounts. The Court decided that the Commissioner was estopped by his conduct.[300]

*422.* The Employees Deposit-Linked Insurance Scheme. 1976 is an added social security for members of the EPF and the Coal Mines Provident Fund. Under this scheme an 'assurance benefit' linked to the average balance in the PF account of the employee is payable to the family in the event of death while being a member of the fund. Employees do not pay any premia, but employers are required to contribute at such rate as the central government may decide, but not exceeding 1 per cent of the aggregate pay of members of the provident fund every month. In addition, the employers have also to contribute one-fourth of the aforesaid contribution as the further sum for meeting the administrative expenses of the insurance scheme. The central government, likewise contributes one-half of the contribution which employers are required to make. The insurance cover is equal to the average balance in the provident fund account of the deceased during the preceding 12 months, subject to a maximum of Rs 60,000 (with effect from June 2000). If the average balance exceeds this amount the assurance benefit is raised by 12 per cent subject to the above ceiling. The pay ceiling in respect of this scheme as well as other schemes under the Act was Rs 6,500 per month and it can be raised as the government may decide. By an amendment to the scheme in 2010, on the death of the member, the person entitled to receive the provident fund accumulations shall, in addition to such sum, be paid an amount equal to 12 months, except where the balance exceeds Rs 50,000 the addition made will be 40 per cent subject to a ceiling of Rs one lakh. The members of the relevant provident funds are automatically insured. The assurance benefit is payable to the nominee of the deceased named in this provident fund

299. LLJ, 2006, Vol. 1, *Sunanda, Widow of Shrikant Dhote* v. *Regional Provident Fund Commissioner*, Aurangabad and Another, High Court of Bombay, pp. 984–986.

300. LLJ, 2009, Vol. 3, *Regional Provident Fund Commissioner, Karnal* v. *Gurnam Singh and Others*, High Court of Haryana and Punjab, pp. 33–35.

account. The scheme has a stated procedure to be followed for establishing the shares of family members, if the nomination does not relate to the whole amount.

*423.* The Cine-Workers and Cinema Workers Act, 1981, provides, under Section 16, that the EPF shall apply to every cine-worker who has worked in not less than three feature films with one or more producers, as if he was an employee. Similarly, Section 24 provides that the EPF Act shall apply to every cinema theatre in which five or more workers are employed on any day, as if it was an establishment to which this Act applied and each such worker was an employee under the Act. The EPF scheme was notified in April 1986 but with effect from October 1984. Soon another Scheme called the Family Pension Fund Scheme was also launched. In respect of the latter class of establishments a dispute arose because both the employer and the employees were required to make their respective contributions retrospectively with effect from the date of notification. The cinema theatre owner contended that some workers had already retired; moreover, it would be inequitable to deduct PF contributions retrospectively from the meager wages of existing employees. The High Court gave relief by directing the cinema theatre owners to pay the contributions with effect from the date of judgment. The matter was then raised before the Supreme Court. The Court, while upholding the High Court's Order in respect of workers, directed that there was no justification in granting the same relief to the employers who were accordingly ordered to bear the liability in respect of their share of contributions to the PF from the date on which they filed the writ petitions in the High Court.[301]

*424.* The EPF Act provides for exemption for an establishment from its provisions, for a period of three years from the date it is set up, as an infancy benefit. An existing company installed a factory at another location. The EPF authorities decided that the new unit was a branch of the existing company and so was not entitled to the infancy benefit. The Authorities relied on an agreement between the two units which required the new factory to produce cloth exclusively for its promoter and not for any other establishment. However, the High Court decided that the new factory was not a branch or department of the promoter company, but a different factory and was entitled to the benefit of infancy period. The Court held that there was no supervisory, managerial or financial control or functional integrality between the two units. The nature of goods manufactured was different and both paid their respective taxes separately; indeed, both units were owned by different companies, so even on the test of ownership the two could not be clubbed together to from one establishment. Even if there was common ownership, and all the companies were in the same line of manufacturing there was no functional integrality between them. Each unit could survive without the other.[302]

---

301. Supreme Court Cases, 1996, *Union of India and Another* v. *Murugon Talkies*, Supreme Court of India, pp. 504–506.

302. 2000, LLJ, Vol. 1, *Niton Industries* v. *Union of India and Others*, High Court of Bombay, pp. 151–155.

*425.* The Kerala High Court had to decide a writ by a Temple Trust against the order of Regional Provident Fund Commissioner to pay Rs 9,871,227.85 as the EPF dues, because on the basis of an enquiry it was found that the Trust was a composite establishment under the Act and engaged in many notified activities. This followed a complaint against the Trust by the employees for denying them, the benefits of having provident fund. In an earlier complaint the press and Newspaper owned by the Trust were viewed as District and separate industrial units under the ID Act. The petitioner contended that the Trust had a hospital, an Industrial Training Institute, a rubber estate. The hospital was covered under the Act since 30 April 1991. The Industrial Training Institute and the estate never employed more than 20 persons at any time, so they were not required to be covered under the Act. The petitioner said that all the activities of the trust were separate entities, having no functional integrality, therefore the staff of all the establishments cannot be treated as a single entity and they do not constitute one establishment. The orders passed as per Exhibit P-3 and Exhibit P-6 are totally baseless and illegal. Exhibit P-3 was the original order and Exhibit P-6 was the confirmatory order following a review under Section 7B. The Court relied on the Apex Court's judgements and the tests, like, unity of ownership, unity of management and control, unity of finance, unity of labour and employment leading to functional integrality to decide the issues raised. It held that a proper enquiry was not conducted in the matter. Whether one establishment can be run without the other establishments, whether all the entities are maintaining the same accounts relating to financial matters, or whether the employees can be transferred from one unit to others, are matters to be considered in order to treat separate units as a single establishment for the purpose of the Act. None of the above features had been found out by the authority in Exhibit P-3. Exhibit P-5 would show that every unit was independent with no functional integrality. It can never be said that a Hospital is dependent on industrial training centre or an estate. 'The nature of employment differs and there is no unity of employment. So is the case of STD Booth, sale of cassettes, auditoriums, renting of bus, etc. There is no material to indicate that a single account is being maintained. This feature by itself is sufficient to set aside P-3 and P-6.' The writ petition was allowed and exhibits P-3 and P-6 were quashed.[303]

## §5. GRATUITY

*426.* Gratuity is a form of retirement benefit, but in India it is payable on the completion of five years of service and so it may also take the form of termination of service benefit. The Payment of Gratuity Act, 1972 was enacted to provide for payment of gratuity to the employees in every factory, mine, oil-field, plantation and railway and also to every shop and establishment or classes of establishments in which ten or more persons are employed. Such other establishments or classes of establishments in which ten or more persons are employed can also be notified

303. LLJ, 3, 2012, *Attukal Bhagavathy Temple Trust, Thiruvananthapuram, rep by its Secretary* v. *Regional Provident Fund Commissioner, E.P.F.O, Thiruvananthapuram and Another*, Kerala High Court, pp. 736–739.

under the Act. The Act applies to educational institutions even though they are exempted from the operation of Shop and Establishments Act of the State. The term 'employee' has been broadly defined to include those employed on wages and who do any skilled, semi-skilled, or unskilled, manual, supervisory, technical or clerical work, whether or not such person is employed in a managerial or administrative capacity, but excludes all government employees. By the 1987 amendment it is provided that all private employers must obtain an insurance in the prescribed manner from the Life Insurance Corporation of India for their liability towards the payment of gratuity. However, any employer who has already established an approved gratuity fund may be exempted. Employers must now register themselves with the controlling authority and it is now a condition of registration that an insurance cover should have been obtained or an approved gratuity fund established. For this purpose a board of trustees must be constituted. Following a Supreme Court judgment in 2004 in which the court held, 'that if it was extended to cover in the definition of 'employee' all kinds of employees, it could have as well used such wide language as is contained in clause (f) of Section 2 of the Employees Provident Funds and Miscellaneous Provisions Act 1952, which defines 'employee' to mean any person who is employed for wages in any kind of work, manual or otherwise, in or in connection with the work of the establishment. It had been held that non-use of such wide language in the definition of 'employee' under clause (e) of Section 2 of the Payment of Gratuity Act, 1972 reinforces the conclusion that teachers are clearly not covered in the said definition.[304]

*427.* The payment of Gratuity (Amendment) Act, 2009 has widened the definition of 'employee' in order to extend the benefit of gratuity to teachers and give effect to this amendment retrospectively from April 1997, the date on which the government of India vide its notification had extended the provisions of the Act to the educational institutions employing ten or more persons. The new definition of 'employee' means any person (other than an apprentice) who is employed for wages, whether the terms of such employment are express or implied, in any kind of work, manual or otherwise, in or in connection with the work of a factory, mine, oilfield, plantation, port, railway company, shop or other establishment to which this Act applies, but does not include any such person who holds a post under the central government or state government and is governed by any other Act or by any rules providing for gratuity. The Amendment Act provides that the 3 April 1997 notification shall be valid and shall be deemed always to have been valid as if the Payment of Gratuity (Amendment) Act, 2009, had been in force at all material times and the gratuity shall be payable accordingly.[305]

*428.* In a case the widow of a medical officer was denied the gratuity payable to her husband. She received family pension. But the state government withheld the gratuity on the ground of wrong fixation of pay and decided to deduct the excess amount paid to the deceased from the amount of gratuity payable. This happened

304. 2004, LLJ, Vol. 1, *Ahmadabad (P) Primary Teachers' Association* v. *Administrative Officer*, Supreme Court of India, p. 596.
305. LLJ, July 2010, 'Statutes', p. 17 (st.).

because the relevant procedures laid down in government orders were not followed. He was wrongly granted the promotional pay scale. The excess amount was calculated at Rs 368,719 while the gratuity payable was Rs 350,000 The Court decided that the excess amount paid was not due to any misrepresentation or fraud on the part of the deceased, nor did he have any knowledge that the amount being paid was in excess of what he was entitled to receive. The widow cannot be held responsible for wrong interpretation of rules. The officials did not take care to correct the mistake in the lifetime of the doctor. He was ultimately regularized. The excess amount cannot be withdrawn after his death, and in any case not from the widow. The state government was directed to pay the gratuity. The petition succeeded.[306]

*429.* Gratuity is payable to an employee after he had rendered continuous service for not less than five years, on his superannuation, or retirement, or resignation, or death, or disablement due to an accident or disease. In the event of death the condition of five years of service is waived. For every completed year of service or part thereof in excess of six months gratuity is payable at the rate of 15 days of wages as last drawn by the employee. The amount of gratuity payable is not to exceed Rs 350,000. The Act clarifies that in the case of monthly rated employees, the 15 days' wages shall be calculated by dividing the monthly rate of wages by 26 and multiplying the quotient by 15. The term 'continuous service' has been defined to include an interruption caused by sickness, accident, leave, absence from duty without leave, (not being an absence in respect of which an order treating the absence as a break in service has been passed in accordance with the standing orders, or rules, etc.), lay-off, strike or lockout, or cessation of work not due to any fault of the employee. The Act does not permit any break in service due to punishment or penalty to interrupt the continuity of service. Gratuity can also be claimed at the higher rate than provided for in the Act under a settlement. The Payment of Gratuity (Amendment) Act, 2010 has increased the sum of gratuity payable from the maximum of Rs 350,000 of (rupees ten lakhs) or one million. The amendment came into force from 24 May 2010. The enhancement of benefit is expected to compensate the retiring employees from the erosion of value of rupee due to persistent inflationary conditions. The substantial rise in the level of salaries also necessitated the enhancement of the maximum gratuity payable at retirement.

*430.* In one case a single judge of the High Court decided that the employer was liable to pay interest at 12 per cent on the delayed payment of gratuity. Interest would be payable on each of the three installments of gratuity paid. This was challenged before the High Court. It was argued that the claim of interest was hit by the principles of constructive prejudice, since he had not claimed interest in the earlier writ petition. The Court rejected the plea. This Court had not adjudicated the claim regarding payment of gratuity earlier. The award of interest of 12 per cent cannot

306. LLJ, December 2010, *Ramawati Devi (Smt.)* v. *State of UP and Others*, High Court of Allahabad, pp. 718–720.

be said to be illegal. The order passed by the Single judge was upheld and the interest payable. The appeal failed.[307]

*431.* Under the Act wages include all emoluments but not bouns, commission, house rent allowance, overtime and any other allowance. For piece rated workers, daily wages are computed on the average of total earnings for three months preceding the termination of employment, but excluding overtime wages. The Act provides that in the case of a disabled employee who is employed on reduced wages the wages for the period preceding his disablement shall be taken as the wages received by him during that period, but for the subsequent period the wages as so reduced will be taken into account. Another important change is that the seasonal industries/establishments which work throughout the year have been brought at par with the non-seasonal establishments. However, for employees who are not employed in seasonal establishment throughout the year, the rate of gratuity will continue to be paid at the rate of seven days for each season. If an employee changes his job from government service to another employer, he cannot claim continuity of service with the state government. He was given an option and he chose to leave the government service. Hence gratuity was payable only for the period he was in government service.[308]

*432.* In a case the Apex Court had to decide whether dearness allowance is required to be merged or added to the basic pay on par with the state government employees for the purpose of determining the gratuity amount in the light of the government orders of 1995 and 1999 and also the settlement. It held that the dearness allowance is also included in wage and gratuity has to be calculated by taking into account 30 days of wages for every completed year. The Court observed that what was contemplated by the parties was that the rate of dearness allowance would be at par with the rate sanctioned by the state government to its employees from time-to-time and from the same date. It was never contemplated that a different amount of gratuity shall be payable to an employee who retired prior to the revision of scale of pay, although the terms of settlement were applicable to his case. The decision of the Apex Court was binding on the Corporation as well as all its employees who were similarly placed. Some other employees who had retired and filed the writ petition later to secure the same benefit did not succeed. The Apex Court, considering that they had not worked and they were not in service and by the time they filed the petition they had retired, held that such persons were not entitled to the benefit. This happened due to extension of age of retirement from 58 years to 60 years. Those who retired at 58 years were not entitled to relief because they had not worked in service. The judgment of the Apex Court was applicable not only to the petitioners, but also to such of the employees who have not approached the Court. In the light of the above, all the employees who are at par with the *Krishna Reddy*

307. LLJ, October 2010 *U.P.S.R.T.C. Through its Managing Director and Others* v. Mohd. *Rais Khan*, High Court of Allahabad, pp. 279–288.
308. LLJ, June 2010, *Rajkot District Cooperative Dairy Employees Union* v. *State of Gujarat and 7 Others*, High Court of Gujarat, pp. 788–789.

case will become entitled for consideration of their cases by the Corporation irrespective of whether they have approached the court or not.[309]

*433.* In a case the employee was not paid gratuity on retirement. The Labour Court granted him relief though the employer pleaded that the workman had not given either the store clearance or vacated the quarters. The employer was directed to pay the gratuity after deducting the store amount and full pay for the period subsequent to the date of the employee's superannuation and other consequential benefits and also pay Rs 500 as costs. His writ petition was dismissed by the High Court. The Apex Court found the Labour Court in error in treating the retired employee to be in service merely because gratuity had not been paid. The reliance on a notification dated 15 July 1982 was misplaced, partly because it remained in force until 31 December 1983, though the employee retired on 5 November 1986. Moreover, the notification is in four parts. The first part says: The Management shall pay the amount of gratuity to a retiring workman as may be found due to him on receipt of a clearance slip in respect of articles of stores, advance, etc. The workman shall simultaneously vacate his quarters and hand over its possession to the management. The second part says, The retiring workman shall be deemed to be in service and shall be entitled to full wages and all fringe benefits as long as the employer does not tender the due amount of gratuity to him. The notification was applicable to the Sugar Industry.

The Court held that only if the first clause was satisfied, would the second clause come into operation. Only then, if the gratuity was not paid, the employee would be deemed to be in service. The impugned order was set aside. The appellant was directed to withdraw the undisputed amount due to the employee and to pay the same immediately upon his vacating the quarters in question.[310]

*434.* A *beedi* company owning the trade mark 'Seyadu Beedi' was aggrieved by the common order of the appellate authority under the payment of gratuity Act to pay gratuity to the *beedi* workers. since their services were no longer required. They clamed gratuity in respect of the services rendered by them. The management took the plea that the liability to pay gratuity should be fastened, not on them, but the person, known as Shahul Hameed, who supplied the raw materials. The Apex Court had already enquired and decided that the Gratuity Act was a special law and whether in the special circumstances it was not fair that the entire amount be paid by the appellant to the employees without driving them to a separate proceeding. This was cited to clarify the question of the jurisdiction of the Dy. Labour Commissioner who passed the order and not the Joint Commissioner of Labour. The question of lack of jurisdiction did not merit court's attention. The Court noted that

---

309. LLJ, August 2010, *Amar Singh H.B. and Other* v. *Karnataka State Road Transport Corporation, Bangalore and Others*, High Court of Karnataka, pp. 386–398; the judgment in the case LLJ, 2007, Vol. 1, *Management of K.S.R.T.C. Through Chief Law Officer* v. *R. Krishna Reddy*, Supreme Court of India, pp. 231–235.

310. LLJ, 2006, Vol. 4, *Ganeshwar Ltd* v. *Sugar Mills Mazdoor Sangh and Another*, Supreme Court of India, pp. 750-51. A similar case was decided along the same laws in 2008, LLJ, 2008, Vol. 3, *UP State Sugar Corporation and Another* v. *Sukhveer Singh and Another*, High Court of Allahabad, pp. 779–782. The case was decided in favour of the appellant by relying on the Standing Orders.

before the enactment of the *Beedi* and Cigar Worker (Conditions of Employment) Act, 1966 the *beedi* owner used to avoid statutory payments. Section 2(g) of the Act defines the term 'employer' in a wider angle. The purpose was to hold the trade-mark owner as the ultimate authority to pay gratuity and other amounts. This makes the owner of trade mark, the appellate, liable for payment of gratuity. At this stage the Court took notice of the communication of the Appellate Authority that in the absence of an interim order the amounts deposited by the appellants have been paid to the employees. In this light the writ petition was misconceived and the same was dismissed.[311]

*435.* The petitioner bank adjusted a sum of about Rs 1.61 lakhs due to an employee on account of gratuity in respect of a housing loan payable by him. This was not considered proper by the Appellate Authorities under the Act. The petition challenged their orders. The loan amount was about Rs 600,000 and the employee who was an officer with the bank was compulsorily retired on the proven charge of causing the loss to the bank to the tune of Rs 790,366 The Appellate authority had directed the bank to pay a sum of gratuity of Rs 161,700 and further a sum of Rs 50,193 as interest for delayed payments. Other authorities had confirmed the order. Meanwhile all other terminal dues were released to the employee. The gratuity amount was appropriated towards partial satisfaction of the outstanding housing loan. Still his liabilities were much more than the terminal benefits and he was liable to pay the same. The pension was being released regularly. The Court held that, in view of the facts and circumstances of the case, there was no hesitation to hold that the bank was well within its right to adjust the amount of gratuity towards the outstanding housing loan amount of the employee. His conduct was most reprehensible and unbecoming of an officer and he was not entitled to any relief from this Court. The writ petition succeeded and the orders passed by the Controlling Authority and the Appellate Authority were quashed.[312]

*436.* In one case the petitioner challenged the order of the state government to make deductions from the gratuity amount without granting him a hearing and no records or materials produced before the Court in support of their contentions. The petitioner retired as an assistant teacher in a high school. The government deducted Rs 65,125 from the gratuity, as evident from the Pension Payment Order. The deduction was an account of overdrawal of pay. As mistakes were detected by the audit department in the fixation of pay, the authorities were competent to recover the said sum from the pension or gratuity or both within four years after the date of retirement under the relevant scheme. The government took the plea that a mistake did not confer any right to any party and it could be corrected. The Court held that since the action of deduction was detrimental to the petitioner, it was incumbent upon the state of afford him an opportunity to present his case. The unilateral action of deducing a sum of Rs 65,125 cannot be sustained. Moreover, the affidavit filed

311. LLJ, 2009, Vol. 3, *Management, Seyadu Beedi Co. Tirunelveli* v. *Appellate authority, Payment of Gratuity Act and Another*, High Court of Madras, pp. 35–38.
312. LLJ, 2008, Vol. 2, *Punjab and Sind Bank* v. *Labour Commissioner and Others*, High Court of Punjab and Haryana, pp. 841–844.

by the state is totally bereft of particulars. The assertions made in the petition have virtually gone uncontroverted. The affidavit in opposition is a tell-tale account of how the efficiency of the government department has reached its nadir. The action taken is high handed, arbitrary, mala fide and illegal. The order of deduction cannot be sustained and it was set aside and quashed. The writ sedition succeeded.[313]

*437.* The Payment of Gratuity Act is a complete code. If there is any dispute as to the amount of gratuity or the admissibility of any claim, etc. the employer must deposit the admitted amount with the controlling authority. If the employer raises an objection about maintainability of the application for payment of gratuity to the retired employee, the issue must be adjudicated and decided in the forum provided in the Act. The objection cannot travel to another forum provided by another Act. The benefit of gratuity cannot be denied under Section 22 of the Sick Industrial Companies (Special Provisions) Act, 1985. It is not a bar for recovery of payment of wages or gratuity to workmen though the unit may have been declared sick. Nor can the gratuity payment be withheld from an employee on the ground that disciplinary proceedings were still pending. These lapse on superannuation. If under the Rule, disciplinary proceedings cannot be continued after the superannuation of the employee, there is no question of withholding his retiral dues.[314]

## §6. Maternity Benefits

*438.* The Maternity Benefit Act, 1961 has been amended several times, in 1970, 1972, 1973, 1988, 1995 and 2007. Gradually this Act has extended to the whole of India. It applies to every establishment being a factory, mine, the circus industry or plantation and to every shop and establishment which is engaged in equestrian, acrobatic and other performances in which 10 or more persons are employed, except the employees covered under the ES Insurance for certain periods before and after child birth and provides for maternity and other benefits. The Act empowers the state governments, on obtaining the approval of the central government, to notify it in respect of any other establishment or class of establishments, industrial, commercial, agricultural or otherwise. Thus the Act is of potentially universal coverage. The Municipal Corporation of Delhi which employed a large number of woman workers, though not regularized, was ordered to provide them all the benefits conceived under the Act, though the provisions of the Act had not been applied to it. The Apex Court decided to scrutinize the claim of working women by bringing in the directive principles of the Constitution and the UN convention on discrimination against

313. LLJ, 2009, Vol. 1, *Dhirendra Nath Purkait* v. *State of West Bengal and Others*, High Court of Calcutta, pp. 685–687.

314. LLJ, Vol. 1, 2000, *Dholpur Kraya Vikaraya Sahkari Samiti Ltd.* v. *Controller under Payment of Gratuity Act, Bharatpur and Others*, High Court of Rajasthan, pp. 663–664; LLJ, Vol. 1, 2000, *Swadeshi Cotton Mills* v. *Asstt. Labour Commissioner (Central) and Controlling Authority under Payment of Gratuity Act, Allahabad and Others*, High Court of Allahabad, pp. 1221–225; LLJ, Vol. 1, 2000, *Krishnendu Narayan Ghosh* v. *Union of India and Others*, High Court of Calcutta, pp. 1543–1556.

women. This Act has been made applicable to *beedi* and cigar workers with the proviso that Sec. 8 and 10 have been omitted. Section 8 provides for the payment of a medical bonus if no pre-natal confinement and post-natal care is provided by the employer free of charge. Section 10 provides for additional leave with wages for a maximum period of one month in cases of illness arising out of pregnancy, delivery, premature birth of the child, miscarriage, medical termination of the pregnancy or a tubectomy operation. The 2007 Amendment substituted a new Section 8 for the existing one to provide for payment of medical bonus of one thousand rupees from the employer, if no pre-natal confinement and post-natal care is provided by the employer free of charge. The central government is authorized to increase this amount by notification subject to the maximum of Rs 20,000. The government raised the medical bonus from Rs 1,000 to Rs 2,500 vide notification dated 11 August 2008.

*439.* Employment of women is prohibited during the six weeks immediately following the day of delivery, miscarriage or medical termination of pregnancy; and no pregnant woman, on a request being made by her, can be required to do any work of an arduous nature which might interfere with her pregnancy, or the normal development of the foetus, or is likely to cause a miscarriage, or to adversely affect her health during the period of one month preceding the period of six weeks before the date of expected delivery, and during the period of six weeks if she does not avail of leave of absence under Section 6 of the Act, (which provides for the claim for maternity benefit and payment thereof). The maternity benefit to which a woman is entitled will be calculated on the basis of average daily wage payable to her during the period of three calendar months immediately preceding the date on which she takes maternity leave. To be eligible the woman should have worked for not less than 80 days in the 12 months immediately preceding the date of her expected delivery. The maternity benefit is payable at the rate of average daily wage for the period of actual absence up to 12 weeks due to delivery. In cases of illness arising due to pregnancy, they are entitled to additional leave with wage for a period of one month. In one case a woman employee working on a contract basis was denied maternity leave on the ground that she was employed on a consolidated salary. She had entered the State Medical and Health Services after being found fit and eligible by a selection committee. The Court admitted her writ petition against the impugned communication added 27 April 2006, denying her maternity leave since there was no provision for maternity leave in the rules. This was opposed to the normal practice of the Rajasthan government on providing maternity leave to its women employees. The Court held the communication as neither justified nor bonafides. It referred to Article 42 of the Constitution and to the judgments of the Apex Court. The impugned communication was quashed. The respondents were required to take up for consideration the sanctioning of maternity leave as applied for and all the consequential benefits thereto within 30 days from today.[315]

315. LLJ, 2008, Vol. 3, *Dr Mrs. Hemlata Saraswat* v. *State of Rajasthan and Others*, High Court of Rajasthan, pp. 423–429.

*440.* A woman who has been deprived of maternity benefit or medical bonus, or both, or discharged or dismissed during her pregnancy or on account of her being absent from work for this reason, has the right to appeal to the Authority under the Act, and the decision of the Authority shall be final. The Act makes an extraordinary provision of empowering the Inspector to direct payments to be made to any woman who claims that maternity benefit or any other amount to which she is entitled have been improperly withheld or that she has been discharged or dismissed on account of absence from work. The Act has made stringent provisions of penalty, including fines and imprisonment for the employer who may contravene the Act in respect of providing maternity benefit to eligible women. However, if a woman works in any establishment during the periods of maternity leave she shall forfeit the claim for maternity benefit for such period. In a case, a maternity benefit case was seen to be languishing in the High Court ever since the Labour Court passed its award in 1999. It was heard in April 2006. The services of a lower division clerk were terminated when she proceeded on maternity leave. The Labour Court held the termination as illegal, but instead of reinstatement she was granted 3 months' salary. She petitioned the High Court. In fact she was sanctioned leave as requested, but, while on leave she received a communication that her services stood terminated from the date of commencement of leave, no reasons were assigned. The Court in a lengthy judgment propounded the law on maternity leave and decided to reinstate her to her job with continuity of service, but during the long period she had remained unemployed, denied her full back salary 50 per cent of back wages were awarded from the date of termination of her job. She was awarded cost of litigation at Rs 10,000 to be paid within four weeks.[316]

316. LLJ, 2007, Vol. 1, *Chandrika K.* v. *Indian Red Cross Society and Another*, High Court of Delhi, pp. 289–299.

# Chapter 5. Unemployment Compensation

## §1. Introduction

*441.* In India there is no system of providing social security in the event of unemployment. A limited amount of unemployment security is provided under the Industrial Disputes Act. This will be described under the statutory provisions for lay-off, retrenchment and closure. It was the practice among the progressive employers to pay voluntarily such amounts as they considered reasonable and fair to reduce the hardships caused by lay-off or retrenchment, and for the tribunals to award compensation after taking several factors into consideration. This was not a satisfactory way of handling a general dispute on which unions had taken a strong position. The matter took a serious turn in 1953 when the cotton textile industry, faced with accumulated stocks, decided to reduce shifts and to lay-off or retrench a large number of workers. In order to forestall this possibility and the consequent industrial unrest the government promulgated an ordinance in October 1953 making it obligatory to pay lay-off and retrenchment compensation to the affected workmen in all establishment covered by the ID Act and followed it up with an amendment to the Act.

## §2. Lay-off Compensation

*442.* Lay-off means the failure, refusal or inability of an employer to give employment to a worker, whose name is borne on his muster-rolls, within two hours of his presenting himself on account of:

- shortage of coal, power or raw materials: or
- the accumulation of stock; or
- the breakdown of machinery; or
- natural calamity; or
- any other connected reasons.

*443.* In respect of chapter VA, the provisions of lay-off and retrenchment do not apply to industrial establishments in which less than 50 workmen are employed on an average per working day in the preceding month or those which are of a seasonal character or in which work is performed only intermittently. These provisions apply only to those workmen who meet the definition of 'continuous service' which refers to rendering continuous service for a period of 240 days in a year preceding the date on which lay-off or retrenchment occurs and over a period of six months, it is 120 days. The period of 240 days need not be in the same service or same type of service. This period includes paid holidays and leave with full wages or absence caused by temporary disablement due to an accident arising out of and in the course of employment, as well as the days on which he has been laid-off, and in case of a female, the period of maternity leave.

*444.* In respect of Chapter VB, the provisions relating to lay-off, retrenchment and closure are applicable to industrial establishments, as in Chapter VA, in which not less than 100 workmen were employed on an average per working day in the preceding 12 months. Under this chapter lay-off is prohibited of a workman (other than a *badli* workman or a casual workman), whose name is borne on the muster-rolls, except with the prior written permission of the appropriate government. No permission is required if such lay-off is due to shortage of power or natural calamity and in the case of a mine if it is due to fire, flood, excess of inflammable gas or explosions. Financial stringency is not a cause for which a lay-off could be given. If power is disconnected due to financial difficulties and workers are laid off without prior permission it would be illegal.

*445.* The employer is required to make an application stating the reasons for the intended lay-off with a copy served on the concerned workmen. Where a lay-off has already occurred due to valid reasons, the employer must apply for permission within 30 days, if the lay-off is to continue. On receiving such as application the concerned authority may either grant such permission or refuse it but only after giving the employer and the workmen the opportunity of being heard and for reasons to be recorded in writing. If the government does not communicate the order within 60 days of making the application, it shall be deemed to have been granted. If an order has been issued, it shall be final and binding for one year. However, the government on its own motion, or on the application made by either the employer or any workman, refer the order and the matter to a tribunal for adjudication. Where a reference has been made to a tribunal, it shall pass an award within 30 days from the date of such reference.

*446.* A lay-off can occur only in a business that continues and the laid off worker remains on the muster-rolls. The employer has the duty to recall the worker as soon as the circumstances that gave rise to the inability to provide work have been removed. Workmen can be laid off due to purely trade reasons. It cannot be used as a weapon of collective bargaining or for exerting unfair pressure upon workers. In one case 38 workers were asked to quit, but they refused and raised an industrial dispute. Thereupon they were laid-off without payment of compensation and after 45 days they were retrenched. During the period of lay-off workers resorted to the tactics of *gherao* officers and pelted stones. Retrenchment compensation when offered was refused. In this case the management action was not faulted.[317]

*447.* Under Chapter VA, the lay-off compensation is payable at 50 per cent of the total of basic wages and DA for all days of lay-off, except for such weekly holidays as may intervene. There must be an agreement between the employer and workmen for nonpayment of compensation for lay-off beyond 45 days. After the period of 45 days the employer may retrench workers in accordance with the provisions of the Act and when he does so the compensation paid for lay-off may be set-off against the compensation payable for retrenchment. The employer is required

317. LLJ, 1995, Sh. *Satya Prakash Giri and Other* v. *Presiding Officer, Industrial Tribunal Haryana and Another*, High Court of Punjab and Haryana, pp. 437–441.

to serve a notice of commencement of lay-off to the authorities within seven days. Similarly a notice of termination of lay-off should be sent within seven days.

*448.* Under both Chapter VA and VB, particularly the latter, a workman is not deemed to be laid off if he is offered any alternative employment in the same establishment or in any other belonging to the same employer situated in the same town or village or near about, provided that no special skills are required, and it does not involve any loss of wages. If the workman refuses to accept an alternative employment which is reasonable, and it would not cause any hardship, he loses his claim to compensation under Chapter VA. Similarly no compensation is payable if he does not present himself for work at the appointed time at least once a day. If the lay-off has been caused by a strike or a slow down in another part of the establishment the effected workmen will not be entitled to any compensation (Section 25E).

*449.* A number of points pertaining to the law may be noted. First, the lay-off compensation payable under Section 25(C) is controlled by the definition of lay-off under Section 2(kkk) and by the SO of the establishment. The right to lay-off does not exist outside of the Act and the SO. Second, an employer can declare a lock-out and, when this action is justified, lay-off compensation cannot be claimed during the period of involuntary unemployment. Third, it is better to incorporate the statutory provisions on lay-off in the SO. The right to lay-off can be exercised only if it is legal and matched by the obligation to pay compensation.

*450.* Chapter VA qualifies the right to lay-off compensation only in respect of the employer who owns an 'industrial establishment', and the level of employment is 50 or more on any days but less than 100 when Chapter VB takes over. What happens to workmen who are not covered by Chapter VA but are laid off? Are they entitled to any compensation? Section 25J can be invoked if a workman is entitled to benefits which are more favorable than those provided in Chapter VA or elsewhere in the ID Act. Ordinarily the workman who are not covered by Chapter VA would be entitled to their full wages, but if a reference is made to a tribunal/Labour Court, a lesser sum may be awarded should the lay-off be found to be justifiable.

## §3. Retrenchment Compensation

*451.* Under the 1984 amendment, under S(00) (bb), retrenchment means the termination of the service of a workman for any reason other than as a punishment, excluding:

- voluntary retirement; or
- retirement on superannuation; or
- termination of service as a result of the non-renewal of contract of employment on its expiry; or
- such contract being terminated under a stipulation contained in the contract; or
- termination on the ground of continued ill health.

In West Bengal the last point has been omitted by an amendment. Hence termination on grounds of continued ill health is also retrenchment. Termination of service not covered by the excluded categories amount to retrenchment. The termination of the service of a workman whose appointment was void *ab initio* would not amount to retrenchment and such a person would not be entitled to retrenchment compensation. A contract of appointment which comes to an end by passing of time does not amount to retrenchment. A temporary workman whose employment is terminated for the reason that work is not available is a case of retrenchment. But in this case, since the mandatory provisions of the Section 25F were not complied with, though retrenchment compensation was paid and accepted, the order of termination was not legal, nor was it a proper order of termination. It was set aside and the company was directed to reinstate the workman with back wages.[318]

*452.* The workmen who are eligible for lay-off compensation are also entitled to retrenchment compensation. Chapters VA and VB make common provisions for lay-off and retrenchment. The former provides that no workman who has been in continuous service for not less than one year can be retrenched until:

- he has been given one month's notice in writing stating the reasons for retrenchment and the notice period has expired or wages paid in lieu of the notice period;
- the retrenchment compensation calculated at the rate of 15 days of average pay for every completed year of service or any part thereof in excess of six months has been paid; and
- notice in the prescribed manner has been served on the appropriate government.

These provisions also apply in cases involving transfer of ownership (Section 22FF), or change in management of an undertaking resulting in termination of service of some workmen. All such cases should be treated as if they had been retrenched. On the other hand, if the service of any workman is not interrupted by the transfer of ownership and he is reemployed on the terms and conditions of service which are not less favourable, the new employer, under the terms of transfer, is legally liable to pay retrenchment compensation on the basis that the service of any workman has been continuous and has not been interrupted by the transfer. Retrenchment without complying with the conditions precedent (Section 25F) would be void *ab initio*.

*453.* In establishments employing 100 or more workmen, Chapter VB has provided for conditions precedent to retrenchment. No workman who has been in continuous service for not less than one year can be retrenched until:

- the workman has been given three months notice in writing or has been paid wages in lieu thereof; and
- the prior permission of the government has been obtained on an application made in this behalf.

318. LLJ, Vol. 1, 2001, *ANZ Grindlays Bank* v. *General Secretary, Grindlays Bank Employees' Union and Others*, High Court of Bombay, pp. 1238–1241.

Where permission of retrenchment has been granted, every workman who is to be retrenched must be paid compensation at the rate of 15 days of wages for every completed year of service or any part thereof in excess of six months. But a company lacking in bonafides may obtain the government's permission to make retrenchment and pay compensation and the same accepted by workman, yet the retrenchment order is liable to be set aside because a proper retrenchment must be for bonafide reasons.[319]

*454.* If retrenchment compensation has not been paid, the notice of retrenchment becomes inoperative. Whether a workman has completed 240 days of service or not in a period of 12 months preceding the date of termination should be established. The workman is bound to prove that he had been in continuous service of 240 days during twelve months preceding the order of termination. In a case where he invokes the provisions of S25G and 25H thereof, he may not have to establish the said fact. S25G provides that in the absence of an agreement between the employer and the workman in this behalf, the employer shall retrench the last person to be employed unless for reasons to be recorded the employer retrenches any other workman. S25H provides that where any workmen are retrenched and the employer proposes to take any other person in his employ, he must give an opportunity to the retrenched persons to offer themselves and they will have preference over other persons. These provisions have no application where S(00) (bb) is attracted. Termination of service due to non-renewal of the contract of employment or termination of such contract of employment would not be retrenchment.

Ordinarily, the employers should effect retrenchment on the principle of 'last in come, first out', but for sufficient reasons a departure can be made. Each branch of a company can be regarded as a distinct establishment for the purpose of retrenchment and the junior-most should go first. Industrial tribunals are not competent to question the reorganization scheme that gives rise to surplus workers, hence retrenchment.[320]

*455.* Where a workman fails to prove 240 days of service in a year preceding termination, he could not claim violation of Section 25F (Conditions precedent to retrenchment). In one case the cook's attendance record was not up to the mark. He was paid wages and benefits as per the rules. His termination was discharge *simpliciter.* He worked in a temporary capacity and was dismissed as such. In all he had worked for 221 days, including Sundays and other holidays. Consequently Sections 2(00) and 25F of the ID. Act were not attracted. The Court held that no legal right accured to the workman under labour laws. His writ petition was dismissed.[321]

*456.* In a case a project employee's service was terminated on the termination of the project. He claimed that he had put in 1000 days of continuous service and that

---

319. LLJ, Vol. 2, 2000, *Gordon Woodroffe and Staff Union* v. *Joint Commissioner of Labour, Madras and Another*, High Court of Madras, pp. 1150-1168.
320. LLJ, 2007, Vol. 1, *Bhogpur Coop. Sugar Mills Ltd* v. *Harmesh Kumar*, Supreme Court of India, pp. 488–490.
321. LLJ, 2007, Vol. 1, *Gurjeet Singh Bhatia* v. *Management of Narang International Hotel (P) Ltd*, High Court of Delhi, pp. 403-404.

the principle of 'last come, first go' was not complied with. His claim was upheld by the High Court, which led the Railway Administration as the appellant to the Supreme Court. The Court noted that he was paid retrenchment compensation in terms of Section 25F of the ID Act. However, his plea was that he should have been placed much higher in the seniority list and thus could not have been retrenched. The Court said that if a casual employee is employed in different establishments, may be under the same employer e.g. the Railway Administration as a whole, the concept of continuous service could not be applied. There are different requirements and different projects, so it would not be possible to claim higher status on the basis of continuous service. Moreover, if the project came to a close, the requirement of Section 25N were not required to be complied with.The impugned judgment could not be sustained and was set aside accordingly. The appeal was allowed.[322]

*457.* In a case several employees lost their jobs on the closure of a company under Section 25FFA of the ID Act. The Industrial Court held the closure as valid and legal. Almost all workers accepted their dues and in respect of the unclaimed balance the closed company deposited the amount with the Maharashtra Labour Welfare Board. The union challenged the closure successively at the Industrial Court, the High Court and the Supreme Court and met with dismissal of its petition at every stage. Thereafter 65 workmen who used to work in the closed unit made a complaint at the Industrial court that the employer had started another unit at another location, 11 years later and in terms of Section 25H they were entitled to be offered employment in the new unit and some other relief. The complaint was of unfair labour practices under the MRTU & PULP Act, 1971 and that the employer be directed to desist from the same. In addition he should be directed to take the necessary steps to collect the amounts from the Maharashtra Labour Welfare Board and pay them 50 per cent of the wages from the date of filing the complaint till passing of the order and pay full wages till the revival of employment at the rate of wages being paid at the new factory. The judgement incorporated the above noted part of the complaint and two months of time was granted for compliance with the order. Aggrieved by this order the employer appealed to the High Court, the Single Judge modified the order of the Industrial Court and set aside the order of payment of 50 per cent of back wages. The employer appealed against the order that the employees were entitled to relief under Section 25 H, the complaint that it was an unfair labour practice, that the employer showed favour to some of the older workers by giving the employment in the new factory. The Court relied on an earlier judgement of the Supreme Court on Section 25 H. 'Once a valid transfer or a valid closure comes into effect, the relationship of employer and employee does not survive and ceases to exist.' Section 25H has no application in such an event when there is a closure of an undertaking. The court decided,

> In our opinion, if the effect of valid closure is cessation of relationship between the employer and the employee, there is no question of application of S25H, in

322. LLJ, 2007, Vol. 1, *Union of India and Others* v. *Jummasha Diwan*, Supreme Court of India, pp. 225–227.

> such a situation. 'Closure may be of a unit or part of an undertaking, it need not be the closure of the entire plant. The closure maybe of an industrial undertaking and not necessarily of the entire business of the employer S25H will get attracted only in a case the employer wants to start the same undertaking which is closed down. It cannot be extended to a case where after a valid closing down of an undertaking, the employer wants to set up an industrial undertaking at some other places. The argument of unfair labour practice has no substance. Once the relationship of employer and employee comes to an end, there is no question of the employer committing an unfair labour practice of the nature specified in items of the MRTU & PULP Act.

The appeal filed by the employer succeeded and Schedule 4 the order of the single judge was set aside. The complaint filed by the workmen was dismissed and so was the appeal filed by them.[323]

*458.* Retrenchment is not complete unless the compensation has been paid. If the workman refuses to accept the payment, the employer cannot be faulted.However, it is not a valid argument to advance that the compensation was kept ready, but it could not be paid because the workman deliberately absented himself from work. In a case, 173 workers, who had been retrenched without following the provisions of Section 25F (conditions precedent of retrenchment) and Section 25G (last come first go) were reinstated with back wages. The union had claimed that the retrenchment was unauthorized, invalid and illegal and it was done for false reasons. The Court found that compensation had not been paid on or before the date of retrenchment, nor was the notice served to all workman.

*459.* An employee employed as a gardener-cum-watchman than was retrenched after working for more two and a half years without giving him a notice or pay in lieu thereof or retrenchment compensation and complying with the mandate of law. Several persons junior to him were retained,though no seniority list was prepared. This was in the wake of government instructions on the need to cut back on expenditure due to a financial crisis. It appears that as per Section 25F of the ID Act a demand draft of compensation money was sent at his address, but the employee declined to accept it and left the station. It was sent again and was accepted. As recorded by the Labour Court, the total number of employees was about 400, so Section 25N of the Act was applicable. There was no evidence furnished by the management that compensation was refused. It decided that the workman was entitled to reinstatement with full back wages. This award was challenged in a writ petition. The court allowed it and set aside the award of the Labour Court. One reason was that the employee could not be reinstated in service because he was not employed against any sanctioned post and his initial employment was made without complying with the statutory provisions. There were judgments of the Supreme Court, that a person who has taken entry illegally by the back door cannot be reinstated. The Apex Court noted that the Labour Court had taken a similar stand in the

323. LLJ, January 2011, *Somayya S. Bhandari and Others* v. *Oriental Rubber Industries Ltd*, High Court of Bombay, pp. 193–200

case of several other employees whose services were terminated. The writ petitions filed against the award were dismissed by the High Court, though this judgment was not kept in view by the Bench which admitted the writ petition. It assumed that the initial employment was not legal and that the conditions precedent to retrenchment were complied with. The Apex Court held that the approach adopted by the Division Bench was contrary to the judicially recognized limitations of the High Court's power to issue the writ of *certiorari* under Article 226 of the Constitution. Moreover, if the mandatory provisions of Section 25F were not followed, the retrenchment of an employee would be a nullity. No documents were produced to prove that compensation was offered at the time of termination. There was no pleading that the employee was engaged without following statutory rules. The High Court was not justified in setting aside the award. The Apex Court restored the award and allowed the appeal. If the appellant has not been reinstated, the respondent shall do so within one month of receipt of this order.[324]

*460.* In a case the Courts had to deal with an order of retrenchment under Section 25N of the Act. 'The gradual souring of relations between the workers and the management commenced with a strike call given by the workers on 3 April 2001 and got aggravated when the management purported to take a decision to jettison 90 permanent workers and moved an application before the government on 12 September 2002 for permission to retrench them under Section 25N of the Industrial Disputes Act. During the strike the management outsourced the making of seat covers for Maruti Udyog Ltd, India's biggest car manufacturer. They then decided to close the stitching unit and depend for it on an independent contractor. The workers' response was that it was an act of victimization and the permission ought not be granted. The government granted the permission on 10 October 2002, but limited the number to be retrenched to 82 workmen. The union made an application for a review of the decision but failed. It then filed a writ petition against the order passed by the government, the bonafides of management were questioned; victimization was alleged; workmen were illegally employed through a contractor, and the primary motive was to close down the stitching unit, and the appropriate procedure was to seek permission under Section 25O of the Act. Hence the application for retrenchment was not competent. The management's its defence was purely legalistic and formal compliance with the procedure. Moreover, in the altered scheme of production and meeting the demand of the principal, to reduce the cost of production and price, at first by 4.5 per cent, followed by a further reduction of 25 per cent, left no other option. The scaling down of operation and reduced economies of scale necessitated reorganization of the assembly line, the PU department, the stitching department, the maintenance department and quality control. The Court examined all the issues in the light of the scope of judicial review. The management's rights to organize his business was subject only to the bonafides. If it was accepted on the

324. LLJ, July 2010, *Anoop Sharma* v. *Executive Engineer, Public Health Division, Panipat (Haryana)*, Supreme Court of India, pp. 1–9.

basis of facts and arguments, the tribunal cannot question its propriety. The law provides for exit. The government decision has been taken on due consideration of all the relevant facts. The petition was dismissed.[325]

*461.* The Tamil Nadu Khadi and Village Industries Board employed 2200 employees all over the state. The government directed it to retrench 86 employees on making a one time payment of Rs 4 crore. It worked on subsidy from the government and was turning in losses year after year. Following the order, the Board decided to abolish 862 posts and to retrench the employees holding these posts. The employees chose to approach the High Court with a writ appeal. The Court had to decide whether the board was an industry and whether the Board had violated Section 25N of the ID Act. There was also the question of maintainability of the petition since it questioned an administrative policy decision. The Court referred to the ideology of the Father of our Nation, Gandhi, and the directive principles of the Constitution on promotion of *Khadi* and rebutted the issue of maintainability. It held that the Board had several manufacturing units producing *Khadi* yarn and cloth, soap, paper, honey, leather products, food products, pottery, toys, etc which aim at improving the economic activities at the village level. These fitted the definition of the term, 'industry', in the Act. The Court held that the Board was covered by the Industrial Disputes Act, 1947 and that it was an industry. It was bound to observe the mandatory prohibitions imposed by the Act in regard to retrenchment. The Board should have made an application for permission to the government, giving reasons for the proposed retrenchment and serve a notice on all of the concerned workmen. On receiving the permission the Board should comply with the Section 25F pertaining to the conditions precedent to retrenchment, and accordingly pay the compensation. This procedure was not followed. Hence the Court held that the impugned action was in violation of Section 25N of the ID Act, and it was deelared void and illegal. The government no doubt provided funds to the Board, but it could not direct it to act in violation of the statutory provisions. The 862 employees who held regular and permanent positions in the Board could not be ousted and sent out without complying with the provisions of law. The employees would be entitled to continue in service, but during the period of unemployment they would not be entitled to wages. They will be taken back in service within a period of four weeks from today. The writ petitions were allowed.[326]

*462.* A workman claimed that his termination was without notice or notice pay and retrenchment compensation, therefore illegal. The Labour Court came to the conclusion that the termination occurred after the workman had put in a service of about three years and he drew the salary of a machine man, not of a helper as claimed by the employer. The court ordered his reinstatement with full back wages. This led the petitioner employer to the High Court. One of the pleas was that the

---

325. LLJ, October 2010, *Bharat Seats Employees Union* v. *Specified Authority Under S-25N of the ID Act and Another,* High Court of Punjab and Haryana, pp. 87–92.

326. LLJ, Vol. 1, 2007, *Madheswaran A.* v. *State of Tamil Nadu represented by the Secretary to the Government, Handloom, Handicrafts, Textiles and Khadi Crafts Deptt. Chennai,* High Court of Madras, pp. 28–40.

workman had abandoned his job and it was not a case of termination. This was rejected by the court on the ground that it cannot reappraise the evidence which was examined by the Labour Court. No enquiry was conducted by the employer on the unauthorized absence of the workman; the workman's contention that he had gone to join duty but was not allowed to join remain unrefuted. Another plea was that the reference was not legal. This was not examined by the Labour Court, but on this ground the award could not be set aside. The writ petition was dismissed with cost of Rs 10,000 payable by the petitioner to the workman.[327]

*463.* Retrenchment compensation is payable as per Section 25F of the Act. An employer cannot hope to save his retrenchment order by offering compensation on a higher scale. However, compensation paid as part of a voluntary retirement plan, or on the basis of a settlement that is more beneficial to workers than the statutory scheme, would be beyond question. Accordingly, it is a common practice for managements seeking reduction in their labour force to arrive at agreements with their unions which include voluntary retirement plans or schemes of retrenchment. The compensation may be paid at the rate of one month of pay for every year of service plus three months of pay in lieu of the notice period. In this manner the provisions of the ID Act are wholly avoided.

*464.* According to the new definition, termination on the expiry of contract does not amount to retrenchment. Taking this plea, the Allahabad University terminated the service of some daily-wage earners who had worked continuously for five years without any break and did not pay them any compensation. The contract has been renewed after every three/six months and the university took the plea that they were not regular employees. The plea fell before the Allahabad High Court. The Court took the view that if contractual employment was used as a mechanism to frustrate the claim of employees to become regular or permanent against jobs which were permanent in nature, such contract/agreement would have to pass the test of fairness and bona fides. An agreement for arm twisting or to perpetuate the policy of hire and fire cannot be deemed to be included in the relevant clause of the definition of retrenchment. In another case, however, it was held that once an appointment is for a fixed period. Section 25F would not apply, because it would be covered by the exclusions listed in the definition of the term 'retrenchment'. Termination of an employment can be examined by the court only if there is a finding that the power was misused or vitiated by its malafide exercise. In another case, the court held that, unless the appointment of a workman on casual or daily wages was in terms of relevant rules and due process of selection, he could not claim to be made permanent. The concept of 240 days of services had to be read in the light of the above rule and not *dehors* the same. As the appointment as a temporary, casual and daily rated workman was otherwise illegal, he was not entitled to be reinstated, on ground of non-compliance with Section 25F of the ID Act. Consequently the award directing

327. LLJ, Vol. 1, 2007, *Emsons Radio Corporation and Another* v. *Secretary (Labour) Government of NCT, Delhi and Another*, High Court of Delhi, pp. 140–142.

the workman to be reinstated with full back wages was held to be not sustainable. It was set aside and quashed.[328]

*465.* In a case the question was whether Section 25N was applicable to the Haryana Land Reclamation and Development Corporation Ltd. The single judge of the High Court had answered the question in the affirmative which led to a writ petition. The Court held that prima facie it could not be said that the Corporation was an industrial establishment since the packages of gypsum and pesticides received by it were sold in 'as it is' condition at its various sales points. Its entire activity was in the nature of trading. The Corporation's main object was to undertake, assist, aid, finance, execute and promote measures for land development, conservation and improvement of soil and water resources. The Corporation had declared 11 clerks-cum-typists as surplus who were later retrenched. Section 25F was complied with, but not Section 25N. The Court said that the proper course for deciding whether a particular Corporation was an industrial establishment or not was to secure the reference of such a dispute under the ID Act, so that the issue could be decided on the basis of evidence on record. The finding of the single judge was set aside.[329]

## §4. Closures

*466.* In several cases it was alleged that Section 25G and Section 25H of the ID Act were violated by the employer and the Court had to decide whether the provisions of these two sections were complied with or in a given situation, they were required to be complied with. It was contended that the requirement of continuous work in terms of Section 25B was not necessary in so far as the statutory requirements under Sections 25G and 25H were concerned. According to the Supreme Court, Section 25H is capable of application to all retrenched workmen and not merely those covered by S25F. The provision for reemployment of retrenched workmen in the matter of reemployment gives preference to a retrenched workman. It is enacted for their benefit, but without causing any prejudice to a better placed retrenched workman. On Section 25G, the Court said that the rule of first come last go, could be deviated from by the employer, if he belongs to a particular category of workmen in the absence of any agreement between the employer and the workmen in this behalf, for reasons to be recorded. This rule can be deviated from in cases of lack of efficiency or loss of confidence, etc., but the burden will then be on the employer to justify the deviation. On the question of reinstatement with entire back wages, this court time and again has held that the jurisdiction under Section 11A must be exercised judiciously. The workman must be employed by a state within the meaning of Article 12 of the Constitution of India having regard to public employment. It is also required to recruit employees in terms of the provisions of the rules for recruitment framed by it. In the given case, the workman had not

---

328. LLJ, November, 2010, *New India Assurance Co. Ltd* v. *Narender Kumar*, High Court of Delhi, pp. 498–502.
329. LLJ, Vol. 2 1994, *Haryana Land Reclamation and Development Corp. Ltd* v. *Pawan Kumar*, High Court of Punjab and Haryana, pp. 1198–1204.

regularly served under the appellant. The job was not of perennial nature. There was nothing to show that when his services were terminated any person junior to him in the same category had been retained. The Court held that it would not be proper to direct his reinstatement with back wages. 'We, therefore, are of the opinion that interest of justice would be sub-served, if instead of and in place of reinstatement of his services, a sum of Rs 75,000 is awarded to the respondent by way of compensation as has been done by this Court in a number of judgements.'[330]

*467.* Under Ch. VA, the provisions on closure are applicable to an industrial establishment in which less than 50 workmen are employed or were employed on an average per working day in the preceding 12 months and to an undertaking set up to do construction work. Section 25FFA provides that a notice of at least 60 days must be served upon the appropriate government, if the employer intends to close down an undertaking. If the undertaking employs 100 or more workers a notice of 90 days must be served under Section 25O of Chapter VB. Whereas in the former case, the employer may serve notice and proceed to close down his undertaking and pay compensation under Section 25FFF without waiting for permission to be given, under Section 25O, he cannot do so until permission has been received from the government, Closures may not be always permanent and irrevocable. A change of circumstances may encourage an employer to revive the industrial activity, and this leads to the question whether any closure is for bona fide reasons or just a devise to terminate the services of workmen. It is for the industrial court to determine whether, in a given case, it is a genuine case of closure or a lock-out in the guise of closure. Where an undertaking is closed down, every workman who has been in continuous service for not less than one year is entitled to receive before such closure a notice and compensation in accordance with the provisions of Section 25F, as if the workman has been retrenched.

*468.* Section 25O(2) provides that permission for closure may be granted having regard to the genuineness and adequacy of the reasons stated by the empoyer. These are to be tested in the light of the interest of the general public and other relevant factors. The bona fides of the employer is a relevant factor and the government may probe into all the circumstances to arrive at a conclusion. The government is empowered to refer the matter to the industrial tribunal for reviewing the decision, after a decision to give effect to closure had been given either on an application received from workmen or the employer or on its own motion. The decision to effect closure is valid for one year. An order passed by the appropriate government under Section 25O(2) shall be final and binding on all parties unless it is reviewed by the government, or is disturbed by the Tribunal upon a reference made to it in terms of Section 25O(5). An order passed earlier, upon reference for a review, may be affirmed, modified or set aside, but it does not mean that the order passed under

330. LLJ, Vol. 1, 2007, *Jaipur Development Authority* v. *Ram Sahai and Another*, Supreme Court of India, pp. 429–434. Also, LLJ, Vol. 3, 2009, *Divisional Forest Officer (SFP), Hisar*, v. *Bharat Singh @ Bharta and Anothers*, High Court of Punjab and Haryana, pp. 268–271.

Section 25O(2) becomes inoperative, dead or irrelevant for all purposes, upon invoking of the remedy under Section 25O(5).[331]

*469.* In a case the company was engaged in the small scale industry of manufacturing crank shaft, vibration dampers etc. faced financial and other constraints and decided to close the factory and paid the workmen notice pay and closure compensation. Thirty-five workmen received the notice and accepted the payment. The company obtained stamped receipts from the workmen. The signed receipt has the declaration. 'I have no further or other claim monetary or otherwise including that of reinstatement/reemployment'. Subsequent to this the trade union contended that the closure was illegal, company was carrying on the same work in another name of the same time each of the workers raised an individual dispute under Section 2A(2) of the ID Act before the labour officer, Chennai. Each worker alleged unfair labour practice by the employer in terminating his service without providing any opportunity self defence though he worked faithfully and efficiently. Each worker had joined the trade union affiliated to CITU while the employer close to chose the factory. The matter went before the conciliation officer. The workers claimed that it was only a temporary closure and they were eligible for reinstatement with other benefits. On receiving the failure report, the dispute was referred to the Labour Court for adjudica. The issues raised pertained to Sections 25F and 25G of the ID Act. The Labour Court registered each dispute and conducted separate trial for each industrial dispute and recorded evidence of each workman. He could have grouped them but respecting them as individual disputes chose not to do so. The Labour Court passed awards on different dates. It took notice of two exhibits produced by workers showing delivery notes to Hindustan Motors subsequent to closure notice. The management accepted that the company had sister concerns and that the factory premises have not been vacated and they were paying electricity charges, but these were being used by a sister company. The court failed to notice the fact that the enforcement officer of the Provident Fund Organization had reported that the establishment was closed. The company had surrendered their registration license and the Inspector of Factories knew about its closure. Yet the Labour Court found that there was no real closure in the eye of law and the retrenchment of workers was illegal, since Section 25 H and Section 25 O were not complied with. The company continue to function; moreover, since Section 25F of the ID Act was not complied with, the notice of closure was invalid. Each worker was entitled to reinstatement with 50 per cent of back wages. This award was challenged in a writ petition before the High Court. The single judge who heard the petition found that the findings made by the Labour Court were not in consonance with the materials produced before it. It was an erroneous finding that the muster rolls were not produced. Further, having received full and final payment and giving up any further claim, and without protesting against closure, indeed, accepting closure under Section 25 FFF of the ID Act, the question of individual non-employment does not arise. Moreover, before the conciliation officer workers had said that it was a case of termination, though

---

331. LLJ, Vol. 3, 2009, *Brittania Industries Ltd* v. *Maharashtra General Kamgar Union and Another*, High Court of Bombay, pp. 275–301. This judgment undid other court orders on the subject and became the law in Maharashtra as per the court order.

later they claimed it to be a case of retrenchment. The judge found it startling that the Labour Court had observed that closure means the closure of the company itself. It showed that the Labour Court did not understand the concept of closure. It does not mean that the company should be wound up. It means the permanent closing down of a place of employment or part thereof. The foremost fundamental flaw in the impugned award was that, in the absence of a collective industrial dispute challenging the closure, could the Labour Court, in a dispute under Section 2A(2) of th ID Act go into the real nature of closure? 'If it is held that it was not an industrial establishment covered by chapter V-B, then the question will be, in the absence of a closure held to be invalid, an individual dispute claiming to be non-employment will not arise. There cannot be individual non-employment, because the entire work force is sent out of service on account of closure. Section 25 F applies only for the purpose of computation of compensation and for no other. Once a valid transfer or a valid closure comes into effect, the relationship of employer and employee does not survive and ceases to exist. Compensation is required to be paid to the workman as a consequence thereof and for no other purpose. The position in law is that if the entire establishment of an employer is not closed down, but only a unit is closed which does not have functional integrity with other units of the undertaking, the provision of Section 25 FFF of the Act will get attracted, and the workmen will be entitled to compensation as provided in Section 25 FFF of the Act, which has to be calculated in accordance with Section 25 F of the Act. The disputes raised by the workmen are not maintainable for more than one reason. First, there cannot be individual non-employment in case of a closure. Second, when the workmen have received closure compensation, then it cannot be said that the petitioner management was carrying on its business and the resultant non-employment had deprived them of their legitimate rights. The Labour Court did not take note of the closure compensation received by the workmen. Under the circumstances, this Court is obliged to interfere with the impugned awards. The writ petitions are allowed and the impugned awards will stand set aside.[332]

*470.* The Court order on the sub Section (5) of S25O has caused considerable confusion. Several High Courts decided that as soon as the decision to permit closure has been referred to the tribunal for a review, the principal order taken under Section 25O(2) is stayed and eclipsed and has no force whatsoever. The Tribunal, not being a court of appeal and clothed with quasi-judicial power, could not possibly review the order made by the competent Authority under Section 25O(2), but was empowered by the reference under Section 25O(5) to review the entire matter, as if the application was made to it for full consideration and make an award under this sub-section. The tribunal can not travel beyond Section 25O, because it is a complete code. This was assailed and rejected by the Bench of there judges of Bombay High Court referred to in paragraph 431.[333]

---

332. LLJ, 3, 2012, *Management of Holwart Engineering Company rep. by its sole proprietor, Mr. Ramamoorthy, Chennai* v. *S. Dhanasekar and another*, Madras High Court, pp. 400-412.

333. LLJ, Vol. 2, 2003, *Voltas Employees Union* v. *Voltas Ltd*, High Court of Bombay (referred to by the bench in its judgment).

*471.* In one case the petitioner company challenged the order to review the order giving permission to for closure of one of its divisions. The Authority reviewing its earlier order referred the matter to the industrial tribunal. The challenge was on the ground that no reasons were given. The plea was that the Authority could not have taken the decision without full consideration of facts and reasons recorded for the purpose. The order of reference is a non-speaking order and there is no application of mind. The Court held that the government is clothed with the power to review its own order or to refer the matter to the Tribunal for adjudication with the purpose to examine the legality and validity of the decision under Section 25O(2) of the Act. In the first option, the state government would be required to record reasons as a sine qua non to the extent of modifying the earlier order. But in the second option the government does not review its order, but it refers the matter to adjudication. It would be akin to making a reference under Section 10 of the Act.[334]

*472.* A dispute on the interpretation of Section 25O(5) relative to the order passed under Section 25O(2) came up before the Bombay High Court in 2008 and was decided in favour of workman pleading for an embargo on the implementation of the permission to close down the factory till the matter was adjudicated by the tribunal. Under the Section 25O, the employer is required to apply for permission to effect closure at least 90 days in advance of the intended date of closure. The government is required to complete its enquiries and issue its orders either granting the permission or declining it within 60 days of the date of application. Thereafter the order is final and binding, but it remains in force for one year only. The Court held that the finality and binding character of the order is kept in abeyance and cannot be acted upon once the closure application is referred to the tribunal for adjudication. The award of the tribunal will replace the original order, as if it was never made and instead the application was directly referred to the Tribunal. To the question whether the order passed under Section 25O(2) can be enforced immediately, or the employer must wait for a reasonable time and in any event for 60 days after the permission is granted, the Court held that, 'Once there is a reference, the Tribunal has to consider the application afresh without having to advert to the order of the appropriate government granting the permission for closure.' The period for disposing of an application under Section 25O is 30 days from the date it is referred. The Court said, 'If the employer is permitted to implement the closure immediately on being granted permission under Section 25O(2), the provisions of subsection (5) of Section 25O would be rendered nugatory. That could not be the legislative intent, in letter and spirit. Nor can this be the object of Section 25O which is contained in a welfare legislation.' The restrictions are provided to deter reckless, unfair, unjust and malafides closures. The mechanism of a review/reference has been provided as a safeguard against unwarranted closures of industrial undertakings.[335]

---

334. LLJ, November 2010, *N.S.P. Straw and Paper Products (P) Ltd* v. *Commissioner of Labour, Gujarat State*, High Court of Gujarat, pp. 356–359.
335. LLJ, Vol. 2, 2009, *Navnath Kanha Naik and Others*, v. *United Breweries Ltd and Others*, High Court of Bombay, pp. 558–569 (the order was passed by a single judge).

*473.* In a pathetic case the workers through their unions espoused the hopeless cause of preventing the closure of seven cement plants owned by the public sector ailing company, the Cement Corporation of India Ltd. The Company had been suffering huge losses since 1996 and had been referred to the Board of Industrial and Financial Reconstruction as a sick company. A draft rehabilitation scheme, approved by the BIFR, proposed the sale of one unit, which was carried out. At this stage all but three units were non-operating and yet paying idle wages to labour. Following the service of a show cause notice in 2001 why the company should not be wound up, the company submitted a proposal in 2004 for closure of seven non-operating units and operating of the three remaining units with capital infusion from the central government. At this the BIFR passed an order in March 2006 approving of the scheme of rehabilitation. From this stage onwards the employees' unions started challenging the closure process in courts at every level that was open to them. These included an appeal before the Appellate Authority of Industrial and Financial Reconstruction, a writ petition before the Delhi High Court, a Special Leave Petition before the Supreme Court of India, a writ petition before the Punjab and Haryana High Court and finally another petition before the High Court of Madhya Pradesh. They met with dismissal or rejection every where, but succeeded in stalling and delaying the closures. In the courts the legal basis was provided by Section 25O(5) of the ID Act which provided for the review of the closure decision. Finally the Ministry vide its order on 27 March 2008 granted permission for closure of the seen units with effect from the date of the issue of the order. As the High Court saw it, 'the attempt of the petitioner looked like flogging a dead horse, as the matter had gone through more than one judicial intervention at the highest level.' The government had agreed to set aside its order before the Delhi High Court in May 2008 and provide yet another hearing to the employees. Finally the Competent Authority issued an order in July 2008 granting permission to closure. The writ petition against this order before the High Court of Madhya Pradesh produced an exasperated response. The Court found no merit in the petitions and was inclined to impose cost, but refrained from it.[336]

*474.* If the proviso made in Section 25FFF(1) is applicable, the workman shall be paid closure compensation equivalent to 15 days of average pay for every completed year of continuous service or any part thereof in excess of six months, but, if it is not applicable, and it is found that the undertaking has closed down on account of unavoidable circumstances beyond the control of the employer, the compensation payable is only three months of average pay. The expression 'unavoidable circumstances beyond the control of the employer' comprehends a situation of continuous industrial strife, strikes, lawlessness, violence and negligence by workmen resulting in heavy losses. In one case it was found that the closure was not due to circumstances beyond the control of the employer. The company was under the winding up order of the liquidator. The issue to be decided was: was this a factor

336. LLJ, Vol. 2, 2009, *Cement Corporation Employees Union* v. *Union of India and Others*, High Court Madhya Pradesh, pp. 347–356.

beyond the control of the employer? The official liquidator had answered the question in the affirmative. The Court, however, said that the winding up orders in a large number of cases, are the result of financial difficulties of the companies or due to their inability to discharge all their debts in due course of business. In these circumstances the appropriate finding would be that the financial difficulties were in fact the result of the company's trading activities and were not on account of unavoidable circumstances, beyond the control of the employer. Thus interpreted, the Court was able to uphold the primacy of Section 25FFF over the provisions of the Companies Act. The Court also said that even in cases of liquidation of companies, Section 25O can be invoked to determine the genuineness of the cause for closure by the appropriate government or on review by the tribunal. In this case the employer had closed the undertaking without serving notice under Section 25FFF and it was only in the course of liquidation proceedings that workers realized that they would not be paid compensation as per the provisions of Section 25F. The employer's action was considered as unreasonable as was the order issued by the official liquidator.[337]

*475.* A transport company closed some of its branches because of indiscipline on the part of employees without complying with the provisions of the law in respect of 60 days of notice to the government and the procedure to be followed for retrenchment under Section 25G. The tribunal directed the management to reinstate the employees in identical posts held by them before terminations. The management filed a writ petition before the High Court. The Court held that due to the indiscipline the matter had got out of hand. The workers withheld the documents relating to day-to-day business; they were not affecting delivery of articles received from other branches; no accounts were maintained; claims of damages were being raised by the customer; and there was a huge loss. This was a case of closure caused by unavoidable circumstances beyond the control of the employer. The court drew a subtle distinction between 'closure of branches and relief to employees' and 'relief to employee's consequent to closure'. Accordingly, payment of compensation and wages for the period of notice are not conditions precedent to closure. Moreover, there was an unavoidable impediment to conducting business and this fitted with subsection (i) of Section 25FFF. With the result the tribunal's award was set aside. The tribunal was directed to arrive at a fresh conclusion scanning the entire evidence and with 'due application of mind'. Similar circumstances occurred in a jute mill where Section 25FFF(i) was also found to be applicable and the closure compensation was limited to three months of wages. Non-compliance with Section 25FFF dose not render the closure illegal.[338]

---

337. LLJ, 1995, Vol. 2, *Anthony Raj* v. *A. Shanmugam and Others,* High Court of Madras, pp. 1208–1223.
338. LLJ, Vol. 2. 1994, *Savani Transport Pvt* v. *Savani Transport Employees' Association and Another*, High Court of Kerala, pp. 269–277; LLJ, Vol. 2, 1994, *Presidency Jute Mills Co. Ltd* v. *Fifth Industrial Tribunal and Others*, High Court of Calcutta, pp. 564–572.

§5. TRANSFERS

*476.* Section 25FF though forming part of Chapter VA is also applicable to Chapter V and Chapter VB. The question arose, whether in a case of transfer of an undertaking the employer was bound to comply with Section 25N and Section 25O. On a certain day in 1992, the Company issued a notice to the effect that on that very day, at 10.15 am the ownership of the sugar factory had been transferred and all the employees were entitled to compensation under Section 25FF and their employment would cease forthwith. This was challenged on the ground that the undertaking was covered by Chapter VB and so Section 25N (viz.conditions precedent to retrenchment), would apply. The challenge failed because Section 25FF was equally applicable to factories covered by Chapter VB; and in such a case Section 25N would be clearly inapplicable. Transfer is not closure, because the factory continued to be in operation under the new management. So Section 25O had no application. The contention that transfer of an undertaking really amounted to closure, or it should be equated with the same was rejected as without any merit.[339]

*477.* A company was transferred to anther firm and continued to function under a new employer. An employee was on leave and on his return decided not to serve under the new employer. He asked the transferor company either to extend him the voluntary retirement scheme or to terminate his employment by granting retrenchment compensation under Section 25FF of the ID Act or under Section 25F of the Act. This was not paid, His grievance was that before transferring his services his consent was not taken and he was not willing to serve under the new employer. He also claimed arrears of wages, He filed a writ petition. The petition was admitted because of the reference to the violation of 25FF of the Act. The Court held that the employees consent is not required in the cases of statutory transfers; Section 25FF does not provide for it. This section operates only if the three conditions in the proviso to the 525FF are violated. In this case the petitioner has no right to his job with the transferor. He can resign from his job with the transferee Company and claim all his dues but the law does not give him the right to seek termination and retrenchment compensation. He was asked to approach the new employer with the order of the Court and he will take appropriate decision in accordance with law.[340]

*478.* A sugar mill was auctioned by the secured creditor,the bank, and the sale proceeds were deposited in the bank. Two questions arose. First, who was liable to clear the dues and pay compensation, as if retrenched, to the workmen under Section 25FF of the Act? Second, up to what date the dues and retrenchment compensationwas payable? On the first question, the Apex Court decided that these are to be paid out of sale proceeds.Those who have acquired the mill by auction have no liability in this regard. Thereafter the computation of wages was taken up and on further direction by the Apex Court it was decided that the computation should be

339. LLJ, Vol 1.1995, *Workmen of Deccan Sugars* v. *Nava Bharat Ferro Alloys Ltd* and *Others*, High Court of Madras, pp. 1211–1214.

340. LLJ, February 2011, *J.V. Sudhakar*, v. *Govt. of Andhra Pradesh rep. by its Principal Secretary and Others*, High Court of Andhra Pradesh. pp. 540–549.

in respect of all amounts due to workmen. On the cut-off date the problem was that the bank took over the mill, under the SARFAESI Act 2002, on 25 November 2004, while the auction was done on 24 March, 2005. Thereafter the sale certificate was issued on 10 August, 2005, but due to other complications of law it was registered on 24 August, 2006. The Court held that the benefit of Section 25FF of the Act shall be computed up to 10 August, 2005, when the sale certificate was issued. The ownership was transferred on this date.[341]

*479.* Very important issues came up for consideration in connection with the amalgamation of a public sector company, the Indian Petrochemicals Corporation Ltd, with the private company, the Reliance Industries Ltd. The latter acquired a commanding position in IPCL pursuant to the policy of disinvestment in selected public sector undertakings. The scheme of amalgamation came up before a Company Court under the Companies Act. The IPCL filed the requisite company petition before the Court seeking sanction of the scheme of amalgamation in 2007. All the legal requirements were met and that the Government of India had no objection to approval of the scheme and it was not against the public policy. The Company judge allowed the petition. An appeal against the Company judge's order of approval was filed in the High Court by the IPCL Employees Association. One contention was that the employees have a right to be informed, to represent, to be heard, to be taken into confidence, to be involved and to participate in amalgamation proceedings. They did not claim the right to veto over the Scheme. Clause 8 of the scheme declares and directly transfers the employees of IPCL to RIL and makes them employees of the latter without any consent or consultation or even a notice to the employees. A transfer of employment can only be by way of a tripartite agreement including the employees. Without it the transfer is illegal. The second issue was that the IPCL employees were not given the option to join or not join the RIL. If the choice existed and the termination of services the by IPCL as a result of transfer took place, it would be considered as deemed retrenchment under Section 25FF of the Act and the workmen entitled to retrenchment compensation. The second part of clause 8 provided by way of clarification that the IPCL workers shall not by virtue of the scheme be eligible for the benefits of any employment policy or other benefits available to RIL employees. This was clearly illegal. The existing terms and rights of the IPCL employees, would be preserved, but there may not be parity with the RIL employees. Hence the IPCL employees would remain as a regimented and marginalized class. These contentions were effectively rebutted. The transferee company undertook to continue to abide by any agreement/settlement, if any, by the transferor company with any union/employee of the transferor company. The Court held that neither the Section 391 to 394 of the Companies Act. 1956 or Section 25FF of the ID Act, provide for consultation with the workers for the purpose of deciding matters of merger or amalgamation. Strictly speaking, there is no requirement of holding any separate meeting or discussion by the transferor company with the workmen or unions. It cannot be said that the interest and rights of IPCL employees did not receive a fair consideration or protection. This submission could not be

341. LLJ, January 2011, *New Horizon Sugar Mill Ltd rep by its Director* v. *Commissioner of Labour, Govt. of Puducherry, and Others*, High Court of Medras,pp 291–296.

accepted. In a case (Management, *MetturBeardsell Ltd* v. *Workmen of MetturBeardsell Ltd* in 2006, Supreme Court of India), the Court held that absence of consent of individual employees cannot invalidate the action of transfer of an undertaking. This was in the context of Section 25FF of the ID Act. We see no reason to take a different view in the matter and accordingly hold that the workmen in the transferor company have no statutory right of holding meetings and to express their opinion on the question of amalgamation, but the workmen of the transferor company do have the *locus standi* to express their views before the Company Court when the proceedings under Sections 391 and 394 are pending. On the question of right to consent before the employees are transferred to the transferee company, the Court took up the question of the right to get retrenchment compensation of those workmen who opt not to join the transferee company. Under Section 25FF such on employee who opts not to joint the transferee company has to voluntarily relinquish his job and take his dues. In fact Section 25FF is enacted for the benefit of workmen by avoiding termination on transfer of a company. The first part of Section 25FF postulates that, on a transfer, the employment of workmen comes to an end and it provides for compensation to them under the terms of Section 25F. But termination of service in law does not amount to retrenchment. The Court held that the proviso to Section 25FF does not take away the freedom of an individual workman of the transferor company to accept retrenchment as the legal consequence of the dissolution of the transferor company, brining to an end the contract of service between them. Those who join the transferor company would not be entitled to retrenchment compensation. All the questions on employee's rights to parity etc. can be raised under the ID Act. and get them adjudicated. They can raise such demands or claims to benefits enjoyed by the RIL employees. The Court confirmed the order of the Company judge sanctioning the Scheme of Amalgamation. The Court directed that the persons who were in employment of IPCL on the date of judgment of Company Court shall be given an option, within one month from today, that those who do not wish to continue with the RIL will be entitled to receive compensation under the previsions of Section 25FF of the ID Act. in accordance with the provisions of Section 25F of the Act. Those who decide to continue in employment of RIL will not be entitled to such compensation. Subject to these directions, the appeal was dismissed.[342]

342. LLJ, Vol. 1, 2009, *IPCL Employees Association and Another* v. *Indian Petrochemicals Corporation Ltd*, High Court of Gujarat, pp. 399–424.

# Part III. Collective Employment Relationship

## Chapter 1. The Law on Trade Unions

### §1. Introduction

*480.* The Trade Unions Act, 1926, was enacted to provide for registration of trade unions and give them basic protection so that they may pursue their legitimate objectives. The statute has not made registration of unions obligatory; however, the registered unions enjoy immunity from criminal or civil conspiracy in conducting trade disputes. The practice of trade unions is further safeguarded by the fundamental right to form associations guaranteed under the Constitution. This right is unrestricted except where the government is the employer and its employees are debarred from forming or joining trade unions. The Trade Unions Act confers a legal and corporate status on every registered trade union. Article 19(I) guarantees the fundamental right to all citizens to form associations or unions. It does not follow, however, that every object for which unions may be formed would be protected by this article. Nor that any legislation which might hamper the fulfillment of any of the objectives for which a union is formed would necessarily offend this article. The Act was amended in 2001 with the object of reducing multiplicity of unions. While Article 19 of the Constitution provides for unrestricted right to form unions,the amended Act seeks to restrict it by making the law on registration more strict. It provides that no trade union of workmen shall be registered unless at least 10 per cent or 100 of the workmen who are members of that union are employed in the establishment. Further, on the date of making the application at least seven members of the union should be employed in the establishment with which it is connected. If these provisos are not satisfied, it would not be registered. Moreover, Section 9A provides that at all times the trade union should continue to have not less than 10 per cent or 100 workmen as members, subject to a minimum of seven employed in the establishment. To enforce it, subsection (C) in Section 10 authorizes the Registrar of Trade Unions to withdraw or cancel the registration of the union, if it ceases to have less than the requisite number of members. Furthermore, not more than one-third of the total number of office bearers or five, whichever's less, should be actually employed in the establishment. It is provided that the retired or retrenched employees would not be considered as outsiders for the purpose of this sub-section. The Court clarified that the requirements placed in the Act do not impinge upon the right of the workmen to form one or more unions, but it regulates the registration. 'Even without registration under the Act, the union is entitled to work for the benefit of its members and take proceedings even under the Industrial Disputes Act and allied laws. Therefore it cannot be said that by imposing certain conditions for registration, which have the arowed purpose, the right to form union is rendered illusory or that those provisions are *ultra vires*.'[343]

*481.* The fundamental right to form unions or associations does not confer the right to collective bargaining or the right to strike. These rights are subject to reasonable restrictions, as provided for in the Industrial Disputes Act, 1947. The government servants' conduct rules usually prohibit strikes and demonstrations and deeply infringe upon freedom of speech, freedom of assembly and freedom of association though all of these are guaranteed under the constitution. The Supreme Court has held that while the conduct rules which prohibit freedom of speech and assembly do offend the fundamental right of speech and assembly, the prohibition of strikes does not. Similarly, the rule, that no government servant may join or continue to be a member of any association which has not been recognized by the government, has been held to be contravening their fundamental right. Employees cannot hold demonstrations in the office premises under its cover. It is a judicial doctrine that no one could exercise this right to cause harm and prejudice the exercise of right of another. On this ground unions have the right of peaceful demonstration and picketing but they may not physically prevent ingress or egress of any willing worker. In one case a razor blade manufacturing company in Maharashtra employed 1260 persons and had three unions to represent them. The company instituted a suit in the High Court making allegations that one of the unions had indulged into criminal and disruptive activities which have no connection with legitimate trade union activity. The union has been terrorizing the employees and the management by resorting to violence, issuing threats, assaulting employees and taking recourse to coercive activities. The plaint contained description of events and incidents on 29 June 2007, 18 July 2007, 9 August 2007 and 21 January 2008. These acts of violence resulted in a cumulative loss of production and damage to property. The loss of reputation and goodwill was estimated at Rs 50 crores. Relief was claimed in two parts: (i) a claim for damage for loss of business and (ii) a claim on account of a loss of reputation and goodwill. The plaintiff claimed an injunction restraining the union from various violent and unlawful activities, including 'preventing ingress and egress of employees and material'. The Court examined the law on the subject, especially on the issues connected with the motion for relief in the form of an injunction. It held the claim for injunction is directly related to and arises from the provisions of Schedule III of the MRTU & PULP Act. Where an unfair labour practice falls within the scope and purview of Schedules II, III and IV of the Act, recourse to the remedy of a civil suit for the grant of injunctive relief would be barred. Moreover, the Industrial Court had granted an injunction on the union, its office bearers, agents, supporters and members by restraining them from agitating within the vicinity of 200 meters of the company premises and preventing or obstructing the ingress or engress of man and materials on 31 January 2004 and it

343. LLJ, Vol. 2, 2009, *Lohia Machines (LML) Karamchari Sangh and Others* v. *Registrar, Trade Unions and Others*, High Court of Allahabad, pp. 29–36.

was still in force. Apparently this injunction was not being observed, but to this the Court said that relief could not be granted at the interlocutory stage, since it must await adjudication at the trial. The Industrial Court where the complaint was pending had not completed the adjudication proceedings.[344]

*482*. The ID Act recognizes under Section 2, the 'office bearer' in relation to a trade union, which includes any member of the executive thereof, as well as the 'trade union', registered under the Trade Unions Act. Under Section 36 of the ID Act a workman is entitled to be represented by any office-bearer of a registered trade union in any proceedings under the Act, whether or not he is a member of the said union. Section 35 of the ID Act imposes a restriction upon the Trade Union Act in as much as it forbids the expulsion of a member from the union or imposition of any penalty or fine, and denial of any right by the union for refusing to take part in an illegal strike. The provision for recognition and its withdrawal is made in the states of Maharashtra and Madhya Pradesh, but not in the Central Act. In a peculiar case the union made a complaint to the High Court in a writ petition that under Section 33A of the ID Act a protected workman was dismissed from service without securing the permission in writing of the industrial tribunal, where a dispute pertaining to him was pending.Under the Bombay Rules, any dispute between the recognized union and the employer on protected workman has to be referred to the conciliation officer, whose decision shall be final. The union selected its joint secretary in March 1998 for protection. The Company did not respond within 15 days as per the rules, so the union approached the conciliation officer. Unlike the Central Rules which provide that, 'the list of workmen be recognized as protected workmen (for the period of 12 months from the date of communication)', the Bombay rules do not provide for it. On 28 September 1998, in a joint meeting called by him, the union learnt that the Company gave its intimation accepting the workman as protected. Thereafter the CO had several hearings and finally on 13 July 1999 he informed the union about acceptance of the list. The Court found that the recognition was granted for the year 1998. Though the CO had communicated to the union on 13 July 1999 that the Company had no objection, in fact the Company gave its no objection on 25 September 1998. This was obviously for the year 1998, when the elections were held. It could not be held that the protection continued after the term of election expired, as new election would be held and a new set of office bearers would be elected. The protection could not be extended to the next year. In February 1999, after the election, the union sent a list of 15 names to the Company but the Company did not accept them. The dispute was referred to the CO. The CO in his order of 14 March 2000 refused to accept the particular workman as protected, since he was already dismissed on August 1999. He was suspended on 8 March 1999, a charge sheet issued to him on March 26, 1999 and it was followed by dismissal. The CO's order was confirmed by the Single Judge of the Court in an earlier, union petition and the same was further confirmed by the Division Bench in an

344. LLJ. Vol. 2, 2009 *Vidyut Metallics Pvt. Ltd* v. *Maharashtra Rajya Rashtriya Kamgar Sangh and Others*, High Court of Bombay, pp. 387-397.

appeal by the union. The Court held that this was not a fit case for interfering with the impugned award of the industrial tribunal. The writ petition was dismissed.[345]

*483.* In a case the petitioner did not grant the status of protected workmen to several workmen as sought for by the union.The union made an application to the management for the purpose on 15 March 2001 for protection of five office bearers. The management asked the union to furnish information on the process of election of the office bearers of union, the date of election and a complete list of office bearers of the union. The management took the stand that four workmen- office bearers were suspended from service on 23 August 1999 for misconduct and disciplinry proceedings initiated against them. Thereafter their services were terminated on 11 July 2001and an application under Section 33(2)(b) of the Act made to the industrial tribunal. Consequently they could not be declared as protected workmen. The union took the stand that it was not necessary to send the information about the conduct of election and other matters asked for by the management. The workmen were suspended out of revenge. The Asstt. Labour Commissioner who heard the dispute decided in favour of the union. By mere suspension the employee–employer relationship does not come to an end, only dismissal or removal from service would do so. Upto the date of dismissal the employees were entitled to be declared as protected workmen. This order was challenged before the Court. The petitioner submitted that no election of office bearers was held after 1998 and no returns with regard to the union and its election were ever filed before the Registrar of Trade Unions. The application for grant of protection to workmen was not supported by any resolution of the union. The action of the union was a gross abuse of process of law with the ulterior motive of protecting the workmen facing serious charges.The union did not file a counter affidavit. The Court held that if the employer has a doubt that the office bearers had not been appointed in accordance with rules, he has every right to ask the trade union to provide him the details of appointment of the office bearers and the manner in which they have been elected or appointed. He has every right to ensure that the status of protected workmen is being sought for by the genuine persons and the shield of protected workmen is not sought to be misused. Compliance with rules of union and appointment of office bearers in accordance with rules is inbuilt into the provisions for granting the status of protected workmen. The union should have provided the information sought by the employer. The court held the ALC's order that the employer had no right to ask for information as contrary to law and express provisions of the Act. The writ petition was allowed and the ALC's order was set aside.[346]

*484.* In a case the Vice-President of the Tata Chemical Staff Union claimed the status of protected workman for the year 2010–11. The company, Tata Chemicals Ltd objected to his inclusion on the ground that he had already enjoyed the benefits of the 'salary revision scheme' meant for all the permanent supervisors working in

345. LLJ, Vol. 3, 2007, *Cipla Employees Union and Others* v. *Cipla Ltd*, High Court of Bombay, pp. 577–583.
346. LLJ, Vol. 2, 2007, *Voltas Ltd* v. *Voltas Employees' Union and Another*, High Court of Delhi, pp. 604–608.

grades S-1 to S-4, the categories, 'mainly working and intending to work in supervisory capacity, either by nature of duties, attached to the office or by reason of the powers rested in him/her, functions mainly of a managerial nature'. The scheme was applicable to only those supervisors who were doing mainly supervisory and administrative work. The employee had the designation Asstt. Fire Officer, yet he claimed to be a workman, not a supervisor. The High Court heard the petition against the order of the Conciliation officer cum Asstt. Labour Commissioner conferring the status of 'protected workman' on him and rejecting the case of the establishment supervisors were members of the staff union. The company pointed out that the employee had accepted an important condition of accepting the Scheme that, 'no employee can claim any benefits of whatsoever nature accrued by an previous or present settlement'. Cases decided by the Apex Court were cited by the respondent that it is not the designation but the nature of work that was decisive in deciding whether an employee was a workman or not. Even a manager or doctor may be Workman. The Court held that a person who obtains and enjoys the benefits flowing from 'Salary Revision Scheme', who knowing very well the contents of the Scheme applied for the grant of benefits of that scheme cannot be allowed to claim that he is a workman. To allow such a person to 'blow hot and cold' and to allow him to obtain a status of 'protected workman' will amount to permitting him to do mockery of justice. That cannot be allowed. Only because he was vice president of the union he seems to be hijacking the union and getting his name listed on the top of the list of protected workman submitted by the union. The petition was allowed and the impugned order was quashed and set aside.[347]

## §2. Legal Definitions and Issues

*485.* The Trade Unions Act defines the trade union as 'any combination, whether temporary or permanent, formed primarily for the purpose of regulating the relations between workmen and employers or between workmen and workmen, or between employers and employers, or for imposing restrictive conditions on the conduct of any trade or business and includes any federation of two or more trade unions'. Thus workers as well as employers can form trade unions. An organization of unions is also a trade union, similarly is a branch of a union. It need not be a permanent organization. A strike committee may be a trade union. The overriding test in deciding whether an organization is a union or not is to ascertain its objectives. If it adheres to the statutory objects, it is a trade union. A registered trade union is a person under law, while an unregistered union is not a juristic person. Under the Maharashtra Recognition of Trade Unions and Unfair Labour Practices Act, 1972, the recognized union is entitled to several privileges and the employer is required to extend them. In one case, the recognized union of the Tata Memorial Hospital and Cancer Research Centre accused it of indulging in unfair labour practices by extending facilities to an unrecognized union, which were reserved exclusively for the recognized union. This was allowed by the trial court. The Tata

347. LLJ. 3, 2012, *Tata Chemicals Ltd.* v. *General Secretary and Another*, Gujarat High Court, pp. 667-672.

Memorial Centre approached the High Court with a writ petition against the order of the trail court. The Court referred to Sections 20 and 22 of the Act, and observed that the petitioners were engaged in an unfair labour practice. The petition was dismissed.[348]

*486.* The Act defines 'trade dispute' to mean any dispute between employers and workmen or between workmen and workmen, or between employers and employers which is connected with the employment or non-employment, or the terms of employment or the conditions or labour, of any person. The term 'workmen' means all persons employed in trade or industry whether or not in the employment of the employer with whom the trade dispute arises. The first definition is almost similar to that of 'industrial dispute' in the ID Act, though in respect of the second, the definitions in the two legislations are quite different. However, in all practical matters it is the ID Act that matters. The importance of the term 'workmen' is in determining who can form or join a union, because it appears that the class of employees who are not workmen cannot do so under this Act. The importance of the term 'trade dispute' in the Trade Unions Act lies in the immunities from civil and criminal conspiracy which unions enjoy under law in conducting their disputes. Under Section 2, 'The appropriate government', means in relation to trade unions whose objects are not confined to one state, the central government, and in relation to other trade unions, the state government. In one case this clause was used to thwart a trade union registered in Maharashtra from participating in a conciliation proceeding in the centrally administered territory of Dadra and Nagar Haveli and with success. This defence of the Labour and Enforcement officer persuaded the CO to refuse permission to the union from participating in the proceedings on behalf of the workmen of M/s IPCA Laboratories Ltd in Dadra and Nagar Haveli. The union petitioned the High Court against the said order. The Court learnt that in 1952, as per the notification of the central government, the Bombay government had appointed its Registrar of Trade Unions to be the Registrar of those unions whose objects were not confined to the state. Moreover, the petitioner union had carried out an amendment to its constitution extending its activities beyond the Maharashtra state. The Court held the CO's order as unsustainable and quashed it.[349]

*487.* 'Workman', as defined in the Act, should be employed in a trade or industry, and the institution in which workmen are employed should be in the nature of an industry. Therefore, if the business is a trade or industry the workmen employed therein are entitled to register themselves as a union. At one stage, a federation of teachers could not register as a trade union because primary school teachers were held not to be in the employment in any trade or industry. The expression 'workmen' must include ex-workmen as well. In one case, a company employing cine-workers and artists had terminated the services of 19 employees. The union secured the boycott of the company by all the bodies and associations of cine artists and the

---

348. LLJ, Vol. 4, 2006 (NOC), *Tata Memorial Centre and Another* v. *Tata Memorial Hospital Workers Union and Another*, High Court of Bombay, pp. 949–950.

349. LLJ, Vol. 1, 2009, *Krantikari Kamgar Union* v. *Labour and Enforcement Officer, Dadra and Nagar Haveli and Others*, High Court of Bombay, pp. 17–22.

company's work came to a standstill. Then it secured an injunction against the union from a civil court on the plea that Section 18, providing for immunity from civil suits, was non-operative as there was no trade dispute pending between the two parties. The union appealed to the High Court which upheld the appeal and quashed the injunction, holding that any breach of contract in furtherance of a trade dispute was protected by Section 18 and the union was within its legal and constitutional rights to obtain support and solidarity for its cause. However, the bar on civil courts under this section ceases to operate, once the union agitation becomes unlawful, tortious and violent; the courts then can entertain the suit for injunction to protect the legitimate right of employers.

*488.* Under the Act, the appropriate government must appoint a Registrar of trade unions to register unions, to receive returns filed by the unions and carry out other prescribed duties. The Registrar has no judicial power; he cannot administer oaths or compel the attendance of witnesses or the production of documents. If a proper application for the registration of a union has been made, the Registrar may satisfy himself that the requirements have been complied with and then issue a certificate of registration. He cannot ordinarily refuse a registration; nor can he cause undue delay in issuing the certificate of registration. Whether or not the activities of the union are lawful and legitimate are of no concern to the Registrar. He cannot oversee the activities of registered unions. The Registrar has no jurisdiction to settle any dispute between rival office-bearers. An employer cannot approach the Registrar and ask for cancellation of a union already registered. Section 7(2) of the Trades Unions Act requires the Registrar not to register a union with a name that is identical to another already registered union. In Maharashtra State, the All India Trade Union Congress is a registered union, yet in December 2004 another union secured registration with the deceptive name of 'AITUC Hawkers Union'. The AITUC objected to it, but failed with the Registrar. AITUC is the abbreviated name of the oldest trade union organization in India. Finally its writ petition to the High Court succeeded. The Court saw through the deception and set aside the registration giving the union the option to seek registration in another name.[350]

*489.* The rules of the union must contain, besides its name and objects, the purposes for which its funds will be applicable, a list of members and facilities for their inspection by members and office-bearers, the provision for the admission of ordinary members as well as honorary or temporary members, and their election as office-bearer, if any, the payment of subscription, entitlement of benefits to the members and the provision for imposition of fine or forfeiture, the procedure for amending or rescinding the rules, the appointment and removal of members of the executive and office bearers, the safe custody of funds, annual audit, facility for inspection of accounts by members, and finally the manner in which the union may be dissolved. The 2001 Amendment provides that the trade union's rules should provide for the manner in which the office bearers of the trade union shall be elected or removed. They cannot be just appointed. Election is mandated for the purpose.

350. LLJ, Vol. 4, 2006, *All India Trade Union Congress* v. *Deputy Registrar of Trade Unions and Others*, Bombay High Court, pp. 398–400.

In UP the Registrar is authorized to issue the order of recognition to the election of office bearers of the trade union in from 'J'. In one case he recalled his order and directed the parties to hold a fresh election to diffuse the controversy among the members of the union. This was challenged on the ground that he did not have the power to recall his order. The Court rejected this contention and held that he had done no wrong by directing the parties to hold a fresh election and since substantial justice had been done, no interference under Article 226 of the constitutions is called for. The Trade Union Act does not provide for deciding internal disputes, and for settling them recourse must be taken to civil courts. The Trade Unions and Bombay Industrial Relations (Amendment) Act, 1967 provides for power of the Industrial Court to decide such disputes, provided the person raising the dispute has been a member of the registered trade union for six months prior to the date of application. A non-member cannot raise an internal dispute.[351, 352]

*490.* The cancellation of registration is possible:

(i) on an application made by the union (which must be verified in the prescribed manner); and
(ii) if the certificate has been obtained by fraud or mistake, or the union has ceased to exist, or it has willfully and after notice from the Registrar contravened any provision of this Act, or allowed any rule to continue in force which is inconsistent with any such provision, or it has rescinded any rule that is required to be made;
(iii) Section 9A provides that a registered union shall at all times continue to have not less than 10 per cent or 100 of the workmen, whichever is less, subject to a minimum of seven engaged or employed in an establishment or industry with which it is connected, as its members. If the Registrar is satisfied that the union ceases to have the requisite number of members, the registration may be withdrawn or cancelled by him.

In the event of withdrawal or cancellation of a certificate of registration there is a provision for appeal and the judicial determination of the dispute. The withdrawal or cancellation of the registration must be preceded by the requisite notice and show cause against the proposed action. An appeal will lie with the Labour Court or an industrial tribunal depending upon where the head office is located. In one case this section was found too inadequate, so the appeal was directed to be heard by a civil court under Section 11(b).[353]

*491.* The powers of the Registrar under the Trade Union Act are sufficient for the performance of his administrative function. He can undertake a reasonable

351. LLJ, January 2011, *Rashtriya Mazdoor Sabha, UP and Another,* v. *State of UP and Others,* High Court of Allahabad, pp. 239–243.
352. LLJ, Vol. 1, 2001, *Borosil Glass Works Ltd Employees Union* v. *D.D. Bambode and Others Supreme Court*, pp. 171–173.
353. LLJ, Vol. 2, 2008, *Starian Employees Union, Noida and Another* v. *P.O. Labour Court (II), U.P. Ghaziabad and Others*, High Court of Allahabad (NOC), pp. 1132.

inquiry under Section 8 (viz. registration of a union) and Section 28 (viz. the power to make regulations in connection with registration, the transfer of the head office of a registered union, audit of union's accounts, inspection of documents kept by the Registrar and the fees to be charged and any other matter that may be prescribed), to ascertain the names of elected office-bearers. But the inquiry cannot go beyond ascertaining facts. No party can lead any evidence before him or cross-examine the witnesses. No detailed inquiry is envisaged under the Act for deciding the controversy between two rival factions of the union. He cannot decide any dispute between them. It is a private dispute which can be adjudicated upon by the civil court only, and not by the Registrar. No provision of law provides for holding of anelection under the supervision of the Registrar. Under the MRTU & PULP Act. the power of determining the majority of the union is vested in the Industrial Court. It is decided by verification of membership, not election. The option of election is not provided in the Act. The High Court of Patna held in a case that the Registrar my not take *suo moto* any decision to hold the election for electing its office bearers, but under the Court's orders it should do so and complete the exercise.[354]

*492*. The Trade Union Act provides for cancellation of registration on several grounds, including fraud or mistake or for violating any statutory provision or rule. But once the union is registered in accordance with the provisions of the Act, the registration cannot be recalled or cancelled except on grounds of fraud or mistake on the part of the applicants. If the mistake is on the part of the Registrar, he is not allowed to recall his order. 'The said act cannot again be nullified by the second decision of the Registrar, who has no power of review under the Act'. This cannot be done in exercise of power under Section 10 of the Act. 'Thus, only the act of obtaining the Registration Certificate by fraud or mistake, that too, by the person applying for registration could only be a reason or ground for cancellation of registration of the Trade Union under Section 10 of the Act.' Only a trade union can apply for cancellation, which must be verified in the prescribed manner. An individual or a group of individuals cannot legally ask for registration. An individual may submit an application under Section 10 (a) of the Act to invite the attention of the Registrar of Trade Union. The Registrar thereafter can *suo moto* take cognizance under Section 10 of the Act. Section 10(a) needs to be read along with Section 10(b), which speaks about the satisfaction of the Registrar about validity of the Certificate.[355] In another case the petitioner filed objections persuading the registrar not to register the union. However, on the application of the trade union through it President/Secretary he recalled his refusal and granted the registration. This became a subject of an appeal to the High Court. The Court found that those who raised the objection were casual labourers and not members, so were not allowed to vote in the election. The Court upheld the Registrar's action of recalling his order of refusal. 'The refusal by the Registrar to register the union on the aforesaid objection of the

354. LLJ, Vol. 1, 2008, *Hasanpur Chini Mill Mazdoor Union* v. *State of Bihar*, High Court of Patna, pp. 927–930.
355. LLJ, Vol. 3, 2009, *D'Souza R.G.* v. *Poona Employees Union,* High Court of Bombay, pp. 466–471; LLJ, Vol. 3, 2007, *Girija Shankar Shukla and Others* v. *Hindustan Aeronautics Ltd, Amethi, Sultanpur and Others,* High Court of Allahabad, pp. 648–651.

petitioners and like persons was itself an act without jurisdiction and authority which has been subsequently corrected by ordering registration.' If any petitioners or like members are aggrieved by their exclusion from election, they could have challenged the election in the appropriate forum as would be available under law. Such an objection is not at all tenable under the Act.

*493.* The 2001 Amendment Act made an important change in the rules a trade union is required to make under Section 6(h), whereby all office bearers shall be elected or removed in accordance with the manner laid down. The Tata Workers Union allowed itself to be guided by the rules adopted in 1956. Accordingly, in the election the President was elected who in turn nominated the office bearers of the Executive Committees. At first, the matter was sent to the Registrar, Cooperative Societies, who refused to register the name of office bearers. In a complaint by a member, it was brought to the notice of the Registrar, Trade Unions. It was learnt that the office bearers were not elected, but nominated by the President and this was not the proper manner. The Registrar, Trade Unions sent an order that the old Executive Committee and its office bearers will continue in office and they should hold an election to elect the office bearers in accordance with law/rules. He issued a notice dated 4 February 2005 as to why the registration be not cancelled on 6 May 2005. In the writ petition the order of the Registrar was challenged as without jurisdiction and not in accordance with Section 10 (b). He should have served two notices before the action of cancellation. The Court decided that to maintain judicial decorum and in conformity with the order passed by this Court in another case, 'I am also not inclined to decide the issues as raised by the petitioner, there being an alternative remedy of appeal available to him.[356] In another writ petition against the Registrar's order on the legal requirement to hold election of office bearers and not recognizing the new office bearers, the Court was informed that since the registration of the union has been cancelled, the petition has become infructious. It was accordingly dismissed. The Court held that once the registration has been cancelled, the Registrar of Trade Unions has no jurisdiction to give any direction in respect of the de-recognized union. The order dated 4 February 2005 cannot be acted upon either for the purpose of election or for the purpose of interim arrangement. Since this order has lost its force, this writ petition has become infructious.

*494.* In Maharashtra, the Trade Unions Act has been amended to provide for the Industrial Court to decide certain disputes. The disputes may pertain as to who is an office bearer of a registered union or wrongful expulsion of members, or relate to the property (including the account books). Then any member with the consent of the Registrar may refer the dispute to the Industrial Court constituted under the Bombay Industrial Relations Act, 1946, for a decision. Accordingly, no civil court shall entertain any suit or other proceedings in relation to the dispute referred to the Industrial Court. The High Court decided in one case, whether a civil court can

---

356. LLJ, Vol. 1, 2006, *Tata Workers Union* v. *State of Jharkhand*, High Court of Jharkhand, pp. 1045–1048. LLJ, Vol. I, 2006, *Tata Workers Union and Others* v. *State of Jharkhand and Others*, High Court of Jharkhand, pp. 813–814. Both appeals were heard by the same judge, decided respectively on 9 and 11 August 2005.

examine a dispute before reference to the Industrial Court, that this would be completely irrational and fallacious, because the Act completely ousts the jurisdiction of the civil court to entertain any dispute at any stage. Earlier the trial court had rejected the objection, holding that the jurisdiction of the civil court was barred only as regards those disputes which were already referred to the Industrial Court.

*495.* In Madhya Pradesh, the Trade Unions Act has been amended to provide for the 'approved list' of unions to be maintained by the Registrar. Any representative union, or where there is none, any registered trade union may apply in the prescribed manner for being entered in the approved list. The Registrar should then conduct an inquiry and enter the name of such union in the approved list and issue a certificate to this effect. The Registrar has the power to refuse to put a union on the approved list, if he is satisfied that the application is not made bona fide in the interests of the employees, but is made in the interests of the employers. The amended Act also provides for the power of a court of civil jurisdiction to be bestowed on the Registrar. Moreover, any dispute regarding (i) the Registrar refusing to register any union, (ii) withdrawing or cancelling a certificate of registration, and (iii) who is the lawful officer of a registered union, and related matters, may be referred to the Industrial Court for adjudication. Section 28J of the Act provides that if there is any dispute as to who is the lawful officer of a registered trade union, 'any person claiming to be such an officer or the Registrar may refer the dispute to the Industrial Court in such manner as may be prescribed'. The Registrar does not have the power to deal with election disputes and any order passed by him to stay the election as a court is without any jurisdiction. When such a dispute arises, it has to be referred to the industrial court. In one case the Registrar interfered in a dispute with regard to office bearers.The Court held that he could not have dealt with it. He could not have encroached upon an area and passed an order of stay relating to the election. The order of the single judge in this connection was unsustainable. The order of the single judge was set aside and the order passed by the Registrar quashed.[357]

*496.* In a case a railway workers union had to be bifurcated following the creation of a new zone for railways administration. Under the rules, the Railway authorities have to grant permission for forming a new union. Consequently the South Eastern Railway Men's Union (SERMU) was bifurcated and the South East Central Railway Men's union (SECRMU) was formed. Soon the problem arose as to who were the legal office bearers of the new union. An election was held which was disputed. A writ petition was filed in the High Court for quashing the election. The Court directed that no office bearer has a right to function unless the Registrar of Trade Union grants such recognition. Accordingly, the Railway Authorities should deal with only those office bearers who are recognized by the Registrar, Trade Unions. However, the respondent, opposed to the petitioner, moved the Industrial Court under Section 28J and the Industrial Court passed an award.This award was challenged in the writ petition. The issue was, when was the new union formed

357. LLJ, Vol. 3, 2008, *Kathal R.K.* v. *Registrar of Trade Unions and Others*, High Court of Madhya Pradesh, pp. 642–651.

and election held. The High Court found serious discrepancy in the Industrial Court's award on the said issue. The Industrial Court had admitted the plea that the office bearers were elected on 11 July 2002, which was very curious since the Railway Board ordered the reorganization of the union on 8 August 2002. No election could have been held on the date claimed. There was no material to show that before 11 July 2002, the SECRMU was formed. The Industrial Court misconstrued another document, the Annexure P/10 as a certificate of registration. The Court found perversity in the reasoning of the Industrial Court and it reached a wrong conclusion. In fact there was no evidence to show that the first respondent was a member of the SECRMU. As such he could not have maintained the application under Section 28J of the Act. Furthermore, in the election held on 26 April 2004, 20 persons were elected as office bearers of the SECRMU, but the first respondent did not implead all the them, only two who were the petitioners. The Industrial Court should have directed the remaining office bearers to be impleaded. Still the Industrial Court decided that the election held on 26 April 2004 was illegal. The High Court held that the order made by the Industrial Court was in utter violation of the principles of natural justice. It extinguished the rights of those office bearers who were not parties to the application without hearing them. The writ petition was allowed and the impugned award of the Industrial Court was quashed. The application filed by the first respondent under Section 28J was dismissed.[358]

*497.* In Madhya Pradesh, Section 28J of the Trade Unions Act provides that, if there is any dispute as to who is the lawful officer of a registered union, any person claiming to be such an officer or the Registrar may refer the dispute to the Industrial Court, which on hearing the parties to such dispute and recording such evidence as necessary will decide the dispute and its order shall be final. In one case the Registrar's order on conducting an election outside the gate of the factory or some other shed, was flouted. The supervision of Asstt. Labour Commissioner was disregarded and the Registrar's order to stay the election without observing his directive was openly ignored. The election was held at another place and officers of the union elected. The petitioner gave intimation to the Registrar to grant approval of elected office bearers. This was not done. Instead he cancelled the election. Against this order the appellant moved the industrial court at Gwalior. The Industrial Court heard the case at Rewa, due to summer vacation, without serving notice to any party, the Registrar and the management or the objectors who had complained against the illegalities being committed by a particular group, and allowed the petition *ex parte* and decided the dispute. The Court heard the writ petition against the award of the industrial court and held that the Industrial Court had acted in a most arbitrary manner and method, without adhering to the basic fundamentals of the judicial procedure and statutory mandate cast under sub-section (2) of Section 28J of the Trade Union Act. It was incumbent upon the Industrial Court to issue a notice to the Registrar and to objectors, etc. and notice was not issued to the opposite faction. 'It passes comprehension how the order could have been passed *ex parte* by the Industrial Court, sitting at camp Rewa, whereas the matter was required to be heard at

358. LLJ, Vol. 3, 2006, *Salis Lawrence and Another* v. *Subrato Mukherjee and Others*, High Court of Chhattisgarh, pp. 744–752.

Gwalior. It appears that an attempt was made to secure the order at Rewa in *ex parte* without the hearing.' The case was earlier heard by the single judge and he found that a caveat was also filed, though the Industrial Court wrongly mentioned in the order that no caveat was filed. The single judge recorded that the filing of the caveat was ignored by the Industrial Court. The Court held the order as a nullity due to the flagrant violation of the rule of audi alteram partum, forming part of the principles of natural justice. 'In the circumstances, we have no hesitation to say that the order passed by the Industrial Court was totally uncalled for, it was a nullity and has been rightly quashed, no right accrued to any person on the basis of the aforesaid order.' There was no merit in the appeal and it was dismissed.[359]

*498.* In West Bengal the Act was amended vide the Trade Union (Amendment) Act, 1983 to incorporate Section 28A, providing for recognition of Trade Union as a bargaining agent and it was enforced by the notification dated 11 November 1992. Any registered trade union may apply to the Registrar for recognition as the bargaining agent. A case arose from union rivalry in a five star hotel in Calcutta before the Registrar.The appellant union, affiliated to CITU (Centre of Indian Trade Unions), raised an industrial dispute in 2003 on payment of bonus. The Hotel Management had already entered into a bipartite settlement with the rival union (affiliated to the INTUC) and claimed that all the employees accepted the benefit derived from the said settlement.The appellant union resorted to demonstrations, at which the management approached the High Court complaining against police inaction. The Single Judge held that the union should instead raise an industrial dispute and have the matter referred to a Labour Court. The appellant union appealed against the Court order and secured a direction that the Registrar on receiving an application, under Section 28A of the Act, should decide the case as per law treating the hotel as an 'industry'. The Registrar held a meeting of the two unions and heard them but did not invite the management. He held that the hotel was neither an 'industrial establishment' nor a 'class of industry'. But following the Court direction he asked the management to recognize the appellant union for two years with effect from 1 January 2006. Against this order two writ petitions were filed. The single judge allowed the writ petition and quashed the said order of the Registrar on the ground that the management was not given a hearing. Again the appellant union field an appeal. The Bench decided to examine the two terms used by the Registrar in describing the hotel as an industry. 'An industrial establishment' as stated in Section 25A of the ID Act. Under this section an 'industrial establishment', is either a factory, or a mine or a plantation. Hotel is neither a mine nor a plantation, while the definition of 'factory', excludes from its purview any hotel, restaurant or an eating place. Therefore, the term, 'industrial establishment' in relation to Section 28A of the Act would exclude a hotel. A 'class of industry' is one as is notified by the state government. But there was no such notification. Hence in this regard too, Section 28A had no application. To come within the mischief of Section 28A, it was not enough that hotel should be viewed as an 'industry', which was correct. The Single Judge was right when he quashed the Registrar's order. The Registrar misconstrued

359. LLJ, Vol. 1, 2009, *Kanwar Singh Mawai* v. *Anoop Singh Tomar and Others*, High Court of Madhya Pradesh, pp. 128–134.

the order of the Division Bench. There was scope for interference. The appeals failed and were dismissed.[360]

*499.* The trade union can maintain a political fund for the promotion of the civil and political interests of its members and can use it for elections, holding of meetings, distributing its literature, maintenance of any person elected to a legislative body and a number of other things. But no member can be compelled to contribute to any political fund, nor can anyone who refuses to do so be denied the benefits of union membership or placed in any disability either directly or indirectly, nor can contributions to the political fund be made a condition of membership.

*500.* Any person who has attained the age of 15 can become a member of a trade union subject to its rules and may derive all the benefits of membership as per the rules. But a member cannot become an office-bearer until he is 18 years of age, or if he had been convicted by any court in India of any offence involving moral turpitude and sentenced to imprisonment, unless a period of five years has elapsed since his release. An office-bearer ceases to hold the office on the commencement of his prison term. No member can claim any immunity for an act which is an offence under the law. In one case the office-bearers were prohibited from holding demonstrations and shouting slogans within the radius of 500 meters from the boundary wall of the hotel. This was later reduced to 300 meters. The union's office was inside the hotel and the executive members claimed it as their legitimate right to visit the office. The Court held that in order to hold the scale of balance and taking the interest of justice in view, a single office-bearer at a time would be allowed to visit the union office. In another case, the petitioner company could not prevent illegal action of the respondent union and its members, despite. filing a civil suit and obtaining interim injunction against them. Its writ petition seeking orders for full police protection was granted. The Court held that the immunity under Section 18(1) the Trade Union Act could not mean that the trade union could achieve its object by a method not permitted in law.[361]

*501.* In a civil suit the Vidya Sagar Institute of Mental Health and Neuro Sciences (VIMHANS) sought a declaration that the strike threatened by the employees union was illegal and an injunction against them from holding demonstrations, slogan shouting, etc. within a distance of 500 meters from the hospital. No one appeared for the employees union, nor was any written statement filed. Suit was proceeded with exparte and it was decreed. The Hospital received a demand letter dated 18 February 2002 from a newly formed union. It filed a claim before the conciliation officer and in the proceedings the management sought to amicably settle the dispute. It was followed by a strike notice dated 29 April 2002 from the newly formed union. It filed a claim before the conciliation officer and in the proceedings the management sought to amicably settle the dispute. It was followed by a strike

360. LLJ, Vol. 1, 2009, *Hotel Hindustan Karamchari Union* v. *Hotel Hindustan and Others*, High Court of Calcutta, pp. 747–752.
361. LLJ, Vol. 3, 2009, (NOC), *Avec Ltd, Power Product division, Poonapally, Hosur*, v. *Suptd. of Police, Krishnagiri Distt. and others*, High Court of Madras, p. 784.

notice dated 29 April 2002 to which the Hospital replied on 14 May 2002. A letter was sent threatening the Hospital to settle their demands by 23 July 2002, failing which the union will take recourse to coercive methods including a strike. On 21 June 2002 by an interim order the union was restrained from holding demonstrations which may in any way obstruct the ingress and egress of any member of the management or any employee or patient or visitor to the hospital and that they will hold demonstration peacefully at least at a distance of 50 meters from the entrance to the hospital. The plaintiff stated and proved that they followed all rules and procedures and by-laws as provided under labour laws and the demand letter of the union dated 18 February 2002 was illegal and arbitrary and without any just cause. The plaintiff said that despite the reference of the dispute for adjudication, the union threatened to take law in its own hands and take recourse to slogan shouting, blockage of passage and disruption of medical facilities. The Court held that the plaintiff has a right to continue its activities without disruption, while the union may have a right to vent their grievances, but they cannot disrupt and cause inconvenience to patients, visitors and the staff. It held that the civil court has the jurisdiction to entertain a suit of this nature. The immunity under Section 18 of the Trade Union Act does not extend to these acts which may amount to an offence. Unions have a right to peaceful demonstrations and go on peaceful and legal strike. But they cannot indulge in acts of violence,physical assault, intimidation, etc. The Court held the threat of strike as illegal and restrained all members of the union from holding demonstration, etc. They may demonstrate at a distance of 200 meters from the outer radius of the Hospital. Cost of suit was awarded to the plaintiff against the defendants. Suit was decreed and a decree sheet would be drawn.[362]

*502.* The right to admit members is assured by the Act, but whether a person is admitted as a member or not depends upon the rules. Membership is strictly voluntary. A union cannot force compulsory membership, not even under a settlement. Similarly, an employer cannot make union membership or non-membership a condition of employment. Such a condition would be constitutionally void. In admitting new members a union may seek to extend the coverage of an award beyond the intended scope, thereby endangering the award itself. In one case the Supreme Court considered the questions:

(i) whether the union could change its constitution and extend its membership; and
(ii) whether the award of the tribunal (allowing overtime payment) could be made operative to workmen employed in other establishments of the company on the basis of extension of union membership.

The Court admitting the appeal agreed with the company that such an extension would be beyond the scope of the award. On the question whether a union can amend the constitution, the answer is in the affirmative provided the procedural formalities are completed and the Registrar should notify that the said amendments

362. LLJ, Vol. 1, 2006, *Vidya Sagar Institute of Mental Health and Neuro Sciences* v. *Vidya Sagar Hospital Employees Union*, High Court of Delhi, pp. 781–784.

have been registered. Until this is done the amended constitution does not come into effect.

*503.* Under the Trade Unions Act an ordinary member or a temporary member of a union can become an office-bearer, but the Act nowhere provides that such a member shall also have the right to negotiate with the management, or that the management would be under an obligation to negotiate with an office-bearer who had retired and was no longer in employment of a industry with which the union was connected. In one case the management decided that it would not negotiate with the office-bearer concerned, since he had already retired. The Court took note of the practice and usage followed by the bank for decades, whereby only serving employees represented the union in bilateral discussions with the bank and this practice had also been recognized by the staff federation. The Court held that the retired employee could not legitimately claim his continuance as an ordinary member of the staff association and general secretary of the union after his retirement and could not claim a right to negotiate with the management as the representative of the staff association. This election was declared as bad in law, and also not in accordance with the staff association's rules.[363]

*504.* Trade union office-bearers are sometime granted duty relief and are given time off to attend to union work and members grievances. In one case, an office-bearer was transferred and this was considered as illegal, arbitrary, discriminatory and violative of the usual norms and procedures of transfer and there were protests. The management claimed that the transfer order was passed due to administrative reasons and exigencies. The Court held that it was for the employer to decide when, where and at what point of time an employee should be transferred. Transfer of a trade union leader does not ipso facto imply that the transfer is an act of victimization. The duties rendered by the office-bearers are not part of the duties rendered to the establishment. The prime duty of an employee is to serve the establishment and then the union. The grant of duty relief is only a concession and it does not pertain to the conditions of service.[364]

## §3. Verification of Membership versus Election

*505.* In one case the union objected to the introduction of the check-off system in the major ports of India, under which each employee upon becoming a member of the union would nominate the union to receive from the employer the subscription deducted from his salary every month. This would enable the government to decide the majority union. Various objections were raised against it including the grounds that it was violative of democratic norms and there might be collusion between a particular union and management agencies. However, a vast majority of

363. Factories Journal Reports, Vol. 89, Part 3, 1996, *State Bank of India Association and Another* v. *State Bank of India and Others*, Supreme Court of India, pp. 61–63.

364. Factories Journal Reports, Vol. 87, Part 12, 1995, *Kishori Lal Verma* v. *Hindustan Zinc Ltd and Another*, Rajasthan High Court, pp. 327–336.

workers returned the forms issued to them for the purpose. In a earlier judgment the Supreme Court had favoured the use of secret ballot for deciding the majority trade union. Considering that the employees had already given their consent to the check-off system, the Court dismissed the writ petition.[365]

*506.* The Managing Director of the Tamil Nadu Cement Corporation Ltd served a notice announcing the holding of election amongst the unions functioning in the factory for the purpose of recognizing one of them for the settlement, under Section 12 (3) of the ID Act, dated 28, October 2005. This notice came under a challenge in a writ petition, which was dismissed on the ground that the notice could not be called in question in a writ petition. On merits, the Court said that 'as for as the recognition of union is concerned, it is by now well settled that it is not recognized by any statute, though the petitioner in his capacity as the General Secretary of the trade union may be entitled to raise an industrial dispute under the provisions of the Industrial Disputes Act, 1947.' Citing another case decided by the Court. it was held that 'the election held for recognition of a trade union is not governed by any statute, or the management exercising any statutory function with regard to the said subject, in order to invoke the constitutional remedy under article 226 of the constitution of India'.[366]

*507.* In another case, the petitioner union, the MRF United Workers Union, took up its quarrel with the management of MRF Ltd (Madras Rubber Factory), on the issue of recognition as a representative union, representing 898 of the 1029 permanent workmen of the Company and that another union, namely, MRF cycle Tyre Unit Employees Association, which was being considered by the management, be not permitted the facility of deduction of membership fees from the wages of the employees. The management did not entertain the request and did not recognize the union. The union filed a civil suit in the court for a declaration that it was the majority union, but the suit was declined by the court on the ground that it did not have the territorial jurisdiction to entertain the suit. The union then wrote to the Commissioner of Labour asking for the determination of the majority union by secret ballot. The Commissioner replied that there was no law providing for any such determination. Meanwhile, the management reached a settlement with the rival union. Following it, the petitioner union raised an industrial dispute and in the conciliation proceedings expressed a willingness to prove its majority by a secret ballot. In May 2006, about two years later the management announced that a secret ballot would be held. The union complained to the court that though its representatives got elected by a huge margin the Management did not like the results and asked the newly elected office bearers to resign. Moreover, in July 2006, the Management extended the check-off facility to another newly registered union. Thereafter, there being no other remedy, the union filed a complaint before the Committee on Freedom of Association of the ILO. Following it, the Tamil Nadu Government

365. LLJ, Vol. 2, 1999, *Visakhapatnam Port of Dock Workers' Union* v. *Board of Trustees, Visakhapatnam Port Trust and Others*, High Court of Andhra Pradesh, pp. 1123–1125.
366. LLJ, Vol. 1, 2007, *Ramchandran A. and Others*, v. *Managing Director, Tamil Nadu Cement Corporation Ltd and Others*, High Court of Madras, pp. 918–919.

asked one of its Labour Officer to inquire into the complaint and report. In the report the union's claim as a majority union was accepted. The union got a copy of the report by invoking the Right to Information Act, 2005. The matter was taken up by the Committee on Freedom of Association. It found that the petitioner union had more than 70 per cent membership of the total permanent workers and recommended that the government should take appropriate steps in that behalf. The state government repeated its stand that there was no law on recognition. That led to a writ petition seeking a direction on the subject. An interim injunction as asked for by the union was granted, restraining the Company from entering into a settlement with a rival union. This was later vacated on an appeal from the said union. In May 2009 the Company declared a lock-out which was lifted within two weeks. It was submitted before the Court that around 765 workmen had signed for the settlement to derive the benefits from it and more were agreeable to do the same. The other union which enjoyed the check-off facility reported that out of 1400 confirmed workmen, its membership was 1249 and that it was the majority union. The management took the position that it was a discretionary mater and that it will recognize the union which fostered peace and not the petitioner union which was disturbing industrial peace in the factory. The Court referred to Section 25U of the ID Act and the Fifth Schedule which provide for unfair labour practices on the part of management and union and, specially item 15, which lists the refusal to bargain in god faith with the recognized union' as an unfair labour practice. The Court laid down detailed instructions on the duty of management in this regard, rejecting the idea of management discretion. The Court asked the government to decide the question on the basis of the Code of Discipline.[367]

*508.* In one case the union at first gave its consent to verification of membership by secret ballot in 1996. The Court found that its statement that it was persuaded by a court order on the subject was false. The minutes were read out to show that the consent was given even before the said writ petition was filed. Moreover, the petition was not filed by the petitioner union. In fact the Oil and Natural Gas Commission had already adopted the policy of verification of membership of trade unions by secret ballot. In the petition there was no challenge to the policy. 'In our opinion, unless the policy adopted by ONGC is challenged and an order is sought for setting aside that policy, the process of secret ballot initiated by the employer pursuant to the policy decision cannot be set aside. The Court noted that the petitioner union was recognized as the majority union pursuant to the secret ballot in 2004 for a period of two years. On the completion of two years, when the process of secret ballot was initiated again, the petitioner union filed this petition and obtained an interim order as a result of which the process of secret ballot was not completed and the petitioner union continued to enjoy the status of the recognized union. 'In our opinion this conduct of the petitioner union disentitles it to any relief at the hands of this Court in its extraordinary jurisdiction. If it was genuinely felt by the petitioner union that the system of secret ballot is invalid, it first should have given up its status as

367. LLJ, Vol. 4, 2009, *MRF United Workers Union rep. by its General Secretary, Arakkonam* v. *Government of Tamil Nadu rep. by its Secretary, Labour and Employment Deptt. and Others*, High Court of Madras, pp. 685–699.

the recognized union and then should have filed this petition'. The petition was rejected. A request was made to order a stay in the process of verification. In fact in the process of verification only the ballots had to be opened now. The request was rejected.[368]

*509.* In the case of a public sector company the government issued a circular proposing to verify the membership of unions operating in Air India Ltd through the secret ballot. The government decided to convene a meeting of the unions to obtain their consent for holding the secret ballot under the Code of Discipline. In a subsequent letter, the Dy. Chief Labour Commissioner said that no consensus could be reached, yet it has been decided to hold the election on 13 April 2004 and 13 May 2004. To this a union filed a writ petition, objecting to the procedure laid out in the notification. The petition referred to a judgement of the Apex Court that under the Maharashtra law, even if secret ballot method is resorted to with the consent of parties, such consent cannot cure the illegality of substitution of a procedure not recognized by law.It was in fact alien to the Act and, therefore, that method or mode could not be accepted as valid for the purposes of recognition'. The petitioners took the stand that the method of secret ballot was struck down and this law would apply irrespective of the enactment, code or agreement that may be applicable in a given case. In another case, the Division Bench held that the procedure should not be completely derogatory to the scheme of the Act. In an important case the Apex Court had agreed to the secret ballot on the basis of consent of rival unions. Having examined the various Court's judgments, the Court decided on an unusual course. 'We do not intend expressing any views on the merits of the rival contentions between the parties.' The questions raised by them are of great importance and arise in a number of matters. 'We are of the view that the matter requires further and detailed consideration by a larger Bench of this Court even if it being held that the ratio of judgements apply only in cases under the MRTP and PULP Act and not where the Code of Discipline applies. The Court framed two questions on the subject, including whether the method of secret ballot in the fact of this case be viewed as arbitrary.[369]

## §4. Approved and Recognized Union

*510.* The Bombay Industrial Relations Act, 1946, provides for the maintenance of a register of approved unions and for a representative union to secure legal recognition in a 'local area'. This Act applies to Maharastra and Gujarat and the same principles are reflected in the Madhya Pradesh legislation. Only a registered union with a membership of not less than 25 per cent of the workforce in any industry in a local area can be recognized as a representative union. Unions which are not representative but have the membership of 25 per cent of the workforce in an industry

368. LLJ, Vol. 4, 2009, *Petroleum Employees Union* v. *Chief Labour Commissioner, (Central) and Others*, High Court of Bombay, pp. 745–748.
369. LLJ, Vol. 1, 2006, *Air India Employees Guild* v. *Air India Ltd and Others* and *Air India Employees Union* v. *Air India and Another*, High Court of Bombay, pp. 666–670.

in a local area are recognized as qualified unions. If a union cannot be recognized as either representative or qualified, there is still scope for a third category, viz. as primary unions which have membership of at least 15 per cent of employees in an undertaking. Each category enjoys certain statutory advantages though the bargaining rights are reserved only for the first. The law is applicable only to those industries which are not covered by the ID Act.

*511.* The Maharashtra Recognition of Unions and Prevention of Unfair Labour Practices Act, 1972, provides for the recognition of a sole bargaining agent in an industry and for union security. Once recognized, the union's status as a sole bargaining agent cannot be challenged for two years. Unrecognized unions are entitled to handle grievances of their members and appear on their behalf in departmental inquiries. This Act applies to all industries that fall outside the jurisdiction of the Bombay Industrial Relations Act. Thus between the two legislation all the industries employing 50 or more persons located in the state are covered. The recognition is conferred by the industrial court set up under the Act. But only unions enjoying the membership of not less than 30 per cent of employees in an undertaking can seek recognition. The government is empowered to declare a group of concerns in an industry in an area as an undertaking for this purpose. This Act has implemented the principle of one trade union in respect of an undertaking. The union seeking recognition should not have called or aided an illegal strike in the six months preceding its application to the industrial court, and, after recognition is granted, it must refrain from unfair practices including supporting an illegal strike. This legislation has made the duty to bargain obligatory for a recognized union; the refusal to do so is an unfair practice.

*512.* Under the Maharashtra Act the method of secret ballot is not the proper method for determining the allegiance of workers; this being alien to the statute. Even if the secret ballot method is resorted to with the consent of the parties, such consent cannot cure the illegality of substitution of a procedure not prescribed in the Act. Section 11 of the Act provides that any union, which has for the whole of the period of six months preceding the month in which it applies for recognition a membership of not less than 30 per cent of the total number of employees in any undertaking, may apply to the industrial court for this purpose. The industrial court then conducts a preliminary scrutiny and puts up a notice giving its intention to consider the applications and inviting objections, etc., as to why the recognition should not be granted. Thereafter the industrial court may conduct such inquiry as it deems fit and if it is satisfied that the requisite conditions are met, it will grant recognition, and issue a certificate to this effect. In one case the industrial court resorted to ballot at the instance of the parties and by their consent. The Bombay High Court declared the method adopted as illegal. The Supreme Court agreed and declined to interfare.[370]

370. Supreme Court Cases, 1995, Supp, *Association of Engineering Workers* v. *Dockyard Labour Union and Others*, Supreme Court of India, pp. 544–546.

*513.* In one case the union did not seek recognition to negotiate as a majority union on behalf of all workmen, but only a limited recognition to discuss the grievances of its members who formed a separate category. The Court held that though the demand for limited recognition was not a fundamental right or a statutory right, yet it could not be denied that fair play required that such recognition should be conceded. The union had filed a petition seeking a writ of mandamus directing the chairman and managing director, Indian Airlines, to give limited recognition and negotiate with it. The Company had already given recognition to seven other unions, though no fresh recognition had been given since 1959. According to the Court the arbitrary decision to close the door against this particular union even with regard to its claim for a limited recognition has given the order a tinge of abuse of power and even raises a doubt about its bona fides. Accordingly the prayer was granted and the Company directed to grant limited recognition as requested.[371]

371. LLJ, Vol. 1, 1995, *Indian Airlines Technical Assistants union, Hyderabad* v. *Chairman and MD Indian Airlines (HQ) and Others*, High Court of Andhra Pradesh, pp. 578–582.

# Chapter 2. Voluntary versus Compulsory Principles of Settlement of Disputes

## §1. Introduction

*514.* The principal legislation for regulation the collective relationship between the employers and workers is the Industrial Disputes Act, 1947. The adoption of this Act gave the industrial relations system a permanent orientation towards tripartitism, ascribing a pivotal role to the Industrial Relations Machinery (IRM). Indeed, several well meaning attempts to change the course of industrial relations towards bipartitism, with a minimum resourse to the IRM, have proved fruitless and even unpopular. No party is prepared for the risks inherent in giving up the very useful crutches the government machinery provides, including the government as the employer, and now it seems that so deep seated has become the habit of depending upon the courts that even voluntary arbitration is not ordinarily accepted as an alternative to adjudication.

*515.* At the time of enactment of the ID Act it was presumed that not all differences between the management and the labour would acquire the colour of formal disputes and it would be possible to settle them within the industry. For this purpose the ID Act made an explicit provision, viz. works committees. These had to be constituted in establishments employing 100 or more workers and were charged with the duty 'to promote measures for securing and preserving amity and good relations between employers and workmen and, to that end, to comment upon matters of their common interest or concern and endeavor to compose any material difference of opinion in respect of such matters'. Where unions are weak the works committees perform the role of representing workers, settling grievances and ensuring reasonable observance of rules and laws. But where the unions are strong it is not always possible for the works committee to be cast in a role that does not rival that of the union. Where inter-union rivalry exists the works committees also become engulfed in their internecine squabbles.

## §2. Code of Discipline

*516.* The Code of Discipline, now largely defunct, is basically an ethical instrument designed to prevent disputes. It reflects the Gandhian principle of essential harmony between labour and capital and, based on it, a tripartite commitment to allow industrialization of the country to proceed in a climate of peace. The many do's and don'ts the Code prescribes are based upon the central premise that 'to maintain discipline in industry (both in public and private sectors) there has to be:

- a just recognition by employers and workers of the rights and responsibilities of either party, as defined by the laws and agreements (including bipartite and tripartite agreements agreed at all levels from time to time); and
- a proper and willing discharge by either party of its obligations consequent on such recognition.

§3. JOINT CONSULTATION

*517.* In India, at the centre there do not exist any statutory provisions, other than works committees under the ID Act, for promoting joint consultation either on a bipartite or tripartite basis. However, the tradition of tripartite consultations at the initiative of the government has been maintained, though at one stage it had been allowed to fall into disuse. The tripartite industrial committees meet more often and 'the issues like strikes, lock-out, sickness of the industries, workers' participation in management and safety and occupational health requirements' are discussed and analysed individually.

*518.* The government is generally committed to workers' participation in management. The concepts discussed in this context include the formulation of a statutory scheme providing for consultative forums at the shop floor, plant and corporate board levels both in the public and private sectors. The other concept involving equity participation – required to be made by the management but optional for employees – has also been mooted. At the state level, under the Bombay Industrial Relations Act, 1946 and the BIR (Gujarat Extension and Amendment) Act, 1961, as amended in 1972, the governments of Maharashtra and Gujarat have made provions for joint councils in industrial undertakings.

*519.* The scheme of joint consultation usually faces two hurdles:

(i) workers' apathy to consultation in disregard of issues that concern them directly. These relate to wages, housing, social security and promotions, etc.;
(ii) managers' hostility and insecurity born out of the apprehension that they would lose such limited powers and role as they have if all the important matters are discussed in the joint bodies.

There also remains the more fundamental opposition of private employers to sharing of prerogatives, and in the public sector of the ministries' reluctance to delegate effective power on the ground of their accountability to Parliament. Moreover, in the public sector, at crucial stages of wage negotiations, the ministers like to play the decisive role, relegating even the top managements of public sector undertakings to secondary importance.

§4. JOINT NEGOTIATIONS

*520.* The government has taken several steps to maintain dialogue with its employees. In a number of cases the same bodies also negotiate and reach agreements. The joint consultative machinery (JCM) now covers the entire general body of employees including the civilians employed in defence installations and the departmental undertakings. The Indian Railways have maintained a permanent negotiation machinery since 1951 and, in addition, have a JCM since 1969. They discuss issues relating to pay and service conditions, as well as safety and the interests of the travelling public.

*521.* The PNM in the railways is the result of an agreement between unions and the ministry of railways and is not subject to any statutory provisions. It functions as a three-tier structure:

(i) the first tier operates at the divisional or workshop level and, at the headquarters, it involves the general manager of the Zonal Railway and the central executive of the recognized union;
(ii) the second tier consists of the Railway Board and the recognized federation of unions; and
(iii) the third tier functions as an ad hoc tribunal consisting of equal number of representatives of unions and the railway administration with a neutral chairman.

As the sphere of the negotiation unit rises, so does the scope of negotiations. Questions concerning pay scales, allowances, etc., are handled at the second tier. At the first level, only matters within the purview and competence of the divisional superintendent may be brought up. At the first level the PNM also functions as a grievance committee. At the second level, matters pertaining to confirmation and creation of posts, amenities, housing, administrative anomalies, etc., are discussed. The tribunal can investigate any dispute between the Railway Board and the recognized federations of unions which may be referred to it. The awards are not binding, and it is open to the government 'to accept, reject or modify the decision of the Tribunal'.

## §5. Voluntary Arbitration

*522.* Settlement of industrial disputes through voluntary arbitration is provided for in the ID Act under Section 10A. The employer and workmen interested in the dispute should take recourse to voluntary arbitration before the dispute is referred to adjudication. They are required to sign an agreement in the prescribed form and include the names of persons who will act as arbitrators. Reference to arbitration is possible during the pendency of conciliation proceedings. The presiding officers of Labour Courts/tribunals can also be appointed as arbitrators. The written agreement must be sent to the conciliation officer and to the appropriate government which will publish the agreement within one month. If the government is satisfied that the persons signing the agreement actually represent the majority of each party, it may issue a notification giving an opportunity to the employees and workmen who are not parties to the arbitration agreements to present their cases before the arbitrators. Further, having investigated the dispute, the arbitrators will submit the award to the government. Publication of arbitration agreements is mandatory and this should be done within one month. The status of the arbitrator is that of a statutory tribunal, so his award is equally binding.

*523.* On issuing the notification the government may prohibit any strike or lockout in connection with such dispute which may be in existence on the date of reference. In such a case (Section 18), the arbitral award is binding on not just the parties to the agreement but also on all the others who had been properly summoned to appear and present their views before the arbitrators. Otherwise it is binding only on the parties to the agreement. Section 33 further provides that, during the pendency of conciliations/adjudication/arbitration proceedings, no employer shall alter the conditions of service to the prejudice of the workmen concerned in the dispute, or for any misconduct connected with the dispute, discharge or punish in any manner such workmen except with written permission of the authority/arbitrator before whom the proceedings are pending. Every award, including an arbitration award, becomes enforceable on the expiry of 30 days from the date of its publication. An award made beyond the terms of reference is illegal. Moreover, if the copy of the arbitration agreement is not forwarded to the appropriate government the award would not come within the purview of the ID Act.

*524.* Can the arbitrator's award become a subject of appeal to higher courts? In one case, where the arbitrator had to decide whether the service of 400 discharged workmen who had taken part in an allegedly illegal strike could be terminated, or whether they should be reinstated, and gave the award in favour of the employer, the High Court admitted the appeal and quashed the award. The case then went to the Supreme Court. The Court held that every wrong order cannot be righted merely because it is wrong. 'It can be quashed only if it is vitiated by the fundamental flaws of gross miscarriage of justice, absence of legal evidence, perverse misreading of facts, serious errors of law on the face of the order, jurisdictional failure, and the like.' Earlier the Court had held that because the arbitrator had the power to bind even those who were not parties to the reference and the force of the award on publication was derived from the statue, he should legitimately be regarded as 'falling within the rainbow of statutory tribunals amenable to judicial review'. Then the Court decided that the arbitrator had as much power to give appropriate relief in cases of discharge or dismissal of workmen (under Section 11A) as do Labour Courts and tribunals. Merely because arbitrators were not named in this section, it did not follow that, being equivalent to tribunals, they did have or could not exercise identical powers. The Court held that 'both culpability and qualification of punishment are within the jurisdiction of the Tribunal/Arbitrator'.

## §6. Collective Bargaining

*525.* Collective bargaining, as understood in the industrially developed countries of the west, is not widely practised in India, nor does it form an important plank of the government's labour policy. The government does not oppose collective bargaining. In any case the government does not get in the way, if the two parties can reach agreements without resource to open conflicts. The ID Act does not promote collective bargaining; it is a statute of compulsory conciliation and adjudication. Though voluntary arbitration rests upon voluntary agreement, it does not form an integral part of the collective bargaining process. It is tied to the procedure and machinery of the ID Act.

*526.* A 'settlement' may be arrived at in the course of conciliation proceedings, or otherwise as a written agreement between the employer and workmen provided it 'has been signed by the parties thereto in such a manner as may be prescribed' and a copy has been duly field with the government and the conciliation officer. If this procedure is not adhered to, the 'settlement' loses legal validity and it may not be enforceable through the courts.

*527.* A settlement can be arrived at even during the pendency of adjudication proceedings. The tribunal cannot veto a settlement; indeed, it is bound to accept it. If a settlement has been signed after the tribunal has given its award, but before its publication by the government, it is binding and preferable to the award. A settlement is completely binding upon the workmen whom the union represents. It cannot be argued that it is binding only upon the union and not on the workmen. A minority union cannot assail a settlement reached between the management and the recognized majority union which acted as the sole bargaining agent. It would be binding on all workmen of the establishment. A settlement accepted by a majority of workmen must be presumed to be just and fair and tribunal's interference with it on the basis of a minority union's opposition would be unwarranted. The High Court should be wary of issuing any writs in such cases.[372]

*528.* Despite the limitations of law, collective bargaining has continued to find wider acceptance and is increasingly practiced at the level of enterprise as well as some industries. Plantwise agreements are more common, but, in the leading industrial centers, collective bargaining is practiced in the cotton textiles, synthetics, silk, jute textiles, plantations, coal, petroleum refining and distribution, steel, aluminum and ports and docks, among others. In some industries all-India settlements have been signed, though it is more common to adhere to industry-cum-region patterns. The ports and docks, and Life insurance Corporation and the nationalized banks have signed all-India agreements and created sound bargaining traditions. The plant-level agreements mostly relate to the plant-level issues, viz. payment of bonus, special allowance, leave and holiday facilities, uniform and liveries, age of retirement, etc. The Apex Court is of the view that the binding nature of settlements arrived at in the course of conciliation proceedings is based on the principle of collective bargaining for resolving industrial disputes and for maintaining industrial peace.[373]

*529.* In the public sector, collective bargaining is commonly practised both at the industry and enterprise levels. On sustentative issues, landmark settlements have been arrived at on productivity-linked bonus schemes in the Indian Railways, the Post and Telegraph Departments, the Air India, etc. Similar agreements have been signed in the hotel industry and in several private organizations. The public sector organizations are expected to function as model employers. Unions demand it and

372. LLJ, Vol. 2, 2000, *Mysore Kirloskar Mazdoor Sangh* v. *Management of Mysore Kirloskar Ltd and Others*, High Court of Karnataka, pp. 1050–1057.

373. LLJ, Vol. 1, 2000, *National Engineering Industries Ltd* v. *State of Rajasthan and Others,* Supreme Court of India, pp. 247–267.

are sometimes led to make exaggerated claims upon managements. On the other hand, the public sector undertakings cannot handle union demands with the same degree of freedom and flexibility as is practised by their counterparts in the private sector. The government issues guidelines on most issues relating to pay and personnel. In respect of the public service undertakings which come within the purview of the ID Act, all the formalities and procedures laid down in the Act apply; disputes are first heard at the level of conciliation, then referred to Labour Courts or tribunals for adjudication, which give awards, etc. Similarly, collective bargaining takes the form of signing the 'settlement' under the Act.

### §7. Wage Boards

*530.* Under the state legislation, the Bombay Industrial Relations Act which is applicable in the states of Maharashtra and Gujarat, provides for setting up statutory wage boards. Accordingly, wage boards have been set up for cotton textiles, artificial silk and sugar industries. Their awards have been implemented according to law. In Uttar Pradesh, the UP Industrial Disputes Act, 1947, provides for legal implementation of any non-statutory wage boards' recommendations after the state government has accepted and notified them. The central government has generally accepted the unanimous recommendations of non-statutory wage boards, though difficulties have arisen when unanimity could not be reached. Then discussions with interest groups must precede decisions.

*531.* The main advantage of the wage board system from the point of view of the government lay in that the representatives of employers and trade unions would negotiate an industry-wide wage structure within the framework of its socio-economic policy and produce recommendation that might find wide acceptance. However, the method adopted by wage boards caused too much delay and in several cases they had to give interim awards which provided immediate relief to workers. Although the wage boards succeeded in standardizing wage structures in the concerned industries by abolishing a number of wage scales and job designations, and merging existing scales, etc., the trade unions became completely disenchanted. So the government discontinued the system, excepting the class of working journalists, for whom wage boards may be appointed under the Working Journalists (Fixation of Rates of Wages) Act, 1958 and the Working Journalists (C. of S.) and Miscellaneous Provisions Act, 1955. An award on wages made by a wage board under these laws is recommendatory and is enforced by the Government under the provisions of these Acts. Any modifications made by the Government should not alter their important recommendations or the basic recommendations.[374]

374. LLJ, Vol. 1, 2006, *Gen Sey. Karnataka Karya Niratha Pathrakarthara Sangha, Banglore* v. *Gen Manager, Printers (Mysore) Projavani and Deccan Herald, Banglore,* High Court of Karnataka, pp. 513–521.

# Chapter 3. Conciliation and Adjudication

## §1. Selected Definitions

### I. Industrial Disputes

*532.* The definition of the term 'industrial dispute' in the ID Act is almost identical to that of 'trade dispute' in the Trade Unions Act and 'means any dispute or difference between employer and employer or between employers and workmen, or between workmen and workmen, which is connected with the employment or non-employment or the terms of employment or with the conditions of labour of any person. This definition has four key elements. First, there should be a dispute or difference of real substance which if not resolved might endanger industrial peace. Second, the dispute should arise between the parties named in the Act, viz:

(i) between employer and employer;
(ii) between employers and workmen; and
(iii) between workmen and workmen.

It is a dispute in which the named parties are interested and one that can be resolved. Third, the subject matter of the dispute should be connected with:

(i) the employment or non-employment;
(ii) the terms of employment; or
(iii) the conditions of labour of any person.

The last part of the third element gives the definition an 'unqualified width'. It must be a dispute that continues and has not ceased. In certain cases, viz. the death of a dismissed workman during the pendency of adjudication proceedings, the dispute would normally cease since the person cannot be reinstated. However, even in such cases, the dispute may be kept alive if the union is interested in seeking an award. The concept of 'employment or non-employment' has three ingredients, viz:

(i) the employer;
(ii) the employee (or workman); and
(iii) the contract of employment.

*533.* A dispute between an employer and a single employee cannot *per se* be an industrial dispute, but it may become one if it is taken up by a union or a number of workmen. Individual settlement of a dispute covered by Section 2A alone is legal. Thus a very wide area of employment and non-employment and the terms of employment is covered. Fourth, an industrial dispute can arise only in an industry. Though this does not form part of the definition, it is of crucial significance because even if an industrial dispute satisfies all the tests of the definition, it will still be outside the scope of the ID Act if it is not located in an industry.

*534.* Workmen may raise industrial disputes but only if they are legally recognized as such. If an employer denies this status to the person raising the dispute and succeeds in it, the Labour Court cannot proceed in the matter. Under the Industrial Employment (Standing Orders) Act, 1946, the employer is required to classify the workmen in his employ. In respect of classification, a dispute can conceivably arise as to whether one or more workmen should be permanent or temporary, because of its connection with the conditions of employment. A minority union or a group of workmen, who are not members of a majority union, can also sponsor a workmen's case. A master-servant relationship should exist. The most essential requirement is the control exercised by the employer in discharge of duties by the employee. The burden of proving it is on the employee or the workman making the claim.[375]

*535.* A formal industrial dispute may come into existence though a written cause may not be there. In the instant case, a clerk had been charge-sheeted and dismissed from service. He had failed to make a demand for reinstatement, instead the union approached the conciliation officer demanding reinstatement. According to the Supreme Court the tribunal was in error for agreeing with the management that, since the workman had not demanded reinstatement, the industrial dispute did not exist. The clerk's appeal to the appellate forum contending that the order of dismissal was wrong and that he should be reinstated in service was sufficient to establish an industrial dispute. In fact once a dispute has been referred to adjudication, the presumption is that it is an industrial dispute. A retired employee is not a workman and cannot raise an industrial dispute. A union of retired employees in a writ petition sought a direction to the conciliation officer (Regional Labour Commissioner), to submit his failure report on the dispute regarding denial of higher persionary benefits to the retired employees of the bank. The Court held that a retired employee could not be a party to an industrial dispute and dismissed the petition.[376]

*536.* For the purpose of raising a dispute a recognized union need not be registered. It is also not necessary that an industrial dispute should be backed by the resolution adopted by a substantial body of workmen. A union can raise an industrial dispute concerning the non-employment of others who are not workmen of the concerned employer at the relevant time. However, where the cause of a workman has been espoused by a union which has nothing to do with the establishment where the workman is or was employed would not be an industrial dispute. On the other hand, industrial disputes subsist even after a closure or takeover of the industry. An industrial dispute can be validity agitated by a group of employees on behalf of others who may be employed in the same organization, though not 'workmen' under the ID Act, on the ground that there is a community of interest between them.[377]

375. LLJ, Vol. 4, 2006, *Bombay Hospital, Trust and Another* v. *Dr. Shailesh Hathi and Another,* High Court of Bombay, pp. 679–684.

376. LLJ, Vol. 2, 2007, *Standard Chartered Grindlays Bank Retired Employees Association and Others,* v. *Union of India and Others*, High Court of Calcutta, pp. 887–893.

377. LLJ, Vol. 1, 2000. The Law on the Subject is Discussed in considerable detail in *Mukand Ltd* v. *Mukand Staff and Officers' Association and Others*, High Court of Bombay, pp. 1583–1602.

*537.* A workman worked as a cook on daily wages in a hotel. He sought regularization because he was not paid equal wages and other benefits as to the regular employees. Despite representation to the management he was not regularized. The two workmen who were similarly placed raised an industrial dispute which was referred for adjudication. The management took the plea that their contract was contingent on getting a contract of catering from the Indian Airlines. When this contract comes to an end, the workmen's services shall not be required. The issue was whether the cause of the workman was properly espoused. Another issue related to his absence from duty. On the first issue, the Labour Court decided against the workman. The Court held that barring a dispute related to dismissal, discharge, retrenchment or termination of an individual workman, to which Section 2A applies, an industrial dispute must be a collective dispute. If there is no industrial dispute, the same cannot be referred. A dispute between an individual and management cannot be an industrial dispute. A valid industrial dispute must be sponsored or espoused by a union or by a number of workmen. The union may be of a minority of workmen. An outside union may be held to be sufficiently representative of workmen in the establishment to espouse a cause. Espousal means that the dispute of an individual workman is adopted by the union as its own dispute. It should be a collective decision of the executive body of the union, though it can be taken in an informal manner. On the date of reference it should be a proper industrial dispute. In this case there was no evidence on record of the espousal of the dispute of the petitioner. Accordingly, it could not be held that an industrial dispute existed between the employer and the workmen. The award of the tribunal was *per se* perverse. On the issue of regularization, the High Courts acting under Article 226 of the constitution should not give direction for absorption, regularization or permanence, unless the recruitment was made regularly and in terms of the constitutional scheme. No right can be founded on an employment on daily wages that such employees should be treated on a par with a regularly recruited candidate and made permanent. The award was set aside as perverse *per se*. The writ petition was dismissed.[378]

## II. Settlement

*538.* Under the ID Act this term'means settlement arrived at in the course of conciliation proceedings and includes a written agreement between the employer and workmen arrived at otherwise than in the course of conciliation proceedings, where such agreement has been signed by the parties thereto in such manner as may be prescribed and a copy thereof has been sent to an officer authorized in this behalf by the appropriate government and the conciliation officer.'

The settlement should be just and reasonable. All the formalities prescribed in the definition must be completed in order to make a settlement binding. However, a memorandum of settlement signed by the office bearers of a union, without being authorized to do so either by the constitution or the executive committee or by the workmen to enter into an agreement with the management, will not pass the test of

378. LLJ, Vol. 2, 2007, *Management of Hotel Samrat* v. *Government of NCT and Others*, High Court of Delhi, pp. 950–956.

a binding settlement. A settlement is legal if it is related to a body of workmen and the employer and not the individual disputes. A compromise document signed under duress and not arrived at before the court but outside the court is not binding. An illegal retrenchment could not be settled in this manner and was set aside, and the workman reinstated with 50 per cent of back wages. An award cannot be made solely on the basis of an existing settlement between the management and a majority of workmen. The Court held in one case that while deciding the main reference, the Industrial Court should frame a specific issue as to the justness, fairness and reasonableness of the settlement.[379]

*539.* Section 18 provides that a settlement arrived at between the employer and workmen otherwise than in the course of conciliation proceedings is binding only on the parties to the agreement, but a settlement arrived at through the process of conciliation shall be binding on:

(i) all parties to the industrial dispute;
(ii) all other parties summoned to appear as parties to the dispute;
(iii) the employer, his heirs, successors or assigns in respect of the establishment to which the dispute relates; and
(iv) all persons who are employed in the establishment as well as all those who subsequently become employed therein.

These provisions are common to arbitration awards and awards made by Labour Courts and tribunals. Individual settlements cannot modify standing orders, nor can they dispense with Section 9A, requiring notice of charge to be served upon the workmen, nor can the office-bearers of a union, who do not have the authority to do so, sign a settlement within the meaning of Section 2(P) of the Act. They must be authorized to do so. A settlement should reflect the spirit of collective bargaining and in such negotiations the individual workman necessarily recedes into the background. A large number of individual settlements (with 500 workmen) for lifting a lock-out were found to be illegal.[380] A settlement reached with one section of workmen is not binding upon workmen of other sections. In one case the Court held that, having obtained the benefit under the settlement, it was not open to the workman to contend that the settlements was not fair.[381]

*540.* In a settlement under Section 18 of the Act, the employees were given pay scales on promotion. Two employees claimed in a writ petition in the High Court that the pay scale given to them was not in existence and they should get the next scale of promotion. The Court allowed the petition and issued the requisite direction. The petitioner Company appealed to the Apex Court. The Court found that the

379. LLJ, Vol. 1, 2000, *Gokulesh Petroleum, P. Ltd* v. *Himalaya R. Shah*, High Court of Gujarat, pp. 1254–1261; LLJ, Vol. 2, 2006, *Franco-Indian Pharmaceuticals Pvt. Ltd*, v. *Franco-Indian Workers Union*, High Court of Bombay, pp. 335–357.

380. LLJ, Vol. 2, 1999, *Hindustan Lever Ltd* v. *Hindustan Lever Employees Union*, High Court of Bombay, pp. 804–825.

381. LLJ, Vol. 2, 2006, *State of Uttaranchal* v. *Jagpal Singh Tyagi*, Supreme Court of India, pp. 10–11.

conclusion that there was no existing pay scale as awarded per the settlement was not correct. There were three settlements, and as per the third settlement, the pay scale was there. This was so at the time the writ petition was filed. Their plea was that the latest settlement, being the fourth, was arrived at after their promotion and so it was not binding on them. The Court held that the last settlement was arrived at during the pendency of the writ petition and it would be binding on the respondents. It is settled law that a settlement, admittedly arrived at in conciliation proceedings, is binding on all. Unfortunately the High Court has not referred to the settlement or dealt with it at all. The impugned order was set aside. The appeal allowed and the writ petition stood dismissed.[382]

*541.* An award may be 'an interim or a final determination of any industrial dispute or of any question relating thereto by any Labour Court, industrial tribunal or national tribunal and includes an arbitration award made under Secton 10A'. According to this definition, an award may be (i) an interim or (ii) final determination of a dispute or any question relating thereto and it may be made by the bodies mentioned therin, including one given by an arbitrator. The purpose of giving an award is to settle the differences or resolve an industrial dispute. An award may be given only after a judicial determination of a dispute has been made. It should reflect the judgment of the tribunal. The High Court cannot give an award, since it is not mentioned in the definition, though it can hear appeals and, if satisfied, set aside an award or require its reconsideration. The High Court can also modity an award, if it rests on incorrect interpretation of facts, or lower a punishment if it is found to be excessive. But it cannot direct the appointment of a dismissed workman on a lesser post on compassionate grounds.[383] Awards and settlements are comparable in the sense that the law in respect of one also holds good in respect of the other. An award for reinstatement of a workman is under an eclipse, if the management makes an appeal and secures an interim stay. The eclipse is cleared once the writ petition is dismissed and the workman is entitled to reinstatement with full wages last drawn by him.[384]

*542.* An award can be enforced in the following three ways:

(i) the appropriate government may be moved to prosecute the defaulting party under Section 29, which lays down the penalty for a breach of a settlement or an award;
(ii) an application under Section 33C (1) and (2), various subsections, can be made to the government for the recovery of money or benefits due to a person under the award;
(iii) finally, a civil suit for obtaining a decree can be instituted.

382. LLJ, Vol. 1, 2006, *Indian Rare Earths Ltd and Another* v. *Pramod Chandra Panigrahi and Others,* Supreme Court of India, pp. 1080–1082.
383. LLJ, Vol. 2, 1999, *A.P.S.R.T.C.* v. *K. Pochaiah and Another*, Supreme Court of India, pp. 976-977.
384. LLJ, Vol. 3, Supp., 2000, *Sirput Paper Mills Ltd* v. *Chairman, Industrial Tribunal-cum-Labour Court and Another*, High Court of Andhra Pradesh, pp. 1212–1221.

However, the last option is the most time consuming and expensive and for most workmen it is not a practical course. When an award goes unimplemented and the government machinery is unable to produce the benefits provided for in it, workers prefer to go on strike or stage demonstrations. Where the employer is a public sector undertaking there is the option of making an appeal to the High Court to issue a writ of mandamus or any other appropriate writ, because the remedy under Section, 29 and 33C(2) is not equally efficacious.

## III. Award

*543.* An award passed completely ignoring the law is grossly illegal and void ab initio. The daily wage employees are excepted by the clause (bb) of Section 2(oo) of the Act. They cannot raise an industrial dispute on termination of their employment. They are not entitled to attract the provisions of Section 25 F of the Act. In one case, the High Court Bench held that its power to interfere may extend to quashing of mistakes apparent on the face of the record and also to ensure that the tribunal functions within the limits of its powers. In a case cited in this judgment,the Supreme Court said, 'the relationship between the parties being contractual, the terms of contract was that the services stood terminated at the end of the day. The Tribunal has not given any reason whatsoever as to what was the obligation on the appellant to employ the respondent. The status of the respondent was at best that of a daily wages. By virtue of his letters of appointment he ceased to be employed at the end of the day. His day's service stood automatically terminated. This being so the decision of the Tribunal in holding that the respondent shall be deemed to have continued in service from 16 June 1977, and would also be entitled to equal pay and allowance is clearly untenable.' The award of the Tribunal, dated 29 May 1980 was set aside as the respondent was neither entitled to demand employment, nor was he entitled to any other relief. In this case the High Court citing the English law held that the invalidity of a void act could not be cured by waiver or acquiescence.[385]

## IV. Industry

*544.* This has proved to be the most controversial term in the ID Act. An industrial dispute can arise only in an industry. If the establishment concerned is not deemed to be an industry, the whole ID Act loses meaning and cannot be invoked for settling the dispute. 'Industry means any business, trade, undertaking, manufacture or calling of employers and includes any calling, service, employment, handicraft, or industrial occupation or avocation of workmen.' This definition is in two parts; the first part defines industry from the standpoint of employers and the second from that of workmen. The two parts have led to conflicting opinions and only recently have the two been combined to give the term its widest meaning. The

385. LLJ, Vol. 2, 2008, *Sanjay Kumar Tiwary and Other,* v. *State of Bihar and Others,* High Court of Patna, pp. 977–984.

Industrial Disputes (Amendment) Act, 1982 has amended the definition of industry to mean:

any systematic activity carried on by cooporation between an employer and his workmen (whether such workmen are employed by such employer directly or by or through any agency including a contractor) for the production, supply or distribution of goods or services with a view to satisfy human wants or wishes (not being wants or wishes which are merely spiritual or religious in nature) whether or not:

(a) any capital has been invested for the purpose of carrying on such activity.
(b) such activity is carried on with a motive to make any gain or profit.'

*545.* Then the definition proceeds to include any activity of the Dock Labour Board as well as any activity relating to the promotion of sale or business or both carried on by an establishment and to exclude agricultural operations other than where they are integrated with any activity listed above and also to exclude plantations covered by the Plantations Labour Act, 1951. The definition explicitly excludes hospitals and dispensaries, educational, scientific and training institutions, institutions owned or managed by charitable, social or philanthropic organizations, *khadi* and village industries, any activity of the government relatable to its sovereign functions including departments of defense research, atomic energy and space, and also any domestic service, any professional activity practised by an individual or body of individuals, if their number is less than ten. However, this definition of 'industry' has not yet been notified.

*546.* The Industrial Disputes Act has two quite distinct definitions of the term 'industry' under Section 2(J). The original definition is in two parts and contains words like, undertaking, calling and service, leaving it to the higher courts to interpret them. In judgements the Apex court found the definition as vague and 'rather clumsy vaporous and tall and dwarf' and found it necessary to invoke the principle of 'noscitur a sociis' to determine if the undertaking was engaged in activities which were analogous to trade or business. If so, it was industry, otherwise not industry and out of reach of the Act. In 1977, the constitutional bench redefined the scope of the term and in 1982 the Act was amended to incorporate a new definition but did not notify it. In the instant case the new definition was incorporated in the judgement to uphold the petition of the Institute of Science, Bangalore that it was not an industry, so the ID Act was not applicable to it. The case arose from the grievance of a woman whose husband was an employee of the Institute on a temporary basis and died in harness. She applied for appointment on compassionate grounds. The Institute appointed her as a temporary clerk since there was no vacancy in the 5 per cent quota for regular posts to which one could be appointed on compassionate grounds. Later she remarried but did not disclose the change in her status from widow to married. This was held against her and the Institute on learning that she had remarried terminated her appointment as per Section 2(oo) (bb) of the ID Act. She raised an industrial dispute by filing a petition before the Labour Court under Section 10(4A) of the ID Act. The Labour Court framed three issues, of which the first was whether she could prove her status as a workman as defined in the Act, the second was on justifiability of reasons for terminating her services, and the third, to what relief was she entitled? In the award the court held that she was a workman, that the termination was not justified and directed reinstatement to the original post with continuity of service but without back wages. The Institute challenged the award in the High Court, while the employee did so to claim back wages. The two writ petitions were heard together. The management said that the Institute was founded in 1901 by an endowment made by J.N. Tata under the charitable endowment Act, 1890 and it functioned as a research institution with financial support from Government of India. The first point the Court raised was, whether the Institute was an 'industry' as defined in the Act. It extracted the definition enacted in 1982. It provides for nine a exclusions in which item 3 reads as, 'educational, scientific, research or training institutions'. The court reviewed all the pertinent cases cited by the lawyers and drew upon the Supreme Court's judgement on, whether the government owned and funded Physical Research Laboratory was an industry or not and held that an institution was an industry if it was analogous to trade or business. Further an activity undertaken by the Government cannot be regarded as 'industry', if it is in discharge of its sovereign functions. One more aspect to be borne in mind is that the aforesaid principles are not exhaustive either as regards what can be said to be sovereign function or as regards the other aspects dealt with by the Court. The Court held that the PRL was not an industry. Applying these principles to the Institute, the Court held that the activity carried on is not for the benefit of any particular individual or an institution, but it is for the benefit of the society as a whole and its objects is as not to render services to others!! In that view of the matter, I am of considered view that the activity carried on by the Institute cannot be held to fall within the definition of industry'. Thus decided, the employee's claim petition was held, not maintainable'. The writ petition of the Institute was allowed and the award of the Labour Court quashed. The Court also considered the issue of compassionate appointment. This is briefly reported in para. 204.[386]

*547.* The position of the Supreme Court is that (i) where there is systematic activity, (ii) it is organized involving the cooperation between the employer and his employers, (iii) for the purpose of production and distribution of goods and services in order to satisfy human wants, but excluding purely spiritual or religious wants, it is industry. The 'absence of profit motive or gainful objective is irrelevant, be the venture in the public sector, joint, private or other sector'. According to the Supreme Court, 'the true focus is functional and the decisive test is the nature of the activity with special emphasis on the employer-employee relations. If the organization is a trade or business, it does not cease to be one because of its philanthropy animating the undertaking'. As a result, the term 'industry' now includes all the activities which satisfy the triple tests, and even professions – clubs, educational institutions, cooperatives, research institutions, charitable projects and organizations lie within the orbit of the ID Act. All the welfare and economic activities of the government and statutory bodies are included; only the strictly understood sovereign functions are excluded. Whether a particular function of the state is or is not a sovereign function, depends on the nature of the power and the manner of its exercise. An activity

386. LLJ, Vol. 3, 2012, *B. vijayakumari Pillai, Bangalore* v. *Management of Indian Institute of Science, rep. by its Registrar*, Banglore, Karnataka High Court, pp. 627-637.

to fulfil bioaesthetic, recreational and educational aspirations of the people has been held to be an industry. A Ramand Home or after-care hospital is not an industry. A sports club is industry. A Central Cattle Breeding Farm is industry, so is the Irrigation Department.

## V. Reference

*548.* Where the parties to an industrial dispute apply to the government, whether jointly or separately, for a reference of a dispute, the reference is to be made on the government being satisfied that the persons applying represent the majority of each party. The terms of reference determine the scope of the tribunal's power and jurisdiction. Given this reference, the Labour Court is competent to grant interim relief to the aggrieved workman. It is for the appropriate government to decide whether to refer or not to refer a dispute. The High Court should not give a direction to make the reference.[387]

*549.* Any reference of matters not involved in an industrial dispute is devoid of competence and an award given pursuant to such a reference is unsustainable. It is not obligatory on the part of the government to make a reference at the instance of the union in each and every case. If it finds that in the interests of industrial peace it is not necessary to do so, it can refuse to make the reference. But the government cannot refuse to refer the dispute and decide the same itself. The government is not competent to decide whether the workers who are raising the dispute are workmen or not. This is a matter which the Labour Court may decide on the basis of facts placed before it. Reference is not adjudication. According to the Supreme Court:

> the government should be very slow to attempt an examination of the demand of workmen with a view to decline reference. It can do so, if it has come to the conclusion that demands made by workmen are perverse or frivolous and so do not merit a reference. But it is not a valid ground to refuse reference that the domestic enquiry was proper and that the punishment was proportionate to the gravity of the offence. Reference cannot be denied because in the opinion of the government the workmen had admitted the charges and it would be unnecessary to seek adjudication on the dispute.

A matter decided earlier by CAT and High Court cannot be raised again. reference should be declined. A reference was set aside on the ground that it revealed no application of mind. A dispute relating to termination of 58 medical representatives was referred to the National Tribunal. This was held to be not of national importance.[388]

*550.* The IPCL (Indian Petrochemicals Corporation Ltd.) was amalgamated with Reliance Industrial Ltd. The new management came out with a voluntary separation scheme on 6, March 2009. About 2400 workmen applied for it within the last two

---

387. LLJ, Vol. 2, 2007, *Rashtriya Chemicals and Fertilizers Ltd* v. *General Employees' Association*, Supreme Court of India, pp. 1032–1038.
388. LLJ, Vol. 2, 2007, *FDC Ltd* v. *Union of India*, High Court of Delhi, pp. 413–417.

days of the scheme, i.e. on 19 and 20 March 2007. Workers alleged that this was done under pressure, and on realization that it was a mistake chose to recall their request for vss applications, rejected the withdrawal requests and paid the VSS on 21 March 2007 and thereafter, but before the cessation of their services. None the less, the company chose to accept all VSS applications rejected the withdrawal requests and paid the VSS dues directly into the bank accounts of workmen. At this they raised an industrial dispute and it sought a reference for conciliation/ adjudication. The Asstt. Labour Commissioner–cum–conciliation officer refused to make the reference on the ground that there was no relationship of employer and employee and they were not workmen. Hence no dispute was in existence. They filed writ petitions against this order which were dismissed by the single judge. Their appeal was heard by a division bench. The Court recalled several judgments of the Supreme Court and restated the law. First, the High Court cannot sit in appeal over a finding of the state on facts. But if there is a disputed question of fact or law which requires determination on the basis of evidence, the issue cannot be decided by the government. If requires adjudication. A reference for adjudication is required. Second, an application for VSS is an offer, which a acceptance by the management will lead to cessation of service. Prior to the date of relieving of the duty, the rural relationship of the employer and employee does not cease. In this case the Asstt. Labour Commissioner had no jurisdiction to look into the evidence to decide the question on reference. The single judge adjudicated the matter on the presumption that all the workman were voluntarily retired, though some workmen had recalled their offers prior to their release. Both judgments were set aside and the case were remitted with a direction to the state to refer the dispute under Section 10(1) of the ID Act. The reference should be couched in a proper manner.[389]

*551.* In order to make a valid order of reference of an industrial dispute the government must satisfy itself:

(i) that on the basis of facts and circumstances an industrial dispute exists or is apprehended;
(ii) and it is expedient to make a reference. In one case, the conciliation officer reported failure, but a settlement outside the conciliation was reached and duly placed before the appropriate authority. Despite this the government made a reference. The High Court quashed the order of reference, because no industrial dispute subsisted at that time. A wrong reference on a mistaken premise that labourers on contract were workmen under the ID Act, led to an award favouring the labourers. It was set aside by the High Court.[390]

If the government does not possess any facts or material, the order of reference is liable to be quashed. Once a reference is made, if cannot be withdrawn, cancelled or superseded. But an existing reference can be amended. The government can also

389. LLJ, 2, 2011, *Thakor Nagjibhai Bhailal* v. *IPCL, Now Amalgamated with Reliance Industries Ltd. and others*, Gujarat High Court, pp. 182–192.
390. LLJ, January 2011, *Airport Authority of India* v. *Indian Airports Kamgar Union*, High Court of Bombay, pp. 211–223.

make a fresh reference, under Section 10 of the Act. The power to make the amendment flows from this section. In a case, the union could not make out a case that engagement of the contractor was a sham and bogus, and the refusal of the government to make the reference could not be challenged.[391]

*552.* The tribunal is required to adjudicate upon the points in a dispute referred to it and to matters incidental thereto. It cannot enlarge the scope of an industrial dispute. Difficulties arise because quite often the orders of reference are not carefully drafted and leave scope for ambiguity or controversy. The tribunal is expected to find out what the real dispute is and to do so not too technically, or in a pedantic manner, but 'fairly and reasonably'. This matter is connected with the question of tribunals exceeding their jurisdiction and interpreting an order of reference to include points that were not specifically stated therein. In one case the dispute pertained to frequent lay-off of badli workers;the demand of the workers was to regulate lay-offs. The tribunal gave the award directing the management to make all badli workers permanent form the date of the award. The management filed a writ petition against it. The Court referred to Section 10(4) the ID Act, that tribunal should confine the adjudication to the points referred to it. It is not open to the tribunal to travel beyond the scope of the reference.The impugned award was set aside.[392]

*553.* In an industrial dispute raised by trade unions representing textile mills of Tamil Nadu, the State Government under Section 10B of the ID Act (as amended in the state) and Section 10(1)(C) of the Act ordered a reference for adjudication of the dispute along with interim relief of Rs.150 per month per worker, to be adjusted with the payment of wages under the adjudicated award. Section 10(B) provides for interim relief in the interest of maintaining industrial peace, public order and supplies and services essential to the life of the community, when industrial disputes are referred under Section 10(1) of the ID Act. In a writ petition the single judge had held, that before passing the order under Section 10(B) the government should have followed the principles of natural justice, but the order of reference was valid. The order under Section 10(B) was set aside as not sustainable. Against this judgment both the mills and the unions filed writ appeals, which were heard together. On the first question, the Division Bench held that the requirement for initiating action under Section 10(1) of the Act is that there ought to be some material before the government to enable it to form an opinion that an industrial dispute exists or is apprehended for the purpose of reference under clause (c) or (d) of the Act, it is enough if the matter connected with or relevant to the dispute relate to any matter specified in second or third schedule. If the government has not applied its mind, then it cannot be said to have formed an opinion. The order of reference follows the formation of an opinion and is an administrative act. The adequacy or sufficiency of

391. LLJ, Vol. 3, Supp., 2000, *Pix Transmission Limited, Nagpur* v. *State of Maharashtra and Others*, High Court of Bombay, pp. 202–203; LLJ, February 2011, *Ladeku Mazdoor Sanghv* v. *Tata Communications Ltd*, High Court of Bombay, p. 539.

392. LLJ, Vol. 2, 2009, *Sree Meenakshi Mills Ltd, Madurai and Another* v. *Workmen represented by its Secretary, Madurai Workers Union (CITU), Madurai and Another*, High Court of Madras, pp. 50–53.

the material on which the opinion is formed is beyond the pale of judicial scrutiny. So far as Section 10(B) is concerned, the government need not provide opportunities to the appellant mills to hear them. The government acts while discharging its sovereign function and is not required to look into the nuances of legal issues, evidence, etc. on the plea taken by the mills that an industry wide reference was not called for, since there were mill based settlements. The government in its reference had not specified which mills were covered under Section 10(1) and which under Section 10(5) of the Act. The Court held that the absence of the same will not is any manner vitiate the order of reference, since the High Court could not act as an appellate authority under Article 226 of the constitution. Moreover, the order cannot be interpreted to rope in the establishments in which a dispute cannot be raised on account of subsisting settlements. Subsection 10(S) of the Act applies to the establishments other than the one or ones which are parties to the industrial dispute in respect to which the reference under Section 10(1) has been made. The single judge held, that an order under Section 10(B) cannot be made applicable to all the mills, unless it is specified which establishment / mill comes under Section 10(1) of the Act, because the 10(B) order of the government is a special or general order, so the question, which mill comes under the arena of dispute under Section 10(1) and which under Section 10(5) of the Act can very well be looked into by the Tribunal and determined by it. The power under Section 10(B) of the Act has to be exercised instantaneously after a reference is made under Section 10(1) read. This opinion was set aside as not correct. A composite reference can be made. It was based on an honest and bonafide opinion on the existence of the industrial dispute. The Court held that both orders were perfectly legal and valid in law and there were no material irregularitie and patent illegalities, so as to cause its interference. In the result the writ appeals filed by the unions were allowed and the order of the single judge regarding interim relief was set aside. The writ appeals of the mills concerning certain charter of demands raised by workmen were dismissed.[393]

## §2. CONCILIATION

*554.* Once an industrial dispute is recognized as a threat to industrial peace by the appropriate government, the conciliation officer may start conciliation proceedings. Conciliation is obligatory when a notice of strike or lock-out is given in respect of a public utility, but in other industries it is left to the discretion of conciliation officers. The conciliation officers are expected to conduct proceedings expeditiously and, in the course of their work, are empowered to:

(i) serve reasonable notice to parties;
(ii) make inspections;
(iii) interrogate any person connected with the subject matter of conciliation; and

393. LLJ, 2, 2011, *Sri Veereshwara Spinning Mills (P) Ltd., Tirupur, rep. by its Managing Director* v. *State of Tamil Nadu rep. by Secretary, Labour and Employment, Chennai and Others*, High Court of Madras, pp. 325–367.

(iv) call for any documents which are deemed to be relevant to the dispute or necessary for the verification of the implementation of any award.

*555.* In these respects, they enjoy the powers of a civil court. Their primary duty is to conciliate in disputes, help the two parties to see the other's point of view and promote settlements. In this respect, the function of a conciliation officer is more than mediatory; he cannot wait to be invited. It is his statutory duty to intervene in a dispute once it is referred to him, and obligatory to do so in disputes affecting public utilities. Conciliation proceedings commence after a notice is served. An employer may not dismiss an employee during the pendency of a conciliation proceeding. In one case, in a public utility there was a prolonged strike and the employer took disciplinary action and dismissed them from service. He was not held to be at fault by the Court since the formal notice by the conciliation officer had not been issued.[394]

*556.* If a settlement is reached, the conciliation officer should send a report thereof to the government along with a memorandum of settlement. The settlement should be in form H, which specifies the names of the parties representing the employer and the workmen, asks for a short recital of the case, the terms of settlement, signatures of the parties, of two witnesses and that of the conciliation officer. If a settlement is not reached, he should file a 'failure report', giving reasons for the inability of the parties to reach a settlement. When no settlement is arrived at, the government has two options. It may either make a reference for adjudication or communicate to the parties concerned its reasons for not making a reference. In one case the absence of the union in the conciliation proceedings vitiated the settlement signed between the employer and a union under Section 12(3) of the Act. It was not binding upon the apellant union. The issue was of the absorption of contract labour. The union representing the contract labour asked for following the rule of seniority and not to decide on the whims and caprices of the employer. The Court declined to interfere with the order of the single judge.[395]

*557.* The importance of conciliation proceedings is best appreciated in the context of Section 33, which imposes a blanket ban upon the employers to make any change in the conditions of service to the prejudice of workmen, 'in regard to any matter connected with the dispute', or likewise punish any workmen, 'for any misconduct connected with the dispute', save with the express permission of the authority concerned. This restriction applies equally to adjudication and arbitration proceedings. Moreover, the employer may not take any action against any protected workman, (union members and officials) connected with a dispute pending before conciliation before an express permission is obtained. The difference between ordinary workman and protected workman is in respect of the employer's prerogative to change the conditions of service of the former, as per the company SO, or the

---

394. LLJ, Vol. 4, Supp. 2006 (NOC), *Gujarat Ambuja Cement Pvt. Ltd* v. *U.B. Gadhe*, High Court of Gujarat, p. 897.

395. LLJ, Vol. 2, 2008, *Neyveli Lignite Corporation and Others* v. *N.L.C. Indco Serve Thezilalar Uzhiyear Sangam*, High Court of Madras, pp. 897–906.

contract of service, if it is not connected with the dispute. In the case of the latter the employers are enjoined not to exercise this right without prior permission.

## §3. Settlements: Procedure and Difficulties

*558.* A 'settlement' is a written agreement between an employer and workmen stating the terms on which the dispute has been settled and it should be signed by the representatives of the two parties. An *ad hoc* agreement which does not settle at least a part of the dispute, or the procedure for resolving it in some manner, and leaves the substance of the dispute unresolved and is silent on what procedure is to be followed would not be a settlement. A settlement arrived at in the course of conciliation means that:

(i) conciliation proceedings are still pending;
(ii) it has concurrence of the conciliation officer;
(iii) and it is considered by him to be fair and reasonable.

As soon as a settlement becomes operative, the contract embodied in it takes effect and the existing terms and conditions of workmen are modified accordingly. The embodied contract continues to govern the relations between the parties concerned, though it may be altered by a fresh settlement, an award or legislation. Legally binding settlements can be reached even during the pendency of adjudication proceedings, indeed even after the award has been made but before its publication. But a settlement relegating the dispute to arbitration is not a settlement.[396]

*559.* Section 36A provides for power to remove difficulties. If in the opinion of the appropriate government any difficulty or doubt arises as to the interpretation of any provision of an award or settlement, it may refer the question to such Labour Court or tribunal as it may think fit. Thereupon the adjudicator will decide the question in accordance with the established procedure and its decision shall be final and binding on all such parties who have been given an opportunity of being heard. In interpreting a settlement it is vital that the intention of the parties as expressed in the language used by them should be found out. Consideration of the context and the setting is indispensable for ascertaining the meaning of an expression.

*560.* A difficult situation may arise if the establishment has more than one union, so that while one union arrives at a settlement with the concurrence of the conciliation officer, the rival union does not agree to it. According to the Supreme Court, the settlement is binding upon everyone including the rival union. But, where there are two identical industrial disputes before the conciliation officer, one cannot assume that a settlement with one union will be automatically binding upon the other unless the two cases are treated as one dispute and either a settlement is jointly reached with both unions, or it should be referred to adjudication and then its award will be binding. A settlement under Section 18(3) is binding on all workmen of the

396. LLJ, Vol. 1, 2000, *Chemplast Sanmar Limited* v. *Mattur Chemicals Podhu Thozhilalar Sangam and Another*, High School of Madras, pp. 1335–1340.

establishment including those belonging to the minority union which opposed it, while a settlement under Section 18(1) is binding only on the parties to the agreement. Negotiated settlements under Section 18(1) are honoured by courts and placed on a pedestal even higher than judicial adjudication.[397]

*561.* In one case the company signed a settlement with the recognized union under Section 18(1) of the Act. Such a settlement is binding on all workmen, present and future. However the benefits and obligations flowing from the settlement applied only to the permanent workmen of the patalganga establishment of the company, the CIPLA Ltd, and not to the trainees, temporary and casual workmen of the company. The settlement provided for an ex gratia payment in lieu of arrears for the period 1 August 2000 to April 2004, proportionate to the attendance of each workman at the rate of Rs 1150 per month after deducting 5 per cent as donation to the Cipla Employees Union. It also provided for individual acceptance by requiring an individual declaration that the terms and conditions were acceptable to him. This particular clause, No. 14, became a bone of contention, since it provided that in case a workman fails to submit the declaration by the due date, but does so at a later date, the benefits in respect of prospective wages would be applicable from the first of the month following the date of submission. If he fails to do so, the Company was at liberty to withdraw the benefits arising from the settlement. A few workmen raised a dispute of unfair labour practice under the MRTU and PULP Act and secured a favourable award from the Industrial Court. The Company filed a writ petition against the award. The Court held that clause 14 of the settlement was redundant and unnecessary because the settlement was binding on all workmen, since the union was recognized as the majority union under the MRTP & PULP Act. The declaration of individual workmen was opposed to public policy as the rights of workmen could not be abrogated by the employer at his whims. It could be severed from the agreement by, 'running a blue pencil through it'. It was an unfair labour practice to deny the benefits of the settlement to the two workmen who had not submitted the individual declaration and made the complaint. The petition was dismissed. Another case was decided on the ground that a settlement under Section 18 of the ID Act with a recognized union was binding on all workmen and the employer engaged in an unfair labour practice by denying wages and bonus rightly due to workmen.[398]

*562.* If no period is agreed upon, a settlement is considered binding for a period of six months from the date on which it is signed by the two parties. At the expiry of this period either party can serve a two months' notice for terminating the settlement, and it would stand terminated at the end of the notice period. A mere submission of a charter of demand by the union may not be viewed as a tacit representation of not wanting to remain bound by the settlement. It must take the

397. LLJ, Vol. 2, 2000, *R. Sekar* v. *Presiding Officer, First Additional Labour Court, Madras and Another,* High Court of Madras, pp. 694–696; LLJ, Vol. 2, 2009 (NOC), *Deonath Majhi* v. *Central Coalfields Ltd*, High Court of Jharkhand, pp. 757–758.

398. LLJ, Vol. 2, 2008, *CIPLA Ltd* v. *Anand Ganapat Patil and Others,* High Court of Bombay, pp. 377-388; LLJ, Vol. 2, 2008 (NOC), *Ruby Coach Builders Ltd* v. *P.S. Ghose,* Member, Industrial Court and Others, High Court of Bombay, pp. 1106–1107.

form of an express representation. When a period is fixed in a settlement, it non the less remains in force thereafter until one party gives a written notice of two months for terminating it. However, it is also possible to give an advance notice of the intention to terminate the settlement well before its expiry though this cannot become the basis for curtailing its life. During the life of a settlement reached under Section 18(3), a fresh dispute cannot be raised by a minority union and it cannot be referred for adjudication. Such an action would destroy the purpose of the Act. If a reference has been yet made, it would be due to non-application of mind and it should be recalled by the government. The law is that a settlement not under Section 18(3) of the ID Act is binding on both the parties and continues to remain in force unless and until the same is altered, modified or substituted by another settlement.[399]

## §4. JURISDICTION OF ADJUDICATION AUTHORTIES

*563.* Under Section 10(4), the jurisdictions of the Labour Court, the Industrial Tribunal and the National Tribunal are established. It is stated therein: 'where in an order referring an industrial dispute to a Labour Court, Tribunal or National Tribunal under this section or in a subsequent order, the appropriate government has specified the points of dispute for adjudication, the Labour Court, or the Tribunal or the National Tribunal, as the case may be, shall confine its adjudication to those points and matters incidental thereto'. The tribunal has the power to decide a dispute and grant relief but without exceeding its authority. This has been a subject of a number of disputes.

*564.* The union made an application before the Industrial Tribunal to implead the principal employer in a reference relating to the validity of retrenchment effected by the contractor. The Tribunal did not grant the prayer. Against this order the union filed a writ petition in the High Court. The Court held that whether the workmen were working under the principal employer and whether they had been retrenched by such employer could not be included in the reference. The Tribunal has to confine its adjudication to points of dispute under Section 10 (4) of the ID Act. Consequently the impugned order was neither improper nor illegal. The petition was dismissed.[400] In another case a daily wages chowkidar was terminated on being surplus, but received support from the award of the Labour Court on a reference, whether the termination of the services of the chowkidar was justified and in order? And if not, to what relief was he entitled? On an appeal, the High Court upheld the award. The Supreme Court noticed three flaws. One, the fact that the Deptt. of Food and Supplies, Punjab was an 'industry'. The Court found that the Labour Court did not consider this aspect, because it did not form part of the reference, while the High Court, which heard the arguments on this aspect, ignored it. The Court held that it

399. LLJ, Vol. 1, 2000, *National Engineering Industries Ltd* v. *State of Rajasthan,* Supreme Court of India, pp. 247-267; LLJ, Vol. 2, 2009, (N.O.C.) *Deonath Majhi* v. *Central Coalfields Ltd*, High Court of Jharkhand, pp. 757–758.

400. LLJ, Vol. 2, 2009, *(N.O.C.), Birla Tyres Workers Union* v. *Industrial Tribunal, Orissa, Bhubaneswar and Others*, High Court of Orissa, p. 762.

was not an 'industry' under the ID Act and, in view of this jurisdictional fact, there could not be an industrial dispute. Second, there was a long delay of nine years in raising the dispute. However, the employer should have made a grievance on a stale claim being made in a writ petition. But this aspect was not considered by the management. Third, the claim of the workman that he worked from June, 1985 to 24 August 1986 was not correct, because his services ended at the end of each day. The daily wage labour's strength increased and decreased with the increase/decrease in the food grains stock. He was found to be surplus. The order of the Labour Court was quashed and the Labour Court was asked to adjudicate the dispute on these aspects.[401]

*565.* To problem of jurisdiction might arise when a local dispute pertaining to an all-India concern is referred to a tribunal by the state government. The dispute raised by the employees controlled by the local office can be validly adjudicated by the state tribunal even through it may raise issues of importance to all the employees. This is so because the Supreme Court has affirmed that as far as possible the adjudication of a dispute should rest upon the industry-cum-region principle and, further, that in applying this principle, 'the tribunal cannot abstain from seeing that fair conditions of service prevail in the industry with which it is concerned', even though the award may cause a deviation in the service conditions on an all-India basis. Such an award will no doubt apply only to local employees and cannot be automatically extended beyond the state boundaries. The Act provides for referring a dispute of an all-India nature to a National Tribunal, but the appropriate government that can do so is the central government. A workman was posted at a project in Rajasthan, though the appointment and transfer order were passed in the Delhi office. He was terminated from services while working in Rajasthan. The High Court held that the substantial cause of action arose within the jurisdiction of Delhi. The Delhi government referred the dispute to the Labour Court. The Labour Court rejected the reference because the employee was working in Rajasthan. The High Court set aside the order of the Labour Court. The company was directed to reinstate the appellant with back wages.[402]

*566.* The tribunal is expected to function as a judge of the dispute and not as an administrator. In the performance of this function, it must reconcile the conflicting interests of employers and workmen and also overcome the clash of basic principles, such as freedom of contract and the right to carry on business with the security of employment, fair wages, etc. The primary duty of tribunals is to promote industrial harmony, secure social justice, improve working conditions and to help the State in maintaining industrial peace. In order to do this, the ID Act has conferred upon them the powers to modify contracts and to go beyond the limits of ordinary law in making new contracts and enforcing them. They can confer new

---

401. LLJ, Vol. 2, 2007, *Director, Food and Supplies, Punjab and Another* v. *Gurmit Singh*, Supreme Court of India, pp. 813–815.

402. LLJ, July 2010, *Bageshwar Maurya* v. *Management, Naveen Projects P Ltd*, High Court of Delhi, pp. 317–320.

rights as well as modify existing rights and are not fettered by an existing agreement or contract between labour and employer. The tribunals cannot alter statutory provisions; nor can they violate judicial principles laid down by the higher courts. Furthermore, in altering an existing obligation, they should act with proper restraint. The tribunal should ascertain facts and based on them give their awards. In one case the Labour Court found that the order of dismissal was justified, but decided to grant Rs 20,000 to the workman by way of social rehabilitation and in the interest of social justice. This was found to be a gross error, perverse and without jurisdiction, and the order was quashed. Labour Courts cannot be benevolent in their awards.[403]

*567.* The tribunals are empowered to grant interim relief, as well as full and adequate relief. An interim relief is granted through an interim award. This is carved out of the main relief sought by the employees and cannot become the whole of it. For example, on a complaint of unjustified and improper dismissal, the tribunal cannot award reinstatement as an interim relief, because thereafter nothing more would remain to be done. Interim relief can be granted in disputes pertaining to back wages, bonus, DA, etc. Ordinarily, the union should make out a case for interim relief and plead for it. Under Section 17B, the Labour Court/tribunal has been given additional powers to direct the employer, who prefers an appeal to the higher courts against its order of reinstatement, to pay such workmen full wages last drawn by them during the pendency of such proceedings. This proviso covers not only cases of reinstatement, but also cases of rejection of employer's applications to permit dismissal under Section 33(2)(b) of the Act. If the award does not order the reinstatement of the workman, Section 17B cannot be invoked. It would have no application.[404]

*568.* The ID Act has empowered the tribunals to entertain specific complaints directly from workmen on changes made in the conditions of service during the pendency of proceedings, or any unauthorized action against the protected workmen (Section 33, various subsections), and to adjudicate upon them (Section 33A). Similarly, complaints under Section 33C can be heard directly on applications from individual workmen, or any person authorized by the complainants. However, while computing the monetary benefit due to the complainant under an award, the Labour Court cannot make a new award. If the award is unambiguous, the tribunal should interpret and execute it and if it is an ambiguous one, it is competent to construe the award to ascertain its precise meaning, and then enforce it. These steps are necessary for computing the monetary benefit due to a worker and they should be taken. The claim for computation of any benefit under this section does not die with the death of the workman.

*569.* Where a party is prevented from appearing at the hearing, under Section 33(2), and is faced with an ex parte award, it is as if the party is visited with an

403. LLJ, Vol. 3, 2000, *Victor F. Parmar* v. *Elecon Engineering Co. Ltd,* High Court of Gujarat, pp. 494–500.
404. LLJ, August 2010 *Arora Combines* v. *Damaji Ganpat Mankav and Another,* High Court of Bombay, pp. 533–534.

award without notice of the proceedings. The High Court in the case held that where the tribunal had proceeded to make an award without notice to a party, the award was a nullity. In this case the applicant before the Labour Court was unable to attend the court due to his wife's illness and the court had dismissed the case for default. He then prayed for the restoration of the case, but it was argued by the opposite party that after passing the final order the Labour Court had no power to review the said order, because no such power was conferred under the Act. The High Court held that though there was no express provision in the ID Act giving the tribunal the jurisdiction to do so, yet it should be considered to be endowed with such ancillary or incidental powers as are necessary to discharge its function effectively for the purpose of doing justice between the parties. It no reference was pending before the Labour Court/tribunal as to the previous punishment imposed, no permission was required to be obtained under Section 33(2)(b) of the ID Act. A writ petition was pending in the High Court, but the High Court is not included in the authorities under Section 33(1). Hence Section 33(2) would not be applicable.[405]

*570.* Although an award is final, once it is published and it cannot be questioned in any court of law, none the less, it remains under the writ jurisdiction of the High courts and the Supreme Court. The award is not 'final', if it can be proved that the order of reference was null and void, or that the tribunal exceeded its jurisdiction, or if one party failed to appear so that the award became *ex parte*. If the material on record shows that the findings of the tribunal are perverse, it would be open to the High Court to set aside these findings. But the Court would not sit in appeal over the judgment of the tribunal. In one case, the petitioner's grievance was that the award was based on acceptance of the settlement in part and not *in toto*. The tribunal ought to have either accepted or rejected the settlement *in toto*, it could not have accepted or rejected it in part. This petition was granted and to that extent the award was rejected. In one case the tribunal enhanced the age of superannuation from 55 years to 58 years. This was found to be illegal and unenforceable. The decision of the employer to roll back the age of retirement from 60 years to 58 years could not be interfered with in the exercise of the Court's power of judicial review. But the said decision should not affect the existing rights of employees under the standing orders.[406]

*571.* An award remains in operation for one year though its life can be extended by the government. Where the government, on its own motion or on an application of any party, is convinced that there has occurred a material change in the circumstances since the award was made, it may refer it to a tribunal to decide whether its life should not be shortened, and the tribunal's decision shall be final. In order to terminate it, a notice of two months beyond the period of operation is required. Even

405. LLJ, August 2010, *General Manager, Karnataka Bank Ltd, Mangalore* v. *Ashok Kumar and Others*, High Court of Karnataka, pp. 506–508.

406. LLJ, July 2010, *ITI Ltd and Others* v. *Venugopalan N and Others*, High Court of Karnataka, pp. 77–87.

after the termination of an award, the rights and obligations created under it remain unaffected. These can be changed only if fresh adjudication leads to a new award or the parties concerned conclude a settlement on their own. Section 19 gives the government the discretion to reduce the period of any award, and fix such period as it thinks fit and, before its expiry, also extend it by a period not exceeding one year at a time up to a maximum period of three years from the date on which it came into operation. For terminating a settlement under Section 19(2), a formal notice is not always considered necessary. Various representations made by the union to the employer could be construed as notice of termination. The mere fact that the workmen went on strike, or that the management participated in conciliation proceedings, would not suffice to show that the previous award had been terminated. A settlement is truly terminated only when it is replaced by another settlement or award. Until altered, the contract so created continues to govern the relations between the parties in respect of the terms and conditions of service. But a union's claim that the previous award is terminated must establish the point of time of termination.

*572.* In one case the High Court had to deal with the problem of a public service undertaking forcing a memorandum of settlement on workers, in which several clauses were contrary to various provisions of law with the obvious motive of depriving the employees of the benefit of the new wage structure for cotton mill workers, the provident fund benefits and other statutory benefits. During the conciliation proceedings, a lock-out was declared, which in pursuance of a bipartite settlement was later lifted. However, it was made clear that the workmen who had been sent notices to resume their duties would have to sign a copy of the bipartite settlement. This provided for voluntary termination of service and to accept temporary service for a period of 59 days. The Court held, first, that the company which was fully owned and controlled by the state government had acted in a clearly unlawful and arbitrary manner and in contravention of Sections 25F and 25G of the ID Act. Second, the company was directed not to compel the workmen to enter into the said agreement in contravention of the law.[407]

*573.* A case arose raising the question, whether the Labout Court was competent to deal with the claims of bonus and differential HRA under Section 33C(2) of the Act. The High Court held that the order giving the benefit to the petitioners was without any basis. On the basis of materials on record, it could not be said to be ancillary or incidental to the dispute but went to the very root of the matter coming within Schedule II of the ID Act, and as such it required to be determined by the industrial tribunal as an industrial dispute under Section 10(1). The right to bonus was never adjudicated upon, nor the claim to the differential HRA. The Labour Court's orders were quashed as suffering from serious infirmities, so these could not be sustained. In another case an application under Section 33C(2) of the Act for

407. LLJ, Vol. 1, 1996, *Pancha Mayurakshi Cotton Mills Employees' Union and Others* v. *The State of West Bengal and Others,* High Court of Calcutta, pp. 132–138.

nursing allowance, etc. of an auxiliary nurse mid wife in government dispensaries was granted the benefits by the Labour Court by enforcing the government order on the subject. This was challenged in the High Court. The Court held that it was permissible for the Labour Court to interpret the government order. On merits there was no error in the award. The petition failed.[408]

408. LLJ, October 2010, *Govt. of NCT of Delhi* v. *Rita Luthra and Others*, High Court of Delhi, pp. 19–23.

# Chapter 4. Strikes and Lock-outs

## §1. Definitions

### I. Strike

*574.* The term 'strike' is defined in the ID Act as 'a cessation of work by a body of persons employed in industry acting in combination, or a concerted refusal, or a refusal under a common understanding, of any number of persons who are or have been so employed to continue to work or to accept employment'. In India the concept of strike is indissolubly bound with that of 'industry'. A strike in an establishment that is not an industry 'would lie outside the scope of the ID Act and cannot be dealt with under its provisions'. Likewise, there can be no strike in an industry that has closed down. The constitution does not have any provision on the right to go on strike; the ID Act also does not provide for this right. None the less, any strike that does not contravene any statutory provisions of any law in force may be deemed to be legal. Strike is to be used as a last resort when all other avenues for settlement of industrial disputes as provided for in the ID Act have proved futile. In a public utility, a strike which is not preceded by 14 days notice is illegal. Strikes are illegal if called or continued despite the order of prohibition under Section 22 of the ID Act.

*575.* The important ingredients of a strike are:

- there should be a cessation of work;
- this should be done by a body of persons acting in combination;
- there should be a concerted refusal to accept work or employment; and there should exist a relationship of employment in an industry.

These ingredients imply that strikes would usually take place for the purpose of enforcing an industrial demand. But whether the employees acted in combination or not could be deduced from the course of their conduct. The duration of a strike has no legal significance. It can be for a few hours or of longer duration. A pen-down strike is included in the scope of this term. A few hours of cessation of work by a group of workmen without prior notice to the employer would be a strike. If workmen, after reporting for duty, stage a demonstration for 15 to 20 minutes, they would not be considered to be on strike. A concerted action by employees to apply for casual leave and the refusal of the employer to grant it might not be a strike. This is a controversial position because all the ingredients of a strike are present, though there may be some doubt whether a concerted cessation of work was intended on the part of employees. When the management substituted the weekly rest day without giving a notice of change under Section 9A, the refusal to work on the substituted holiday did not amount to strike. Therefore a mere refusal to work is not a strike.

*576.* Strike may take many forms. The 'sit-down' or 'stay-in' strike is also a cessation of work, though the workers do not walk out of the work premises. In these forms workers not only cease work but also occupy the property of the employer. This is an act of civil conspiracy and a breach of common law rights of the employer. However, registered unions are immune from this charge. A 'go-slow' may not be a strike because there is no cessation of work; it is a serious misconduct under the MSO. It is like slow poisoning and cannot be permitted. If a majority of workers were to go slow it would present a problem to the employer, but he must take action against all of them. Selecting a few workers for disciplinary action is likely to be viewed as victimization, hence illegal.[409]

## II. Lock-out

*577.* The Amendment Act, 1982 modified the definition of the term, 'lock-out', to mean, 'the (temporary closing of a place of employment) or the suspension of work, or the refusal by an employer to continue to employ any number of persons employed by him'. The way the term is defined, there is no difference between a lock-out caused by an industrial dispute and a temporary closure resulting from 'flood, fire or earthquake', Furthermore, what is the difference between a lock-out and a business closure? Prior to the 1982 amendment there existed practically no difference and even with the amended definition a temporary closure would be identical to a lock-out. The difference is brought out by the facts of the case. A lock-out means that while business continues, work ceases. If used as a weapon of collective bargaining, it is a lock-out, and if for reasons of shortage of raw material or power or recession in trade, etc. it is a closure. If work ceases due to the suspension of a number of workmen it is not a lock-out. A lock-out should be formally declared; otherwise, on the basis of evidence and circumstances, it would be for the Tribunal to decide whether a lock-out had occurred and whether it was justified or not. In a lock-out the employer refuses to employ the workmen who are in his employment though the business activity has not closed down, nor is it intended to close down. So, if work is ordered to be suspended, it would amount to a lcok-out. A closure implies the closing of industrial activity as a consequence of which the workmen concerned are rendered jobless. In one case the High Court held that the Section 7 of the ID Act read together with the Second Schedule, item 5, empowers the Labour Court to adjudicate the illegality or otherwise of a strike or lock-out. The government lacks the jurisdiction to declare a lock-out as illegal and direct the employer to allow workers to perform their duties, because it cannot adjudicate an industrial dispute.

*578.* A lock-out should be differentiated from a 'lay-off'. The points of distinction are:

- a lay-off occurs in a continuing business, whereas a lock-out is a temporary closure; it is a temporary discharge of workmen;

409. LLJ, Vol. 1, 2001, *Mysore Wine Products and Allied Co. Ltd Bangalore* v. *Presiding Officer, Industrial Tribunal, Bangalore and Another*, High Court of Karnataka, pp. 1166–1181.

- a lay-off affects one or more workmen, but a lock-out amounts to a wholesale discharge of all workmen;
- lay-offs are actuated purely by trade reasons, whereas a lock-out is a weapons of collective bargaining.

These differences are important because laid off workers are entitled to receive compensation and have a right to recall according to their seniority, but locked out workers cannot claim any compensation unless the lock-out is considered to be 'unjustified and illegal'. If there is a strike or slow down in production in one part of the establishment, then the subsequent lay-off of workers in other parts would be covered by the term 'lay-off'. But in one case the High Court held that, if a lay-off occurs as a result of deliberate 'go-slow', the laid of workers would loss their claim for compensation.[410]

## III. Public Utility

*579.* In the ID Act (Section 2(n), 'public utility service' is described to include those industries and activities which not only usually fit this term but also 'any industry specified in the First Schedule which the appropriate government may, if satisfied that public emergency or public interest so requires, by notification in the Official Gazette, declare to be a public utility service for the purpose of this Act, for such period as may be specified in the notification'. In the ID Act the First Schedule includes 20 industries, but the State Governments have amended it to include several more on a permanent basis. The advantage of getting an industry declared as a public utility is that the management's anxiety about having to face a strike is substantially lowered and the government is required to act promptly as soon as a serious threat to industrial peace is apprehended. Under the MRTU and PULP Act,a strike which is illegal can become legal if it is withdrawn within 48 hours after the Court declares it to be illegal. Thus the illegality at the inception of a strike can be cured and a legal fiction created. Under the ID Act, Section 24(2), an illegal lock-out becomes legal subsequent to the expiry of the period of 14 days of notice. On the expiry of the notice period the lock-out is in compliance with the provisions of law.[411]

## IV. 'Unfair Labour Practice'

*580.* In respect of strikes and lock-outs, 'unfair labour practices', have found a place in the ID Act since the 1982 Amendment Act, in which it was defined in Section 2(ra). The Fifth Schedule enumerates them. The act of threatening a lock-out or

410. LLJ, Vol. 1, 2001, the Madras High Court judgment cited in the Karnataka High Court judgment cited in para. 533.
411. LLJ, Vol. 2, 2001, *Otis Elevator Company (India) Ltd* v. *G.S. Baj & Others*, High Court of Bombay, pp. 298–302.

closure is an unfair labour practice on the part of the employer and so is discharging or dismissing a workman for taking part in a strike which is not illegal. He cannot insist on individual workmen to sign a good conduct bond as a precondition of allowing them to resume work; nor can he recruit workmen during a strike, which is legal. If an employer proposes or continues a lock-out which is deemed to be illegal, it would be an unfair labour practice.

*581.* On the part of workmen and trade unions, it is an unfair labour practice to actively support or instigate a strike that is deemed to be illegal. They cannot take part in picketing in such a manner as to physically bar the non-striking 'workmen form entering the workplace'. To indulge in acts of force or violence or to hold threats of intimidation against non-striking workmen or the managerial staff is also an unfair labour practice. All forms of coercive actions, such as go-slow, squatting on the work premises during the working hours and *gherao* (encircling) any member of the managerial staff are unfair labour practices. Section 25T prohibits employers and workmen from committing any unfair labour practice and Section 25U prescribes penalties in the form of fines and imprisonment in respect of anyone who commits an unfair labour practice. The provisions on unfair labour practices in the MRTU and P ULP Act are frequently invoked in the Maharashtra state.

## §2. Justified Strikes and Lock-outs

*582.* The whole purpose of industrial legislation in India has been to define strikes and lock-outs in order to prevent them and canalize the industrial disputes into the conciliation and adjudication channels. The law may be said to provide the definition of an illegal strike, stating the conditions in which they can be declared illegal. Strikes and lock-outs, though recognized as inevitable in the collective bargaining process, are not considered justifiable unless all avenues of peaceful settlement of disputes are exhausted. A strike may be justified by the circumstances that preceded it, but it should remain strictly peaceful, within law, and preferably of short duration. This philosophy has left the task of defining what is a justified strike to the higher courts. According to the Supreme Court, whether a strike is justified or not must be determined by facts. In order to entitle the workmen to wages for the period of strike, the strike should be legal as well as justified. In one case the strike was considered as justified, because, before the conclusion of conciliation proceedings, the company had retrenched 93 workmen without bothering to go give the intimation to the Labour Commissioner; it was also not considered to be illegal. Whether the go-slow tactics of workers amount to a strike and the lock-out that followed was legal, under Section 24(3) of the ID Act, and whether it was justified under the circumstances, are questions of facts to be decided on the evidence on record by the labour/industrial court. It is not for the High Court to give its findings on these issues.

*583.* The law treat lock-outs on a par with strikes. A lock-out is legal if there is no contravention of any statutory provisions and it has not been prohibited, yet it may not be justified. A lock-out declared in response to a spontaneous but illegal strike, or a persistent demonstration on the premises of the establishment which amounted to a strike, would be a justified one. Similarly, if a lock-out is necessitated by the go-slow tactics and improper conduct of workers, it is justified. Likewise, a lock-out declared as a result of a hunger strike by some workers, under the circumstances was considered to be justified. In another case, the management declared the Saturday to be the day off instead of the Sunday, which the workers did not accept and refused to work. The management concluded that a strike had commenced which had brought the factory to a stand-still and declared a lock-out and this was considered to be justified.

*584.* The Aluminium Industries Ltd, a public limited company, faced financial difficulties and the payment of incentive wages was delayed and it put up a notice that these would be paid as soon as funds were available. For about a month the unionized workers entered the factory, punched their cards, but did not attend to their work. This was a tool down strike. The management issued several notices over a period of one month warning of disciplinary action and asking workers to resume work. Thereafter, the management declared a lock-out. On receipt of the lock-out notice, the unions represented to the management that they had not gone on a strike and they were willing to work. This was followed by protracted negotiations and an understanding was reached before the Joint Commissioner of Labour that the management would lift the lock-out and the issue of wages for the period of lock-out would be referred to adjudication. The Tribunal, ruling out objections, decided to consider whether the lock-out was justified or not as a part of the reference. It held that the workers had resorted to a tool-down strike, which came within the definition of strike and it was illegal. The workers would lose wages for this period. It also held that the management did nothing it avoid a lock-out, not even after receiving a letter from the unions to lift the lock-out, call a meeting to negotiate and reach an amicable settlement, or invoke the assistance of the conciliator. Hence the lock-out was justified in the beginning, but due to its long duration, became unjustified. However, meanwhile, the wages for the strike period were already paid. Accordingly this issue was excluded from the reference. On the question of wages for the lock-out period, the Tribunal decided to apportion the blame between the management and the workers on the basis of 50 per cent each. Workers would get wages for only half the period of the lock-out. The Company filed a writ petition in the High Court against this award. The Court observed that there could not be an inflexible formula for apportioning the blame and declined to interfere. The petition was dismissed.[412]

*585.* In one case the workers demanded that a fellow workman be taken back in service. This was followed by a regular notice. Since the demand was not conceded, the workmen went on a strike. When the strike was continuing the management charge-sheeted them and an inquiry officer was appointed. An industrial dispute was raised and the Labour Court found that while the strike was legal, the

412. LLJ, Vol. 1, 2006, *Aluminum Industries Ltd Hyderabad* v. *Industrial Tribunal, Hyderabad and Others*, High Court of Andhra Pradesh, pp. 16–20.

termination of a workman was illegal, unjustified and an act of victimization. However, according to the High Court, which heard the writ petition of the employer, there could not be any doubt that the striking workmen were not ordinarily entitled to wages for the strike period, even if the strike was legal but not justified, or if the strike was illegal though justified. Despite this position in law, in the present case, the claim of workmen for wages was upheld by the Court, because the strike was called after giving a notice. Their participation in the strike could not be visited by the termination of their services.

*586.* In one case the government of India decided to recover the salary paid to the Health Scheme employees during a strike. A settlement between the parties used the period of strike as, *dies non*. It was not agreed between the parties that for the period of strike, the principle, 'no-work-no-pay', was to be applied and the employees were paid salary for the months of May and June 1992. In a writ petition, the Employees Association questioned the circular seeking to recover the salary paid for the strike period. The Court decided to translate the meaning of the words 'dies non It means that the said period is to be treated as without business and therefore, non-existent for both the employer and the employees. The impugned notice clearly stated that the employees were not entitled to any salary during the strike period. Given this position the argument advanced by the petitioners had no substance. However, in view of the fact that all the employees were class IV employees and could not afford to live without any income if the recovery of salaries was made in one lumpsum, the Court directed that the government, as the respondent, should make the recovery in four equal instalments. The writ petition was partly allowed.[413]

*587.* In one case the Essorpe Mills Ltd was declared a public utility service and Section 22 of the ID Act and the rules pertaining to it were applicable if a strike was called. In November 1990 the workers went on an illegal strike. Disregarding the requirement of serving a six weeks notice and not to commence the strike as announced due to Section 20 of the Act, which provides for 'deemed conciliation' to commence on receipt of a strike notice under Section 22(1), the union served a notice on 14 March 1991. The Act provides for stalling a strike by giving the conciliation officer the time needed to resolve the dispute. A legal strike cannot be called during the conciliation proceeding, provided a formal notice has been served on the employer and the union. An illegal strike had been called on 8 November 1990 and 55 workmen were charged of misconduct and suspended, 34 workmen apologized and were allowed to join duty, three more workmen apologized and were forgiven. But the rest did not relent and on 8 April, 24 April and 13 May they were dismissed from service following a disciplinary enquiry. They filed petitions under Section 2A of the Act against the order of dismissal and the Labour Court, while holding the strike as illegal, invoked the powers under Section 11A of the Act, to substitute the punishment of discharge for the dismissals and a compensation of Rs 50,000 to each workmen. The award was challenged by the Company as well as the

413. LLJ, Vol. 1, 2006, *All India Central Government Health Scheme Employees Association, Nagpur and Another* v. *Union of India and Others*, High Court of Bombay, pp. 798–799.

workmen. It was heard by the Single judge and on an appeal by the Division Bench. The Court admitted the appeal of workmen and ordered their reinstatement with back wages, while dismissing that of the Company. This led the Company to the Supreme Court. The Apex Court examined the salient facts of the case and held that the High Court had totally failed to act under the law, on the notice period and deemed conciliation. Conciliation was not pending when workmen were dismissed. In the absence of a valid notice period, 'deemed conciliation' could not have commenced. The earlier illegal strike could not be remedied by a subsequent strike. If no notice is served on the employer, the effect is that he is not aware of the proceedings. The judgments of the Single Judge and that of the Division Bench were set aside. Earlier in March 2006 the Apex Court had proposed certain terms for an amicable settlement, which the employer accepted and the workmen had refused. This was revived by the Apex Court and given effect to.[414]

## §3. Legal Strikes and Lock-outs

*588.* A legal and justified strike called for the betterment of the service conditions of workers may become unjustified, if workers turn unruly and violent and it is prohibited by the government under the provisions of the ID Act. Likewise, a legal lock-out can be declared, if it does not contravene any law and is meant to save the factory from anticipated sabotage or violence or any other serious labour difficulties. But a lock-out declared with a view to victimize or intimidate workers is neither legal nor justified. In one case the reference was made under the Payment of Wages Act which was answered by the court, but the High Court found it to be bad in law, because on the question of wages being deducted during the strike period, the PW Act could not be put into service. The reference should have been made under Section 10 of the ID Act. In another very complicated case the token strike was considered unjustified, then the lock-out that followed was justified, but the tribunal's findings were found to be based on conjectures and surmises, hence perverse and illegal.

*589.* In a case the company experienced disturbed industrial relations resulting in demonstrations, *gherao,* assault, tool-down strike, declaring holidays and crippling its functioning. The company suffered huge losses. There was an illegal and unjustified strike from 23 April 1997 to 22 August 1997. In September 1997 the company wrote a letter to the Asstt. Labour Commissioner in this regard. There was nothing like discipline in the company. In October the company addressed a letter to the union on the subject but the disorder continued and in November the company wrote to the Labour Commissioner on the subject. There was a tool down strike in March 1998 and again in July 1998. Another strike followed in December 1999 and the production stopped completely. In January 2000 the company declared a lock-out and informed the Labour Commissioner. A show-cause notice was

414. LLJ, Vol. 3, 2008, *Management, Essorpe Mills Ltd* v. *Presiding Officer, Labour Court and Others,* Supreme Court of India, pp. 614–618.

received from the conciliation officer on a complaint by the union against the lock-out. Thereafter, the government passed two orders, making the reference for adjudication and prohibiting the lock-out. Against the prohibition, the company filed a writ petition. In the counter-affidavit the company was blamed by the union for affecting a closure in the garb of a lock-out and for handing over the work to the contractors. A single judge dismissed the writ petition. The company made an appeal against the judgement. The Court held that the reference under Section 10(1) of the ID Act does not affect the rights of the parties. Therefore, it cannot interfere with the order and the writ petition against this order is liable to be dismissed. The petition was premature. On the order of prohibition of the lock-out under Section 10(2) of the Act, the single judge said that unless and until the petition against the reference to adjudication succeeds, the consequential order prohibiting the lock-out cannot be challenged. The Division Bench disagreed with this observation. Under Section 10(3), the strike or lock-out which can be prohibited must be in connection with the reference of a dispute to the Labour Court or tribunal. The Court observed that the lock-out was in connection with the indiscipline and unjustified activities of the workmen and not with the dispute referred to the Labour Court or tribunal. Hence Section 10(3) of the Act was not attracted. The reference under Section 10(1) of the Act was regarding wages, annual increment, house rent, conveyance allowance and related matters. The terms of reference were not regarding the justification of workmen's conduct in indulging in strike, *gheraos*, abusing, assaulting, slogan shouting and other acts of misconduct. Hence Section 10(3) has no application at all. It is not any kind of strike or lock-out that can be prohibited under Section 10(3) of the Act, but only a strike or lock-out connected with a dispute referred under Section 10(1). If the reference is regarding some other matter, the order under Section 10(3) cannot be validly passed. In the Court's opinion, the order under Section 10(3) has nothing to do with the matters referred to the tribunal and it is not connected with the dispute referred. Conciliation proceedings have nothing to do with the validity of an order under Section 10(3), prohibiting the continuance of a strike or a lock-out. The Court decided that the impugned judgment in so far as it upholds the order under Section 10(3) is not sustainable and is hereby set aside. The appeal was disposed of with the direction that the reference order under Section 10(1) was valid, while the order under Section 10(3) prohibiting the lock-out was illegal.

> If the version of the employer, that the members of the respondent/union had committed grave misconducts, e.g. illegal strikers, abuses, *gherao*, assault on the officials, slogan shouting etc.is well founded in facts on record then prima facie it seems to us that the lock-out was certainly justified, because the lock-out can be used as a retaliatory weapon by the employer, as held by the Supreme Court in the *Express Newspaper* case. However, we are not expressing our final opinion on the validity of lock-out since that can be decided in a reference under Section 10(1) of the Industrial Disputes Act.

Appeal disposed of.[415]

415. LLJ, Vol. 4, Supp. 2006, *D.D. Gears Ltd* v. *Secretary (Labour) and Others*, High Court of Delhi, pp. 387–393.

*590.* The Atul Glass Industries Ltd produced mirrors and other glass articles. Its finances declined and it become a sick unit suitable for reference to the Board for Industrial and Financial Reconstruction in 2000. Alongside its relations with the workmen deteriorated and it declared a lock-out in October 2000. The conciliation proceedings failed and the industrial dispute was referred to adjudication. Continuation of the lock-out was prohibited. Earlier there was a settlement in 1994, operational for three years, but the union raised a demand for higher wages in 1996 and secured a fresh settlement, again valid for three years. On its completion, yet another settlement was signed with a life of two years. During this period, the losses increased and the Company lost more than 50 per cent of its net worth. It was duly registered with the BIFR, but the union resorted to concerted action, disrupting the smooth functioning of the Company. There was a slow down and sabotage and the management issued warming notices to workmen, but did nothing to involve the government's Labour Department. Workers roamed about in the factory premises and wasted time. At this stage the lock-out was declared. The workers' behaviour could be construed as on strike. At around this time, suspicious of managements motives, the union filed a civil suit in Faridabad for a decree of permanent injunction against the company, restraining it from removing plant, machinery and raw materials from the factory. The management had told the workmen that foreign companies had invaded the Indian market and it was difficult to procure sufficient orders. So there was a paucity of work in the company. The civil suit was disposed of by a settlement in October 2000. On the failure of conciliation, only the legality and justifiability of the lock-out was referred for adjudication, not the strike which the union never called, but was acted upon by the workmen inside the factory premises. The company challenged the reference in a writ petition. It pleaded that while a lot of the assertions and allegations made by the union have been accepted, the Company is left defenceless due to there being no reference to the strike behavior of workmen, highlighted in the series of notices served by the management. The Court reduced this matter to the issue, whether the Company has been prejudiced in raising its defence to substantiate its claim before the Labour Court. The Court held that it was open to the Company to lead any evidence within the terms of reference to show on what basis the lock-out declared was legal and justified. The Company has a right to establish that the lock-out was declared on account of activities of the workers/union. The Labour Court shall record its conclusions thereon in accordance with law. There was another contention, that there was no written demand or notice by the union, so the inference of an industrial dispute was not warranted and as such the Government could not make the reference of the presumed dispute to the Labour Court. The Court cited the definition of the term, 'industrial dispute'. It no where contemplates that the dispute would come into existence in any specific or prescribed manner. A written course is not a sine qua non, except in public utility services. This contention was rejected. The Company had also said that the delay in making the reference by six months meant that the Company was all but finished and there was no scope for revival of the Company. The Court held that the delay was due to the management's non-cooperation to engage in the conciliation process. The Company never addressed any notices to the labour Department or any authority in the Government to bring to their notice that the workers were on strike or were indulging in activities which would collectively amount to a strike. The petition was dismissed.[416]

*591.* Under Section 10(3), after a reference has been made to a Board, Labour Court, Tribunal or National Tribunal, the Government may prohibit the continuance of a strike/lock-out in connection with such dispute as existed on the date of reference. Under Chapter V, which deals with strikes and lock-out, Section 22 provides for their prohibition in public utility services unless the specified conditions are fulfilled. Section 23 provides for general prohibition of strikes and lock-outs during the pendency of proceedings before a Board, Court or tribunal and for some time after they have concluded. Section 24 provides for declaration of certain strikes and lock-outs as illegal. Under Section 24(3) it is further provided that a lock-out declared in consequence of an illegal strike, or a strike declared in consequence of an illegal lock-out shall not be deemed to be illegal. It has been held by the Court that once a strike has been declared to be illegal, the question of justifiability would not arise, The employees cannot claim wages for the strike period unless they prove that the strike was legal.

*592.* Whether the strike in a public utility concern is legal or justified are questions of fact which are to be decided on the evidence on record. There was a dispute between the State Bank of India (SBI) and its award staff relating to wage-scale revision and, after serving due notice, the recognized Federation called a strike. The issue was the implementation of a settlement. Being a public utility, conciliation proceedings were started. The SBI management took the stand that it was awaiting the approval of the central government in respect of the settlement, while the Federation contended that this was not a condition specified in the settlement. Meanwhile, the management issued a circular that if the award staff went on strike, their wage for the strike period would be deducted. In a writ petition filed by one of the unions for quashing the circular, the High Court held that, since the strike was called during the conciliation proceedings, it was illegal though it could not be held to be unjustified, and the writ petition was dismissed. Against this decision the union made a writ appeal in the High Court. The Division Bench took the view that there was no valid industrial dispute left for conciliation to resolve, since the issue of wage scale revision was already settled, and further the seeking of approval from the central government was not a legal requirement. On this basis the Court held that the strike was legal and since the management had failed to implement the settlement, it was also justified. The matter then reached the Supreme Court. The Apex Court held that if it was obligatory for the Bank to obtain the approval of the government before implementing the settlement, it mattered very little whether this stipulation was made in it or not. If the approval was necessary, then there did exist a valid industrial dispute between the parties and the conciliation proceedings could not be said to be illegal. The implementation of the settlement could have waited for the conciliation proceedings to be the over and, if necessary, even for the completion of adjudication proceedings. The Court held that a strike could be legal

416. LLJ, Vol. 4, Supp. 2006, *Atul Glass Industries Ltd* v. *State of Haryana and Others*, High Court of Punjab and Haryana, pp. 164–176.

only if was not in contravention of Sections 22, 23 or 24 of the ID act, but the justifiability of the strike would depend upon all the relevant factors and circumstances that gave rise to it, and an inquiry into these aspects was essentially an inquiry into facts of the case. The High Court had exceeded its jurisdiction by examining the facts of the dispute and arriving at a conclusion.

## §4. Sit-down Strike, Stay-in Strike, Etc.

*593.* If workers use unconventional methods of strike, such as, 'cessation of work', while staying in their seats, of places of work, thus occupying the factory premises as an instrument of economic coercion, will this be legal or justified? Two situations may be distinguished, one, in which workers, while refusing to work during duty hours, remain peaceful, and the other, in which they threaten or cause injury to any person or property. These acts, even though peaceful, would clearly violate disciplinary rules and under the SO would ordinarily warrant punishment, including dismissal. Though the police may not be called in, or the management may refrain from ordering workers to vacate the premises, there is no doubt that, even without violence, a stay-in or sit-down strike is an invasion of the rights of the employer in the property of the mill. However, there are instances where the courts have refused to intervene or treat a pen-down or stay-in strike as illegal, if there was no violence. The Court viewed them as strikes and the workmen were deemed to enjoy the same protection under the Trade Unions Act as in any traditional strike. Dismissal can be ordered, if there is a fair and impartial inquiry establishing the guilt of the workmen concerned.

*594.* Although a sit-down strike is not *per se* illegal, it may become illegal, if it is commenced or is continued in contravention of Section 23 of the ID Act. But, in normal conditions, should workers participate in such illegal strike and, as a consequence, if they are dismissed from service, would their claim for reinstatement be upheld? It is for the tribunal to decide whether the strike was justified, though illegal. It may reinstate the dismissed workers though a deduction can be made in wages for the period of strike. Can the employer declare a lock-out in retaliation? In one case the management declared a lock-out following acts of trespass, restraint and illegal confinement by workers of certain officers of the mill.The union complained that the lock-out was illegal and the Labour Court agreed. Aggrieved, the management appealed to the Supreme Court. However, the Court's finding was that the lock-out was in contravention of the provisions of the Bombay Industrial Relations Act, 1946 and so it was illegal.

*595.* In one case the company faced a financial crisis and alongside there was much labour indiscipline and it declared a lock-out. The dispute pertaining to it was referred to the Industrial Tribunal, which came to the conclusion that there was no justification for declaring the lock-out. The Company appealed to the High Court, but the Single Judge affirmed the Tribunal's order and dismissed the writ petition. This became the subject of appeal before the Court's Bench. The Single Judge had held that there were no materials to establish financial difficulties. The notice on lock-out did not say anything on workers' indiscipline, citing financial stringency. On the basis of the materials before the Tribunal any reasonable person could arrive at one or other conclusion and not that of perversity. The lock out was declared just one day before the day of payment of wages. There was the admitted problem of the supply of raw materials not being sufficient to sustain productivity. Hence the level of production, agreed to in the memorandum of settlement, could not be reached. The Court held that in this case, there was no question of jurisdictional error and as such it would not interfere in the same. The conclusions arrived at on the basis of the materials could not be said to be perverse. In the result the appeal failed and was dismissed.[417]

*596.* The employees of a cooperative bank, a public utility undertaking, gave a strike notice proposing to go an a strike after two weeks. The reason was that some employees were suspended and their salaries withheld by the management. The strike call was illegal and the union was asked not to go on a strike. The Labour Officer commenced the conciliation proceedings. But the employees started the strike, though totally illegal. The workmen were served a notice to join duties and tender unconditional apologies. This was accepted and a settlement was arrived at, and 134 employees gave up the strike call and returned to work. But 53 employees refused to join duty and continued to be on strike. They also prevented other employees from joining their duties and threats made of dire consequences. Disciplinary proceedings were initiated and 53 employees were placed under suspension. They did not take part in the disciplinary proceedings. By the order of punishment, the stoppage of increments for 1–4 years with cumulative effect was imposed on them and there would be non-payment of salary for the period of suspension. Later the workmen joined the duty and raised an industrial dispute, which was referred to the Labour Court. The Labour Court held that all the four charges against the workmen were proved, the enquiry was legal and valid, hence the action of the management could not be described as illegal or improper. The demands of workmen were rejected and the reference dismissed. The union appealed against it to the High Court.

*597.* The single judge considered the stoppage of 1–4 annual increments as 'harsh', not valid in law and set it aside. The management was directed to pay the arrears in respect of stoppage of increments without cumulative effect together with 12 percent interest per annum within 60 days. The management made an intra court appeal to the Division Bench. The Bench modified the order by providing for stoppage of increments without cumulative effect for all 53 employees. The payment of interest was set aside. This order was appealed to the Supreme Court. According to the Apex Court, in our considered opinion, the award passed by the Labour Court was perfectly just, legal and proper and required 'no interference' by the High Court, in exercise of power of judicial review under Article 226/227 of the constitution; therefore, should not have interfered with the well considered award by the Labour Court. The Court then dealt with the doctrine of proportionality. Was the

417. LLJ, Vol. 2, 2006, *American Refrigerator Co. Ltd* v. *First Industrial Tribunal, West Bengal and Other*, High Court of Calcutta, pp. 271–275.

penalty imposed on workmen in proportion to the misconduct committed by them? Lack of proportionality is manifest unreasonableness. The doctrine has its genesis in the field of administrative law. The very essence of decision making consists in the attribution of relative importance to the factors and considerations in the case. The doctrine of proportionality thus steps in focus the true nature of exercise of the elaboration of a rule of permissible priorities'. The Court asked, whether in the facts and circumstances of the present case, the High Court was justified in invoking and applying the doctrine of proportionality. 'In our judgment, the answer must be in the negative. Keeping in view the charges proved, the Labour Court, in our opinion rightly held that the punishment imposed on workmen could not be said to be harsh so as to interfere with it. The decision rendered by the single judge and modified by the Division Bench of the High Court must be set aside.' However, the Court noted that the strike and resumption of duty took place more than three decades ago. All the 53 employee were performing their functions and discharging their duties faithfully, diligently and to the satisfaction of the appellant bank. Industrial peace has been restored. If some order will be passed by this Court after so long a period, it may adversely affect the functioning of the bank. The Court in the particular facts and circumstances of the case, therefore, may not interfere with the limited relief granted by the Division Bench of the High Court. The appeal was disposed off with the aforesaid order under Article 142 of the constitution.' While declaring the law on the point, we temper justice with mercy.[418]

## §5. *Gheraos*, Etc., Injunctions by Courts

*598.* Strikes and protest activities in India have not been confined to the definitions provided in the ID Act. For example, if an award is not implemented, the legal remedy is to make an application before the Labour Court or raise a fresh dispute. Sometimes, the implementation of an award is delayed for several years because the employers have secured writs on constitutional grounds and have challenged the award for violating basic legal principles. Outside of the statutory provisions, the government could not be very helpful, though on numerous occasions senior ministers have tried to resolve disputes and used informal pressure to produce acceptable solutions. The epidemic of *gheraos* occurred in a situation in which the managements as well as the unions had lost their authority and respect of workers. It was the manifestation of a complete breakdown of the industrial relations system mainly caused by far too many instances of non-implementation of awards and the government's helplessness in the face of this defiance. These continue to occur.

*599.* In a hospital the union went on strike on the ground that two of its office bearers were suspended from service. The strike was peaceful and had not hampered the functioning of the Hospital. On the charge that they had gone on an illegal and unjustified strike without giving any notice and for obstructing loyal

418. LLJ, Vol. 2, 2007, *Management of Coimbatore District Central Coop. Bank* v. *Secretary, Coimbatore District Central Co-op. Bank Employees Association and Another*, Supreme Court of India, pp. 724–733.

employees, patients and their attenders, seven workmen were dismissed from service. The Enquiry Officer submitted a report holding that the charges were proved. In the reference court the union conceded the fairness of enquiry and the Labour Court found that the strike was illegal and unjustified. However, on the question of proportionality of the punishment, the Labour Court found that the strike had not caused any damage to the property, nor was there any violence and held that the order of dismissal was too harsh. The court modified the punishment by denying two annual increments and directed the management to reinstate the workmen without back wages. The hospital filed a writ petition against this order. The management took the plea that when the strike was found to be 'illegal and unjustified, which caused irreparable hardship to the hospital, the Labour Court was not justified in modifying the punishment. In defence, the union pleaded that the strike lasted for only three days, of which one was a holiday. The Hospital was not covered under the provisions of Section 22 or Section 23 of the ID Act, so the strike was not illegal. The punishment of dismissal was totally disproportionate to the gravity of the charge. Moreover, though 60-70 persons took part in the strike, the memo of charges was issued only against seven members. The High Court found that, unlike the other participants in the strike, these seven employees obstructed the loyal employees, patients and others and threatened other employees with dire consequences. The Court said that a strike in the hospital cannot be appreciated and cannot be compared with any strike in the industry or factory. Though one day was a holiday, there cannot be any holiday in a hospital. Indiscipline in the hospital cannot be tolerated. The Labour Court should have considered the gravity of the charge while exercising the power under Section 11A of the ID Act. In the Court's opinion, the exercise of discretionary power under Section 11A of the Act was not justifiable. The writ portion was allowed and the award of the Labour Court was quashed.[419]

*600.* *Gheraos* are part of the coercive actions of agitating workers against management personnel in the course of regular or irregular strikes. In one case, the employer secured an interim injunction of the court directed at the union and its office-bearers, that it would be prevented from acts of coercion or violence or staging, encouraging, instigating or participating in any *gheraos* of any member of the managerial or other staff, etc. This matter came up for review in a writ petition. The Court drew a distinction between a strike which is peaceful, non-violent and called in pursuit of the legitimate objectives of trade unions and which may be either legal or illegal and another kind which includes indecent language, coercive actions and is patently illegal. In a democratic state workmen have every right to withhold labour in support of their demands and a legal strike is a legitimate weapon in matters of industrial relations. The term 'illegal strike' is a creation of law and cannot be found outside it. *Gheraos* are also classified as an unfair labour practice.

---

419. LLJ, Vol. 1, 2009, *Bangalore Hospital, Bangalore* v. *Workmen of Bangalore Hospital*, High Court of Karnataka, pp. 661–665. For a similar case, see LLJ, Vol. 4, Supp. 2006 (N.O.C.), *Gujarat Ambuja Cement Pvt. Ltd* v. *U.B. Godhera*, High Court of Gujarat, pp. 897.

*601.* The plaintiff heart institute sought in this suit a permanent injunction restraining the union, its president and members from engaging in *dharna* (blocking the passage by squatting at the gate) *gherao* (encircling the management personnel), etc. within a radius of 100 meters of the hospital. The Hospital was duly registered under the Contract Labour (Regulation and Abolition) Act, 1970 and had a valid licence to engage the services of contractors and specialized agencies for providing services mostly for good house keeping. Accordingly, it has engaged two contractors and the workers rendering the services are employed by them. They also render similar services to other establishments and hospitals in Delhi and outside Delhi. The union of contract workers has raised industrial disputes and impleaded the Hospital. There was no question of any absorption of contract workers by the Hospital, since they were in the employ of their contractors. The proceedings are pending before the conciliation officer, but the union has decided to stage demonstration and gherao the officials of the management in the premises of the hospital. They have threatened to hold simultaneous demonstrations at the residences of the two directors of the company. The Court found it a fit case for granting an *ex parte*, ad interim injunction, restraining the defendent union and its members from causing any obstruction in the free ingress and egress of the doctors, medical staff, visitors, patients and other employees and from demonstrating or shouting slogans within the radius of 60 meters of the premises of the hospital. They were also restrained from holding any demonstration at the residences of the directors. The SHO was directed to ensure that the order was duly complied with. The Court held that while it may be the right of the union to hold peaceful demonstrations, they could not under its garb become violent or adopt threatening action to stop the employees or damage the property. Accordingly, a decree of permanent injunction was passed in favour of the plaintiff.[420]

*602.* The petitioner bank sought a direction to the state government to maintain law and order in view of the strike accompanied by *dharna* (squatting to cause obstruction) and *pradarshan* (demonstration) threatened by the employees' federation and officers' association. The employees contended that while they are not to obstruct the normal working of the bank, they are entitled to exercise their right as a trade union. Curtailing their right in any manner would mean taking away their statutory right, as also their fundamental right under Article 19 of the Constitution of India. The Court held that the three stands taken by the three parties resolve the matter. The unions have undertaken not to disrupt banking services. This means that they will not directly or indirectly prevent the customers or members of the management from reaching the bank or leaving the bank. In case the bank finds any obstruction either directly or indirectly, the management would immediately contact the district civil and police administration, who would be legally bound to render all assistance in the matter 'All entrance and exit points from the bank or its branches shall be kept unobstructed and the dharna and pradarshan would be at least

---

420. LLJ, Vol. 1, 2007, *Escorts Heart Institute and Research Centre Ltd* v. *Delhi Mazdoor Sangathan, Regd. and Others*, High Court of Delhi, pp. 366–368.

ten meters away from all such points and premises.' With these directions the petition was disposed off.[421]

*603.* In a case the petitioner corporation sought a writ to get the strike notice issued by the unions declared illegal and consequential relief. The strike notice was violative of Sections 22, 23 and 24 of the Industrial Disputes Act, 1947. The union denied the charge that the proposed strike would be in violation of these sections. The Court held that this issue could not be decided at this stage in this proceeding, because it can be effectively decided in an appropriate proceeding under the Industrial Disputes Act. The single judge had rightly refused to grant interim relief in the present writ petition on the ground that the same would grant final relief to the petitioners. In the present case, the Court could not arrive at a final conclusion that the proposed strike has been called by the unions in contravention of Sections 22, 23 and 24 of the Act. The Court could not issue a writ of mandamus to prevent or restrict the use of strike as a weapon, unless it is established beyond reasonable doubt that the strike has been called in violation of the aforesaid sections. The application for stay was dismissed, as being devoid of any merit.[422]

*604.* In a case the Association of Engineering workers filed a writ petition for direction to the Assistant Commissioner of Labour to initiate conciliation proceedings on its demand for lifting the lock-out. This was declined on the ground that there was a bar under Section 59 of the Maharashtra Recognition of Trade Unions and Prevention of Unfair Labour Practices Act, 1971. The order was that 'since ULP Act invoked, writ petition is rejected.' The Asstt. Commissioner of labour cited three reasons for not intervening. One, that the legality of the lockout with effect from 5 June 1996 was pending before the Labour Court in compliance with the MRTU & PULP Act; second, the workers who were excluded from the notice of lock-out resorted to a strike from 5, June 1996; and three, that there was a bar under Section 59 of the MRTU & PULP Act in respect of any proceeding under the Industrial Disputes Act, 1947, in view of the pending reference. The object is to prohibit duplicating the proceedings in respect of the matter which falls within the purview of the MRTU & PULP Act. It is a bar to entertain any proceeding under the Industrial Disputes Act. Hence the rejection of the writ petition by the Single Judge could not be faulted. The appeal was dismissed.[423]

*605.* In West Bengal there is a Government Scheme for Financial Assistance to workers in locked-out Industrial Units, 1998 (FAWLOI). In one locked-out unit, the Shine Up Fibres Ltd, the Screening Committee of the Labout Department adopted a resolution dated 27 July 2007, that on the facts these workers would not be entitled to financial assistance under FAWLOI scheme with effect from 1 October 2005 at the rate of Rs 500 per month. The government determined that in the Shine Up

---

421. LLJ, Vol. 1, 2009, *Punjab National Bank* v. *State of Bihar and Other*, High Court of Patna, pp. 760–761.
422. LLJ, Vol. 3, 2007, *Bharat Petroleum Corporation Ltd and Another*, v. *State and Others*, High Court of Calcutta, pp. 603–605.
423. LLJ, Vol. 2, 2006, *Association of Engineering Workers* v. *V.K. Date and Others*, High Court of Bombay, pp. 625–627.

Fibres Ltd the lock-out continued and no tangible progress could be achieved towards reopening of the unit, despite intervention of the conciliation machinery. Petitioner workmen, no.2 to 140 were receiving this financial assistance from 1 December 2003 to September 2005, then all of a sudden, without assigning any reason, it was stopped from October 2005. The workmen filed a writ petition in 2007, and it was disposed of with a direction to the Screening Committee to examine the grievances and give an appropriate decision. The decision merely affirmed what had been already decided. Against the impugned decision the union moved the High Court again. The facts were that a large number of workmen accepted the Shine Up offer to resign from their services, take terminal benefits and take up employment under another Corporation which started functioning in the premises of the Shine Up under a bilateral transaction creating a lease According to the Screening Committee these workmen who refused to accept the Shine Up offer would not be entitled to the financial assistance w.e.f. 1 October 2005. The Court considered the question, whether the benefits could be denied on this ground? It held that so long as the government continues to recognize the Shine-Up as an industrial unit under a lock-out and the Scheme remains in force, the benefits thereunder could not be denied to these workers who declined the Shine Up offer. They were still in employment of the Shine Up and their services have not been terminated. The court allowed the writ petition, set aside the impugned decision and issued a mandamus commanding the respondents to give the financial benefit so long as they remain in the Shine Up's employment and the Scheme remains in force, for the period from 1 October 2005 to March 2008, within a fortnight from the date of communication of this order to the respondents.[424]

*606.* A short recital of the history of industrial relations in a textile mill which went into liquidation but restarted as a new company by the state government would show the severe limits to which the labour laws can be stretched. The case brings out the contest of will and resources between management and organized labour in a sick industry. The Mayurakshi Cotton Mills Ltd. functioned normally till it turned sick and was closed in 1986. The mill was referred to BIFR, which in due course decided on winding up the company, and it was wound up on 20 September 1989. The state government decides to step in the auction sale and purchased it from the official liquidator as an individual entity. Thereafter, the government issued a Notification on 4 January 1990 to run the Mill provisionally, and the reborn mill started functioning again from February 1990. The new management rehired the employees and workmen of the erstwhile company on a temporary basis on the same posts they were holding prior to winding up. Soon industrial relations in a pre conflict form revived. In April 1991, one union (among four unions) submitted a charter of demands and the conciliation process started in October 1991 to which all the four unions were asked to participate. The issues were: a new wage structure in 1995, introduction of provident fund, annual leave and other statutory benefits, and other issues. The negotiations failed and law and order in and around the Mill deteriorated, which led to a notice of lock-out on 5 August 1992. The unions challenged

424. LLJ, July 2010, *Shine Up Fibers Ltd Sangrami Shramik Union and Others* v. *Principal Secretary, Deppt of Labour, Government of West Bengal and Another*, High Court of Calcutta, pp. 39–41.

the lockout by a writ application in the High Court. Daring the pendency of writ application, a bipartite settlement was arrived at with one union, (No.4), on 27, February 1993. Thereafter, the lock out was lifted in the manner and on terms agreed in the memorandum of settlement. A legally dubious term of the settlement was that workmen should individually sign a copy of the settlement as a token of acceptance. The writ application was dismissed in August 1993 and the unions filed an appeal in the Court in October 1993. The Court gave an order granting liberty to members of the petitioner unions to sign the settlement and join their duties without prejudice to their rights, and on 20 March 1995 it allowed the appeal. The Management than made an appeal to the Apex Court against the High Court order. The Supreme Court set aside the order of the Division Bench, while restoring that of the Single Judge, but with the modification that a reference shall be made to a Tribunal in respect of all matters arising as to employment, non-employment, the validity of settlement and allied issues, and the relief to be granted to the parties, and the Tribunal should decide it within six months from the date of reference. This was in March 2000. In April 2000 the state government duly made the reference with seven issues to be decided. The unions challenged the order of reference in the High Court which disposed of the writ application, upholding the reference. As directed, the Tribunal gave its award on 14 November 2000. One of the issues (no. 4), on which the award was found contentious was, whether the workmen were entitled to get the benefits of the cotton textile industry-wise settlement of 16 June 1995. The management challenged the award in the High Court with a writ petition and on 15 December the Court stayed the operation of the award on issue no. 4. till the disposal of the writ petition. This was duly incorporated by the government in the revised award as published the entire award on 20 December 2000. The validity of this action was challenged by Management, which was disposed of on 29 March 2001, modifying the published award to the extent as ordered earlier by the court on issue no. 4. This was duly incorporated by the government in the revised award as published afresh. Following more writ application, the Division Bench gave the direction on 21 September 2001 to hear the writ expeditiously while staying the operation of the impugned award. One of the unions appealed against this order in the Apex Court, which heard it and gave fresh directions on 8 May 2002, asking the High Court to dispose of the writ petitions pending before it. The Court did it by remanding the industrial dispute back to the Tribunal, mainly to determine the reasonableness and validity of the bipartite settlement and not the issue of its binding nature. The impugned award dated 14 November 2000 was set aside and the Tribunal was asked to complete the entire exercise within four months, disposing of the writ petitions. Accordingly, the Tribunal passed a new award on 16 September 2003. The bipartite settlement operating in the Mill was reasonable and valid save and except the terms, that the status of the employees would be temporary and that those employees who did not sign the settlement stall be deemed to have given up the job. The issue of confirmation should be decided as per the Model Standing Orders or the service rules, if any. The employee members of the unions must be allowed to join the company without signing, the settlement and their service shall be treated as continuous from the date of their employment in the company, but without back wages. This award was again challenged by the unions. One contention was that the winding up of the company was fictitious, because the company carried on the previous business. Workers could not be treated as temporary and they stayed in service till the lock out in 1992. The age of retirement should not be lowered from 60 to 58, refusal of back wages was incorrect. The management countered all arguments with facts and law. The company was not a member of the Cotton Textile Industries Association and the award passed in their respect has no application to the Mill. The fourth union, which had signed the settlement, adopted all the submissions made on behalf of the company. The single Judge rejected every argument advanced against the award. The Tribunal did not exceed its limit or jurisdiction. The company law was cited, Section 445 with three subsections. The erstwhile company stood dissolved with an order of winding up, and the new company was neither the successor in interest of the erstwhile company, nor its business had been continuing after its closure in 1986 until 8 February, 1990. There was no impropriety or illegality in the finding of the Tribunal on the above issues. In view of stringent financial conditions, it was not unjustified to withdraw the benefits of 15 days of leave with full pay and six days of casual leave with full pay. The company had every right to reorganize and manage its own affairs. The award for Cotton Textile Industries was not binding on the new company. Lowering the age of retirement to 58 years was justified. The decision making process of the Tribunal was proper and valid. The writ application was dismissed.[425]

425. LLJ, 2, 2012, *Mayurakshi Cotton Mills Employees Union and another* v. *9th Industrial Tribunal and others*, Calcutta High Court, pp. 583–590.

# Chapter 5. Employment Relationships in the Unorganized Sector

## §1. The Unorganized Sector

*607.* Under the Unorganized Workers Social Security Act (Section 2(L)), the term 'unorganized sector' means an enterprise owned by individuals or self employed workers and engaged in the production or sale of goods or providing service of any kind whatsoever, and where the enterprise employs workers, the number of such workers is less than ten'. In Section 2(M), the term 'unorganized worker' is defined. It 'means a home-based worker, self-employed worker or a wage worker in the unorganized sector and includes a worker in the organized sector who is not covered by any of the Acts mentioned in Schedule II of this Act'. The Act also defines three other terms to provide greater coverage. These are 'home-based worker', 'self employed worker' and 'wage worker'. The term 'employer; is defined to mean a person or an association of persons, which has engaged or employed an unorganized worker either directly or otherwise for remuneration. 'Under these definitions, an employer exists only in relation to the 'home based workers' and the 'wage worker'. The scope of the Act is defined on a residual basis by excluding the Acts listed in the Schedule II.

*608.* Six Acts are listed in Schedule II. These are (i) The Workmen's (Employees) Compensation Act, 1923, (ii) The Industrial Disputes Act, 1947, (iii) The Employee's State Insurance Act, 1948 (iv) The Employees Provident Funds and Miscellaneous Provisions Act, 1952 (v) the Maternity Benefit Act, 1961, and (vi) The Payment of Gratuity Act, 1972. These are social security laws which provide various forms of social security protection to the workers or the employees covered by them. Each Act operates within the bounds of the definitions laid down in it and the Rules pertaining to it. The workers or employees who are excluded under the definitions but are 'wage workers' as defined in the Unorganized Social Security Act may be brought under its coverage. The procedure is provided in the Rules for registration of unorganized workers. On receiving an identity card from the District Administration, which is the agency for making the registration, he will be entitled to receive the social security benefits.

*609.* The rules and regulations framed under various labour laws require maintenance of registers of periodic submission of returns. There used to be a persistent demand from small businesses and industrial establishments for simplification of rules and reduction in the number of registers and forms as well as the visits made by the Inspectors. Responding to these demands the government enacted the Labour Laws (Exemption from Furnishing Returns and Maintaining Registers by Certain Establishments) Act, 1988. In this Act the term, 'establishment', has the meaning assigned to it in a Schedule of the Act, and the term 'scheduled Act' means the Act as specified in the Schedule. Nine Acts are listed in the Schedule. These are (i) the Payment of Wages Act, 1936, (ii) the Weekly Holidays Act, 1942, (iii) the Minimum Wages Act, 1948, (v) the Plantations Labour Act, 1951, (vi) the Working Journalists and Other Newspaper Employees (Conditions of Service and Miscellaneous Provisions) Act, 1955, (vii) the Contract Labour (Regulation and Abolition) Act,

1970, (viii) the Sales Promotion Employees (Conditions of Service) Act, 1976 and (ix) the Equal Remuneration Act, 1976.

*610.* There are two critically important definitions in this Act. The term 'small establishment' is one in which not fewer than 10 and not more than 19 persons are or were employed on any day in the preceding 12 months. The term 'very small establishment' is one in which not more than nine persons are or were employed on any day in the preceding 12 months. The employers in relation to small establishments now have to furnish a core return (form A), a register of wages (from B), the muster-roll (Form C) and a monthly register of welfare amenities (Form D). In relation to very small establishments, the employers are required to maintain only form D and a monthly register of muster-roll-cum-wages (Form E). These have to be inspected and signed by the Inspector. This Act excludes the entire segment covered by The Unorganized Workers Social Security Act.

## §2. Coverage of Labour Legislation

*611.* Several statutes regulate working conditions in particular unorganized industries. For example.The *Beedi* and Cigar Workers (Conditions of Employment) Act, 1966 has the object of regulating employment conditions in establishments by granting licences for permitting the use of any premises as a factory or industrial premises or godown for making *beedis* or cigars or both with or without the use of power. Typically in this industry machines driven by power are not used and the manufacturing process depends largely on human labour. Three systems are employed:

(i) the factory system where workers are employed and work under the supervision of the employer;
(ii) the contract system, which is the most prevalent, in which a middleman is engaged to manufacture beedis from the materials supplied by the proprietor either by hiring labour directly, or indirectly by distributing the materials amongst the 'home workers'; and
(iii) the out-workers system in which workers receive the materials and manufacture beedis for the proprietor without the intervention of the middlemen.

This law was enacted to provide a measure of protection to all categories of workers regardless of the system of work employed. Accordingly, the employers must take work only in licensed premises and maintain minimum standards of ventilation, lighting and sanitation. Chapter IV (Safety) and Section 85 of the Factories Act (power to apply the Act to certain premises) have been notified so as to bring those premises which run as factories under the umbrella of this Act. The Act also provides for the extension of the Payment of Wages Act, the Maternity Benefits Act, the ID Act and the Industrial Employment (Standing Orders) Act. Women comprise a majority of the workforce and are difficult to unionize. In order to ameliorate their living and working conditions the *Beedi* Workers Welfare Cess Act, 1976 was passed. It provides for the levy and collection of a cess on the excise duty on manufactured beedis and to create a fund under the *Beedi* Workers Welfare Fund Act, 1976. In the Act the Labour Inspectors are allowed to conduct examinations or hold enquiries and issue ID cards for the home workers for ascertaining that the provisions of the Act are complied with in all places. These are legally valid documents whether signed by the owner of the trade mark or the contractor or the Labour Inspector.[426]

*612.* The issue whether any gratuity was payable under the Payment of Gratuity Act had to be decided by the High Court in two cases. The Company claimed that the Payment of Gratuity Act was not applicable to *beedi* and cigar workers because their employment was of various types and most of them were home workers. The Court, however, accepted the argument that the word, 'establishment', employed in the Payment of Gratuity Act was comprehensive in nature; moreover, the *Beedi* and Cigar Workers Act, too, was a law in relation to an establishment as contemplated in the Payment of Gratuity Act, and so this beneficial legislation was applicable to the *beedi* and cigar workers. Accordingly, it was held that the management would be liable to pay gratuity as specified in this statue and the rules made there under. The workers would be entitled to invoke the jurisdiction of the controlling authority under the Payment of Gratuity Act to seek the relief due to them under its provisions. The widow of a home worker was also entitled to receive gratuity payable under the Act. A 'home worker' is an employee. The liability for payment of gratuity is that of the principal employer and not of the person who supplies the raw materials.[427]

*613.* The Tamil Nadu government amended the rules under the *Beedi* and Cigar Workers Act to require the employer to issue a service book to every employee and maintain a register of service books. The service book shall be the property of the employee. This rule was challenged in the High Court as imposing an unreasonable restriction on the right of the employer to carry on the business of trade of *beedi* manufacturing, as being *ultra vires* of the Constitution and hence incapable of performance. The Court held that the amended rule safeguarded the interest of the employees and protected them from exploitation by the employer. It cannot be said to suffer from any infirmity, much less violating any of the provisions of the Constitution. The rule in question is only regulatory. The appeal was dismissed. In another case, it was held that the establishment covered by the *Beedi* Workers Cess Act, 1976 could be included in the scope of a notification under the provisions of the ESI Act. The benefits due to the employees protected by the ESI Act cannot be avoided, if the Act is made applicable. The ESI Court had come to the conclusions

426. LLJ, Vol. 1, 2009, *Management of D.C. Diwan Mohideen Beedi, Factory Salem* v. *Appellant authority, B and C Workers (C of E) Act, 1966, Labour Officers Salem* and *Others*, High Court of Madras, pp. 616–622.

427. LLJ, Vol. 3, 2009, *Management Seyadu Beedi Company, Tirunelveli* v. *Appellate Authority, Payment of Gratuity Act and Another*, High Court of Madras, pp. 35–38.

that the Act was applicable to a *beedi*-making establishment and it was liable to pay the contribution. This was upheld by the Court.[428]

*614.* The Cine-workers and Cinema Theatre Workers (Regulation of Employment) Act, 1981 was enacted because existing labour laws did not provide the necessary safeguards to the low paid artists and technicians engaged in the production of feature films with regard to conditions of employment and social security benefits. The Act requires every producer of a feature film to enter into a written agreement with each cine-worker in the prescribed form and to have it registered with the Competent Authority. The Act provides for conciliation and, if necessary, adjudication of disputes by reference to a single-member cine-workers tribunal. The object of this Act is to ensure that the cine-workers are protected from exploitation without imposing too harsh a set of regulations on this creative industry. The principal Act is backed by the Cine-Workers Welfare Fund Act, 1981, which provides for the levy and collection of a cess on feature films as an excise duty. So far as the cinema theatre workers are concerned, the main Act in Chapter III provides for the application of the EPFMP Act, 1952 and the Payment of Gratuity Act, 1972, to every cinema theatre in which five or more workers are employed on any day, as if such cinema theatres met the definition of the term 'establishment', to which these Acts were applied by a notification of the Central Government. Sections 24 and 25, have been challenged on various grounds, but without success. The most serious challenge which the High Court heard was in respect of the provision that a cinema theatre employing five or more workers would be bound to pay gratuity, though the Payment of Gratuity Act, under its provisions was applicable only to an establishment employing 10 or more workers. The Court held that the Cine-Workers Act has carved out a special class of establishments with regard to the cinema theatres. This is a special enactment, while the provisions in the Payment of Gratuity Act can be construed as a general enactment. The principle, 'special prevails over general', will apply to this case and, therefore, there is no inconsistency between the two provisions. A legal fiction is introduced by Sections 24 and 25 by virtue of which the workers mentioned in the two sections are deemed to be employees within the meaning of the other two Acts, viz. the EPFMP Act, 1952 and the Payment of Gratuity Act, 1972. A challenge against the notification of the EPFMP Act, 1952 to include cinema theatres employing five or more workers also failed. The cine workers and the cinema workers are a kind of unorganized workers to whom social security protection could be provided under a special law enacted for their benefit.

*615.* There are a number of laws, mostly at the state level, which are directed at specific industries and employments and provide protection to the people employed therein. Examples are the Maharashtra Employees of Private School (Conditions of Service) Regulations Act, 1977, Tamil Nadu Industrial Establishment (Conferment of Permanent Status to Workmen) Act, 1981 and Kerala Industrial Employees Payment of Gratuity Act. 1970. In the shops and establishments sphere, there are special legislation, viz., the Madras Catering Establishment Act, 1958, the Maharashtra

428. LLJ, Vol. 2, 2000, *Muruga Home Industries* v. *Employees' State Insurance Corporation*, High Court of Madras, pp. 590–593.

Grocery Market Shops Unprotected Workers (Regulation of Employment and Welfare Scheme) Act, 1973, the Gujarat Shops and Establishments Employees' Wages in Kind (Computation of Cash Value) Rules, 1984, etc., which have specific purposes and are meant to confer greater benefits upon the target groups. The main advantage of these laws is that, once enforced, an authority is appointed with the responsibility for implementation of laws, receive complaints, and, if necessary, prosecute the defaulting employers. Around these laws and the enforcement machinery unions become active and gradually the employees' statutory rights are accepted and also established in practice. There is also stringent state legislation which severely restricts the right to strike and refusal to work overtime. The Maharashtra Essential Service Maintenance Act, 1999 is one such Act.

*616.* In respect of school teachers and other employees hired by private schools in Maharashtra, several questions of law were decided in one case. The school maintained two muster books, one for the permanent employees and another for the temporary employees. The temporary employees were hired through a contractor, called Mithila Azad Security Force, and as per the management, at all material times they were the employees of Mithila, which raised the bills in respect of the services provided and were paid by the School. All the employees, who raised a dispute on the issue of permanency on completion of two years of service, were not included in the muster for temporary employees. The Mumbai Labour Union took up their case with appeals before the School Tribunal under Section 9 of The Maharashtra Employees of Private Schools (conditions of Service) Regulation Act, 1977. The tribunal decided in favour of one employee and directed the school to reinstate him with all the service benefits from the date of termination. The termination order was set aside. This order led the management of the school to file a writ petition in the High Court. The first issue was whether the right forum was the civil court, not the tribunal. This was rejected in view of Section 9 (b) which provides for a right to appeal to the tribunal constituted under Section 8 of the Act. The Court held that the right to appeal was full and complete and untrammeled by procedural or substantive limitations. It is an appellate Tribunal over the decisions of the management is respect of matters covered by Section 9. The Court also rejected the plea that the employees cannot be treated as employees of the School since their appointments were not approved by the Education Department. This was not a correct position in law as the Full Bench had decided. The requirement of approval related to the disbursement of grants-in-aid, not on appointment of teachers and other staff. For want of approval an appointment would not be rendered invalid. The Court further held that

> if a person, duly qualified, is appointed by the management as a member of the staff and if it is not disputed that such person has worked for two years, on a permanent vacancy, he is deemed to have been confirmed as provided for under Section 5(2) and consequently entitled for all the benefits of permanent staff, even if his appointment is not approved and a formal order of appointment was not issued.

It also held that the school was not within the purview of the Contract Labour Act. Its provisions are not at all attracted in so far as the School is concerned. In fact contract labour cannot be allowed to enter the field of education. The Court decided that the reinstated employees would be entitled to 50 per cent of back wages. To this extent the tribunals order was modified and the petition disposed of.[429]

*617.* Under the Maharastra Mathadi Hamal and Other Manual Workers (Regulation of Employment and Welfare) Act, 1969, the workers needed for particular jobs are indented by registered contractors to work for their principal employers, who are also duly registered with a Board constituted under the Act. Under the Act and the Schemes framed under it, all the parties are registered and function in accordance with the rules and Court's direction. The Rashtriya Chemicals and Fertilizers Ltd was the principal employer in a case and there were several contractors who worked for it for transporting, loading and unloading the imported goods for the RCF on the arrival of ships in the does. The Board allotted about 360 *mathadi* workers, constituted into different groups, for carrying out the required work at Chembur for the RCF under its supervision and control. The wages payable to them were under a settlement signed with the unions, though the settlement had expired. The Board made a unilateral wage increase in the year 2000 without a hearing. The RCF filed a writ petition and secured a direction to the Board to grant a hearing to the Company as well as the unions and pass a reasoned order. This was done and a 10 per cent increase in wages came into effect. There was a second round of pay increase of 6 per cent on the existing monthly wages and this led to a second writ petition. Directions were issued to all the parties and the second wage increase was rendered ineffective in so far as the petitioner RCF was concerned. Following another unilateral order, without giving any reasons for the same, the Court had to issue yet more directions. Fresh orders backed by proper reasons should be issued, but the Company preferred an appeal against them. During its pendency, an agreement was signed between the RCF and the unions limiting the overall wage increase to 16 per cent. The contractor to the RCF filed a writ petition against the order of wage increase on two grounds. One that he was not given a hearing and two, that his financial capacity was not considered. The responsibility for making wage payments was his and his concerns should have been heard. The Court rejected both pleas. The first, because the Board had sent notices to the contractors along with the principal employer and the second, that it is the financial capacity of the principal employer that is taken into account and not that of the contractor. The petition was summarily rejected.[430]

*618.* The Maharashtra Mathadi, Hamal and Other Manual Workers (Regulation of Employment and Welfare) Act, 1969, employs several schemes framed under it. The terms 'unprotected worker' and 'worker' gave rise to interpretations by the

---

429. LLJ, Vol. 2, 2008, *Hindi Vidya Bhavan and Others* v. *Presiding Officer, School Tribunal, Mumbai and Others*, High Court of Bombay, pp. 138–152.

430. LLJ, Vol. 3, 2007, *Zulash Clearing and Shipping Agency* v. *Chairman, Railway Goods Clearing and Forwarding Establishments Labour Board for Greater Bombay and Others*, High Court of Bombay, pp. 894–896.

Court which required a review by a full Bench. The question was, whether 'unprotected workers' in Section 2(11) of the Act was confined to casually engaged workers or not. Two judges of the Bench answered in the negative and that, this,interpretation was not correct and proper. The employer's view was that though their establishments may fall within the purview of the term, 'scheduled employment', their workers who do manual work are protected by more than one central legislation and the Act does not deal with them or those employees engaged on the monthly basis and protected under the Shops and Establishment Act. Read together with the definition of 'worker', it means that the 'unprotected worker' is someone engaged other than directly, indirectly or by a simple agreement. The rival contention was that the term referred to mean, manual workers, as defined in the Act, and not restricted to workers not protected by other legislation. The Supreme Court in a judgment had given a wider meaning to the term. 'A mathadi worker is an unprotected worker in the scheduled employment in connection with loading, unloading, stacking weighing, measuring, sewing, stitching, sorting, cleaning or such other work preparatory or incidental to such operations.'[431] This was undisputed. Accordingly, the 'unprotected workers' means (i) a person who is engaged or to be engaged directly, (ii) a person who is engaged or to be engaged through any agency and (iii) a person who works with the permission of or under on agreement with the employer or the contractor, to do any manual work in any scheduled employment, whether for wages or not and only the members of the employer's family are excluded. In a separate judgment the third member of the Bench said that going by the natural meaning of the words employed in the Act, it is clear that all manual workers who are either engaged or are to be engaged in scheduled employments are called 'unprotected workers' irrespective of whether their conditions of service are regulated or protected by any other labour legislation or not. 'Unprotected workers', within the meaning of the Act are definitely not only those manual workers who are casually engaged.

*619.* The Kerala State has enacted a number of laws for the protection and welfare of workers engaged in unorganized employments. The Kerala Headload Workers Act, 1978 was enacted to provide for registration of workers and, as a logical necessity, of every employer or contractor who may employ or engage for an establishment any head load worker. This was followed by the Kerala Loading and Unloading (Regulation of Wages and Restriction of Unlawful Practices) Act, 2002. Under the 1978 Act, the Kerala Workers (Regulation of Employment and Welfare) Scheme, 1983 was promulgated. Under the scheme the government notifies the areas in which the establishments are brought under its operation. In one case, the trade unions raised a demand upon an employer that he should employ only the registered workers for loading and unloading and the fact that neither his establishment nor his workers were registered, meant that he was disabled by law from engaging them. He refused to come to their terms, then use of force commenced and there was trespass and obstruction. The police did not come to his help and in the end he sought a direction from the High Court in a writ petition. The petitioner said that

431. LLJ, Vol. 1, 2007, *Kay Kay Embroideries Pvt. Ltd* v. *Cloth Markets and Shops Board and Others*, High Court of Bombay, pp. 865–901.

the workmen on regular pay roll predominantly attended to packing work and other incidental activities and on some occasions when lorry loads arrive they also attended to unloading work. His workers attend to inflammable and toxic chemicals and the establishment is answerable in respect of injuries that may result from inept handling of such materials. These questions were earlier referred to the full Bench, as to whether the provisions of The Headload Workers Act, Rules or Scheme may not apply to an establishment. The full Bench observed that,

> if the worker is doing loading and unloading work regularly in the establishment, he cannot be taken out of the purview of the Act only for the reason that he is discharging some other duties also. On the other hand, if he is principally employed to carry on the work other than loading and unloading and if occasionally he does the work of loading and unloading, it may not be possible to treat him as a headload worker coming within the definition.

In the light of this judgment, the Court held that, it did not intend to snatch away a portion of work from regular workmen, and in fact dealt hardly with any issues in respect of such group. The demand for grant of work as coming from the unions has no legal basis. The petitioner will have the right to carry on the work, including unloading work, by engaging his own workmen. Neither he, nor his workmen are obliged to register under the Act or the Scheme. The Police will render adequate assistance when required. The petition was allowed.[432]

*620.* In another case of unions' high handedness in invoking the Kerala Headload Workers Act, 1978, the owners of paddy fields faced a demand of the union to give the headload workers the work of loading paddy to the exclusion of his permanent workers. He sought police protection, but could not get it. He filed a writ petition. The Court observed that under Section (J) of the Act the word 'establishment' is defined. Under Section 1(3), the Act restricts the operational field to the establishments. The Scheme lists the group of activities that come within the definition. Plantations, such as, coffee, rubber, etc. come within the purview of the Act, but agricultural operations relating to paddy are not included in the Schedule. Another law, the Kerala Agricultural Workers Act, applies to them. Headload work is incidental to agricultural work, including harvesting, threshing, bagging and at times transport. Under the Scheme, in a notified area, the headload workers have to be pooled by a Committee, which is considered the employer of the workers. The owner of the establishment is required to register himself under the Act and pay a levy and remit the equivalent amount of wages in advance. The Committee alone is authorized to depute the workers. The union representing workmen cannot gate crash and demand work, even from an establishment registered under the Scheme. It has been done in the authorized manner. It would be preposterous to suggest that an agriculturalist has to register himself under the Act, pay levy and make a request for deputation of workers, when year round he engages regular workmen and they are entitled to attend to every work relating to agricultural activities. The workers registered under the Headload Workers Act have no legally enforceable right for

432. LLJ, Vol. 1, 2006, *Venkatraman* v. *Sub-Inspector of Police*, High Court of Kerala, pp. 471–476.

insisting that any such work is to be reserved for them. The Court held that the petitioners have the right to engage their own employees for the works relating to agricultural operations, namely, loading and unloading paddy, also the work of straw, seeds, manure and the like. No purpose would be served by requiring the regular workmen to keep idle and available work is to be farmed out to third parties. The proposition is an absurdity viewed from an economic angle. Police protection must be provided as required.[433]

*621.* The Building and Other Construction Workers (Regulations of Employment and Conditions of Service) Act, 1996 provides for safety, health and welfare and for other matters connected thereto and applies to every establishment which employes or had employed on any day of the preceding 12 months 50 or more workers in any building or other construction work. The Act provides for registration of every establishment and also to the 'effect of non-registration', which is to prohibit such an employer of an establishment who has not registered from employing building workers. The Act also provides for the registration of building workers as beneficiaries who shall be entitled to the benefits provided by the Building and Other Construction Workers' Welfare Board from its fund under the Act. Every beneficiary worker will get an identity card with his photograph duly affixed thereon, with enough space of entering the details of the building or construction work done by him. The Board may provide immediate assistance to a beneficiary in case of an accident, payment of pension on the beneficiary completing the age of 60 years, pay premiums towards group insurance schemes, meet medical expenses, payment of maternity benefit to female beneficiaries, sanction loans/advances for construction of a house, The Authority for determining the hours of work and making Rules will be exercised by the appropriate government. The Act provides for safety committees to be constituted and safety officers to be appointed in every establishment in which 500 or more building workers are employed. The responsibility of employers for providing constant and adequate supervision of any building or construction work and for payment of wages and compensation is prescribed by Sections 44 to 45 respectively. It is a complete code framed along the lines of the Factories Act and accordingly provides for penalties and procedure for contravention of provisions made in the Act. The Building and Other Construction Workers Welfare Cess Rules, 1988 have been notified by the central government. Under the Rules the key authorities are the Cess Collector, the Assessing Officer and the Appellate Authority, which have to be appointed by the state governement.

*622.* In a case the contractors questioned the levy of cess under the Building and Other Construction Workers Welfare Cess Act, 1996 on the ground that they were not the employer, but were employed by a Company and therefore they were not liable for the cess which is levied on the employer. The Court observed that under clause (i), (iii) of sub-Section 2 of the Construction Workers Act, 1996 the term 'employer' is defined in relation to a building or other construction work carried on by or through a contractor, or by the employment of building workers supplied by

433. LLJ, Vol. 2, 2006, *Jaya Prakash and Another* v. *Suppt. of Police*, High Court of Kerala, pp. 995–997.

a contractor. The definition leaves open the option of collection of the cess from the class of persons who owe the liability, whether it would be the Head of Department, the Chief Executive or the contractor, as the case may be. This provision binds the government or the public sector undertaking to deduct or cause to be deducted the cess payable. The Bharat Oman Refineries Ltd, a joint venture of Bharat Petroleum Corporation Ltd and Oman Oil Co. Ltd constructed a refinery and engaged 37 contractors for various buildings and other construction works. They were held liable to pay cess at 1 per cent of the cost of the construction incurred. They took the plea that the construction workers Act excluded construction work under the Factories Act. The company argued that the liability for cess was that of the contractors and the joint liability imposed by the order was bad and should be set aside. The question posed by the Court was, whether the contractors can be said to be the employer under the Act. The Court cited the Act and its definitions and observed that the Act was a piece of beneficial legislation, whereas the cess Act of 1996 was in the nature of taxing statute, making compulsory imposition of cess. The Court held that the sub rule (3) of rule 4 binds the government or the public sector undertaking to deduct the cess or cause to be deducted from the bills paid for such works. The Company is liable to realize the cess for the bills of the contractors and account for the same. This case disposed of 14 writ petitions challenging the order for payment of cess under the Construction Workers Welfare Cess Act, 1996.[434]

## §3. Contract Labour

*623.* If contract labour has not been prohibited, it may be permitted in an establishment provided it is registered under the Act. The contractor who employs contract labour must have a license. The subcontractors are equally responsible for obtaining licenses and implementing the provisions of the Act and the Rules. In one case, it was found that the principal employer had not obtained the licence to engage contract labour through one or more contractors, nor had the particular contactor had a licence to supply labour. The two parties had clearly flouted the mandatory provisions of the Act. The Contractor is responsible for paying wages, if fewer than 1,000 contract workers are employed, before the expiry of seven days, and in other cases before the expiry of ten days. If employment of a worker is terminated, wages due to him must be paid before the expiry of the second day after the termination of employment. No deductions from wages other than those authorized by the government are permitted. The principal employer is required to ensure the presence of his authorized representative at the place and time of disbursement of wages. He should also sign on the wages register certifying that the amounts shown as paid to workmen have been paid in his presence. On prohibition of contract labour, the Act does not provide for automatic absorption of contract labour, the workmen go with the contractor, and he may either retain them in his employ or retrench them in accordance with law. There is no provision in Section 10 which stipulates automatic

434. LLJ, June 2010, *Gannon Dunkerley and Co. Ltd* v. *State of Madhya Pradesh and Others,* High Court of Madhya Pradesh, pp. 809–818, also see LLJ, January 2011, *Adani Agri Logistics Ltd and Another* v. *State of Haryana and Others,* High Court of Punjab and Haryana, pp. 307–312.

absorption of contract labour, subsequent to its prohibition notification. Contract labour is a species of workman. But where the contractor is a mere camouflage, the workmen concerned become the direct employees of the principal employer. Such person should fit the definition of the term 'workman' in the Act.[435]

*624.* In a case, the *Airports Authority of India*, Mumbai challenged a reference made by the central government regarding the sham character of the contract through which the workmen were employed as well as the merits of the award. The Division Bench of the Court in a writ petition had decided to pass an order by consent of the parties to the effect that the central government was directed to make a reference to industrial tribunal on three issues: (i) whether the contract between the Airport Authority of India and the contractors was a sham and bogus and a mere camouflage to deprive workers the benefits of permanent workers? (ii) Whether the workers be declared permanent in the Airport Authority of India? And (iii) what are the wages and consequential benefits to be paid to the workers concerned with the petition? These questions were adjudicated and an award made. This was challenged in the writ petition. The points of law raised by the petitioners were on the legality of the reference. The contract workers who individually filed the petitions were excluded by the Industrial Disputes Act, since they were not workmen as defined under Section 2(S) of the Act. Hence they could not make a reference, only a union of workmen under the Act can espouse the cause of contract workers. This has not happened, hence the reference is not maintainable. Secondly, only the government can abolish contract labour, and not the Court. However, if the contract was a sham and a camouflage the contract workers would become the deemed employees of the principal employer and in that capacity they would be entitled to raise an industrial dispute. The Court observed that the culture of contract labour has thrown open the doors of contractual and commercial establishments to unqualified and unskilled workers who would otherwise not be able to obtain any employment in an industry. The contract labourers' action was misdirected and ill-advised. They cannot be *ipso facto* regularized, if they are found to be lacking in the requisite qualifications and if they are not employed as per procedure established by law, under which permanent employees doing similar work are employed, even if they are held to be the workmen of the petitioner. The Court held that the basis of the award coming to such conclusions in favour of contract workers proceeded on a fundamentally erroneous premise. The contract workers cannot be brought within the scope of 'workmen' under the ID Act. The award was set aside.[436]

*625.* In a case the single judge had to decide, whether the MP Industrial Relations Act, 1960 was applicable to electricity generation and distribution in which the National Thermal Power Corporation was engaged. The judge decided that the workers could not enforce their claim as the Company's employees and also not as

435. LLJ, Vol. 2, 2001, *Hindustan Coca Cola Bottling S/W.P. Ltd and Another* v. *Narayan Rawal and Others*, High Court of Bombay, pp. 502–510. The Court directed the Industrial Court to frame proper issues and decide them on the basis of the evidence and materials adduced by the parties.
436. LLJ, January 2011, *Airports Authority of India, Mumbai* v. *Indian Airports Kamgar Union and Others*, High Court of Bombay, pp. 211–223.

contract workers. On the prayer that a direction be issued to the NTPC to absorb them as their workmen, the single judge held that there was no notification issued by the appropriate Government abolishing the contract labour, so there was no scope for granting any relief. Overruling this judgment, the Division Bench held that the object of the Act was to regulate the employment of contract labour and to provide for its abolitions in certain circumstances and the matters connected therewith and gave a judgment in favour of worker. This was appealed in the Supreme Court of India. The Apex Court recalled its earlier judgments. The Apex Court said, 'in view of the provisions of Section 10 of the Act, it is only the appropriate Government which has he authority to abolish genuine labour contract in accordance with the provisions of the said section. No court including the industrial adjudicator has jurisdiction do so.' The industrial adjudicator, after receipt of the reference of such dispute will have first to direct the workmen to approach the appropriate government for abolition of the contract labour under Section 10 of the Act and keep the reference pending. If the contract labour is abolished, the adjudicator will give opportunity to the parties to place the necessary material before him to decide whether the workmen of the erstwhile contractor should be absorbed by the principal employer, how many of them and on what terms? If contract labour is not abolished, the industrial adjudicator has to reject the reference. In another judgment the Apex Court observed that, neither Section 10 of CLRA Act, nor any other provision in the Act, whether expressly or by necessary implication, provides for automatic absorption of contract labour on issuing a notification prohibiting employment of contract labour in any process, operation or other work in any establishment. Consequently the principal employer cannot be required to order absorption of the contract labour working in the establishment. The High Court could not have appropriately adjudicated on the issue, whether the contract was a sham and bogus on the basis of material on record. The material could not be the foundation or basis to say that the contract was a sham and a camouflage. The Division Bench was not justified in its conclusion, and on the contrary the single judge had correctly analysed the law. The civil appeals were allowed.[437]

*626.* An entirely new set of issues arose in a case-in which the State Government issued a notification on 11 April 1997 prohibiting contract labour in industrial canteens in factories employing 250 workers in Karnataka State. This had followed the unanimous recommendation of the State Contract Labour Advisory Board, as provided in Section 4 of the Act. More than 700 factories in the state came under its purview. This was challenged in the High Court by some 40 managements which were aggrieved by the notification. The writ petitions were heard by a Division Bench, which dismissed them. The matter was then agitated before the Supreme Court, where again the petition was dismissed. Thereafter, a review petition was filed which met the same fate. The validity of notification was upheld and reached finality on 19 April 2001. The workmen then asserted the right to be treated as the employees of the principal employers from the date of the notification, while the

437. LLJ, Vol. 1, 2009, *National Thermal Power Corporation and Others* v. *Badri Singh Thakur*, Supreme Court of India, pp. 198–208.

managements decided not to implement it. One of the trade unions initiated proceedings against the employers under Section 23 of the Act. At this the Karnataka Employers Association submitted a representation to the Commissioner of Labour requesting him to withdraw the notification. The state government took cognizance of the representation and, ignoring its statutory obligation and disregarding the decisions of the Supreme Court and despite opposition of the Labour Ministry, issued another notification on 4 August 2001, rescinding the earlier notification. This led to writ petitions being filed by the trade unions praying for quashing the second notification and to uphold the claim of workmen that they be treated as employees of the principal employers. In the statement of objections the state government relied upon the Supreme Courts view, that prohibition of contract labour was a matter of government's policy and it could decide on prohibiting contract labour in an establishment, irrespective of whether workmen were engaged in core activity or peripheral activity. The state government is required to consult the state advisory board, but is not bound by the advice given. The substance of employers representation was that in the context of the market oriented globalised new economic policy of the government and in the changed situation, industrial establishments have to focus an their core competencies for survival and growth of business, for which use of outside specialized services was essential. The focus on peripheral activities, such as, security, housekeeping, gardening, transportation, food preparation, etc, will cause immense strain on the establishments distracting their attention from the core activates. Diversion of business resources to peripheral activities would make the establishments ineffective and inefficient. The measure was retrograde in that the local industry would find it impossible to face competition from China and South Asia countries, which were manufacturing quality goods and offering them at considerably power prices. the prohibition of contract labour in the state would result in shifting of industries to other states where contract labour is not prohibited. Taking these views into account, the notification was withdrawn; it was legal and valid. It was a policy decision. The single judge, who had heard the writ petitions, held that the government failed to see the earlier proceedings, the judicial approval by the Apex Court, the object of the Act, the divided opinion in the government and the discussion the Secretary had with the Chief Minister. The impugned notification ran contrary to the very object of the Act and set aside the second notification. Moreover, contract labour engaged in canteens stood on a different footing composed to other contract laborers and were entitled to regularization. Further, by quashing the second notification, the earlier notification came into operation. Aggrieved by this order appeals were filed and heard by the Division Bench. The Court formulated four issues to be decided entitled to regularization. Further by quashing the second notification, the earlier notification came into operation. Aggrieved by this order appeals were filed and heard by the Division Bench and formulated four issues to be decided:

(1) Whether the government has the power to in rescind the earlier notification which was upheld by the Apex Court.
(2) Is the state has the power, whether the said power is exercised in accordance with law?

(3) Whether the single judge was justified in declaring that all persons employed as contract labourers in statutory canteens would become employees of the principal employer by virtue of the notification dated 11 April 1997?
(4) If the subsequent notification dated 1 August, 2001 is held to be invalid and set aside, would it have the effect of reviving the earlier notification?

*627.* On the first issue, the court noted that the power conferred by Section 10 of the contract Labour Act was read with Section 21 of the General Clauses Act, 1897 to rescind the earlier notification. First, in the contract Labour Act there is no power vested in the government to withdraw, rescind or revoke a notification issued under Section 10 of the Act. The scheme of the Act does not provide for it but Section 21 of the General Clauses Act provides for 'power to issue, to include power to add to, amed, vary or rescind notification, orders, rules or bye laws'. This is applicable to every statute to which it applies. The Court cited laws under which the General clauses Act did not apply. It cannot be invoked to withdraw or cancel an order under Section 10(1) of the Industrial Disputes Act to refer a dispute to adjudication. Nor can't be invoked once the process of election has started, except by an order of the Court. Similarly, the rule embodied in Section 21 cannot be invoked under the Commission of Enquiry Act. A detailed reviewed of judicial decision led the Court to hold that 'broadly stated Section 21 of the Act applies as rule, non application is an exception'. The power to create includes the power to destroy and also the power to alter what is created. 'This legal position is in no way denuded merely because the notification issued under an enactment was the subject matter of litigation and the validity of such notification has been upheld by a court.' Therefore, the government which earlier defended the notification, after it reached finality on a second thought being convinced that the said notification was not in public interest, rescinded it for good reasons.

*628.* The second point was the charge that instead of implementing the notification the government rescinded it. This is malice in law. The state which is expected to unhold the rule of law is a party to violation of law and the power to exercised is vitiated. The single judge had granted an interim stay and it was in force when the matter went before the Apex Court. Therefore, the earlier notification could not have been given effect to and the government could not be blamed for inaction. Later as a policy decision the notification was withdrawn. The prescribed procedure was followed. In the absence of any specific allegation of mala fides against any official, the mere fact of withdrawing the notification after it was upheld by the Apex Court would not constitute malice in law so as to vitiate the notification. The Court did not see any substance in the said contention. Insofar as violation of principles of natural justice is concerned, the views of the Advisory Board were considered and workmen were represented on the Board. The labour unions clearly and unequivocally expressed their views opposing such withdrawal. However, their views were not accepted and the government proceeded to issue the second notification. Therefore, it cannot be said that principles of natural justice were violated. The record shows that the labour minister was totally opposed to withdrawing the earlier notification and the Chief Minister was in a fix. After due consultations, the government took the decision to withdraw the earlier notification. The single judge erred in sitting over the judgement of the views of the members, the notes which were made in the course of proceedings and other materials on record as if he is an appellant authority. The High Court cannot sit in appeal over the decision, all that the Court has to look into is whether the decision making process was just, in accordance with law and reasonable. It cannot sit in judgement over the correctness of the decision of the government. It is not in the domain of the Court to embark upon the unchartered ocean of public policy. This must be left to the discretion of the executive and the legislative authority, as the case may be.

*629.* The running of canteens is regarded as a business. It is a specialized activity. The second notification recognizes it as a growing service sector. It is the expert bodies which can organize canteen like activity. Practical difficulties in running canteens have been pointed out by the employers. If the cook does not turn up, it would be practically impossible for management to make alternate arrangement. The contractor can do this better. The obligation of employing permanent labour to run canteens should not be forced on the employers. It is not an incentive to new investment. 'Therefore, we do not see any illegality committed by the Government is issuing the second notification'. Contract labour employed in factory canteen is entitled to all the welfare measures provided in the Factories Act. But this Act does not provide for appointment of workers, fixation of pay scales. There is nothing in the Act to suggest that on abolition of the system of contract labour, workers become permanent employees of the employer. They do not acquire any special right. Her Neither the Factories Act, nor the Contract Labour Act provide for automatic absorption of contract labour. The employer is under no obligation to absorb such contract labour in his establishment. In the instant case, we declare the notification withdrawing the earlier notification as valid and uphold the same. The learned single judge was not justified in granting such declaration, (automatic absorption of contract labour), and the said declaration is liable to be set aside. The writ appeals are allowed. Writ petition is dismissed. The order of the single judge setting aside the notification dated 1 August, 2001 is set aside and the notification is upheld. Whatever rights the contract labour possesses under the Factories Act are intact.[438]

## §4. Decasualization Schemes

*630.* Under the Dock Workers (Regulation of Employment) Act, 1948, labour decasualization schemes have been formulated and implemented in major Indian ports. The Schemes provide for the registration of dock workers and employers 'in order to ensure greater regularity of employment and to regulate the employment of dock workers, whether registered or not, in a port'. The management of these Schemes is vested in tripartite dock labour boards (DLB) for different ports constituted under the Rules of 1962. These Rules require that a statutory tripartite advisory committee, comprising equal numbers of members representing the central

438. LLJ, 3, 2012, *L and T Komatsu Ltd., (Earlier known as Larsen and Tourbo Ltd.) Bangalore works rep. by its Asstt. G.M. HR. and others* v. *All India Trade Union Congress, Karnataka State Committee, rep. by its General Manager, Bangalore,* Karnataka High Court, pp. 187–230.

government, the employers and dock workers, may advise the government in matters arising out of the administration of the Act or any Scheme made thereunder. The main Act provides for the appointment of Inspectors, for establishing the procedure for lodging complaints with the Inspectors, for conducting an enquiry and for cognizance of offences, etc. The Dock Labour Board is not an industry under the ID Act, so any reference of disputes regarding pay-scales and profit bonus between stevedores and their monthly workmen is barred under the ID Act. The relationship of employer and employee does not exist as between a DLB and dock workers. The Board is not a factory and the dock workers are not engaged in a manufacturing process. So the Factories Act does not apply to the DLB.

*631.* Under the Madras Unregistered Dock General Workers (Regulation of Employment) Scheme, 1988, some employees were retrenched by their employer on the ground of fall in business. The employees along with the employer made a joint request to the Madras Dock Labour Board to place them on list B (general pool) until they were reallocated to another employer. The DLB declined to do so on the ground that only list A employees of completely closed stevedoring business could be placed on list B until their case the employer was continuing in business, so they could not be placed on list B, till they were reallocated to another employer. The High Court held that clause 18 of the Scheme shows that in addition to closing of business, the Chairman of the Board may transfer the retrenched employees to list B temporarily until they are reallocated to another registered employer for any other compelling reasons found valid by him. Clause 22(3) also empowers him for valid and sufficient reasons to transfer to the general pool a monthly rated worker, on a request in writing of the employer explaining fully the reasons for the transfer, provided that such transfer shall be subject to the fulfilment of any condition regarding termination of employment. The Board was under an obligation to consider the request and examine whether there were sufficient and valid reasons to transfer the retrenched employees to list B and send them a suitable reply. The principles of natural justice are to be complied with and the retrenched employees were entitled to have an opportunity to meet the objection, if any, on the part of the Board for declining to place them on list B.

*632.* In the unprotected sector, a distinction may be made between employments such as handlooms, which are predominantly run on the basis of self-employment and receive support and subsidy from the government, and others in which wage labour has come to stay. The former must of necessity remain excluded from the scope of protective labour legislation except insofar as it may better reflect their collective interests, whereas it should be possible for the latter to be gradually brought within its scope. Legislation regulating hours of work, rest period, weekly day off, mode of wage payment, deduction from wages, overtime, etc., would prove to be beneficial without impairing the employment potential. The basis for unionization, or the formation of other voluntary organizations, is also laid when legislation provides them the needed legitimacy as well as a day-to-day need to get the grievances settled.

*633.* The weakest of all segments in the urban labour force are the home workers or the out-workers who are deemed to be self-employed persons and, therefore, lie completely outside the purview of the entire labour statue. The legal distinction between 'a contract of service' and 'a contract for service' separates all those who are employed directly or indirectly, (the first category), from the self-employed who work to do a job on contract, (the second category). The actual control exercised over the out-workers by the contracting employer maybe as close as that of a master over his servants and the hours of work may be just as long as existed before the enactment of the Factories Act, but in law they remain independent contractors, free to choose and to lay down their terms and then execute the contract, as per the agreement, explicit or implied, no matter how one-sided, exploitative or unreasonable the terms may be. In practical terms most of the home workers do not have direct access to the judicial system under labour laws.

# Chapter 6. Migrant Labour, Bonded Labour, Female and Child Labour

## §1. Interstate Migrant Labour

*634.* The Interstate Migrant Workers (Regulation of Employment and Conditions of Service) Act, 1979 was enacted to protect the greatly exploited migrant labour force, mostly unskilled, and recruited from amongst the very poor, landless, often tribal people of certain states, mainly Orissa. The basic administrative notification for the appointment of officers who can register the establishments and license the contractors was issued by the Centre in 1985. The Act applies to the whole of India: the appropriate government is the Centre if the establishment is under its authority or control, and for all others it is the state government. The laws which have been made applicable to the ISM workmen are (i) the Workmen's Compensation Act, (ii) the Payment of Wages Act, (iii) the Industrial Disputes Act, (iv) the ESI Act, (v) the EPFMP Act, and (vi) the Maternity Benefit Act.

*635.* This enactment applies to every establishment in which five or more interstate migrant workmen are employed, whether or not in addition to other workmen in a day, and to every contractor who employs, or employed, five or more workers on any day in the preceding 12 months. Every such establishment which proposes to employ interstate migrant labour must be registered with either the central or the state government and obtain a licence from the specified authority, both of the state to which the workman belongs, (home state), and the state in which he is proposed to be employed (host state). The contractor is required to furnish the particulars of migrant workers to both the home state and the host state and to issue to every workman a passbook containing the details of the employment. The *kedars* and *jamadars* engaged to recruit workers are contractors and the persons so recruited are interstate migrant workmen who are accordingly entitled to all the benefits of the Act. It has been held that every state and union territory of India is obliged to permit officers of the originating states to hold appropriate inquiries within the limits of the recipient state for enforcement of this Act and no embargo or hindrance shall be placed in such process. Under Section 21, the interstate migrant workmen shall be deemed to be in employment from date of recruitment for the purposes of certain enactments. These include the Payment of Wages Act, 1936.

*636.* Wages must be paid according to the specific guidelines, and from the day of recruitment. 'Wages' has the same meaning as in the Payment of Wages Act. In no case can an interstate migrant workman be paid less than the wages fixed under the Minimum Wages Act, and wages payable shall be paid regularly in cash. All such workmen are entitled to a displacement allowance and a journey allowance in addition to their wages. The amenities that are required to be provided include, 'provision of suitable residential accommodation, adequate medical facilities, protective clothing to suit varying climatic conditions and suitable conditions of work'.

*637.* An important provision of this legislation is that, in addition to the Inspector appointed by the appropriate government, the home state can also appoint

Inspectors for visiting the establishments where its workmen are employed to see whether the provisions of this Act are being complied with. Moreover, the migrant workmen have been given the right to raise an industrial dispute either in the host state or the home state after their return on completion of the contract of employment. They are permitted to apply for the transfer of proceedings in relation to an industrial dispute to their home state on the ground that they have returned to that state after the completion of their contracts. They are deemed to be in employment and to have actually worked in the establishment from the date of their recruitment. This Act provides that the wage rates, holidays, hours of work and other conditions of service of an interstate migrant workman should be the same or similar as for 'any other workman in that establishment' or 'in any other case be such as may be prescribed by the appropriate government' In addition, the law also provides for equal pay for equal work irrespective of sex, thereby enforcing the Equal Remuneration Act, 1975. Under Section 22, the migrant workmen on returning to the home State or the State where the recruitment was made, can raise an industrial dispute or institute the proceedings in the said State within a period of six months from the date of return after completing their employment.

*638.* In a case the contractor residing in Gujarat secured a contract to execute certain works in Surat for which he needed to recruit labour. He appointed a subcontractor residing in Andhra Pradesh to recruit the labourers for work in Surat. He recruited them in Andhra Pradesh who on completion of the works returned to their home state. As per the records, the workers alleged that they were not completely paid all the wages due to them and filed a group of applications under the Payment of Wages Act in Andhra Pradesh. The labourers made a huge claim of Rs 24 lakhs and secured the registration of the dispute. The authorities served a show cause notice on 10 August 2006, to which the contractor as the principal employer replied and urged that the notice may be dropped in view of the contentions raised by him, but the proceedings were not dropped and the contractor received another notice dated 13 September 2007 from the Asstt. Commissioner of Labour, in Andhra Pradesh to which he again replied. The petitioner filed a writ petition in the High Court of Gujarat pleading that since the cause of action arose in Gujarat, the applications cannot be maintained in Andhra Pradesh, that the said applications under the Payment of Wages Act are mala fide to extract the amounts that are not due and payable. The Court went though the Inter-State Migrant Workmen (Regulation of Employment and Conditions of Service) Act, 1979 and also reviewed the law on cause of action. The Court observed that even if this High Court had parallel jurisdiction, in propriety, it can and would refuse to exercise its jurisdiction. Propriety demanded that the applicants were poor migrant workmen who cannot be asked to attend the proceedings in Gujarat. Moreover, the adjudicating authority has taken cognizance of the dispute and issued notices and its jurisdictions lies within that of the High Court of Andhra Pradesh. Then the objections against the workmen's claim should be raised before the High Court of Andhra Pradesh, because the cause of action is also located there. The petitioner has already raised his objections before the authority and he can invite it to decide the said objections as a preliminary issue.

The Court clarified that the observations made were prima facie and not to be construed as final conclusions. The petition was dismissed with the clarifications and observation made in the judgment.[439]

## §2. The Bonded Labour System

*639.* The Bonded Labour System (Abolition) Act, 1976, was enacted to provide for its abolition with a view to preventing the economic and physical exploitation of the weaker sections of the people and for matters either connected or incidental thereto. The system rested upon a written or oral agreement, or partly written and partly oral agreement, to provide labour in return for a debt. The debtor worked for the creditor:

(i) in consideration of an advance obtained by him or any of his lineal ascendants or descendants and in consideration of the interest;
(ii) in pursuance of:
    (a) any customary or social obligation; or
    (b) an obligation devolving by succession;
(iii) or for any economic consideration received by him or by any of his lineal ascendants or descendants; or
(iv) by reason of his birth in any particular caste or community.

He not only rendered labour/service himself but also committed members of his family or dependents to do so for either a specified or unspecified period and also forfeit the freedom of employment or other means of livelihood for this specified or unspecified period. He could not travel freely or appropriate or sell any of his property or produce of labour or those of his family members. The system included a surety who on behalf of the debtor entered, or is presumed to have entered, into an agreement with the creditor to the effect, that in the event of non-payment of debt he would render bonded labour on behalf of the debtor. Under the Amendment Act, 1985, the contract labour and the interstate migrant labour are also treated as bonded labuor as defined in the Act. This Act is administered by the state governments. The implementation consists of identification, release and rehabilitation of bonded labourers. It is held that the existence of forced labour will give rise to a presumption that the labourer is required to work for some economic consideration and is a bonded labourer.

*640.* Section 4 stipulates that the aforesaid bonded labour system shall stand abolished and every bonded labour be freed and discharged from any obligation to render any bonded labour. The making of advances in pursuance of the bonded labour system or compelling any person to render any form of forced labour have been abolished under Section 5. Any custom, tradition, contract or agreement which stipulates any kind of bonded service or labour has also been rendered void and

---

439. LLJ, Vol. 4, 2009, *Khalid A. Hakim* v. *Asstt. Commissioner of Labour and Others,* High Court of Gujarat, pp. 431–444.

inoperative. Under Section 6, the obligation of a bonded labourer to pay any bonded debt is deemed to have been extinguished. No suit can lie for the recovery of such debts; and any decree or order issued for recovery of bonded debt, and not fully satisfied, shall be deemed to have been fully satisfied. Every attachment stands vacated and any moveable property seized and kept under the control of any court must be restored to the person. Similarly, if any property had been seized by the creditor, it should be restored, 'as soon as practicable', after the commencement of the Act. If this was not done within 30 days, the aggrieved party would have the right to make an application and seek the restoration of the property. Furthermore, if any property was seized and sold, the freed bonded labourer would have the right to deposit the amount of sale proceeds less any amount on profits the decree holder has received in the court and get the sale nullified and secure the restoration of the property. If any suit or proceeding for the enforcement of a bonded obligation was pending in any court at the time of enactment it would stand dismissed. Moreover, every bonded labourer detained in a civil prison, 'whether before or after judgment, shall be released from detention forthwith'. An order made by any prescribed authority in respect of the above (Section 6), shall be deemed to be an order of the civil court and may be executed by the court of the lowest pecuniary jurisdiction within the local limits of whose jurisdiction the creditor resides or carries on business. The bonded labourer must be identified and released, and on release he should be suitably rehabilitated.

*641.* Section 7 of the Act frees and discharges all property, 'vested in a bonded labourer', which was under any mortgage, charge, lien or other encumbrances, insofar as these may be relatable to the bonded debt. Section 8 stipulates that no freed bonded labourer can be evicted from any homestead or other residential premises which he has been occupying and, if he had been evicted, it is the duty of the executive magistrate in charge of the subdivision to restore to him the premises. Section 9 makes the complementary provision that, 'no creditor shall accept any payment against any bonded debt which has been extinguished'; and anyone contravening this provision is liable to be punished with imprisonment of up to three years and also with a fine. In addition, the court may direct the convicted creditor to deposit the amount accepted by him in contravention of law, 'for being refunded to the bonded labourers'. The authorities may take steps for formation of cooperative societies, allocation of land, and location of homestead for building new residential accommodation for the freed bonded labourers.

*642.* The principal implementing authority under the Act is the district magistrate, and the state governments may confer such powers and impose such duties upon him as may be necessary. The district administration has the additional responsibility of promoting the welfare of the freed bonded labourers and for protecting their economic interest so that they may not contract any further bonded debt. In addition, the state governments are required to set up vigilance committees in each district and in each subdivision. A vigilance committee will function as an advisory body to the district magistrate and is charged with a number of specific responsibilities which include authorizing one of its members to defend a suit against a freed bonded labourer and to act as his authorized agent. The Act also provides under Section 15 that if any debt is claimed by a bonded labourer, the burden of proving that, 'such debt is not a bonded debt shall lie on the creditor' (Section 15).

*643.* The petitioner sought an a application under Section 482 of the Criminal Procedure Code, 1973, to quash an order passed by the Sub-Divisional Magistrate who took cognizance under Section 4(1) and (2) of the Bonded Labour System (Abolition) Act 1976 against him. The main ground of this application was that under Section 21 of the Act, the authority with the power of taking cognizance of a complaint is the Executive Magistrate who has been expressly conferred with the power of judicial magistrate. He shall conduct the trial of offences falling within the Act. The general provision of the Criminal Procedure code (Cr. P.C.), shall also be applicable for initiating a criminal case under the Act. The Court reviewed the relevant sections of the Cr. P.C. and observed that the SDM was not empowered to take cognizance of the offences under the Bonded Labour Act. 'However, only because of it, the order of cognizance cannot deemed to be illegal. It is merely an irregularity which does not vitiate the proceedings'. The Court cited the Section 460 of Cr. P.C. in support of the conclusion. This section lists the irregulaties which do not vitiate the proceedings if any magistrate not empowered by law did the listed things. Thus the ground taken by the petitioner was not sufficient under law to quash the order of cognizance in question. The application was dismissed.[440]

## §3. Abolition of Sex Discrimination

*644.* Until 1976, there existed no statutory provision that enforced the constitutional guarantee of equality of sexes. An employer who discriminated against women violated no law and risked no punishment. This rather serious lacuna was removed by the enactment of the Equal Remuneration Act 1976. The Act provides, 'for the payment of equal remuneration to men and women workers and for the prevention of discrimination on the grounds of sex against women in the matter of employment and for matters connected therewith or incidental thereto'. The provisions of this Act override anything that may be inconsistent with any other law or in the terms of any award, agreement or contract of service. By the 1987 amendment, the Act also prohibits discrimination in relation to conditions of service, such as promotions, training and transfers. The amended Act (Section 15), specifically disallows the continuance of discriminatory practices against women workers. It is held that the Act providing equality of pay for equal work between men and women is a part of the constitutional principle, 'equal pay for equal work'.

*645.* The Equal Remuneration Act, under Section 4, establishes an employer's duty to pay equal remuneration to men and women for the same work or work of a similar nature. This is defined to mean that:

---

440. LLJ, Vol. 2, 2007, *Chhote Shukla @ Vijay Kumar Shukla* v. *State of Bihar and Others,* High Court of Patna, pp. 1018–1019.

(i) no employer shall pay any worker at rates that are less favourable than those payable to the opposite sex;
(ii) in order to comply with this provision no employer shall reduce the rate of remuneration of any worker; and
(iii) Where different rates of remuneration are paid to men and women for the same work, the higher of the two rates will be payable.

Section 5 requires that, from the commencement of this Act, no employer will make any discrimination against women at the time of recruitment, except where their employment is prohibited or restricted under any law. However, this provision would not affect any priority or reservations made in favour of scheduled castes, scheduled tribes, etc. The term, 'employer', has the same meaning assigned to it as in the Payment of Gratuity Act, 1972. It has been held that a settlement arrived at between a management and the employees cannot be a valid ground for effecting discrimination of remuneration between male and female employees performing the same work or work of a similar nature. The term, 'same work or work of a similar nature', has been defined in the Act and the stress is upon the similarity of skill, efforts and responsibility when performed under similar conditions.

*646.* The rules specify that a register be maintained which will give information on the category of workers, a brief description of work, the numbers of men and women employed and details of their remuneration. Second, the Inspectors have wide powers to enter the premises, inspect documents, take evidence and, where necessary, to initiate proceedings against an employer in accordance with the provisions of the Act. The provision in respect of registers (Section 8), has been amended by the Labour Laws (Exemption from Furnishing Returns and Maintaining Registers by Certain Establishments) Act, 1988 applicable to small and very small establishments. In a case, the Managing Director of ICICI Bank was prosecuted for failure to maintain the register of workers at a branch. This led to a writ petition. The Court held that under the definition of the term, 'employer', The Branch Manager would fit the definition, not the Managing Director, who did not have ultimate control over the establishment. He did not come within the term, 'employer'. The proceedings were quashed.[441]

*647.* Section 6 provides for the constitution of one or more Advisory Committees to advise the appropriate government on increasing employment opportunities for women. It may also tender advice on the nature of work, hours of work, suitability of women for employment and such other factors as the committee may think fit, and the government may, after considering the advice, issue such directions in respect of employment of women workers as may be feasible under the law.

*648.* If any question arises as to whether two or more jobs are of the same nature, or of a similar nature, it shall be decided by the authority appointed under the Act. The authority has the power to give orders on payment of wages to women

441. LLJ, Vol. 1, 2007, *Kamath K.V.* v. *Labour Enforcement Officer (Central), Kolkata,* High Court of Calcutta, pp. 936–939.

at equal rates with men and also to direct the employer to ensure that there is no contravention of any provision of this Act. For the purpose of recoveries of money, Section 33C(1) of the ID Act will apply. The definitions have made it clear that 'words' and expressions used in the Act and not defined, but defined in the Industrial Disputes Act, 1947' shall have the same meaning as in that Act. Where there is an employment relationship, this Act applies. It will not apply, however, if the government notifies that the differences in remuneration are not due to sex discrimination but to factors other than sex, or where the terms and conditions of women will be adversely affected by compliance with the law, or where any special treatment is accorded to women in connection with birth or expected birth.

*649.* In Maharastra, two female sweepers were employed on compassionate grounds on the death of their husbands who were employed as male sweepers, and at a fixed consolidated pay. They lodged a complaint of unfair labour practice against their employer under the MRTU and PULP Act. The complaint was referred to the Industrial Court, which allowed it under items 5 and 9 of Schedule IV of the MRTU & PULP Act. The Industrial Court directed the institution which managed the educational institution where the female sweepers where employed to pay them the salary in the pay scale on which regular male sweepers were employed. Against this order a writ petition was filed. The High Court observed that though the Industrial Court had not considered the Equal Remuneration Act, the said Act has an overriding effect under Section 3. Section 4 prohibits the employer from paying remuneration to women employees at lower rates than paid to the male employees doing the 'some work or work of similar nature'. This Act fully governs the dispute which was referred to the Industrial Court. Moreover, the workload was available and the work done by male and female sweepers was of similar nature. The Court applied the doctrine of, 'equal pay of equal work', and held that as an unfair labour practice under the MRTU & PULP Act, this finding cannot be said to be either erroneous or perverse. The Equal Remuneration Act applied to educational institutions. Though grant of employment by showing compassion is an exception to the normal mode of recruitment, discrimination against women employees violated the Equal Remuneration Act. There was no case made out to interfere in the award of the Industrial Court and the writ petition was dismissed.[442]

## §4. CHILD LABOUR

*650.* The first important legal step was the enactment of the Employment of Children (Amendment) Act, 1985 which amended the Act of 1938 to provide for heavier fines and imprisonment for violating the prohibitory provisions in respect of employment of children. The Schedule to the Act listed the employments and occupations in which children were forbidden from working, viz. *beedi*-making, carpet weaving, cement manufacture including bagging of cement, cloth printing, dyeing, weaving, manufacture of matches, explosives and fireworks, mica-cutting

442. LLJ, July 2010, *Janta Shikshan Prasarak Mandal, Pusad and Another* v. *Industrial Court, Yavatmal and Others,* High Court of Bombay, pp. 114–118.

and splitting, shellac and soap manufacture, tanning, wool-cleaning and the building and construction industry. With the enactment of the Child Labour (Prohibition and Regulation) Act, 1986, the Act of 1938 was repealed. The 1986 Act includes all the progressive features of the 1985 amendment Act and in addition it overrides a number of other laws. Additionally it empowers, any person to seek the enforcement of the law'. Part III of the Act, dealing with the regulation of conditions of work of children, was enforced on 26 May 1993.

*651.* In this Act a child is a person who has not reached 14 years of age. This Act prohibits the employment of children in any employment or workshop listed in either Part A or Part B of the Schedule. The government has the power to amend the Schedule through administrative notification by giving not less than three months' notice and may add any occupation or process to it. Part A lists seven occupations, viz. transport by railway, cinder picking, clearing of an ashpit, or building operation in the railway premises, catering jobs at a railway station, construction work at a railway station or with any other work in close proximity to it, or between the railway lines, and a port authority within the limits of any port and also work relating to crackers and fireworks and slaughterhouses. The government has thus prohibited employment of children in two of its largest activities. This Act has simultaneously amended the Minimum Wages Act, the Plantations Labour Act, the Merchant Shipping Act, and the Motor Transport Workers Act to bring their definitions of child, adolescent and adult at par with it. The government amended the Schedule in May 2001 to include under the 'process', seven more types of employment. Earlier in 1988 it had been amended to include a large number of occupations. From time-to-time the central government notifies a small number of occupations added to the Schedule.

*652.* The Act provides for regulation of conditions of work in Part III and these include occupations and processes in which child labour is not prohibited. Section 7 regulates hours and periods of work and prescribes that no child will work for more than three hours at a time and must have an interval of rest of one hour before working again. The child's total working day including the rest interval should not exceed six hours, and, furthermore, no one should be allowed to work between 7.00 pm and 8.00 am. Over time work for children is forbidden. No child may be allowed to work in two establishments on any day. Section 8 prescribes one whole day's holiday in a week. The health and safety provisions of the Act, (Section 13), require that detailed rules should be prescribed about cleanliness, freedom from nuisance, disposal of wastes and effluents, ventilation and temperature, dust and fumes, etc., and in respect of safety measures pertaining to work on dangerous machines, protection of eyes, explosives or inflammable gas and other related matters. The Act defines a 'workshop', as any premises where any industrial process is carried on, but excludes the factories to which the Factories Act, Section 67, prohibiting the employment of children below the age of 14 years, applies. The Act requires occupiers of workshops to display notices in the local language and English stating the prohibition of employment of children as well as the notification of the weekly holiday. The regulatory provision of the Act (Sections 7, 8 and 9), are not applicable to any workshop wherein any process is carried on by the occupier with the aid of his family. Every occupier who employs children must maintain a register listing the name and date of birth of every child, the hours of work and rest intervals and other related matters as prescribed.

In one case for an offence of violation of Sections 67 of the Factories Act a fine of Rs 200 was imposed. The state government appealed to the High Court to impose a fine under Section 14 of the Child Labour (Prohibition and Regulation) Act 1986. The Court upheld this contention and raised the find to Rs 10,000.[443]

*653.* In a case the petitioner employers were directed to pay Rs 20000/- for each child labour employed by them or face legal action. The order was passed by the Mamlatdar cum *ex officio* Labour Inspector who made the inspection of the factory premises and saw several child labourers at work. On receiving the notice, the employer replied, denying that children were below 14 years of age. Some of them though present had come to serve tiffin to the labourers. The inspection note was wrong and persons who were not their employees were shown as engaged in labour. This explanation was rejected by the Mamlatdar in view of the Supreme Court's judgment and sought to recover a sum of Rs 140,000 from the employer. The Asstt. Labour Commissioner in his counter affidavit said that no satisfactory evidence was provided for the age of five workers, therefore the action taken against the petitioner was legal and valid. The Court observed that Section 14 of the Act would not authorize a Mamlatdar or an Inspector to hold a person guilty of the offences, nor would they be entitled to award any punishment to the alleged wrong doer. Once a prima facie case was established, he should file a complaint before the competent Judicial Magistrate to secure a conviction and then a penalty could be imposed. In the present case the prosecution was still pending before the judicial magistrate. The Court held that an Inspector or Mamlatdar or Asst. Labour Commissioner cannot take action at their whims, caprice or arbitrariness. They cannot say that the reply to the show cause notice did not satisfy them, therefore the recovery would be made in the case. The defence could not be rejected as bogus. The Asstt. Labour Commissioner filed a false affidavit to mislead the Court. Such an approach could not be protected under the judgement of the Supreme Court in the case of *M.C. Mehta* v. *State of Tamil Nadu and Others,* reported in 1997. The orders passed by the Mamlatdar/Inspector and Asstt. Labour Commissioner were quashed. Eash of the petition was allowed with costs of Rs 10,000 in each case to be paid by the Labour Deptt. to the petitioners within 15 days from today.[444]

*654.* The applicant had a motor cycle repair shop and was proceeded against for engaging one child labour. He was served a show-cause notice as to why compensation of Rs 20,000 should not be recovered from him. A criminal case was also registered against him. He was directed to deposit the said sum in the District Child Labour Rehabilitation and Welfare Fund, failing which it would be recovered by way of land revenue. The appellant did not pay the amount and instead moved the

443. LLJ, Vol. 2, 2001, *State of Gujarat* v. *Bhupendra Kumar Jagjivandas Patel*, High Court of Gujarat, pp. 1517–1519.

444. LLJ, Vol. 1, 2008, *Haria Ginning and Pressing Factory* v. *Mamlatdar and Others*, High Court of Gujarat, pp. 104-108.

High Court. The single judge dismissed the writ petition. He made a writ appeal before a Bench. The judgement of the Supreme Court was placed before the Bench in which the following observation was made. Citing Article 39 of the Constitution, the Court said,

> It seems to us that the least we ought to do is see to the fulfillment of legislative intendment behind enactment of the Child Labour (Prohibition and Regulation) Act, 1986. Taking guidance there from, we are the view that the offending employer must be asked to pay compensation for every child employed in contravention of the provisions of the Act, a sum of Rs 20000/- and the Inspectors, whose appointment is visualized by Section 17 to secure compliance with the provisions of the Act, should do this job. The Inspectors appointed under Section 17 would see that for every child employed in violation of the provisions. of the Act, the concerned employer pays Rs 20000/- which sum could be deposited in a fund to be known as Child Labour Rehabilitation-cum Welfare Fund. The liability of the employer would not cease even if he would desire to disengage the child presently employed.

The single judge followed this judgment. The Bench of the Court said,

> and we the Judges now in the Division Bench have to bow our heads to the law declared by the Supreme Court and in doing so we are of the considered view that the impugned order passed by the learned Single Judge here under challenge is perfectly in order and in consonance with law declared by the Supreme Court, and as such, the same cannot be interfered with by us in the appeal.

The appeal was dismissed.[445]

*655.* In an appeal before the Supreme Court the appellant Company impugned an order of the Inspector to pay Rs 60,000 as penalty to the Child Labour Wefare Fund. The point raised in the appeal was whether the Inspector appointed under the Act had the power to pass an order holding that the labour employed by the appellant were below the age limit prescribed under the Act and also to direct the appellant to pay the compensation. The Inspector in his inspection of the construction site had seen three child labourers working there. The appellant relied upon two age certificates, one by the Sarpanch, Gram Panchayat and the other by the medical officer that the child labourers were above 14 years of age. The Inspector issued the order demanding Rs 20,000 per child to be deposited with the Child Labour Welfare Fund, failing which the recovery would be made as arrears of land revenue. This was affirmed by the High Court with the direction that the appellant should be given a

445. LLJ, Vol. 1, 2008, *Hayat Khan* v. *Dy Labour Commissioner, Regional Office, Belgaum and Others*, High Court of Karnataka, pp. 284–288 and LLJ, Vol. 4, Supp-2006, *Hayat Khan* v. *Dy Labour Commissioner, Belgam and Others*, High Court of Karnataka, pp. 101–104 (judgment given by the single judge)

hearing. The Labour Officer heard the appellant and reiterated his order. The certificates produced by the appellant were rejected on the ground that they were not issued by the prescribed medical authority under Section 16(2) of the Act. This order was challenged in a writ petition, which the High Court rejected and he was ordered to pay Rs 60,000 within four weeks, failing which it would carry interest at 12 per cent annum. The appellant deposited the sum. The Apex Court read Section 16(2) of the Act and decided that the jurisdiction of the Inspector did not extend to trying of the complaint, which can be done only by courts not inferior to the Metropolitan Magistrate or Magistrate, First class. Besides, Section 16(2) does not make the production of age certificate mandatory. In fact, under Section 10 of the Act, a dispute can be raised on the age of the child employed. The Inspector should have referred the age certificates to the prescribed medical authority for a decision. He did not have the jurisdiction to impose a fine. The young persons in employment should produce the age certificate from a competent medical authority, under Rule 17. This was not the obligation of the employer. The impugned order of the Inspector and the order of the High Court were set aside and the appeal allowed. The appellant was at liberty to withdraw the amount deposited.[446]

*656.* A single judge at High Court of Allahabad said that a large number of cases pertaining to recovery certificate were being issued, wherein the Labour Court as the Authority was issuing notice to the occupier for payment of Rs 2000 on the basis of inspection report without getting the said child medically examined for determination of age by an appropriate Medical Authority. The impugned proceeding of issuance of notice or recovery certificate without determination of the age of the child labour according to the provision of Section 10 and Rule 17 of the Act is clearly illegal. He also held that from a conjoint reading of Section 10 and Rule 17, it is apparent that:

1. It is the duty of the occupier/employer to provide a certificate in respect of all young persons in his employment in any occupation given in Schedules A and B of the Act, and
2. Charges of issuance of such certificate by the medical authority shall be borne by the employer of young persons whose age is disputed.

In the present case, the Recovery Certificate dated 26 May 2008 was quashed. 'It is directed that Labour Inspector will first get age determined by medical examination of young person/child labour, allegedly to be the employee of the petitioner, through the prescribed Medical Officer under the Act and only then necessary orders may be passed pursuance to the notice dated 24 April 2008.' In another case the High Court of Rajasthan quashed an order for recovery of the alleged amount of penalty by resorting to the provisions of the Rajasthan Land Revenue Act, even without imposing a penalty or fine in accordance with law. This was like putting the cart before the horse. It also indicates the reckless and casual manner in which the concerned

446. LLJ, Vol. 4, Supp. 2006, *Anant Construction Co.* v. *Government Labour Officer and Inspector*, Supreme Court of India, pp. 738-740.

authority under the Act has acted in the present case against the petitioner. Meanwhile, the proceedings initiated under Section 14 of the Act were terminated by way of acquittal. 'It is clear that no penalty amount or fine can be recovered from the petitioner in the present case.' Therefore the proclamation issued by the Tehsildar was quashed.[447]

447. LLJ, Vol. 3, 2008, *Rahul Kumar, Proprietor of Sheetal Hotel* v. *State of U.P. and Others*, High Court of Allahabad, pp. 881–883; LLJ, Vol.3, 2008, *Bhanwar Lal Solanki* v. *State of Rajasthan and Others*, High Court of Rajasthan, pp. 909–911.

# Selected Bibliography


Agarwal P.K., *Naxalism, Causes and Cure*, New Delhi, Manas Publications, 2010.

*Business India*, 29 November-12 December, 2010.

Chandra Bipan *et al., India after Independence*, Viking, 1999, Ch. 37.

*Economic and Political Weekly*, 4 December, 2010, Paranjoy Guha Thakurta and Akshat Kaushal, 'Underbelly of the Great Telecom Revolution'.

*Economic Survey*, 2007-08.

*Economic Survey*, 2008-09.

*Economic Survey, 2009-10*, New Delhi, OUP, 2010.

*The Economist*, 2 January 2010 'Comments on Copenhagen'.

*The Economist* – 25 September October, 2010.

*Eleventh Five-Year Plan, 2007-2012*, Vol. II, 'Social Sector' and Ch. 1, 'Education'.

*Eleventh Five-Year Plan*, Vol. III, Ch. 'Urban Infrastructure, Housing, Basic Services and Poverty Alleviation'.

*Frontline*, 6 November 2009.

*Frontline*, 7 May 2010.

*Frontline*, 7 May 2010 also 6 November, 2009, 'Flawed Operation'.

*Frontline*, 27 August 2010, Suhrid Sankar Chattopadhyay, 'Resisting Maoists'.

Mahadevia, Darshini, 'Urban Land Market and Access to the Poor', in *Urban Poverty Report*, 2009.

Mehra, Ajay K. (ed.), *Emerging Trends in Indian Politics: 'The 15*th *General Election*, New Delhi, Routledge, 2010. Articles by Jyoti Srivastava. 'Contemporary Indian Politics and the Corporate Sector' and Girijesh Pant, 'Diaspora in Indian Politics: Issues before the 15th General Election'.

*Mid-Term Appraisal of 10th Five-Year Plan*, June 2005.

Muchkund, Dubey, 'School Education, a Constraint to the Sustainability of Growth Rate in India', in Manmohan Agarwal (Ed.) *India's Economic Future ,Education, Technology, Energy and Environment,* New Delhi, Social Science Press, 2009.

Muralidharan, Sukumar, 'Media: Stenographer to Power'.

NCEUS, Government of India, The Challenge of Employment in India, An Informal Economy Perspective.

Ninan, T.N., 'The Newspaper Capital of the World', in *Business Standard, India 2009*, New Delhi, B.S. Books, 2009.

Planning Commission, Annual Report, 2009-10.

Sankar, T.L., 'India's Energy Crisis: Threat or Opportunity' in S. Mahendra Dev and N. Chandrasekhar Rao (eds.), *India: Perspectives on Equitable Development*, New Delhi, Academic Foundation, 2009.

Seminar, February 2010, 'Symposium on Climate Change Conundrum', esp. Sanjay Joshi, 'The Shaping of Discourse'.

**Selected Bibliography**

Singh, D.P., 'Poverty and Migration: Does Moving Help' in India Urban Poverty Report 2009, New Delhi, OUP, 2009.

*South Asia Politics*, October 2010, Madhumita, 'Naxalism-Development or Discontent: A study in Jharkhand'.

*Tenth Five-year Plan*, 2002-2007, Vol. 1.

The World Bank, *India's Employment Challenge, Creating Jobs, Helping Workers*, New Delhi, World Bank OUP, 2010.

# Laws Mentioned in the Text

**Laws Mentioned in the Text**

## Laws Mentioned in the Text

# Table of Cases

*A.P. S. R. T.C.* v. *Pochaiah and Another*, Supreme Court of India, pp. 976–977, LLJ, Vol. 2, 1999

*A.B.C Ltd Durgapur, Burdwan* v. *Radha Gobinda Ghatak and Others*, High Court of Calcutta, pp. 686–694, LLJ, Vol. 1, 2000

*A.P. Foods* v. *S. Samuel and Others*, Supreme Court of India, pp. 18–22, LLJ, Vol. 3, 2006

*Adani Agri, Logistics Ltd and Another* v. *State of Haryana and Others*, High Court of Punjab and Haryana, pp. 307–312, LLJ, January 2011

*Adarsh Gupta* v. *State of Haryana and Others*, High Court of Punjab and Haryana, pp. 751–756, LLJ, June 2010

*Ahmadabad (P) Primary Teachers Association* v. *Administrative Officer*, Supreme Court of India, p. 596, LLJ, Vol. 1, 2004

*Ahmedabad Industrial and Other Employees' Union* v. *State of Gujarat*, High Court of Gujarat, pp. 1424–1438, LLJ, Vol. 1, 2000

*Air India Employees Guild* v. *Air India Ltd and Others,* and *Air India Employees Union* v. *Air India and Another*, High Court of Bombay, pp. 666–670, LLJ, Vol. 1, 2006

*Airport Authority of India* v. *Indian Airports Kamgar Union*, High Court of Bombay, pp. 211–223, LLJ, January 2011

*Airports Authority of India, Mumbai* v. *Indian Airports Kamgar Union and Others*, High Court of Bombay, pp. 211–223, LLJ, January 2011

*All India Central Government Health Scheme Employees' Association, Nagpur and Another v. Union of India and Others*, High Court of Bombay, pp. 798–799, LLJ, Vol. 1, 2006

*All India General Mazdoor Trade Union (Regd)* v. *Delhi Administratiion and Others*, Supreme Court of India, pp. 101–103, LLJ, Vol. 3, 1999

*All India State Bank of Indore Officers Coordination Committee* v. *State Bank of Indore*, High Court of Madhya Pradesh, pp. 859–861, LLJ, September 2010

*All India Trade Union Congress* v. *Deputy Registrar of Trade Unions and Others*, High Court of Bombay, pp. 398–400, LLJ, Vol. 4, 2006

*Allied Industries* v. *Mool Chand and Another*, High Court of Rajasthan, pp. 737–742, LLJ, Vol. 3, 2007

*Aluminium Industries Ltd., Hyderabad v. Industrial Tribunal, Hyderabad and Others*, High Court of Andhra Pradesh, pp.16–20, LLJ, Vol. 1, 2006

*Amal Kanti Bose* v. *West Bengal State Cooperative Bank Ltd and Others*, High Court of Calcutta, pp. 171–176, LLJ, Vol. 2, 2000

*Amar Singh H.B. and Others* v. *Karnataka State Road Transport Corporation, Bangalore and Others*, High Court of Karnataka, pp. 386–388, LLJ, August 2010

## Table of Cases

*Amar Singh* v. *Himachal Pradesh State Electricity Board and Others*, High Court of Himachal Pradesh, pp. 34–38, LLJ, January 2011

*American Refrigerator Co. Ltd* v. *First industrial Tribunal, West Bengal and Others*, High Court of Calcutta, pp. 271–275, LLJ, Vol. 2, 2006

*Anant Constructiion Co.* v. *Government Labour Officer and Inspector*, Supreme Court of India, pp. 738–740, LLJ, Vol. 4, Supp. 2006

*Andhra Bank through Regional Manager* v. *Industrial Tribunal- cum- Labour Court and Another,* Supreme Court of India, pp. 957–959, LLJ, Vol. 2, 2008

*Andhra Bank, Vishakhapatanam* v. *Industrial Tribunal-cum- Labour Court and Another*, Supreme Court of India, pp. 957-759, LLJ, Vol. 2, 2008

*Andhra Pradesh State Forest Development Corporation Ltd Employees' Union* v. *Government of Andhra Pradesh, Environment, Forests, Science and Technology Department and Another,* High Court of Andhra Pradesh, pp. 1002–1003, LLJ, Vol. 1, 2001

*Anil Kumar Jaggi* v. *Industrial Tribunal–Cum–LabourCourt, Chandigarh and Another*, High Court of Punjab and Haryana, pp. 193–199, LLJ, Vol. 1, July 2010

*Anoop Sharma* v. *Executive Engineer, Public Health Division, Panipat (Haryana),* Supreme Court of India, pp.1–9, LLJ, July 2010

*Anthony Raj* v. *A. Shanmugam and Others*, High Court of Madras, pp. 1208–1223, LLJ, Vol. 2, 1995

*ANZ Grindlays Bank* v. *General Secretary, Grindlays Bank Employees Union and Others,* High Court of Bombay, pp. 1238–1241, LLJ, Vol. 1, 2001

*Arora Combines* v. *Damaji Ganpat Mankav and Another*, High Court of Bombay, pp. 533–534, LLJ, August 2010

*Ashok Leyland Ltd Ennore* v. *Industrial Tribunal, Madras and Another*, High Court of Madras, pp. 1234–1247, LLJ, Vol. 1, 2000

*Ashok Tiwari* v. *M.P. Text Book Corporation and Another*, High Court of Madhya Pradesh, pp. 589–595, LLJ, November 2010

*Association of Engineering Workers* v. *Dockyard Labour Union and Others*, Supreme Court of India, pp. 544–546, Supreme Court Cases, 1995, Supp.

*Association of Engineering Workers* v. *V. K. Date and Others*, High Court of Bombay, pp. 625–627, LLJ, Vol. 2, 2006

*Atul Glass Industries Ltd* v. *State of Haryana and Others*, High Court of Punjab and Haryana, pp. 164–171, LLJ, Vol. 4, 2006

*Avinash Anant Vaidya* v. *Regional Provident Funds Commissioner, Thane and Others*, High Court of Bombay, pp. 489–493, LLJ, Vol. 1, 2006

*Avtec Ltd, Power Product Division, Poonapally, Hosur* v. *Suptd. of Police, Krishnagiri Distt and Others*, High Court of Madras, p. 784, LLJ, Vol. 3, 2009 (NOC)

*Bagalkot Cement Company Workers Union* v. *Management of Kanoria Industrial Ltd*, High Court of Karnataka, pp. 656–662, LLJ, Vol. 3, 2006

*Bageshwar Maurya* v. *Management, Naveen Projects (P) Ltd* High Court of Delhi, pp. 317–320, LLJ, July 2010

*Bangalore Hospital Bangalore* v. *Workmen of Bangalore Hospital*, High Court of Karnatka, pp. 661–665, LLJ, Vol. 1, 2009

*Bank of India and others* v. *K. Mohandas and Others*, Supreme Court of India, pp. 609–623, LLJ, Vol. 1, 2009

*Bank of Maharashtra* v. *Bank of Maharashtra Karamchari Sangh*, High Court of Bombay, pp. 579–589, LLJ, Vol. 1, 2009

*Best Workers Union and Another* v. *Best Undertaking and Another*, High Court of Bombay, pp. 1058–1061, LLJ, Vol. 1, 2008

*Bhanwar Lal Solanki* v. *State of Rajasthan and Others*, High Court of Rajasthan, pp. 909–911, LLJ, Vol. 3, 2008

*Bharat Petroleum Corporation Ltd and Another* v. *State and Others*, High Court of Calcutta, pp. 603–605, LLJ, Vol. 3, 2007

*Bharat Seats Employees' Union* v. *Specified Authority Under S.25N of the ID Act and Another*, High Court of Punjab and Haryana, pp. 87–92, LLJ, October 2010

*Bhogpur Coop. Sugar Mills Ltd* v. *Harmesh Kumar*, Supreme Court of India, pp. 488–490, LLJ, Vol. 1, 2007

*Biddle Sawyer Ltd* v. *Chemical Employees' Union*, High Court of Bombay, pp. 749–757, LLJ, Vol. 3, 2009

*Birla Tyres Workers Union* v. *Industrial Tribunal, Orissa, Bhubaneshwar and Others,* High Court of Orissa, p. 762, LLJ, Vol. 2, 2009 (NOC)

*Bisumal Nagraj Oswal (Jain)* v. *Kunda Ashok Shinde and Others*, High Court of Bombay, pp. 1382–1386, LLJ, Vol. 3, 2000

*Board of Trustees of Chennai Port Trust, Chennai* v. *Asstt. Labour Commissioner and Another*, High Court of Madras, pp. 544–552, LLJ, November 2010

*Bombay Hospital Trust and Another* v. *Dr. Shailesh Hathi and Another*, High court of Bombay, pp. 679–684, LLJ, Vol. 4, 2006

*Bombay Labour Union* v. *Bhartiya Arogya Nidhi and Others*, High Court of Bombay, pp. 783–785, LLJ, December 2010

*Borosil Glass Works Ltd. Employees Union* v. *D.D. Bambode and Others*, Supreme Court of India, pp. 171–173, LLJ, Vol. 1, 2001

*Branch Manager Oriental Bank of Commerce, Karimnagar* v. *Shaik Madar and Others*, High Court of Andhra Pradesh, pp. 705–711, LLJ, September 2010

*Bridge and Roof Co. (India) Ltd* v. *Union of India*, Supreme Court of India, LLJ, Vol. 2, 1965

*Brittania Industries Ltd* v. *Maharashtra General Kamgar Union and Another*, High Court of Bombay, pp. 275–301, LLJ, Vol. 3, 2009

*Carona Ltd* v. *Sitaram Atmaram Ghag and Others*, High Court of Bomaby, pp. 296–304, LLJ, Vol. 2, 2000

*Cement Corporation Employees Union* v. *Union of India and Others*, High Court of Madhya Pradesh, pp. 347–356, LLJ, Vol. 2, 2009

*CFFP Employees Association (AITUC) and Another* v. *Chairman and Managing Director and Others*, Supreme Court of India, pp. 685–686, Supreme Court Cases, 1995 Supp. (3)

*Chanchal Kumar Tiwari and Others* v. *Hari Shankar and Others,* High Court of Allahabad, pp. 581–587, LLJ, February 2011

*Chandra Pal Shukla* v. *Labour Court (V) Kanpur and Others*, High Court of Allahabad, pp. 588–589, LLJ, Vol. 2, 2007

*Chandra Shekhar* v. *State of Haryana and Others*, High Court of Punjab and Haryana, pp. 855–859, LLJ, September 2010

*Chandrika K.* v. *Indian Red Cross Society and Another*, High Court of Delhi, pp. 289–299, LLJ, Vol. 1, 2007

## Table of Cases

*Chemplant Employees' Union* v. *Government of Tamilnadu*, High Court of Madras, pp. 824–826, LLJ, June 2010

*Chemplast Sanmar Ltd* v. *Mettur Chemicals Podhu Thozilalar Sangam and Another*, High Court of Madras, pp. 1335–1340, LLJ, Vol. 1, 2000

*Chhote Shukla @ Vijay Kumar Shukla* v. *State of Bihar and Others*, High Court of Patna, pp. 1018–1019, LLJ, Vol. 2, 2007

*Cipla Employees' Union and Others* v. *Cipla Ltd* High Court of Bombay, pp. 577–583, LLJ, Vol. 3, 2007

*CIPLA Ltd*, v. *Anand Ganapat Patil and Others*, High Court of Bombay, pp. 377–388, LLJ, Vol. 2, 2008

*Cochin Mazdoor Sangh* v. *Bobby*, High Court of Kerala, pp. 702–707, LLJ, Vol. 3, 2006

*Cochin Shipyard Ltd* v. *Iqbal*, High Court of Kerala, pp. 1095–1099, LLJ, Vol. 2, 2006

*Consumer Education and Research Centre and Others* v. *Union of India and Others*, Supreme Court of India, pp. 768–789, LLJ, Vol. 2, 1995

*Crescent Catalyst and Chemicals* v. *Employees' State Insurance Corp., Hyderabad,* High Court of Andhra Pradesh, pp. 147–154, LLJ, Vol. 3, 2007

*D. D. Gears Ltd* v. *Secretary (Labour) and Others*, High Court of Delhi, pp. 387–393, LLJ, Vol. 4, Supp. 2006

*D. Hanumantha Rao* v. *A. P. State Agro Industries Development Corporation Ltd*, High Court of Andhra Pradesh, pp. 96–98, LLJ, Vol. 4, 2009

*D'Souza R.G.* v. *Poona Employees Union*, High Court of Bombay, pp. 466–471, LLJ, Vol. 3, 2009

*Dalmia Cement (Bharat) Ltd* v. *Regional Provident Funds Commissioner*, High Court of Madras, p. 257–263, LLJ, Vol. 1, 2009

*Damodaran P. and Others* v. *M. K Krishnan Kutty*, High Court of Kerala, pp. 407–408, LLJ, Vol. 3, 2006

*Davendra Sahu* v. *Industrial Tribunal–Labour Court, Vishakhapatanam and Another*, High Court of Andhra Pradesh, pp. 466–470, LLJ, Vol. 3, 2008

*Deccan Merchant Corporation Bank Ltd* v. *Avdhoot Marutrao Rane and Another*, High Court of Bombay, pp. 40–41, LLJ, Vol. 2, 2008

*Deendayalam S. and Other* v. *Chairman, Port Trust, Chennai and Others*, High Court of Madras, pp. 776–777, LLJ, Vol. 2, 2007

*Delhi Transport Corporation* v. *Harpal Singh*, High Court of Delhi, pp. 475–487, LLJ, Vol. 2, 2006

*Dena Bank* v. *D. Kundalia and Another*, High Court of Bombay, pp. 682–686, LLJ, June 2010

*Deonath Majhi* v. *Central Coalfields Ltd,* High Court of Jharkhand, pp. 757–758, LLJ, Vol. 2, 2009 (NOC)

*Deputy Director, ESI Corp., Hyderabad* v. *Amrutanjan Ltd, Hyderabad and Others*, High Court of Andhra Pradesh, pp. 16 7–179, LLJ, Vol. 4, 2009

*Deputy Regional Director* v. *Virgilio Velho*, High Court of Bombay, pp. 355–364, LLJ, Vol. 2, 2000

*Dhananjay Kumar Singh* v. *State of Bihar and Others*, High Court of Patna, pp. 759–760, LLJ, December 2010

*Dhirendra Nath Purkait* v. *State of West Bengal and Others*, High Court of Calcutta, pp. 685–687, LLJ, Vol. 1, 2009

*Dholpur Kraya Vikraya Sahkari Samiti Ltd* v. *Controller, Under Payment of Gratuity Act, Bharatpur and Others*, High Court of Rajasthan, pp. 663–664, LLJ, Vol. 1, 2000

*Director, Food and Supplies, Punjab and Another* v. *Gurmit Singh*, Supreme Court of India, pp 813–815, LLJ, Vol. 2, 2007

*Divisional Forest Officer (SFP), Hisar* v. *Bharat Singh @ Bharta and Another*, High Court of Punjab and Haryana, pp. 268–271, LLJ, Vol. 3, 2009

*Dr. Mrs. Hemlata Saraswat* v. *State of Rajasthan and Others*, High Court of Rajasthan, pp. 423–429, LLJ, Vol. 3, 2008

*Dutta (Hiramanya Datta)* v. *State of Jharkhand and Another*, High Court of Jharkhand, pp. 561–564, LLJ, August 2010

*Emson Radio Corporation and Another*, v. *Secretary (Labour), Government of NCT, Delhi and Another*, High Court of Delhi, pp. 140–142, LLJ, Vol. 1, 2007

*Escorts Heart Institute and Research Centre Ltd* v. *Delhi Mazdoor Sangathan Regd. and Others*, High Court of Delhi, pp. 366–368

*ESI Corporation Indore* v. *Siara (Smt) and Another*, High Court of Madhya Pradesh, pp. 394–397, LLJ, Vol. 2, 1999

*ESI Corporation* v. *Sainaba* High Court of Kerala, pp. 320–323, LLJ, Vol. 1, 2006

*ESIC* v. *ESIC Officers Association and Others* High Court of Bombay, pp. 383–384, LLJ, Vol. 2, 2006

*Essel Mining Industries Ltd and Another* v. *Union of India* High Court of Orissa, pp. 316–324, LLJ, Vol. 2, 1989

*F D C Ltd* v. *Union of India*, High Court of Delhi, pp. 413–417, LLJ, Vol. 2, 2007

*Factory Manager, CIMMCO Wagon Factory* v. *Virendra Kumar Sharma and Another*, Supreme Court of India, pp.773–775, LLJ, Vol. 2, 2000

*Franco–Indian Pharmaceuticals Pvt. Ltd* v. *Franco Indian Workers Union*, High Court of Bombay, pp. 335–357, LLJ, Vol. 12, 2006

*G. B. Pant University of Agriculture and Technology, Nainital* v. *State of Uttar Pradesh and Others*, Supreme Court of India, pp. 1109–1115, LLJ, Vol. 2, 2000

*G.M. Singareni Collieries Co. Ltd* v. *Presiding officer, Industrial Court –1, Hyderabad and Another*, High Court of Andhra Pradesh, pp. 760–762, LLJ, Vol. 2, 2006

*Ganeshwar Ltd* v. *Sugar Mills Mazdoor Sangh and Another*, Supreme Court of India, pp. 750–751, LLJ, Vol. 4, 2006

*Gannon Dunkerley and Co. Ltd* v. *State of Madhya Pradesh and Others*, High Court of Madhya Pradesh, pp. 809–818, LLJ, June 2010

*Gen Secy. Karnataka Karya Niratha Pathrakarthara Sangha, Bangalore* v. *Gen. Manager, Printers (Mysore) Projavani and Deccan Herald, Banglore,* High Court of Karnataka, pp. 513–521, LLJ, Vol. 1, 2006

*General Manager, Karnataka Bank Ltd, Mangalore* v. *Ashok Kumar and Others*, High Court of Karnataka, pp. 506–508, LLJ, August 2010

*General Manager, Punjab and Sind Bank and Others* v. *Daya Singh*, Supreme Court of India, pp. 255–261, LLJ, January 2011

*General Manger, EID Parry (India) Ltd, Rampet* v. *Presiding Officer, Labour Court and Others*, High Court of Madras, pp. 757–769, LLJ, Vol. 1, 1995

*General Secretary BEST Workers Union, Mumbai* v. *General Manager BEST Undertaking and Another*, High Court of Bombay, pp. 924–928, LLJ, Vol. 3, 2006

*German Remedies Ltd* v. *Presiding Office*, *Labour Court, Bhopal*, High Court of Madhya Pradesh, pp. 8–13, LLJ, Vol. 2, 2006

*Gokulesh Petroleum (P.) Ltd* v *Himalaya R. Shah,* High Court of Gujarat, pp. 1254–1261, LLJ, Vol. 1, 2000

*Goltumukkala Appala Narsimha Raju and others* v. *National Insurance Co. Ltd.*, Supreme Court of India, pp. 531–536, LLJ, Vol. 2, 2007

*Good Year India Ltd* v. *D. N. Trickchija and Another*, High Court of Punjab and Haryana, pp. 476–486, LLJ, August 2010

*Gordon Woodroffe and Staff Union* v. *Joint Commissioner of Labour, Madras and Another*, High Court of Madras, pp. 1150–1168, LLJ, Vol. 2, 2000

*Government of Andhra Pradesh and Others* v. *Jaya Prasad Rao and Others*, Supreme Court of India, pp. 2030–2045, *A I R Supreme Court Weekly*, 17 April 2007

*Govt of N CT of Delhi* v. *Rita Luthra and Others*, High Court of Delhi, pp. 19–23, LLJ, October 2010

*Gujarat Agricultural University* v. *All Gujarat Kamdar Karamchari Union*, Supreme Court of India, pp. 382–391, LLJ, Vol. 4, 2009

*Gujarat Ambuja Cement Pvt Ltd* v. *U.B. Gadhe*, High Court of Gujarat, pp. 897, LLJ, Vol. 4, Supp 2006 (NOC)

*Gujarat State Fertilizers and Chemicals Ltd and Another* v. *Industrial Tribunal and Another*, High Court of Gujarat, pp. 225–238, LLJ, January 2011

*Gujarat State Road Transport Corp.* v. *Narmadashanhanker G. Joshi*, High Court of Gujarat, p. 1033 (NOC), LLJ, Vol. 4, 2006

*Gujarat Water Supply and Sewage Board and Another* v. *Bipin Chandra N. Ramanuj*, High Court of Gujarat, pp. 84–86, LLJ, January 2011

*Gurjeet Singh Bhatia* v. *Management of Narang International Hotel (P) Ltd*, High Court of Delhi, pp. 403–404, LLJ, Vol. 1, 2007

*H.P. State Electricity Board and Another* v. *Ranjeet Singh and Others*, Supreme Court of India, pp. 629–632, LLJ, Vol. 2, 2008

*Haria Ginning and Pressing Factory* v. *Manilatdar and Others*, High Court of Gujarat, pp. 104–108, LLJ, Vol. 1, 2008

*Haryana Land Reclamation and Development Corporation Ltd* v. *Pawan Kumar*, High Court of Punjab and Haryana, pp. 1198–1204, LLJ, Vol. 2, 1994

*Hasanpur Chini Mill Mazdoor Union* v. *State of Bihar*, High Court of Patna, pp. 927–930., LLJ, Vol. 2, 2008

*Hayat Khan* v. *Dy Labour Commissioner, Belgaum and Others*, High Court of Karnataka, pp. 101–104, LLJ, Vol. 4, 2006

*Hayat Khan* v. *DyLabour Commissioner, Regional office, Belgaum and Others*, High Court of Karnataka, pp. 284–288, LLJ, Vol. 1, 2008

*Himachal Pradesh State Electricity Board and Others* v. *KrishanDutt,* High Court of Himachal Pradesh, pp. 115–119, LLJ, January 2011

*Hindi Vidya Bhawan and Others* v. *Presiding Officer, School Tribunal, Mumbai and Others*, High Court of Bombay, pp. 138–152, LLJ, Vol. 2, 2008

*Hindustan Aeronautics Ltd* v. *State of U.P. and Others*, High Court of Allahabad, pp. 340–343, LLJ, Vol. 2, 1993

*Hindustan Coca Cola Bottling S / W. P. Ltd and Another* v. *Narayan Rawal and Others,* High Court of Bombay, pp. 502–510, LLJ, Vol. 2, 2001

*Hindustan Lever Ltd* v. *Hindustan Lever Employees' Union*, High Court of Bombay, pp. 804–825, LLJ, Vol. 2, 1999

*Hindustan Lever Ltd, Bombay,* v. *B. N. Dongre*, Supreme Court of India, Reported in 1994 III SC. 141 and *Cases on Indian Labour Law*, Vol. 1, New Delhi, Friedrich Ebert Stiftung, 1995, pp. 466–502.

*Hindustan Machine Tools Ltd, Ajmer* v. *Labour Court and Another*, High Court of Rajasthan, pp. 1219–1224, LLJ, Vol. 2, 1993

*HLL Life Care Ltd* v. *Hindustan Latex Labour Union, (AITUC) and Another*, High Court of Kerala, pp. 811–815, LLJ, September 2010

*Hotel Hindustan Karamchari Union* v. *Hotel Hindustan and Others,* High Court of Calcutta, pp. 747–752, LLJ, Vol. 1, 2009

*I.T.I. Ltd and Others* v. *Venugopalan and Others*, High Court of Karnataka, pp. 77–87, LLJ, July 2010

*Indian Airlines Technical Assistants Union, Hyderabad* v. *Chairman and Managing Director, Indian Airlines (H.Q.) and Others*, High Court of Andhra Pradesh, pp. 578–582, LLJ, Vol. 1, 1995

*Indian Couneil for Enviro-legal Action and Others* v. *Union of India*, Supreme Court of India, pp. 212–252, Supreme Court Cases, Vol. 3, 1996

*Indian Oil Corporation* v. *Presiding Officer, Central Government Industrial Tribunal and Others*, High Court of Gauhati, pp. 597–603, LLJ, Vol. 2, 2007

*Indian Overseas Bank* v. *Workmen, All India Indian Overseas Bank Employees' Union*, Supreme Court of India, pp. 253–257, LLJ, Vol. 2, 2006

*Indian Potash Ltd* v. *State of Assam and Others*, High Court of Gauhati, pp. 673–677, LLJ, Vol. 1, 2009

*Indian Rare Earths Ltd and Another* v. *Pramod Chandra Panigrahi and Others*, Supreme Court of India, pp.1080–1082, LLJ, Vol. 1, 2006

*IPCL Employees' Association and Another* v. *Indian Petrochemicals Corporation Ltd*, High Court of Gujarat, pp. 399–424, LLJ, Vol. 1, 2009

*ITI Ltd and Others* v. *Venugopalan N. and Others*, High Court of Karnataka, pp. 77–87, LLJ, July 2010

*J.V. Sudhakar* v. *Government of Andhra Pradesh rep. by its Prinicpal Secretary and Others*, High Court of Andhra Pradesh, pp. 540–549, LLJ, February 2011

*Jaipur Development Authority* v. *Ram Sahai and Another*, Supreme Court of India, pp. 429–434, LLJ, Vol. 1, 2007

*Janta Shikshan Prasarak Mandal, Pusad and Another* v. *Industrial Court,Yavatmal and Others,* High Court of Bombay, pp.114–118, LLJ, July 2010

*Jaswinder Singh* v. *Regional Manager, Punjab National Bank, Karnal and Another*, High Court of Punjab and Haryana, pp. 702–704, LLJ, September 2010

*Jaya Prakash and Another* v. *Supt. of Police*, High Court of Kerala, pp, 995–997, LLJ, Vol. 2, 2006

*Jayapandi T.* v. *State Express Transport Corp. Ltd and Others*, High Court of Madras, p.744 (Brief Resume), LLJ, Vol. 2009

*Jeychandran K.* v. *Special Officer, V. Kurumtapatti Agriculatural Coop. Bank and Others*, High Court of Madras, pp. 609–610, LLJ, Vol. 2, 2006

*Joginder Chand* v. *Punjab Electricity Board*, High Court of Panjab and Haryana, pp. 113–115, LLJ, Vol. 1994

*Jyothi Ademma* v. *Plant Manager, Nellore*, Supreme Court of India, pp. 324–326, LLJ, Vol. 3, 2006

*K. Narayanaswamy* v. *Government of Tamilnadu and Others*, High Court of Madras, pp. 437–439, LLJ, February 2011

*Kamath K. V.* v. *Labour Enforcement Officer (Central), Kolkata*, High Court of Calcutta, pp. 936–939, LLJ, Vol. 1, 2007

*Kanhaiya Lal* v. *State of Rajasthan and Others*, High Court of Rajasthan, pp. 474–488, LLJ, Vol. 1994

*Kanta Kumari Banfal (Smt.) and Others* v. *RICO and Others*, High Court of Rajasthan, p. 795, (NOC), LLJ, Vol. 3, 2009

*Kanwar Singh Mawai* v. *Anoop Singh Tomar and Others*, High Court of Madhya Pradesh, pp. 128–134, LLJ, Vol. 1, 2009

*Karnataka State Road Transport Corporation, Bangalore* v. *S.D. Bandi*, High Court of Karnataka, pp. 352–356, LLJ, Vol. 4, 2006 Supplement

*Kathal R.K.* v. *Registrar of Trade Union and Others,* High Court of Madhya Pradesh, pp. 642–651, LLJ, Vol. 3, 2008

*Kay Kay Embroideries Pvt. Ltd* v. *Cloth Markets and Shops Board and Others*, High Court of Bombay, pp. 865–901, LLJ, Vol. 1, 2007

*Kerala Electrical and A E O Ltd* v. *Leemns D'Cruze*, High Court of Kerala, p.104, LLJ, Vol. 2, 2009,

*Kerala State Civil Supplies Corporation* v. *Industrial Tribunal*, High Court of Kerala, pp. 884–887, LLJ, Vol. 2, 2007

*Khalid A. Hakim* v. *Asstt. Commissioner of Labour and Others,* High Court of Gujarat, pp. 431–444, LLJ, Vol. 4, 2009

*Khandu Krishna Bhogade* v. *Kalyani Steel Ltd and Others*, High Court of Bombay, pp. 314–318, LLJ, Vol. 2, 1995

*Khetriya Sri Gandhi Ashram, Gorakhpur* v. *Dy. Labour Commissioner /Preseribed Authority and Another*, High Court of Allahabad, pp. 866–870, LLJ, Vol. 4, 2009

*Kishori Lal Verma* v. *Hindustan Zinc Ltd and Another*, High Court of Rajasthan, pp. 327–336, *Factories Journal Reports*, Vol. 87, Part 12, 1995

*Kolandhayee* v *Deputy Commissioner of Labour (Commissioner for W.C. Act)*, High Court of Madras, pp.768–773, LLJ, September 2010

*Krantikari Kamgar Union* v. *Labour and Enforcement Officer, Dadra and Nagar Haveli and Others,* High Court of Bombay, pp. 17–22, LLJ, Vol. 1, 2009

*Krishnakutty Nair P.B* v. *Regional Director, ESI Corporation and Another*, Supreme Court of India, pp. 997–1000, LLJ, Vol. 2, 2008

*Krishnendu Narayan Ghosh* v. *Union of India and Others*, High Court of Calcutta, pp. 1543–1556, LLJ, Vol. 1, 2000

*Kumaon Mandal Vikas Nigam Ltd.* v. *Girija Shankar Pant and Others*, Supreme Court of India, pp. 583–594, LLJ, Vol. 1, 2001

*Ladaku Mazdoor Sangh* v. *Tata Communications Ltd*, High Court of Bombay, p. 53, LLJ, February 2011

*Laxmibai K.* v. *Provident Funds Commissioner, Hyderabad,* High Court of Andhra Pradesh, pp. 27–32, LLJ, Vol. 1, 2006

*Lohia Machines (LML) Karamchari Sangh and Others* v. *Registrar, Trade Unions and Others,* High Court of Allahabad, pp. 29–36, LLJ, Vol. 2, 2009

*Lokesh Kumar Pareek and Another* v. *State of Rajasthan and Another,* High Court of Rajasthan, pp. 1219–1221, LLJ, Vol. 1, 1993

*M. Gopalakrishnaiah* v. *Union of India and Another*, High Court of Delhi, pp. 933–947, LLJ, Vol. 2, 1995

*Madheswaran A.* v. *State of Tamilnadu represented by the Secretary to the Government, Handlooms, Handicrafts, Textiles and Khadi Crafts Deptt. Chennai,* High Court of Madras, pp. 28–40, LLJ, Vol. 1, 2007

*Madhukar G. Wagh* v. *Union of India, Secretary, Deptt. of Atomic Energy, Mumbai and Another*, High Court of Bombay, pp. 359–370, LLJ, February 2011

*Madras Labour Union* v. *Binny Ltd. (Backingham and Carnatie Mills) and Others*, High Court of Madras, pp. 516–601, *Indian Factories Journal* and *Factories Journal Reports* Vol. 89, parts 17, 19, 1996

*Mahanagar Telecom Nigam Ltd* v. *M. Nikam and Others High Court* of Bombay, pp. 597–599, LLJ, August 2010

*Maharashtra General Kamgar Union* v. *State of Maharashtra and Others*, High Court of Bombay, pp. 841–844

*Maheswari* v. *Tamilnadu Manual Labour Social Security Board Chennai and Others,* High Court of Madras, pp. 963–968, LLJ, Vol. 2, 2007

*Mahindra Gujarat Traetor Ltd, Gujarat* v. *Shabana w/o Abdul Rauf Pathan and Others,* High Court of Bombay, pp. 445–448, LLJ, November 2010

*Mala Bhandari Dr. (Mrs.)* v. *Authority under Delhi Shops and Establishments Act and Another,* High Court of Delhi, pp. 464–466, LLJ, Vol. 2, 2007

*Malla C. N.* v. *State of Jammu and Kashmir and Others*, Supreme Court of India, pp. 667–669, LLJ, Vol. 4, 2009

*Management 2 of Madura Cement Pvt. Ltd* v. *Presiding officer, Principal Labour Court, Madurai and Others*, High Court of Bombay, pp. 955–959, LLJ, Vol. 3, 2006

*Management of APSRTC* v. *Workmen of APSRTC and Another,* High Court of Andhra Pradesh, pp. 439–456, LLJ, Vol. 1, 2009

*Management of Cipla Ltd* v. *R. Jaya Kumar*, p. 503, Yearly Supreme Court Civil Digest, 1999

*Management of Coimbatore District Central Coop. Bank* v *Secretary,District Central Coop. Bank Employees Association, Coimbatore and Another,* Supreme Court of India, pp. 724–733, LLJ, Vol. 2, 2007

*Management of D.C. Diwan Mohideen Beedi Factory, Salem* v. *Appellate Authority, Beedi and Cigar Workers (Conditions of Employment) Act, 1966, Labour officer, Salem and Others*, High Court of Madras, pp. 616–622, LLJ, Vol. 1, 2009

*Management of Dayang Tea Estate* v. *Secretary, Assam Chah Karamchari Sangha,* High Court of Gauhati, pp. 622–626, LLJ, September 2010

*Management of Hardy Exploration and Production, India Inc.* v. *Presiding Officer, II Additional Labour Court, Chennai and Others*, Madras High Court, pp. 553–554, LLJ, Vol. 3, 2009

*Management of Hotel Samrat* v. *Government of NCT and Others,* High Court of Delhi, pp. 950–956, LLJ, Vol. 2, 2007
*Management of Jyothi Home Industries and Others* v. *State of Karnataka and Others,* High Court of Karnataka, pp. 596–609, LLJ, Vol. 1, 2000
*Management of KSRTC Through Chief Law Officer* v. *R. Krishna Reddy,* Supreme Court of India, pp. 231–235, LLJ, Vol. 1, 2007
*Management of Premier Mills Ltd* v. *Labour Court, Coimbatore and Others*, High Court of Madras, pp. 757–761, LLJ, June 2010
*Management of Salem District Cooperative Milk Producers Union Ltd* v. *Industrial Tribunal and Another*, High Court of Madras, pp. 436–438, LLJ, August 2010
*Management of Thekkalur Primary Coop. Bank (K–2019) represented by President* v. *Asstt. Commissioner of Labour, Combatore and Others,* High Court of Madras, pp. 610–615, LLJ, Vol. 2, 2006
*Management, Broadcasting Corp. of India, Chennai* v. *Presiding Officer, Central Government Labour Court, Chennai and Another,* High Court of Madras, pp. 541–544, LLJ, August 2010
*Management, Seyadu Beedi Co. Tirunelveli* v. *Appellate Authority, Payment of Gratuity Act* and *Another,* High Court of Madras, pp. 35–38, LLJ, Vol. 3, 2009
*Management, Essorpe Mills Ltd* v. *Presiding officer, Labour Court and Others,* Supreme Court of India, pp. 614–618, LLJ, Vol. 3, 2008
*Manager, Ore (India) Ltd* v. *Chandi Lal Saha and Others,* Supreme Court of India, pp. 1537–1542, LLJ, Vol. 3, 1999, Supp.
*Manager, Umashankar Agarwal* v. *Regional Labour Commissioner*, High Court of Bombay, pp. 800–804, LLJ, Vol. 1, 1993
*Managing Director, Hassan Cooperative Milk Producers' Society, Union Ltd* v. *Astt. Regional Director, ESIC,* Supreme Court of India, pp. 860–869, LLJ, June 2010
*Managing Director, Kannad Sahkari Sakhar Karkhana Ltd* v. *Vishwanath Jagannath Khirsagar*, High Court of Bombay, pp. 342–344, LLJ, Vol. 4, 2009
*Managing Director, Tamilnadu State Transport Corporation* v. *Ezhilarasan and Another*, High Court of Madras, pp. 151–154, LLJ, Vol. 3, 2009
*Mangatu J. Verghese* v. *Daulatram Dyeing and Bleaching Mills*, Bombay, High Court of Bombay, pp. 421–426, LLJ, Vol. 1, 2001
*Mining Engineer, Mines and Geology Deptt.* v. *Malu Ram and Another*, High Court of Rajasthan p.854 (NOC), LLJ, Vol. 4, 2006
*Mishra Dhatu Nigam Ltd., Hyderabad* v. *Industrial Tribunal Andhra Pradesh, Hyderabad and Another,* High Court of Andhra Pradesh, pp. 1189–1194, LLJ, Vol. 3, 1999, Supp.
*Mohd. Ibrahim* v. *State of U.P. and Others*, High Court of Allahabad, p. 827 (NOC), LLJ, Vol. 3, 2009
*Morinda Sugar Mills Ltd* v. *Morinda Cooperative Sugar Mills Workers Union,* Supreme Court of India, pp. 559–563, LLJ, Vol. 3, 2006
*MRF United Workers Union represented by its General Secretary, Arakkonam* v. *Government of Tamilnadu represented by its Secretary, Labour and Employment Deptt and Others,* High Court of Madras, pp. 685–699, LLJ, Vol. 4, 2009
*Ms. Bakarupanda Padmavathi* v. *Bank of India*, High Court of Andhra Pradesh, pp. 463–466, LLJ, Vol. 3, 2008

*Mukand Ltd* v. *Mukand Stafff and Officers' Association and Others,* High Court of Bombay, pp. 1583–1602, LLJ, Vol. 1, 2000

*Municipal Academy of Higher Education* v. *Provident Funds Commissioner,* Supreme Court of India, pp. 667–671, LLJ, Vol. 2, 2008

*Muruga Home Industries* v *Employees State Insurance Corporation,* High Court of Madras, pp.590–593, LLJ, Vol. 2, 2000

*Mysore Kirloskar Mazdoor Sangh* v. *Management of Mysore Kirloskar Ltd and Others,* High Court of Karnataka, pp. 1050–1057, LLJ, Vol. 2, 2000

*Mysore Paper Mills Officers Association* v. *State of Karnataka*, High Court of Karnataka, pp. 228–230, LLJ, Vol. 2, 1995

*Mysore Wine Products and Allied Co Ltd, Bangalore* v. *Presiding Officer, Industrial Tribunal, Bangalore and Another,* High Court of Karnataka, pp. 1166–1181, LLJ, Vol. 1, 2001

*N.S. Hospital and Maternity Home, Kollam* v. *The Industrial Tribunal, Kollam and Another,* High Court of Kerala, pp. 60–62, LLJ, Vol. 1, 2001

*N.S.P. Straw and Paper Products (P) Ltd* v. *Commissioner of Labour, Gujarat State,* High Court of Gujarat, pp. 356–359, LLJ, November 2010

*Nagsrathinam A. (Deceased) and Others* v. *Commissioner, Corporation of Madurai and Others*, High Court of Madras, pp. 803–806, LLJ, September 2010

*Narmada Bachao Andolan* v. *Union of India*, Supreme Court of India, p. 1271, Supreme Court Annual Digest 2000

*National Airport Authority* v. *Sudershan Kumar and Others*, High Court of Delhi, pp. 557–562, LLJ, November 2010

*National Aviation Co.* v. *S. M. K. Khan*, Supreme Court of India, pp. 40–44, LLJ, Vol. 3, 2009

*National Council of Cement and Building Materials* v. *State of Haryana and Others,* Supreme Court of India, pp. 206–210, Supreme Court Cases Vol. 3, 1996

*National Engineering Industries Ltd* v. *State of Rajasthan,* Supreme Court of India, pp. 247–267, LLJ, Vol. 2, 2000

*National Engineering Industries Ltd* v. *State of Rajasthan and Others,* Supreme Court of India, pp. 247–267, LLJ, Vol. 1, 2000

*National Federation of Telecom Employees, (BSNL) and Another* v. *Bharat Sanchar Nigam Ltd,* High Court of Calcutta. pp. 877–881, LLJ, Vol. 2, 2007

*National India Rubber Works Ltd* v. *ESI Corporation through its Regional Director and Another,* High Court of Madhya Pradesh, pp. 1014–1017, LLJ, Vol. 3, 2007

*National Insurance Co. Ltd* v. *Mubasir Ahmed and Another,* Supreme Court of India, pp. 1035–1038, LLJ, 2007

*National Thermal Power Corporation and Others* v. *Badri Singh Thakur,* Supreme Court of India, pp. 198–208, LLJ, Vol. 1, 2009

*Navnath Kanha Naik and Ohters* v. *United Breweries Ltd and Others,* High Court of Bombay, pp. 558–569, LLJ, Vol. 2, 2009

*Nepal Chandra Das* v. *State of Tripura and Others,* High Court of Gauhati, pp. 877–879, LLJ, Vol. 2, 2008

*Neyveli Lignite Corporation and others* v. *N.L.C. Indco Serve Thozilalar Uzhiyear Sangam,* High Court of Madras, pp. 897–906, LLJ, Vol. 2, 2008

*New Horizon Sugar Mills Ltd* v. *Commissioner of Labour, Government of Puducherry and Others,* High Court of Madras, pp. 291–296, LLJ, January 2011

*New Horizon Sugar Mills Ltd represented by its Director* v. *Commissioner of Labour, Govt. of Puducherry and Others,* High Court of Madras, pp. 291–296, LLJ, January 2011

*New India Assurance Co. Ltd Vishakhapatanam* v. *T. Narsimha Murthy Raju and Another,* High Court of Andhra Pradesh, pp. 925–927, LLJ, Vol. 1, 2007

*New India Assurance Co. Ltd* v. *Narender Kumar,* High Court of Delhi, pp. 498–502, LLJ, November 2010

*Niton Industries* v. *Union of India and Others,* High Court of Bombay, pp. 151–155, LLJ, Vol. 1, 2000

*Nutrine Confectionery Co. Ltd Chittoor* v. *Government of Andhra Pradesh and Others*, High Court of Andhra Pradesh, pp. 655–659, LLJ, Vol. 1, 2000

*Om Prakash Batish* v. *Rannjit @ RanbirKaur and Others,* Supreme Court of India, pp. 599–603, LLJ, Vol. 3, 2008

*Oriental Insurance Co. Ltd* v. *Bimla Devi @ Bindu and Another,* High Court of Himachal Pradesh, pp. 457–462, LLJ, February 2011

*Orissa Power Generation Corp. Ltd* v. *Conciliation Officer–Cum–Asstt Labour Commissioner and Another*, High Court of Orissa, pp. 467–476, LLJ, February 2011

*Otis Elevator Company (India) Ltd* v. *G. S. Baj and Others,* High Court of Bombay, pp. 298–302, LLJ, Vol. 2, 2001

*P. V. K . Distillery Ltd* v. *Mahendra Ram*, Supreme Court of India, pp. 513–517, LLJ, Vol. 2, 2009

*Pan Network Ltd, Bangalore* v. *B. Balakrishna*, High Court of Karnataka, pp. 596–599, LLJ, February 2011

*Pancha Mayurakshi Cotton Mills Employees' Union and Others* v. *The State of West Bengal and Others,* High Court of Calcutta, pp. 132–138, LLJ, Vol. 1, 1996

*Parle Products Ltd* v. *Subir Mukerjee,* High Court of Calcutta, pp. 864–868, LLJ, Vol. 1, 2000

*Patel Pravin Kumar Somnath and Others* v. *Gujarat State Land Development Corporation Ltd and Others*, High Court of Gujarat, pp. 916–931, LLJ, Vol. 1, 1993

*Petroleum Employees' Union* v. *Chief Labour Commissioner (Central) and Others,* High Court of Bombay, pp. 745–748, LLJ, Vol. 4, 2009

*Pix Transmission Ltd., Nagpur* v. *State of Maharashtra and Others,* High Court of Bombay, pp. 202–203, LLJ, Vol. 3. Supp. 2000

*Pondicherry Housing Board Employees' Union and Another* v. *Government of Pondicherry and Another,* High Court of Madras, pp. 359–364, LLJ, Vol. 4, 2009

*Prakash Match Industries* v. *Employees' State Insurance Corporation,* High Court of Madras, pp. 49–52, LLJ, Vol. 2, 2000

*Presidency Jute Mills Co. Ltd* v. *Fifth Industrial Tribunal and Others,* High Court of Calcutta, pp. 564–572, LLJ, Vol. 2, 1994

*Principal, St. Sebastian Industrial Training Institute, Madras, and Another* v. *Principal Labour Court Madras and Another*, High Court of Madras, pp. 333–339, LLJ, Vol. 1, 2000

*Punjab and Sind Bank* v. *Labour Commissioner and Others,* High Court of Punjab and Haryana, pp. 841–844, LLJ, Vol. 2, 2008

*Punjab National Bank* v. *State of Bihar and Others,* High Court of Patna, pp. 760–761, LLJ, Vol. 1, 2009

*Punjab State Electricity Board and Another* v. *Industrial Tribunal and Another, Punjab and Haryana High* Court, pp. 381–385, *Factories Journal Reports*, Vol. 89, Part 12 and 13, 1996

*Purushothaman V.N.* v. *State Bank of Travancore and Others*, High Court of Kerala, pp. 635–637, LLJ, Vol. 2, 2000

*R. Pattabhi (Deceased) and Others* v. *Tamilnadu Minerals Ltd*, High Court of Madras, pp. 555–566, LLJ, February, 2011

*R. Sekar* v. *Presiding Officer, First Additional Labour Court Madras and Another,* High Court of Madras, pp 694–696, LLJ, Vol. 2, 2000

*Rahul Kumar Proprietor, Sheetal Hotel* v. *State of U.P. and Others,* High Court of Allahabad, pp. 881–883, LLJ, Vol. 3, 2008

*Rajasthan State Road Transport Corporation* v. *Labour Court and Others*, High Court of Rajasthan, pp. 542–545, LLJ, Vol. 1, 1994

*Rajkot District Cooperative Dairy Employees' Union* v. *State of Gujarat and 7 Others,* High Court of Gujarat, pp. 788–789, LLJ, June 2010

*Ram Avtar* v. *Bank of Baroda and Others*, High Court of Allahabad, pp. 298–313, LLJ, July 2010

*Ram Dev Puri* v. *Trishla Devi and Others,* High Court of Himachal Pradesh, pp. 652–657, LLJ, June 2010

*Ramany S.* v. *Hotel Pondicherry Ashok and Another*, High Court of Madras, pp. 135–142, LLJ, October 2010

*Ramawati Devi (Smt.)* v. *State of U.P. and Others,* High Court of Allahabad, pp. 718–720, LLJ, December 2010

*Ramchandran A. and Others* v. *Managing Director, Tamilnadu Cement Corporation Ltd and Others,* High Court of Madras, pp. 918–919, LLJ, Vol. 1, 2007

*Rashtriya Chemicals and Ferilizers Ltd* v. *General Employees Association,* Supreme Court of India, pp. 1032–1038, LLJ, Vol. 2, 2007

*Rashtriya Mazdoor Sabha U.P. and Another* v. *State of U.P. and Others,* High Court of Allahabad, pp. 239–243, LLJ, January 2011

*Regional Director ESI Corporation and Another* v. *Ran Singh and Another,* High Court of Madhya Pradesh, pp. 791–793, LLJ, Vol. 1, 2000

*Regional Director, Employees State insurance Corporation* v. *K.D. Gopi and Another,* High Court of Karala, pp. 235–237, LLJ, Vol. 2, 1995

*Regional Director, Employees' State Insurance Corporation* v. *Narsabai, w/o NaranPantji,* High Court of Gujarat, pp . 1488–1490, LLJ, Vol. 1, 2001

*Regional Director, ESI Corp.* v. *Kerala Drugs and Pharmaceuticals Ltd and Others,* Supreme Court of India, pp. 148–149, Supreme Court Cases 1995, Supp. 3

*Regional Director, ESIC, Bangalore,* v. *Falcon Trading Association, Mangalore and Another,* High Court of Karnataka, pp. 81–82, LLJ, Vol. 3, 2007

*Regional Direetor ESI Corporation* v. *Shakeenabibi Munarash Khan Pathan and Another,* High Court of Gujarat, pp. 571–584, LLJ, August, 2010

*Regional Provident Fund Commissioner* v. *Wipro Ltd, and Another,* High Court of Madras, pp. 513–521, LLJ, Vol. 4, 2009

*Regional Provident Funds Commissioner* v. *Bhavani,* Supreme Court of India, pp. 1079–1083, LLJ, Vol. 2, 2008

*Regional Provident Funds Commissioner, Karnal* v. *Gurnam Singh and Others,* High Court of Haryana and Punjab, pp. 33–55, LLJ, Vol. 3, 2009

*Roha Dye Chemicals Ltd, Mumbai* v. *State of Maharashtra Industries and Labour Deptt,* High Court of Bombay, pp. 929–934, LLJ, Vol. 2, 2007
*Ruby Coach Builders Ltd* v. *P. S Ghose, Member, Industrial Court and Others,* High Court of Bombay, pp. 1106–1107, LLJ, Vol. 2, 2008 (NOC)
*S.G. Pharmaceuticals* v. *Sarabhai Chemicals Staff Association and Others,* High Court of Gujarat, pp. 436–441, LLJ, Vol. 2, 1999
*Sadashivam S.* v. *Managing Director, Head office, Tamilnadu State Transport Corporation Ltd and Another*, High Court of Madras, pp. 635–637, LLJ, September 2010
*Sahkari Ganna Vikas Samiti Ltd, Hardwar* v. *Dy. Labour Commissioner, Dehradun and Others,* High Court of Uttarakhand, pp. 657–659, LLJ, September 2010
*Salis Lawrence and Another* v. *Subroto Mukherjee and Others,* High Court of Chhatisgarh, pp. 744–752, LLJ, Vol. 3, 2006
*Sanjay Kumar Tiwari and Others* v. *State of Bihar and Other,* High Court of Patna, pp. 977–981, LLJ, Vol. 2, 2008
*Sarabibi Usman Khan Pathan* v. *Supt. Engineer, Gujarat Electricily Board and Others*, High Court of Gujarat, pp. 776–780, LLJ, Vol. 1, 1995
*Satija J. K* v. *Indian Oil Corporation and Another*, High Court of Delhi pp. 484–488, LLJ, November 2010
*Savani Transport (Pvt.) Ltd* v. *Savani Transport Employees Association and Another,* High Court of Kerala, pp. 269–277, LLJ, Vol. 2, 1994
*Secretary, Chennai Corporation Societies Employees Cooperative Thrift and Credit Society* v. *R. Paneerselvam and Others*, High Court of Madras, pp. 128–131, LLJ, July 2010
*Seshashayee Paper Mills and Others* v. *Seshashayee Paper and Boards Ltd,* High Court of Madras, pp. 617–624, LLJ, Vol. 3, Supp. 2000
*Sh. Satya Prakash Giri and Others* v. *Presiding Officer, Industrial Tribunal, Haryana and Another,* High Court of Punjab and Haryana, pp. 437–441, LLJ, Vol. 1, 1995
*Shalimar Tanning Co.* v. *ESI Corporation and Another,* High Court of Madras, pp. 937–941, LLJ, Vol. 2, 2000
*Sheikh Jahangir Ali and Others* v. *Calcutta Port Trust and Others*, High Court of Calcutta, pp. 381–386, LLJ, Vol. 3, 1999
*Shine Up Fibres Ltd, Sangrami Shramik Union and others* v. *Principal Secretary, Deptt of labour, Government of West Bengal and Another,* High Court of Calcutta, pp. 39–41, LLJ, July 2010
*Shiva Anand* v. *Indian Airlines Ltd and Others*, Supreme Court of India, pp. 666–667, LLJ, Vol. 1, 2008
*Shyam Babu Bhatnagar* v. *UP Power Corporation Ltd and Others*, High Court of Allahabad, pp. 833–834, LLJ, September 2010
*Shyam Bouri* v. *Eastern Coalfields Ltd and others*, High Court of Calcutta, pp.588–589, LLJ, Vol. 2, 2009
*Simplex Electronics* v. *Vimalaben Atmaram Yadav and Another*, High Court of Gujarat, pp. 841–848, LLJ, Vol. 1, September 2010
*Sirput Paper Mills Ltd* v. *Chairman, Industrial-Cum- Labour Court and Another,* High Court of Andhra Pradesh, pp. 1212–1221, LLJ, Vol. 3, Supp. 2000

*Somayya S. Bhandari and Others* v. *Oriental Rubber Industries Ltd*, High Court of Bombay, pp. 193–200, LLJ, January 2011

*South Indian Bank Ltd* v. *V.G. Krishna Kumar and Another*, High Court of Kerala, pp. 661–669, LLJ, Vol. 2, 2006

*Sree Meenakshi Mills Ltd Madurai and Another* v. *Workmen represented by Secretary, Madurai Workers Union (CITU), Madurai and Another,* High Court of Madras, pp. 50–53, LLJ, Vol. 2, 2009

*Standard Chartered Grindlays Bank Retired Employees' Association* v. *Union of India and Other*, High Court of Calcutta, pp. 887–893, LLJ, Vol. 2, 2007

*Starian Employees Union, Noida and Another,* v. *P.O. Labour Court (II) U.P., Ghaziabad and Others,* High Court of Allahabad, p. 1132, LLJ, Vol. 2, 2008, (NOC)

*State Bank of India Staff Association and Another* v. *State Bank of India and Others,* Supreme Court of India, pp. 61–63, *Factories Journal Reports*, Vol. 89, Part 3, 1996

*State Government of M.P. and Others* v. *Shankar Lal,* Supreme Court of India, pp. 289–293., LLJ, Vol. 2, 2008

*State of Andhra Pradesh* v. *S. Venkateswara Rao and Another*, High Court of Andhra Pradesh, pp. 396–400, LLJ, February 2011

*State of Assam* v. *Barak Upatyaka D.U. Karamchar Sanshtha*, Supreme Court of India, pp. 279–286, LLJ, Vol. 4, 2009

*State of Gujarat* v. *Bhupendra Kumar Jagjivandas Patel,* High Court of Gujarat, pp. 1517–1519, LLJ, Vol. 2, 2001

*State of Gujarat* v. *Dilip Kumar Dahyabhai Patel and Another*, High Court of Gujarat, pp. 109–115, FJR, Vol. 87, Parts 4 and 5, 1995

*State of Gujarat* v. *Dinesh S. Raval c/o All Gujarat General Mazdoor Sangh*, High Court of Gujarat, pp. 27–29, LLJ, Vol. 2, 2008

*State of Gujarat* v. *Fatlufakru Bhuria and Others,* High Court of Gujarat, pp. 427–432, LLJ, November 2010

*State of Gujarat* v. *Ishwarbhai Harkhabhai Patel*, High Court of Gujarat, pp. 793–797, LLJ, Vol. 1, 1995

*State of Gujarat* v. *Maganlal Gordhandas Merchant*, High Court of Gujarat, pp. 206–213, LLJ Vol. 1, 1995

*State of Haryana and Others* v. *UmeshKumar and Nagpal and Anil Malik*, Supreme Court of India, pp. 798–800, LLJ, Vol. 1, 1995

*State of Madhya Pradesh and Others* v. *Omkar Prasad Patel*, Supreme Court of India, pp. 681–683, LLJ, Vol. 2, 2006

State of Orissa and Others v. Kailas Chandra Nayak and others, High Court of Orissa, pp. 675–678, LLJ, Vol. 2, 2007

*State of Orissa through its Principal Secretary, Home Department* v. *Bimal Kumar Mohanty*, Supreme Court of India, pp. 568–573, LLJ, Vol. 1, 1995

*State of Rajasthan* v. *Umrao Singh*, Supreme Court of India, pp. 908–910, LLJ, Vol. 1, 1995

*State of Uttaranchal* v. *Jagpal Singh Tyagi,* Supreme Court of India, pp. 10–11, LLJ, Vol. 1, 2006

*Steel Authority of India Ltd and Others* v. *Authority under Minimum Wages Act, 1948 and Another,* High Court of Madhya Pradesh, pp.750–764, LLJ, Vol. 2, 2007

*Steel Plant Canteen Employees' Union, Vishakhapatanam and Others* v. *Chairman–Cum–Managing Director Vishakhapatanam Steel Project and Others*, High Court of Andhra Pradesh, pp. 1270–1278, LLJ Vol. 2, 2009

*Sumer Singh* v. *Chief Conservator of Forests, Haryana and Others*, High Court of Punjab and Haryana, pp. 834–836, LLJ, September 2010

*Sunanda, Widow of Shrikant Dhote* v. *Regional Provident Funds Commissioner, Aurangabad and Another,* High Court of Bomaby, pp. 984–986, LLJ, Vol. 1, 2006

*Suresh Mahato* v. *G.E. Industrial Pvt. Ltd and Others*, High Court of Calcutta, pp. 489–491, LLJ, Vol. 4, 2009

*Suttokati V. (Smt)* v. *Chief Manager, Syndicate Bank and Others*, High Court of Karnataka, pp. 232–234, LLJ, .Vol. 1, 2008

*Swadeshi Cotton Mills* v. *Asstt. Labour Commissioner (Central) and Controlling Authority Under Payment of Gratuity Act, Allahabad and Others,* High Court of Allahabad, pp. 1221–1225, LLJ, Vol. 1, 2000

*Swaraj Yadav, Alias Suraj Yadav* v. *ESI Corporation and Another,* High Court of Haryana and Punjab, pp. 273–275, LLJ, Vol. 4, 2009

*Swastik Textile Engineers Pvt. Ltd* v. *Vrijbhai Mavjibhai Rathod and Another,* High Court of Gujarat, pp. 533–536, LLJ, Vol. 2, 2008

*T.V.S. Finance and Services Ltd* v. *S. H Shiva Kumar*, Supreme Court of India, pp. 679–680, LLJ, December 2010

*Tata Engineering and Locomotive Co. Ltd* v. *Ishwarchand and Tarachand Jain and Another*, High Court of Bombay, p.1146 (Brief Resume), LLJ, Vol. 2, 2008

*Tata Memorial Centre and Another* v. *Tata Memorial Workers Union and Another,* High Court of Bombay, pp. 949–950, LLJ, Vol. 4, 2006 (NOC)

*Tata Power Co. Ltd. and Others* v. *Regional Provident Funds Commissioner,* High Court of Bombay, pp. 992–996, LLJ, Vol. 1, 2008

*Tata Tea Ltd and others* v. *State of Tamil Nadu and Others*, High Court of Madras, pp. 762–778, LLJ, June 2010

*Tata Workers Union and Others* v. *State of Jharkhand and Others,* High Court of Jharkhand, pp. 813–814, LLJ, Vol. 1, 2006

*Tata Workers Union* v. *State of Jharkhand,* High Court of Jharkhand, pp. 1045–1048, LLJ, Vol.1, 2006

*Tej Singh Manavat* v. *Bank of Rajasthan Ltd*, High Court of Rajasthan, pp. 153–154, LLJ, Vol. 3, 2000

*Textile Technical Tradesmen Association and Others* v. *Union of India represented by Secretary, Ministry of Labour, New Delhi and Others*, High Court of Madras, pp. 297–304, LLJ January 2011. Also referred to *Kesavananda Bharthi* v. *State of Kerala*, Supreme Court of India

*Textile Traders Cooperative Bank Ltd* v. *Jagdishbhai Natwarlal Patel*, High Court of Gujarat, pp. 235–241, LLJ, Vol. 1, 2000

*Thiru Arooram Sugars Ltd* v. *Asstt. Provident Funds Commissioner (ENF), Trichirapalli and Another,* High Court of Madras, pp. 806–813, LLJ, Vol. 1, 2008

*Triveni Engineering and Industries Ltd, Khatauli* v. *1st Additional District Judge, Muzaffarnagar and Others,* High Court of Allahabad, pp. 491–494, LLJ, Vol. 3, 2007

*U.P State* v. *Brahm Singh and Another*, High Court of Allahabad, p. 980 (NOC), LLJ, Vol. 4, 2006

*U.P. State Road Transport Corporation and Another* v. *Suresh Chand Sharma and Another*, Supreme Court of India, pp. 278–283, LLJ, July 2010
*U.P. State Sugar Corporation and Another* v. *Sukhveer Singh and Another,* High Court of Allahabad, pp. 779–782, LLJ, Vol. 3, 2008
*U.P.S.R.T.C. Through its Managing Director and Other,* v. *Mohd. Rais Khan,* High Court of Allahabad, pp. 279–288, LLJ, October 2010
*Ujjain Charitable Trust Hospital and Research Centre* v. *State of M.P. and Another*, High Court of Madhya Pradesh, pp. 345–349, LLJ, November 2010
*Union Bank of India through its Chairman and Managing Director* v. *Union Bank of India Employees' Union, Pune and Another,* High Court of Bombay, pp. 692–695, LLJ, June 2010
*Union Bank of India* v. *M. T.Lathesh*, Supreme Court of India, pp. 4626–4639, *AIR Supreme Court (Weekly)* Vol. 5, 2006
*Union Bank of India, Mumbai* v. *Union Bank of India Employees' Union, Pune and Another*, High Court of Bombay, pp. 692–695, LLJ, June 2010
*Union of India through the Secretary, Government of India* v. *Secretary, the Staff Union of India Security Press*, High Court of Bombay, pp. 78–83, LLJ, January 2011
*Union of India and Another* v. *Muragan Talkies,* Supreme Court of India, pp. 504–506, Supreme Court Cases 1996
*Union of India and Others* v. *Jummasha Diwan,* Supreme Court of India, pp. 225–227, LLJ, Vol. 1, 2007
*Union of India through Secretary, Government of India* v. *Arun Vithal Bande and Others*, High Court of Bombay, pp. 535–540, LLJ, August 2010
*Uttar Pradesh Pollution Control Board* v. *Mohan Meakins Ltd*, Supreme Court of India, pp.859–860, The Supreme Court Annual Digest, 2000
*Vector Vero* v. *State of Nagaland and Others*, High Court of Gauhati, pp. 851–852 (NOC), LLJ Vol. 4, 2006
*Venkatraman* v. *Sub–Inspector of Police,* High Court of Kerala, pp. 471–486, LLJ, Vol. 1, 2006
*Victor F. Parmar* v. *Elecon Engineering Co. Ltd*, High Court of Gujarat, pp. 494–500, LLJ, Vol. 3, 2000
*Vidya Sagar Institute of Mental Health and Neuro Sciences* v. *Vidya Sagar Hospital Employees' Union,* High Court of Delhi, pp. 781–784, LLJ, Vol. 1, 2006
*Vidyut Matallics Pvt. Ltd* v. *Maharastra Rajya Rashtriya Kamgar Sangh and Others,* High Court of Bombay, pp. 387–397, LLJ, Vol. 2, 2009
*Vijay Kumar and Others* v. *State T.B. Control Society Haryana and Another*, High Court of Punjab and Haryana, pp. 918–922, LLJ, Vol. 3, 2007
*Vijaya Diagnostic Centre and Another* v. *Employees' State Insurance Corp., Hyderabad,* High Court of Andhra Pradesh, pp. 443–448, LLJ, Vol. 2, 2006
*Visakhapatanam Port and Dock Workers Union* v. *Board of Trustees, Visakhapatanam Port Trust and Others,* High Court of Andhra Pradesh, pp. 1123–1125, LLJ, Vol. 2, 1999
*Vittal Venkatesh and Others* v. *Patheja Forging and Auto Parts Manufacturers Pvt. Ltd and Others,* High Court of Bombay, pp. 1015–1021, LLJ, Vol. 2, 1994
*Voltas Employees Union* v. *Voltas Ltd.* High Court of Bombay (referred to by the Bench) in the case on pp. 428, LLJ, Vol. 2, 2003

*Voltas Ltd* v. *Voltas Employees Union and Another,* High Court of Delhi, pp. 604–608, LLJ, Vol. 2, 2007
*Voltas Switchgear Plant Employees' Union* v. *Voltas Switchgear Ltd*, High Court of Bombay, pp. 1242–1246, LLJ, Vol. 1. 2001
*Workmen of Ashok Leyland Ltd and Ashok Leyland Cooperative Canteen Ltd* v. *Ashok Leyland Ltd and Others*, High Court of Madras, pp. 2–3, Digest of Labour Cases, January 1992
*Workmen of Calcutta Electric Supply Corporation Ltd* v. *Calcutta Electric Supply Corporation*, Supreme Court of India, pp. 251–261, LLJ, Vol. 2, 1973
*Workmen of Deccan Sugars* v. *Nava Bharat Ferro Alloys Ltd and Others,* High Court of Madras, pp. 1211–1214, LLJ, Vol. 1, 1995
*Workmen of Kettlewell Bullen & Co. Ltd* v. *Kettlewell Bullen and Co. Ltd. and Others,* Supreme Court of India, pp. 1201–1209, LLJ, Vol. 1, 1995
*Zulash Clearing and Shipping Agency* v. *Chairman, Railway Goods Clearing and Forwarding Establishment's Labour Board for Greater Bombay and Others,* High Court of Bombay, pp. 894–896, LLJ, Vol. 3, 2007

# Index

*Numbers refer to paragraphs.*

## Index

www.ingramcontent.com/pod-product-compliance
Lightning Source LLC
Chambersburg PA
CBHW071414230926
51846CB00001B/82
*9789041153265*